Pattern Recognition Theory and Applications

NATO ASI Series

Advanced Science Institutes Series

A series presenting the results of activities sponsored by the NATO Science Committee, which aims at the dissemination of advanced scientific and technological knowledge, with a view to strengthening links between scientific communities.

The Series is published by an international board of publishers in conjunction with the NATO Scientific Affairs Division

A **Life Sciences** B **Physics**	Plenum Publishing Corporation London and New York
C **Mathematical and Physical Sciences**	D. Reidel Publishing Company Dordrecht, Boston, Lancaster and Tokyo
D **Behavioural and Social Sciences** E **Applied Sciences**	Martinus Nijhoff Publishers Boston, The Hague, Dordrecht and Lancaster
F **Computer and Systems Sciences** G **Ecological Sciences** H **Cell Biology**	Springer-Verlag Berlin Heidelberg New York London Paris Tokyo

Series F: Computer and Systems Sciences Vol. 30

Pattern Recognition Theory and Applications

Edited by

Pierre A. Devijver

Philips Research Laboratory
Avenue Em. Van Becelaere 2, Box 8
B-1170 Brussels, Belgium

Josef Kittler

Department of Electronic and Electrical
Engineering, University of Surrey,
Guildford GU2 5XH, United Kingdom

Springer-Verlag
Berlin Heidelberg New York London Paris Tokyo
Published in cooperation with NATO Scientific Affairs Divison

Proceedings of the NATO Advanced Study Institute on Pattern Recognition Theory and Applications held in Spa-Balmoral, Belgium, June 9–20, 1986.

ISBN-13:978-3-642-83071-6 e-ISBN-13:978-3-642-83069-3
DOI: 10.1007/978-3-642-83069-3

Library of Congress Cataloging in Publication Data. NATO Advanced study Institute on Pattern Recognition and Applications (1986 : Spa, Belgium) Pattern recognition theory and applications. (NATO ASI series. Series F, Computer and systems sciences ; v. 30) "Proceedings of the NATO Advanced Study Institute on Pattern Recognition Theory and Applications held in Spa-Balmoral, Belgium, June 9–20, 1986"—Copr. p. 1. Pattern perception—Congresses. I. Devijver, Pierra A., 1936- . II. Kittler, Josef, 1946- . III. Series: NATO ASI series. Series F, Computer and systems sciences ; vol. 30. Q327.N22 1987 006.4 87-9635
ISBN-13:978-3-642-83071-6

Softcover reprint of the hardcover 1st edition 1987

2145/3140-543210

To King Sun Fu

PREFACE

This book is the outcome of a NATO Advanced Study Institute on Pattern Recognition Theory and Applications held in Spa–Balmoral, Belgium, in June 1986. This Institute was the third of a series which started in 1975 in Bandol, France, at the initiative of Professors K.S. Fu and A. Whinston, and continued in 1981 in Oxford, UK, with Professors K.S. Fu, J. Kittler and L.-F. Pau as directors. As early as in 1981, plans were made to pursue the series in about 1986 and possibly in Belgium, with Professor K.S. Fu and the present editors as directors. Unfortunately, *le sort en décida autrement:* Professor Fu passed away in the spring of 1985. His sudden death was an irreparable loss to the scientific community and to all those who knew him as an inspiring colleague, a teacher or a dear friend. Soon after, Josef Kittler and I decided to pay a small tribute to his memory by helping some of his plans to materialize. With the support of the NATO Scientific Affairs Division, the Institute became a reality. It was therefore but natural that the proceedings of the Institute be dedicated to him.

The book contains most of the papers that were presented at the Institute. Papers are grouped along major themes which hopefully represent the major areas of contemporary research. These are:

1. Statistical methods and clustering techniques
2. Probabilistic relaxation techniques
3. From Markovian to connectionist models
4. Graph theory and geometry
5. Structural methods
6. Hybrid methods and fuzzy sets
7. Knowledge-based recognition techniques
8. Machine vision and image processing

Each theme is introduced by one – or more – tutorial presentations, and illustrated by more specialized, advanced or applied contributions. Whenever feasible, we have attempted to present applications of one methodology in several, different domains. Thus a paper on speech recognition neighboring one on image processing is no accident. In so doing, our goal was to promote cross-fertilization between apparently unrelated areas.

In essence, the book provides an up-to-date account of the state of the art in pattern recognition, and in many places it suggests directions for future research. Therefore, it should be not only a useful reference, but also a stimulus to researchers interested in the advancement of the subject. It is only regrettable that one aspect of the Institute could not be captured within this book: the spirit and conviviality of the many informal interactions between the participants. The "information channel" established between individuals with varied orientation towards the field will hopefully lead to increased interdisciplinary applications of pattern recognition in the future.

The major funding of the Institute was through a grant from the NATO Scientific Affairs Division. However, substantial additional support was obtained from

1. Philips Belgium
2. IBM Belgium
3. The Philips Research Laboratory, Brussels

to whom we are most indebted.

I also wish to thank a number of individuals for their active support and help. Ms. Vinciane Lacroix participated actively in the preparation of both the Institute and the proceedings. The typing of about half of the book was accomplished diligently and skilfully by Mrs. Edith Moes. The layout of the book owes much to Mr. Frans Heymans who responded with his usual good will and competence to my many requests, up to the point of designing one of the type fonts used in the text. Finally, my most sincere thanks to my colleague and friend Michel Dekesel who shared with me all the burden of the organizer's and editor's duties.

Brussels
Christmas 1986

Pierre A. Devijver

CONTENTS

ADVANCES IN STATISTICAL PATTERN RECOGNITION

Anil K. Jain

Department of Computer Science
Michigan State University
East Lansing, Michigan 48824, U.S.A.

Abstract

Statistical pattern recognition is now a mature discipline which has been successfully applied in several application domains. The primary goal in statistical pattern recognition is classification, where a pattern vector is assigned to one of a finite number of classes and each class is characterized by a probability density function on the measured features. A pattern vector is viewed as a point in the multidimensional space defined by the features. Design of a recognition system based on this paradigm requires careful attention to the following issues: type of classifier (single-stage vs. hierarchical), feature selection, estimation of classification error, parametric vs. nonparametric decision rules, and utilizing contextual information. Current research emphasis in pattern recognition is on designing efficient algorithms, studying small sample properties of various estimators and decision rules, implementing the algorithms on novel computer architecture, and incorporating context and domain-specific knowledge in decision making.

Keywords: pattern recognition, training samples, features, class-conditional density, Bayes decision rule, clustering, error probability, bootstrap technique, computational complexity, computational geometry, VLSI design, contextual information, domain-specific knowledge.

1. Introduction

Pattern recognition techniques assign a physical object or an event to one of several prespecified categories. Thus, a pattern recognition system can be viewed as an automatic decision rule; it transforms measurements on a pattern into class assignments. The patterns themselves could range from agricultural fields in a remotely sensed image from Landsat satellites to a speech waveform or utterance from an individual; the associated recognition or classification problems are to label an agricultural field as wheat or non-wheat and to identify the spoken word. Patterns are recognized based on some features or measurements made on the pattern. In remote sensing applications, the features are usually the reflected energies in several wavelength bands of the electromagnetic spectrum, whereas in word identification or speech recognition problems, one common set of features are the LPC's (Linear Predictive Coefficients) computed from the speech waveform. Recent concerns over productivity and quality control have led to

NATO ASI Series, Vol. F30
Pattern Recognition Theory and Applications
Edited by P. A. Devijver and J. Kittler

an upsurge in the application of pattern recognition techniques to new domains. Pattern recognition techniques are now used in industrial inspection, document processing, remote sensing, personal identification, and various other scientific applications. Fu (1982) gives a detailed account of many of these applications.

The pattern recognition problem is difficult because various sources of noise distort the patterns, and often there exists a substantial amount of variability among the patterns belonging to the same category. The end result of this is that the features or measurements on patterns belonging to the same category are different. Hopefully, this difference will be small compared to the differences between patterns belonging to different categories. For example, the speech waveform associated with the utterance of the word "computer" by different speakers will be different. Even the same speaker uttering the same word at different times will generate slightly different speech waveforms. A successful recognition system must be able to handle these pattern variabilities. To recognize complex patterns in noisy and unconstrained environments, we often need to use symbolic features rather than numeric features and incorporate additional constraints and knowledge about the problem domain (Chandrasekaran, 1986; Nagao, 1984; Nandhakumar and Aggarwal, 1985). But this demands substantial computational resources for the recognition system to operate in "real time". Recent developments in VLSI design have resulted in special purpose hardware to speed up the recognition algorithms (Fu, 1984).

There are essentially two basic paradigms to classify a pattern into one of several different categories or pattern classes.

In a geometric or statistical approach, a pattern is represented in terms of N features or properties and viewed as a point in N-dimensional space. We wish to select those features such that pattern vectors belonging to different categories will occupy different regions of this feature space. Given certain sample patterns from each pattern class (training samples), the objective is to establish decision boundaries in the feature space to separate patterns belonging to different classes. In the statistical approach, the decision boundaries are determined by the statistical distributions of the patterns which must be specified. One can also take a "non-statistical" approach, where first the form of the decision boundary (linear, quadratic, etc.) is specified and then the "best" decision boundary of the specified form is found. A large number of books (See, for example, Duda and Hart, 1973; Devijver and Kittler, 1982) cover this approach. The choice of features is data dependent and is crucial to the performance of the recognition system. Defining appropriate features requires interaction with a person who is an expert in the application area. In many recognition problems involving complex patterns, the number of features required to establish a reasonable decision boundary is very large. In such situations it is more appropriate to view a pattern as being composed of simple subpatterns (Pavlidis, 1977). A subpattern itself could be built from yet simpler subpatterns. The simplest subpatterns to be recognized are called primitives and the given complex pattern is represented in terms of the interrelationships among these primitives. Thus we need to define primitives and rules of constructing patterns from those primitives. In syntactic pattern recognition, an analogy is drawn between the structure of patterns and the syntax of a language. The patterns are viewed as sentences belonging to a language, primitives are viewed as the alphabet of the language, and the sentences are generated according to a grammar. Thus a large set of complex patterns can be described by a small number of primitives and grammatical rules. The grammar for each pattern class must be inferred from the available training samples.

Structural pattern recognition is intuitively appealing. The main advantage of the structural approach over the geometric approach is that, in addition to classification, it also provides a description of how the given pattern is constructed from the primitives. This paradigm has been used in situations where the patterns have a definite structure which can be captured in terms of a set of rules (*e.g.*, EKG waveforms, textured images, shape analysis of contours). See the book by Fu (1982) for a discussion on these applications. The implementation of a syntactic approach leads to many difficulties which primarily have to do with the segmentation of noisy patterns to detect the primitives and inference of the grammar. While there are some problems with the statistical approach also, it is better understood and relies on more firmly established elements of statistical decision theory. Perhaps this is why most commercial recognition systems utilize decision-theoretic approaches. Fu (1986) has introduced the notion of attributed grammars which unifies the syntactic and statistical pattern recognition. We will now concentrate on the statistical approach.

2. Statistical Pattern Recognition

The paradigm of statistical pattern recognition can be summarized as follows. A given pattern is to be assigned to one of C categories $w_1, w_2, \ldots, w_c$ based on its feature values $(x_1, x_2, \ldots, x_N)$. The features are assumed to have a density function conditioned on the pattern class. Thus a pattern vector $\underline{x}$ belonging to class w_i is viewed as an observation drawn randomly from the class-conditional density $p(\underline{x} \mid w_i)$. Well-known concepts from statistical decision theory are utilized to establish decision boundaries between the pattern classes. For example, the Bayes decision rule, which minimizes the average risk or probability of misclassification, involves the class-conditional densities $p(\underline{x} \mid w_i)$, a priori probabilities $p(w_i)$, and the loss function $L(w_i, w_j)$. The class-conditional densities are never known in practice and must be "learned" from the training samples. We now discuss some design considerations and practical issues which a pattern recognition system designer faces. The answers to these questions depend on the amount of available data, prior information about the underlying class-conditional densities, guidance from an expert in the domain of application, and computational realities.

2.1. Design Considerations

Various strategies utilized to design a classifier in statistical pattern recognition depend on what kind of information is available about the class-conditional densities. If it is assumed that the form of the class-conditional densities is known but some of the parameters of the densities are unknown then we have a parametric decision problem. A common strategy for this kind of problem is to replace the unknown parameters in the density functions by their estimated values. If the form of the densities is not known then we operate in nonparametric mode. In that case, we must either estimate the density function (*e.g.*, Parzen window approach) or use some nonparametric decision rule (*e.g.*, k-nearest neighbor rule). The estimation of parameters or the density function requires the availability of learning or training samples. Another dichotomy in statistical pattern recognition is that of supervised learning (labeled training samples) versus unsupervised learning (unlabeled training samples). The label on each training pattern represents the category to which that pattern belongs.

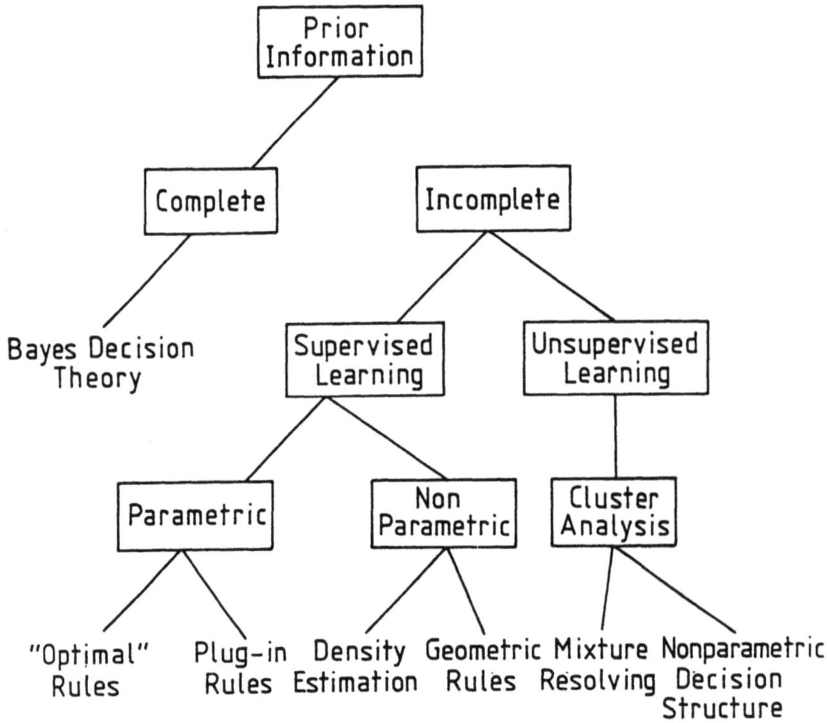

Figure 1: Breakdown of problems in pattern recognition

These various dichotomies which appear in statistical pattern recognition are shown in the tree structure of Figure 1. The classification problems get more difficult as one traverses the tree from top to bottom and left to right. The field of cluster analysis essentially deals with decision making problems in the nonparametric and unsupervised learning mode (Dubes and Jain, 1980). Further, in cluster analysis no prespecified categories are supplied; the task is to discover a reasonable categorization of the data (if one exists).

The choice of a specific design for a recognition system is also dictated by the number of pattern classes, number of features, number of training samples, and the desired recognition speed. We now discuss three important design criteria.

2.1.1. Single-stage versus hierarchical (tree) classifier

A single-stage or one-shot classifier makes class assignments based on a single decision using a fixed set of the features. Typically, a discriminant function is determined for each class and a pattern is assigned to the class with the maximum discriminant function value. This may not be the most appropriate scheme, if the number of pattern classes is large; in order to achieve a satisfactory separation of all the pattern classes, a single-stage classifier requires a large number of features.

An alternative classification structure is a multistage or tree classifier where the most obvious or natural discriminations are done first, postponing the more subtle distinctions until a later stage (Dattatreya and Kanal, 1985). A decision tree consists of a root node, nonterminal nodes, and terminal nodes. A nonterminal node corresponds to intermediate or partial decisions so a subset of pattern classes is associated with it. A single pattern class is associated with a terminal node. Starting with the root node, a test sample is directed to a terminal node through a sequence of decisions. This results in a higher processing speed since the average number of features per node is substantially less than the number of features required by a single-stage classifier. Multistage classifiers are more adept than single-stage classifiers at handling pattern classes that are multimodal in nature. They are also useful when the features are of mixed type (*e.g.*, nominal and ratio) or if some of the feature values are missing. Several systems for the classification of white blood cells (for example, HEMATRAK) use this classification strategy.

The design of a hierarchical classifier requires decisions about the following components:

i) The choice of a tree skeleton or hierarchical ordering of pattern classes.

ii) The choice of features to be used at each nonterminal node.

iii) The decision rule for performing the classification at each nonterminal node.

These are difficult issues to resolve and there are no "optimal" solutions. Mui and Fu (1980) propose an interactive scheme for tree design. A straightforward approach to partitioning the feature space at each nonterminal node is to use hyperplanes parallel to the feature axes. The choice of feature subset to use at each node is then reduced to choosing a single feature and a corresponding threshold which give an "optimal" division at that node. Sethi and Sarvarayudu (1982) determine the optimal division based on maximizing the amount of average mutual information gain at a node. Li and Dubes (1986) propose a statistical test to determine whether a node should be further split.

2.1.2. Parametric versus nonparametric approach

Most of the popular parametric techniques are optimal if the class-conditional densities happen to be Gaussian. However, verifying the normality of multivariate data is a difficult problem (Smith and Jain, 1985; Fukunaga and Flick, 1986). Even though statistics based on Gaussian distributions are robust, it is wise to consider nonparametric techniques, *e.g.*, nearest-neighbor classifier, if the data substantially departs from normality. Van Ness (1980) does an extensive Monte Carlo study to compare the performance of four different decision rules (linear, quadratic, average linkage, and nonparametric with Parzen window based density estimates) on high dimensional Gaussian data. The standard linear and quadratic algorithms assume that the means and covariances are unknown. The average linkage algorithm computes the average distance of a test pattern to all the training patterns for each class. The surprising result of this study is that the nonparametric algorithm using Parzen estimates of the density function performs better than linear and quadratic classifiers in high dimensions. The dominance of the nonparametric decision rule occurs even when the given data is ideal for the linear and quadratic decision rules.

The superiority of nonparametric decision rules over parametric decision rules in high dimensions can be explained by the poor estimates of the covariance matrices when the ratio of number of training samples to the number of features is small. For this reason, Van Ness (1982) suggests the use of shrinkage estimators of the covariance matrix over the commonly used unbiased estimator. Keating and Mason (1985) and Morgera (1986) also propose alternate estimators of the covariance matrix for vectorcardiogram data and remote sensing data, respectively.

The nonparametric decision rules also require a careful choice of some parameters. For example, a key question in using K-NN decision rule is: what value of K should be selected? For finite number of training samples increasing K does not monotonically increase the recognition accuracy (Bailey and Jain, 1978). A useful guideline in practice is to select K proportional to $\sqrt{n}$, where n is the number of training samples. What distance metric should be used for computing the nearest neighbors? Euclidean metric is most commonly used, but recent results by Fukunaga and Flick (1984) indicate that under certain conditions (Gaussian assumption) a quadratic distance metric results in a lower error rate than the Euclidean metric.

Similarly, there are two main decisions to be made before using the kernel-based density estimator: *i)* choice of the functional form of the kernel, and *ii)* choice of the window width. While some asymptotic results on "optimal" kernels are available, in practice Gaussian or uniform kernels are used (Postaire and Vasseur, 1982). The choice of window-width parameter is more critical because it is influenced by the number of features and the number of training samples. A window width proportional to $n^{-c/d}$ is recommended, where n is the number of training samples, d is the number of features, and c is a constant in the interval $(0,1)$. Recently, cross validation procedure has also been utilized for window width selection (Van Ness, 1980; Hall,1983; Smith, 1986).

2.1.3. Supervised versus unsupervised learning

In many applications of pattern recognition it is difficult or expensive to label the training samples. Consider, for example, an application in remote sensing. In order to get 'ground truth' information, the physical site associated with the pixel must be visited to determine its land-use category. Similar problems exist in nondestructive evaluation. Often the labels are not very reliable. This is especially true in some medical decision-making applications where different experts may give different opinions about, say, an EKG waveform.

Unsupervised learning refers to situations where training samples are not labeled. This is a difficult problem and, in practice, one often has to rely on techniques of cluster analysis (Dubes and Jain, 1980) to identify natural groupings (categories) present in the data. Cluster analysis attempts to assess the interaction among patterns by organizing them into groups or clusters. The results of cluster analysis are useful for forming hypotheses about the data, classifying new data, testing for the homogeneity of the data, and for compressing the data. Fukunaga and Short (1978) use clustering for problem localization. The recently proposed technique of conceptual clustering (Michalski and Stepp, 1983) is being touted as capable of aiding machine learning and knowledge representation in artificial intelligence (Cheng and Fu, 1984; Chiu and Wong, 1986).

A large number (hundreds) of clustering algorithms have been developed and implemented. But there is no 'best' clustering algorithm — the performance of a clustering algorithm is data dependent. This points to the difficulty of interpreting the results of a clustering algorithm, particularly in high dimensions. Only a few statistical tests are available to assess cluster tendency (Smith and Jain, 1984) and cluster validity (Dubes and Jain, 1979) in practical situations.

2.2. Practical Issues

Once an overall strategy has been decided upon to design a recognition system, many practical issues still need to be considered. The performance of the recognition system critically depends on the choices made. Nagy (1983) discusses how pattern recognition researchers often ignore these issues in practice.

2.2.1. Dimensionality and sample size relationship

The well-known phenomenon of the curse of dimensionality cautions a system designer to use a limited number of features when only a small number of training samples are available (Jain and Chandrasekaran, 1982). In practice the performance of a classifier based on estimated densities quite often improves up to a point, then starts deteriorating as further measurements are added, thus indicating the existence of an optimal measurement complexity when the number of training samples is finite. Trunk (1979) provides a simple example to highlight this dimensionality problem. It is recommended that the number of training samples per class be at least five to ten times the number of features to avoid this peaking in performance. In a different but related context, Kalayeh and Landgrebe (1983) also provide the guideline that the number of training samples should be about five times the number of features in order to have a reliable maximum likelihood estimate of the covariance matrix.

2.2.2. Feature selection and extraction

One of the fundamental problems in statistical pattern recognition is to determine which features should be employed for the best classification result. The purpose of feature selection and extraction is to identify the features which are important in discriminating among pattern classes. The need to retain only a small number of "useful" or "good" features in designing a classifier arises due to computational reasons, cost considerations, and existence of optimum measurement complexity. Given an $n \times d$ pattern matrix, one row per pattern or sample, two general strategies have been used for dimensionality reduction and generating an $n \times p$ matrix, $p < d$.

i) Feature Selection: Choose the "best" subset of size p from the given set of d features.

ii) Feature extraction: Apply a transformation to the pattern matrix and select the p best features in the transformed space. Thus each new feature is a combination of all the d features.

The terms "feature selection" and "feature extraction" have been used interchangeably in the literature. Feature selection is more useful when the objective is to minimize the overall cost of measurement acquisition. Feature extraction is considered a process of mapping original features into more effective features. These mapping techniques can be either linear or nonlinear (Biswas *et al.*, 1981). What should be the value of p or how many features are adequate? Intrinsic dimensionality (Wyse *et al.*, 1980) of the data provides a lower bound on the value of p.

Cover and Van Campenhout (1977) show that to determine the best feature subset of size p out of d features, one needs to examine all possible subsets of size p. Therefore, to guarantee the optimality of a subset of size 10 out of 20 given features, all 184,756 feature subsets of size 10 must be evaluated. For practical considerations, some heuristics must be employed to avoid the exhaustive search. These heuristics, for example, "sequential forward selection", "sequential backward selection", and "plus l – take away r" strategies (Devijver and Kittler, 1982), do not guarantee that the best feature subset will be found. How do we evaluate the feature subsets for their classification performance? Several performance indices have been proposed to measure the class separability of feature subsets and can be divided into two main categories.

i) Probability of error: The error can be estimated either under a parametric model or nonparametrically.

ii) Distance measure: A number of probabilistic distance and information measures between the class-conditional densities, which are "related" to the error probability, can be used to measure feature set effectiveness.

The heuristic search strategy used for obtaining the "best" feature subset is independent of the separability criterion used. Narendra and Fukunaga (1977) show that if the feature separability criterion used satisfies the "monotonicity" property then the branch and bound search strategy guarantees the optimal feature subset without explicitly evaluating all possible feature subsets.

In linear feature extraction, each new feature is a linear combination of the given d features. If no category information is available for the training patterns then the eigenvectors of the sample covariance matrix define the best (from a minimum mean-square error point of view) linear transformation. This is the well known principal component method or the Karhunen-Loeve expansion. If p features are to be extracted then we choose those p eigenvectors which correspond to the p largest eigenvalues of the sample covariance matrix. When category information for training patterns is available then the classical discriminant analysis is more appropriate. Discriminant analysis defines a linear transformation in terms of the eigenvectors corresponding to the $C-1$ non-zero eigenvalues of $S_W^{-1}S_B$, where C is the number of pattern classes, S_W is the within-class scatter matrix, and S_B is the between-class scatter matrix. The desired p new features, $p < (C-1)$, are the p eigenvectors of $S_W^{-1} S_B$ corresponding to the p largest eigenvalues.

The classical discriminant analysis has two serious limitations. First, the maximum number of features which can be extracted is $(C-1)$. Fukunaga and Mantock (1983) and Okada and Tomita (1985) propose new discriminant analysis techniques where up to d features can be extracted. The second limitation of the classical discriminant analysis is that the Fisher criterion (Duda and Hart, 1973), which it maximizes, does not take into consideration the difference of class covariance matrices. Several attempts have been made to extend the Fisher criterion (Malina, 1981). A related feature extraction method represents each pattern class in terms of its own linear subspace of the Euclidean feature space (Oja and Kuusela, 1983).

Classical discriminant analysis is ideal for multivariate Gaussian distributions with common covariance matrices. For other distributions, linear feature extraction may not retain sufficient discriminatory information. Nonlinear feature extraction techniques may be useful in such situations. The drawback of these techniques is that they are data dependent and cannot be represented by a simple mapping function. If no category information on the patterns is available then the nonlinear mapping algorithm of Sammon (1969) is useful to project high dimensional patterns to two or three dimensions. In supervised learning case, Fukunaga and Ando (1977) show that in many situations, the a posteriori probability density functions constitute the optimum feature space.

2.2.3. Error estimation

The probability of misclassification or error is the most effective measure of the performance of a recognition system. Competing designs for a classification problem can also be compared based on their error probabilities. It is very difficult to obtain an analytic expression of the probability of error for a particular classification problem unless, of course, the class-conditional densities are Gaussian with common covariance matrices. If an analytic expression for the probability of error were available, it could be used to study the effect of parameters such as the number of features, number of training samples, and prior probabilities.

In practice, the probability of misclassification of a recognition system must be estimated from the available samples. That is, the classifier is first designed using training samples, and then the test samples are fed in one at a time to the classifier. The percentage of misclassified test samples is usually taken as the estimate of the probability of error. In order for this error estimate to be reliable in predicting the future classification performance of the recognition system, the training and test samples must be statistically independent or at least be different (Devijver and Kittler, 1982). It is important to note that the error estimate of a classifier is a random variable. Thus we can define properties like bias, variance, and confidence interval of an error rate estimator, which depend on the number of available samples. These properties are useful in comparing different estimators.

Various methods available to estimate the probability of error depend on how the available samples are divided into training and test sets.

i) Resubstitution Method: This method uses the same set of samples to train as well as test the classifier. It is well known that the resulting error estimate is optimistically biased (Foley, 1972).

ii) Holdout Method: The available samples are randomly partitioned into two groups. One of these groups is used to design the classifier and the other one is used to test the classifier. For a given total number of samples, how should one divide it into design sets and test sets? Should one use more test samples or more training samples? This method gives a pessimistically biased error estimate.

iii) Leave-One-Out Method: In this method each sample is used for design and test, although not at the same time. The classifier is designed using $(n-1)$ samples and then tested on the remaining sample, where n is the total number of available samples. This is repeated n times with different design sets of size $(n-1)$. The error estimate is the total number of misclassified samples divided by n. While the leave-one-out estimator is unbiased, it does have large variance and requires the implementation of n classifiers.

A substantial amount of literature on error estimation in pattern recognition has dealt with deriving asymptotic properties of various error rate estimators, and establishing relationship between Bayes error and the error rate of K-nearest neighbor rule (Devijver and Kittler, 1982). But very little attention has been given to the properties of these estimators in small sample size situations, particularly when the dimensionality of the data is high. For example, while the expected error of the nearest neighbor rule converges asymptotically (as the sample size approaches infinity) to a value between the Bayes error and twice the Bayes error, the nearest neighbor error may exceed twice the Bayes error when a finite number of samples is available. One would hope that increasing the sample size would reduce both the bias and the variance of the error estimate. Fukunaga and Hummels (1985) demonstrate that the reliability of the estimated error rate of the popular nearest neighbor rule cannot be increased for high dimensional patterns by simply increasing the sample size. Their results show that increasing the number of samples from 1,000 to 10,000 reduces the bias in the near neighbor error estimate by only 6.9% in 64 dimensions.

3. Recent Developments in Pattern Recognition

The fundamentals of the statistical decision theory are now quite well understood. Early work in pattern recognition was concerned with demonstrating asymptotic properties and error rates of decision rules, convergence of parameters and density estimators, and establishing bounds on Bayes error rate. Most of these results were quite useful but others were of purely academic interest. For example, several papers were written in the early seventies which established the relationship between the asymptotic Bayes error and various distance and information measures. In practice, when the number of samples is small these bounds are of very little value.

The current interest in pattern recognition is to expand the domain of applications of this methodology. This has resulted in more careful attention to practical issues such as reliable estimates of error rate, computational complexity, robustness of classifiers, implementation of decision algorithms into hardware, and utilizing contextual or expert information in the decision rules. These are difficult problems and we do not yet know all the answers. For example, we do not know how to measure and specify the robustness of a classifier. In several recognition problems, an object can be viewed by different sensors (*e.g.*, IR, Radar, TV). A practical issue is at what level should the information derived from different sensors be merged? Suppose a separate classifier is designed for each type of sensor. What happens if different classifiers give contradictory results? Several techniques from artificial intelligence literature are available to handle this problem of integrating information provided by a collection of disparate knowledge sources (*e.g.*, Cohen, 1984; Garvey *et al.*, 1981). Exploratory pattern analysis, which deals with topics like two-dimensional projections, testing for multivariate normality, intrinsic dimensionality, and clustering tendency, should constitute the first stage in the design of a recognition system. If the data do not have enough "classifiability" then there is no need to do feature selection and classifier design. A cursory look at recent issues of leading pattern recognition journals and conference proceedings indicates that a majority of papers now deal with these practical issues. We briefly review some of the recent developments in these areas.

3.1. Bootstrap Techniques

Bootstrap sampling refers to a class of procedures that resample given data with replacement (Efron, 1982). It permits determining the properties of an estimator when very little is known about the underlying distribution and no additional samples are available. The bootstrap procedure provides nonparametric estimates of the bias and standard error of an estimator from a single set of samples. The name bootstrap reflects the fact that the patterns available generate other sets of patterns. Bootstrapping is similar to other resampling schemes such as cross-validation and jackknifing. The difference lies in the manner in which additional or fake data sets are generated. Since its invention in 1977, bootstrap techniques have been useful in many statistical estimation and inference problems. Bootstrapping techniques are by nature computationally intensive; the more resamplings that can be processed, the more reliable will be the results. In fact, these techniques have only become practical with the advent of more powerful computers.

Estimating the error rate of a classifier is one area in pattern recognition where bootstrap techniques have been found to be superior to other commonly used techniques. Efron (1983) and Chernick *et al.* (1985) have used bootstrapping to estimate the bias of the apparent error rate (resubstitution method), obtained by reclassifying the design samples, of a linear discriminant function. Their experiments were limited to two and three pattern classes, two- and five-dimensional Gaussian feature vectors, and training sample sizes of 14, 20, and 29. The bootstrap estimate of the bias of the apparent error rate was somewhat smaller than the true bias, but was far less variable than the jackknife estimate or the cross-validation estimate. Jain *et al.* (1986) extended these results to the nearest neighbor and quadratic classifiers. The utility of bootstrapping is also being explored in other areas of pattern recognition, including feature selection, feature extraction, window width selection for Parzen density estimates, and estimating number of clusters.

3.2. Computational Complexity

Sometimes the algorithms used in designing a classifier are computationally so demanding that only problems of moderate size (in terms of the numbers of features and samples) can be solved in a reasonable amount of time. Day and Wells (1984) show that simply changing the metric used to measure distances between partitions of a set can drastically change the computational complexity of the algorithm. In such cases, a careful, and sometimes clever, analysis of the problem can often lead to a more efficient algorithm which can be used with large pattern matrices. Optimal feature selection is one such case. The branch and bound algorithm for feature subset selection (Narendra and Fukunaga, 1977) explored only 5,646 subsets compared to 2,704,156 subsets under exhaustive search to find the best 12 features out of 24 features. Although this required the use of a monotonic criterion function. A similar strategy has been used to design an efficient algorithm to identify the nearest neighbor of a test pattern (Kamgar-Parsi and Kanal, 1985). A parallel scheme for performing branch and bound search is given by Kumar and Kanal (1984). Miclet and Dabouz (1983) propose a $O(n \log n)$ algorithm to find an "approximate" nearest neighbor of a test pattern, where n is the number of training patterns.

A novel scheme to reduce the processing time of a maximum likelihood classifier is proposed by Feivson (1983). Usual implementations of maximum likelihood classifiers require the evaluation of a probability density function for each pattern class for every pattern to be classified. When the number of pattern classes and the number of patterns to be classified is large (*e.g.*, in remote sensing), the computation time for such a scheme is very large. Feivson computes a set of fixed thresholds $\{T_{ij}\}, i, j = 1, \ldots, C, i \neq j$, such that for a given pattern vector $\underline{x}$ if $p(\underline{x} \mid w_i) > T$ then $p(\underline{x} \mid w_i)$ "dominates" $p(\underline{x} \mid w_j)$ and there is no need to evaluate the density function for class w_j. If the underlying densities are continuous, unimodal, and quasi-concave then these thresholds are optimal. For a nine-class classification problem in remote sensing, the average number of densities evaluated per pattern vector was equal to 3.99.

3.3. Computational Geometry

In pattern recognition, decisions often have to be made about patterns residing in a spatial region. For example, the decision of whether a given pattern is the Kth nearest neighbor of another given pattern is used frequently in cluster analysis and decision making. In addition to classification, we are also interested in the spatial distribution of point patterns. For example, epidemiologists may collect the locations of occurrences of some rare disease over some time interval to determine whether there may be some regions of unusually high incidence (Ripley, 1981). Graph-based techniques are useful to capture the spatial relationship and the distribution of patterns. In this context the most frequent use of graphs is as a criterion for selecting a subset of interpoint distances for clustering or to define a neighborhood function on the points for K-nearest neighbor decision rule.

There has been considerable recent development and interest in the discipline of computational geometry, which concerns itself with the implementation and complexity of geometric decisions. Through these efforts, more efficient algorithms are now available for computing nearest neighbors, minimal spanning tree, convex hull etc. which are useful both in pattern recognition and image processing (Lee and Preparata, 1984; Toussaint, 1980). For example, a naive approach to constructing the Gabriel graph of a set of patterns in two dimensions has complexity $O(n^3)$, where n is the number of patterns. However, by initially constructing, the Delaunay triangulation of the data and pruning its edges, it is possible to obtain the Gabriel Graph in $O(n \log n)$ time (Supowit, 1981). Urquhart (1982) presents a method for clustering data which utilizes the relative neighborhood graph and Gabriel graph. Chaudhuri (1985) investigates the use of hierarchical data structures such as binary tree, quadtree, octree, and their generalizations for pattern recognition applications.

Many useful geometrical tasks are NP-complete. For such problems the general approach involves either developing algorithms that approximately solve the task in polynomial time, or algorithms which will provide exact solutions and yet run quickly most of the time. As an example, Kallay (1986) has expressed the problem of determining if a target point lies in the convex hull of a set of points in terms of a linear programming problem, which can be implemented to provide an exact solution in essentially polynomial time.

Computational complexity is an important factor in the investigation of graph structures. While efficient algorithms are available for computing these graph structures in two and sometimes in three dimensions, they are not practical to use for high dimensional data. Thus most of the recent developments in computational geometry are applicable only to two- or three-dimensional patterns. Various problems in two-dimensional image processing such as texture modeling, shape analysis, and point pattern matching have benefited substantially from new developments in computational geometry.

3.4. Use of VLSI Systems

Many pattern classification algorithms are inherently time consuming and require large amounts of storage. In order for a recognition system to operate in "real time" mode, these algorithms have to be implemented in hardware. Special VLSI chips can now be designed and built for a specific algorithm which speed-up the operation by taking advantage of pipelining and parallelism (Fu, 1984, Bhavsar *et al.*, 1985). VLSI designs are now available for matrix operation, minimum-distance classification, clustering, string matching, and several graph algorithms. This will have the effect that the designers of a pattern recognition system need no longer discard an algorithm or an approach just because it takes too much time.

Several special computer architectures have also been implemented to solve pattern recognition problems in real-time. One such system, called Massively Parallel Processor (MPP), is being tested at NASA Goddard (Tilton and Strong, 1984) to analyze remotely sensed data. The MPP is a Single Instruction, Multiple Data Stream (SIMD) computer containing 16,384 processors connected in a 128×128 array. With a parallel computer like MPP it is now more practical to incorporate contextual and spatial information in decision making. Preliminary analysis indicates that a contextual classifier (Swain *et al.*, 1981) implemented on a MPP will result in a speed-up factor of at least 500 over a serial processor. A 512×512 multispectral image containing 4 channels of LANDSAT D data can be partitioned into 16 clusters using the ISODATA clustering algorithm

(100 iterations) in 18 seconds on the MPP compared to 7 hours on a VAX-11/780 computer. Ni and Jain (1985) also report similar speed-up with a two-level pipelined systolic pattern clustering array. Conventional maximum likelihood classifier has also been implemented on the MPP.

3.5. Utilizing Context And Domain-Specific Knowledge

Recent experience with the design of complex recognition systems indicates that maximum similarity alone is not adequate to recognize patterns. A satisfactory solution to most recognition problems requires the utilization of context and domain-specific knowledge in decision making (Toussaint, 1978). The role of context is to resolve ambiguities in the class assignment of a pattern based on the labelings of the "neighboring" patterns. It has been successfully used as a post-processing step in text recognition (regular occurrences of a particular combination of letters qu, ee, est, tion; Hull *et al.*, 1983) and remote sensing (no wheat fields in residential areas; Swain *et al.*, 1981). Context is often incorporated through the use of compound decision theory or Markovian models (Haslett, 1985).

Domain-specific knowledge has always played an important role in designing a classifier. The choice of features, and the grouping of pattern classes in forming a decision tree are based on this knowledge. This knowledge is especially important when the difficulty of the classification problem increases (contrast the situation when only the machine printed numerals have to be recognized against the recognition of two thousand hand written chinese characters). In several recognition problems, such as speech understanding, it is not necessary that individual "items", either phonemes or words, be correctly classified as long as the intent of the utterance is understood. In order to achieve this level of performance, higher level constraints in the form of syntactic and semantic knowledge is needed. The recognition accuracy can be substantially improved if both bottom-up (data driven) and top-down (knowledge driven) approaches are implemented (Smith and Erman, 1981).

Lately there has been an emphasis on building expert systems to make difficult decisions in a specific domain (*e.g.*, medical diagnosis, geology). An expert system is generally knowledgeable about the actions it must take to achieve one of its goals in a restricted environment. This knowledge, which is acquired from experts in the field, consists of domain facts and heuristics. While pattern recognition systems also utilize this same information, an expert system stores this information explicitly in a Knowledge Base so that it can be easily accessed and modified. Further, these facts and heuristics are often stored as "rules" in terms of symbolic information rather than strictly numerical information. Thus a cell can be described as "abnormal" if it is "dark blue, not round, has coarse texture, and is unusually large compared to neighboring cells". A confidence score, between 0 and 1, can also be assigned to this rule. A rule can be viewed as one path from the root to a leaf node in the hierarchical classifier. Techniques from artificial intelligence are used for acquiring and efficiently storing this knowledge. An expert system also contains an inference procedure or a control structure to utilize the facts and heuristics stored in the Knowledge Base to a given situation or a pattern. This module of the expert system determines the order in which rules should be applied in a given situation and how to merge evidence provided by different rules.

Bayes decision theory is one of the techniques used for this purpose. But other inference techniques from artificial intelligence (*e.g.*, automatic theorem proving) are also used.

Many of the expert systems currently available (*e.g.*, MYCIN, PROSPECTOR) essentially solve the classification problem. However, they differ from traditional pattern recognition systems in the use of symbolic information rather than numerical information (Chandrasekaran, 1986). Conventional pattern recognition techniques will continue to play an important role, but they will need to be augmented by new techniques from artificial intelligence as the application domains get more complex and the emphasis shifts from classification to description.

4. Summary

Pattern recognition has emerged as a mature discipline over the past twenty-five years. The earliest applications of pattern recognition included character recognition and classification of white blood cells. Since then pattern recognition techniques have been successfully applied to remote sensing, speaker identification, non-destructive testing (X-ray, eddy current, ultrasound), target identification, and various biomedical applications [32,33]. There are several approaches to classification, none of them 'optimal'. Therefore, it is important to try out various approaches when designing a classification system for a new application.

Current research emphasis in pattern recognition is on designing efficient algorithms, studying the small sample properties of various estimators and decision rules, implementing the algorithms on novel computer architectures, and incorporating context and domain-specific knowledge in decision making.

Acknowledgment

This research was supported by NSF Grant ECS-8603541

References

[1] T. Bailey and A.K. Jain, "A note on distance-weighted K-nearest neighbor rules," IEEE Trans. Systems, Man, and Cybernetics, Vol. 8, 1978, pp. 311-313.

[2] V.C. Bhavsar, T.Y.T. Chan and L. Goldfarb, "On the metric approach to pattern recognition and VLSI implementation," Proceedings IEEE Computer Society Workshop on Computer Architecture for Pattern Analysis and Image Data Base Management, Miami Beach, 1985, pp. 126-136.

[3] G. Biswas, A.K. Jain and R. Dubes, "Evaluation of projection algorithms," IEEE Trans. Pattern Analysis and Machine Intelligence, Vol. 3, 1981, pp. 701-708.

[4] B.B. Chaudhuri, "Application of quadtree, octree, and binary tree decomposition techniques to shape analysis and pattern recognition," IEEE Trans. Pattern Analysis and Machine Intelligence, Vol. 7, 1985, pp. 652-661.

[5] B. Chandrasekaran, "From numbers to symbols to knowledge structures: Pattern recognition and artificial intelligence perspectives on the classification task," in Pattern Recognition in Practice, Vol. 2, E.S. Gelsema and L.N. Kanal (Eds.), North Holland, 1986.

[6] Y. Cheng and K.S. Fu, "Conceptual clustering in knowledge organization," Proceedings First IEEE Conference on Artificial Intelligence Applications, Denver, 1984, pp. 274-279.

[7] M.R. Chernick, V.K. Murthy and C.D. Nealy, "Application of bootstrap and other resampling techniques: Evaluation of classifier performance," Pattern Recognition Letters, Vol. 3, 1985, pp. 167-178.

[8] D.K.Y. Chiu and A.K.C. Wong, "Synthesizing knowledge: A cluster analysis approach using event covering," to appear in IEEE Trans. Systems, Man, and Cybernetics, 1986.

[9] P.R. Cohen, Heuristic Reasoning About Uncertainty: An Artificial Intelligence Approach, Pitman, 1985.

[10] T. M. Cover and J. M. Van Campenhout, "On the Possible orderings in the measurement selection Problem," IEEE Trans. Systems, Man and Cybernetics, Vol. 7, 1977, pp. 657-661.

[11] G.R. Dattatreya and L.N. Kanal, "Decision trees in pattern recognition," Technical Report TR-1429, Machine Intelligence and Pattern Analysis Laboratory, University of Maryland, 1985.

[12] W.H.E. Day and R.S. Wells, "Extremes in the complexity of computing metric distances between partitions," IEEE Trans. Pattern Analysis and Machine Intelligence, Vol. 6, 1984, pp. 69-73.

[13] P.A. Devijver and M. Dekesel, "Insert and delete algorithms for maintaining dynamic Delaunay triangulations," Pattern Recognition Letters, Vol. 1, 1982, pp. 73-77.

[14] P. Devijver and J. Kittler, Statistical Pattern Recognition, Prentice Hall, 1982.

[15] L. Devroye and F. Machell, "Data structures in kernel density estimation," IEEE Trans. Pattern Analysis and Machine Intelligence, Vol. 7, 1985, pp. 360-366.

[16] R. Dubes and A. K. Jain, "Clustering methodology in exploratory data analysis," in Advances in Computers, Vol. 19, M. Yovits (Ed.), Academic Press, 1980.

[17] R. Dubes and A. K. Jain, "Validity studies in clustering methodology," Pattern Recognition, Vol. 11, 1979, pp. 235-254.

[18] R. O. Duda and P. E. Hart, Pattern Classification and Scene Analysis, Wiley, New-York, 1973.

[19] B. Efron, "Estimating the error rate of the prediction rule: Improvements on cross validation, JASA, Vol. 78, 1983, pp. 316-331.

[20] B. Efron, "The jackknife, the bootstrap and other resampling plans", Society for Industrial and Applied Mathematics, Philadelphia, 1982.

[21] A. H. Feiveson, "Classification by thresholding," IEEE Trans. Pattern Analysis and Machine Intelligence, Vol. 5, Jan. 1983, pp. 48-54.

[22] D.H. Foley, "Consideration of sample and feature size," IEEE Trans. Information Theory, Vol. 18, 1982, pp. 618-626.

[23] K.S. Fu, "A step towards unification of syntactic and statistical pattern recognition," IEEE Trans. Pattern Analysis and Machine Intelligence, Vol. 8, 1986, pp. 398-404.

[24] K.S. Fu (Editor), VLSI for Pattern Recognition and Image Processing, Springer Verlag, 1984.

[25] K.S. Fu (Editor), Applications of Pattern Recognition, CRC Press, 1982.

[26] K.S. Fu, Syntactic Pattern Recognition and Applications, Prentice Hall, 1982.

[27] K. Fukunaga and D.M. Hummels, "Bias of nearest neighbor error estimates," to appear in IEEE Trans. on Pattern Analysis and Machine Intelligence, 1986.

[28] K. Fukunaga and T.E. Flick, "A test of the Gaussian-ness of a data set using clustering," IEEE Trans. Pattern Analysis and Machine Intelligence, Vol. 8, 1986, pp. 240-247.

[29] K. Fukunaga and T.E. Flick, "Classification error for a very large number of classes," IEEE Trans. Pattern Analysis and Machine Intelligence, Vol. 6, 1984, pp. 779-788.

[30] K. Fukunaga and T. Flick, "An optimal global nearest neighbor metric," IEEE Trans. Pattern Analysis and Machine Intelligence, Vol. 6, 1984, pp. 314-318.

[31] K. Fukunaga and J.M. Mantock, "Nonparametric discriminant analysis," IEEE Trans. Pattern Analysis and Machine Intelligence, Vol. 5, 1983, pp. 671-678.

[32] K. Fukunaga and S. Ando, "The optimum nonlinear features for a scatter criterion in discriminant analysis," IEEE Trans. Information Theory, Vol. 23, 1977, pp. 453-459.

[33] K. Fukunaga and R.D. Short, "Generalized clustering for problem localization," IEEE Trans. Computers, Vol. 27, 1978, pp. 176-181.

[34] T.D. Garvey, J.D. Lawrence and M.A. Fishler, "An inference technique for integrating knowledge from disparate sources," Proceedings IJCAI, Vancouver, 1981, pp. 319-325.

[35] R.C. Gonzalez and M.G. Thomason, Syntactic Pattern Recognition: An Introduction, Addison-Wesley, 1978.

[36] P. Hall, "Large sample optimality of least squares cross-validation in density estimation," Annals of Statistics, Vol. 11, 1983, pp. 1156- 1174.

[37] J. Haslett, "Maximum likelihood discriminant analysis on the plane using a Markovian model of spatial context," Pattern Recognition Journal, Vol. 18, 1985, pp. 287-296.

[38] J.J. Hull, S.N. Srihari and R. Choudhari, "An integrated algorithm for text recognition: Comparison with a cascaded algorithm," IEEE Trans. Pattern Analysis and Machine Intelligence, Vol. 5, 1983, pp. 384-395.

[39] A. K. Jain and B. Chandrasekaran, "Dimensionality and sample size consideration in pattern recognition practice," in Handbook of Statistics, Vol. 2, P. R. Krishnaiah and L. N. Kanal (Eds.), North Holland, 1982, pp. 835-855.

[40] A.K. Jain, R.C. Dubes and C.C. Chen, "Bootstrap techniques for error estimation," submitted to IEEE Trans. Pattern Analysis and Machine Intelligence, 1986.

[41] M.M. Kalayeh and D.A. Landgrebe, "Predicting the required number of training samples," IEEE Trans. Pattern Analysis and Machine Intelligence, Vol. 5, November 1983, pp. 664-667.

[42] M. Kallay, "Convex hull made easy," Information Processing Letters, Vol. 22, 1986, pp. 161.

[43] B. Kamgar-Parsi and L.N. Kanal, "An improved branch and bound algorithm for computing k-nearest neighbors," Pattern Recognition Letters, Vol. 3, 1985, pp. 7-12.

[44] J.P. Keating and R.L. Mason, "Some practical aspects of covariance estimation," Pattern Recognition Letters, Vol. 3, 1985, pp. 295-298.

[45] V. Kumar and L.N. Kanal, "Parallel branch-and-bound formulation for AND/OR tree search," IEEE Trans. Pattern Analysis and Machine Intelligence, Vol. 6, 1984, pp. 768-778.

[46] D. T. Lee and F. P. Preparata, "Computational geometry: A survey," IEEE Trans. Computers, Vol. 33, 1984, pp. 1072-1101.

[47] X. Li and R. Dubes, "A new statistic for tree classifier design," to appear in Pattern Recognition, 1986.

[48] W. Maline, "On an extended Fisher criterion for feature selection," IEEE Trans. Pattern Analysis and Machine Intelligence, Vol. 3, 1981, pp. 611-614.

[49] L. Miclet and M. Dabouz, "Approximative fast nearest-neighbor recognition," Pattern Recognition Letters, Vol. 1, 1983, pp. 277-285.

[50] R.S. Michalski and R.E. Stepp III, "Automated construction of classification: Conceptual clustering versus numerical taxonomy," IEEE Trans. Pattern Analysis and Machine Intelligence, Vol. 5, 1983, pp. 396-410.

[51] S.D. Morgera, "Linear, structured covariance estimation: An application to pattern classification for remote sensing," Pattern Recognition Letters, Vol. 4, 1986, pp. 1-7.

[52] J. K. Mui and K. S. Fu, "Automated classification of nucleated blood cells using binary tree classifier," IEEE Trans. Pattern Analysis and Machine Intelligence, Vol. 2, 1980, pp. 429-443.

[53] M. Nagao, "Control strategies in pattern analysis," Pattern Recognition, Vol. 17, 1984, pp. 45-56.

[54] G. Nagy, "Candide's practical principles of experimental pattern recognition," IEEE Trans. on Pattern Analysis and Machine Intelligence, Vol. 5, 1983, pp. 199-200.

[55] N. Nandhakumar and J.K. Aggarawal, "The artificial intelligence approach to pattern recognition—a perspective and an overview," Pattern Recognition, Vol. 18, 1985, pp. 383-389.

[56] P. M. Narendra and K. Fukunaga, "A branch and bound algorithm for feature subset selection," IEEE Trans. Computers, Vol. 26, 1977, pp. 917-922.

[57] L.M. Ni and A.K. Jain, "A VLSI systolic architecture for pattern clustering," IEEE Trans. on Pattern Analysis and Machine Intelligence, Vol. 7, 1985, pp. 80-89.

[58] E. Oja and M. Kuusela, "The ALSM algorithm—An improved subspace method for classification," Pattern Recognition, Vol. 16, 1983, pp. 421-427.

[59] T. Okada and S. Tomita, "An optimal orthonormal system for discriminant analysis," Pattern Recognition, Vol. 18, 1985, pp. 139-144.

[60] T. Pavlidis, Structural Pattern Recognition, Springer Verlag, 1977.

[61] R. Peck and J. Van Ness, "The use of shrinkage estimators in linear discriminant analysis," IEEE Trans. Pattern Analysis and Machine Intelligence, Vol. 4, 1982, pp. 530-537.

[62] J.G. Postaire and C. Vasseur, "A fast algorithm for nonparametric probability density estimation," IEEE Trans. Pattern Analysis and Machine Intelligence, Vol. 4, 1982, pp. 663-666.

[63] B.D. Ripley, Spatial Statistics, Wiley, 1981.

[64] I.K. Sethi and G.P.R. Sarvarayudu, "Hierarchical classifier design using mutual information," IEEE Trans. Pattern Analysis and Machine Intelligence, Vol. 4, 1982, pp. 441-445.

[65] A.R. Smith and L.D. Erman, "Noah—A bottom-up word hypothesizer for large-vocabulary speech understanding systems," IEEE Trans. Pattern Analysis and Machine Intelligence, Vol. 3, 1981, pp. 41-51.

[66] S.P. Smith, "A window-width selection rule for kernel-based density estimation," Technical Report, Northrop Research and Technology Center, Palos Verdes Peninsula, CA, 1986.

[67] S.P. Smith and A.K. Jain, "An experiment on using the Friedman-Rafsky test to determine the multivariate normality of a data set," Proceedings IEEE CVPR Conference, San Francisco, 1985, pp. 423-425.

[68] S.P. Smith and A.K. Jain, "Testing for uniformity in multidimensional data," IEEE Trans. Pattern Analysis and Machine Intelligence, Vol. 6, 1984, pp. 73-81.

[69] K.J. Supowit, "Topics in computational geometry," Ph.D. thesis, Department of Computer Science, University of Illinois, Urbana, 1981.

[70] P. H. Swain, S.B. Vardeman and J.C. Tilton, "Contextual classification of multispectral image data," Pattern Recognition, Vol. 13, 1981, pp. 429-441.

[71] J.C. Tilton and J.P. Strong, "Analyzing remotely sensed data on the massively parallel processor," Proceedings Seventh International Conference on Pattern Recognition, Montreal, 1974, pp. 398-400.

[72] G. T. Toussaint, "The use of context in pattern recognition," Pattern Recognition, Vol. 10, 1978, pp. 189-204.

[73] G.T. Toussaint, "Pattern recognition and geometrical complexity," Proceedings 5th International Conference on Pattern Recognition, Miami Beach, 1980, pp. 1324-1327.

[74] G.V. Trunk, "A problem of dimensionality: A simple example," IEEE Trans. Pattern Analysis and Machine Intelligence, Vol. 1, 1979, pp. 306-307.

[75] R.B. Urquhart, "Graph theoretical clustering based on limited neighborhood sets," Pattern Recognition, Vol. 15, 1982, pp. 173-187.

[76] J. Van Ness, "On the dominance of non-parametric Bayes rule discriminant algorithms in high dimensions," Pattern Recognition Journal, Vol. 12, 1980, pp. 355-368.

[77] N. Wyse, A.K. Jain and R. Dubes, "A critical review of intrinsic dimensionality algorithms," in Pattern Recognition in Practice, E.S. Gelsema and L.N. Kanal (eds.), North Holland, 1980, pp. 415-425.

TEXTURE SUBSPACES

Erkki Oja and Jussi Parkkinen

Department of Computer Science and Mathematics
Kuopio University
POB 6, 70211 Kuopio, Finland

Abstract

The subspace method of pattern recognition has been developed for fast and accurate classification of high-dimensional feature vectors, especially power spectra and distribution densities. The basic algorithms for class subspace construction are statistically motivated, and the classification is based on inner products. In texture analysis, this method has been previously applied for two-dimensional spatial frequency spectra. In this work we show that a feasible method for texture window classification is to use a smoothed cooccurrence matrix as the feature vector and to define texture classes for such representations by the subspace method. These texture subspaces seem to capture the characteristic second-order properties of texture fields. Results are given using various natural and synthetic textures.

1. Introduction

Texture features are known to contain significant discriminatory information for image segmentation in a variety of applications like terrain classification from remote sensing images and biomedical image analysis. Statistical methods in texture analysis use statistical classification algorithms applied on features derived from the preprocessed image. Some of the commonly used features in this category are based on Fourier spectra, grey value cooccurrence matrices and difference histograms, run length matrices, spatial domain filter masks or texture field models like autoregression or Markov random field models [9]. The popularity of features based on second order statistics originates from studies on the human visual system, especially the well-known conjecture by Julesz [12] which seems to be valid for natural textures despite some counterexamples [3].

One of the most successful second-order statistical representations for texture is the grey-level cooccurrence matrix, defined as a sample estimate of the joint probability density of the grey levels of two pixels separated by a given distance and given direction. Haralick *et al.*, [10] gave a now classical set of scalar features to be extracted from the cooccurrence matrix. Five of them are generally used in texture analysis: energy, entropy, correlation, homogeneity and inertia. Because these features do not seem to take into account enough of the information contained in the cooccurrence matrix, some new features have been added to the list [5].

For frequency domain texture analysis, some suggested features are integrals over ring- or wedge-shaped subsets of the spatial frequency space [16]; various heuristic peak

NATO ASI Series, Vol. F30
Pattern Recognition Theory and Applications
Edited by P. A. Devijver and J. Kittler

position and shape characteristics [6]; and descriptions of closed planar curves obtained from contours of optical Fourier spectra [8]. Since many of such features are chosen on a rather *ad hoc* basis, it is not easy to see which statistical classifier would be optimal for such a feature space. However, the experimental results seem to point out that the spatial frequency domain should not be abandoned in the search for efficient classification of texture fields.

The usual approach in classifying textures by either frequency spectra or cooccurrence histograms is to first compute some set of scalar features and then classify these by some standard classification algorithm. A considerable part of the literature in the field suggests new and often quite elaborate sets of texture features, with much less emphasis and few comparisons on the classification algorithm itself. A recent survey is [24].

The approach to texture classification and clustering advocated in this paper is based on two objectives: first, the feature set should preserve as much of the discriminatory information of the texture as possible, and second, the classifier applied on the feature set should be somehow adapted to take optimal advantage of this information. The solution that we propose and test to the information loss problem is to use the cooccurrence matrix as such, with a suitable number of grey level pairs, in classification and clustering. No explicit features are extracted. In this manner little texture information is lost when going from the raw digital image to the texture representation. Another advantage is a computational one: once the cooccurrence matrix estimate is obtained for a texture window, the time-consuming step of computing values for the features is totally omitted.

A suitable classifier for such a relatively large feature matrix is then the subspace method of pattern recognition [17]. With this technique, good results have been obtained earlier in classifying spectral phonemes in speech recognition [15]. In an earlier paper [21], the present authors showed that this approach works well for texture power spectra, too.

Related approaches to the texture feature extraction proposed here are [23] and [25] in which the cooccurrence matrix is also used as such. However, the data compression and classification methods in those references are quite different.

The subspace method essentially combines feature extraction and classification into one algorithm by finding an optimal set of linear features for each texture class separately, the optimality being defined in terms of the classification rule of the method. Such linear features work well for discrete distribution densities, e.g., frequency spectra and grey-level cooccurrence histograms, and the resulting classification rule is very fast to compute. This is essential because 2-D discrete densities may have a large number of value pair categories, each of which adds one dimension to the feature vector.

Section 2 gives an overview of the subspace method of pattern recognition, with emphasis on the two algorithms applied to textures. An iterative clustering algorithm, a special case of the *Dynamic Clusters Algorithm* [7], discussed by the present authors in [20], represents the clusters by subspaces of fixed dimensions and rotates these subspaces until they converge to optimal representations of the clusters. An iterative classification algorithm called the *ALSM*, introduced by one of the authors [18] on the basis of the *Learning Subspace Method* [15], optimizes the classification for a design sample by learning from erroneous classifications.

In Section 3, these algorithms are applied to texture classification and clustering and the results are compared to those obtained with some standard methods. In Section 4, some conclusions are drawn.

2. An Overview of the Subspace Method

2.1. Subspaces as Representations for Classes

Subspace methods are statistical vector space methods. They assume a Euclidean multidimensional pattern space in which each object can be represented as a point, and hence they belong to the low-level feature classification stage of the general pattern recognition paradigm. By statistical we simply mean that the measurements contain uncertainty, which is almost always the case in analyzing real-world objects.

A subspace in the n-dimensional pattern space, denoted $\mathcal{L}(a_1, a_2, \ldots, a_p)$, is defined as the vector set

$$\mathcal{L} = \mathcal{L}(a_1, a_2, \ldots, a_p) = \{z | z = \sum_1^p \zeta_i a_i \text{ for some scalars } \zeta_1, \ldots, \zeta_p\}. \tag{1}$$

The number p of linearly independent vectors a_i spanning the subspace is its dimension. For a p-dimensional subspace, there always exists an orthonormal basis of p vectors.

Geometrically, a subspace restricts the possible directions of the vectors in it, while the lengths remain undetermined. For some object representations, such a property is very natural. One- or multi-dimensional discrete histograms or densities are an example. Consider a noisy acoustic signal comprised of p basic frequencies with randomly varying amplitudes and phases. The power spectral density is spanned by p functions with sharp peaks at the basic frequencies. Any linear combination lies in the subspace spanned by these basis functions.

Another example, to be discussed more thoroughly in Section 3, is the cooccurrence matrix of a digital image region, whose entries give the numbers of pixel pairs at a given spatial displacement and with given grey values. If the cooccurrence matrix is plotted as a histogram, each peak reveals a feature of the underlying texture. When the cooccurrence matrix is stacked row by row into a vector, this vector is roughly in a subspace which is characteristic of the texture. The length of the vector has no significance, which is revealed by the fact that histograms are routinely normalized by dividing each entry by their sum.

Assume, then, that each of the K classes $\omega^{(1)}, \ldots, \omega^{(K)}$ in a classification problem is represented by a subspace of the n-dimensional pattern space. These are denoted $\mathcal{L}^{(1)}, \ldots, \mathcal{L}^{(K)}$ with $p^{(i)} = \dim(\mathcal{L}^{(i)}), i = 1, \ldots, K$. Each subspace is spanned by $p^{(i)}$ orthonormal vectors $u_j^{(i)}, j = 1, \ldots, p^{(i)}$. Often each $p^{(i)}$ is considerably smaller than n. For a pattern vector x, the classification rule is

$$\text{if } \delta(x, \mathcal{L}^{(i)}) < \delta(x, \mathcal{L}^{(j)}) \text{ for all } j \neq i, \text{then classify } x \text{ in class } \omega^{(i)}, \tag{2}$$

where $\delta(x, \mathcal{L})$ denotes the distance of vector x from a subspace $\mathcal{L}$. In terms of the orthonormal basis vectors $u_1, \ldots, u_p$ of $\mathcal{L}$ the distance is computed as

$$\delta(x, \mathcal{L}) = \sqrt{\|x\|^2 - \sum_1^p (x^T u_i)^2}. \tag{3}$$

Equivalently, squared distances can be used in eq. (2). Since $\|x\|^2$ is then the same for each class, it can be dropped. This means that for the classification rule (2), all we need is the inner products of x and all the basis vectors of all the classes. If the sum of dimensions of all the subspaces is relatively small, the classification rule is fast to compute. Furthermore, since the basis vectors have unit norm and, due to the insensitivity of the subspace classifier to vector lengths, also vector x can be similarly normed, integer arithmetic can often be used. This property is very useful in real-time applications like speech recognition. In [22], a microprocessor implementation is reported in which the classification is performed by an array processor.

In some cases, a similarity measure or distance between two subspaces are needed. One example is a short-cut method to compute rule (2) in which all the distances need not be computed [22]. Another example is subspace clustering in which merging and splitting of clusters defined by subspaces becomes necessary [20]. For the distance of a lower-dimensional subspace $\mathcal{L}$ from a higher-dimensional subspace $\mathcal{M}$, a natural generalization of (3) is

$$\rho(\mathcal{L},\mathcal{M}) = \max_{x\in\mathcal{S}} \delta(x,\mathcal{M}), \tag{4}$$

with $\mathcal{S}$ the compact unit sphere in $\mathcal{L}$. If $\mathcal{L}$ and $\mathcal{M}$ have equal dimensions, then it can be shown that (4) is a metric in the set of subspaces, often called the "aperture" or "gap" between the two subspaces [1]. In [20], a method has been given to compute (4) in terms of the orthonormal basis vectors of the two subspaces, producing as a side result the canonical angles between the subspaces.

An essential question in the subspace method of pattern recognition is how to actually construct all the class subspaces in order to obtain an optimal performance in practical data classification. An overview of this problem is given in [17, chapter 4]. The *CLAFIC* method [26] is based on a minimum mean square criterion. The class subspace $\mathcal{L}^{(i)}$ or, equivalently, the orthonormal basis vectors of subspace $\mathcal{L}^{(i)}$, corresponding to the class $\omega^{(i)}$, are determined from

$$\text{minimize } E\{\delta^2(x,\mathcal{L}^{(i)})|x\in\omega^{(i)}\}. \tag{5}$$

This reduces to the problem

$$\text{maximize } \textstyle\sum_1^{p^{(i)}}(u_j^T C u_j) \tag{6}$$

where $u_1,\ldots,u_{p^{(i)}}$ are the $p^{(i)}$ orthonormal basis vectors of $\mathcal{L}^{(i)}$. Matrix C, defined as

$$C = E\{xx^T|x\in\omega^{(i)}\}, \tag{7}$$

is the autocorrelation matrix of class $\omega^{(i)}$. The solution, based on Lagrange multipliers, gives the vectors $u_1,\ldots,u_{p^{(i)}}$ as the $p^{(i)}$ eigenvectors of C corresponding to the largest eigenvalues. If the data vectors x have been statistically normalized to zero mean, these vectors are the Karhunen-Lòeve basis vectors. Such a normalization, however, should not be performed unless the class means are taken into account separately in the classification. For unnormalized data, the first eigenvector corresponding to the largest eigenvalue is in some cases quite close to the class mean, depending on the eigenvalue distribution.

Some variations and generalizations to the basic *CLAFIC* procedure have been given by [11], [13], and [17]. An iterative method called *ALSM*, resulting in improved discrimination in a multiclass situation, will be briefly reviewed in section 2.2.

The subspace formalism may also be suitable to represent clusters in nonsupervised classification. Such an approach has been suggested in [7] as part of the *Dynamic Clusters Method* and further discussed in [20]. A subspace representation is a compromise between representing a cluster either by the set of all its members, or by the mean vector only. In the first case information loss is minimal, but distance measures based on the nearest-neighbor or furthest-neighbor principles are computationally heavy. The mean vector, although easy to use to define distances, may not contain enough information for e.g. merging schemes. A subspace representation of a cluster provides a natural set of parameter vectors whose number can be freely adjusted to achieve a trade-off between computational requirements and the accuracy of representation. The subspaces will be adjusted automatically to correspond to the most important feature dimensions of each underlying class, and they provide compact descriptions of the clusters.

In cluster analysis, no unique general-purpose algorithm exists, and the methods must be developed in interaction with the applications at hand. Subspace clustering, too, assumes an underlying structure of the object representations, of which frequency spectra and density histograms are an example.

In many practical cases the number of clusters is known at least approximately, or a sensible estimate of both the number of clusters and a relevant partition can be made based on the result of hierarchical clustering. In the following, an algorithm for the iterative formation of a set of subspaces with given dimensions and a given number of clusters is given. The procedure has been shown to converge to a local optimum in terms of a criterion function; see [7] and [20]. It is an extension of the basic *ISODATA*-type iteration to the case of subspace clustering.

Algorithm for iterative subspace clustering

> **begin**
> *form initial subspaces* $\mathcal{L}^{(1)}, \ldots, \mathcal{L}^{(K)}$ *with given dimensions;*
> **for** *each data vector* x **do**
>   *classify* x *in subspaces according to eq. (2);*
> **endfor**;
> **repeat until** *classification is stable;*
>   *based on current classifications, compute sample correlation*
>   *matrices* $C^{(i)}$ *and their eigenvectors;*
>   *form subspaces* $\mathcal{L}^{(i)}$ *from the eigenvectors;*
>   **for** *each data vector* x **do**
>   *classify* x *in subspaces according to eq. (2);*
>   **endfor**;
> **endrepeat**;
> **end**.

The algorithm has been tested on EEG spectra in a biomedical application and on texture power spectra in digital image analysis. The latter application is explained in Section 4.

2.2. The ALSM Algorithm

A drawback of the *CLAFIC* method is that each class subspace, although depending on the statistics of that class through the optimization criterion (5) or (6), is formed independently of the statistical properties of the *other* classes. This means that two classes which are partly overlapping can be very difficult to separate by this subspace method. A crude improvement was suggested in [19]: instead of criterion (5), one could try

$$\text{maximize} \sum_{j \neq i}^{K} E\{\delta^2(x, \mathcal{L}^{(i)})|x \in \omega^{(j)}\} - E\{\delta^2(x, \mathcal{L}^{(i)})|x \in \omega^{(i)}\} \tag{8}$$

This criterion tends to define the subspace $\mathcal{L}^{(i)}$ so as to maximize the average squared distances of all vectors of the other classes and at the same time minimize those of the vectors of the i-th class itself. Eq. (8) leads to the choice of the dominant eigenvectors of matrix

$$\bar{C}^{(i)} = C^{(i)} - \sum_{j \neq i} C^{(j)} \tag{9}$$

as the basis vectors of subspace $\mathcal{L}^{(i)}$. However, when tested, this method yields only a minor improvement over *CLAFIC* [17]. Intuitively, it seems to be too crude a way to maximize the average squared distances of all the vectors in the other classes from the present subspace, since most of these vectors would never be misclassified anyway. In a multiclass situation, the sum matrix on the right hand side of eq. (9) tends to be rather similar for all i, and it dominates over matrix $C^{(i)}$, which has the effect of blurring the differences between class subspaces. A better way would be to include in the average in eq. (8) only those vectors that are misclassified for the present class $\omega^{(i)}$. This is a starting-point for the *Averaged Learning Subspace Method (ALSM).*

In that algorithm, an iterative approach is taken using a representative training sample from each class. This is necessary because the class regions getting misclassified cannot be found from any close-form expression in a non-parametric method like the subspace method. The *ALSM* algorithm was motivated by the *LSM* algorithm introduced earlier [14],[15]; in fact, it could be derived from the *LSM* using averaging techniques [18].

In *ALSM*, sample estimates of *conditional correlation matrices* are used, where the conditioning events are the two types of misclassification: either a sample vector of class $\omega^{(i)}$ is misclassified into another class, say $\omega^{(j)}$, or a sample vector of another class, say $\omega^{(k)}$, is misclassified into class $\omega^{(i)}$. Denote the unnormalized conditional correlation matrix estimate by

$$S^{(i,j)} = \sum_{x} \{xx^T | x \in \omega^{(i)}, x \mapsto \omega^{(j)}\} \tag{10}$$

with $\mapsto$ denoting "gets classified into" . At each step of the iteration, there exist *current subspaces* for all the classes, and based on them all data vectors x can be classified and all matrices $S^{(i,j)}, i, j = 1, \ldots, K$ can be computed.

Algorithm ALSM for constructing the classification subspaces

begin
compute (unnormalized) class correlation matrix estimates $\hat{C}^{(1)}, \ldots, \hat{C}^{(K)}$;

form initial subspaces $\mathcal{L}^{(1)}, \ldots, \mathcal{L}^{(K)}$ *with given dimensions*
using CLAFIC procedure of eq. (6);
repeat until *classification is stable or given number of steps;*
for *each data vector* x **do**
classify x *in current subspaces according to eq. (2);*
if x *is classified incorrectly* **then**
update the respective conditional correlation matrix $S^{(i,j)}$;
endif;
endfor; **for** $i = 1$ **to** K **do**
$\hat{C}^{(i)} := \hat{C}^{(i)} + \sum_{j \neq i} \alpha S^{(i,j)} - \sum_{k \neq i} \beta S^{(k,i)}$;
form new subspace $\mathcal{L}^{(i)}$ *from the dominant eigenvectors of* $S^{(i)}$;
endfor;
endrepeat;
end.

Note that the (unnormalized) conditional correlation matrices representing the misclassified vectors of class $\omega^{(i)}$ are *added* to matrix $\hat{C}^{(i)}$, while the matrices corresponding to the vectors of the other classes, misclassified into $\omega^{(i)}$, are *subtracted* from matrix $\hat{C}^{(i)}$. Both α and β are positive coefficients, which can in fact be chosen equal.

Good results have previously been obtained for the classification of phoneme spectra, when the *ALSM* algorithm was used to construct the class subspaces [18]. In a typical situation (18 classes, 30 dimensional spectral vectors, 3861 training vectors) the correct classification rate for an independent equally sized test sample was about 94 per cent, 10 per cent higher than the result using *CLAFIC*. In some cases for a smaller sample the algorithm in fact converged to a 100 per cent correct classification. More details can be found in [17].

3. Subspaces for Texture Clustering and Classification

3.1. Test Material

To test the applicability of the subspace method to texture analysis using cooccurrence matrices, we used 3 different texture sets in our experiments: 12 natural textures from Brodatz album [2], 4 real textures from paper industry and the two synthetic textures defined in [4].

The feature extraction method was as follows. The original images in all experiments were 256×256 images consisting of one type of texture only. The first-order grey value statistics were normalized by histogram flattening. From each image, $N \times N$ subimages were taken at random locations. The size of the subimage windows N was varied according to the experiment. From these subimages, unsymmetric cooccurrence matrices of size $G \times G$ were then computed, where G was the number of grey levels in the image. The cooccurrence matrix was smoothed by dividing it into $n \times n$ equally sized submatrices, and the average value of the matrix elements in each submatrix formed one component of the feature vector. This is equivalent to first representing the image obtained from histogram flattening with the resolution of n grey levels and then computing the cooccurrence matrix for this lower-resolution image in the usual manner.

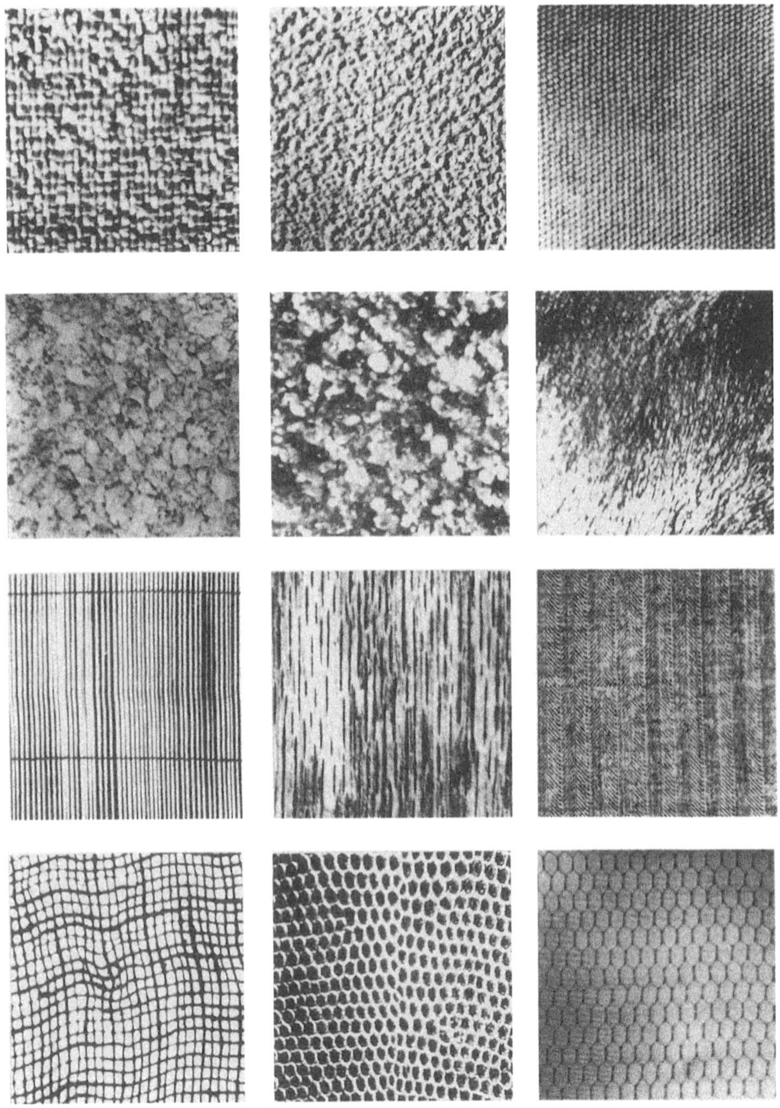

Figure 1: The Brodatz textures used

Geometrically, each feature vector is then in the positive octant of the n^2-dimensional Euclidean space. The feature vector thus obtained was classified or clustered by the subspace method.

In the first experiment we used natural textures from Brodatz album [2] (from top left to bottom right in Fig. 1, texture numbers 84,57,77,33,28,93,49,68,16,103,3,and 34). The value for window size N was either 64 or 32. The feature vector was a 16-component vector, *i.e.*, the cooccurrence matrices of preprocessed images with uniform histograms were divided into 16 submatrices of size 16×16 whose average values were computed. In fact the information loss in such averaging of the original 256×256 cooccurrence matrices is not as severe as it seems, since the histograms of the original texture images were peaked and concentrated on a rather narrow range of grey values. The displacement vector in the cooccurrence matrices was chosen as $\Delta x = 1$, $\Delta y = 0$, i.e. one pixel difference in the horizontal direction.

In the second experiment the 4 different textures shown in Fig. 2 were used. These textures look rather similar and rather random. 16 component cooccurrence feature vectors were formed in the sane manner as for the Brodatz textures. Different shift vectors were tried, but the change of the shift had a rather small effect on the accuracy of classification or clustering. The shift was chosen as $\Delta x = 2, \Delta y = 0$.

In the last experiment the method was tested with two synthetic textures, which cannot be separated by the five usual cooccurrence features described earlier in Section 1. The textures were synthetized in the same manner as in [4]. The Markov matrices for these textures are given in Table 1. There were only three grey levels in the images, and the feature vector was the whole cooccurrence matrix having 9 components. The shift vector was $\Delta x = 1, \Delta y = 0$, which should be suitable for these Markov matrices.

$$\begin{pmatrix} 0.8 & 0.0 & 0.2 \\ 0.0 & 0.4 & 0.6 \\ 0.2 & 0.6 & 0.2 \end{pmatrix} \qquad \begin{pmatrix} 0.2 & 0.6 & 0.2 \\ 0.6 & 0.4 & 0.0 \\ 0.2 & 0.0 & 0.8 \end{pmatrix}$$

Table 1. Synthetic texture field Markov matrices

3.2. Results

We have earlier [21] reported results on a comparison study of different texture feature sets, in which we used thirteen of Haralick's cooccurrence matrix features, four difference statistics histogram features, five run length matrix features, and six Fourier power spectrum features, which were compared to the use of the smoothed power spectrum as such as the feature vector. In those experiments, several clustering methods (nearest neighbor, farthest neighbor, average linkage, weighted average linkage, median method, centroid method, Ward's method, flexible strategy and subspace clustering) as well as two classification methods (multiple discriminant analysis based on Wilks'lambda criterion and the *ALSM* subspace algorithm) were tried. The data were five Brodatz textures . In that comparison the cooccurrence matrix features in general turned out to be the best, and for some values of the displacement vector and for some clustering and classification methods the result was 100% correct. Also the combination of the subspace method and the direct power spectrum over a window gave equally good results. As for the other feature sets, the results were worse.

Experiments were first made on a subset of eight of the Brodatz textures of Fig. 1 (numbers 3,16,28,33,34,49,68,77). Using the cooccurrence matrix as a 16 component feature vector in the way indicated above, resulted in 100% correct discrimination in subspace classification, where the whole sample consisted of 45 randomly located texture windows for each texture. For the classification 10 feature vectors were used in the design set and the remaining 35 comprised the test set for each texture, and all subspace dimensions were equal to five. This result was obtained for 64×64 windows. For all the twelve textures, the corresponding result was 90.2%. The subspace clustering results for the 64×64 Brodatz texture windows were 94.4% for the subset of eight textures

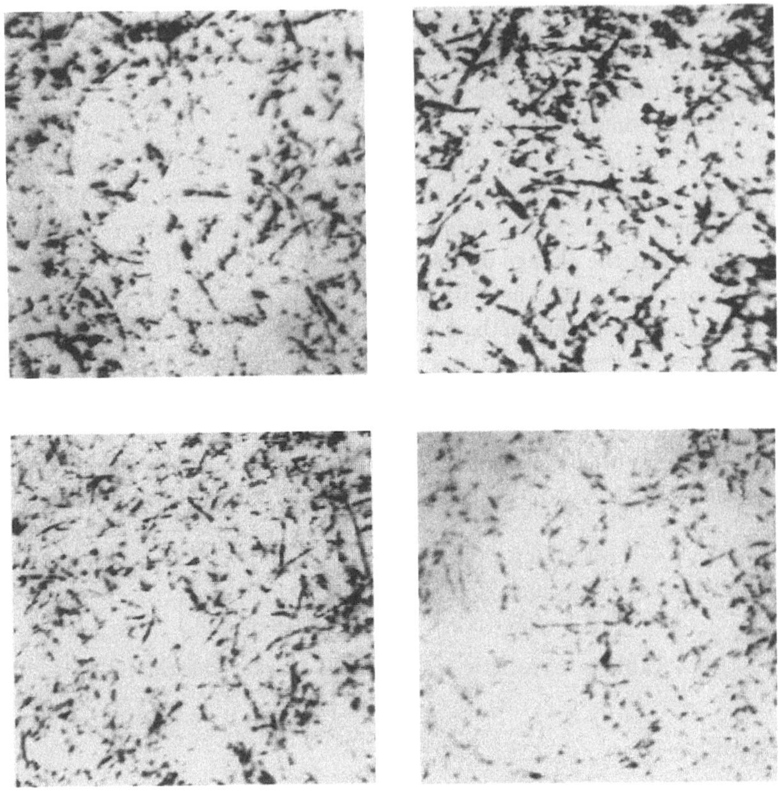

Figure 2: Paper industry textures

and 85.7% for all twelve textures, respectively. Using 32×32 windows and slightly larger sample size (80 design windows and 20 test windows for each texture), the eight textures were classified with 88.1% accuracy.

A comparison result using two classification methods is shown in the confusion matrices of Table 2. In this experiment, the texture window size was 64×64. Again, 10 samples for each of the eight textures given above were used as the design set to compute the five basis vectors of the subspaces, and 15 other samples were the test set. The number of training samples is inadequate to form any reliable statistical correlation estimates. Still, texture subspaces classify the test set without errors as shown in Table 2a (left).

For comparison, Table 2b (right) shows the result obtained using the five standard cooccurrence matrix features and linear discriminant analysis for classification. The window size and the training and test samples were exactly the same as in Table 2a.

As for the computational complexity of the two methods of feature extraction (averaged cooccurrence matrix *vs* the five features), the difference in practical CPU time is nearly 2 decades in favour of the averaged matrix.

For paper industry textures (Fig. 2) the subspace classification algorithm gave 91.3% correct results for texture window size 64×64. Both training and test set sizes were 20 for each texture. Subspace dimensions were either four or five. For the synthetic

Table 2. Classification results (see text).

15	0	0	0	0	0	0	0	7	0	0	0	0	0	0	0
0	15	0	0	0	0	0	0	0	15	0	0	0	0	0	0
0	0	15	0	0	0	0	0	1	0	13	0	0	0	1	0
0	0	0	15	0	0	0	0	0	0	0	15	0	0	0	0
0	0	0	0	15	0	0	0	0	0	0	0	15	0	0	0
0	0	0	0	0	15	0	0	0	0	0	0	0	15	0	0
0	0	0	0	0	0	15	0	5	0	2	0	0	0	14	0
0	0	0	0	0	0	0	15	2	0	0	0	0	0	0	15

Horizontal: correct class, vertical: classification result

textures and 3×3 cooccurrence matrices, 16×16 texture windows were used. 80 windows from both images were taken and either clustered or split in two, the first 40 samples being used to compute the *ALSM* subspaces and the last 40 samples being classified. Both clustering and classification resulted in 100% errorfree results.

4. Conclusions

The subspace method is a pattern recognition method through which high-dimensional feature vectors, especially spectral or probability densities, can be classified accurately and fast. The purpose of this work was to demonstrate the feasibility of this classifier in texture analysis.

For texture classification, second-order statistics are generally believed to yield the best discriminating features. Especially, the grey level cooccurrence matrix seems to capture a large amount of the texture information in a digital image. The practical problem is that the cooccurrence matrix even for one choice of the displacement between the pixel pairs is often larger than the texture window itself. It has to be reduced to a manageable set of scalar features which are subsequently classified.

In this work we used cooccurrence matrix information to classification and clustering essentially without deriving any features from the matrix. The matrix itself with a desired grey level resolution was the feature vector for texture analysis. For all images, at first preprocessed to have a uniform first-order grey level distribution, the reduction of the cooccurrence matrix to 16 submatrices of equal sizes was sufficient. In principle, any grey level resolution could be used. The motivation was that such smoothing of the matrix tends to decrease the effect of noise on the pixel grey levels, without losing too much of texture information. The computational complexity of the smoothing is small; equivalently, the cooccurrence matrix might be computed with the desired low resolution in the first place. Especially if the cooccurrence estimate must be computed from a very small texture window, which might be the case in segmentation problems, it is to be expected that the smoothed cooccurrence matrix itself has less variation than some features computed from the total cooccurrence matrix.

This particular choice of the texture representation was also motivated by the subsequent classification phase, for which the subspace method was used. The subspace classification and clustering algorithms were briefly reviewed. The classification and clustering efficiency of the subspace method applied to smoothed cooccurrence matrices turned out to be good. The classification phase is also very fast to compute even for high-dimensional feature vectors. The clustering results especially indicate that the method will be suitable also for segmentation.

References

[1] Akhiezer,N.I. and Glazman,I.M.: Theory of Linear Operators in Hilbert Space, *Vol. I, Pitman Adv. Publ. Progr., Boston, 1981.*

[2] Brodatz, P.: Textures: A Photographic Album for Artists and Designers, *Reinhold, New York, 1968.*

[3] Caelli,T. and Julesz, B.: On Perceptual Analyzers Underlying Visual Texture Discrimination: Part I, Part II, *Biol. Cyb.* **28**, 1978, pp. 167-175 and **29**, 1978, pp. 201-214.

[4] Conners,R.W. and Harlow,C.A.: A Theoretical Comparison of Texture Algorithms, *IEEE Trans. on Patt. Anal. and Mach. Intel., PAMI-***2**, 1980, pp. 204-222.

[5] Conners,R.W., Trivedi,M.M., and Harlow,C.A.: Segmentation of a High Resolution Urban Scene Using Texture Operators, *Comp. Vision, Graphics and Image Proc.* **25**, 1984, pp. 273-310.

[6] D'Astous,F. and Jernigan,M.E.: Texture Discrimination Based on Detailed Measures of the Power Spectrum, *Proc. 7th ICPR, Montreal, July 30 - Aug. 2, 1984*, pp. 83-86.

[7] Diday,E. and Simon,J.C.: Clustering Analysis, in K.S.Fu (Ed.), *Digital Pattern Recognition*, Springer, Berlin-Heidelberg-New York, 1976, pp. 47-94.

[8] Duvernoy,J.: Optical-Digital Processing of Directional Terrain Textures Invariant under Translation, Rotation, and Change of Scale, *Appl. Optics* **23**, No. 6, 1984, pp. 828-837.

[9] Haralick,R.M.: Statistical and Structural Approaches to Texture, *Proc. IEEE* **67**, 1979, pp. 786-804.

[10] Haralick,R.M., Shanmugam,K., and Dinstein,I.: Textural Features for Image Classification, *IEEE Trans. Syst. Man Cybern., SMC-***3**, 1973, pp. 610-621.

[11] Iijima,T.: A Theory of Pattern Recognition by Compound Similarity Method (*in Japanese*), *Trans. IECE Japan, PRL* **74-25**.

[12] Julesz,T.: Visual Pattern Discrimination, *IRE Trans. Inform. Theory IT-* **8**, 1962, pp. 84-92.

[13] Kittler,J. and Young,P.C.: Discriminant Function Implementation of a Minimum Risk Classifier, *Biol. Cyb.***18**, 1975, pp. 169-179.

[14] Kohonen,T., Nemeth,G., Bry,K.-J., Jalanko,M., and Makisara,K.: Spectral Classification of Phonemes by Learning Subspaces, *Proc. 1979 IEEE Int. Conf. on Acoust., Speech and Signal Proc., April 2-4, 1979, Washington, DC*, pp. 97-100.

[15] Kohonen,T., Riittinen., Jalanko,M., Reuhkala,E., and Haltsonen,S.: A 1000 Word Recognition System Based on the Learning Subspace Method and Redundant Hash Addressing, *Proc. 5th Int. Conf. on Pattern Recognition, Miami Beach, FL, Dec. 1.-4., 1980*, pp. 158-165.

[16] Lendaris,G. and Stanley,G.: Diffraction Pattern Samplings for Automatic Pattern Recognition, *Proc. IEEE* **58**, 1970, pp. 198-216.

[17] Oja,E.: Subspace Methods of Pattern Recognition, *Research Studies Press, Letchworth and J. Wiley, New York, 1983.*

[18] Oja,E. and Kuusela,M.: The ALSM Algorithm - an Improved Subspace Method of Classification, *Patt. Rec.* **16**, No. 4, 1983, pp. 421-427.

[19] Oja,E. and Karhunen,J.: An Analysis of Convergence for a Learning Version of the Subspace Method, *J. Math. Anal. Appl.***91**, 1983, pp. 102-111.

[20] Oja,E. and Parkkinen,J.: On Subspace Clustering, *Proc. 7th. Int. Conf. on Pattern Recognition, Montreal, Canada, July 30.- Aug. 2., 1984*, pp. 692-695.

[21] Parkkinen,J. and Oja,E.: Texture Classification by the Subspace Method, *Proc. 4th. Scand. Conf. on Image Analysis, Trondheim, Norway, June 17.-20.,1985*, pp. 429-436.

[22] Riittinen,H.: Recognition of Phonemes in a Speech Recognition System Using Learning Projective Methods, *Dr.Tech. Thesis, Helsinki University of Technology*, 1986.

[23] Unser,M.: A Fast Texture Classifier Based on Cross Entropy Minimization, *in H.W. Schüssler (Ed.), Signal Processing II: Theories and Applications*, Elsevier Sci. Publ., 1983, pp. 261-264.

[24] Van Gool,L., Dewaele,P. and Oosterlinck,A.: Texture Analysis Anno 1983, *Comp. Vision, Graphics and Image Proc.* **29**, 1985, pp. 336-357.

[25] Vickers,A.L. and Modestino,J.W.: A Maximum Likelihood Approach to Texture Classification, *IEEE Trans. on Pattern Anal. and Machine Intelligence, PAMI-4*, 1982, pp. 61-68.

[26] Watanabe,S.: Knowing and Guessing - a Quantitative Study of Inference and Information, *J. Wiley, New York, 1969.*

AUTOMATIC SELECTION OF A DISCRIMINATION RULE BASED UPON MINIMIZATION OF THE EMPIRICAL RISK[1]

Luc Devroye

School of Computer Science, McGill University
805 Sherbrooke Street West, Montréal
Canada H3A 2K6

Abstract

A discrimination rule is chosen from a possibly infinite collection of discrimination rules based upon the minimization of the observed error in a test sample. For example, the collection could include all k nearest neighbor rules (for all k), all linear discriminators, and all kernel-based rules (for all possible choices of the smoothing parameter). We do not put any restrictions on the collection.

We study how close the probability of error of the selected rule is to the (unknown) minimal probability of error over the entire collection. If both training sample and test sample have n observations, the expected value of the difference is shown to be $O(\sqrt{\log(n)/n})$ for many reasonable collections, such as the one mentioned above. General inequalities governing this error are given which are of a combinatorial nature, *i.e.*, they are valid for all possible distributions of the data, and most practical collections of rules.

The theory is based in part on the work of Vapnik and Chervonenkis regarding minimization of the empirical risk. For all proofs, technical details, and additional examples, we refer to Devroye (1986).

As a by-product, we establish that for some nonparametric rules, the probability of error of the selected rule converges at the optimal rate (achievable within the given collection of non-parametric rules) to the Bayes probability of error, and this without actually knowing the optimal rate of convergence to the Bayes probability of error.

1. Introduction

In pattern recognition, we normally use the data, either directly (via formulas) or indirectly (by peeking), in the selection of a discrimination rule and/or its parameters. For example, a quick inspection of the data can convince us that a linear discriminator is appropriate in a given situation. The actual position of the discriminating hyperplane is usually determined from the data. In other words, we choose our discriminator from a class $\mathbf{D}$ of discriminators. This class can be small (*e.g.*, "all k-nearest neighbor rules")

[1]Research of the author was sponsored by NSERC Grant A3456 and by FCAR Grant EQ-1678

NATO ASI Series, Vol. F30
Pattern Recognition Theory and Applications
Edited by P. A. Devijver and J. Kittler

or large (*e.g.*, "all linear and quadratic discriminators, and all nonparametric discriminators of the kernel type with smoothing factor $h > 0$"). If we knew the underlying distribution of the data, then the selection process would be simple: we would pick the Bayes rule. Unfortunately, the Bayes rule is not in **D** unless we are incredibly lucky. Also, the underlying distribution is not known. Thus, it is important to know how close we are to the performance of the best discriminator in **D**. If **D** is large enough, then hopefully, the performance of the best discriminator in it is close to that of the Bayes discriminator. There are two issues here which should be separated from each other.

A. The closeness of the best element of **D** to the Bayes rule.

B. The closeness of the actual element picked from **D** to the best element in **D**.

The former issue is related to the consistency of the estimators in **D**, and will only be dealt with briefly. Our main concern is with the second problem: to what extent can we let the data select the discriminator, and how much are we paying for this luxury? The paper is an exercise in compromises: on the one hand, **D** should be rich enough so that every Bayes rule can be asymptotically approached by a sequence of rules picked from a sequence of **D**'s, and on the other hand, **D** should not be too rich because it would lead to trivial selections, as any data can be fit to some discriminator in such a class **D**. One of the biggest advantages of the empirical selection is that the programmer does not have to worry about the choice of smoothing factors and design parameters.

Statistical model. Data-split technique

Our statistical model is as follows. The *data* consists of a sequence of $n + m$ iid $R^d \times \{0,1\}$-valued random vectors $(X_1, Y_1), \cdots, (X_{n+m}, Y_{n+m})$. The X_i's are called the *observations*, and the Y_i's are usually called the *classes*. The fact that we limit the number of classes to two should not take anything away from the main message of this paper. Note also that the data is artificially split by us into two independent sequences, one of length n, and one of length m. This will facilitate the discussion and the ensuing analysis immensely. We will call the n-sequence the training sequence, and the m-sequence the testing sequence. The testing sequence is used as an impartial judge in the selection process. A *discrimination rule* is a function $\psi : R^d \times (R^d \times \{0,1\})^{n+m} \to \{0,1\}$. It classifies a point $x \in R^d$ as coming from class $\psi(x, (X_1, Y_1), \cdots, (X_{n+m}, Y_{n+m}))$. We will write $\psi(x)$ for the sake of convenience.

The *probability of error* is

$$L_{n+m}(\psi) = L_{n+m} = P(\psi(X) \neq Y \mid (X_1, Y_1), \cdots, (X_{n+m}, Y_{n+m}))$$

where (X, Y) is independent of the data sequence and distributed as (X_1, Y_1). Of course, we would like L_{n+m} to be small, although we know that L_{n+m} cannot be smaller than the *Bayes probability of error*

$$L_{Bayes} = \inf_{\psi : R^d \to \{0,1\}} P(\psi(X) \neq Y) .$$

Minimization of the empirical risk

In the construction of a rule with small probability of error, we proceed as follows: **D** is a (possibly infinite) collection of functions $\phi : R^d \times (R^d \times \{0,1\})^n \to \{0,1\}$, from which a particular function ϕ' is picked by minimizing the *empirical risk* based upon the testing sequence:

$$\hat{L}_{n,m}(\phi') = \frac{1}{m} \sum_{i=n+1}^{n+m} I_{[\phi'(X_i) \neq Y_i]} = \min_{\phi \in D} \frac{1}{m} \sum_{i=n+1}^{n+m} I_{[\phi(X_i) \neq Y_i]} \,.$$

Here it is noted that

$$\begin{aligned} \phi(X_i) &= \phi(X_i, (X_1, Y_1), \cdots, (X_n, Y_n)) \,, \\ \phi'(X_i) &= \phi'(X_i, (X_1, Y_1), \cdots, (X_n, Y_n)) \,, \end{aligned}$$

i.e., the discriminators themselves are based upon the training sequence. Let us formally write

$$\begin{aligned} \psi(x) &= \psi(x, (X_1, Y_1), \cdots, (X_{n+m}, Y_{n+m})) \\ &= \phi'(x, (X_1, Y_1), \cdots, (X_n, Y_n)), \quad x \in R^d. \end{aligned}$$

It is necessary to do this because ψ depends upon both the training sequence and the testing sequence. Since $\hat{L}_{n,m}(\phi)$ is an unbiased binomial estimate of $L_n(\phi)$, it is not unlikely that $L_{n+m}(\psi)$ is close to $\inf_{\phi \in D} L_n(\phi)$, yet this has to be proven rigorously. It is this closeness that is under investigation here. We observe that the idea of minimizing the empirical risk in the construction of a rule goes back to Vapnik and Chervonenkis (1971, 1974).

Why split the data?

If we define our empirical risk entirely in terms of the training sequence, *i.e.*, if we count the number of errors committed by a rule on the training sequence itself, then we can end up with strange rules. Consider for example the problem of the data-based choice of k in a k-NN rule. It is obvious that no errors are committed on the training sequence itself when $k = 1$, yet, $k = 1$ can but does not have to be the optimal choice in a given situation. Glick (1972, 1976) has shown however that for many nonparametric rules such as the kernel rule, counting the errors on the training sequence is essentially harmless provided that the nonparametric rule is consistent. Unfortunately, we want to choose the best discriminator from huge collections of discriminators from which it is possible to draw many nonconsistent sequences. The presence of nonconsistent rules is practically appealing (one can mix parametric and nonparametric discriminators; recall also that we can include all k NN rules in **D** without restriction on k), but dangerous since we surely don't want our procedure to lead to nonconsistency.

Cover (1969) suggested taking $m = 1$, and counting the number of errors committed by considering $n+1$ training sets, each time leaving one of the observations (X_i, Y_i) out, and verifying whether the rule classifies the deleted X_i as Y_i. This, at least, reduces the anomaly observed when our collection of discriminators includes the 1-NN rule and no deletion is employed. Our approach is nothing more than an attempt to obtain an alternative to Cover's suggestion for which we can obtain good analytical guarantees of the performance. Not separating a training set from a testing set works in some cases, but it seems that good bounds on the probability of error can only be obtained when the collections are very nice or simple.

A last word about our split into a training sequence and a testing sequence. This split is primarily aimed at deriving results that are valid for many classes **D**. There are well-known tricks of the trade such as cross-validation (or leave-one-out) (Lunts and Brailovsky, 1967; Stone, 1974), holdout, resubstitution, rotation, and bootstrap (Efron, 1979, 1983) which can be employed to construct an empirical risk from the training sequence, thus obviating the need for a testing sequence (see Kanal (1974), Cover and Wagner (1975) and Toussaint (1976) for surveys, and Glick (1978) for a discussion and empirical comparison). This works well in many important situations (see Vapnik and Chervonenkis (1974), Vapnik (1982), Devroye and Wagner (1979)), but can fail miserably in other circumstances. This would then force us to restrict **D** to such an extent that our results would be less powerful. We will make a case for the split-data method by showing just how good the empirical choice is for most popular discrimination rules. This universality seems more difficult to obtain with other methods. In addition, we will argue that the testing sequence can often be taken much smaller than the training sequence ($m = o(n)$). It seems probable that more sophisticated methods such as cross-validation would be equally good or better than the split-data method, but we haven't been able to show this thus far.

The size of the class of rules

When **D** contains all rules, selection is like a lottery. Even though the Bayes rule itself is in **D**, it is impossible to let the testing sequence pick a good rule, since the error committed on the testing sequence for the selected rule is zero, and thus has no relationship to the actual probability of error with that rule. When **D** is large but not gigantic, $\inf_{\phi \in D} L_n(\phi)$ is probably close to L_{Bayes}: this is the case when **D** contains all k-NN rules, or when it contains all kernel-type rules. On the other hand, **D** can be so small that there is no hope of getting close to L_{Bayes}. A point in case is the class **D** of all linear discrimination rules.

The selection error

Good automatic selection is impossible without good error estimates, and thus, it should come as no surprise that the estimate on which the automatic selection is based can serve as an estimate of the probability of error of the selected rule. This relationship is captured in

The Fundamental Inequalities

$$\begin{aligned} L_{n+m}(\psi) - \inf_{\phi \in D} L_n(\phi) &\leq 2 \sup_{\phi \in D} |\hat{L}_{n,m}(\phi) - L_n(\phi)|. \\ |\hat{L}_{n,m}(\phi') - L_{n+m}(\psi)| &\leq \sup_{\phi \in D} |\hat{L}_{n,m}(\phi) - L_n(\phi)|. \end{aligned}$$

We see that upper bounds for $\sup_{\phi \in D} |\hat{L}_{n,m}(\phi) - L_n(\phi)|$ provide us with upper bounds for two things simultaneously:

A. An upper bound for the suboptimality of ψ within **D**, $L_{n+m}(\psi) - \inf_{\phi \in D} L_n(\phi)$. We will call this difference the *selection error* SE.

B. An upper bound for the error $|\hat{L}_{n,m}(\phi') - L_{n+m}(\psi)|$ committed when $\hat{L}_{n,m}(\phi')$ is used to estimate the probability of error $L_{n+m}(\psi)$. This could be called the *error estimate's accuracy EEA*.

In other words, by bounding the *worst-case deviation* $W = \sup_{\phi \in D} |\hat{L}_{n,m}(\phi) - L_n(\phi)|$, we kill two flies at once. It is particularly useful to know that even though $\hat{L}_{n,m}(\phi')$ is usually optimistically biased, it is within given bounds of the unknown probability of error with ψ, and that no other test sample is needed to estimate this probability of error. Whenever our bounds indicate that we are close to the optimum in **D**, we must at the the same time have a good estimate of the probability of error, and vice versa.

Conditional upper bounds

To make the random variable W small, m should be large so that we may benefit from the healthy averaging effect captured for example in the central limit theorem. Unfortunately, the size of **D** works against us. We will now derive bounds for $E(W|$ training data) that are functions of n, m and a quantity measuring the size of **D** only.

All the probabilities and expected values written P_n and E_n are conditional on the training sequence of length n, whereas P and E refer to unconditional probabilities and expected values. The bounds derived below refer to conditional quantities, and do not depend upon the training sequence. In other words, they are valid uniformly over all training sequences. The important consequence of this is that, although the testing sequence should have the right distribution and be iid, the training sequence can in fact be arbitrary. In particular, annoying phenomena such as dependence between observations, noisy data, etcetera become irrelevant for our bounds — they could have a negative impact on the actual value of the probability of error though.

2. Finite Classes

We consider first finite classes **D**, with cardinality bounded by N_n. We have

Theorem 1. (Devroye, 1986) Let **D** be a finite class with cardinality bounded by N_n. Then

$$E_n W \leq \sqrt{\frac{\log(2N_n)}{2m}} + \frac{1}{\sqrt{8m\log(2N_n)}} .$$

Size of the bound

If we take $m = n$ and assume that N_n is large, then Theorem 1 shows that on the average we are within $\sqrt{\log(N_n)/(2n)}$ of the best possible error rate, whatever it is. Since most common error probabilities tend to the Bayes probability of error at a rate much slower than $1/\sqrt{n}$, the loss in error rate studied here is asymptotically negligible in many cases relative to the difference between the probability of error and L_{Bayes}, at least when N_n increases at a polynomial rate in n.

Distribution-free properties

Theorem 1 shows that the problem studied here is purely combinatorial. The actual distribution of the data does not play a role at all in the upper bounds.

The k-nearest neighbor rule

When **D** contains all k nearest neighbor rules, then $N_n = n$, since there are only n possible values for k. It is easily seen that

$$E_n W \leq \sqrt{\frac{\log(2n)}{2m}} + \frac{1}{\sqrt{8m\log(2n)}} .$$

Since $k/n \to 0$, $k \to \infty$ imply that $E(L_n) \to L_{Bayes}$ for the k-nearest neighbor with data-independent (deterministic) k, for all possible distributions (Stone, 1977), we see that our strategy leads to a universally consistent rule whenever $log(n)/m \to 0$. Thus, we can take m equal to a small fraction of n, without losing consistency. That we cannot take $m = 1$ and hope to obtain consistency should be obvious. It should also be noted that for $m = n$, we are roughly within $\sqrt{\log(n)/n}$ of the best possible probability of error within the given class. The same remark remains valid for k nearest neighbor rules defined in terms of all L_p metrics, or in terms of the transformation-invariant metric of Olshen (Olshen, 1977; Devroye, 1978).

3. Consistency

Although it was not our objective to discuss consistency of our rules, it is perhaps worth our while to present Theorem 2. Let us first recall the definition of a *consistent* rule (to be more precise, a consistent sequence of ϕ's): a rule is consistent if $E(L_n) \to L_{Bayes}$ as $n \to \infty$. Consistency may depend upon the distribution of the data. If it does not, then we say that the rule is universally consistent.

Theorem 2. Consistency Assume that from each **D** (recall that **D** varies with n) we can pick one ϕ such that the sequence of ϕ's is consistent for a certain class of distributions. Then the automatic rule ψ defined above is consistent for the same class of distributions (*i.e.*, $E(L_{n+m}(\psi)) \to L_{Bayes}$ as $n \to \infty$) if

$$\lim_{n\to\infty} \frac{m}{\log(1+N_n)} = \infty .$$

If one is just worried about consistency, Theorem 2 reassures us that nothing is lost as long as we take m much larger than $\log(N_n)$. Often, this reduces to a very weak condition on the size m of the training set.

4. Asymptotic Optimality

Let us now introduce the notion of *asymptotic optimality*. A sequence of rules ψ is said to be asymptotically optimal for a given distribution of (X, Y) when

$$\lim_{n\to\infty} \frac{E(L_{n+m}(\psi)) - L_{Bayes}}{E(\inf_{\phi\in D} L_n(\phi)) - L_{Bayes}} = 1 .$$

Now, by the triangle inequality,

$$1 \leq \frac{E(L_{n+m}(\psi)) - L_{Bayes}}{E(\inf_{\phi\in D} L_n(\phi)) - L_{Bayes}} \leq 1 + \frac{E(SE)}{E(\inf_{\phi\in D} L_n(\phi)) - L_{Bayes}}$$

When the selected rule is asymptotically optimal, we have achieved something very strong: we have in effect picked a rule (or better, a sequence of rules) which has a probability of error converging at the optimal rate attainable within the sequence of **D**'s. And we don't even have to know what the optimal rate of convergence is. This is especially important in nonparametric rules, where some researchers choose smoothing factors in function of theoretical results about the optimal attainable rate of convergence for certain classes of problems. For the k-nearest neighbor rule with the best possible sequence of k's, the rate of convergence to the Bayes error is often of the order of $n^{-2/5}$ or worse. In those cases the selection rule is asymptotically optimal when $m = \varepsilon n$ for any $\varepsilon > 0$.

Mixing parametric and nonparametric rules

We are constantly faced with the problem of choosing between parametric discriminators and nonparametric discriminators. Parametric discriminators are based upon an underlying model in which a finite number of unknown parameters is estimated from the data. A point in case is the multivariate normal distribution, which leads to linear or quadratic discriminators. If the model is wrong, parametric methods can perform very poorly; when the model is right, their performance is difficult to beat. Our method chooses among the best discriminator depending upon which happens to be best for the given data. We can throw in **D** a variety of rules, including nearest neighbor rules, a few linear discriminators, a couple of tree classifiers and perhaps a kernel-type rule. Theorems 1 and 2 should be used when the cardinality of **D** does not get out of hand.

5. Infinite Classes

Theorem 1 is useless when $N_n = \infty$. It is here that we can apply the inequality of Vapnik and Chervonenkis (1974) or one of it modifications. Fortunately, the bound remains formally valid if N_n, the bound on the cardinality of **D**, is replaced by $2e^8$ times the *shatter coefficient* S, which in turn depends upon n, m and the "richness" of **D** only. The shatter coefficient is always finite, regardless of the "size" of **D**.

The shatter coefficient

Let **C** be the collection of all sets

$$\{\{x : \phi = 1\} \times \{0\}\} \cup \{\{x : \phi = 0\} \times \{1\}\}, \quad \phi \in \mathbf{D} .$$

Thus, every ϕ in **D** can contribute at most one member to **C**. Then the shatter coefficient is defined as the maximum over all possible testing sequences of length m^2, and all possible training sequences of length n, of the number of possible misclassification vectors of the testing sequence. (The misclassification vector is a vector of m^2 zeroes and ones, a one occurring if and only if the corresponding testing point has been incorrectly classified.) Note that $S \leq N_n$. Also, S is not random by virtue of the definition in terms of maxima. Generally speaking, S increases with the size of **D**. It suffices now to compute a few shatter coefficients for certain classes of discrimination rules. For examples, see Cover (1965), Vapnik and Chervonenkis (1971), Devroye and Wagner (1979), Feinholz (1979), Devroye (1982), and Massart (1983).

Smorgasbords of rules

For a collection $\mathbf{D}$ of the form $\mathbf{D} = \cup_{j=1}^{k}\mathbf{D}_j$, we have

$$S \leq \sum_{j=1}^{k} S_j ,$$

where S_j is computed for $\mathbf{D}_j$ only. This allows us to treat each homogeneous subcollection of $\mathbf{D}$ separately.

Linear discrimination

Consider all rules that split the space R^d in two by virtue of a halfplane, and assign class 1 to one halfspace, and class 0 to the other. Points on the border are treated as belonging to the same halfspace. Because the training sequence is not even used in the definition of the collection, S can't possibly depend upon n.

There are at most

$$2\sum_{k=0}^{d}\binom{m^2-1}{k} \leq 2m^{2d}+1$$

ways of dichotomizing m^2 points in R^d by hyperplanes (see *e.g.*, Cover, 1965) (this takes into account that there are two ways of attaching 0's and 1's to the two halfspaces). We see that

$$S \leq 2\left(\sum_{k=0}^{d}\binom{m^2-1}{k}\right) \leq 2(m^{2d}+1) .$$

A rule ϕ in which the set $\{x : \phi(x) = 1\}$ coindices with a set of the form

$$\{a : a_0 + \sum_{j=1}^{d^*} a_j f_j(x) \geq 0\}$$

for given fixed functions $f_1, \cdots, f_{d^*}$ and some real numbers $a_0, \cdots, a_{d^*}$ is called a *generalized linear discrimination rule* (see Duda and Hart, 1973). These include for example all quadratic discrimination rules in R^d when we choose all functions that are either components of x, or squares of components of x, or products of two components of x. In all, $d^* = 2d + d(d-1)/2$. The counting argument of the previous paragraph remains valid, provided that d is replaced by d^*.

Kernel-based rules

Kernel-based rules are derived from the kernel estimate in density estimation originally studied by Parzen (1962), Rosenblatt (1956) and Cacoullos (1965). A point x is assigned class 1 if

$$g(x) = \sum_{i=1}^{n}\left(Y_i - \frac{1}{2}\right) K\left(\frac{x - X_i}{h}\right) \geq 0$$

and to class 0 otherwise, where K is a fixed function called the kernel, and $h > 0$ is a smoothing factor. It is easy to verify that this is a voting scheme in which the i-th observation carries weight $K\left(\frac{x-X_i}{h}\right)$. Thus, K is usually decreasing along rays. For particular choices of K, rules of this sort have been proposed by Fix and Hodges (1951, 1952), Sebestyen (1962), Bashkirov, Braverman and Muchnik (1964), Van Ryzin (1966), and Meisel (1969).

We begin by considering the collection $\mathbf{D}$ of all kernel rules for all values of h, but fixed kernel $K = I_A$ where I is the indicator function, and A is any star shaped set of unit Lebesgue measure (a set A is star- shaped if $x \notin A$ implies that $cx \notin A$ for all $c \geq 1$). We vary h monotonically from 0 to ∞. For fixed X_j in the testing sequence, the function $g(X_j)$ on which the decision is based can at most take n values. Therefore, $S \leq nm^2 + 1$.

A typical star-shaped set is the centered unit cube. In the class $\mathbf{D}$ considered above, only one parameter was varied. In d-dimensional pattern recognition, it is often necessary to adjust the scales of many component variables. Thus, it seems natural to classify $x = (x_1, \cdots, x_d)$ in class one if

$$g(x) = \sum_{i=1}^{n} \left(Y_i - \frac{1}{2}\right) \prod_{l=1}^{d} K\left(\frac{x_l - X_{il}}{h_l}\right) \geq 0 ,$$

where now K is a one-dimensional kernel, $h_1, \cdots, h_d$ are d positive numbers, and X_{il} is the l-th component of X_i. It should be noted that this is certainly not the only way of introducing d different smoothing factors, one for each component. Let $\mathbf{D}$ be the collection of all rules of this type considered over all possible values $h_1, \cdots, h_d$. For this class, we have $S \leq (nm^2)^d + 1$ for all kernels K that are indicators of centered hypercubes.

The *consistency* of the class $\mathbf{D}$ is insured when K is the uniform kernel on the unit hypercube, by applying the universal consistency theorem of Devroye and Wagner (1980) and Spiegelman and Sacks (1980) (see also Greblicki, Krzyzak and Pawlak, 1984), provided that $m/\log(n) \to \infty$. The standard bounds for relating the probability of error to the L_1 error in density estimation (see *e.g.*, Devroye and Gyorfi, 1985), combined with well-known results about the best possible expected error with any kernel density estimate (*i.e.*, the best possible expected L_1 error is about equal to a constant times $n^{-2/(4+d)}$, see Devroye and Gyorfi, 1985), give us lower bounds for $E(L_n(\phi) - L_{Bayes})$ that decrease as $n^{-2/(4+d)}$, where ϕ is the kernel discrimination rule in which the h is chosen in an optimal way for the underlying densities. Since this tends to 0 slower than $\sqrt{\log(n)/n}$, it seems plausible that the automatic selection rule with $m = n^{1-\epsilon}$ (with an appropriately picked small ϵ) is asymptotically optimal for large classes of distributions.

Binary tree classifiers

Binary tree classifiers have become increasingly important because of their conceptual simplicity and computational feasibility. Many strategies have been proposed for constructing the binary decision tree (in which each internal node corresponds to a cut, and each terminal node corresponds to a set in the partition: see for example Sethi and Chatterjee (1977), Payne and Meisel (1977), Sethi and Sarvarayudu (1981), Lin and Fu (1983), Breiman, Friedman, Ohlsen and Stone (1983), and Casey and Nagy (1984).

If we consider all binary trees in which each internal node corresponds to a split perpendicular to one of the axes, and the space is partitioned into k hyperrectangles, then $S \leq (1 + d(n + m^2))^{k-1}$.

Here we have an example of a class that is too large to be practical for the present procedure, since k is typically a polynomially increasing function of n.

References

[1] O. Bashkirov, E.M. Braverman, and I.E. Muchnik, "Potential function algorithms for pattern recognition learning machines," *Automation and Remote Control*, vol. 25, pp. 692-695, 1964.

[2] L. Breiman, J.H. Friedman, R.A. Olshen, and C.J. Stone, *Classification and Regression Trees*, Wadsworth International, Belmont, CA., 1984.

[3] T. Cacoullos, "Estimation of a multivariate density," *Annals of the Institute of Statistical Mathematics*, vol. 18, pp. 179-190, 1965.

[4] R.G. Casey and G. Nagy, "Decision tree design using a probabilistic model," *IEEE Transactions on Information Theory*, vol. IT-30, pp. 93-99, 1984.

[5] T.M. Cover, "Geometrical and statistical properties of systems of linear inequalities with applications in pattern recognition," *IEEE Transactions on Electronic Computers*, vol. EC-14, pp. 326-334, 1965.

[6] T.M. Cover, "Learning in pattern recognition," in *Methodologies of Pattern Recognition*, ed. S. Watanabe, pp. 111-132, Academic Press, New York, N.Y., 1969.

[7] T.M. Cover and T.J. Wagner, "Topics in statistical pattern recognition," *Communication and Cybernetics*, vol. 10, pp. 15-46, 1975.

[8] L. Devroye, "A universal k-nearest neighbor procedure in discrimination," in *Proceedings of the 1978 IEEE Computer Society Conference on Pattern Recognition and Image Processing*, pp. 142-147, 1978.

[9] L. Devroye and T.J. Wagner, "Distribution-free performance bounds for potential function rules," *IEEE Transactions on Information Theory*, vol. IT-25, pp. 601-604, 1979.

[10] L. Devroye and T.J. Wagner, "Distribution-free performance bounds with the resubstitution error estimate," *IEEE Transactions on Information Theory*, vol. IT-25, pp. 208-210, 1979.

[11] L. Devroye and T.J. Wagner, "Distribution-free inequalities for the deleted and holdout error estimates," *IEEE Transactions on Information Theory*, vol. IT-25, pp. 202-207, 1979.

[12] L. Devroye and T.J. Wagner, "Distribution-free consistency results in nonparametric discrimination and regression function estimation," *Annals of Statistics*, vol. 8, pp. 231-239, 1980.

[13] L. Devroye, "Bounds for the uniform deviation of empirical measures," *Journal of Multivariate Analysis*, vol. 12, pp. 72-79, 1982.

[14] L. Devroye and L. Gyorfi, *Nonparametric Density Estimation: the L_1 View*, John Wiley, New York, 1985.

[15] L. Devroye, "Automatic pattern recognition: a study of the probability of error," Technical Report, School of Computer Science, McGill University, 1986.

[16] R.O. Duda and P.E. Hart, *Pattern Classification and Scene Analysis*, John Wiley, New York, N.Y., 1973.

[17] B. Efron, "Bootstrap methods: another look at the jackknife," *Annals of Statistics*, vol. 7, pp. 1-26, 1979.

[18] B. Efron, "Estimating the error rate of a prediction rule: improvement on cross validation," *Journal of the American Statistical Association*, vol. 78, pp. 316-331, 1983.

[19] L. Feinholz, "Estimation of the performance of partitioning algorithms in pattern classification," M.Sc.Thesis, Department of Mathematics, McGill University, Montreal, 1979.

[20] E. Fix and J.L. Hodges, "Discriminating analysis, nonparametric discrimination, consistency properties," Report 21-49-004, USAF School of Aviation Medicine, Randolph Field, Texas, 1951.

[21] E. Fix and J.L. Hodges, "Discriminatory analysis: small sample performance," Report 21-49-004, USAF School of Aviation Medicine, Randolph Field, Texas, 1952.

[22] N. Glick, "Sample-based classification procedures derived from density estimators," *Journal of the American Statistical Association*, vol. 67, pp. 116-122, 1972.

[23] N. Glick, "Sample-based classification procedures related to empiric distributions," *Transactions on Information Theory*, vol. IT-22, pp. 454-461, 1976.

[24] N. Glick, "Additive estimators for probabilities of correct classification," *Pattern Recognition*, vol. 10, pp. 211-222, 1978.

[25] W. Greblicki, A. Krzyzak, and M. Pawlak, "Distribution-free pointwise consistency of kernel regression estimate," *Annals of Statistics*, vol. 12, pp. 1570-1575, 1984.

[26] L.N. Kanal, "Pattern in pattern recognition," *IEEE Transactions on Information Theory*, vol. IT-20, pp. 697-722, 1974.

[27] Y.K. Lin and K.S. Fu, "Automatic classification of cervical cells using a binary tree classifier," *Pattern Recognition*, vol. 16, pp. 69-80, 1983.

[28] A.L. Lunts and V.L. Brailosvsky, "Evaluation of attributes obtained in statistical decision rules," *Engineering Cybernetics*, vol. 5, pp. 98-109, 1967.

[29] P. Massart, "Vitesse de convergence dans le théorème de la limite centrale pour le processus empirique," Ph.D. Dissertation, Université de Paris-Sud, Orsay, France, 1983.

[30] W. Meisel, "Potential functions in mathematical pattern recognition," *IEEE Transactions on Computers*, vol. C-18, pp. 911-918, 1969.

[31] R.A. Olshen, "Comments on a paper by C.J. Stone," *Annals of Statistics*, vol. 5, pp. 632-633, 1977.

[32] E. Parzen, "On the estimation of a probability density function and the mode," *Annals of Mathematical Statistics*, vol. 33, pp. 1065-1076, 1962.

[33] H.J. Payne and W.S. Meisel, "An algorithm for constructing optimal binary decision trees," *IEEE Transactions on Computers*, vol. C-26, pp. 905-916, 1977.

[34] M. Rosenblatt, "Remark on some nonparametric estimates of a density function," *Annals of Mathematical Statistics*, vol. 27, pp. 832-837, 1956.

[35] G. Sebestyen, *Decision Making Processes in Pattern Recognition*, Macmillan, New York, N.Y., 1962.

[36] I.K. Sethi and B. Chatterjee, "Efficient decision tree design for discrete variable pattern recognition problems," *Pattern Recognition*, vol. 9, pp. 197-206, 1977.

[37] I.K. Sethi and G.P.R. Sarvarayudu, "Hierarchical classifier design using mutual Information," *IEEE Transactions on Pattern Analysis and Machine Intelligence*, vol. PAMI-4, pp. 441-445, 1981.

[38] C. Spiegelman and J. Sacks, "Consistent window estimation in nonparametric regression," *Annals of Statistics*, vol. 8, pp. 240-246, 1980.

[39] C.J. Stone, "Consistent nonparametric regression," *Annals of Statistics*, vol. 8, pp. 1348-1360, 1977.

[40] M. Stone, "Cross-validatory choice and assessment of statistical predictions," *Journal of the Royal Statistical Society*, vol. 36, pp. 111-147, 1974.

[41] G.T. Toussaint, "Bibliography on estimation of misclassification," *IEEE Transactions on Information Theory*, vol. IT-20, pp. 474-479, 1974.

[42] J. VanRyzin, "Bayes risk consistency of classification procedures using density estimation," *Sankhya Series A*, vol. 28, pp. 161-170, 1966.

[43] V.N. Vapnik, *Estimation of Dependences Based on Empirical Data*, Springer-Verlag, 1982.

[44] V.N. Vapnik and A. Ya. Chervonenkis, "Theory of uniform convergence of frequencies of events to their probabilities and problems of search for an optimal solution from empirical data," *Automation and Remote Control*, vol. 32, pp. 207-217, 1971.

[45] V.N. Vapnik and A. Ya. Chervonenkis, "On the uniform convergence of relative frequencies of events to their probabilities," *Theory of Probability and its Applications*, vol. 16, pp. 264-280, 1971.

[46] V.N. Vapnik and A. Ya. Chervonenkis, "Ordered risk minimization. I," *Automation and Remote Control*, vol. 35, pp. 1226-1235, 1974.

[47] V.N. Vapnik and A. Ya. Chervonenkis, "Ordered risk minimization. II," *Automation and Remote Control*, vol. 35, pp. 1043- 1412, 1974.

[48] V.N. Vapnik and A. Ya. Chervonenkis, *Theory of Pattern Recognition*, Nauka, Moscow, 1974.

[49] V. N. Vapnik and A. Ya. Chervonenkis, "Necessary and sufficient conditions for the uniform convergence of means to their expectations," *Theory of Probability and its Applications*, vol. 26, pp. 532-553, 1981.

LINEAR MODELS IN SPATIAL DISCRIMINANT ANALYSIS

J. Haslett, G. Horgan

Department of Statistics, Trinity College
Dublin 2, Ireland

1. Introduction

This paper reports on developments of a linear model, proposed in Haslett and Horgan (1985), for the reconstruction of binary (2 colour) images corrupted by additive Gaussian noise. The proposed method involved constructing a simple linear filter of the image, and thresholding the result. This very simple method was competitive with others, much more complicated, in terms of accuracy and speed. Further, by virtue of its close affinities with classical statistical methods of multivariate linear discriminant analysis, it yielded important and easily interpretable qualifications to any given reconstruction, notably (a) an estimated value for the proportion of pixels correctly classified and (b) posterior probabilities for the colour of each pixel.

There are a number of potential developments. We shall, for reasons of space, confine ourselves to outlining the extension to the general k-colour case — where the "true colour" of each pixel, before corruption, is one of k colours, for each of which the mean spectral response, in each of p bands, is known. Related methods, in that they employ formal ideas from the field of statistics and probability, include Besag (1986), Haslett (1985), Geman and Geman (1984). The closest methods are that proposed by Switzer (1980) and developed by Mardia (1984), and the recent work on mixed pixels by Kent and Mardia (1986) which employs linear algebra with some success to a related problem. In Section 2 we give the outlines of the application of the methods of classical linear discriminant analysis to the k-colour problem. Its detailed properties and interrelationships with other approaches will be presented elsewhere. Section 3 presents some results, and the position is reviewed in Section 4.

2. Linear Discriminant Analysis on the Plane

We briefly state the general principles of conventional linear discriminant analysis (LDA) in the context of allocating a pixel to a colour solely in terms of its spectral response. We then outline the general approach.

2.1. Notation, and LDA

Let $c(x)$ denote the "true colour" of pixel x, where x denotes a pixel on a finite rectangular lattice, and $c(x) \in \{1, 2, \ldots, k\}$. Let $z(x)$ denote the p-dimensional signal at x.

NATO ASI Series, Vol. F30
Pattern Recognition Theory and Applications
Edited by P. A. Devijver and J. Kittler

Suppose that when $c(x) = c$, $z(x)$ may be taken as a realization of a r.v. Z_c, with $\mathrm{E}\ Z_c = \mu_c$ and $\mathrm{Var}\ Z_c = \Sigma_c = \Sigma$, where μ_c and the (common) variance covariance matrix Σ are known. Unconditionally, $z(x)$ is a realization of Z, where $Z = Z_c$ with probability $p_c = Pr\{c(x) = c\}$ for a randomly chosen x. $\mathrm{E}\ Z = \sum p_c\mu_c = \mu$.

In LDA, the allocation of a pixel to one of the colours, given $z(x)$, often proceeds on the basis of allocating to that class c to which $z(x)$ is closest in the sense of the Mahalanobis squared distance

$$D_c^2(x) = (z(x) - \mu_c)^T\Sigma^{-1}(z(x) - \mu_c) \tag{2.1}$$

(Seber 1984, Section 6.9, Mardia *et al.* 1979, Chapter 11), or equivalently to that c which has maximum "discriminant function"

$$L_c(x) = \lambda_c^T z(x) - \frac{1}{2}\lambda_c^T \mu_c \tag{2.2}$$

where $\lambda_c^T = \Sigma^{-1}\mu_c$. In fact, this is maximum likelihood classification when Z_c has a Multivariate Normal (MVN) distribution. When this is so, the maximum a posteriori allocation (map) which has maximum possible overall probability of correct allocation, proceeds via $L_c^*(x) = L_c(x) + \log p_c$. Although the MVN is formally necessary for optimality, the method is known to be robust (*e.g.* Seber, 1984, Section 6.11) and has been widely used in practice for many years, even where there may be some departures from this classical position, and is possessed of a huge literature.

2.2. LDA and the Neighbourhood

Let $(x + x_s)$ denote the sth neighbour of x on the lattice, where all neighbours lie within $\pm n$ pixels, vertically and horizontally, of x. We refer to this as the n-neighbourhood of x, $N_n(x)$. To avoid ambiguities at the image edges we arbitrarily take the image to be wrapped on a torus (Besag and Moran (1975)). The labelling $s = 1, 2, \ldots, (2n+1)^2$ is arbitrary, but we take $x_0 = 0$. We write $z(x + x_s) = z_s(x)$ and $z_0 = z(x)$, and for notational simplicity we write $\nu = (2n+1)^2$. Let $z^V(x) = (z^T(x), z_1^T(x), \ldots, z_\nu^T(x))^T$. $z^V(x)$ contains the complete signal information in $N_n(x)$.

We regard $z^V(x)$ as a realization of Z_c^V, when $c(x) = c$ where Z_c^V is a $(\nu+1)p$ dimensional r.v. with $\mathrm{E}\ Z_c^V = \mu_c^V$ and $\mathrm{Var}\ Z_c^V = W_c = W$ for all c. We propose the allocation rule, for pixel x, given $z(x)$: allocate x to colour c which has maximum value of

$$L_c^V(x) = \lambda_c^T z^V(x) - \ell_c \tag{2.3}$$

where $\lambda_c^T = W^{-1}\mu_c^V$ and $\ell_c = \frac{1}{2}\lambda_c^T\mu_c^V + \log p_c$.

This rule is clearly motivated by the map MVN rule. Note, however, that even if Z_c is MVN, Z_c^V is not (except in the degenerate case of $\mu_c = \mu$). Nevertheless we shall presume that the MVN is a sufficiently adequate approximation, not only to motivate (2.3) but to provide us later with some ancillary results. The application of the rule requires a choice of n, and the image parameters $\mu_c^V (c = 1, \ldots, k)$ and W.

2.3. Image Parameters

The above rule was proposed by Switzer (1980). His proposals for image parameters were, however, unnecessarily over-simple, and relied on a concept he called "local continuity". He proposed that E $[Z(x + x_s) \mid c(x) = c] \equiv \mu_c(x_s) \simeq \mu_c$, at least for close neighbours of x, and hence that $\mu_c^V \simeq \mu_c \otimes 1$. The approximation implicit here restricted him to the simplest neighbourhood $N_1(x)$. Mardia (1984) developed this idea for a larger neighbourhood.

We avoid such approximations. In this paper we make the following assumptions:

(a) A "true image" of colours $c(x)$ or, more formally with a view to applications, a large sample of "true image" is available from the population of such images for which reconstruction from corresponding "noisy images" is to be attempted.

(b) The spatial correlation structure of the assumed stationary spatial stochastic noise process $\varepsilon(x) = \{Z_c(x) - \mu_c\}$ is available. Here we take this as "white noise" with Var $\varepsilon(x) = \Sigma_\epsilon$ and $\text{Cov}(\Sigma(x_1), \Sigma(x_2)) = 0$ if $x_1 \neq x_2$.

Given (a) and $\mu_c(c = 1, \ldots, k)$ we have a "clean image" $\{y(x)\}$. We may simply compute

$$\mu_c(x_s) = \text{E}[Z(x + x_s) \mid c(x) = c] = \text{Avg}[y(x + x_s) \mid c(x) = c] \tag{2.4}$$

where the average is over all pixels $(x+x_s)$ such that $c(x) = c$. Equivalently we may form $y^V(x)$ for each x (*i.e.* the complete population) and compute the conditional average of this vector as μ_c^V. Similarly, we may compute W_c, the conditional variance/covariance matrix for $y^V(x)$ and hence form the "pooled within group matrix of sums of squares and cross products" (see Mardia *et al.*, (1978), Section 11.1)

$$W = \sum_1^k p_c W_c \tag{2.5}$$

As this corresponds to a "noisy image" with $\Sigma_\epsilon = 0$ we emphasize this by writing this as $W(0)$.

The "parameters" $\mu_c^V(c = 1, \ldots, k)$ and $W(0)$ constitute our parametrization of the "clean image" $\{y(x)\}$. It is acknowledged that this is a large number of parameters, but there is, on the assumption above, no shortage of data with which to compute it. More parsimonious parametrizations are available if the Markov random field model (as, for example, Besag 1986) is available, and implicitly these would define μ_c^V and W; no explicit relation is available however to exploit this.

The data image $\{z(x)\}$ is clearly parametrized by

$$\mu_c^V \quad \text{and} \quad W(\Sigma) = W(0) + \Sigma_\epsilon \otimes I_{(\nu+1)\times(\nu+1)}.$$

The above parametrization requires assumption (a) above. If this is not available then these parameters need to be estimated. This is straightforward, but will be presented elsewhere.

2.4. The Neighbourhood Discriminant Functions and Symmetries

The application of (2.3) is, in principle, straightforward. However if, for example, we have selected the neighbourhood $N_5(x)$ and $p = 3$, there are 363 terms in μ_c^V and the matrix $W(\Sigma)$ is extremely large. Fortunately however, there are many symmetries to be exploited. In particular, if we seek an isotropic method, every x_s in, say, the first quadrant, has 3 other points symmetric with it, by successive rotation of x_s through 90°. Let $\overline{z}(x_s) = \frac{1}{4}\sum z(x + x_s)$ where the summation is over these symmetries, and define $\overline{z}^V(x) = \{z^T(x), \overline{z}_1^T(x), \ldots, \overline{z}_{\overline{\nu}}^T(x)\}^T$ where $\overline{\nu} = n(n+1)$, and consider discriminant functions based on linear combinations of $\overline{z}^V(x)$. The above theory is modified rather simply to yield isotropic discriminant functions

$$\overline{L}_c^V(x) = \overline{\lambda}_c^T \overline{z}^V(x) + \overline{\ell}_c \tag{2.6}$$

where $\overline{\lambda}_c^T = \overline{W}^{-1}(\Sigma)\overline{\mu}_c^V$, with an obvious notation.

For the above example this results in 93 terms only. Further considerable savings can be made by the application of classical variable selection routines (Seber (1984), Section 6.10) wherein only certain elements of $\overline{z}^V(x)$ are selected for the purpose of discrimination. These will be reported elsewhere.

The above theory is the simple generalization of the binary ($c = 2$) case previously reported (Haslett and Horgan, 1985). In that approach the strictly equivalent regression approach was used to compute equivalents of $\{\overline{L}_1^V(x) - \overline{L}_2^V(x)\}$ (see, for example, Flury (1985)).

2.5. Some Ancillary Results

The above method yields an allocation method with performance, as is reported in Section 4, comparable to the many other methods available. Its interest lies in the fact that, via the MVN approximation for the distribution of Z^V we have access to probabilistic measures based on the fact that $\overline{L}_c^V(x)$ itself has a univariate normal distribution.

Overall Performance

The probability of correct classification is PCC $= \sum p(c \mid c)p_c$ where

$$\begin{aligned} p(c_1 \mid c) &= Pr(\text{Classify as } c_1 \mid c(x) = c) \\ &= Pr(\overline{L}_{c_1}^V(x) - \overline{L}_{c_2}^V(x) \geq 0;\ c_2 = 1, \ldots, k \mid c(x) = c) \end{aligned} \tag{2.7}$$

Such probabilities may be computed straightforwardly from the MVN distribution functions with $(k-1)$ dimensions. The details need not concern us here. PCC may in particular be used to select the neighbourhood size n (see below).

Posterior Probabilities

From classical theory

$$Pr(c(x) = c \mid \overline{z}^V(x)) \propto \exp\{\overline{L}_c^V(x)\} \tag{2.8}$$

This may be used to decide that there is not enough evidence to allocate a pixel with confidence, or to qualify the reconstruction.

Distance and Outliers

From classical theory

$$D_c^{2^V}(x) = (\bar{z}^V(x) - \bar{\mu}_c^V)W^{-1}(\Sigma)(\bar{z}^V(x) - \bar{\mu}_c^V) \tag{2.9}$$

The Mahalanobis distance of $\bar{z}^V(x)$ from $\bar{\mu}_c^V$, has a χ^2 distribution with $(\bar{\nu}+1)p$ degrees of freedom, if $c(x) = c$. Thus extreme values of $D_c^{2^V}(x)$ may be used to suggest that the pixel x should not be allocated to any of the categories $c = 1, \ldots, k$, for the minimum distance is too large to be accepted. This would indicate that this pixel is an *outlier*, worthy perhaps of rather careful attention. More subtly, it indicates a discrepancy between the model and the data near pixel x. We develop this in Section 3.

Saebo *et al.* (1986) have shown how both "doubters" and "outliers" do arise in practice in remotely sensed imagery.

3. Results

The practical application of the method requires the prior choice of neighbourhood $N_n(x)$. The natural solution is: (a) to select initially some (possibly large) value of n and construct μ_c^V and $W(\Sigma)$; and (b) to choose a subset of these for actual reconstruction of the image. The choice of subset can be guided by the (estimated) PCC associated with this subset, from (2.7). (It can also be assisted by conventional stepwise methods not critically dependent on MVN: to be reported elsewhere). In (3.1) below we relate claimed and achieved PCC in different circumstances and contrast the "appearance" of the LDA-reconstructed image and that achieved by other methods. Finally in (3.2) we examine the application of the results on posterior probabilities and distances.

3.1. Overall Accuracy - Claimed and Achieved

Table 2 presents results via probability of correct classification PCC for two 3-colour images, shown in Figure 1. The isotropic variant has been used for differing neighbourhood sizes. Table 1 gives the values of $\{\mu_c\}$ and $\{p_c\}$ for these images. The signal has been taken as two-dimensional, with "noise" in each band independently having variance σ^2. Examples of such reconstructions with increasing neighbourhood size are also shown in Figure 1. These, and the "achieved" figures below, have been obtained by simulating additive Gaussian noise, and subsequently reconstructing the result. The results for a neighbourhood of 0 (*i.e.* the naïve method, involving the central pixel only) are included for comparison. Figure 2 compares a reconstruction using LDA with a 7×7 neighbourhood with three alternatives.

The conclusion corresponds very well to that already drawn in the previous paper: that achieved accuracy is very similar to that attained by other methods, and that predicted accuracy somewhat overestimates achieved accuracy, but provides quite clear guidelines on the neighbourhood size required in practice, as it asymptotes quite fast. In appearance the reconstruction corresponds closely with the symmetric methods of Besag's ICM and "probabilistic relaxation" (Rosenfeld (1977)).

FIGURE 1 (a) CAT

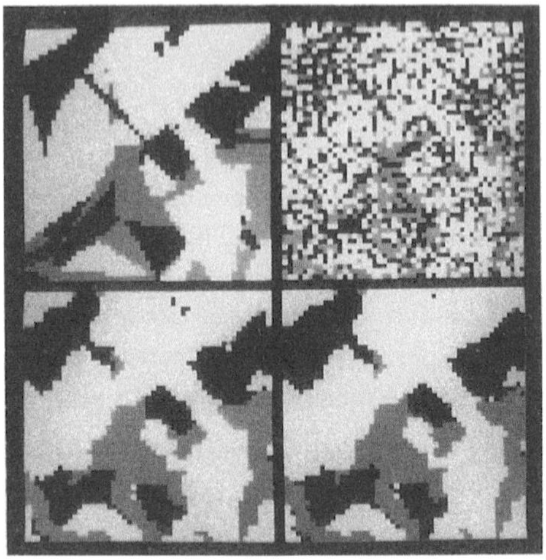

FIGURE 1 (b) TRIANGLE

Image and Reconstrictions
in LDA with ±n neighbourhood

Image	n = 0
n = 2	n = 5

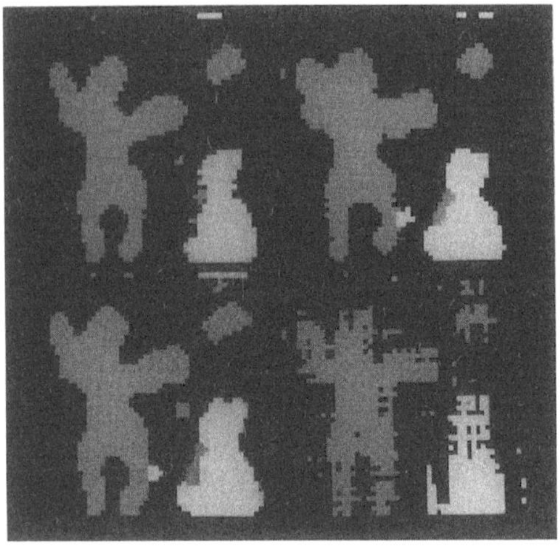

FIGURE 2

LDA (n=3)	Besag's ICM
Relaxation	Pickard's Model

FIGURE 3

Image	LDA (n=3)
Doubters	Outliers

		Class 1	Class 2	Class 3
CAT	Mean	(0,0)	(1,0)	(0,1)
	Proportions	.647	.242	.111
	PCC by naïve method	$\sigma^2 = 1.0$	0.68	
		$\sigma^2 = 0.5$	0.73	
TRI	Mean	(0,0)	(1,0)	(0,1)
	Proportions	.280	.185	.535
	PCC by naïve method	$\sigma^2 = 1.0$	0.62	
		$\sigma^2 = 0.5$	0.70	

Table 1: Class Conditional Means and Probabilities for Images CAT and TRIANGLE

			$\sigma^2 = 0.5$		$\sigma^2 = 0.1$	
			Claimed	Achieved	Claimed	Achieved
CAT	Neighbourhood size	3×3	.93	.90	.86	.84
		5×5	.97	.93	.92	.89
		7×7	.97	.93	.94	.91
		9×9	.98	.93	.95	.90
		11×11	.98	.94	.95	.91
	Besag's ICM		–	.94	–	.89
	Haslett's "Pickard Model"			.94	–	.87
	Rosenfeld's Relaxation		–	.94	–	.90
TRI	Neighbourhood size	3×3	.89	.87	.81	.81
		5×5	.92	.89	.86	.85
		7×7	.92	.89	.87	.86
		9×9	.93	.90	.87	.86
		11×11	.93	.90	.87	.86
	Besag's ICM		–	.89	–	.85
	Haslett's "Pickard Model"		–	.88	–	.81
	Rosenfeld's Relaxation		–	.89	–	.86

Table 2: Values of PCC - Claimed and Achieved

3.2. Doubters and Outliers

In Figure 3 we present a binary image which has been corrupted, before adding univariate Gaussian noise, by a small area of a quite distinctive texture. Class means are taken as 0 and 1. A reconstruction, following LDA with neighbourhood 7×7 is shown, when the noise SD was 0.4. In these circumstances the method claims very high accuracy, and would achieve it without such "textural corruption". However LDA, as described in Section 2.5, can provide quite clear guidelines as how to view such a reconstruction. Highlighted are "doubters" (bottom left) and "outliers" (bottom right). In this context a "doubter" is a pixel whose posterior probability (of either black or white) lies in (.4,.6). Edges are sometimes doubtful, though less often than might be expected, and there is a significant patch, corresponding to the corruption, where a number of pixels are in doubt.

However there is a dramatic path of outliers in this region, as well as a few elsewhere. These outliers are those which exceed the 1% level of the appropriate χ^2 distribution. Note that all pixels, viewed singly, are indeed black or white. Further, without this additional corruption, about 25 pixels in the complete 50×50 image would be expected to be designated as outliers in any case. Outlier status, in this example, indicates that the signals in the neighbourhood of x, taken as a set, do not accord with the model. It indicates "lack of fit" in a statistical context. Equivalently, in more traditional image processing language, LDA incorporates, in a natural way, a texture measure.

4. Conclusions

This paper has developed ideas proposed in an earlier paper. That paper included a plea that methods of contextual classification of images, particularly those proposed by statisticians, should carry with them the sort of second order information which distinguishes statistical from non-statistical estimation elsewhere. In particular, one should expect to be able, *in the context of a given image*, to provide the client with at the least some statement of overall performance, and preferably some guidance as to which parts of the reconstruction should be viewed with caution. Some suggestions were also made as to how that might be achieved, and by quite simple methods, for binary images. We have demonstrated that these ideas may be generalized to multi-coloured images, and have shown how the basic method naturally incorporates textural information. A number of tasks remain; notably these include the estimation of the parameters of the model from a given noisy image, the implementation of efficient stepwise algorithms to further simplify implementation and the interrelating of this method and others (Besag (1986), Kent and Mardia (1986)) which view the problem, with some success, as a spatial stochastic process. All of these ideas seem to flow naturally however, from their equivalent in our first paper and will be reported elsewhere.

Acknowledgements

This work has received the support of NBST grant SRP 36/84. It has benefited greatly from the continued association with Environmental Resource Analysis Ltd., Dublin.

References

[1] Besag, J., "On the Statistical Analysis of Dirty Pictures", read to the Royal Statistical Society, May 1986, and to appear in JRSS(B).

[2] Besag, J. and P.A.P. Moran, "On the Estimation and Testing of Spatial Inter-Action in Gaussian Lattice Processes" Biometrika 62, pp. 555- 562, 1975.

[3] Flury, B.N. and H. Riedwyl, " T^2-Tests, the Linear Two-Group Discriminant Function and their Computation by Linear Regression", The American Statistician 39, pp. 20-25, 1985.

[4] Geman, S. and D. Geman, "Stochastic Relaxation, Gibbs Distributions and the Bayesian Restoration of Images", IEEE Trans. PAMI-6, pp. 271-741, 1984.

[5] Haslett, J., "Maximum Likelihood Discriminant Analysis on the Plane, Using a Markovian Model of Spatial Context", Pattern Recognition 18 3/4, pp. 287-296, 1985.

[6] Haslett, J. and G. Horgan, "Spatial Discriminant Analysis - A Linear Function for the Black/White Case", presented to SERC Workshop "Statistics and Pattern Recognition", Edinburgh 1985, and submitted for publication.

[7] Kent, J.T. and K.V. Mardia, "Spatial Classification Using Fuzzy Membership Models", preprint, 1986.

[8] Mardia, K.V., "Spatial Discrimination and Classification Maps, Comm. Statist. Theor. Meth. 13(18), pp. 2181-2197, 1984.

[9] Mardia, K.V., J.T. Kent and J.M. Bibby, "Multivariate Analysis", Academic Press, 1979.

[10] Rosenfeld, A., "Interactive Methods in Image Analysis", Pattern Recognition 10, pp. 181-187, 1978.

[11] Saebo, H.V., K. Braten, N.L. Hjort, B. Llewellyn and E. Mohn, "Contextual Classification of Remotely Sensed Data : Statistical Methods and Development of a System", Rept. 768, Norwegian Computing Centre, 1985.

[12] Seber, G.A.F., "Multivariate Observations, Wiley, 1984.

[13] Switzer, P., "Extensions of Linear Discriminant Analysis for Statistical Classification of Remotely Sensed Imagery", J. Int. Ass. Math. Geol. 12, pp. 367-376, 1980.

NON SUPERVISED CLASSIFICATION TOOLS ADAPTED TO SUPERVISED CLASSIFICATION

R. Fages, M. Terrenoire, D. Tounissoux and A. Zighed

Université Lyon 1, UA 934
F-69622 Villeurbanne
France

1. Introduction

Let X be some set of individuals. We consider the following two mappings:

$$R : X \longrightarrow \mathbf{R}^p$$
$$\Omega : X \longrightarrow \{\omega_1, \cdots, \omega_n\}$$

For an individual x, $x \in X$, $R(x)$ is its representation ($\mathbf{R}^p$ being the feature-space) and $\Omega(x)$ is its class. A training set in a supervised classification problem consists in the data $(R(x), \Omega(x))$ for any x belonging to a subset T of X.

Using clustering methods — the Percolation Method in Section 2 and the Non-Hierarchical Divisive Method in Section 3 — we shall build a partition $(G_0, \cdots, G_r)$ of T, by taking into account both the proximity of the representation of the individuals x, and their class $\Omega(x)$. Then, we will define one partition $(Z_0, Z_1, \cdots, Z_n)$ of $\mathbf{R}^p$, induced by $(G_0, \cdots, G_r)$ and the following classification rule: For any $x \in X$, $x \notin T$,

i) $R(x) \in Z_j$, $(j \neq 0)$, we assign x to class ω_j;

ii) $R(x) \in Z_0$, we don't take any decision.

Each domain Z_j will be obtained by considering one or many groups G_i.

2. An Adaptation of the Percolation Method

2.1. The Percolation Method

First, we briefly review the basic principles of the percolation method, [1]. To any x, $x \in X$, we associate an ε-neighborhood of x, $V(x, \varepsilon) \doteq \{y \in T : d(R(x), R(y)) < \varepsilon\}$ where d is a distance measure on $\mathbf{R}^p$, and ε a positive threshold; and a *local density coefficient* $\delta(x, \varepsilon)$, $\delta(x, \varepsilon) \doteq \mathrm{card}\{y \in T : y \in V(x, \varepsilon)\}$. The percolation method is an agglomerative technique in which the elements x of T are considered successively according to decreasing density coefficients.

NATO ASI Series, Vol. F30
Pattern Recognition Theory and Applications
Edited by P. A. Devijver and J. Kittler

For the purposes of this presentation, let $\tilde{T}$ designate the subset of elements of T, considered previously at some stage of the process, and let $(G_0, G_1, \cdots, G_q)$ be the currently existing groups. Let y be the next element to be considered (y is such that $\delta(y, \varepsilon) = \max(\delta(x, \varepsilon) \mid x \in T - \tilde{T})$). Then,

i) if $V(y, \varepsilon) \cap G_i = \emptyset$, $i = 1, \cdots, q$, we create a new group G_{q+1}, and y is its unique element;

ii) if there exists one (and only one) group G_i ($i \neq 0$) such that $V(y, \varepsilon) \cup G_i \neq \emptyset$, then y is assigned to G_i;

iii) if $V(y, \varepsilon) \cup G_i \neq \emptyset$ for more than one group, y is assigned to G_0 (y is called a *boundary point*).

2.2. Supervised Classification with the Percolation Method

We first substitute a *local homogeneity* coefficient $I(x, \varepsilon)$, for the local density coefficient $\delta(x, \varepsilon)$ of the previous section:

$$I(x, \varepsilon) \doteq h\left(\frac{1}{n}, \cdots, \frac{1}{n}\right) - h\left(f_1(x, \varepsilon), \cdots, f_n(x, \varepsilon)\right)$$

where h is an entropy function defined on Γ_n, $\Gamma_n \doteq \{p \in \mathbf{R}^p : \sum_{j=1}^n p_j = 1,\ p_j \geq 0,\ j = 1, \cdots, n\}$ (for instance we can choose the quadratic entropy $h(p_1, \cdots, p_n) \doteq \sum_j p_j(1 - p_j)$), and

$$f_j(x, \varepsilon) = \frac{\operatorname{card}(\omega_j \cap V(x, \varepsilon))}{\operatorname{card}(V(x, \varepsilon))}$$

By the virtue of this modification, the partition $(G_0, \cdots, G_r)$ given by the percolation method takes into account not only the notion of proximity in $\mathbf{R}^p$, but also the notion of homogeneity with respect to the classes ω_j. The partition $(G_0, \cdots, G_r)$ of T will now serve as a basis for defining a two-step classification process:
Step 1: We define a partition $(Y_0, \cdots, Y_r)$ of $\mathbf{R}^p$, as follows: For any $x \in X$,

$$R(x) \in Y_i, \quad i \neq 0, \quad \text{if} \begin{cases} V(x, \varepsilon) \cap G_i \neq \emptyset \\ V(x, \varepsilon) \cap G_k \neq \emptyset, \quad k \in \{1, \cdots, r\} - \{i\} \end{cases}$$
$$Y_0 = \mathbf{R}^p - \cup_{i=1}^r Y_i \quad \text{(doubtful area)}$$

Step 2: To each group G_i we associate its majority ($m(i) \in \{1, \cdots, n\}$):

$$\operatorname{card}(\omega_{m(i)} \cap G_i) = \max(\operatorname{card}(\omega_k \cap G_i)/k = 1, \cdots, n)$$

Then, using the notation of Section 1, we can define the Z_j as follows:

$$Z_j = \cup_i \{Y_i / m_i = j\},\ j = 1, \cdots, n$$
$$Z_0 = Y_0$$

Two remarks should be made:

- In the algorithm just defined, the choice of ε is obviously very important. Experimental evidence shows that a good way to proceed consists in selecting the value of ε that minimizes the number of classification errors on the training set.

- Step 2 of the classification process may be modified as follows. For each group G_i, we compute the ratio q_i

$$q_i \doteq \frac{\operatorname{card}(\omega_\ell \cap G_i)}{\operatorname{card}(G_i)} = \max\left(\frac{\operatorname{card}(\omega_k \cap G_i)}{\operatorname{card}(G_i)} / k = 1, \cdots, n\right)$$

Let s be a threshold, $s \in]1/2,\ 1[$, then we put: $m(i) = \ell$, if $q_i > s$ and $m(i) = 0$ if $q_i < s$. The doubtful area Z_0 becomes $Z_0 = Y_0 \cup \{\cup_i Y_i / m(i) = 0\}$.

3. A Non–Hierarchical Divisive Approach

3.1. The Non–Hierarchical Divisive Method

First, we briefly review the non-hierarchical divisive method proposed by Fages [2]. This clustering method uses a set function called *scattering measure* suggested by Emptoz and Fages [3]. A scattering measure with respect to R is a mapping

$$D : \mathcal{T} \longrightarrow \mathbf{R}^+$$

($\mathcal{T}$ is the collection of all subsets of T) which satisfies the following properties: for any $A \subset T$ and $B \subset T$, we have $D(A) = 0$, if $R(A)$ is an atom, and $D(A \cup B) > D(A) + D(B)$, if $A \cap B = \emptyset$. For example the *inertia* of $R(A)$ is a scattering measure for A (see Section 3.2).

Let $P_r = (G_1, \cdots, G_r)$ be a partition of T, then the quantity $D[P_r] = \sum_{i=1}^{r} D(G_i)$ is called the scattering measure of the partition P_r.

A *weak element* of A, ($A \subset T$), is an element $a \in A$ such that $D(A - \{a\}) = \min(D(A - \{x\})/x \in A)$.

Let r denote the maximum of the desired numbers of groups. The non-hierarchical divisive method builds a sequence of locally optimum partitions $P_1 \cdots P_q \cdots P_r$. These partitions are not necessarily compatible (nested) as in the case of a standard hierarchy. The algorithm operates as follows:

Step 1: Set $q = 1$ and $G_1 = T$.

Step 2: Determine the group whose scattering measure is maximal and determine the weak element α of this group. Set $a := q + 1$ and constitute a new group $G_q = \{\alpha\}$.

Step 3: An element x from G_i is moved to G_j if this entails a strict decrease of $D[P_q]$. This step is repeated until convergence.

Step 4: Edit the partition $P_q = \{G_1, \cdots, G_q\}$. If $q < r$ then go to Step 2.

3.2. Supervised Classification with the Non–Hierarchical Divisive Method

Let us consider the following two scattering measures defined on $\mathcal{T}$ with respect to $R \times \Omega$. For $A \subset T$:

$$I(A) = \min\left(\sum_{a \in A} \| R(a) - y \|^2 / y \in \mathbf{R}^p\right) = \sum_{a \in A} \| R(a) - g \|^2$$

where g is the weighted mean of $R(A)$; and

$$H(A) = \text{card}(A) \sum_{i=1}^{n} p_i(1 - p_i)$$

where $p_i = \text{card}(A \cap \omega_i)/\text{card}(A)$.

We will make use of the following property: If D_1 and D_2 are two scattering measures defined on the same space, then $D = (1-\lambda)D_1 + \lambda D_2$, $0 < \lambda < 1$, is a scattering measure. This property allows us to work with the following measure:

$$D^*(A) = (1 - \lambda)\frac{I(A)}{I_0} + \lambda\frac{H(A)}{H_0}, \qquad A \subset T,$$

where $I_0 = I(T)$, and $H_0 = H(T)$. The parameter λ permits to give more or less importance to the notion of homogeneity with respect to Ω.

For given values of the parameters λ, r, and using the non-hierarchical divisive method with scattering measure D^*, we build a partition $P_r = (G_1, \cdots, G_r)$ of T. We then define a classification process similar to the one in Section 2 but for
Step 1': We define a partition $(Y_0, Y_1, \cdots, Y_r)$ of $\mathbf{R}^p$, induced from $G_1, \cdots, G_r$, as follows: for any $x \in X$,

$$\begin{aligned} R(x) \in Y_i,\ i \neq 0, \quad & \text{if } I(G_i + \{x\}) - I(G_i) \\ & = \min\left[I(G_k + \{x\}) - I(G_k) \mid k = 1, \cdots, r\right] \\ Y_0 = \mathbf{R}^p - \cup_{i=1}^{r} Y_i \quad & \text{(doubtful area)} \end{aligned}$$

Two comments are in order. First, for what concerns the choice of parameters, given λ, it is easy to find the corresponding optimal r, due to the sequential nature of the method. Then, the search for an optimal value of λ is done by minimizing the number of classification errors on the training set. Second, as far as computational aspects of the classification rule are concerned, we can directly assign an individual x, $x \in X - T$, to the group G_k according to

$$\frac{t_k}{1 + t_k} \parallel R(x) - g_k \parallel^2 = \min\left[\frac{t_i}{1 + t_i} \parallel R(x) - g_i \parallel^2 / i = 1, \cdots, r\right]$$

where g_i denotes the weighted mean of $R(G_i)$, and $t_i = \text{card}(G_i)$. Then, x will be assigned to class $\omega_m(k)$. This result leads to quite an easy classification process; as soon as the partition $(G_1, \cdots, G_r)$ is at hand, it is sufficient to save three data, *viz.*, (g_k, t_k, and $m(k)$) for each group G_k. (Recall that $m(k)$ is defined in Section 2.2.)

4. Experimental Results

The "Burn Center" of the Hôpital E. Herriot (Lyon, France) has been addressing a statistical approach to septic risk in burnt patient [4]. Three possible evolutions have been distinguished for burnt patients:

- alive without infection (this type of evolution will correspond to class ω_1),
- alive with infection (class ω_2),
- death (class ω_3).

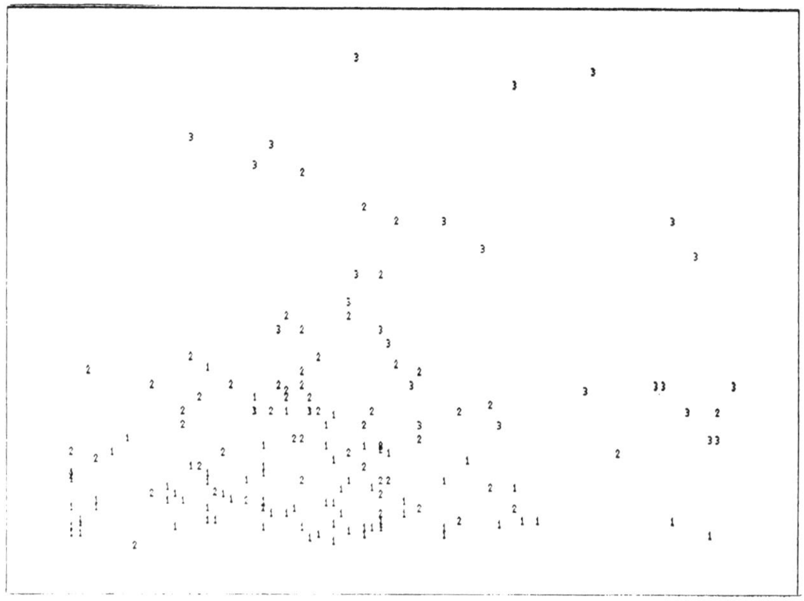

Figure 1: see text for explanation.

In Figure 1 a population of 174 burnt patients is represented:

- the horizontal axis shows the age of the patient,
- the vertical axis shows the burn extent measured in Burn Units (BUS),
- a patient denoted by "i" belongs to class ω_i, $i = 1, 2, 3$.

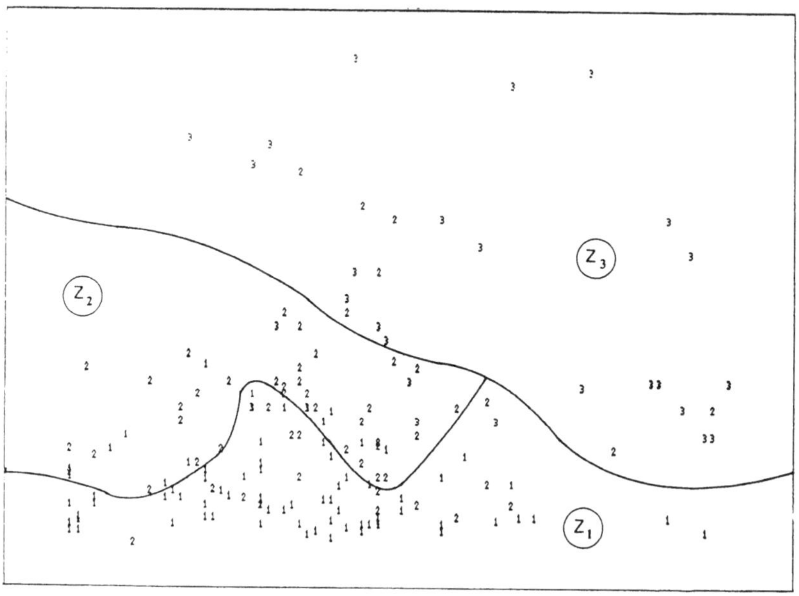

Figure 2: see text for explanation.

Using the pair Age-BUS, as the representation of the patients, the supervised classification algorithm issued from the non-hierarchical divisive method produced the results shown in Figure 2. The value of the miss-classification rate was equal to 0.23; (it should be noted that the linear discriminant analysis led to a miss-classification rate of 0.28). The optimal values for λ and r were $\lambda = 0.1$ and $r = 14$ respectively.

References

[1] Tremolière, R., "The percolation method for an efficient grouping of data," *Pattern Recognition*, vol. 11, no. 4, 1979.

[2] Fages, R., Emptoz, H., "Une approche ensembliste des problèmes de classification," Journées Internationales: Développements Récents en Reconnaissance des Formes, Lyon, 1979 - Actes édités par le C.A.S.T.

[3] Emptoz, H., Fages, R., "A set function for clustering and Pattern Recognition," IEEE International Symposium on Information Theory, Grignano, Italy, 1979.

[4] Marichy, J., Buffet, F., "Statistical approach of septic risk in burnt patient," First Sino-American Conference on Burn Injuries, Chongquing, China, 1985.

THE BOOTSTRAP APPROACH TO CLUSTERING

Jean Vincent Moreau and Anil K. Jain

Department of Computer Science
Michigan State University
East Lansing, Michigan 48824, U.S.A.

1. Introduction

A very difficult problem in cluster analysis is to determine the number of clusters present in a data set. Most clustering algorithms can partition a data set into any specified number of clusters even if the data set has no cluster structure. Unfortunately, it is very hard to decide if a K-cluster structure makes sense for the given data set.

Numerous procedures for determining the number of clusters have been proposed. Dubes and Jain [3] provide a general description of cluster validity techniques. A recent study by Milligan [7] conducts a Monte-Carlo evaluation of 30 indices for determining the number of clusters. We propose a new approach to this problem, using the bootstrap technique [4], [2]. A similar approach was suggested in [8] for the particular case of univariate data sets. Our approach can be used in any dimension. Our aim is not to present a new statistic for problems of cluster validity, but to extract new kinds of information from existing statistics. The proposed method can be integrated with any cluster analysis method and, therefore, can be useful in two other related issues: the problem of clustering tendency and the choice of clustering algorithm. We present experiments with four different clustering algorithms on both artificial and real data sets.

2. General Description of the Method

Let E be a set of data containing n patterns. We suppose that a clustering algorithm is available which permits us to obtain a K-cluster partition P_K of E. We assume that E is clustered, and we denote as K^* the real or true number of clusters in E. Our problem is to determine the value of K^*.

Our algorithm is based on the following intuitive idea:

NATO ASI Series, Vol. F30
Pattern Recognition Theory and Applications
Edited by P. A. Devijver and J. Kittler

- a K*-cluster solution will be stable. By stability we mean that the cluster memberships of the patterns will stay the same, even with moderate variations or perturbations of the data in E.

- any other K-cluster solution, $K \neq K^*$, will not be stable. In that case the memberships of the clusters in P_K could be completely changed if some patterns in E are modified.

Our aim is thus to implement this intuitive idea via a bootstrap technique [4], [2]. Bootstrapping is a resampling technique (sampling with replacement) which permits the generation of several "fake" data sets from the original data. Each data set is different from the original in that some patterns are missing, and we get multiple copies of some others. Let $B_1, B_2, \cdots, B_p$ be p sets of n patterns obtained from E by a classical bootstrap process. $P_{K,i}$ is the K-cluster partition obtained on B_i. We also need to define a criterion $W_K : \mathcal{P}_K \longrightarrow \Re$ to characterize the structure of $P_{K,i}$, where $\mathcal{P}_K$ is the set of all K-cluster partitions of E, and $\Re$ is the set of real numbers. Many different statistics can be used for this purpose [7]. $W_K(P_{K,i})$ is then a real value associated with partition $P_{K,i}$. Our criterion to measure the stability of the partition P_K is ΔW_K, the 68% confidence interval of variation of $W_K(P_{K,i})$ over the p bootstrap samples. The 68% interval is used to remove the outliers of W_K : 68% interval contains those values which are within one standard deviation of the mean value, assuming a normal distribution for W_K. The value of K which minimizes ΔW_K is taken as an estimate of K^*.

Let us illustrate this algorithm on a simple example. We consider a set of 20 two-dimensional patterns arranged in 3 clusters, as shown in Figure 1 (a). Figures 1 (b), 1 (c) and 1 (d) gives the partitions obtained for 2, 3 and 4 clusters, respectively, on three different bootstrap data sets derived from E. A K-means algorithm was used to generate these partitions. Note the stability of the 3-cluster solution and the instability of the partitions for 2 and 4 clusters. W_K in this example is the within-cluster scatter, which is defined as:

$$W_K = \sum_{k=1}^{K} \sum_{x_i \in C_k} D^2(x_i, g_k) \tag{1}$$

where K is the number of clusters, C_k the kth cluster, and g_k the cluster center of C_k. D is the Euclidean distance metric in $\Re^2$. Table 1 gives the values of ΔW_K (based on 100 bootstrap samples) for $K = 2, 3, 4$, and 5. The smallest value of ΔW_K is clearly obtained for $K = 3$.

K	ΔW_K
2	0.092
3	0.078
4	0.110
5	0.137

Table 1: Values of ΔW_K for data in Figure 1 (a).

Figure 1 (a): a data set E .

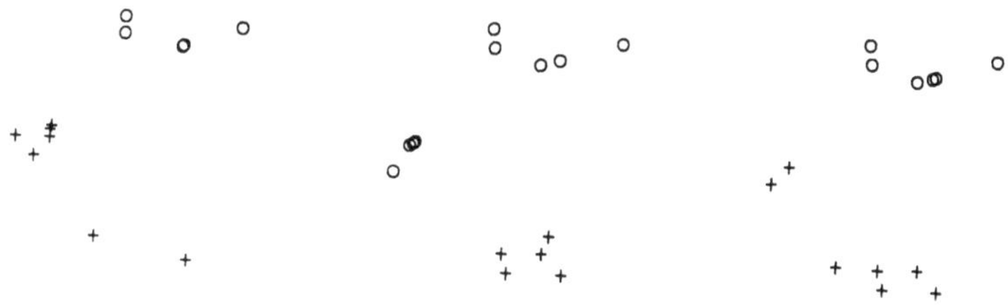

Figure 1 (b): 2-cluster partition of three bootstrap samples derived from E.

Figure 1 (c): 3-cluster partition of three bootstrap samples derived from E.

Figure 1 (d): 4-cluster partition of three bootstrap samples derived from E.

3. The Clustering Methods

The clustering technique is a user-specifiable parameter in our bootstrap process. Four different techniques are used in this paper:

- The first method, K-means [6], is a partitional clustering algorithm. To obtain the first partition in the iterative process, an initialization procedure is required. This initialization is often done by choosing K patterns at random as initial cluster centers in the data set. The probability of obtaining the near-optimal partition with a single initialization is not very high. Thus, the clustering is repeated with several different initializations. Table 2 gives the percentage p of correct clustering obtained on 100 Monte-Carlo data sets generated by a Neyman-Scott process [9]. The number of clusters ranges from 2 to 10 and the average deviation of patterns in each cluster is 0.02. The number i of initializations necessary to obtain correct clusters 95% of the time is shown in the same table. Note the small percentage of correct clustering when K is high. Additional experiments indicate that we generally need fewer initializations as the dimensionality increases, for a given cluster spread.
- The three other clustering techniques we use, *i.e.*, single-link, complete-link, and Ward's methods, are hierarchical in nature. The output is a set of nested partitions in the dendrogram. A practical advantage of these techniques over the K-means method is that all the partitions are obtained with only a single run of the hierarchical program.

K	2	3	4	5	6	7	8	9	10
p	100	71	38	25	15	9	6	6	4
i	1	3	7	11	19	32	49	49	74

Table 2: % of correct partitions versus number of clusters, on Neyman-Scott data.

4. The Clustering Statistic

The statistic W_K used in our experiments takes into account both within and between cluster distances. This is the Davies and Bouldin [1] criterion defined as follows:

$$W_K = \frac{1}{K}\sum_{i=1}^{K} R_i \quad \text{with} \quad R_i = \max_{\substack{j \\ j \neq i}} \frac{S_i + S_j}{T_{i,j}} \tag{2}$$

$$S_i = \frac{1}{|C_i|}\sum_{x_j \in C_i} |x_j - g_i|$$

$$T_{i,j} = \left\{\sum_{l=1}^{d} |g_i^l - g_j^l|^2\right\}^{1/2}$$

where d is the dimensionality of the data, g_i is the center of cluster C_i, and $|C_i|$ is the number of patterns in C_i.

Initial experiments with this statistic tend to illustrate the fact that the size of the 68% bootstrap confidence interval ΔW_K is generally a better criterion to detect those K-clusterings for which $K > K^*$ than those for which $K < K^*$. In general, the values of ΔW_K for all clusterings with $K < K^*$ are similar to the value for $K = K^*$; K-cluster partitions, often obtained by merging together some of the clusters in the K*-cluster partition, can also provide well-separated clusters and therefore stable clusterings. A good way to distinguish the K*-partition from the K-partitions, with $K < K^*$, is to measure its compactness. The compactness of the partition in a K^*-cluster solution is generally higher compared to that of K-cluster solution with $K < K^*$. The measure of compactness, M, that we use for our experiments is the within-cluster scatter, defined in equation (1). We denote by δM_K the average decrease in the value of M from the K to $K+1$ partitions. Note that within-cluster scatter is not a very good choice for W_K because its values decrease monotonically as K increases.

For each K-clustering we measure δM_K which characterizes the compactness of the partition P_K relative to that of P_{K+1}, and ΔW_K which measures the stability of P_K. Our clustering statistic is then defined as

$$R = a \times (\Delta W_K / \|\Delta W\|) + b \times (\delta M_K / \|\delta M_K\|), \tag{3}$$

where

$$\|\Delta W\| = \sqrt{\sum_k (\Delta W_k)^2}, \quad \|\delta M\| = \sqrt{\sum_k (\delta M_k)^2}, \quad K_1 \leq k \leq K_2,$$

and K_1 and K_2 are respectively the minimum and maximum number of clusters tested. The weighting parameters a and b are empirically determined. After many preliminary experiments, $a = 0.75$ and $b = 0.25$ appear to provide the best results, but other values of a and b also give reasonable results. ΔW_K and δM_K are normalized in equation (3) to make them of comparable magnitude. The number of clusters which minimizes R is taken as K^*.

5. The Algorithm

Our algorithm to detect the number of clusters is given below:

- Select a clustering algorithm C (see Section 3).
- If C is K-means, input i the number of initializations.
- Input K_1 and K_2 , the minimum and maximum number of clusters to be tested.
- Input the number p of bootstrap data sets ($p = 100$ in our experiments).
- Apply the clustering algorithm (with i initializations if K-means) on each bootstrap data set B_j, $j = 1, \ldots, p$, for $K_1 \leq K \leq K_2$.
- Compute $W_K(P_{K,j})$, for each j and each K.

- Compute ΔW_K, the 68% confidence interval of variation of $W_K(P_{K,j})$ on the p bootstrap samples, for each number K of clusters.

- Compute δM_K the average variation of M from K to $K+1$ clusters on the bootstrap samples.

- Compute $R = a \times (\Delta W_K/\|\Delta W\|) + b \times (\delta M_K/\|\delta M_K\|)$, with $a = 0.75$, $b = 0.25$ for each K.

- The value of K which minimizes R is taken as K^*.

6. Experiments

We have demonstrated the performance of our algorithm on both synthetic and real data.

a) Synthetic data:

Experiments were conducted on data sets consisting of hyperspherical shaped clusters. We generated 3-clustered data with 100 patterns in the unit hypercube, in 2 and 5 dimensions. The Neyman-Scott process [9] with control of minimum overlap between clusters was used for this purpose, with different values of σ (average deviation of the patterns in each cluster). Figure 2 shows some of these data sets in two dimensions. Note that as σ increases, the clusters get more diffuse. Values of R are computed from two to ten clusters. Table 3 gives some of the results obtained with K-means, for $K = 2$ to $K = 5$. Values of R are significantly smaller for 3 clusters, except for data with very diffuse clusters. For two-dimensional data, the values of R for $K = 2, 3$ are very close when $\sigma = 0.017$, and a 4-cluster solution is found for $\sigma = 0.26$. In 5 dimensions, the 3-cluster solution is the overwhelming choice until $\sigma = 0.26$.

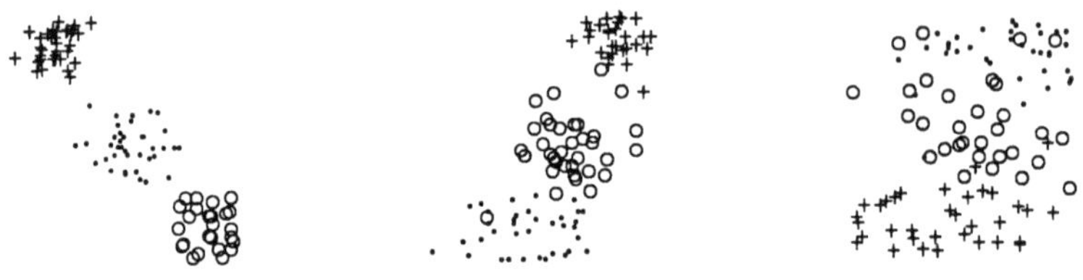

(a) $\sigma = 0.09$ (b) $\sigma = 0.13$ (c) $\sigma = 0.17$

Figure 2: Data with 3 clusters

Table 4 gives the optimal number of clusters obtained for these data with the four clustering algorithms. Numbers in the parentheses correspond to other values of K giving values of the R statistic very close to the optimal one. The K-means and Ward algorithms generate the true number of clusters for most of the data sets. These methods are known to be well suited for hyperspherical clusters. Results are also reasonable with

K \ σ		0.09	0.11	0.13	0.15	0.17	0.26
dim=2	2	0.249	0.212	0.242	0.223	0.202	0.270
	3	*0.094	*0.115	*0.141	*0.211	*0.196	0.257
	4	0.158	0.179	0.152	0.220	0.220	*0.222
	5	0.283	0.205	0.267	0.327	0.229	0.258
dim=5	2	0.247	0.231	0.257	0.250	0.254	0.255
	3	*0.059	*0.061	*0.052	*0.077	*0.092	*0.231
	4	0.129	0.144	0.253	0.222	0.163	0.232
	5	0.212	0.237	0.246	0.291	0.238	0.252

Table 3: Values of statistic R for 3-clustered data in 2 and 5 dimensions, using K-means program. * identifies the value of K for which R is minimum.

the complete-link method. However, the single-link method finds the true number of clusters only if these clusters are very well separated; it tends to merge clusters as soon as a few patterns form a bridge between them (see, for example, Figures 2 (b) and 2 (c)).

	σ	K-means	Single Link	Complete Link	Ward
dim=2	0.09	3	3	3	3
	0.11	3	2	3	3
	0.13	3	2	3	3
	0.15	3	2	2	2
	0.17	3 (2)	2	3 (2)	2
	0.26	4	2	2	3 (4)
dim=5	0.09	3	3	3	3
	0.11	3	3	3	3
	0.13	3	3	3	3
	0.15	3	2 (3)	3	3
	0.17	3	2 (3)	3	3
	0.26	3 (4)	2	3 (2,4)	3

Table 4: Optimal number of clusters based on minimum value of R for 3-clustered data, in 2 and 5 dimensions.

b) Real data:

Several different real data sets have been evaluated by our technique. Here we report results for IRIS data. It consists of 150 4-dimensional patterns from three species of iris. Two of our four methods, K-means and Ward, find a three-cluster solution and the resulting partitions correspond to the categories. Single-link provides a 2-cluster solution in which two of the three categories are merged into one cluster. This solution seems reasonable because the 3-cluster solution does not correctly separate the two other categories. Finally, the complete-link method provides a 4-cluster solution and this solution mixes up the two close categories (as does the 3-cluster solution).

Another series of applications to real data is in computer vision. Range images are described by the sensed 3-D coordinates and estimated normal vectors for each pixel on the surface of the object [10]. Data are therefore 6-dimensional and each pattern corresponds to a pixel in the range image. These images can be segmented to find natural object faces. The problem is to find the number of clusters that best partitions or segments the image. The K-means program is used for these experiments. An image of a disk, bent along a diametral line, is generated synthetically with added noise. Results show clearly a 3-cluster partition, 2 of them corresponding to the two half-circles, and the third one to the median line over which the normal is not well defined (see grey-level description of the solution in Figure 3 (a)). For the cup image, obtained by a laser scanner, two and three clusters appear to be very close for the best choice, (see Figures 3 (b) and 3 (c)). The 2-cluster solution isolates the bottom and handle from the side of the cup. The 3-cluster solution splits the side of the cup into concave and convex surface regions. Note that the handle is still merged with the bottom of the cup, because the normal vectors at the pixels in these two regions are oriented roughly the same way. In the 6-cluster solution, which is ranked third, the handle forms one cluster, the bottom a second one, and the side of the cup is partitioned into four sections.

(a) Bent disk with 3 clusters (b) Cup with 2 clusters (c) Cup with 3 clusters

Figure 3: Optimal partitions of range images.

7. Summary and Conclusions

We have presented a method to determine the number of clusters in a data set, using a bootstrap technique. Our results show good performances of this approach in several dimensions, for both synthetic and real data. As we have seen, the choice of clustering algorithm is very crucial for the results and the user must ensure that the clustering algorithm used is well matched to the data. Our method can be useful to compare the performances of several clustering algorithms. We are also evaluating the variance of R to assess clustering tendency.

Acknowledgement

We thank Richard Hoffman for providing the range images and a careful reading of the manuscript.

References

[1] Davies D.L. and Bouldin D., "A cluster separation measure," *IEEE Transactions on Pattern Analysis and Machine Intelligence*, Vol. PAMI-1, no.2, 224-227, 1979.

[2] Diaconis P. and Efron D., "Computer intensive methods in statistics," *Scientific American*, Vol. 248, 116-130, 1983.

[3] Dubes R. and Jain A.K., "Validity studies in clustering methodologies," *Pattern Recognition*, Vol. 11, 235-254, 1979.

[4] Efron B., "Bootstrap method: another look at the jacknife," *The Annals of Statistics*, Vol. 7, no.1, 1-26, 1979.

[5] Fisher R.A., "The use of multiple measurements in taxonomic problems," *Machine Recognition of Patterns*, A.K. Agrawala, Ed., New York: IEEE Press (1976).

[6] Hartigan J.A., "A K-means clustering algorithm," *Applied Statistics*, Vol. 28, 100-108, 1979.

[7] Milligan G.W and Cooper M.C., "An examination of procedures for determining the number of clusters in a data-set," *The Psychometric Society*, Vol. 50, no.2, 159-179, 1985.

[8] Peck R., Fisher L., Van Ness J., "Bootstrap confidence interval for the number of clusters in cluster analysis", (unpublished paper).

[9] Ripley B.D., *Spatial Statistics*, New-York: Wiley, 1981.

[10] Hoffman R.L. and Jain A.K., "Segmentation and classification of range images," Technical Report MSU-ENGR-86-002, Department of Computer Science, Michigan State University, 1986.

ON THE DISTRIBUTION EQUIVALENCE IN CLUSTER ANALYSIS

Helena Bacelar Nicolau

Department of Statistics
Faculty of Sciences — University of Lisbon
58 Rua da Escola Politecnica
1294 LISBOA Codex — PORTUGAL

1. Introduction

One of the first problems to be solved in cluster analysis particularly when using hierarchical clustering methods is to choose adequate measures of comparison between entities to be clustered.

Most packages for cluster analysis give indeed the possibility of trying a lot of coefficients. Comparing the results by different methods is in principle a good thing. But for common users the knowledge, rules and ability for choosing the right coefficients and criteria and getting finally some kind of consensus in classifications may be a difficult problem too.

Thus doing comparative studies and finding robust similarity coefficients became an essential task in cluster analysis. See for instance the classic Sokal and Sneath (1963), Sibson (1972) and Anderberg (1973). Lerman (1973) also studied the subject searching for general coefficients in order to obtain general patterns, and proposed a probabilistic coefficient p_{xy}. In this area also see Nicolau (1983), Nicolau and Bacelar-Nicolau (1981), Bacelar-Nicolau (1972, 1980, 1985) and Lerman (1981).

In this paper we take the general probabilistic coefficient p_{xy} and explain the notion of distribution equivalence between coefficients. *Distribution equivalent (d.e.) coefficients* will associate to each pair of entities (x, y) the same value p_{xy}. So we don't have to choose among coefficients in the same class of equivalence, due to the uniqueness of p_{xy}. In the special case of binary data a very general theorem of uniqueness (exact or asymptotic) is derived. A simple application to psychiatric data is presented too, illustrating the notions we talk about.

2. Distribution Equivalence

We are interested in the problem of measuring the similarity between variables. Let E be the set of variables to be clustered. Let $x, y \in E$, and $C = C(x, y)$ be a basic similarity coefficient, taking the numerical value c_{xy} for each particular case (that is, each particular pair (x, y) and data set). Under general assumptions (see next paragraph), the mean μ_C and variance σ_C^2 of the random variable (r.v.) C can be evaluated and the

NATO ASI Series, Vol. F30
Pattern Recognition Theory and Applications
Edited by P. A. Devijver and J. Kittler

cumulative distribution function (c.d.f) of C will provide a new similarity coefficient p_{xy} given by the integral transformation

$$p_{xy} = \text{Prob}(C \le c_{xy}) = \text{Prob}(C^* \le c^*_{xy})$$

where C^* is the standard r.v. $C^* = (C - \mu_C)/\sigma_S$, and c^* its numerical value for the pair (x, y).

This probabilistic coefficient p_{xy} can be calculated either exactly or at least asymptotically, because it can be proved that C^* has the standard normal distribution as limit law and in that case $p_{xy} \cong \Phi_{xy} = \Phi(c^*_{xy})$, where Φ is the c.d.f. of N(0,1) random variables. It is called "VL similarity coefficient" (V for validity, L for link) because it measures in a probabilistic sense the validity of the basic similarity coefficient: the lesser is the probability of exceeding the numerical value c_{xy}, the greater is its validity or confidence given to the decision of merging entities x and y.

Note that a VL-similarity coefficient can be built for any type of data, assuring its universality. On the other hand properties of p_{xy} and extensions to agglomerative criteria have been studied by Lerman (1970, 1981), Nicolau (1983, 1985), Nicolau and Bacelar-Nicolau (1981) and Bacelar-Nicolau (1972, 1980, 1985). These methods are now currently used in practice, applications on various fields assuring the goodness of the methodology, either on real or simulated data. Agglomerative criteria based on the notion of VL similarity are called the VL family of clustering methods.

Now comes the definition for distribution equivalence: We say that two coefficients C_1 and C_2 are *equivalent* (respectively, *asymptotically equivalent*) *in distribution* if they assign the same value p_{xy} (respectively, the same limit value $\Phi_{xy} \cong p_{xy}$) to each pair (x, y); (C_1, C_2) are then *distribution equivalent (d.e.) coefficients*.

It is obvious that coefficients associated to the same class of equivalence will produce exactly the same tree of classification whatever the agglomerative criteria is used.

In the next paragraph we will study in more detail the case of binary data.

3. Distribution Equivalence in Binary Data Case

It is well known that the similarity coefficients for binary data are all defined from the 2×2 contingency table crossing each pair (x, y):

x \ y	1	0	
1	s	u	n_x
0	v	t	$n - n_x$
	n_y	$n - n_y$	n

where n is the dimension of the set of objects scored; s and t are the number of common presences and absences respectively; and $u(v)$ is the number of times that $x(y)$ is present and $y(x)$ is absent. Of course $n_x = s + u$, $n_y = s + v$, $n = s + u + v + t$. Combining the elements of this table a great number of coefficients has been proposed (Jaccard, Ochiai, Sokal, Kulezinski, Yule, Russel and Rao, Dice, Pearson, ...). For a rather complete compilation of the usual binary coefficients see for instance Bacelar-Nicolau (1980). Let us now introduce some probabilistic notions.

Let X and Y be two discrete Bernouilli r.v.:

$$X = \begin{cases} 0 & 1 \\ q_X & p_X \end{cases} \qquad Y = \begin{cases} 0 & 1 \\ q_Y & p_Y \end{cases}$$

where $p_X = \text{Prob}(X = 1)$, $q_X = 1 - p_X = \text{Prob}(X = 0)$, and similarly for Y, p_Y, q_Y.

Now the presence or absence of two attributes x and y over some particular object can be interpreted as a realization of values 1/0 of r.v. X and Y; so that the 2×2 table of last page consists of observed values of the table:

$X \backslash Y$	1	0	
1	S	U	N_X
0	V	T	$n - N_X$
	N_y	$n - N_Y$	n

where $S, U, \ldots$ are r.v.'s associated to values $s, u, \ldots$; in this way a comparison coefficient C can always be interpreted as a statistic, $C = C(S, U, V, T)$, so that the particular value c_{xy} of C for a fixed pair (x, y) and given data set is the observed value of a random variable. The problem it is now to get the probability distribution of C, and that depends of course on the distribution of r.v.'s S, U, V, T. We shall consider here only the hypothesis of fixed marginal totals for the table 2×2 above. Under this assumption only one of the four cells is free, say S, the others being linear functions of n, $N_X = n_X$, $N_Y = n_Y$, and S.

Now, because of our "ignorance 'a priori' about the structure of relationship among variables", we will assume the independence as reference hypothesis H_R; so that S will become an hypergeometric r.v. and we can exactly evaluate p_{xy}, under H_R. Besides S is asymptotically normal distributed with mean and variance given by $\mu_S = n_x n_y / n$ and $\sigma_S^2 = n_x n_y (n - n_x)(n - n_y)/[n^2(n-1)]$ and thus the distribution of:

$$S^* = \frac{(nS - n_x n_y)\sqrt{n-1}}{\sqrt{n_x n_y (n - n_x)(n - n_y)}} = \frac{(S/n - p_x p_y)\sqrt{n-1}}{\sqrt{p_x p_y (1 - p_x)(1 - p_y)}}$$

where $p_x = n_x/n$ and $p_y = n_y/n$, approaches the standard normal distribution as n approaches infinity.

So $p_{xy} = \text{Prob}(S \leq s) = \text{Prob}(S^* \leq s^*) \cong \Phi(s^*)$.

Theorem

> Under the reference hypothesis H_R all the usual similarity coefficients for binary data are d.e. coefficients or at least asymptotically d.e. coefficients.

Sketch of proof.

It is easy to prove that those coefficients can be grouped into two classes. In the first one we place all the coefficients that are linear functions of S; and in the second class we include coefficients that are ratio of linear functions of S or, more generally, that are continuous functions of S.

For the first group all coefficients C are d.e. coefficients, since that Prob $(C \leq c_{xy})$ = Prob $(S \leq s) = p_{xy}$.

For the second group similarity coefficients are continuous functions of S, with continuous first derivatives.

From the expressions given above for S^* we can write

$$\frac{S}{n} = p_x p_y + \sqrt{\frac{p_x p_y (1-p_x)(1-p_y)}{n-1}} S^* = \alpha + \beta_n S^*$$

where $\alpha = p_x p_y$ and $\beta_n = \sqrt{p_x p_y (1-p_x)(1-p_y)/(n-1)}$.

Furthermore, S/n converges in probability to α and β_n converges to zero.

S^* is asymptotically normal distributed as we saw above.

Then, by the so-called limit theorem of δ method (see for instance, Tiago de Oliveira (1982)) we have, for any continuous function $C = g(S/n)$ with continuous first derivative g' such that $g'(\alpha) > 0$, the following result:

$$\frac{g(S/n) - g(\alpha)}{\beta_n g'(\alpha)} = C^* \simeq S^*$$

that is, C^* and S^* have the same asymptotic distribution. In other words, if $C = g(S/n)$ represents any coefficient in the second group, we have:

$$\text{Prob}(C \leq c_{xy}) = \text{Prob}\left(g(\frac{S}{n}) \leq g(\frac{s}{n})\right) \cong \text{Prob}(S^* \leq s^*).$$

Thus

$$\text{Prob}(C \leq c_{xy}) \cong \Phi(s^*) \cong p_{xy}$$

In conclusion, all those coefficients are d.e. in limit.

4. Using Distribution Equivalence - An Example

A set of schizophrenic patients described by a set of attributes (sex, age group, time of disease, symptoms, ...) is submitted to cluster analysis searching for typical patterns of suicide behaviour. We expect that those patterns will define pre-suicide syndromes, essential in preventive diagnosis. Thus we will classify the set of attributes.

As the structure of relationship underlying data is 'a priori' unknown, we will take the independence as reference hypothesis H_R. The basic similarity to measure resemblance between two given attributes (x, y) will then be the number s of common presences over the set of patients; in this way two attributes will be as much similar as the probability of observed values of S being lesser or equal to s is larger, and we know that the r.v. S is hypergeometric distributed $H(n, n_x, n_y)$ under H_R. Therefore, the similarity of (x, y) will be evaluated, as explained before, by the value $p_{xy} = \text{Prob}(S \leq s) \cong \Phi_{xy}$.

The set of VL similarity values $[p_{xy} \mid x \neq y]$ will now be submitted to agglomerative criteria searching for hierarchic clustering. We could use classic methods such as single linkage, complete linkage or any other method and the hierarchies got in this way will have properties of consensus among the hierarchies built with the set of the usual binary coefficients. In fact it was easily confirmed on the present data that any other basic binary coefficient gave exactly or approximately (close approximation) the same set of p_{xy} values. But we prefer to present briefly the condensed tree resulting of one of the VL-family of cluster methods (see Nicolau (1983), for some details). In this application our choice goes to AVL tree (Lerman (1970), Bacelar Nicolau (1972)), for the goodness of results of this method. In the sequel we will comment quickly the hierarchical clustering tree presented below.

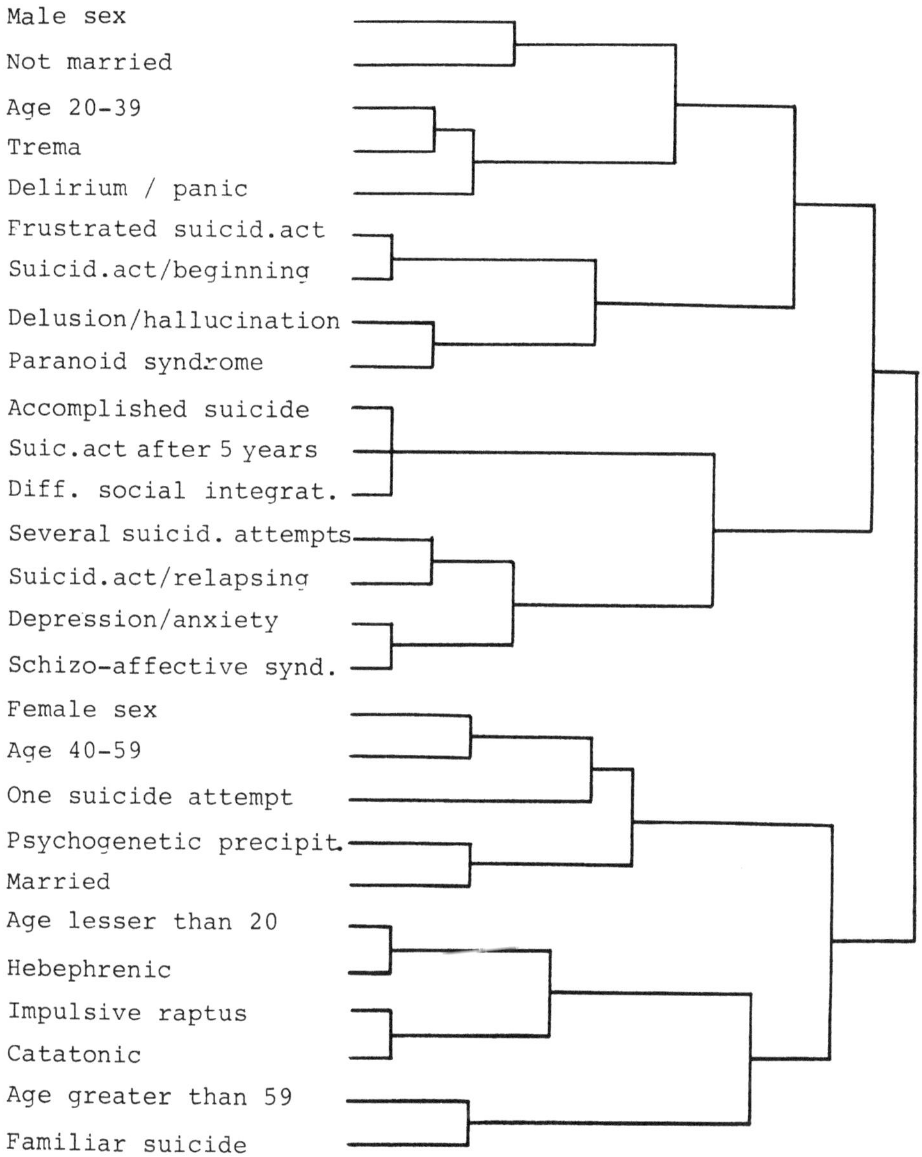

Tipology of suicidal acting — AVL condensed clustering tree

Three general patterns were found, characterizing patients at the moment they have attempted suicide, either with success (death) or not:

▷ A class of patients presenting a general paranoiac syndrome and also symptoms of trema, delirium/panic, delusion and hallucinations; they attempt suicide a short time after the beginning of the disease.

▷ A second class defining a chronic class of patients, with difficult social integration; a general schizo-affective syndrome is present as well as symptoms of depression and anxiety; they accomplished suicide after several suicide attempts and five or more years of disease.

▷ Finally we observe a class of patients for whom the duration of disease is not very important, including hebephrenic patients with catatonia, psychogenetic precipitation; they commit suicide abruptly and unconsciously.

The basic data was also submitted to correspondence analysis. The specialist found however that results of AVL cluster tree were more comprehensive and refined (see Mendes *et. al.* (1979)).

5. Conclusions

We explained here the property of distribution equivalence and analysed the case of binary similarity coefficients. Under the reference hypothesis of fixed total margins for the 2×2 contingency table crossing two attributes a general theorem was stated, proving the exact or at least asymptotic distribution equivalence for all the usual binary similarity coefficients. If we take the free total margins assumption for the 2×2 table as reference hypothesis the d.e. can only be stated for some coefficients. In any case we can always define for each coefficient C the corresponding probabilistic coefficient p_{xy} and its approximation Φ_{xy} by using the multivariate version of limit theorem of δ method.

Acknowledgements

We thank F. Costa Nicolau for advice and help in preparing this paper. This work was supported in part by the Project on Multivariate Data Analysis/Center of Statistics and Applications (I.N.I.C.) - University of Lisbon.

References

[1] Anderberg, M.R., *Cluster Analysis for Applications*, Acad. Press, New York, 1973

[2] Bacelar-Nicolau, H., "Analyse d'un Algorithme de Classification Automatique," Thèse de Doctorat de 3ème Cycle, Univ. Paris VI (Pierre et Marie Curie), 1972.

[3] Bacelar-Nicolau, H., "Contributions to the Study of Comparison Coefficients in Cluster Analysis," (in Portuguese), Ph. D. Thesis, Fac. Ciências Univ. Lisboa, 1980.

[4] Bacelar-Nicolau, H., "The affinity coefficient in cluster analysis," Meth. Oper. Res., 53, 507-12, 1985.

[5] Lerman, I.C., "Sur l'analyse des données préalables à une classification automatique, proposition d'une nouvelle mesure de classification," Rapport n.32, 8ème année, MSH, Paris, 1970.

[6] Lerman, I.C., "Etude distributionnelle de statistiques de proximité entre structures finies de même type, application à la classification automatique," Cahiers du B.U.R.O., n.19, Paris, 1973.

[7] Lerman, I.C., *Classification et Analyse Ordinale des Données*, Dunod, Paris, 1981.

[8] Mendes, J. Fragoso and Figueira, M.L. and Bacelar-Nicolau, H., "Suicidal behaviour in schizophrenia," (in Port.), J.O Med., 1439, vol. XC, 563-580, 1979.

[9] Nicolau, F. Costa, "Cluster analysis and distribution function," Meth. Oper. Res., 45, 431-434, 1983.

[10] Nicolau, F. Costa, "Analysis of a non-hierarchical clustering method based on VL-similarity," Meth. Oper. Res., 53, 603-610, 1985.

[11] Nicolau, F. Costa and Bacelar-Nicolau, H., "Nouvelles méthodes d'agrégation basées sur la fonction de répartition," Coll. Séminaires INRIA, Class. Perc. Ordin., 45-60, 1981.

[12] Sibson, R., "Order invariant methods for data analysis," JRSS, B, 34, n.3, 1972,

[13] Sokal, R.R. and Sneath, P.H., *Principles of Numerical Taxonomy*, Freeman, San Francisco, 1963.

[14] Tiago de Oliveira, J., "The δ method for obtention of asymptotic distributions; applications," Publ. Inst. Statist. Univ. Paris, vol. XXVII, 49-70, 1982.

SPATIAL POINT PROCESSES AND CLUSTERING TENDENCY IN EXPLORATORY DATA ANALYSIS[1]

Erdal Panayırcı[2] and Richard C. Dubes[3]

[2] Faculty of Electrical Engineering
Istanbul Technical University, and
Marmara Research Institute, Istanbul
Turkey
[3] Department of Computer Science
Michigan State University
East Lansing, Michigan, 48823,
U.S.A.

Abstract

Discriminating among random, clustered and regular arrangements of multidimensional patterns (data) is an important problem in exploratory data analysis, statistical pattern recognition and image processing. Clustering methods have been used extensively for this purpose. However, clustering algorithms will locate and specify clusters in data even non are present. It is therefore appropriate to measure the clustering tendency or randomness of a pattern set before subjecting it to a clustering algorithm. Spatial point process models are alternatives to structures obtained from cluster analysis and are a means for objectifying observed data. We survey the work that has been done in developing measures of clustering tendency, with special attention to distance-based methods. We review several models for spatial point processes with an eye towards identifying potential research problems in applying such models to clustering tendency. The successes and failures of these methods are discussed as well as suggestions and directions for future study.

1. Introduction

The goal of Exploratory Data Analysis is to understand the structure of a given pattern set. We consider pattern sets in which n objects, called "patterns", are given in d-dimensional space, $d << n$, whose axes represent the measurements made on each object and are called "features". The word "structure" is difficult to define in a useful way for such a pattern set but the key factors are the interactions among patterns and among features and sample size considerations. Cluster analysis has been used extensively to examine structure by organizing the patterns into natural disjoint groups, called clusters. A wide collection of clustering algorithms is known, each operating

[1]This work was supported in part by a NATO Collaborative Research Grant No. 286/84.

NATO ASI Series, Vol. F30
Pattern Recognition Theory and Applications
Edited by P. A. Devijver and J. Kittler

under various criteria. Some surveys include Anderberg [1], Everitt [2], and Hartigan [3]. Computationally, clustering algorithms are relatively expensive, and their run time increases with the number of patterns and number of features. A serious drawback of these algorithms is that they will find clusters even if the pattern set is entirely random according to various definitions which we explore at length. See Dubes and Jain [4] for some examples of this phenomenon. It is therefore appropriate to measure the "clustering tendency" or "randomness" of a pattern set before subjecting it to a clustering algorithm. The issue of clustering tendency has virtually been ignored in the literature and this makes it difficult to interpret the results of a clustering algorithm [5].

This paper examines techniques that assess the general nature of the spatial arrangement of the patterns and determine which, if any, of the following descriptions fits the given pattern set.

i) The patterns are arranged randomly;

ii) The patterns are aggregated, or clustered;

iii) The patterns are regularly spaced.

This problem of examining the global nature of the spatial arrangement of patterns will be termed the clustering tendency problem. We wish to pose the clustering tendency problem in a hypothesis testing framework. Our null hypothesis will always be that the given pattern set is random. If the null hypothesis fails to be rejected at some significance level then we will say that the pattern set does not exhibit a tendency to cluster and it is not worth while to apply a clustering algorithm to this pattern set. A number of techniques for the analysis and modeling of two-dimensional patterns is available in the literature [1,6,7,8]. The development of these techniques was motivated by a need to interpret and analyze large amounts of two-dimensional data collected in various ecological and socio-geographic studies. These tests have not been tried out on high-dimensional data and it is not known whether a direct generalization (to $d > 2$ dimensions) of these statistics would lead to useful tests.

Spatial point process models are alternatives to structures obtained from cluster analysis and are a means for objectifying observed data. The main purpose of this paper is to summarize several models for spatial processes with an eye towards identifying potential research problems in applying such models to pattern analysis and to survey the work that has been done in developing measures of clustering tendency, to see whether some of the test statistics known to be powerful in 2-dimensions can be generalized to $d > 2$ dimensions, and to discuss the successes and failures of these methods as well as suggestions and directions for future study.

2. Models For Generation of Patterns

When encountering a clustering tendency problem, we are given a set of "training" patterns, or realization of the process being studied. The training patterns are given, in the form of "pattern matrix" whose rows denote patterns, or points in a d-dimensional space, and whose columns consist of measurements made on each pattern. The techniques and models with which we are concerned focus on the relative positions of the patterns in the pattern space. Ideally, a model for a pattern matrix should provide the following information.

i) A likelihood function for the positions of the patterns that establishes a probabilistic model for all possible pattern matrices;

ii) A summary function, or an easily computed function that describes important characteristics of the pattern matrix, such as nearest neighbor information;

iii) A means for sampling the model, or generating pattern matrices that resemble the given pattern matrix;

iv) A practical measure of goodness-of-fit between the model and the given pattern matrix;

v) Parameters from the model which are understood well, which have intuitive appeal, and which can be estimated.

A model description should be simple enough to facilitate parameter estimation and goodness of fit testing but complicated enough to be sensitive to the needs of particular applications. This paper argues that models based on spatial point process can be used to advantage in pattern analysis. The most popular clustering algorithms in practice assume an underlying Gaussian model. This is done for mathematical tractability and because there is often a correspondence between this model and real data. For instance, square error clustering algorithms seek hyperellipsoidal clusters. The statistical model implied by square error creates clusters sprinkling patterns around a cluster center according to a multidimensional normal distribution. Adding the assumption that the positions of the patterns are independent and identically distributed means that a Gaussian mixture model is being fitted to the training patterns. The parameters of the model are the mean vectors for the clusters, which are the estimates of the cluster centers, and the covariance matrices for the clusters which model the spreads of the clusters. If a mixture with k clusters is fit to d-dimensional data, $kd(d-1)/2$ parameters must be estimated, which requires large numbers of patterns for accurate estimates. Many practical clustering problems involve only a few hundred patterns. The multivariate normality of each cluster can be tested [9], but this is a difficult and unrewarding task when both mean vector and covariance matrix are estimated. The most important assumption under a Gaussian mixture model is that the cluster centers and spreads have real significance. That is, if the experiment that generated the sample patterns were repeated, another set of patterns with the same centers and spreads would appear. The patterns would not be the same, but the cluster centers would be in about the same positions. In other words, the cluster centers have actual meaning. Another assumption is that second order statistics will completely characterize the data. The Gaussian mixture model is defined over a pattern space that extends to infinity along all coordinates, even though patterns are observed only in a finite subspace.

A spatial point process model is a mechanism for generating a countable number of points, or patterns, over a pattern space that satisfy some structural requirements. Examples of structures are "purely random", "clustered", and "regularly spaced". Patterns in clustered models can be seen as attracting one another while patterns repel one another in regular models. Randomness can mean neither attraction nor repulsion. Ripley [10], Diggle [11] and Cox and Isham [12] provide excellent summaries and applications of spatial point processes that suit our purposes. This section examines spatial point process models with the problems of exploratory data analysis in mind. A major concern is extending results to an arbitrary number of dimensions.

Spatial point processes are stochastic processes. Thus, the spatial locations of clusters in a clustered spatial point process can vary from one realization to another even though the character of the clusters remains fixed. One must concentrate on the general character of the process, not on the positions of the cluster centers. This is a major difference between a Gaussian mixture model assumed in cluster analysis and a spatial point process model. A second important difference between the two models is that the pattern generated by a spatial point process are not generally independent, while the Gaussian mixture model assumes independent and identically distributed patterns.

The assumptions of independence and fixed cluster centers inherent in the Gaussian mixture model are not satisfied in a number of important applications of pattern recognition. Consider the analysis of satellite imagery. Each pixel or a group of pixels, is described by a pattern. Neighboring pixels are certainly not independent. Images taken over the same terrain on different days vary because of clouds, temperature, season of the year, and growth stages of crops causing cluster centers achieved by ordinary cluster analysis to change from day to day. A spatial point process model is particularly appropriate for such applications.

3. Spatial Point Processes

This section reviews some of the basics of spatial point processes with an eye to application in exploratory data analysis and pattern recognition. Point processes are a special type of stochastic process in which each realization consists of a set of points scattered around some Euclidean space. One-dimensional stochastic process usually have a time parameter so point processes in one dimensions can be pictured as points along a line. One application is queueing, which models the arrival and processing of calls in a telephone exchange or jobs in a batch processing computer. A point then denotes the arrival of a call or a job. The points are not labelled in any way, although "marked" processes have been studied in which each point is assigned a value of a random variable.

Our application in d-dimensions requires that the axes, or features, be comparable so distance has meaning. Planar examples include the locations of towns and the locations of bird nests. Only the location is important. This requirement is also imposed on cluster analysis. Data are usually normalized into an abstract space in which Euclidean distance is meaningful.

We usually extend the interpretation of a time-dependent process by labelling the training patterns as $\mathbf{x}_1, \mathbf{x}_2, \cdots$ and imagining that $\mathbf{x}_1$ was the first pattern generated, $\mathbf{x}_2$ was the second pattern generated, etc. Any ordering will do, but random variables representing the patterns must be numbered in some specific way. We imagine that the process is generated over the entire d-dimensional Euclidean space, even though we can only observe the patterns within a *sampling window*. The assumption made about a sampling window are crucial to the success of model fitting procedures. The next two sections present the background needed for understanding the problems involved in modelling with spatial point processes. The last three sections define three classes of spatial point processes that are applicable to exploratory data analysis.

Some notation for explaining models is now introduced. The word "pattern" will be used for a training pattern, or an observation, while "point" refers to a point in the pattern space, which may not be a pattern. The phrase "spatial point process" will be abbreviated to "process". The random variable $N(A)$ is the number of patterns in the region A of the pattern space; region A often refers to the sampling window. The volume of A is denoted by $|A|$. All processes are assumed to be *orderly*, which means that the possibility of multiply coincident patterns can be ignored.

Processes can be characterized by random variables $\{N(A_i)\}$ where $\{A_i\}$ is a suitable class of sets in the pattern space and by *intensity* functions. The (first order) intensity function for a process is:

$$\lambda(\mathbf{x}) = \lim_{|\Delta\mathbf{x}|\to 0} \{E[N(\Delta\mathbf{x})]/|\Delta\mathbf{x}|\}$$

where E denotes the expectation operator with respect to the underlying probability measure. For stationary processes, $\lambda(\mathbf{x})$ is the same at all locations $\mathbf{x}$. The second order intensity function, $\lambda_2(\cdot)$, depends on the locations of two points.

$$\lambda_2(\mathbf{x},\mathbf{y}) = \lim_{|\Delta\mathbf{x}|,|\Delta\mathbf{y}|\to 0} \{E[N(\Delta\mathbf{x})N(\Delta\mathbf{y})]/|\Delta\mathbf{x}||\Delta\mathbf{y}|\}$$

For stationary processes, $\lambda_2(\mathbf{x},\mathbf{y})$ depends on the points $\mathbf{x}$ and $\mathbf{y}$ only through the difference between the vectors. For stationary and isotropic processes, $\lambda_2(\mathbf{x},\mathbf{y})$ depends on its arguments only through the scalar $|\mathbf{x}-\mathbf{y}|$ and is abbreviated to $\lambda_2(|\mathbf{x}-\mathbf{y}|)$. The value of $\lambda_2(\mathbf{x},\mathbf{x})$, or of $\lambda_2(0)$ in the stationary and isotropic case, might not be defined.

Moments of the counting random variable $N(A)$ can be expressed in terms of intensity functions as follows for stationary and isotropic process.

$$E[N(A)] = \lambda|A| \text{ and } E[N^2(A)] = \lambda|A| + \int_A\int_A \lambda_2(|\mathbf{x}-\mathbf{y}|)d\mathbf{x}\, d\mathbf{y}$$

so that the variance of the number of patterns in region A is:

$$\text{Var}\,[N(A)] = \lambda|A|(1-\lambda|A|) + \int_A\int_A \lambda_2(|\mathbf{x}-\mathbf{y}|)d\mathbf{x}\, d\mathbf{y}\,.$$

Three important functions are now defined which can serve as summary distributions for a process. They can be measured directly and can be derived for some standard models. The *radial distribution function* is defined for a stationary and isotropic process as the ratio of the second order intensity to the square of the first intensity and might not be defined at 0: $r(t) = \lambda_2(t)/\lambda^2$. The *conditional intensity* of a pattern at $\mathbf{x}$, given a pattern at $\mathbf{y}$ has a similar definition: $h(\mathbf{x}|\mathbf{y}) = \lambda_2(\mathbf{x},\mathbf{y})/\lambda(\mathbf{y})$. The conditional intensity depends only on the distance between $\mathbf{x}$ and $\mathbf{y}$ for a stationary and isotropic process and is denoted $h(|\mathbf{x}-\mathbf{y}|)$. The third function is referred to as "Ripleys's $K(t)$" and is a popular summary description of a process. Let $b_{\mathbf{x}}(t)$ denote a sphere of radius t centered at point $\mathbf{x}$.

$$K(t) = \int_{\mathbf{y}\in b_{\mathbf{x}}(t)} h(\mathbf{x}|\mathbf{y})d\mathbf{y}$$

This function does not depend on $\mathbf{x}$ for a stationary and isotropic process. The product $K(t)$ can be interpreted as the expected number of patterns within distance t of an arbitrary pattern, not counting this arbitrary pattern.

The character of a process is reflected in a number of ways. The first and second order intensities establish the first and second moments of the pattern-counting random variable $N(A)$ and this may be a sufficient description of the process for some purposes. The radial distribution function and the $K(t)$ function can also be determined from the first and second order intensities and can provide summary descriptions of the process. The nearest neighbor distribution summarizes a different aspect of the data. A complete description of the process is much more complicated and requires that the *likelihood function* of the process be defined. Several specific processes are discussed in the next sections.

3.1. Simple Poisson Process

The simple Poisson process is a model of pure randomness and has the most easily understood mathematical structure of any nontrivial spatial point process. Its likelihood function is developed in this section along with summary descriptions. Other Poisson processes can reflect clustering and regularity and are discussed in Sections 3.3 and 3.4.

The Poisson process is assumed to exist over the entire d-dimensional pattern space but we observe the locations of patterns only in the sampling window A, a region in the pattern space with finite volume $|A|$. The first order intensity of the process is denoted by the constant ρ. The key characteristic of a Poisson process is that the chance of finding exactly n patterns inside region A is

$$P[N(A) = n] = \frac{(\rho|A|)^n}{n!} e^{-\rho|A|}$$

The joint density function f for the random variables $\{X_1, \cdots, X_n\}$, conditioned on $N(A) = n$, is uniform under a Poisson model.

$$f(\mathbf{x}_1, \cdots, \mathbf{x}_n | N(A) = n) = 1/|A|^n$$

The likelihood function of the Poisson process can then be stated as follows. It is understood that the only patterns inside A are the n patterns already involved.

$$f(\mathbf{x}, \cdots, \mathbf{x}_n) = \frac{\rho^n}{n!} e^{-\rho|A|} .$$

The independence of locations means that when regions A and B have no points in common, the random variables $N(A)$ and $N(B)$, which count the numbers of patterns in the two regions, are statistically independent.

The second order intensity function for a stationary and isotropic Poisson process can be determined from the independence of the n random variables $\lambda_2(t) = \rho^2$ if $t > 0$. The radial distribution function is then, $r(t) = 1$ if $t > 0$. The $K(t)$ function is the volume of a sphere of radius t in d-dimensions, or

$$K(t) = \pi^{d/2} t^d / \Gamma[(d/2) + 1]$$

so $K(t)$ varies with t as t^d.

The Poisson process serves as a reference process and represents pure randomness. Many of its properties can be derived so the Poisson process is a popular reference model. For example, the distribution of the distance from a pattern to its kth nearest neighbor is known and is the same as the distribution from an arbitrary point in the pattern space to the kth closest pattern.

3.2. Gibbs and Markov Point Processes

Applications of spatial point processes in physics have led to a rich source of models that may be exploited for pattern recognition in d- dimensions. The Gibbs process (Cox and Isham, [12], p. 155) is an important illustration. This class of models can be seen as a modification to the Poisson process. Suppose that the non-negative functions $\{g_n(\mathbf{x}_1, \cdots, \mathbf{x}_n)\}$ are given and have "reasonable" properties. The nth function in the set modifies the likelihood function for n locations of the Poisson process as follows.

$$f(\mathbf{x}_1, \cdots, \mathbf{x}_n) = c\, g_n(\mathbf{x}_1, \cdots, \mathbf{x}_n)(\rho^n/n!)\, e^{-\rho|A|}$$

The constant c is a normalizing constant defined to make $f(\cdot)$ a density function. The difficulty of evaluating this constant is one of the major drawbacks to the application of this type of model (Diggle and Gratton, [13]). The distribution of the counting random variable $N(A)$ can be obtained by integrating these functions. The conditional density of the random variables $\{X_1, X_2, \cdots, \mathbf{X}_n\}$, given that region A holds exacting n points is, then,

$$f(\mathbf{x}_1, \cdots, \mathbf{x}_n | N(A) = n) = \frac{g_n(\mathbf{x}_1, \cdots, \mathbf{x}_n)}{\int \cdots \int f(\mathbf{x}_1, \cdots, \mathbf{x}_n) d\mathbf{x}_1 \cdots d\mathbf{x}_n}$$

where the integrals in the denominator all cover the region A. The Gibbs process is obtained by specifying the g functions in terms of the *potential function* Φ as follows.

$$g_n(\mathbf{x}_1, \cdots, \mathbf{x}_n) = \exp\left[\sum_{i<j} \Phi(r_{ij})\right]$$

where $r_{ij} = |\mathbf{x}_i - \mathbf{x}_j|$ is the distance between vectors $\mathbf{x}_i$ and $\mathbf{x}_j$ in a suitable metric, such as Euclidean distance. The sum is over all pairs of vectors, counting each pair once. This form has been used in a number of models in physics where the interaction between pairs of particles determined the behavior of a mass of particles (Kindermann and Snell, [14]) and is especially important in processes defined on a lattice (Spitzer, [16]).

This model is also called a Markov random field. Various models can be defined by specifying the form of the potential function. Examples are given by Cox and Isham, [12], [14] and Ogata and Tanemura, [14-15]. To simplify the notation, let $\mathbf{X}$ denote the set $\{\mathbf{x}_1, \cdots, \mathbf{x}_n\}$ where the number n, of variables is understood. Let $f_n(\mathbf{X})$ denote the conditional density $f(\mathbf{x}_1, \cdots, \mathbf{x}_n | N(A) = n)$. The likelihood function can be written in this shorthand notation as:

$$f_n(\mathbf{X}) = \frac{\exp[-U_n(\mathbf{X})]}{Z(\Phi;\ n, A)}$$

where the denominator integral has been abbreviated to $Z(\Phi;\ n, A)$.

This model has a number of attractive features. Only a single potential function need be specified to define the model. A monotonically increasing potential function Φ tends to make the pattern attract one another, or cluster, while a monotonically decreasing potential function implies a model of repulsion among patterns. Such models are based on the local properties of nearest neighbor distances. For example, the Poisson process is equivalent to setting $\Phi(r) = 0$ for all r. A family of parameterized potential functions $\{\Phi_\theta, \theta \in \Theta\}$ can be specified so the model fitting problem becomes the problems of estimating the parameters θ in the parameter space Θ. Given a potential function of this sort, the process can be sampled on a computer (Metropolis et al. [17]) which provides the opportunity to apply procedures for comparing models based on Monte Carlo sampling. However, the problem of realizing a sample of a Gibbs process is not trivial. For example, Gates and Westcott [49] demonstrated that samples of processes published by Ogata and Tanemura [15] and by Strauss [18] are extremely atypical which casts doubt on the generating algorithm.

An important example is the *Strauss* process (Strauss, [18]; Kelly and Ripley, [19]) for which $f_n(\mathbf{X}) = ab^n c^{s(\mathbf{X})}$, where $s(\mathbf{X})$ is the number of distinct pairs of neighbors in $\mathbf{X}$. That is, $s(\mathbf{X})$ counts the number of pairs of patterns in A that are within the neighborhood of one another. The constants a, b, and c define the characteristics of the process; $b > 0$ reflects the intensity of the process and c, $0 \le c \le 1$, defines the interaction between neighbors. For example, $c = 1$ gives a simple Poisson process. Kelly and Ripley [19] establish the bounds on the parameters in a formal manner.

Pairwise interaction processes constitute a class of processes that contains the Strauss process as a special case and are defined by the local properties of the patterns. The form of the likelihood function is $f_n(\mathbf{X}) = a\, b^n \prod g[\|\mathbf{x}_i - \mathbf{x}_j\|]$ and the product covers all pairs of distinct patterns in $\mathbf{X}$. The function $g(\cdot)$ is restricted to be non-negative, bounded, and identically zero for small enough values of its argument. This last restriction ensures that no two patterns can get too close and that the process is orderly. (Ripley, [7], Diggle [11], p. 64) show how these processes can be sampled when the function g is specified.

3.3. Poisson Cluster Processes

The simple Poisson process in Section 3.2 can be extended in several ways to describe spatial point processes that exhibit clustering, or attraction among patterns, and regularity, or repulsion among patterns. This section discusses Neyman Scott processes, doubly stochastic processes, and inhomogeneous processes as models of clustering.

A Poisson processes can be defined by specifying intensity functions or by specifying the distribution of counting random variables. The Neyman Scott [20] process is defined by describing a model for generating the process, then deriving the intensity functions, from which the counting random variables can be examined. The likelihood function is not known. The generation model for a Neyman Scott process is defined below.

i) Generate "parents" by sampling a simple Poisson process with intensity ρ in some sampling window A.

ii) Let random variable S denote the number of offsprings about each parent so that $P(S = k) = p_k$. Sample this distribution independently for each parent to determine the number of offsprings for that parent. The usual choice is a Poisson distribution with mean μ.

iii) Distribute the offsprings around the corresponding parent according to the density $h(\cdot)$. The usual choice here is a Gaussian distribution with diagonal covariance matrix having σ^2 in all diagonal entries.

The realization of the cluster process consists only of the offsprings. Each offspring is a pattern. The distributions required in *ii)* and *iii)* can be parameterized. These parameters, such as μ and σ, along with ρ, define the process, assuming that the sampling window A has been taken into consideration. The offsprings scattered about each parent define a cluster. The locations of the parents are the cluster centers when $h(.)$ is symmetric.

The Poisson cluster process is stationary with intensity $\lambda = \rho\,\mu$. If $h(\cdot)$ is radially symmetric, the process is isotropic. The second order intensity is known (Diggle, [11]). Baudin [21] provides likelihood functions for certain Poisson cluster processes.

The positions of the cluster centers change from one realization of the Neyman Scott process to another but the character of the clusters remains the same. If the cluster centers were fixed, the process could not be stationary or isotropic. Neyman Scott processes are special case of *compound* process (Cox and Isham, [12]). The Neyman Scott cluster process is an example of a process created by superimposing processes on top of one another to achieve attraction among patterns. Another way of achieving clustering among patterns is to let the intensity function itself by a stochastic process. This approach is called a *doubly stochastic process.*

3.4. Hard Core Processes

Regularity is the opposite of clustering. The patterns in a realization of a regular process are spread somewhat evenly throughout the sampling window so the patterns tend to repulse some another. One can imagine a hard sphere surrounding each pattern and the patterns located so the spheres do not intersect. Regularity can be modelled in several ways. Examples are a decreasing potential function in a Gibbs process and as functions $g(\cdot)$ that are identically zero for small arguments in a pairwise interaction model. Models of regularity can also be stated in terms of the process used to generate the patterns, as shown in this section.

The simplest type of hard core model is *simple sequential inhibition* (Diggle, [11], p.60). This process is similar to a Poisson process except that no pair of patterns is allowed to be closer than some threshold, τ. The *packing intensity* of a simple sequential inhibition process is an important parameter, since it expresses the proportion of the sampling window, A, that can be filled. If λ is the intensity of the process, the packing intensity is the proportion of the pattern space covered by non-overlapping spheres of radius τ, or $\lambda b(\tau)$ where $b(t)$ is the volume of a sphere of radius t. The maximum packing intensity in the plane is known to be about 0.907 while the maximum packing intensity in d-dimensions is unknown (Sloane, [22]).

Matern [23] defined two models for simple sequential inhibition. The first simply thins a sample of a Poisson process until no pair of patterns are too close. The second is a type of birth and death process. The simplest way to sample a hard core model is to place patterns into the sampling window one at a time. Each pattern is located uniformly in the space not covered by spheres of patterns already selected and, of course, the hard sphere around the new pattern is not allowed to intersect the hard sphere around any existing pattern.

The larger the packing intensity, the more difficult it is to establish a realization of the process. The next pattern is usually selected by picking a point in the sampling window A and seeing if the hard sphere will fit. If not, a new point is tried. The process is repeated until a position is found. Inserting the last few patterns can take thousands of trials. Ogata and Tanemura [24] and Shapiro et al. [50] propose a variety of models for regularity from hard core to very soft core.

4. Tests For Clustering Tendency

A test for clustering tendency based on a set of N patterns in a d-dimensional pattern space can be stated as a statistical test of the following null hypothesis.

H_0: The patterns are generated by a Poisson process with intensity λ patterns per unit volume.

We seek test statistics whose distributions are known, at least asymptotically, under H_0, which have large power against various alternatives, and which do not depend on λ.

The size of a statistic is the probability of rejecting H_0 when H_0 is active and is fixed a-priori. The power is the probability of rejecting H_0 when some alternative hypothesis is active. In general, it is extremely difficult to derive distributions for test statistics under realistic alternative hypothesis. A rich source of such tests is the ecological literature where the occurrence of plant species, trees, moon craters, or contagious organisms are observed. Almost all ecological applications are processes in two dimensions, for obvious reasons, while pattern analysis requires d-dimensional tests. Our main objectives will be to determine which procedures can be usefully generalized to d-dimensions, state clearly the form of each test, review the determination of size, and list what is known about power. Statistical tests for clustering tendency based on spatial point process model can be grouped into three main categories: quadrat methods, techniques based on model fitting, and distance-based methods. Several ad-hoc and heuristic procedures can also be proposed. Each of the following sections treats one of these categories.

4.1. Quadrat Methods

Quadrad methods test for randomness by partitioning the pattern space into regions of equal volumes and forming test statistics from the numbers of patterns in each region. In two dimensions, quadrats are squares and a count is made of the number of points of the spatial process observed in each square formed by a grid imposed on the data.

If all counts are roughly the same, we suspect regularity; several small and a few large counts suggest aggregation; a particular distribution of counts indicates randomness. Tests use a chi-squared goodness of fit statistic, or an index of dispersion such as the ratio of the variance to the mean of quadrat counts. Distributions of dispersion statistics under alternative hypothesis of clustering and regularity have also been determined [25]. Cross [26] has analyzed quadrad-based tests for clustering tendency. The major defect of such tests is their inability to detect and test spatial arrangements at more than one scale, set by the quadrat mesh. The Greg-Smith [27] approach attempts to remedy this deficiency.

One serious drawback to extending quadrats to general spaces is the selection of quadrat size. Non-randomness may not be detected unless the number of patterns and the number of quadrats are large. We normally work with sparse data, such as a few hundred patterns, in pattern analysis, so the standard chi-square tests for evaluating the quadrat counts would be statistically useless. A variation is the scan statistic which selects the most populous subregion of the sampling window (Conover et al. [44]) or some other extreme value (Darling and Waterman [45]). These tests are not easy to extend beyond two dimensions.

4.2. Techniques Based on Model Fitting

A promising source of tests for the clustering tendency is the technique of spatial modelling developed by Ripley [7]. Ripley's procedure requires estimating two parameters, namely, λ and $K(t)$. The intensity λ, is the expected number of patterns per unit volume, so $E[Z(A)] = \lambda\nu(A)$, where $\nu(A)$ can be taken as the volume $A \subset \chi$. The parameter $K(t)$ as defined in Section 3.1, involves second moment information.

Both parameters λ and $K(t)$ are invariant under translations and rotations of the pattern space. Specifying λ and $K(t)$ creates a family of models. In two dimensions, it can be shown that the Poisson process is specified by its intensity λ and $K(t) = \pi t^2$. The intensity and $K(t)$ function are also known for the Neyman Scott cluster process and the Matern [23] hard core process (Diggle [11]). Ripley [7] proposes estimators $\hat{\lambda}$ and $\hat{K}(t)$ for λ and $K(t)$, respectively.

The actual process of fitting a model to a given set of n patterns starts with the computation of $\hat{\lambda}$ and $\hat{K}(t)$. The main strategy is to simulate the proposed model, compute several estimates of $K(t)$ on a Monte Carlo basis, and see if $K(t)$ for the given pattern set lies within the average $K(t)$ for the simulations. Note that $K(t)$ need not be known for the process, although other parameters of the process are required to define the model being simulated. If $K(t)$ is known, to within a few parameters, it can also be plotted and compared to $\hat{K}(t)$.

The technique of fitting a model to a given set of n patterns provides source of tests for the clustering tendency problem. If the null hypothesis is that the patterns were generated by a Poisson process, the intensity, λ, is the only parameter and can be estimated by $\hat{\lambda}$. The Poisson process with intensity $\hat{\lambda}$ is then simulated m times. The values of $\hat{K}(t)$ for these simulated realizations are observed and the upper and lower envelopes are plotted over the m samples. We can define the acceptance region of a test by requiring $\hat{K}$ for the given pattern set to be within the envelope of $\hat{K}$ for the simulations throughout this range. Thus, if the observed $K(t)$ stays inside the envelope for any t, then we accept the null hypothesis of Poisson process.

Computational realities are key considerations in extending Ripley's procedures to high dimensions ($d > 3$). In principle, Ripley's models are applicable to any bounded set in d-dimensional space. However, an unreasonable amount of computation is required when $K(t)$ is estimated by known methods and there is a considerable computational burden in doing Monte Carlo simulations to test the goodness of the fit even in the low dimensional cases ($d < 4$). A fundamental theoretical problem is the adequacy of models based on second-order statistics in describing multidimensional phenomena. Procedures based on high-order statistics might be needed to fit a variety of models to multidimensional data.

A fundamental problem in using the models proposed above, such as the Neyman-Scott model, is the large number of parameters involved in each model. The number of cluster centers, the number of patterns per cluster, and the parameters of parent and daughter processes must all be hypothesized or estimated. In practice, one needs information about some of these parameters from prior studies. Testing the global fit of these models is especially troublesome because the form of the model must be specified before observing the data. One practical suggestion is to project a subset of the patterns to two dimensions with a standard technique [28] and infer some of the gross parameters from the projection.

4.3. Distance Based Methods

Distance-based methods present a rich source of potential tests for clustering tendency. A great deal of work has been reported in the literature on distance-based tests. Most of these tests were first suggested in the ecological literature, where two-dimensional spatial point processes provide reasonable models for the growth of trees in a forest, the scattering of plants in a field, or the spread of a contagious organism. We consider several d-dimensional generalizations of these tests in the context of clustering tendency.

Perhaps the most obvious test involving only inter-pattern distance is based on the knowledge of the distribution of distance between two points chosen at random in a bounded set in d-dimension. The most obvious test for clustering tendency would compare the empirical, or observed, distribution of inter-pattern distances to the theoretical distribution under a randomness hypothesis. The test statistics would be either a chi-square or a Kolmogorov-Smirnov statistic which compares the theoretical distribution to the observed distribution. Cross [18,26] demonstrated some difficulties inherent in estimating the inter-pattern distributions in scaling the data and in estimating the sampling window.

Near-neighbor distance based methods present a rich source of potential tests for clustering tendency. They are computationally attractive and have been extensively applied to forestry and plant ecology in two dimensions. The performances of several statistics, including the Hopkins [31], Holgate [32] T-square [33] and Eberhard [34] statistics have been compared but no one test has consistently dominated the others [36]. The T-square statistics are difficult to compute in d-dimensions while little is known about the theoretical properties of the Eberhard statistic. Cross [26] states them in d-dimensions and compares their performances under H_0. Cox and Lewis [36] proposed a test statistic having a known distribution under the randomness hypothesis, as well as under alternative hypotheses of clustering and regularity. Panayırcı and Dubes [37-38] examined a d-dimensional extension of the Cox-Lewis statistic and investigated its power as a function of dimensionality in discriminating among random, aggregated, and regular arrangements of patterns in d-dimensions. We now give the details of two of the most powerful distance-based methods, namely, Hopkins test and Cox-Lewis test.

Hopkins Method

The n patterns, or locations, are d-dimensional vectors denoted $\mathbf{x}_1, \mathbf{x}_2, \cdots, \mathbf{x}_n$. The m sampling origins or "posts" are points randomly selected in the sampling window $E \subset X$ and are denoted by the d-dimensional vectors, $\mathbf{y}_1, \mathbf{y}_2, \cdots, \mathbf{y}_m$. Let u_i be distance from $\mathbf{y}_i$ to its nearest pattern, and let w_i be a random sample of m near neighbor distances between patterns for $i = 1, 2, \cdots, m$. We require $m << n$ because we assume that origin-to-pattern nearest neighbor distances $\{u_i\}$ are represented by independent random variables. That is, no pattern should be the neighbor of more than one origin. Under the null hypothesis of Poisson, u_i and w_i have an identical distribution given by $f(r) = \lambda v d r^{d-1} \exp(-\lambda v r^d)$ where v is the volume of a d-dimensional sphere of radius 1. The Hopkins' statistics is defined as,

$$h = \frac{\sum u_i^d}{\sum (u_i^d + w_i^d)}$$

where all sums are from 1 to m. Under the null hypothesis, the distances from origins to nearest patterns should, on the average, be the same as the inter-pattern nearest neighbor distances so h should be about 1/2. If the patterns are clustered, h should be larger than 1/2 and h is expected to be less than 1/2 for regularly spaced patterns. Thus we can form one-sided or two-sided statistical test of H_0. Assuming that all $2m$ random variables representing nearest neighbor distances are statistically independent, the Hopkins statistic can be shown to have a Beta distribution with parameters (m, m) under H_0.

Recently, Zeng and Dubes [39] have proposed a modified version of the Hopkins method. They used the k-th NN distances rather than first NN in the Hopkins statistic. It was concluded that the modified Hopkins statistic is more powerful for larger k when distinguishing aggregated from random data. However, it was noted that as k gets larger, the problems in dealing with the reality of a finite sampling window become more severe and the independence conditions of the k-NN distances from sampling origins and from marked patterns become more difficult to justify since the number of sampling origins is limited

Cox-Lewis Method

The Cox-Lewis statistic is defined in terms of the pairs of distances $\{u_i, v_i\}$, $i = 1, 2, \cdots, m$. Here, u_i denotes the distance from ith sampling origin to its nearest pattern and v_i denotes the distance from the pattern to its nearest pattern. We again assume randomly located origins and $m << n$ for statistical independence.

Cormack [40] showed that $(2U_i/V_i)^2$ has a uniform distribution when conditioned on the event $2U_i < V_i$, no matter what the spatial distribution of patterns. The random variables U_i and V_i represent the measurements u_i and v_i, respectively. Thus, pairs of measurements satisfying this condition cannot contribute to an assessment of clustering tendency and can be ignored, and the information about spatial patterns resides essentially in the remaining $m' < m$ pairs of measurements. Re-labelling the sampling origins, the near-neighbor distances can be expressed as $\{u_i, v_i, i = 1, 2, \cdots, m'$, where $v_i < 2u_i\}$. For simplicity of notation, m will denote the number of sampling origins actually used so that $2u_i/v_i > 1$ for $i = 1, 2, \cdots, m$. When m is small, the pairs of random variables U_i, V_i, representing the observations $\{u_i, v_i\}$, can be taken to be independent and identically distributed. For convenience, the index i is dropped and the test for clustering tendency will be based on a ramdom variable R_i that depends on v_i/u_i.

Panayırcı and Dubes [41] proved that under randomness, the random variables $\{R_i\}$, $i = 1, 2, \cdots, m$, are independent and identically distributed with uniform distributions over the unit interval so the testing schemes defined for two dimensions can also be applied in d-dimensions. They also derived the distribution of R, under an idealization of a regular arrangement of patterns in which all patterns occur at the vertices of a d-dimensional lattice with side length a, and under a modified Thomas process, which is a simple model for the extreme clustering [35]. The powers of Neyman-Pearson tests of hypotheses are based on the average Cox-Lewis statistic, $\overline{R} = (1/m) \sum_{i=1}^{m} R_i$. The power is a unimodal function of dimensionality in the test of lattice regularity with the minimum occurring at 12 dimensions.

The power of the Cox-Lewis statistic is also examined under hard-core regularity and under Neyman-Scott clustering with Monte Carlo simulations. The Cox-Lewis statistic leads to one-sided tests for regularity having reasonable power and provides a sharper discrimination between random and clustered data than other statistics. The choice of sampling window is a critical factor. The Cox-Lewis statistic shows great promise for assessing the gross structure of a pattern set.

Panayırcı and Dubes [41] compared the powers of the Hopkins and Cox-Lewis test under clustered and regular alternative hypotheses; the Cox-Lewis statistic exhibited some advantages under regularity but the Hopkins statistic was better under clustering. Zeng and Dubes [42] exhibited the difficulties in assuming the wrong sampling window and showed experimentally that the Hopkins statistic dominated the Cox-Lewis statistic in tests of randomness against clustering. Dubes and Zeng [43] proposed a "percentile" frame, which is a hypersphere covering 5% of the patterns, for cases when the sampling window is unknown.

4.4. Other Methods

Our survey is not exhaustive. This section mentions a few other approaches to clustering tendency. Silverman and Brown [30] and Ripley and Silverman [46] base tests on the number of "small" inter-point distances. A clustered process should have an abundance of small distances while a regular process should have none. One problem is to define a threshold for "small". These tests have not been extended to d-dimensions.

Structures from graph theory, such as the minimum spanning tree (MST), Delaunay tessellation, and relative neighborhood graph, capture more "global" information than nearest neighbor distances. Hoffman and Jain [47] found that the edge length distribution in the MST under randomness is useful in d dimensions. Smith and Jain [48] applied the Friedman-Rafsky test to the clustering tendency problem. The test statistic is the number of edges in the MST of a "pooled" sample consisting of the n patterns and n randomly generated sampling origins. Their statistic outperformed the Hopkins and Cox-Lewis statistics in tests against aggregation.

An objective comparison of all methods is extremely difficult because all methods do not require the same assumptions. The method used should be matched to the information available about the data.

5. Conclusions and Directions for Further Research

In this paper, we have reviewed several models of spatial point processes in d-dimensions with an eye towards employing such models for clustering tendency. We have also reviewed several methods for measuring clustering tendency.

A most promising source of tests for clustering tendency is the technique of spatial modelling discussed in Section 3. A strong trust of future research should be in the development of multidimensional versions of Ripley's spatial modelling approach using summary function such as $K(t)$. Higher order covariance structures may be needed to distinguish the various processes in dimensions greater than two. In addition, significant computational problems are present in high dimensions.

Near-neighbor distance based methods provide practical test for clustering tendency. We investigated two of the most powerful methods, namely, Hopkin's method and the Cox-Lewis method. These methods were extended to multidimensional patterns and their powers as a function of dimensionality in discriminating among random, aggregated, and regular arrangements of patterns were examined. The d-dimensional Hopkins and Cox-Lewis statistics were defined and their distribution under a randomness hypothesis of a Poisson spatial point process were given. The powers of the Cox-Lewis statistic and the Hopkins statistic were also examined under hardcore regularity and under Neyman-Scott clustering with Monte Carlo simulations.

Finally we note that further study is needed for the following:

i) Techniques for estimating the sampling window

ii) Extension of spatial point process models such as Gibbs processes to d-dimension and development of algorithms for sampling these models as well as for verifying the samples

iii) The extensions of the work of Ripley [7] to high dimensions

iv) Further research on the distribution of small inter-pattern distances.

References

[1] Anderberg, M.R., *Cluster Analysis for Applications*, Academic Press, New York, 1973.

[2] Everitt, B., *Cluster Analysis*, John Wiley and Sons, New York, 1974.

[3] Hartigan, J.A., *Clustering Algorithms*, John Wiley and Sons, New York, 1975.

[4] Dubes, R.C. and A.K. Jain, "Clustering methodologies in exploratory data analysis," *Advances in Computers*, Vol. 19, pp. 113-228, Academic Press, New York, 1980.

[5] Dubes, R.C. and A.K. Jain, "Validity studies in clustering methodologies," *Pattern Recognition*, Vol. 11, pp. 235-254, 1979.

[6] Pielou, E.C., *An Introduction to Mathematical Ecology*, Wiley, New York, 1963.

[7] Ripley, B.D., "Modelling spatial patterns (with discussion)," *Journal of Royal Statistical Society*, Series B, 39, pp. 172, 1977.

[8] Cliff, A.D. and J.K. Ord, *Spatial Processes, Models and Applications*, Pion Limited, 207 Brondesbury Park, London, 1981.

[9] Smith, S.P. and A.K. Jain, "Test for multivariate normality," *Proc. IEEE CVPR Conf.*, San Francisco, pp. 423-425, 1985.

[10] Ripley, B.D., *Spatial Statistics*, John Wiley and Sons, New York, 1981.

[11] Diggle, P.J., *Statistical Analysis of Spatial Point Patterns*, Academic Press, New York, 1983.

[12] Cox, D.R. and V. Isham, *Point Processes*, Chapman and Hall, London, 1980.

[13] Diggle, P.J. and R.J. Gratton, "Monte Carlo methods of inference for implicit statistical models," *J. Royal Statistical Society*, 46, pp. 193-227, 1984.

[14] Kindermann, R. and J.L. Snell, *Markov Random Fields and their Applications*, American Mathematical Society, Providence, 1980.

[15] Ogata, T. and M. Tanemura, "Estimation of interaction potentials of spatial point patterns through the maximum likelihood procedure," *Annals of the Institute of Statistical Mathematics*, 33, 315-338, 1981.

[16] Spitzer, F., "Markov random fields and Gibbs ensembles," *American Mathematical Monthly*, 78, pp. 142-154, 1971.

[17] Metropolis, N., A.W. Rosenbluth, M.N. Rosenbluth and A.H. Teller, "Equation of state calculations by fast computing machines," *J. Chemical Physics*, 21, pp. 1087-1092, 1953.

[18] Strauss, D.J., "A model for clustering," *Biometrica*, Vol. 62, pp. 467-475, 1975.

[19] Kelly, F.P. and B.D. Ripley, "A note on Strauss's model for clustering," *Biometrika*, 63, pp. 357-360, 1976.

[20] Neyman, J. and E.L. Scott, "Processes of clustering and applications," in *Stochastic Point Processes*, (P.A.W. Lewis, ed.) pp. 646-681, Wiley, New York, 1972.

[21] Baudin, M., "Note on the determination of cluster centers from a realization of a multidimensional Poisson cluster process," *J. Applied Probability*, 20, pp. 136-143, 1983.

[22] Sloane, N.J.A., "The packing of spheres," *Scientific American*, 250, (Jan.) pp. 116-125, 1984.

[23] Matern, B., "Spatial variations," *Medd Fran Statens Skogforskningsinstitut.*, Vol. 49, pp. 1-144, 1960.

[24] Ogata, Y. and M. Tanemura, "Likelihood analysis of spatial point patterns," *J. Royal Statistical Society*, 46, pp. 496-518, 1984.

[25] Rogers, A., *Statistical Analysis of Spatial Dispersion*, Pion, London, 1974.

[26] Cross, G.R., "Some approaches to measuring clustering tendency," Technical Report TR-80-03, Computer Science Dept., Michigan State University, 1980.

[27] Greig-Smith, P., *Quantitative Plant Ecology*, 2d ed., Butterworths, London, 1964.

[28] Biswas, G., A.K. Jain and R.C. Dubes, "Evaluation of projection algorithms," *IEEE Trans. Pattern Anal., Machine Intell.*, Vol. PAMI-3, pp. 701-708, 1981.

[29] Saunders, R. and G.M. Funks, "Poisson limits for a clustering model of Strauss," *Journal Applied Probability*, Vol. 14, pp. 795-805, 1977.

[30] Silverman, B. and T. Brown, "Short distances, flay triangles and Poisson limits," *Journal Applied Probability*, Vol. 15, pp. 815-825, 1978.

[31] Hopkins, B., with an Appendix by J. Skellam, "A new method for determining the type of distribution of plant individuals," *Annals of Botany*, Vol. 18, pp. 213-226, 1954.

[32] Holgate, P., "Tests of randomness based on distance methods," *Biometrica*, Vol. 52, pp. 345-353, 1965.

[33] Besag, J.E. and J.T. Gleaves, "On the detection of spatial pattern in plant communities," *Bulletin of the International Statistical Institute*, Vol. 45, pp. 153-158, 1973.

[34] Eberhardt, L.L., "Some developments in distance sampling" *Biometrics*, Vol. 23, pp. 207-216, 1967.

[35] Diggle, P.J., J. Besag and J.T. Glaves, "Statistical analysis of spatial point patterns by means of distance methods," *Biometrics*, 32, pp. 659-667, 1967.

[36] Cox, T.F. and T. Lewis, "A conditional distance ratio method for analyzing spatial patterns," *Biometrica*, Vol. 63, pp. 483-491, 1976.

[37] Panayırcı, E. and R.C. Dubes, "A new statistic for assessing gross structure of multidimensional patterns," Technical Report, TR-81-04, Computer Science Dept., Michigan State University, 1980.

[38] Panayırcı, E. and N.C. Dubes, "A test for multidimensional clustering tendency," *Pattern Recognition*, Vol. 16, No. 4, pp. 433-444, 1983.

[39] Zeng, E. and R.C. Dubes, "A test for spatial randomness based on k-NN distances," *Pattern Recognition Letters*, 3, pp. 85-91, 1985.

[40] Cormack, R.M., "The invariance of Cox-Lewis's statistic for the analysis of spatial data," *Biometrica*, Vol. 64, pp. 143-144, 1977.

[41] Panayırcı, E. and R.C. Dubes, "Generalization of the Cox-Lewis method to d ($d > 2$) dimensions" ,Technical Report, TR-03, Marmara Research Institute, Gebze, Turkey, 1983, (Also Submitted to Biometrics).

[42] Zeng, G. and R.C. Dubes, "A comparison of tests for randomness," *Pattern Recognition*, Vol. 18, pp. 191-198, 1985.

[43] Dubes, R.C. and G. Zeng, "A test for spatial homogeneity in cluster analysis," to be published, *J. of Classification*, 1986.

[44] Conover, W.J., T.R. Bement and R.L. Iman, "On a method for detecting clusters of possible uranium deposits," *Technometrics*, Vol. 21, pp. 277-282, 1979.

[45] Darling, R.W.R. and M.S. Watermann, "Extreme value distribution for the largest cube in a random lattice," *SIAM J. Applied Math.*, Vol. 46, pp. 118-132, 1986.

[46] Ripley, B.D. and B.W. Silverman, "Quick tests for spatial interaction," *Biometrika*, Vol. 65, pp. 641-642, 1978.

[47] Hoffman, R.L. and A.K. Jain, "A test of randomness based on the minimal spanning tree," *Pattern Recognition Letters*, Vol. 1, pp. 175-180, 1983.

[48] Smith, S.P. and A.K. Jain, "Testing for uniformity in multidimensional data," *IEEE Trans. Pattern Anal., Machine Intell.*, Vol. PAMI-6, pp. 73-81, 1984.

[49] Gates, D.J. and M. Mestcott, "Clustering estimates for spatial point distributions with unstable potentials," *Ann. Inst. Statistical Mathematics*, Vol. 38, pp. 123-135, 1986.

[50] Shapiro, M.B., S.I. Schein and F.M. de Monasterio, "Regularity and structure of the spatial pattern of blue cones of macague retina," *J. Amer. Stat. Assoc.*, Vol. 80, No. 392, pp. 803-813, 1985.

RELAXATION LABELLING

Josef Kittler

Department of Electronic and Electrical Engineering,
University of Surrey, Guildford GU2 5XH
United Kingdom

Abstract

This paper attempts to provide a theoretical basis for probabilistic relaxation. First the problem of a formal specification is addressed. An approach to determining support functions is developed based on a formula for combining contextual evidence derived in the paper. A method of developing relaxation labelling schemes using these support functions is briefly described.

1. Introduction

An important problem in the interpretation of sensory data (e.g. image, speech, etc.) is to name objects or phenomena the data characterises. Depending on the level of representation entities that we may wish to label for instance in image data might be pixels, line segments, regions, shape primitives, and in speech they might be phonemes or words. The principle source of information on which a labelling decision is based is normally a set of measurements associated with each object. For example, in edge detection where the task is to label every pixel in the image either as edge or non-edge, the measurements could be the x and y derivatives of the image function. In shape classification, the role of measurements could be played by Fourier descriptors, moments or random cord distributions. In general, a suitable representation of objects at any level of interpretation would be extracted from the outcome of previous stages of processing of the sensory data.

Due to noise and distortions the classification of objects based simply on such measurements will be prone to errors and inconsistencies. However, as objects in the universe do not exist in isolation, the labelling performance can be meliorated by taking into account extraneous information usually referred to as context. The contextual information that can be exploited is of two basic types: a priori knowledge about the domain in which the sensory data interpretation task is specified, and the information conveyed by other objects in the data.

Contextual information can be exploited in various ways using for instance post processing techniques [10], contextual decision rules [11], and relaxation labelling [1] (for a recent literature survey see e.g. [3]). In this paper we shall concentrate on the relaxation labelling approach in which constraints imposed on object label interactions are used to obtain a consistent labelling for all the objects captured by the data.

NATO ASI Series, Vol. F30
Pattern Recognition Theory and Applications
Edited by P. A. Devijver and J. Kittler

The task of relaxation labelling can be formulated as either unambiguous or ambiguous labelling problem [1]. In the former case the goal is to assign a single label per object which is consistent with the labels of the other objects in the data and the data interpretation is globally optimal in some sense [2]. A wide range of problems in computer vision can be formulated in this way including image restoration, image segmentation, shape from shading, the correspondence problems in stereo vision and motion analysis, etc [3].

In contrast, in the ambiguous labelling problem each object conceptually admits simultaneously all the labels from an associated label set but with a probability distribution defined over them. If the probability of a label at some object is unity, then the probabilistic labelling as far as that object is concerned will be unambiguous. In general, however, the probability distribution over object labels may be such that nonzero probability values are allocated to several labels, thus giving rise to ambiguous interpretation.

The above conceptual differences lead to important differences between ambiguous and unambiguous labelling. For instance, applying the maximum selection operation to the label probability assignment at each object will not necessarily guarantee that the resulting object labelling will be consistent.

Labelling consistency in the ambiguous labelling sense will be assured if the reinforcement of label probabilities via the probability updating scheme of a relaxation process leads to a hard labelling of all the objects. Generally speaking probabilistic relaxation will enhance a more likely interpretation of an object at the expense of less likely ones unless the combined available evidence lends a balanced support to more than one label for that object. An evidence for the existence of such instances which probabilistic relaxation furnishes may be an important factor in the subsequent decision making and in controlling the data interpretation process.

As examples of the unambiguous labelling approach will be discussed elsewhere in this volume, here we shall concentrate on probabilistic relaxation. In Section 2 we shall give a formal statement of the ambiguous labelling problem and identify its main components. In Section 3 an evidence combining formula is developed which is used in Section 4 as a basis for deriving support functions for probabilistic relaxation schemes. Section 5 discusses how suitable schemes which aim of achieving given label probability assignment objectives can be developed.

2. Problem Formulation

Let us consider a set of N objects a_r, $r = 1, 2, \cdots, N$. With each object a_r we associate a set of labels $\Omega_r = \{\omega_{ri}\}_{i=1}^{m_r}$ where m_r denotes the cardinality of Ω_r. In general, label sets Ω_r, $r = 1, 2, \cdots, N$ can differ but for the sake of notational simplicity here we shall assume that they are identical, *i.e.* $\Omega_r = \Omega$ and $m_r = m$, $\forall r$.

We shall denote by $\mathbf{P}_r^n$ the initial assignment of probabilities to the labels in set Ω_r. These may be based on a set of measurements $\mathbf{x}_r$ characterising object a_r. In that case the i-th component of vector $\mathbf{P}_r^n$ represents the probability that, given $\mathbf{x}_r$, the label θ_r of object a_r is ω_{ri}, *i.e.*

$$\mathbf{P}_r^n = [P(\theta_r = \omega_{r1} \mid \mathbf{x}_r), \cdots, P(\theta_r = \omega_{rm} \mid \mathbf{x}_r)]^T \tag{1}$$

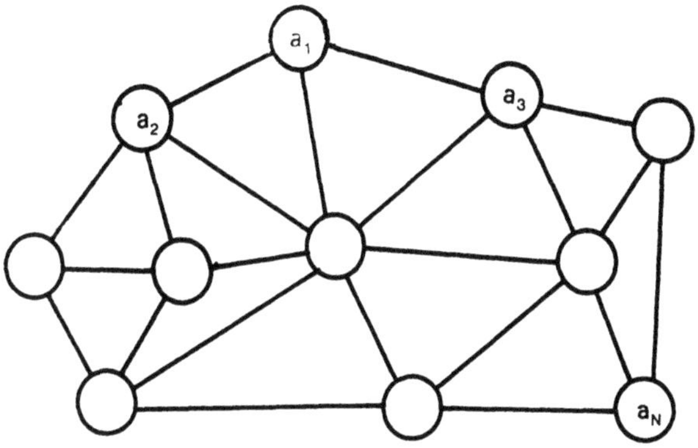

Figure 1: Contextual dependency graph.

The superscript n signifies that these label probabilities do not take into account any contextual information, that is they are "no-context" label probabilities.

Interactions between objects are described by an interaction relation which for each object a_r identifies the objects directly interacting with it. Object a_r is considered not to interact directly with object a_j if the "with context" label probabilities satisfy

$$P^c(\theta_r = \omega_{ri}) = P(\theta_r = \omega_{ri} \mid \mathbf{x}_\ell,\ \forall_\ell) = P(\theta_r = \omega_{ri} \mid \mathbf{x}_\ell,\ \forall \ell \neq j) \tag{2}$$

Let I_r designate the index set of objects a_ℓ which interact directly with object a_r, *i.e.*

$$P(\theta_r = \omega_{ri} \mid \mathbf{x}_\ell,\ \forall \ell) = P(\theta_r = \omega_{ri} \mid \mathbf{x}_\ell,\ \ell \in I_r) \tag{3}$$

The notion of direct interaction does not mean that object a_r is independent of object a_j, $j \notin I_r$. However, given the relevant information about the objects directly interacting with a_r, the contextual interpretation of a_r is conditionally independent of objects a_j, $j \notin I_r$. In other words the directly interacting objects convey all the contextual information contained by all the objects. In Figure 1 direct interaction between two objects is indicated by an arc connecting the two objects. Thus a set of objects and an interaction relation over the objects define a graph or network where the objects are the nodes of the network.

The a priori world knowledge is encoded in the probabilistic relation over labels of interacting objects. In other words it is modelled by the conditional probability that the label θ_r of object a_r takes value ω_{ri}, given the labels θ_j of the directly interacting objects a_j, $j \in I_r$.

Given

- a set of objects a_r, $r = 1, \cdots, N$
- a set Ω_r of labels for each object
- interaction relation over objects
- probabilistic relation over labels of interacting objects (compatibility functions)
- initial label probability assignment and
- global criterion of labelling,

probabilistic relaxation is a process which aims at finding a label probability assignment for all the objects in the network that is optimal in the sense of the labelling criterion. Note that the above formulation of the ambiguous relaxation labelling problem differs from the conventional formulations in an important point. Here an independent explicit formulation of a support function which evaluates the contextual information is not required. This function will be shown to be already imbedded in the above specification. Hence in order to develop a relaxation labelling algorithm, it first has to be made explicit.

The solution of the relaxation labelling problem therefore, has two main components. The first involves the determination of the support function which corresponds to the given specification. The second is concerned with optimization of the labelling criterion. These subproblems will be addressed in detail in Sections 4 and 5 respectively. First in Section 3 we shall develop a general approach to combining evidence which will serve as a starting point for deriving specific support functions in Section 4.

3. Combining Evidence

Let us consider just one node in a network such as the one illustrated in Figure 1 and its directly interacting neighbours. For the simplicity of notation we shall re-index these nodes as shown in Figure 2 with the node in the centre of attention having index 0.

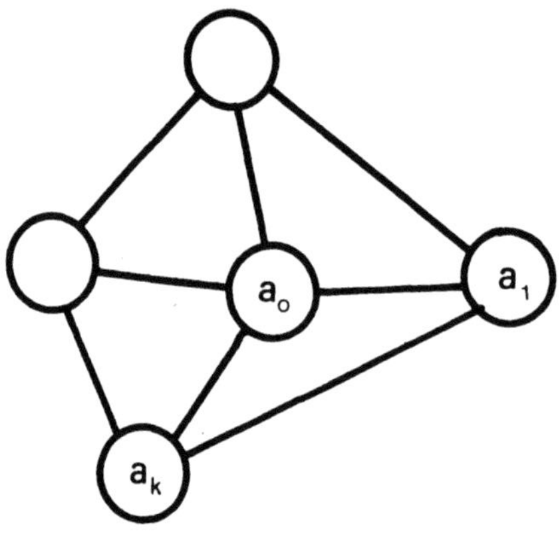

Figure 2: An object and its directly interacting neighbours.

In order to label object a_0, we need to determine the a posteriori, "with context" probabilities of θ_0 taking values ω_{0i}, $i = 1, 2, \cdots, m$, given all the information conveyed by the network. Owing to our assumption about the role of the directly interacting nodes stated in (3), the actual probability we need to compute is $P(\theta_0 = \omega_{0i} \mid \mathbf{x}_0, \cdots, \mathbf{x}_k)$, $\forall i$. Using the Bayes formula and expanding the joint mixture density in the denominator this can be expressed as

$$P(\theta_0 = \omega_{0i} \mid \mathbf{x}_0, \cdots, \mathbf{x}_k) = \frac{p(\mathbf{x}_0, \cdots, \mathbf{x}_k \mid \theta_0 = \omega_{0i}) P(\theta_0 = \omega_{0i})}{\sum_{r=1}^{m} p(\mathbf{x}_0, \cdots, \mathbf{x}_k \mid \theta_0 = \omega_{0r}) P(\theta_0 = \omega_{0r})} \tag{4}$$

where $P(\theta_0 = \omega_{0r})$ denotes the a priori probability of label ω_{0r} at node 0. It is reasonable to assume that the observations, $\mathbf{x}_j$, are conditionally independent, that is given label

θ_j the outcome of observation $\mathbf{x}_j$ is not affected by any other node in the network, *i.e.*

$$p(\mathbf{x}_0, \cdots, \mathbf{x}_k \mid \theta_0 = \omega_{0r}, \cdots, \theta_k = \omega_{k\ell}) = p(\mathbf{x}_0 \mid \theta_0 = \omega_{0r}) \cdots p(\mathbf{x}_k \mid \theta_k = \omega_{k\ell}) \tag{5}$$

to take advantage of this property we shall expand the joint conditional density function $p(\mathbf{x}_0, \cdots, \mathbf{x}_k \mid \theta_0 = \omega_{0r})$ over all possible values of the labels for the objects $a_i, \cdots a_k$, *i.e.*

$$\begin{aligned} & p(\mathbf{x}_0, \cdots, \mathbf{x}_k \mid \theta_0 = \omega_{0r}) \qquad (6) \\ = & \sum_{\theta_1 \in \Omega_1} \cdots \sum_{\theta_k \in \Omega_k} p(\mathbf{x}_0, \cdots, \mathbf{x}_k \mid \theta_0 = \omega_{0r}, \theta_1, \cdots, \theta_k) \cdot P(\theta_1, \cdots, \theta_k \mid \theta_0 = \omega_{0r}) \\ = & \; p(\mathbf{x}_0 \mid \theta_0 = \omega_{0r}) \cdot \sum_{\theta_1 \in \Omega_1} \cdots \sum_{\theta_k \in \Omega_k} \left\{ \prod_{\ell=1}^{k} p(\mathbf{x}_\ell \mid \theta_\ell) \right\} P(\theta_1, \cdots, \theta_k \mid \theta_0 = \omega_{0r}) \end{aligned}$$

which can be rewritten in terms of the "no context" probabilities as

$$\begin{aligned} & p(\mathbf{x}_0, \cdots, \mathbf{x}_k \mid \theta_0 = \omega_{0r}) \qquad (7) \\ = & \frac{p(\mathbf{x}_0) P(\theta_0 = \omega_{0r} \mid \mathbf{x}_0) \cdot \sum_{\theta_1 \in \Omega_1} \cdots \sum_{\theta_k \in \Omega_k} \left\{ \prod_{\ell=1}^{k} P(\theta_\ell \mid \mathbf{x}_k) p(\mathbf{x}_\ell) \right\} P(\theta_1, \cdots \theta_k \mid \theta_0 = \omega_{0r})}{P(\theta_0 = \omega_{0r}) \cdot \prod_{\ell=1}^{k} P(\theta_\ell)} \end{aligned}$$

Substituting for $p(\mathbf{x}_0, \cdots, \mathbf{x}_k \mid \theta_0 = \omega_{0r})$ in (4) from (7) we find that

$$\begin{aligned} & P(\theta_0 = \omega_{0i} \mid \mathbf{x}_0, \cdots, \mathbf{x}_k) \qquad (8) \\ = & \frac{P(\theta_0 = \omega_{0i} \mid \mathbf{x}_0) \sum_{\theta_1 \in \Omega_1} \cdots \sum_{\theta_k \in \Omega_k} \left\{ \prod_{\ell=1}^{k} \frac{P(\theta_\ell \mid \mathbf{x}_\ell)}{P(\theta_\ell)} \right\} P(\theta_1, \cdots, \theta_k \mid \theta_0 = \omega_{0i})}{\sum_{r=1}^{m} P(\theta_0 = \omega_{0r} \mid \mathbf{x}_0) \sum_{\theta_1 \in \Omega_1} \cdots \sum_{\theta_k \in \Omega_k} \left\{ \prod_{\ell=1}^{k} \frac{P(\theta_\ell \mid \mathbf{x}_\ell)}{P(\theta_\ell)} \right\} P(\theta_1, \cdots, \theta_k \mid \theta_0 = \omega_{0r})} \end{aligned}$$

Thus using a probability theoretic framework we have derived an evidence combining formula for computing the contextual label probability $P(\theta_0 = \omega_{0,i} \mid \mathbf{x}_0, \cdots, \mathbf{x}_k)$ in terms of the initial "no context" label probabilistic $P(\theta_\ell \mid \mathbf{x}_\ell)$ at a_0 and at its directly interacting neighbours, and the world knowledge modelled by the a priori probabilities $P(\theta_1, \cdots, \theta_k \mid \theta_0 = \omega_{0r})$, $\forall r$.

In general, if the initial "no context" label probabilities $P^n(\theta_\ell)$ are not based on observations $\mathbf{x}_\ell$ but instead are determined in an alternative manner, by

$$\begin{aligned} & P^c(\theta_0 = \omega_{0i}) \qquad (9) \\ = & \frac{P^n(\theta_0 = \omega_{0i} \mid \mathbf{x}_0) \sum_{\theta_1 \in \Omega_1} \cdots \sum_{\theta_k \in \Omega_k} \left\{ \prod_{\ell=1}^{k} \frac{P^n(\theta_\ell)}{P(\theta_\ell)} \right\} P(\theta_1, \cdots, \theta_k \mid \theta_0 = \omega_{0i})}{\sum_{r=1}^{m} P^n(\theta_0 = \omega_{0r}) \sum_{\theta_1 \in \Omega_1} \cdots \sum_{\theta_k \in \Omega_k} \left\{ \prod_{\ell=1}^{k} \frac{P^n(\theta_\ell)}{P(\theta_\ell)} \right\} P(\theta_1, \cdots, \theta_k \mid \theta_0 = \omega_{0r})} \end{aligned}$$

The evidence combining formula in (9) exhibits a number of interesting properties. As it computes probabilities, it requires no further heuristic normalization. It involves a priori label probabilities $P(\theta_\ell = \omega_{\ell r})$. The formula is unbiased in both the no information experiment and node independent cases [4].

It will be convenient to view the evidence combining formula as a mechanism for updating the initial probabilities $P^n(\theta_0 = \omega_{0r})$, $\forall r$ in the light of contextual information, or support, provided by other objects in the network. Denoting by $q^n(\theta_0 = \omega_{0r})$ and $Q^n(\theta_0 = \omega_{0r})$ the unnormalized and normalized supports lent for label ω_{0r} at a_0 by directly interacting nodes respectively, *i.e.*

$$q^n(\theta_0 = \omega_{0r}) = \sum_{\theta_1 \in \Omega_1} \cdot \sum_{\theta_k \in \Omega_k} \left\{ \prod_{\ell=1}^{k} \frac{P^n(\theta_\ell)}{P(\theta_\ell)} P(\theta_1, \cdots, \theta_k \mid \theta_0 = \omega_{or}) \right\} \tag{10}$$

and

$$Q^n(\theta_0 = \omega_{0r}) = \frac{q^n(\theta_0 = \omega_{0r})}{\sum_{\ell=1}^{m} P^n(\theta_0 = \omega_{0\ell}) q^n(\theta_0 = \omega_{0\ell})} \tag{11}$$

we can rewrite (9) as

$$P^c(\theta_0 = \omega_{0i}) = P^n(\theta_0 = \omega_{0i})\, Q^n(\theta_0 = \omega_{0i}) = \frac{P^n(\theta_0 = \omega_{0i})\, q^n(\theta_0 = \omega_{0i})}{\sum_{r=1}^{m} P^n(\theta_0 = \omega_{0r})\, q^n(\theta_0 = \omega_{0r})} \tag{12}$$

Note that it would be possible to use the evidence combining formula in (12) in an iterative fashion to generate a relaxation labelling scheme in which the contextual probabilities determined during one iteration are used as the initial probabilities in the next iteration. Such a scheme would be essentially identical to the relaxation labelling algorithm of Rosenfeld, Hummel and Zucker [1].

As the general evidence combining formula in (9) is of exponential complexity, in the next section we shall consider how it can be simplified for specific interaction relations of practical significance.

4. Support Functions

The derivation of specific support functions will be illustrated for the three types of neighbourhood of directly interacting units shown in Figure 3.

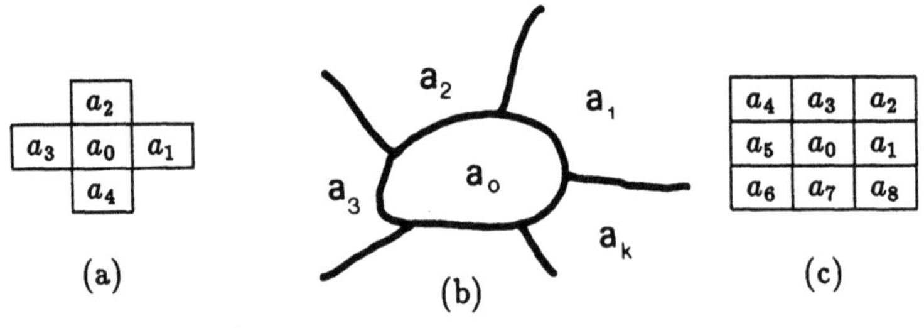

Figure 3: a) 4-pixel neighbourhood b) region neighbouhood
c) 8-pixel neighbourhood

In Figures 3.a and 3.c the objects to be labelled are pixels while in figure 3.b they are regions. Objects are considered to interact directly if they are physically adjacent. In figure 3.a and 3.b objects are physically adjacent only if they share a common boundary.

In figure 3.c physical adjacency is in addition defined in terms of a shared vertex. Thus pixel a_0 directly interacts also with the corner pixels a_ℓ, $\ell = 2,4,6,8$.

The simplifying assumption we shall make use of to derive the support functions for these neighbourhoods is that probabilistic relation functions satisfy

$$P(\theta_\ell = \omega_{\ell j} \mid \theta_r = \omega_{ri}, r \in I) = P(\theta_\ell = \omega_{\ell j} \mid \theta_r = \omega_{ri}, r \in I_d) \tag{13}$$

where I is a node index set and $I_d \in I$ contains only those indices in I which correspond to the nodes directly interacting with a_ℓ. This assumption will enable us to factorize the a priori conditional joint probability $P(\theta_1, \cdots, \theta_k \mid \theta_0 = \omega_{0i})$ in (9) and to develop computationally feasible support functions.

4-Neighbourhood

In this simple neighbourhood system pixels a_j, $j = 1,2,\cdots,4$ interact directly only with the centre pixel, not with each other. Thus using (13), $P(\theta_1, \cdots, \theta_4 \mid \theta_0 = \omega_{0i})$ can be factorized as

$$\begin{aligned} P(\theta_1,\cdots,\theta_4 \mid \theta_0 = \omega_{0i}) &= P(\theta_1 \mid \theta_2,\cdots,\theta_4,\ \theta_0 = \omega_{0i}) \cdots P(\theta_4 \mid \theta_0 = \omega_{0i}) \\ &= \prod_{\ell=1}^{4} \frac{P(\theta_0 = \omega_{0i} \mid \theta_\ell)}{P(\theta_0 = \omega_{0i})} P(\theta_\ell) \end{aligned} \tag{14}$$

Substituting (14) into (10) and rearranging yields the support function

$$q^n(\theta_0 = \omega_{0i}) = \prod_{\ell=1}^{4} \sum_{\theta_\ell \in \Omega_\ell} \frac{P(\theta_0 = \omega_{0i} \mid \theta_\ell)}{P(\theta_0 = \omega_{0i})} P^n(\theta_\ell) \tag{15}$$

This is essentially the product rule support function advocated by other authors [5-9].

The widely use arithmetic average support function [1,3] can be obtained from (15) under the additional assumption of a low contextual information content of the nodes in the 4-neighbourhood, that is when $P(\theta_0 = \omega_{0i} \mid \theta_\ell)$ is close to $P(\theta_0 = \omega_{0i})$. Then expressing the ratio

$$\frac{P(\theta_0 = \omega_{0i} \mid \theta_\ell)}{P(\theta_0 = \omega_{0i})} = 1 + \alpha(\theta_\ell) \tag{16}$$

we can rewrite $q^n(\theta_0 = \omega_{0i})$ in (15) as

$$q^n(\theta_0 = \omega_{0i}) = \prod_{\ell=1}^{4} \left\{ 1 + \sum_{\theta_\ell \in \Omega_\ell} \alpha(\theta_\ell)\, P^n(\theta_\ell) \right\} \tag{17}$$

Since $\alpha(\theta_\ell)$ is small we can approximate the product in (17) by the first order terms only which results in

$$\begin{aligned} q^n(\theta_0 = \omega_{0i}) &= 1 + \sum_{\ell=1}^{4} \sum_{\theta_\ell \in \Omega_\ell} \alpha(\theta_\ell)\, P^n(\theta_\ell) \qquad (18) \\ &= 1 + \sum_{\ell=1}^{4} \sum_{\theta_\ell \in \Omega_\ell} \frac{P(\theta_0 = \omega_{0i} \mid \theta_\ell) - P(\theta_0 = \omega_{0i})}{P(\theta_0 = \omega_{0i})} P^n(\theta_\ell) \end{aligned}$$

Note that q^n in (18) is equivalent in form to the heuristic compatibility and support function of Rosenfeld, Hummel and Zucker [1]. If in addition $[P(\theta_0 = \omega_{0i} \mid \theta_\ell) - P(\theta_0 = \omega_{0i})]/P(\theta_0 = \omega_{0i})$ assumes the role of the compatiblity coefficient used in [1], for the 4-neighbourhood these support functions become identical. However in contrast to [1] where it is suggested that the compatibility coefficient should take values from the interval [-1,1], here it turns out that perhaps more appropriate range is from -1 to ∞.

From the above discussion it would appear that the commonly used support functions have only a very limited applicability. Specifically, they are appropriate for problems with interaction relations represented by the 4-neighbourhood. Moreover, the arithmetic average rule for combining evidence (18) is appropriate only if the network conveys relatively low contextual information.

Region neighbourhood

In the case of the neighbourhood depicted in Figure 3.b the a priori probability factorises as

$$P(\theta_1, \cdots, \theta_k \mid \theta_0 = \omega_{0i}) = \left\{ \prod_{\ell=2}^{k} P(\theta_\ell \mid \theta_{\ell-1}, \theta_0 = \omega_{0i}) \right\} = P(\theta_1 \mid \theta_0 = \omega_{0i}, \theta_k) \tag{19}$$

i.e. it is expressible in terms of a priori probabilities for triplets which form the largest sets of pixels being all adjacent to each other — cliques. The support function for this neighbourhood, which then becomes

$$q^n(\theta_0 = \omega_{0i}) = \sum_{\theta_1 = \Omega_1} \frac{P(\theta_1 \mid \theta_0 = \omega_{0i}, \theta_k)}{P(\theta_1)} P^n(\theta_1) \cdots \sum_{\theta_k \in \Omega_k} \frac{P(\theta_k \mid \theta_{k-1}, \theta_0 = \omega_{0i})}{P(\theta_k)} P^n(\theta_k) \tag{20}$$

is of complexity km^2.

8-Neighbourhood

For the 8-neighbourhood the largest cliques are quartets. By analogy, the a priori probability simplifies as follows

$$\begin{aligned} P(\theta_1, \cdots, \theta_8 \mid \theta_0 = \omega_{0i}) &= P(\theta_2, \theta_3 \mid \theta_1, \theta_0 = \omega_{0i}) \times P(\theta_4, \theta_5 \mid \theta_3, \theta_0 = \omega_{0i}) \\ &\times P(\theta_6, \theta_7 \mid \theta_5, \theta_0 = \omega_{0i}) \times P(\theta_8, \theta_1 \mid \theta_7, \theta_0 = \omega_{0i}) \end{aligned} \tag{21}$$

The substitution of (21) into (10) would yield the corresponding support function whose computational complexity is of the order of km^3.

It is apparent that despite all the simplifying assumptions, even for the relatively simple 8-neighbourhood, the derived support function is considerably more complicated than (15) and (18) which are normally used indiscriminantly regardless of the actual form of node interaction.

5. Probability updating schemes

We shall now return our attention to the whole network of objects a_r, $r = 1, \cdots, N$, in Figure 1. For a current label probability assignment $P^s(\theta_r = \omega_i)$, $\forall r, i$, at the nodes of the network we can apply the results of the previous sections to compute the corresponding supports $q^s(\theta_r = \omega_i)$, $\forall r, i$, lent to the respective node labels by the rest of the network. The question we shall address now is how the label probability assignment at each node should be modified to improve labelling consistency for the network.

A number of global criteria of labelling have been suggested in the literature including the labelling consistency and ambiguity measures in [12] and the average local consistency [13]. Here we shall adopt the latter because of its close relationship with the notion of consistent labelling in discrete relaxation [13]. Accordingly, we shall seek a label probability assignment which maximizes objective function F

$$F = \sum_{r=1}^{N} \sum_{i=1}^{m} P^s(\theta_r = \omega_i)\, q^s(\theta_r = \omega_i) \tag{22}$$

subject to the constraints

$$\sum_{i=1}^{m} P^s(\theta_r = \omega_i) = 1 \qquad \forall r \tag{23}$$

$$P^s(\theta_r = \omega_i) \geq 0 \qquad \forall r, i \tag{24}$$

The criterion function in (22) has a number of interesting properties in conjunction with the arithmetic average support function defined in (18). In this case a local optimum of F implies that the probability assignment is consistent at each and every node in the network. Moreover the function can be optimized using the probability updating formula given in (12), although the speed of convergence may be somewhat limited [14].

In general, however, it is more appropriate to optimize function F using a projected gradient ascent method described in [13]. The method is discussed in detail in [14] in this volume in the context of an arithmetic average support function but it is of course equally applicable to other support functions. The probabilities are updated using a formula of the form

$$P^{s+1}(\theta_r = \omega_i) = P^s(\theta_r = \omega_i) + \alpha \cdot G^s(\theta_r = \omega_i) \tag{25}$$

where $G^s(\theta_r = \omega_i)$ is the component of the gradient vector projected onto the subspace of the feasible region defined by the constraints in (23) and (24), corresponding to node r and label ω_i, α is a step size.

6. Conclusion

Probabilistic relaxation offers an important tool for exploiting contextual information in image interpretation. In this paper a theoretical basis for the probabilistic relaxation labelling approach has been developed. The main contributions include a formal specification of the ambiguous labelling problem, an evidence combining formula developed in the framework of the statistical decision theory, and a model for the probabilistic relationships over labels of interacting objects which leads to support functions commonly used in probability updating schemes. A method of developing such schemes has been briefly described.

References

[1] Rosenfeld, A., R.A. Hummel and S.W. Zucker, "Scene labeling by relaxation operations," *IEEE SMC*, **SMC–6**, pp. 420–433, 1976.

[2] Waltz, D.L., "Understanding line drawings of scenes with shadows" in *The Psychology of Computer Vision*, ed. P.H. Winston, McGraw-Hill, New York, 1975.

[3] Kittler, J. and J. Illingworth, "A review of relaxation labelling algorithms," *Image and Vision Computing*, **3**, pp. 206–216, 1985.

[4] Kittler, J., "Compatibility and support functions in probabilistic relaxation," *Proc. 8th ICPR*, Paris, 1986.

[5] Haralick, R.M., "An interpretation for probabilistic relaxation," *CGVIP*, **22**, pp. 388–395, 1983.

[6] Peleg, S., "A new probabilistic relaxation scheme," *IEEE PAMI*, **PAMI–2**, pp. 362–369, 1980.

[7] Kittler, J. and J. Föglein, "On compatibility and support functions in probabilistic relaxation," *CVGIP*, 1986.

[8] Kirby, R.L., "A product rule relaxation method," *CGIP*, **13**, pp. 158–189, 1980.

[9] Zucker, S.W. and J.L. Mohammed, "Analysis of probabilistic labeling processes," *Proc. IEEE PRIP Conf.*, Chicago, pp. 307–312, 1978.

[10] Brayer, J.M., P.H. Swain and K.S. Fu, "Modelling of earth resources satellite data," in *Applications of Syntactic Pattern Recognition*, K.S. Fu, ed., New York, Springer, 1982.

[11] Kittler, J. and J. Föglein, "Contextual classification of multispectral pixel data," *Image and Vision Computing*, **2**, pp. 13–29, 1984.

[12] Faugeras, O.D. and M. Berthod, "Improving consistency and reducing ambiguity in stochastic labeling: an optimization approach," *IEEE PAMI*, **PAMI–3**, pp. 412–424, 1981.

[13] Hummel, R.A. and S.W. Zucker, "On the foundations of relaxation labeling processes," *IEEE PAMI*, **PAMI–5**, pp. 267–287, 1983.

[14] Illingworth, J. and J. Kittler, "Optimisation algorithms in probabilistic relaxation labelling" (in this volume).

OPTIMISATION ALGORITHMS IN PROBABILISTIC RELAXATION LABELLING

John Illingworth[1] and Josef Kittler[2]

[1]SERC Rutherford Appleton Laboratory
Chilton, Didcot, OXON OX11 0QX
and
[2]Department of Electronic and Electrical Engineering
University of Surrey, Guildford GU2 5XH

Abstract

The use of optimisation approaches for relaxation labelling is reviewed and its relationship to earlier heuristic schemes is considered. The fixed points of optimisation schemes are determined by the constraint relationships and for simple examples can be predicted. Optimisation techniques ensure faster convergence of the relaxation process and can incorporate a wider class of constraints than the heuristic methods. These properties are illustrated using simple "toy" problems.

1. Introduction

High level knowledge about a system can often be expressed as a set of constraining relations which must hold among the constituent entities of the system. The identification and correct utilisation of these constraints is essential in situations, such as image interpretation, where data concerning the entities of the system are either uncertain or corrupted. Relaxation techniques are a class of parallel iterative algorithms for such problems.

In general terms, relaxation methods use information concerning the local context of entities to iteratively improve the global consistency of the data. Clearly, this is an optimisation procedure. However, symbolic interpretation or labelling problems were initially addressed by more heuristic methods and the study of standard optimisation methods for their solution is a more recent advance. In this paper we will review and make comparisons between the two approaches.

2. The Probabilistic Labelling Problem

The general labelling problem involves a system of n objects or nodes, $a_1 \ldots a_n$ to which we would like to assign any of m possible labels from a set $\Lambda = \{\lambda_k \mid k = 1, m\}$. We can perform a series of experiments to obtain a measurement vector, X_i, of properties of each of the n objects and based on this measurement vector, we can tentatively estimate the probability, $p_i^0(\lambda)$, that object a_i has label λ. However, we may believe that many of our initial measurements were uncertain or corrupted and this

NATO ASI Series, Vol. F30
Pattern Recognition Theory and Applications
Edited by P.A. Devijver and J. Kittler

uncertainty will be reflected in the computed $p_i^0(\lambda)$. In the absence of specific knowledge concerning data accuracy we must resort to using general contextual constraints to improve the estimation of the $p_i(\lambda)$. The influence of the assignment of label λ' to node a_j on the interpretation of object a_i by label λ is summarised by a compatibility coefficient $r_{ij}(\lambda, \lambda')$. Large values of this measure represent strong supporting evidence for such simultaneous label assignments while low values suggest highly unlikely or totally incompatible assignments.

In order to have a workable relaxation scheme it is necessary to make several important decisions about how the initial probability estimates $p_i^0(\lambda)$ and the contextual or real world knowledge can be combined. Several schemes have been suggested but we will develop and study optimisation within the most standard scheme. We will limit ourselves to pairwise compatibility functions. This is appropriate for many applications but some problems may require higher order dependencies [5]. The total support, $Q_i(\lambda)$, of nodes in a neighbourhood N_i, for the label assignment λ at node a_i will be defined by

$$Q_i(\lambda) = \sum_{j \in N_i} C_{ij} \sum_{\lambda'=1}^{m} r_{ij}(\lambda, \lambda') p_j(\lambda') \tag{1}$$

i.e., a simple average of pairwise supports with the node weights C_{ij} chosen to sum to unity. The next step in specifying the relaxation scheme is to define the interaction of the current probability assignment $p_i(\lambda)$ and the total support $Q_i(\lambda)$, provided by constraints with its neighbours. In the heuristic scheme suggested by Rosenfeld, Hummel and Zucker [8], henceforth referred to as the RHZ method, $p_i(\lambda)$ for iteration k+1 is given by the values at previous iteration k using the rule

$$p_i^{k+1}(\lambda) = \frac{p_i^k(\lambda) Q_i^k(\lambda)}{\sum_{\mu} p_i^k(\mu) Q_i^k(\mu)} \tag{2}$$

The RHZ rule was derived by plausible reasoning but is in a form which makes calculation of the convergence properties of the algorithm difficult and therefore it was natural to look for a better motivated formalism which would be more amenable to formal analysis. This led to the consideration of optimisation approaches.

3. Optimisation Algorithms

3.1. Choice of Functional

In order to apply standard optimisation algorithms to the relaxation problem we must choose a suitable criterion to gauge the consistency of the data with respect to the constraints. Several classes of functions have been suggested but the measure that we shall minimise as a function of the total labelling $\bar{p}$ is

$$F(\bar{p}) = -\sum_{i=1}^{n} \sum_{\lambda=1}^{m} p_i(\lambda) Q_i(\lambda) \tag{3}$$

This was suggested and motivated by Hummel, Mohammed and Zucker [4] and relates to a definition of consistency in which both the largest $p_i(\lambda)$ and $Q_i(\lambda)$ values agree on the label which should be assigned to the node. Loosely speaking, this means that for all nodes both the node and its contextual neighbours agree on the label assignments. This definition of F is called the average local consistency and relaxation should find a fixed point of this functional which is close to the initial labelling estimate.

3.2. Geometric Interpretation

It is instructive when considering relaxation as an optimisation process to view it as the movement of a vector in a multi-dimensional label probability space. The possible values of label probabilities $p_i(\lambda)$ at a particular node a_i can be envisaged as the basis vectors of an m dimensional space. The probability normalisation condition $\sum_\lambda p_i(\lambda)$ restricts label values to a diagonal hyperplane. Each of the n objects in the labelling problem must be represented by a similar m dimensional space and the relaxation process consists of simultaneously moving in these constrained subspaces subject to the contextual relationships with other nodes.

Within the geometric framework a general class of iterative optimisation algorithm can be expressed by the equation

$$\bar{p}^{k+1} = \bar{p}^{k} + \alpha\bar{u} \tag{4}$$

where $\bar{u}$ is a vector which is called the probability update *i.e.*, $\bar{u}$ is a direction in probability space which leads to a reduction in $F(p)$, and α is a scalar which determines how large a step to take in each probability direction. To determine $\bar{u}$ and α we need to consider the specific form of F and the restrictions imposed by the normalisation and positivity of probabilities.

3.3. Calculation of Update Direction

The gradient direction ∇F of the criterion is that direction in which $F(p)$ increases most rapidly. The direction opposite to this *i.e.*, $-\nabla F$ would seem to be a good direction for u. This is called the steepest descent direction and its components are given by

$$\frac{\partial F}{\partial p_i(\lambda)} = \sum_{j\in N_i} \sum_{\lambda'} [r_{ji}(\lambda',\lambda) + r_{ij}(\lambda,\lambda')]\ p_j(\lambda') \tag{5}$$

This direction will generally not lie in the constraining plane defined by $\sum_\lambda p_i(\lambda)$ so it is necessary to project it into this plane. If the constraint plane is defined by its normal vector $n^T = [1,\ldots,1]$ then the projection operator, P, is

$$P = I - \frac{nn^T}{|n|^2} \tag{6}$$

3.4. Calculation of Optimal Step Size

To calculate the optimal step size α we must consider the change in the functional as we move away a distance ϕ. It can be easily shown that $F(p) - F(p+\phi u)$ is given by

$$\begin{aligned} \phi\ &\left[\textstyle\sum_i \sum_\lambda p_i(\lambda) \sum_j \sum_{\lambda'} r_{ij}(\lambda,\lambda') u_j(\lambda') + \sum_i \sum_\lambda u_i(\lambda) \sum_j \sum_{\lambda'} r_{ij}(\lambda,\lambda') p_j(\lambda')\right] \\ &+ \phi^2\ \left[\textstyle\sum_i \sum_\lambda u_i(\lambda) \sum_j \sum_{\lambda'} r_{ij}(\lambda,\lambda') u_j(\lambda')\right] \end{aligned} \tag{7}$$

The distance to the minimum is therefore a quadratic function of ϕ *i.e.*, $A\phi^2 + B\phi$. If $A > 0$ the optimal step size ϕ' is $-B/2A$. It is also necessary to ensure that no probabilities become negative and this entails determining s which is defined by

$$s = \min\left\{\frac{-p_i(\lambda)}{u_i(\lambda)} \mid u_i(\lambda) < 0\right\} \quad \forall i, \lambda \tag{8}$$

In summary, the step size is given by

$$\alpha = \begin{cases} s & \text{if } A \leq 0\ ; \\ \min(s, \phi') & \text{otherwise} \end{cases} \tag{9}$$

3.5. Steepest Descent Method Algorithms of Faugeras and Hummel

Both Faugeras *et. al.*, [2] and Hummel *et. al.*, [4] have used projected steepest descent methods in relaxation labelling. Their algorithms differ in the treatment of components, $p_i(\lambda)$, which are zero *i.e.*, when one or more lower range constraints are active. Projection of the full gradient may lead to negative update of an already zero probability component. This update is said to be infeasible. In the Hummel algorithm the components corresponding to such infeasible updates are removed from consideration and the remaining components are reprojected into a subspace. This process of removing components and reprojecting is continued until either a totally feasible update direction is found or all components are removed. In contrast, the Faugeras algorithm begins by identifying zero probability components and removing them from the gradient vector. If their projection into the reduced subspace is non zero then it is used as the update direction. If the projection is zero the subspace dimension is increased by the addition of one of the zero probability components. This enlarged vector is projected into the new subspace and the size of update in the added component direction is noted. Each of the zero probability components is added to the non zero probability set in turn and their updates are compared. The update finally chosen is that which leads to the largest positive update in the direction of added zero probability component. If no positive projection exists then a local minimum has been reached.

3.6. Relationship Between RHZ and Projected Gradient Methods

We can see the relationship between the heuristic RHZ method and optimisation approaches if we rewrite the RHZ update rule as

$$p_i^{k+1}(\lambda) = p_i^k(\lambda) + \frac{p_i^k(\lambda)\left(Q_i^k(\lambda) - \sum_\mu p_i^k(\mu)Q_i^k(\mu)\right)}{\sum_\mu p_i^k(\mu)Q_i^k(\mu)} \tag{10}$$

The second term of this expression obviously represents an update direction. The step size factor α is 1. It can be shown [6] that the RHZ update direction is a descent direction of the average local consistency criterion and will lead to a fixed point if

$$r_{ij}(\lambda, \lambda') = r_{ji}(\lambda', \lambda) \tag{11}$$

It is important to note that the update in the RHZ method is proportional to $p_i^k(\lambda)$ and therefore if this becomes zero this component cannot be made non zero. The steepest descent methods do not suffer from this undesirable feature.

Lloyd [6] suggests that the convergence speed of the RHZ method might be greatly improved by using a step size calculated as for the projected gradient approaches.

4. The Fixed Points of F(p)

The necessary and sufficient conditions of fixed points of optimisation schemes are well known [9]. Elfving and Eklundh [1] have presented a characterisation of these conditions for a common class of criterion used in relaxation labelling while Haralick *et. al.*, [3] have studied the specific case of fixed points of the average local consistency if symmetric compatibilities are used. Haralick utilises a matrix equation based on the necessary condition that, at a fixed point

$$p_i(\lambda)\left(Q_i(\lambda) - \sum_{\mu} p_i(\mu)Q_i(\mu)\right) = 0 \quad \forall i, \lambda \tag{12}$$

This is trivially obeyed at nodes where the labelling is unambiguous but is a powerful constraint at an ambiguous labelling. It demands that when the labelling at a fixed point is ambiguous the support for all non zero probability labels at the node is the same. However, in many cases the matrix formulation of Haralick, which demands only a knowledge of the compatibility coefficients, is beset by computational problems and therefore only provides a method for the identification of some of the fixed points of the optimisation process. In principle though the fixed points are specified by the choice of compatibilities.

Once fixed points have been identified their stability can be determined by performing an eigenvalue analysis of their derivative evaluated at the fixed point. If the optima is stable then the absolute size of all the eigenvalues should be less than one [3].

5. Determination of Compatibility Coefficients

The influence of label assignments on one another are expressed by the compatibility coefficients r_{ij} and we have seen that these determine the set of possible fixed points of the optimisation process. Their choice is therefore crucial to the success of the relaxation process. The most widely used quantities are appropriately normalised measures of conditional probabilities, correlation or mutual information. In cases where we have a complete model of the domain of interest, we can estimate them from the probability of individual events $P(A)$ and the joint probability of pairs of events $P(A, B)$.

6. The Two Node – Two Label Case [7]

The simplest network on which to try relaxation is the case of two interacting objects each of which can assume labels from a two element set.

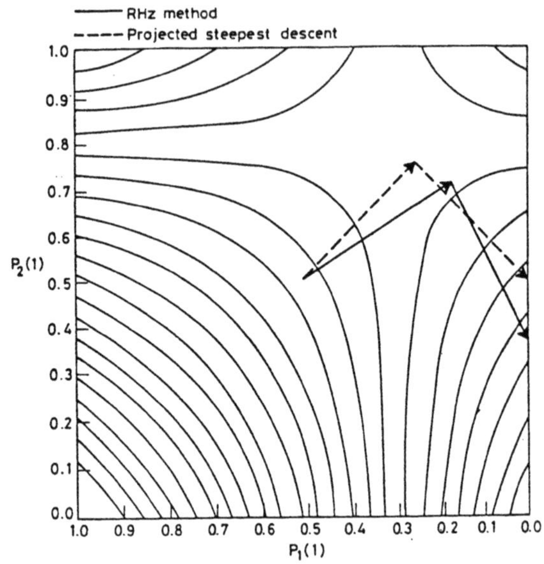

Figure 1: Two node – two label relaxation

The compatibility coefficients form a matrix which has the form

$$R = \begin{pmatrix} 0 & 0 & r_{12}(1,1) & r_{12}(1,2) \\ 0 & 0 & r_{12}(2,1) & r_{12}(2,2) \\ r_{21}(1,1) & r_{21}(1,2) & 0 & 0 \\ r_{21}(2,1) & r_{21}(2,2) & 0 & 0 \end{pmatrix} \tag{13}$$

Possible unconstrained fixed points can be found by calculating the gradient of F and equating it to zero. This yields

$$p_1(1) = \frac{r_{12}(2,2) + r_{21}(2,2) - (r_{12}(2,1) + r_{21}(1,2))}{\det|R_{12}| + \det|R_{21}|} \tag{14}$$

and

$$p_2(1) = \frac{r_{12}(2,2) + r_{21}(2,2) - (r_{12}(1,2) + r_{21}(2,1))}{\det|R_{12}| + \det|R_{21}|} \tag{15}$$

where $\det|A|$ is the determinant of the matrix A. The unconstrained optimum is a saddle point. If it lies within the unit square defined by the variables $(p_1(1), p_2(1))$ then it is accompanied by two local minima at opposite corner points. The other corners of the square are local maxima. Figure 1 shows contours of equal function value for the case where a saddle point exists at (0.3,0.8) and minima exist at the (0,0) and (1,1) corners. Typical paths of convergence are shown for both the heuristic RHZ method and the steepest descent algorithms. The step size in both cases is determined optimally. It should be noted that neither path moves directly to the minima. The topology of the space is determined by both the functional and the values for compatibility. As the update directions differ, cases may occur where the two methods converge to different fixed points. The result of relaxation depends on the initial evidence.

If r_{ij} are chosen so that the saddle point is infeasible then only one minima and maxima exist at the corners and therefore the result of relaxation becomes independent of the initial evidence. This illustrates the crucial role of correct compatibility selection.

7. Toy Triangle Example

This example requires a 3–D interpretation to be given to a 2–D image of a triangle. Each line can arise from one of 4 situations: two surfaces meet forming either a concave, $-$, or convex, $+$, dihedral angle or one surface occludes a second surface, $\rightarrow$, or $\leftarrow$. If the lines represent a triangular object in relation to a transparent background plane, then lines meeting at a vertex should have compatible labellings. The relaxation problem consists of using information concerning compatible labellings of adjacent edges to augment initial estimates of the labelling of each side.

The eight possible triangle labellings provide a model from which we can calculate the contextual relationships of adjacent labels. If we count the number of cases where labels are found on adjacent edges we obtain a joint probability matrix of the form

	$\rightarrow$	$\leftarrow$	$-$	$+$
$\rightarrow$	0.25	0	0.125	0
$\leftarrow$	0	0.25	0	0.125
$-$	0.125	0	0	0
$+$	0	0.125	0	0

Using this, and assuming that the two adjacent edges of the triangle provide contextual information, we can derive compatibility measures. The probabilistic labelling of the triangle can be represented by a 3×4 matrix in which the rows represent the three edges and the columns represent labels in the order $\rightarrow, \leftarrow, -, +$. Table 1 shows the convergence point of several of the methods for a selection of initial probabilities. Correlation coefficients were used to build a symmetric compatibility matrix.

Table 1 shows that there is a dramatic improvement in the rate of convergence of the RHZ method if we use the optimal step size formula of equations (7) to (9). In the case of unit step size the convergence rate is so slow that the relaxation is stopped before a true fixed point is reached. This condition can be checked for by ensuring that equation (12) holds at the point of convergence. The bias introduced by selection of compatibility coefficients is clearly seen in the solution to the first case i.e. the "no information" labelling case, where the $\rightarrow$ and $\leftarrow$ labels are preferred. It is also seen that not all fixed points are unambiguous labellings. The convergence point is a local minima which depends on the initial probability matrix. Case five illustrates the inadequacy of the RHZ method when some label probability values hit the zero probability constraint. The projected gradient algorithms of Faugeras and Hummel are able to give a sensible solution for this case. The two projected gradient algorithms were found to yield identical results in all our experiments but on more complex problems they may yield different answers or follow different paths to fixed points.

Initial probabilities	RHZ step size = 1	RHZ optimal step	Steepest descent
0.25 0.25 0.25 0.25	0.29 0.29 0.21 0.21	0.30 0.30 0.20 0.20	0.30 0.30 0.20 0.20
0.25 0.25 0.25 0.25	0.29 0.29 0.21 0.21	0.30 0.30 0.20 0.20	0.30 0.30 0.20 0.20
0.25 0.25 0.25 0.25	0.29 0.29 0.21 0.21	0.30 0.30 0.20 0.20	0.30 0.30 0.20 0.20
	F = -1.50, N = 20	F = -1.50, N = 1	F = -1.50, N = 1
0.50 0.00 0.50 0.00	1.00 0.00 0.00 0.00	1.00 0.00 0.00 0.00	1.00 0.00 0.00 0.00
0.40 0.00 0.60 0.00	0.08 0.00 0.92 0.00	0.00 0.00 1.00 0.00	0.00 0.00 1.00 0.00
0.50 0.00 0.50 0.00	1.00 0.00 0.00 0.00	1.00 0.00 0.00 0.00	1.00 0.00 0.00 0.00
	F = -2.22, N= 392	F = -2.22, N = 2	F = -2.22, N = 2
0.50 0.00 0.50 0.00	0.95 0.00 0.05 0.00	0.97 0.00 0.03 0.00	0.97 0.00 0.03 0.00
0.50 0.00 0.50 0.00	0.95 0.00 0.05 0.00	0.97 0.00 0.03 0.00	0.97 0.00 0.03 0.00
0.50 0.00 0.50 0.00	0.95 0.00 0.05 0.00	0.97 0.00 0.03 0.00	0.97 0.00 0.03 0.00
	F = -2.20, N= 65	F = -2.20, N = 1	F = -2.20, N = 1
0.30 0.20 0.30 0.20	1.00 0.00 0.00 0.00	1.00 0.00 0.00 0.00	1.00 0.00 0.00 0.00
0.25 0.25 0.25 0.25	1.00 0.00 0.00 0.00	1.00 0.00 0.00 0.00	1.00 0.00 0.00 0.00
0.20 0.20 0.40 0.20	0.08 0.00 0.92 0.00	0.00 0.00 1.00 0.00	0.00 0.00 1.00 0.00
	F = -2.22, N = 265	F = -2.22, N = 9	F = -2.22, N = 9
0.00 0.00 0.50 0.50	0.00 0.00 0.50 0.50	0.00 0.00 0.50 0.50	1.00 0.00 0.00 0.00
0.00 0.00 0.50 0.50	0.00 0.00 0.50 0.50	0.00 0.00 0.50 0.50	1.00 0.00 0.00 0.00
0.00 0.00 0.50 0.50	0.00 0.00 0.50 0.50	0.00 0.00 0.50 0.50	1.00 0.00 0.00 0.00
	F = -1.29, N = 1	F = -1.29, N = 1	F = -2.20, N = 1

Table 1. Triangle convergence points for symmetric compatibilities
F = final function value, N = number of iterations

Initial probabilities	RHZ optimal step	Steepest descent
0.50 0.00 0.50 0.00	1.00 0.00 0.00 0.00	1.00 0.00 0.00 0.00
0.40 0.00 0.60 0.00	1.00 0.00 0.00 0.00	0.90 0.00 0.10 0.00
0.50 0.00 0.50 0.00	1.00 0.00 0.00 0.00	1.00 0.00 0.00 0.00
	F = -2.00, N = 2	F = -2.20, N = 1

Table 2. Triangle convergence points for asymmetric compatibilities
F = final function value, N = number of iterations

If compatibility coefficients are calculated from the joint probability matrix as conditional probabilities then the compatibility matrix is asymmetric and there is no assurance that the RHZ update will be a descent direction. In most cases the RHZ method seems to converge to the ambiguous labelling shown in the example of Table 2 whereas the projected steepest descent methods are more sensitive to the initial probabilities and converge to sensible local minima. Many problems require non symmetric compatibility coefficient matrices and therefore the optimisation approach is the only way to correctly approach them.

8. Conclusions and Future Work

We have presented a brief summary of current optimisation algorithms for relaxation labelling and experimented with their use on several well defined toy problems. Heuristic updating methods suffer from slow convergence and cannot correctly cope when label probabilities become zero. They are also unable to handle asymmetric compatibilities. These poor features can be overcome using optimisation methods. Current methods use a constrained version of the steepest descent method but this is well known to be a method which often exhibits a slow rate of convergence. More sophisticated algorithms based on generating constrained conjugate gradient directions may lead to superior performance.

There remains much work to be done on testing relaxation on larger world problems and on comparing different functionals.

References

[1] Elfving T. and Eklundh J.O., "Some properties of stochastic labeling procedures", Computer Graphics and Image Processing, Vol 20, pp 158-170 (1982)

[2] Faugeras O.D. and Berthod M., "Improving consistency and reducing ambiguity in stochastic labeling : an optimisation approach", IEEE PAMI-3, No 4, pp 412-424 (1981)

[3] Haralick R.M., Mohammed J.L. and Zucker S.L.W., "Compatibilities and the fixed points of arithmetic relaxation processes", Computer Graphics and Image Processing, Vol 13, pp 242-256 (1980)

[4] Hummel R.A. and Zucker S.L.W., "On the foundations of relaxation labelling processes", IEEE PAMI-5, No 3, pp 267-287 (1983)

[5] Kittler J. and Hancock E.R., "A contextual decision rule based on triplets of object-labels", Alvey Vision Club Conference, Bristol, U.K. September 1986.

[6] Lloyd S.L., "An optimisation approach to relaxation labelling algorithms", Image and Vision Computing, Vol 1, No 2, pp 85-91 (1983)

[7] O'Leary D.P. and Peleg S., "Analysis of relaxation processes : the two node – two label case", IEEE SMC-13, No 4, pp 618-623 (1983)

[8] Rosenfeld A., Hummel R.A. and Zucker S.W., "Scene labelling by relaxation operations", IEEE SMC-6, No 6, pp 420-433 (1976)

[9] Ostrowski, Solutions of Equations and Systems of Equations, Academic Press, New York

FEATURE POINT MATCHING USING TEMPORAL SMOOTHNESS IN VELOCITY

I.K. Sethi, V. Salari and S. Vemuri

Department of Computer Science
Wayne State University,
Detroit, MI-48202, U.S.A.

Abstract

One of the vital problems in motion analysis is to match a set of feature points over an image sequence. In this paper, we solve this problem by relying on continuity of motion which is known to play an important role in motion perception in biological vision systems. We propose a relaxation algorithm for feature point matching where the formation of smooth trajectories over space and time is favored. Experimental results on a laboratory generated as well as a real scene sequence are presented to demonstrate the merit of our approach.

1. Introduction

One of the vital problems in motion analysis is to match a set of physical points over an image sequence representing a dynamic scene. This problem is called the correspondence problem and the physical points are often referred to as tokens or feature points. The correspondence problem is an integral part of many important vision tasks such as object tracking [23], event detection and motion interpretation [5,16], and the token based recovery of object structure from motion [22].

Traditionally the correspondence problem has been solved using two frames of the dynamic scene [1,13,15]. Invariably these approaches impose a rigidity constraint on the feature point configuration to obtain the correct correspondence. This is due to the fact that these approaches implicitly assume a situation analogous to the long range motion process of the human visual system [2,3]. Under the long range motion process, the motion stimuli has a large separation in space and time. Consequently the rigidity of objects provides a powerful constraint on possible solutions for correspondence. The assumption of rigidity allows the use of the spatial smoothness of disparity vectors, thus providing a supporting hypothesis for relaxation algorithms to converge to the correct correspondence [1,13,15]. In fact some of the correspondence algorithms using only two frames and the rigidity constraint are also applicable to stereo matching. This clearly indicates that although these algorithms have a much wider applicability, the real use of motion information is not made. Sethi and Jain [17] refer to two frame approaches as quasi-dynamic scene analysis approaches and argue in favor of more realistic dynamic scene analysis techniques.

NATO ASI Series, Vol. F30
Pattern Recognition Theory and Applications
Edited by P. A. Devijver and J. Kittler

For a more realistic use of motion information it is required that we would look at an image sequence acquired over a period of time by sampling the scene at a fairly rapid rate. There are numerous psychological studied [10,14,21] which support the use of motion information over an extended period of time. With continuous motion of physical objects and rapid scene sampling we obtain a situation similar to the short range motion process of the human visual system. This is the motion perception phenomenon which is exploited in cinematography. Continuity of motion is the dominant factor in short range motion perception and it even allows the human visual system to fill-in the gaps when the notion stimuli is presented in a discrete manner [20]. Recent works of Jenkin [8], Jenkin and Tsotsos [9], and Sethi and Jain [17] are examples of exploiting motion continuity to establish correspondence of feature points in a dynamic environment. Input to the system in the case of Jenkin and Tsotsos is a pair of stereo images captured at regular short time intervals. The objective is to match feature points in stereo as well as in time. Because of the use of a stereo pair, Jenkin and Tsotsos use the temporal smoothness of the velocity of feature points in three dimensional space to guide the matching process. A spatial proximity rule is used to help the matching process by limiting the set of possible matches. Sethi and Jain address the problem of feature point correspondence in a monocular image sequence and the smoothness of velocity in the temporal domain in their case refers to the projected two dimensional velocities of the feature points. Smoothness of velocity in the image plane is used by Sethi and Jain to look for an optimal set of smooth trajectories by way of solving an optimization problem. Hildreth's work [7] on the computation of optic flow vectors along moving contours is another example of motion measurement under the short range motion process. Since the line constraints equation for optic flow provides a single equation involving two unknowns at each point on the moving contour, Hildreth suggests a minimization procedure to obtain optic flow vectors. The criterion function for minimization is based on the assumption of spatial smoothness of velocity vectors which Sethi and Jain [18] have shown to be equivalent to the assumption of temporal smoothness of velocity under the short range motion process.

One important issue which is often overlooked in all the correspondence work is the reliability of the feature point detection algorithms. Our experience with laboratory and real scene image sequences indicates that none of the feature point detectors currently available in the literature [4,11,12,19,24] are capable of yielding a satisfactory set of feature points consistently. Thus, if we want a correspondence algorithm to work well, we should either look for a rugged and reliable feature point detector for real images or the correspondence algorithm should be tailored to meet the vagaries of the real scene data. It is the second approach that we have adopted in the present work. Using the hypothesis of smoothness in motion in time as in [17], we present in this paper a relaxation algorithm for obtaining feature point correspondence. Initial confidence match values for feature points are computed using the path coherence function of Sethi and Jain. These match values are then iteratively updated to obtain a smooth set of trajectories indicating the feature point matches. The updating is done using the support provided by the temporal smoothness of motion hypothesis described in Section 2 of the paper. Section 3 describes the relaxation algorithm using this hypothesis. Experimental details are given in Section 4 to indicate the merit of the hypothesis.

2. Temporal Smoothness of Motion

The temporal smoothness of motion hypothesis has its roots in the inertia of moving objects. Because of inertia, a moving object will follow a smooth path in 3-space. The projection of such a smooth path in the image plane will yield a smooth trajectory. In a scene there may be several objects undergoing motion in assorted fashions and each object may have many feature points. Thus in an extended image plane over time we will have an ensemble of smooth trajectories, one for each feature point. Based upon this observation, the temporal smoothness of motion hypothesis states that [17]:

> *If a set of elements undergoing a 2-D transformation can be given a unique assignment as a set of elements following smooth 2-D trajectories, then such an assignment should be preferred over all possible assignments.*

Sethi and Jain use this hypothesis to solve the correspondence problem as an optimization problem in the following way:

Let us consider a trajectory, T_{i_k}, for a feature point P_i in an image sequence of n frames. Let X_i^k denote the spatial position of P_i in the k-th frame of the sequence. Trajectory T_i then can be represented as

$$T_i = \langle X_i^1, X_i^2, \cdots, X_i^n \rangle \tag{1}$$

Now let us consider the deviation d_i^k in the trajectory T_i in the k-th frame. This deviation measures the change in the observed motion characteristics over successive frames and is defined as

$$d_i^k = \phi(\overline{X_i^{k-1} X_i^k}, \overline{X_i^k X_i^{k+1}}) \tag{2}$$

where ϕ stands for any suitable function measuring changes in the observed motion. This function is called the path coherence function. The total deviation for the trajectory T_i can be written as

$$D_i = \sum_{k=2}^{n-1} d_i^k \tag{3}$$

If there are m feature points giving rise to m trajectories, then the total deviation for the set of trajectories can be written as

$$D = \sum_{i=1}^{m} D_i = \sum_{i=1}^{m} \sum_{k=2}^{n-1} d_i^k \tag{4}$$

Given a set of m feature points over n frames, the smoothness of motion hypothesis states that we should favor the correspondence leading to the minimal value of the total deviation of (4) over all possible correspondences. The greedy exchange algorithm proposed by Sethi and Jain determines such a set of trajectories using an iterative optimization procedure. This algorithm requires the same number of feature points to be available in all the frames of a sequence, however. As a consequence, the greedy algorithm cannot be used in those scenes where feature points cannot be detected very reliably. The proposed relaxation algorithm described in the next section is designed to overcome this difficulty of the number of feature points being different in different frames.

3. Relaxation Algorithm for Matching

The relaxation algorithm starts by computing an initial confidence measure of match for all possible triplets of feature points taken one from each of the three consecutive frames. Instead of defining the match over two frames, we define it over at least three frames. This is due to the fact that in order to determine the change in motion characteristics we require at least three frames. Moreover, our computation of the initial confidence measure of match uses only the positional information of feature points as opposed to the use of pictorial or geometrical information. These initial confidence values are then updated by two distinct support processes. One of these processes is a local support process which looks at the evidence available in the current three frames only. The other support process is based on the continuity of evidence and hence derives its updating rule from previous frames. The continuity support process is applied first except in the case of the first three frames of the sequence, where the continuity information is not available. The algorithm goes through the updating process many times in an iterative fashion till it reaches a stage where all the confidence values are either 1 or 0.

Let us consider three feature points P_i, P_j, and P_k from three consecutive frames numbered r, $r+1$, and $r+2$ respectively. This set of frames indexed by r will be called the current frame set while a set of frames indexed by $r-1$ will be referred to as the past set of frames. We will use the notation $C^m_{ijk}(r)$ to represent the confidence value of match for the three feature points P_i, P_j and P_k from the current frame set r at the m-th iteration of the updating process. The trajectory formed by these three feature points over the frame set r will be denoted by $T_{ijk}(r)$. The steps of the algorithm are as follows.

3.1. Initial Confidence Value Computation.

Let X^r_i, X^{r+1}_j, and X^{r+2}_k represent the positions of feature points P_i, P_j, and P_k in the respective frames. Let ϕ_{ijk} define the deviation of the trajectory $T_{ijk}(r)$ obtained by joining P_i, P_j, and P_k. Let the following path coherence function be used to measure ϕ_{ijk}.

$$\begin{aligned}\phi_{ijk} &= W_1\left[1-\frac{\overline{X^r_iX^{r+1}_j}\cdot\overline{X^{r+1}_jX^{r+2}_k}}{\|\overline{X^r_iX^{r+1}_j}\|\cdot\|\overline{X^{r+1}_jX^{r+2}_k}\|}\right]\\ &+ W_2\left[1-\frac{2(\|\overline{X^r_iX^{r+1}_j}\|\cdot\|\overline{X^{r+1}_jX^{r+2}_k}\|)^{1/2}}{(\|\overline{X^r_iX^{r+1}_j}\|+\|\overline{X^{r+1}_jX^{r+2}_k}\|)}\right]\end{aligned} \tag{5}$$

The first component in the above expression measures the change in the direction of the trajectory while the second component reflects the change in the speed. These two components are combined using two weights W_1 and W_2.

Using the path coherence function ϕ_{ijk} we define the initial confidence value of match $C^0_{ijk}(r)$ as

$$C^0_{ijk}(r) = 1/(A+B\phi_{ijk}) \tag{6}$$

where A and B are two constants to limit the initial confidence values in some suitable range. It can be seen easily from (6) that for a triplet of feature points forming a smooth trajectory a relatively large value will be obtained for the initial confidence measure indicating a good match possibility.

3.2. Updating Using Continuity Support Process.

The purpose of this support process is to enhance all those confidence values which lead to the continuation of smooth trajectories over more than three frames. Let us consider two frame sets, the current frame set r and the past frame set $r-1$. Suppose that during the local support process for the frame set $r-1$, confidence value $C^m_{qij}(r-1)$ was incremented indicating a support for the trajectory $T_{qij}(r-1)$. Clearly then any matching in the frame set r which favors the continuation of above trajectory should be supported. Thus for $r > 2$

$$C^m_{ijk}(r) = \text{Min}\,\{1, C^m_{ijk}(r) + C_1\} \text{ for all } k; \tag{7}$$

if there exists the trajectory $T_{qij}(r-1)$ for which $C^m_{qij}(r-1)$ was incremented due to the local support process. Since $T_{qij}(r-1)$ can provide continuity support to many possible trajectories from frame set r, we choose the amount of updating C_1 relatively smaller than the updating C_2 of the local support process described below.

3.3. Local Support Process Updating.

This process examines all possible trajectories from the frame set r. Each of these possible trajectories is classified into one of the following four categories to determine the nature of its local support. This updating process is designed to enhance those matches which correspond to non-conflicting locally smooth trajectories.

a. *Trajectory having definite positive support:* Let $T_{ijk}(r)$ represent the trajectory having the best confidence value at the m-th iteration among the set of all possible trajectories from the frame set r which pass through the feature point P_i of frame r. Let $T_{i'j'k'}(r)$ represent the similar best trajectory for the feature point $P_{i'}$ also of frame r. As long as $j \neq j'$ and $k \neq k'$, we say that $T_{ijk}(r)$ and $T_{i'j'k'}(r)$ are locally supporting each other. If the trajectory $T_{ijk}(r)$ is found to have the local support of all such best trajectories for all possible values of $i' \neq i$, we say that the trajectory $T_{ijk}(r)$ has definite positive support in the current frame set r. In this case, the confidence value associated with the trajectory $T_{ijk}(r)$ is incremented by an amount C_2. Thus

$$C^{m+1}_{ijk}(r) = \text{Min}\,\{1, C^m_{ijk}(r) + C_2\} \tag{8}$$

if $C^m_{ijk}(r) \geq C^m_{ipq}(r)$ for all p and q except when both $p = j$ and $q = k$; and for all $i' \neq i$, there exist $j' \neq j$, $k' \neq k$ such that $C^m_{i'j'k'}(r) \geq C^m_{i'p'q'}(r)$ for all p' and q' except when both $p' = j'$ and $q' = k'$.

b. *Trajectory having definite negative support:* Suppose $T_{ijk}(r)$ represents a trajectory whose confidence value is not the highest over the set of all possible trajectories passing through the feature point P_i. Let $T_{i'j'k'}(r)$ represent the best trajectory for the point $P_{i'}$. If $j' = j$ or $k' = k$ or both, then we say that the trajectory $T_{i'j'k'}(r)$ is giving negative support to $T_{ijk}(r)$. As long as there exists at least one feature point $P_{i'}$ whose best trajectory gives negative support to $T_{ijk}(r)$, we say that $T_{ijk}(r)$ has local definite negative support. In this case, the confidence value associated with $T_{ijk}(r)$ is decremented by an amount C_2. Thus

$$C_{ijk}^{m+1}(r) = \text{Max}\{0, C_{ijk}^{m}(r) - C_2\} \tag{9}$$

if $C_{ijk}^{m}(r) < C_{ipq}^{m}(r)$ for some $p \neq j$ or $q \neq k$; and for some $i' \neq i$, there exists $j' = j$ or $k' = k$ such that $C_{i'j'k'}^{m}(r) \geq C_{i'p'q'}^{m}(r)$ for all $p' \neq j'$, $q' \neq k'$.

It may be noted here that for a trajectory to be classified as having definite positive support, local support of all the best trajectories is required. However, a single negative support is enough to label a trajectory having definite negative support.

c. *Clashing trajectory:* It is quite likely that in some cases the two best trajectories, one for P_i and another for $P_{i'}$, may be sharing the feature points P_j or P_k or both. We then say that the two trajectories are in a clash with each other. In such a case the updating is done by looking at the second best trajectories for P_i and $P_{i'}$ in the following fashion.

Once again let $T_{ijk}(r)$ and $T_{i'j'k'}(r)$ be the best trajectories for points P_i and $P_{i'}$ respectively. For these two trajectories to clash, we must have either $j = j'$ or $k = k'$ or both. Let $T_{ipq}(r)$ be that second best trajectory for point P_i which is not having negative support from $T_{i'j'k'}(r)$, *i.e.* neither $p = j'$ nor $q = k'$. Similarly let $T_{i'p'q'}$ be the second best trajectory for point $P_{i'}$ with similar restrictions. Let

$$D_i = \phi_{ijk} + \phi_{i'p'q'}$$

and

$$D_2 = \phi_{i'j'k'} + \phi_{ipq}$$

The quantity D_1 above defines the contribution to the overall deviation of (4) if we were to favor $T_{ijk}(r)$. Similarly D_2 denotes the contribution when $T_{i'j'k'}(r)$ is favored. Therefore the updating rule for a clashing trajectory $T_{ijk}(r)$ is

if $D_1 < D_2$ then

$$C_{ijk}^{m+1}(r) = \text{Min}\{1, C_{ijk}^{m}(r) + C_2\};$$

otherwise

$$C_{ijk}^{m+1}(r) = \text{Max}\{0, C_{ijk}^{m}(r) - C_2\}.$$

d. *Uncertain case:* A trajectory $T_{ijk}(r)$ may not be the best trajectory for the point P_i and it may not be in receipt of negative support from any of the best trajectories present for different $P_{i'}$. In such a situation we say that not enough evidence is present locally at the time of iteration for the trajectory $T_{ijk}(r)$. Such trajectories are classified as uncertain and no updating of the confidence values are done for these trajectories.

As mentioned before, the updating process loops through the frame sets with continuity and local processes being applied in succession. The updating procedure terminates when all the confidence values reach either 1 or 0. Most of the trajectories which are classified as having definite positive or negative support during the initial iteration will in general maintain the same classification over the entire procedure. Consequently most of the confidence values will monotonically increase or decrease. Trajectories that are labelled initially as uncertain will move on to other classifications as the updating progresses. To see how this might happen, let us consider that $T_{ijk}(r)$ and $T_{ipq}(r)$ are the only two possible trajectories at some point of the iteration involving the feature point P_i. Let $C^m_{ijk}(r) > C^m_{ipq}(r)$. Suppose $T_{ijk}(r)$ is found to be a clashing trajectory, say with $T_{i'j'k'}(r)$, and as a result of this clash the confidence value $C^m_{ijk}(r)$ is decreased. At the same point of time let us assume that $T_{ipq}(r)$ is labelled as uncertain case. In the next iteration, it is possible to have $C^{m+1}_{ipq} > C^{m+1}_{ijk}$. In that case the trajectory $T_{ipq}(r)$ will now be classified as having definite positive support. Because of the two support processes, increments or decrements in the confidence values are not identical for all trajectories. As a result of this, the second best trajectory in the clash cases can change over the iterations. Consequently in some cases a confidence value may increase (decrease) intially but later on it may start decreasing (increasing). However such changes in the direction of updating of a particular confidence value cannot go on indefinitely and therefore all the confidence values will be reaching either the maximum or the minimum value in finite number of iterations.

4. Experimental Results

We have conducted several experiments for matching using synthetic and real scene sequences. In this part of the paper we present details of two of our experiments. In all the experiments we used the same set of values for different constants and thresholds. We first discuss the choice of these values.

The computation of the path coherence measure of (5) involves two weights W_1 and W_2. We used W_1 as 0.1 and W_2 as 0.9. The reason for choosing W_2 much greater than W_1 is that the speed component of the path coherence measure falls off less rapidly compared to the direction component for reasonable changes in speed and direction, respectively. In order to speed up the computation and limit the number of possible matches, we use separate thresholding on the speed and direction components of the path coherence measure. Only those trajectories are considered for matching that have an angle change of less than 50 and speed change ratio of less than 5 over a frame set. The values of constants A and B were selected to be 1.6 and 2.0. Assuming the best possible trajectory, *i.e.* one with no change in speed and direction, the value of the path coherence measure turns out to be 0. A choice of A equal to 1.6 then implies that no initial confidence measure can be beyond a value of 0.625. Similarly for the worst possible trajectory, a choice of B equal to 2.0 ensures that the minimum initial confidence value will be at least about 0.45. This range of initial confidence values along with the choice of C_1 equal to 0.04 and C_2 equal to 0.05 allows the continuity and local support processes to play their part in the updating process. In our implementation we also immediately set rest of the competing confidence values to 0 whenever a particular confidence value attains the maximum value of 1. This helps in reducing the number of iterations.

Our first experiment to be discussed here involves a laboratory generated sequence of seven frames. This sequences consists of three moving blocks. One of these blocks is rotating as well as translating. The other two blocks are simply translating. Feature points in this experiment were taken to be the time-varying corner points. Using the successive frames for differencing, time-varying corner points were detected for the first six frames of this sequence using Shah and Jain's corner detector [19]. Since the response

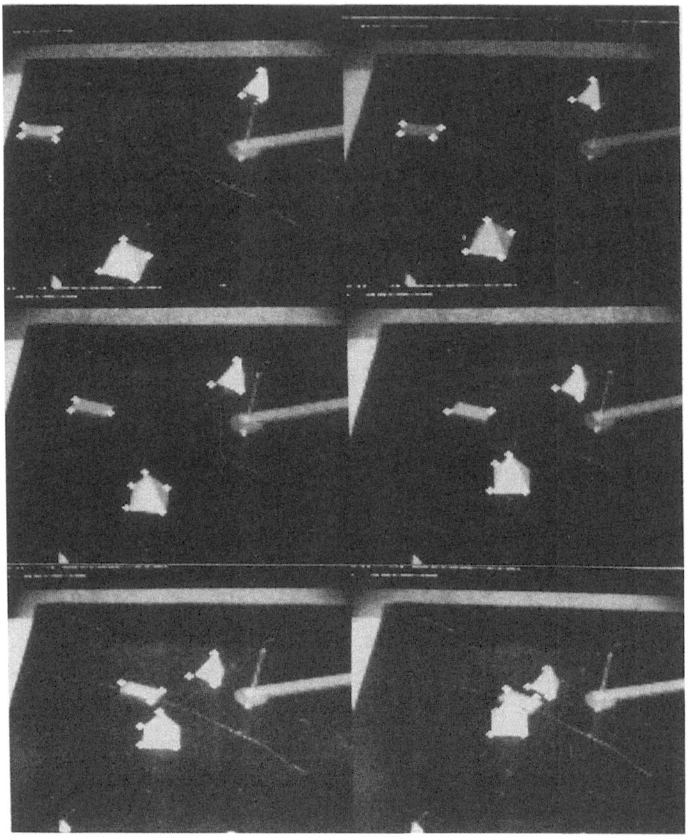

Figure 1: Sequence of moving blocks with the detected corners superimposed.

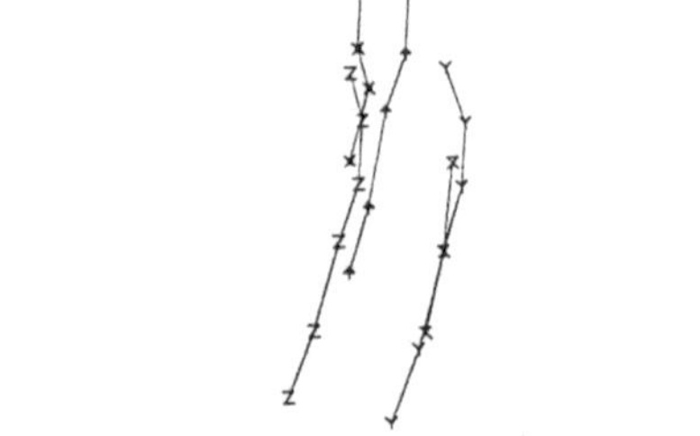

Figure 2: Trajectories of the detected corner points.

of the corner detector does not fall off rapidly as the corner detector is moved away from true corner positions, it was found that the corner detector yielded many more corners than were actually present. Getting false responses at positions close to true corner positions is typical of most corner detectors. It was therefore decided to perform a filtering operation on the output of the corner detector. In our implementation we used a maxima filter of size 9×9. This filter is iteratively placed at the remaining corner of maximum strength and all other corners lying within the filtering window are removed. The filtering process continues till we have no more remaining corners for placing the filtering window. Figure 1 shows the results of corner detection after filtering. The detected corners are superimposed on the original frames of the sequence in this figure. Because of the rotational motion and the thresholding involved in the corner detection process, the number of detected corners was found to be 11, 11, 11, 9, 10, and 9 respectively. The positional information of these corners constituted input to our relaxation algorithm. Figure 2 shows the matching of these corners in the form of trajectories. These were obtained after 8 iterations. Because of the change in number of feature points, only 8 complete trajectories are obtained. These correspond to those feature points which are visible all through the sequence. The three partial trajectories represent those feature points which either appear later or disappear, either due to motion or due to the thresholding of the corner detector output.

Our second experiment was performed on a real scene sequence taken from the movie *Superman*. This sequence consists of four frames and is shown in Figure 3. For our experimentation we picked up a window around the soldier in the front and extracted only those feature points which are present in this window. The feature points were obtained by applying the following steps.

a. Each image frame is convolved with the two dimensional Laplacian of Gaussian operator [6]. We use a σ value of 3 and mask size of 17.

b. Zero crossings in the convolved image are determined by scanning along the rows and looking for pair of adjacent pixels having opposite sign.

c. Only those zero crossing points are retained which are under motion. This is done by differencing two consecutive frames.

d. Local orientation of the zero crossing contour at the zero crossing points detected above is determined by using Sobel's operator.

e. The orientation is quantized into four directions. We select one point from each of the quantized directions over a small neighborhood. The points having larger gradient magnitude are preferred in this selection.

It should be evident from above processing steps that this processing is designed to pick up a sparse set of points from moving contours. The processing of the frames of Figure 3 yielded 17 feature points from frame 1 and 2 and 19 feature points from frame 3. Figure 4 shows these feature points superimposed on the corresponding frames. Also shown in Figure 4 is the result of steps (a) and (b) on the first frame of the sequence. Our algorithm for matching obtained the 11 trajectories of Figure 5 in 13 iterations. Figure 5 also shows those feature points which could not be matched. It must be remembered here that our algorithm defines matches over three frames. Hence, even if a feature point is present over two frames, its correspondence will not be established. Out of 11 matches obtained, two matches were found to be incorrect after visually examining these

Figure 3: Four frames of a real scene sequence from the movie *Superman*.

Figure 4: (a) Zero crossing contours for the first frame of the sequence. (b) Detected feature points in the first frame. (c) Same as (b) for the second frame. (d) Same as (b) for the third frame.

matches on the screen. The error in two matches is not surprising when one takes into account the nature of human movement and lack of use of any distinguishable geometric features in the processing.

5. Conclusion

We have presented an algorithm for feature point matching using motion information alone. Our results indicate that the temporal smoothness of motion provides a powerful constraint for establishing correspondence. We intentionally did not use pictorial or geometrical characteristics of feature points in our matching process as we wanted to demonstrate the strength of the smoothness of motion hypothesis. The additional information through the use of pictorial or geometrical characteristics of feature points can play an important role in the initial confidence value computation by eliminating unlikely groupings of points even if they form smooth trajectories.

Acknowledgement

We gratefully acknowledge the support of the National Science Foundation (DCR-8500717) and the Institute of Manufacturing Research at Wayne State University. We thank Dr. Ramesh Jain and Dr. William Grosky for their interest in our work.

References

[1] Barnard, S.T. and W.B. Thompson, "Disparity analysis of images," *IEEE Trans. on PAMI*, Vol. 2, 1980, pp. 333–340.

[2] Braddick, O.J., "A short-range process in apparent motion," *Vision Research*, Vol. 14, 1974, pp. 519–527.

[3] Braddick, O.J., "Low-level and high-level processes in apparent motion," *Philo. Trans. of the Royal Soc. of London*, Vol. 290, Part B, 1980, pp. 137–151.

[4] Dreschler, L. and H. Nagel, "Volumetric model and 3-D trajectory of a moving car derived from monocular TV-frame sequence of a street scene," *Proc. IJCAI*, 1981, pp. 692–697.

[5] Haynes, S.M. and R. Jain, "Event detection and correspondence," *Optical Engineering*, Vol. 25, 1986, pp. 387–393.

[6] Hildreth, E.C., "The detection of intensity changes by computer and biological vision systems," *CVGIP*, Vol. 22, 1983, pp. 1–27.

[7] Hildreth, E.C., *The Measurement of Visual Motion*, MIT Press, Cambridge, Mass., 1984.

[8] Jenkin, M., "Tracking three dimensional moving light displays," *Proc. Workshop on Motion: Representation and Control*, Toronto, 1983, pp. 66–70.

[9] Jenkin, M. and J.K. Tsotsos, "Applying temporal constraints to the dynamic stereo problem," *CVGIP*, Vol. 33, 1986, pp. 16–32.

[10] Johansson, G., "Spatio-temporal differentiation and integration in visual motion perception," *Psych. Research*, Vol. 38, 1976, pp. 379–383.

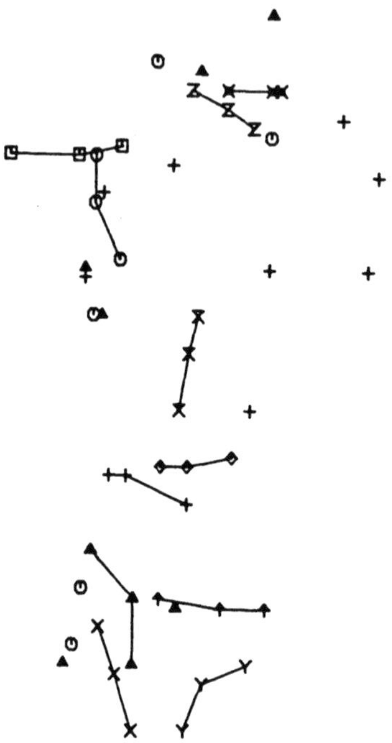

Figure 5: Trajectories of the feature points of Figure 4. Feature points which could not be matched are also shown. 0: Unmatched feature points of frame 1, Δ: unmatched feature points of frame 2, + unmatched feature points of frame 3.

[11] Kitchen, L. and A. Rosenfeld, "Gray-level corner detection," *Pattern Recognition Letters*, Vol. 1, 1982, pp. 95–102.

[12] Kories, R. and G. Zimmermann, "Motion detection in image sequences: an evaluation of feature detectors," *Proc. 7th IJCPR*, 1984, pp. 778–780.

[13] Prager, J.M. and M.A. Arbib, "Computing the optic flow: the MATCH algorithm and prediction," *CVGIP*, Vol. 24, 1983, pp. 271–304.

[14] Ramachandran, V.S. and S.M. Anstis, "Extrapolation of motion path in human visual perception," *Vision Research*, Vol. 23, 1984, pp. 83–85.

[15] Ranade, S. and A. Rosenfeld, "Point pattern matching by relaxation," *Pattern Recognition*, Vol. 12, 1980, pp. 269–275.

[16] Rashid, R.F., "Towards a system for the interpretation of moving light display," *IEEE Trans. PAMI*, Vol. 2, 1980, pp. 574–581.

[17] Sethi, I.K., and R. Jain, "Finding trajectories of feature points in a monocular image sequence," *IEEE Trans. on PAMI*, in press.

[18] Sethi, I.K. and R. Jain, "Smoothness of motion and correspondence," *Motion Understanding*, Eds. J.K. Aggarwal and W. Martin, in Press.

[19] Shah, M.A. and R. Jain, "Detecting time-varying corners," *CVGIP*, Vol. 28, 1984, pp. 345–355.

[20] Shaw, G.L. and V.S. Ramachandran, "Interpolation during apparent motion," *Perception*, Vol. 11, 1982, pp. 491–494.

[21] Todd, J.T., "Visual information about rigid and nonrigid motion: A geometric analysis," *Jour. of Expt. Psych.: Human Perception and Performance*, Vol. 8, 1982, pp. 238–252.

[22] Ullman, S., *The Interpretation of Visual Motion*, MIT Press, Cambridge, Mass., 1979.

[23] Yachida, M., M. Asada and S. Tsuji, "Automatic analysis of moving images," *IEEE Trans. on PAMI*, Vol. 3, 1981, pp. 12–19.

[24] Zuniga, O.A. and R. Haralick, "Corner detection using facet model," *Proc. CVPR Conf.*, 1983, pp. 30–37.

MULTIRESOLUTIONAL CLUSTER SEGMENTATION USING SPATIAL CONTEXT

Jan J. Gerbrands, Eric Backer, Xiang S. Cheng

Delft University of Technology
Department of Electrical Engineering
P.O.Box 5031, 2600 GA DELFT, The Netherlands

Abstract

A multiresolutional cluster/relaxation image segmentation algorithm is described. A preliminary split-merge procedure generates variable-sized quadtree-blocks. These multiresolutional units are used in the subsequent clustering. A probabilistic relaxation procedure conducts the final labeling. A large reduction in data processing is attained by processing blocks rather than pixels, while still yielding good segmentation results.

1. Introduction

Clustering/relaxation image segmentation methods have been discussed in the literature over the past decade [1,2]. Most methods are pixel-based and therefore bear some inevitable drawbacks and limitations: only a limited number of pixels may attend the clustering/relaxation process to keep computational complexity and memory requirement within limits, and the representativity of individual pixels may be quite poor because of noise. The work reported here is an attempt to break these limitations. The concept is the following:

1. Generate a number of image primitives (sets of connected pixels) so that the uniformity within each primitive is satisfactory. Primitives are not necessarily equally sized.

2. Select "dominant" primitives and apply a clustering process to these primitives exclusively.

3. Assign initial class memberships to all primitives.

4. Conduct a relaxation process on the primitives using locally dependent compatibility coefficients.

The above concept bears two obvious merits:

a. Replacing single pixels by larger primitives reduces the number of operational data units drastically.

NATO ASI Series, Vol. F30
Pattern Recognition Theory and Applications
Edited by P. A. Devijver and J. Kittler

b. By allowing only dominant primitives to attend the clustering process, the resulting clusters will be much more reliable.

Certainly, the fundamental assumption is that Step 1 can be realized satisfactorily. Here, a quadtree based split-merge procedure is used. The resulting quadtree blocks (QT-blocks) are considered as the (multiresolutional, variable-sized) primitives. Typically, in a quadtree-based split-merge procedure QT-block dominancy can be related to block area.

2. Design of the Multi-resolutional Segmentation Approach

2.1. The Iterative Split-merge Scheme

Contrary to the general split-and-merge approach introduced by Horowitz and Pavlidis [3] the procedure here does not include the grouping operation. The segmentation predicate is based on the within-block variance [4]. Suppose we have k input images of a scene, which are presumably in registration. Assuming mutual independence among the input images, we adopt the following uniformity predicate:

$$PRE(X) = TRUE \quad \text{iff } S_i(X) < r_i \quad \text{for } i = 1, 2, \ldots, k$$

for each connected subset X from the image domain, where $S_i(X)$ is ith image's sample variance within X. Fixing a particular input image and supposing N regions present, each obeying some probability distribution and having an occurrence probability p_j, the total image variance σ^2 will satisfy

$$\sigma^2 = \sum p_j \sigma_j^2 + \sum p_j p_l (u_j - u_l)^2$$

where σ_j^2 and u_j are the variance and expectation of jth region. The first sum stands for the contribution of the individual variances while the second one represents the spread in the means. The fact that σ^2 will increase/decrease because of the first sum whenever any individual σ_j^2 increases/decreases suggests us to choose the thresholds r_i proportional to the image variances S_i as follows:

$$r_i = hS_i \quad \text{for } i = 1, 2, \ldots, k$$

where h is a common scaling parameter.

Clearly, the smaller h the finer the resulting segmentation quadtree will be. This indicates the existence of an adequate h-value corresponding to a satisfactory output quadtree. We introduce a feedback facility letting the process itself iteratively improve its output in terms of two "goodness" measures:

a. AP-Area Preserve : this measure is defined as the total areal percentage of blocks which are larger than a size threshold;

b. RP-Region Preserve : this measure is defined as the ratio of the sample variance among the weighted means within all individual blocks larger than a size threshold to the sample variance in the input image.

The size threshold is chosen a priori, based on the expected size of the region(s) and the minimum size of a block required to obtain a reasonably accurate variance estimate. A small value of AP will indicate that the chosen h-value is too small. An excessively large value of AP will suggest that h is chosen too large. If we do acknowledge the suitability of the variance predicate, a proper value for AP should be within some interval [Alow,Ahig]. The behaviour of RP is characteristic for preserving the original region structure. The higher RP, the more representative the set of large QT-blocks is for this structure, consequently RP should exceed some lower bound Rlow.

2.2. The Clustering Process

QT-blocks participating in the clustering process are called active. Only blocks with a size not below some prescribed threshold are set active. Normally, for images of size 256×256, we can fix this threshold at, say, 8×8. Each block is represented by its k-dimensional feature vector of graylevel mean values. In accordance with the segmentation predicate, the only metric in the feature space is the so-called supmetric:

$$d_\infty(X,Y) = \max\{|x_i - y_i|\}$$

Each dimension is normalized with respect to its sample variance. As no outliers are expected and clusters are assumed to be well-shaped, MacQueen's k-means method [5] has been adopted. The number of clusters is generally not known in advance. Therefore, "coarsening" and "refining" parameters are used to control merging and splitting clusters (largely similar to ISODATA, [6]). By selecting the largest M QT-blocks from the active blocks, the initial cluster centroids will be highly representative for the entire data. The major difference between the procedure used here and ISODATA is that we do not split current clusters. The procedure reads as follows:

- a1. Take the largest M active QT-blocks as initial clusters of one block each.
- a2. Compute all pairwise distances among the centroids of current clusters. If the smallest distance is less than a "coarsening" parameter C, then the two associated clusters are merged. Repeat this until no merging is possible.
- a3. For each of the remaining active blocks perform the following operations sequentially:
  - Find the cluster with nearest centroid to the block under consideration,
  - If the nearest distance exceeds a "refining" parameter R, then take the block as a new cluster of one block only; otherwise, assign the block to the nearest cluster and perform a2.
- b1. Fix the centroids of the current clusters as a set of seed points and reassign each active block to its nearest seed. Replace the set of seed points by the centroids of all newly formed clusters. Repeat this, controlled by tolerable displacement and/or number of iterations.
- c1. Perform a2; discard all clusters of sizes smaller than a given threshold.

For any active QT-block, its feature vector results in a single point E while the feature mappings of all its pixels would generally exhibit a cloud with E as a concentration spot. Such a cloud may facilitate us with some means to talk about the family sphere of each block. In our experimental approach we have used the family spheres of the individual active blocks to assign the "coarsening" and "refining" parameters properly.

2.3. The Relaxation Process

The final segmentation is obtained by a probabilistic relaxation process which iteratively updates the segmentation towards improved local consistency [7,8]. Let $P_i^{(k)}\{a\}$ be the probability about block i belonging to label $\{a\}$ in kth iteration, then the modificating operation is as follows:

$$P_i^{(k+1)}\{a\} = P_i^{(k)}\{a\}\left[1 + Q_i^{(k)}\{a\}\right]/A_i^{(k)}$$

where $A_i^{(k)}$ is a normalization factor. $Q_i^{(k)}\{a\}$ is the support for labeling $\{a\}$ at block i from its spatial neighborhood. Typically, it takes the following form:

$$Q_i^{(k)}\{a\} = \sum_{j\in N_i} w_{ij} \sum_{b\in V} r_{ij}(a,b)P_j^{(k)}\{b\}$$

where N_i is the neighborhood of block i, V is the label set, w_{ij} is the neighborhood weighing factor ($\sum_j w_{ij} = 1$) and $r_{ij}(a,b)$ is the so-called compatibility coefficient within $[-1,1]$. The very meaning of the compatibility coefficient $r_{ij}(a,b)$ can be seen as some context-dependent and intuitive (in the sense of a priori knowledge and intended goal) measure about to what extent labeling $\{b\}$ at some neighboring j is compatible with labeling $\{a\}$ at i when the labeling for i is facing reconsideration. It is hardly possible to comment on the (in)consistences among neighboring blocks without some knowledge of regional properties. Assuming that the regions are at least locally convex, $r_{ij}(a,b)$ should behave in the following way. If j is smaller than i, it is reasonable that little or no action should be taken on adjusting the labeling at i due to the following:

a. j may lie between two larger and unaligned blocks (i is one of them) from two adjacent regions and therefore the current labeling at j is not yet stable on its own,

b. j is certainly more likely to be a border element of a region than i. If they belong to a common region, there is obviously a necessity for j to be compatibly labeled with i and not the other way round. Otherwise, any current labeling at i is clearly not incompatible with that at j.

It is quite natural to choose a relatively small magnitude for $r_{ij}(a,b)$ according to some nonnegative function $F(SIDE_j, SIDE_i)$ with F somehow proportional to $SIDE_j$ and inversely proportional to $SIDE_i$. Under a similar idea, we tend to let $r_{ij}(a,b)$ also vary according to $F(SIDE_j, SIDE_i)$ when $SIDE_i \leq SIDE_j$. So, an obvious choice will be:

$$r_{ij}(a,b) = c_i(2\delta_{ab} - 1)F(SIDE_j, SIDE_i)$$

where δ_{ab} is the Kronecker delta and c_i is a positive scaling factor which also ensures $r_{ij}(a,b)$ within $[-1,1]$. Clearly, c_i should never exceed $1/F(L, SIDE_i)$ with L being the largest existing block length. Thus, we obtain:

$$r_{ij}(a,b) = c(2\delta_{ab} - 1)F(SIDE_j, SIDE_i)/F(L, SIDE_i)$$

where $c \in (0,1]$ is now independent of any specific i. Some obvious and simple choices for F are the following:

$$F(x,y) = (x/y)^p \quad \text{or} \quad F(x,y) = (\ln x / \ln y)^p$$

with $p > 0$. As a result, we obtain:

$$|r_{ij}| = c2^{(g-s)p} \quad \text{or} \quad |r_{ij}| = c(g/s)^p$$

with $SIDE_j = 2^g$ and $L = 2^s$.

3. Preliminary Experiments

The experiments here are restricted to a single input. In the present example two 256×256 test images are used (see Figure 1), which are GLD-textural images out of some originally heavily textured graylevel images. Based on some a priori judgements we fixed [Alow,Ahig] at [50,85] and constrained the scaling parameter h to [0.1,0.4]. All blocks larger than 4×4 take part in the calculation of AP and RP. Rlow was set at 30.

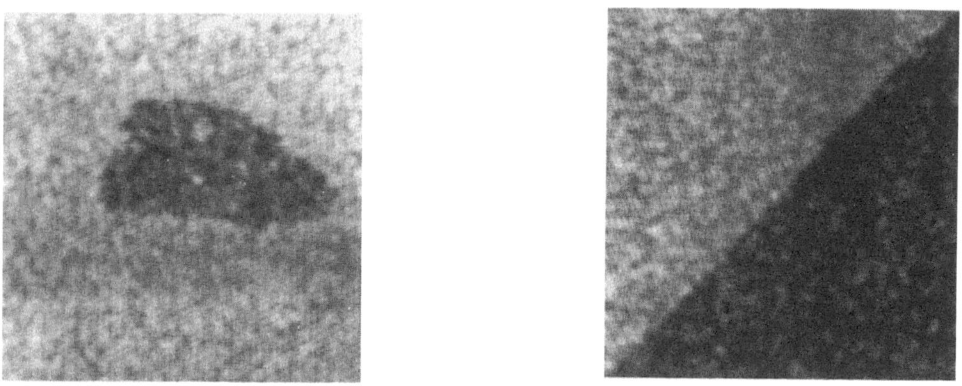

Figure 1: Input test images

The split-merge pre-segmentations are shown in Figure 2. The results of the clustering stage are given in Figure 3. For the relaxation process we adopted the following initialization of the label distribution:

$$P_i^{(0)}\{a\} = \left[1 - d_i\{a\}/\sum d_i\{b\}\right]/(N-1)$$

where $d_i\{a\}$ is the feature distance between block i and cluster $\{a\}$ and N is the number of clusters. For all QT-blocks of a single pixel we applied an uniform initialization.

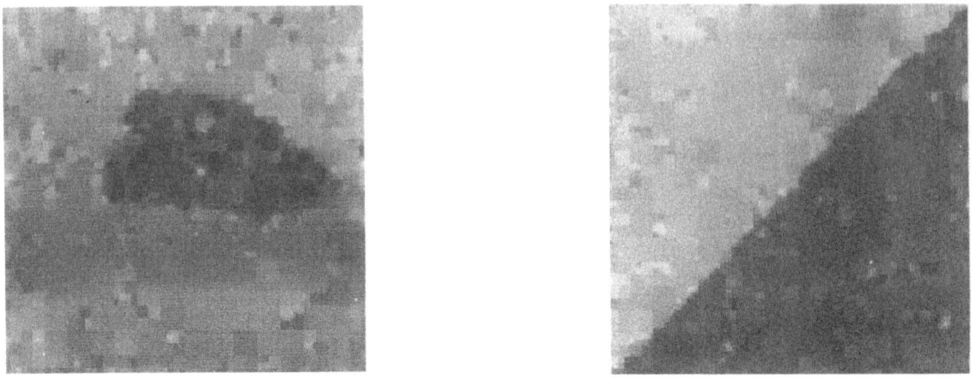

Figure 2: Outputs of the split-merge process

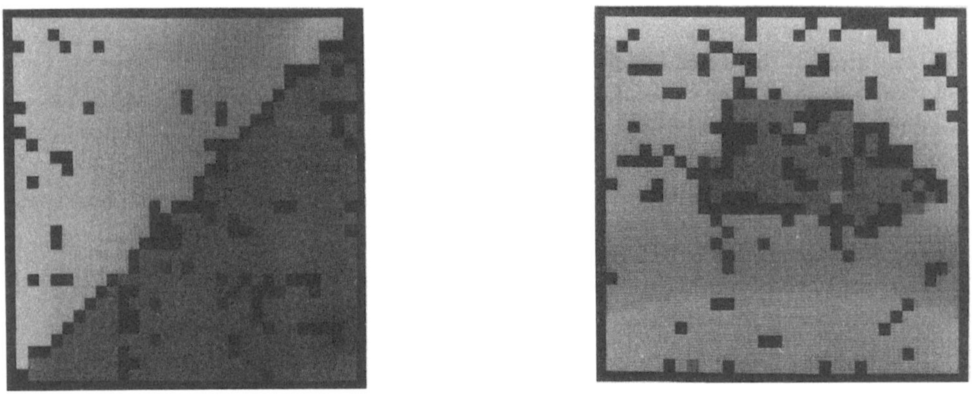

Figure 3: Results of the clustering stage: dark blocks are non-active blocks

Furthermore, all blocks larger than 32×32 are excluded from the relaxation process. To reduce artifacts we set $p = 1$ and $c = 1$ for the compatibility coefficients. The final results are shown in Figure 4 and Figure 5.

We observe some artifacts within the actual regions. However, the detected boundaries of the regions are quite satisfactory.

4. Conclusions

From the preliminary results so far, we come to the following conclusions:

a. The iterative split-merge scheme is a feasible approach and a fully automated scheme seems to be possible;

b. determination of the clustering parameters C and R can be based on the cluster sphere's width of all active QT-blocks together, and

Figure 4: Final segmentations

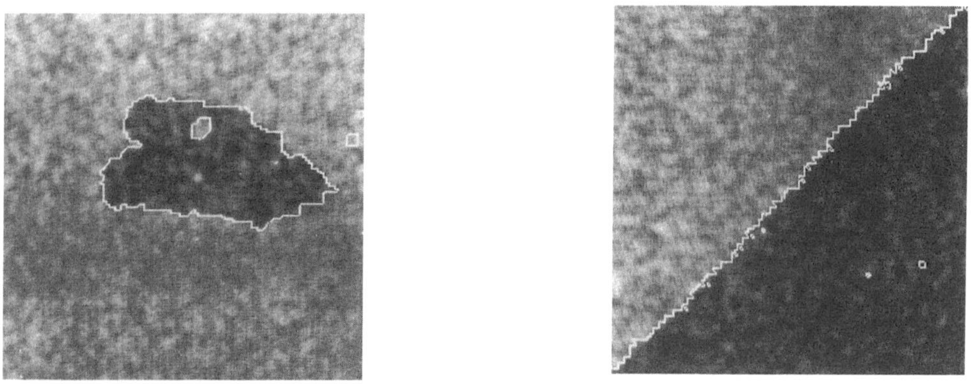

Figure 5: Overlays with the original inputs

c. the final segmentation approximates the true segmentation quite reasonably.

We expect that the proposed approach can be developed into a well-behaved method to tackle segmentation problems for a wide range of purposes.

References

[1] Coleman G.B., Andrews H.C., "Image Segmentation by Clustering," *Proc. IEEE*, Vol. 67, No. 5, May 1979, pp. 773-785.

[2] Nagin P.A., "Segmentation Using Spatial Context and Feature Space Cluster Labels," Univ. of Massachusetts, COINS Techn. Report 78-8, May 1978.

[3] Pavlidis T., *Structural Pattern Recognition*, Springer-Verlag, Berlin, 1977.

[4] Gerbrands J.J., Backer E., "Split-and-merge Segmentation of SLAR-imagery: Segmentation Consistency," *Proc. 7ICPR*, Montreal, Canada, 1984, pp. 284-286.

[5] Anderberg M.R., *Cluster Analysis for Applications*, Acad. Press, New York, 1973.

[6] Ball G.H., Hall D.J., "ISODATA — A Novel Method of Data Analysis and Pattern Classification," Techn. Report SRI, California, 1965.

[7] Rosenfeld A., Hummel R.A., Zucker S.W., "Scene Labeling by Relaxation Operations," *IEEE Trans. SMC*, Vol. SMC-6, No. 6, June 1976, pp. 420-433.

[8] Zucker S.W., Hummel R.A., Rosenfeld A., "An Application of Relaxation Labeling to Line and Curve Enhancement," *IEEE Trans. Comp.*, Vol, C-26, No. 4, April 1977, pp. 394-403.

LEARNING THE PARAMETERS OF A HIDDEN MARKOV RANDOM FIELD IMAGE MODEL : A SIMPLE EXAMPLE

Pierre A. Devijver and Michel M. Dekesel

Philips Research Laboratory
Avenue Em. Van Becelaere 2, Box 8
B-1170 Brussels, Belgium

Abstract

The paper outlines a unified treatment of the labeling and learning problems for the so-called hidden Markov chain model currently used in many speech recognition systems and the hidden Pickard random field image model (a small but interesting, causal sub-class of hidden Markov random field models). In both cases, labeling techniques are formulated in terms of Baum's classical *forward-backward* recurrence formulae, and learning is accomplished by a specialization of the EM algorithm for mixture identification. Experimental results demonstrate that the approach is subjectively relevant to the image restoration and segmentation problems.

1. Introduction

In the recent past, there has been considerable interest in *image segmentation and restoration* using maximum a posteriori (MAP) estimation and (strict sense) Markov random field image models, see [9], [15], [17], [20], [24]–[26], [29], [48] and the references therein. These techniques are based on a variety of image models and optimality criteria, and are scattered over a wide range of the complexity scale. Image models that have been proposed are : hidden Markov random fields [35] in *e.g.*, [9] and [24], hidden Markov mesh random fields [3], [33] in [15], [17] and [20], and Pickard random fields [40], [41] in [29]. It is probably fair to say that the most successful techniques and conceptually complete ideas for treating problems of image processing via MAP estimation in Markov random fields were presented by Geman and Geman [24]. However, [24], as well as all of the works alluded to above, leave an important problem unanswered, namely, that of estimating the parameters of a hidden Markov model from real image data. The difficulty of the problem is elaborated upon and the desirability of "simple, data-driven [estimation] methods based on solid statistical principles" is acknowledged by Geman, Geman and Graffigne elsewhere in this volume, [25].

NATO ASI Series, Vol. F30
Pattern Recognition Theory and Applications
Edited by P. A. Devijver and J. Kittler

A substantially different situation arises in *speech recognition* where the so-called "hidden Markov chain model" has been used quite extensively — and very successfully — over the last decade. In this problem domain various labeling (classification) and learning (parameter estimation) techniques have been developed and well documented, see *e.g.*, [2], [4]–[6], [10], [16], [18], [23], [28], [31], [32], [43]. (In addition references [37] and [42] provide a clear and comprehensive introduction to the subject matter.)

As far as "learning" is concerned, one might conceive that the techniques and ideas developed for speech recognition purposes could provide a good starting point for attacking the problem arising in image processing. However, to the best of our knowledge, this has not proved to be the case so far, for the simple reason that the models assumed in both areas of research differ in an number of significant respects. In particular, the "hidden Markov chain model" for speech is a *causal* process while the most popular "Markov random field" model for images is a *non-causal* process. Loosely speaking, this statement reflects the property that samples of speech signal are "time-ordered" while there is no natural ordering for pixels in an image. This has a number of important consequences: *e.g.*, causality entails recursivity while non-causality is somehow synonymous with iterative treatment.

There exists a notable exception to the rule: Pickard random fields [40], [41] are a (fairly) small but interesting subclass of 2-D random fields which are simultaneously causal and non-causal (see Section 2.2). Therefore they enjoy some of the properties of the 1-D Markov chain model for speech while providing legitimate image models. Moreover, we will see hereafter that rows (columns) in each set of k consecutive columns (row) of a Pickard random field form a k-dimensional vector Markov chain, $k = 1, 2, \cdots$. Haslett [29] is to be credited for being the first at taking advantage of these properties for deriving MAP recursive labeling techniques for images modelled by a hidden Pickard random field. It should come as no surprise that Haslett's method bears a close resemblance to the methods currently used in speech recognition programs.

It is one of the purposes of this paper to extend Haslett's work and to outline learning techniques applicable to the Pickard random field image model. As for labeling, our learning technique owes much to the body of knowledge available in speech recognition circles, viz., it is based on the so-called EM algorithm [44], [19] for mixture identification in a Markovian context [5], [6], [37].

Throughout the paper, 1- and 2-D hidden Markov models are treated in parallel. Section 2 introduces the models of interest. Labeling techniques based on Baum's *forward-backward* algorithm [5], [6], [18] are outlined in Section 3. The learning problem is discussed in Section 4 where the emphasis is on the 2-D problem. In Section 5, experimental results on artificial and real imagery demonstrate that the approach is subjectively relevant to the image restoration and segmentation problem. Comments and suggestions for possible extensions of the work presented here are collected in Section 6. The presentation has a definite tutorial flavor. Both the speech recognition problem (1-D) and the image processing problem (2-D) are treated in the same formalism. In doing so, one of our goals was to demonstrate the possibility of cross-fertilization of both fields.

2. Hidden Markov Models

2.1. The Hidden Markov Chain Model

In this section, we briefly review the definition and main properties of Markov chains that will be needed in the sequel, and we introduce the so-called "hidden Markov chain Model".

Let $\Omega \doteq \{\omega_1, \cdots, \omega_\vartheta\}$ designate the state-space of a discrete parameter, discrete time, first order, homogeneous Markov chain. We write $\omega^\tau = \omega_j$ to indicate that the process is in state ω_j at time τ. The Markov chain is specified in terms of an *initial* state distribution $P_j = P(\omega^1 = \omega_j)$, $j = 1, \cdots, \vartheta$, and a matrix of stationary *state transition probabilities* $P_{jk} = P(\omega^{\tau+1} = \omega_k / \omega^\tau = \omega_j)$, $\tau \geq 1$, and $j, k \in \{1, \cdots, \vartheta\}$. Let us recall that a (first order) Markov chain is defined by the property that for any $\tau > 1$, $P(\omega^\tau / \omega^1, \cdots, \omega^{\tau-1}) = P(\omega^\tau / \omega^{\tau-1})$. There follows that the probability for an arbitrary finite realization $\{\omega_{i_\tau}\}_{\tau=1}^T$ is given by a standard factorization:

$$P(\omega_{i_1}, \cdots, \omega_{i_T}) = P(\omega^1 = \omega_{i_1}) \prod_{\tau=2}^{T} P(\omega^\tau = \omega_{i_\tau} / \omega^{\tau-1} = \omega_{i_{\tau-1}}) = P_{i_1} \prod_{\tau=2}^{T} P_{i_{\tau-1} i_\tau} \qquad (1)$$

In what follows, we shall assume that we are dealing with a *regular* Markov chain, *i.e.*, one that has no transient set and has a single ergodic set with only one cyclic class.

It will prove useful to recall that a Markov chain observed in reverse order, *i.e.*, for decreasing values of τ, is also a Markov process. However, it does not always qualify as a Markov chain in the sense that, in general, the *backward* transition probabilities are dependent on time. Among the Markov chains which remain Markov chains in the reverse direction, we shall be particularly interested in *reversible* chains when we discuss the class of Markov random fields suggested by Pickard [40], [41] and exploited by Haslett [29]. Roughly speaking, a reversible chain is one which looks the same in both directions. Formally, let $[\pi_1 \cdots \pi_\vartheta]$ designate the stationary vector of a regular Markov chain. A chain is said to be *reversible* if $P(\omega^\tau = \omega_i / \omega^{\tau-1} = \omega_j) = P(\omega^\tau = \omega_i / \omega^{\tau+1} = \omega_j)$, uniformly in τ, or equivalently, $\pi_i P_{ij} = \pi_j P_{ji}$. Every two-state ergodic chain is reversible, and every ergodic chain which has a symmetric transition matrix is also reversible, [34].

We assume that the Markov chain cannot be observed. What can be observed is a random variable X which is related to ω through ϑ probability distributions $p_j(\mathrm{X}) = p(\mathrm{X}/\omega_j)$, $j = 1, \cdots, \vartheta$. Moreover, given a sequence $\overline{\boldsymbol{X}}_1^T \doteq \{X^1, \cdots, X^T\}$ of observations of the random variable X — where X^τ is the observation at time τ — we make the assumption that $X^1, \cdots, X^T$ are state-conditionally independent (or that X's are observed in memoryless noise). In other words, we assume that, given ω^τ, X^τ is independent of $\omega^{\tau'}$ and $X^{\tau'}$ for any $\tau' \neq \tau$. There follows a second factorization:

$$p(X^1, \cdots, X^T / \omega^1, \cdots, \omega^T) = \prod_{\tau=1}^{T} p(X^\tau / \omega^\tau). \qquad (2)$$

By combining the factorizations in (1) and (2) and invoking the theorem of the total probability, the likelihood $\tilde{\mathcal{L}}$ of a T-sequence of observations $X^1, \cdots, X^T$ is given by

$$\begin{aligned} \tilde{\mathcal{L}} = p(X^1, \cdots, X^T) &= \sum_{\omega^1, \cdots, \omega^T = \omega_1}^{\omega_\vartheta} P(\omega^1) p(X^1/\omega^1) \prod_{\tau=1}^{T-1} P(\omega^{\tau+1}/\omega^\tau) p(X^\tau/\omega^\tau) \\ &= \sum_{i_1, \cdots, i_T = 1}^{\vartheta} P_{i_1} p_{i_1}(X^1) \prod_{\tau=1}^{T-1} P_{i_\tau i_{\tau+1}} p_{i_{\tau+1}}(X^{\tau+1}). \end{aligned} \tag{3}$$

In what follows, we shall be interested in computing expressions like $\tilde{\mathcal{L}}$ in (3). However, it should be noted that, according to (3), the computation of $\tilde{\mathcal{L}}$ involves $2T\vartheta^{T+1}$ multiplications. For most applications, this would prove intractable. Fortunately, a number of researchers were able to devise clever methods for computing such expressions with a work factor linear in T, [4]–[6], [16], [18], [23], [28]. One of these methods will be reviewed hereafter.

As an illustration of the model just defined, let us take the case of a Markov chain with six states $\omega_1, \cdots, \omega_6$, each of which is equally probable a priori ($P_i = 1/6, \ i = 1, \ldots, 6$). We assume that the transition probabilities are given by

$$\begin{aligned} P_{ij} \ = \ & p > 0 \quad \text{if } j = i, \\ & q > 0 \quad \text{if } j = i+1 \bmod 6, \\ & r > 0 \quad \text{if } j = i+2 \bmod 6, \\ & 0 \qquad\ \ \text{otherwise}, \end{aligned}$$

with $p + q + r = 1$. Thus, the transition matrix is

$$[P_{ij}] = \begin{bmatrix} p & q & r & & & \\ & p & q & r & & \\ & & p & q & r & \\ & & & p & q & r \\ r & & & & p & q \\ q & r & & & & p \end{bmatrix}$$

(Transition probabilities not shown are equal to zero.)

There are various ways to represent Markov chains graphically. Here, we shall adopt the trellis representation, which is introduced in Figure 1. Each node in the figure corresponds to a distinct state at a given time, ($\tau_1 \le \tau \le \tau_{10}$), and each branch represents a transition to some new state at the next instant of time. In Figure 1 is shown one *state-sequence* starting at state $\omega^{\tau_1} = \omega_3$ and ending at state $\omega^{\tau_{10}} = \omega_3$. To every possible state-sequence, there corresponds a unique path through the trellis and vice versa. Note that the presence of zeroes in the transition matrix reduces the number of possible paths through the trellis. We assume that, at any time τ, the system generates (emits) the observable X^τ with a probability $p(X^\tau/\omega^\tau)$ that depends only on the current state ω^τ. Then, by the Markov and memoryless properties, the joint probability of the observation sequence, $X^{\tau_1}, \cdots, X^{\tau_{10}}$, and the state-sequence, say, $\omega^{\tau_1} = \omega_3, \cdots, \omega^{\tau_{10}} = \omega_3$, illustrated in Figure 1, is the product of the initial, transition, and conditional probabilities encountered along the path through the trellis. This product is one of the terms of the sum in Eq. (3).

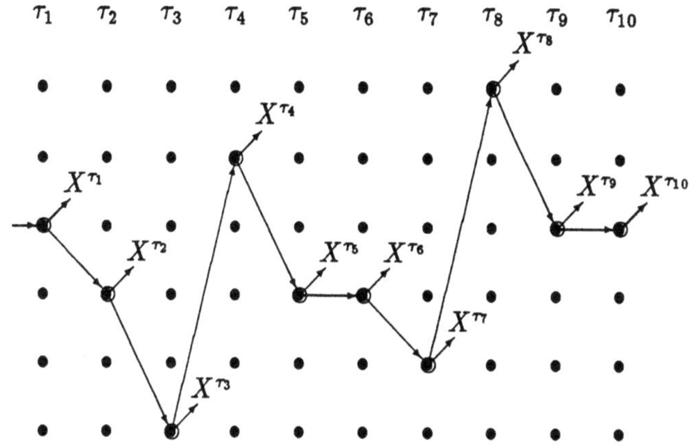

Figure 1: One path through the trellis representation of a six-state Markov chain

A few words are in order about the practical interpretation for the abstract model just defined. In a word, states ω^τ should be interpreted as pattern classes or labels and observations X^τ as feature vectors. For instance, in a text reading machine, states would serve to identify alphabetic characters while observations could be multidimensional vectors of Fourier descriptors of character contours. In a speech recognition application, states could designate phonetic labels of speech segments while observations could be vectors of spectral coefficients of the corresponding segments. In any case, X's are assumed to be observable, but ω's are not. Thus, every X^τ is a probabilistic function of an unseen Markov process—and is in no way Markov[1]. Hence, the term *hidden Markov chain model.*

A number of standard properties of Markov chains can be generalized quite straightforwardly in terms of the (X,ω) process. For instance, it is well known that, given ω^τ, the sequences $\{\omega^t\}_1^{\tau-1}$ and $\{\omega^t\}_{\tau+1}^T$ are mutually independent. Similarly, for the hidden Markov chain model, it holds that

$$P(X^{\tau+1}/\omega^\tau = \omega_j, \overline{\boldsymbol{X}}_1^\tau) = P(X^{\tau+1}/\omega^\tau = \omega_j), \tag{4}$$

and

$$P(\overline{\boldsymbol{X}}_{\tau+1}^T/\omega^\tau = \omega_j, X^\tau) = P(\overline{\boldsymbol{X}}_{\tau+1}^T/\omega^\tau = \omega_j), \tag{5}$$

or, more generally,

$$P(\overline{\boldsymbol{X}}_1^\tau, \overline{\boldsymbol{X}}_{\tau+1}^T/\omega^\tau = \omega_j) = P(\overline{\boldsymbol{X}}_1^\tau/\omega^\tau = \omega_j)P(\overline{\boldsymbol{X}}_{\tau+1}^T/\omega^\tau = \omega_j). \tag{6}$$

2.2. The Hidden Pickard Random Field Model

Presently, we briefly turn to the consideration of random fields defined on the 2-D integer lattice. Let $V_{M,N} = \{(i,j) : 1 \le i \le M, 1 \le j \le N\}$ designate the finite $M \times N$

[1]See [24] and the paper by Geman, Geman and Graffigne (in this volume) for a model in which labels and observables are individually Markov distributed and jointly Markov distributed.

integer lattice. Equivalently, let (m,n) be the pixel at the intersection of row m and column n in a digitized $M \times N$ image. In accordance with standard practice, we assume that the first axis is pointing downwards and the second axis is pointing rightwards. Thus, pixel $(1,1)$ is the upper left pixel of the image. Associated with pixel (m,n) are a label[2] $\lambda_{m,n}$ and a feature vector or image measurement $X_{m,n}$. The interpretation of the model is straightforward : For an arbitrary pixel in the image, a binary label (λ) could indicate presence versus absence of an edge, a multivalued label could designate the region the pixel belongs to, and observations (X) could be vectors of multispectral reflectance measurements as well as vectors of texture descriptors.

The generalization of the Markov property from one to two dimensions is a difficult problem due to the lack of natural ordering of lattice points. This problem has been extensively discussed in the literature, see. e.g., [7], [8], [30], [34], [36]. For the purposes of the present discussion it will be sufficient to recall that, under 8-connectedness, the natural (non-causal) generalization of the Markov property reads

$$P(\lambda_{m,n}/\lambda_{i,j} : (i,j) \neq (m,n)) = P\left(\lambda_{m,n} \Big/ \begin{matrix} \lambda_{m-1,n-1} & \lambda_{m-1,n} & \lambda_{m-1,n+1} \\ \lambda_{m,n-1} & & \lambda_{m,n+1} \\ \lambda_{m+1,n-1} & \lambda_{m+1,n} & \lambda_{m+1,n+1} \end{matrix}\right), \tag{7}$$

with necessary adjustments at the boundaries. A random field satisfying (7) is called a *Markov random field.* Contrasting with (7), Kanal and his co-worker have proposed a kind of (causal) Markov property which reproduces, in terms of lattice sites, the notion of *past*, *present*, and *future* [3], [33]. Their definition (for a *third order* field) reads

$$P(\lambda_{m,n}/\lambda_{i,j} : i \leq m \text{ or } j \leq n) = P\left(\lambda_{m,n} \Big/ \begin{matrix} \lambda_{m-1,n-1} & \lambda_{m-1,n} \\ \lambda_{m,n-1} & \end{matrix}\right). \tag{8}$$

A random field satisfying (8) is called a *Markov mesh random field.* It should be emphasized that (8) implies (7), but the converse is not true in general.

The Pickard random field [40], [41] enjoys the property of being simultaneously a Markov field and a Markov mesh. To simplify the presentation, we shall consider the case of a *binary* random field only, but it should be stressed that this restriction is otherwise unnecessary.

The Pickard random field is a spatially homogeneous random field which is generated from the joint distribution for the vertices of a unit cell

$$\begin{pmatrix} (m-1,n-1) & (m-1,n) \\ (m,n-1) & (m,n) \end{pmatrix}.$$

This distribution is taken to be invariant under the symmetries of the square, and is required to satisfy the condition

$$P\left(\lambda_{m-1,n} \Big/ \begin{matrix} \lambda_{m-1,n-1} \\ \lambda_{m,n-1} \end{matrix}\right) = P(\lambda_{m-1,n}/\lambda_{m-1,n-1}). \tag{9}$$

[2]For the sake of clarity we use different symbols for labels in 1- and 2-D random processes.

Pickard remarked [40] that this distribution is specified by three parameters only,[3] namely,

$$\theta = P(\lambda_{m,n} = 1), \qquad a = P(\lambda_{m,n} = 1/\lambda_{m,n-1} = 1),$$
$$d = P\left(\lambda_{m,n} = 1/ \begin{array}{cc} \lambda_{m-1,n-1} = 1 & \lambda_{m-1,n} = 1 \\ \lambda_{m,n-1} = 1 & \end{array}\right). \tag{10}$$

(Note that the *causality* of the Pickard random field is apparent form the last equation in (10)). However, to get hold of the parameter space is a rather awkward problem because that space turns out to be a peculiar subspace of the unit cube.

If we let $b = P(\lambda_{m,n} = 1/\lambda_{m,n-1} = 0)$, we get $b = \theta(1-a)/(1-\theta)$. Now, from the viewpoint of our subsequent discussion, the interesting thing about Pickard random fields is that the rows (and columns) of the image constitute segments of stationary, homogeneous and reversible Markov chains with transition matrix $\begin{pmatrix} a & 1-a \\ b & 1-b \end{pmatrix}$. Thus, it follows that $P(\lambda_{m,n}/\lambda_{m,n'}; n' \neq n) = P(\lambda_{m,n}/\lambda_{m,n\pm1})$, where $(m, n\pm 1)$ is a short for $\{(m,n-1),(m,n+1)\}$, and similarly for columns. Moreover,

$$P(\lambda_{m,n}/\lambda_{k,\ell} : k = m \text{ or } \ell = n, (k,\ell) \neq (m,n)) = P(\lambda_{m,n}/\lambda_{m,n\pm1}, \lambda_{m\pm1,n}). \tag{11}$$

The binary Pickard random field constitutes one of the rare examples of Markov random fields where the correlation structure is quite easy to uncover. Specifically, with the transition matrix given above, the correlation $\rho_{k,\ell}$ between $\lambda_{m,n}$ and $\lambda_{m+k,n+\ell}$ is given by $\rho_{k,\ell} = (a-b)^{|k|+|\ell|}$, thereby demonstrating that there is no *long-range* correlation, [40].

As in the preceding section, we shall assume that the observable random process associated with the states is represented by ϑ probability distributions $p_\lambda(X)$. In other words, we assume that the distribution of the observation $X_{i,j}$ is $p_q(X_{i,j})$ when $\lambda_{i,j} = q$. Furthermore, we assume that conditionally upon $\lambda_{i,j}$, $X_{i,j}$ is independent from $\lambda_{k,\ell}$ and $X_{k,\ell}$ for any $(k,\ell) \neq (i,j)$[4]. It is then a straightforward matter to generalize the conditional independence properties (4) through (6) in this two-dimensional situation : By writing, e.g., $\overline{X}_{m,1}^{m,n-1}$ for $\{X_{m,1}, \cdots, X_{m,n-1}\}$ it can readily be shown that

$$\begin{aligned} & p(X_{k,\ell} : k = m \text{ or } \ell = n, (k,\ell) \neq (m,n)/\lambda_{m,n}) \\ = \; & p(\overline{X}_{m,1}^{m,n-1}/\lambda_{m,n})\, p(\overline{X}_{m,n+1}^{m,N}/\lambda_{m,n})\, p(\overline{X}_{1,n}^{m-1,n}/\lambda_{m,n})\, p(\overline{X}_{m+1,n}^{M,n}/\lambda_{m,n}). \end{aligned} \tag{12}$$

This observation provides the basis for the work of Haslett [29] we shall refer to in Section 3.2.

As a final remark about Pickard random fields, let us note that they constitute a very small subclass only of Markov random fields, even after extension past the binary case [15]. For this reason, they are of fairly limited practical interest. For our present

[3]This statement can be interpreted as a corollary of the Hammersley–Clifford theorem [8] for an isotropic Markov random field satisfying (9).

[4]In Geman and Geman [24], it is shown that a blurring transformation can be accounted for in a hidden Markov random field image model

purposes, however, they are of definite theoretical interest for they provide a convenient framework for introducing a powerful learning technique that can be extended to the richer class of Markov mesh random fields.

3. The Labeling Problem

The first problem that we wish to address is that of deriving computationally efficient procedures for computing the joint likelihoods of labels and observations under the assumption that the parameters of the underlying model (*i.e.*, initial and transition probabilities for Markov chains, the parameters θ, a and d for Pickard random fields and the conditional distributions for the observation X) are known to us. The problem of estimating these parameters from sample realizations will be the subject matter of the following section. As above, Markov chains and Pickard random fields are treated separately.

3.1. Labeling in Hidden Markov Chains

The labelling problem for hidden Markov chain models has received considerable attention from researchers in speech recognition, see *e.g.*, [10], [13], [32], [37], [42]. Our brief presentation of Baum's *forward-backward* decomposition is based on [18].

Let us first address the problem of computing the joint likelihood $\tilde{\mathcal{L}}_\tau(\omega_j) = P(\omega^\tau = \omega_j, \overline{\boldsymbol{X}}_1^T)$, of being in state ω_j at time τ and observing the sequence $\overline{\boldsymbol{X}}_1^T$. Following Baum, the computation will be based on the simple decomposition:

$$\begin{aligned}\tilde{\mathcal{L}}_\tau(\omega_j) \doteq P(\omega^\tau = \omega_j, \overline{\boldsymbol{X}}_1^T) &= P(\omega^\tau = \omega_j, \overline{\boldsymbol{X}}_1^\tau) P(\overline{\boldsymbol{X}}_{\tau+1}^T / \omega^\tau = \omega_j) \\ &= \tilde{\mathcal{F}}_\tau(\omega_j) \tilde{\mathcal{B}}_\tau(\omega_j),\end{aligned} \tag{13}$$

for $j = 1, \cdots, \vartheta$ and $1 \le \tau < T$. It is customary to call $\tilde{\mathcal{F}}_\tau(\omega_j)$ and $\tilde{\mathcal{B}}_\tau(\omega_j)$ the *forward* and *backward* probabilities respectively.

It is easy to show [18] that the forward probabilities can be computed inductively by the recurrence

$$\begin{aligned}\tilde{\mathcal{F}}_\tau(\omega_j) &= P_j p_j(X^1) & \tau &= 1, \\ &= \textstyle\sum_i \tilde{\mathcal{F}}_{\tau-1}(\omega_i) P_{ij} p_j(X^\tau) & \tau &= 2, \cdots, T,\end{aligned} \tag{14}$$

while the backward probabilities can be computed inductively by the recurrence

$$\begin{aligned}\tilde{\mathcal{B}}_\tau(\omega_j) &= 1 & \tau &= T, \\ &= \textstyle\sum_k P_{jk} p_k(X^{\tau+1}) \tilde{\mathcal{B}}_{\tau+1}(\omega_k) & \tau &= T-1, \cdots, 1.\end{aligned} \tag{15}$$

In view of (13), Baum's forward-backward algorithm is quite simple: $\tilde{\mathcal{F}}$'s are computed recursively forward and stored for use during the backward stage which amounts to computing $\tilde{\mathcal{B}}$'s using (15) and using (13) to get the desired likelihoods $\tilde{\mathcal{L}}_\tau(\omega_j)$ for $j = 1, \cdots, \vartheta$ and $\tau = T, \cdots, 1$. Note that an alternative expression for $\tilde{\mathcal{L}} = p(X^1, \cdots, X^T)$ in (3) is $\sum_j \tilde{\mathcal{L}}_\tau(\omega_j) = \sum_j \tilde{\mathcal{F}}_\tau(\omega_j)\tilde{\mathcal{B}}_\tau(\omega_j)$, uniformly in τ. Now, as (14) and (15) can be computed in *linear* time (*i.e.*, with a fixed number of operations per time frame) the recurrences (14) and (15) have enabled us to overcome the exponential complexity of computing $\tilde{\mathcal{L}}$ in (3).

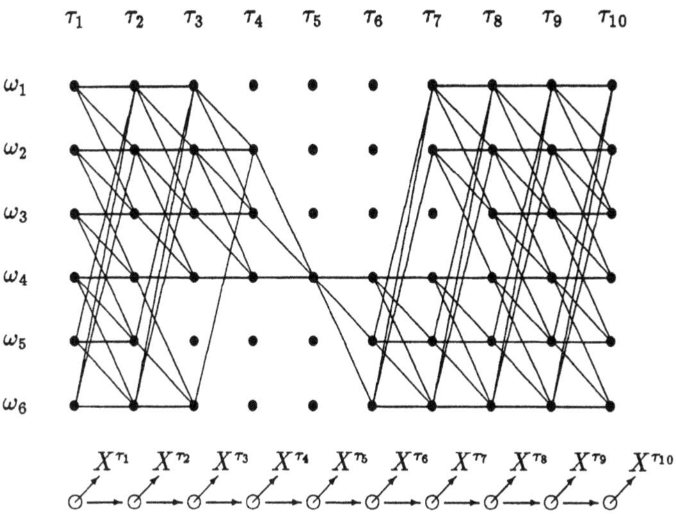

Figure 2: $\hat{\mathcal{F}}_{\tau_5}(\omega_4)\hat{\mathcal{B}}_{\tau_5}(\omega_4)$ is the sum of the probabilities of emitting $X^{\tau_1},\cdots,X^{\tau_{10}}$ along of all distinct paths through ω_4 at time τ_5 when the trellis is traversed from left to right.

The trellis representation for Markov chains provides again a fairly intuitive interpretation for the forward-backward decomposition. The forward probability, say, $\tilde{\mathcal{F}}_{\tau_5}(\omega_4)$, is the sum of the probabilities of emitting the sub-sequence $X^{\tau_1},\cdots,X^{\tau_5}$ along all distinct paths leading to the node $\omega^{\tau_5}=\omega_4$ when the trellis is traversed from left to right, as illustrated in Figure 2 for the simple model introduced in Section 2.1. The backward probability as well as the joint likelihood $\tilde{\mathcal{L}}(\omega_j)$ admit of obvious, equally simple interpretations.

Levinson *et al.* [37] pointed out that the implementation of the recurrences in a computer program would be marred by problems of a numerical nature, for $\tilde{\mathcal{F}}_\tau(\omega_j) \overset{T}{\Rightarrow} 0$ and $\tilde{\mathcal{B}}_\tau(\omega_j) \overset{T-\tau}{\Rightarrow} 0$ at an exponential rate, thereby causing underflow on any real computer, and they suggested a rather heuristic way to remedy the situation. Subsequently, it was shown by Devijver [18] that re-formulating the problem in terms of a posteriori probabilities leads to algorithms which are immune to the underflow problem.

Let $\mathcal{L}_\tau(\omega_j) = P(\omega^\tau = \omega_j/\overline{\boldsymbol{X}}_1^T)$. Then, the derivation in [18] was based on the following decomposition, analogous to (13): For $1 \leq \tau < T$,

$$\begin{aligned}\mathcal{L}_\tau(\omega_j) = P(\omega^\tau = \omega_j/\overline{\boldsymbol{X}}_1^T) &= \frac{P(\omega^\tau = \omega_j, \overline{\boldsymbol{X}}_1^\tau)}{p(\overline{\boldsymbol{X}}_1^\tau)} \times \frac{p(\overline{\boldsymbol{X}}_{\tau+1}^T/\omega^\tau = \omega_j)}{p(\overline{\boldsymbol{X}}_{\tau+1}^T/\overline{\boldsymbol{X}}_1^\tau)} \\ &= \mathcal{F}_\tau(\omega_j)\mathcal{B}_\tau(\omega_j), \qquad j = 1,\cdots,\vartheta.\end{aligned} \tag{16}$$

Note that both $\mathcal{L}_\tau(\omega_j)$ and $\mathcal{F}_\tau(\omega_j)$ are posterior probabilities, whereas $\mathcal{B}_\tau(\omega_j)$ does not seem to be amenable to any natural interpretation[5].

[5]The reader should take notice that we use *tilde*d symbols for the decomposition of joint likelihoods,

The forward (posterior) probabilities can again be computed by a simple recurrence, viz.,

$$\begin{aligned}\mathcal{F}_\tau(\omega_j) &= \mathcal{N}_\tau P_j\, p_j(X^1) & \tau = 1\\ &= \mathcal{N}_\tau \textstyle\sum_i \mathcal{F}_{\tau-1}(\omega_i)\, P_{ij}\, p_j(X^\tau) & \tau = 2,\cdots,T,\end{aligned} \tag{17}$$

where

$$\begin{aligned}\mathcal{N}_\tau &= [\textstyle\sum_j P_j p_j(X^\tau)]^{-1} & \tau = 1\\ &= [\textstyle\sum_i \sum_j \mathcal{F}_{\tau-1}(\omega_i) P_{ij} p_j(X^\tau)]^{-1} & \tau = 2,\cdots,T.\end{aligned} \tag{18}$$

For the backward probabilities, we have the decomposition

$$\mathcal{B}_\tau(\omega_j) = \sum_k \frac{P_{jk}\, p_k(X^{\tau+1})}{p(X_{\tau+1}/\overline{X}_1^\tau)} \times \frac{P(\overline{X}_{\tau+2}^T/\omega^{\tau+1} = \omega_k)}{p(\overline{X}_{\tau+2}^T/\overline{X}_1^{\tau+1})} \tag{19}$$

hence the backward recurrence

$$\begin{aligned}\mathcal{B}_\tau(\omega_j) &= 1 & \tau = T,\\ &= \mathcal{N}_{\tau+1} \textstyle\sum_k P_{jk}\, p_k(X^{\tau+1}) \mathcal{B}_{\tau+1}(\omega_k) & \tau = T-1,\cdots,1,\end{aligned} \tag{20}$$

where $\mathcal{N}_{\tau+1}$ is given again by (18).

It can be observed that the recurrences (17) and (20) expressed in terms of posterior probabilities are formally identical to the recurrences (14) and (15) expressed in terms of joint likelihoods, except for the presence of the normalizing factor $\mathcal{N}_\tau$. However, it should be obvious that, as stated in (17) and (18), the forward recurrence does not lead to an efficient implementation. A much more efficient, though equivalent one, is as follows:

$$\begin{aligned}\mathcal{G}_\tau(\omega_j) &= \textstyle\sum_i \mathcal{F}_{\tau-1}(\omega_i) P_{ij} & \tau = 2,\cdots,T,\\ \mathcal{F}'_\tau(\omega_j) &= P_j\, p_j(X^1) & \tau = 1,\\ &= \mathcal{G}_\tau(\omega_j)\, p_j(X^\tau) & \tau = 2,\cdots,T,\\ \mathcal{N}_\tau &= [\textstyle\sum_j \mathcal{F}'_\tau(\omega_j)]^{-1} & \tau = 1,\cdots,T,\\ \mathcal{F}_\tau(\omega_j) &= \mathcal{N}_\tau \mathcal{F}'_\tau(\omega_j) & \tau = 1,\cdots,T.\end{aligned} \tag{21}$$

With this formulation, $\mathcal{G}_\tau(\omega_j)$ is the a priori probability $P(\omega^\tau = \omega_j/\overline{X}_1^{\tau-1})$ of the process being in state ω_j at time τ, given only the sequence of previous observations $\overline{X}_1^{\tau-1}$, and the scheme prescribed by (21) is nothing but the sequential compound algorithm first proposed by Abend [2] and Raviv [43] for computing $\mathcal{F}_\tau(\omega_j) = P(\omega^\tau = \omega_j/\overline{X}_1^\tau)$; (see Devijver and Kittler [21] for a simpler formulation).

At this stage, maximum a posteriori (MAP) estimators for labels are obtained by the rule

$$\hat{\omega}^\tau = \omega_j \text{ if } \mathcal{L}_\tau(\omega_j) = \max_i \mathcal{L}_\tau(\omega_i) \qquad \tau = 1,\cdots,T.$$

This is nothing but the Bayes rule corresponding to the zero-one loss function (see [2] and [43] for a discussion of the optimality of this rule in the present context of compound decision theory.)

---

and un-*tilded* ones for the decomposition of posterior probabilities. We adhere to this convention throughout this paper (except in Eqs. (29)–(31))

3.2. Labeling in Hidden Pickard Random Fields

The discussion in the preceding section has given us all necessary ingredients entering the 2-D labeling technique proposed by Haslett in [29]. He assumes a hidden Pickard random field image model, and capitalizes on the observation that rows (columns) in each set of k consecutive columns (rows) of the random field form a k-dimensional vector Markov chain. Moreover, he makes the additional simplifying assumption that

$$P(\lambda_{m,n} = q/ \text{ all } X_{i,j}) \approx P(\lambda_{m,n} = q/X_{k,\ell} : k = m \text{ or } \ell = n) \doteq {}_H\mathcal{L}_{m,n}(q). \tag{22}$$

In plain words, this amounts to ignoring the dependence of $\lambda_{m,n}$ upon any $X_{k,\ell}$ not in the same row or column. Now, by invoking the conditional independence property in Eq. (13), we can write

$$\begin{aligned} {}_H\mathcal{L}_{m,n}(q) &\propto P(\lambda_{m,n} = q/\overline{\boldsymbol{X}}_{m,1}^{m,n-1})P(\lambda_{m,n} = q/\overline{\boldsymbol{X}}_{1,n}^{m-1,n}) \\ &\times \; p(X_{m,n}/\lambda_{m,n} = q) \\ &\times \; p(\overline{\boldsymbol{X}}_{m,n+1}^{m,N}/\lambda_{m,n} = q)p(\overline{\boldsymbol{X}}_{m+1,n}^{M,n}/\lambda_{m,n} = q). \end{aligned} \tag{23}$$

Readily, the first two factors in the right hand side of (23) have the same probabilistic structure as $\mathcal{G}_\tau(\omega_j)$ in (21), while the last two ones have the same probabilistic structure as $\mathcal{B}_\tau(\omega_j)$ in (20). Therefore, these factors can be computed using Baum's one-dimensional recurrences along the mth row and nth column respectively. If we let ${}_m\mathcal{G}_n(q)$ stand for $\mathcal{G}_n(\lambda_{m,n} = q)$ along row m, ${}_n\mathcal{G}_m(q)$ stand for $\mathcal{G}_m(\lambda_{m,n} = q)$ along column n, and similarly for $\mathcal{B}$'s, (23) becomes

$${}_H\mathcal{L}_{m,n}(q) \propto {}_m\mathcal{G}_n(q){}_n\mathcal{G}_m(q)p_q(X_{m,n}){}_m\mathcal{B}_n(q){}_n\mathcal{B}_m(q). \tag{24}$$

The application of Haslett's approach is quite simple : The computation of $\mathcal{G}$'s and $\mathcal{B}$'s requires four sweeps over the image; in the course of the last sweep, $\mathcal{L}$'s can be computed by (24) and $\text{argmax}_q\{{}_H\mathcal{L}_{m,n}(q)\}$ is used as a labeling criterion for minimum error-rate. See Section 5 and [29] for experimental results.

Many alternative approaches — all of which could be applied to the Pickard random field image model — have been suggested in the recent past. Labeling techniques in hidden Markov mesh random fields haven been outlined in [15], [17] and [20]. There is a growing body of literature on labeling methods for hidden Markov random fields image models; particular mention should be made of [24]; see also [9], [12], [48], and the contributions by Geman, Geman and Graffigne [25], Güler *et al.* [26], and Aarts and van Laarhoven [1] in this volume.

4. The Learning Problem

Until now, we have been concerned with the problem of using the information embodied in Markovian models in efficient ways, under the assumption that the parameters of the models were known to us. Our next problem is that of estimating these parameters. In some cases, the problem is fairly simple. For instance, in text recognition applications, it is frequently assumed that the number of states is the number of characters in the alphabet, and transition probabilities are estimated from tables of bigram frequencies for the language of interest. Next the parameters of class-conditional distributions can be estimated by standard techniques. This approach has been adopted by many in the past [39], [43], [46], [47], however it has sometimes led to deceiving results [27], [45]. One possible reason for this is that the method consisted in deciding a priori what the model ought to be, and hoping that experimental data would fit the model well.

A closely related method can be applied for estimating some of the parameters of Markov random fields image models, provided ground truth information is available. For instance, in their discussion of texture discrimination, [25], Geman *et al.* use maximum pseudo-likelihood [8] for estimating texture parameters from samples of the textures of interest (see also [14]). However, in image processing applications, the availability of ground truth information — in particular, the label to label relationships — is the exception rather than the rule, and the same authors advocate the desirability of simple, data-driven estimation methods based on solid statistical principles [25].

Hereafter, we shall follow quite a different route, one which does not require ground truth information and finds its origins in research on mixture identification as applied in speech recognition. Our goal will be to fit a hidden Markov model to sample data with as little a priori information as possible. For instance, in the picture segmentation application in Section 5, we will specify the number of possible states for the Markov process without specifying "what the individual states ought to be" and we will let the learning algorithm determine what are the states which best describe the data at hand.

Our learning algorithm for hidden Pickard random field image models in Section 4.2. will be a direct generalization of the so-called EM algorithm for mixture identification [44] which we shall review presently. Here again, the essential ideas are due to Baum and his co-workers [5], [6], (see also [19] for more details).

4.1. Mixture Identification in Hidden Markov Chains

Let us first examine how the ideas underlying the EM algorithm can be applied in the case of hidden Markov chains. To simplify the presentation, we will temporarily assume that the random process associated with the states is represented by ϑ *discrete* probability distributions $p_j(\chi_k) = P(X^\tau = \chi_k/\omega^\tau = \omega_j)$, $1 \leq j \leq \vartheta$, $1 \leq k \leq K$, $1 \leq \tau \leq T$. (In any event, we will assume that the conditional distributions we are working with are *identifiable* [49], [50].)

Let us recall from Section 2.1 that the likelihood $\tilde{\mathcal{L}}$ of a T-sequence of observations is given by (3), which combined with (13) and (15) yields

$$\begin{aligned}\tilde{\mathcal{L}} &= p(X^1, \cdots, X^T) \\ &= \sum_{i=1}^{\vartheta} \tilde{\mathcal{F}}_\tau(i)\tilde{\mathcal{B}}_\tau(i) = \sum_{i=1}^{\vartheta}\sum_{j=1}^{\vartheta} \tilde{\mathcal{F}}_\tau(i)P_{ij}p_j(X^\tau)\tilde{\mathcal{B}}_{\tau+1}(j),\end{aligned} \tag{25}$$

identically in τ. Our problem is to find maximum likelihood estimates for the parameters $\{P_i, P_{ij}, p_j(\chi_k)\}$, given the sample $X^1, \cdots, X^T$, subject to the constraints $\sum_j P_j = 1$,

$\sum_k P_{jk} = 1, \forall j$, and $\sum_k p_j(\chi_k) = 1, \forall j$. This problem can be cast in the mould of constrained optimization, and the solution is obtained in terms of implicit equations [5], [37]

$$P_i = \frac{P_i \partial \tilde{\mathcal{L}} / \partial P_i}{\sum_j P_j \partial \tilde{\mathcal{L}} / \partial P_j}, \qquad P_{ij} = \frac{P_{ij} \partial \tilde{\mathcal{L}} / \partial P_{ij}}{\sum_j P_{ij} \partial \tilde{\mathcal{L}} / \partial P_{ij}},$$

$$p_j(\chi_k) = \frac{p_j(\chi_k) \partial \tilde{\mathcal{L}} / \partial p_j(\chi_k)}{\sum_k p_j(\chi_k) \partial \tilde{\mathcal{L}} / \partial p_j(\chi_k)}.$$

By substituting for the partials from (25), we obtain the so-called re-estimation formulae [37], viz.,

$$P_i = \frac{\tilde{\mathcal{F}}_1(i)\tilde{\mathcal{B}}_1(i)}{\sum_j \tilde{\mathcal{F}}_1(j)\tilde{\mathcal{B}}_1(j)} = \frac{P(X^1, \cdots, X^T, \omega^1 = \omega_i)}{\sum_j P(X^1, \cdots, X^T, \omega^1 = \omega_j)}, \tag{26}$$

$$P_{ij} = \frac{\sum_\tau \tilde{\mathcal{F}}_\tau(i) P_{ij} p_j(X^{\tau+1}) \tilde{\mathcal{B}}_{\tau+1}(j)}{\sum_\tau \tilde{\mathcal{F}}_\tau(i)\tilde{\mathcal{B}}_\tau(i)} = \frac{\sum_\tau P(X^1, \cdots, X^T, \omega^\tau = \omega_i, \omega^{\tau+1} = \omega_j)}{\sum_\tau P(X^1, \cdots, X^T, \omega^\tau = \omega_i)}, \tag{27}$$

$$p_j(\chi_k) = \frac{\sum_{\tau | X^\tau = \chi_k} \tilde{\mathcal{F}}_\tau(j)\tilde{\mathcal{B}}_\tau(j)}{\sum_\tau \tilde{\mathcal{F}}_\tau(j)\tilde{\mathcal{B}}_\tau(j)} = \frac{\sum_{\tau | X^\tau = \chi_k} P(X^1, \cdots, X^\tau, \cdots, X^T, \omega^\tau = \omega_j)}{\sum_\tau P(X^1, \cdots, X^T, \omega^\tau = \omega_j)}. \tag{28}$$

Disregarding temporarily the numerical problems arising from using joint likelihoods instead of posterior probabilities, it is essentially these equations which serve as a basis for iteratively updating initial parameter estimates. $\tilde{\mathcal{F}}$'s and $\tilde{\mathcal{B}}$'s are computed using the forward and backward recurrences respectively for the current values of the parameters. They are then used in (26)–(28) to compute updated values of the estimates, and this gradient ascent procedure is continued until convergence at a maximum of the likelihood function.

It might again be helpful to call one's attention to the interpretation of the terms appearing in the re-estimation formulae. For the illustrative example introduced in Section 2.1, each term in the numerator of (27) is the joint likelihood of observing the sequence $X^{n_1}, \cdots, X^{n_0}$ along all distinct paths in the trellis which make the transition ω_i–ω_j in the time interval $[\tau, \tau+1]$, as illustrated in Figure 3. All other terms can be interpreted in the same manner.

The analogy with the standard EM algorithm for iid data (see, *e.g*, Section 6.4 in [22]) becomes even more obvious when we return to mixtures of multivariate normal distributions with distinct variance-covariance matrices. Equation (26) remains essentially unchanged. Using an obvious notation, (27) and (28) become

$$\hat{P}_{ij} = \frac{\sum_\tau \hat{\mathcal{F}}_\tau(i) \hat{P}_{ij} p(X^{\tau+1} | \omega_j, \hat{\theta}_j) \hat{\mathcal{B}}_{\tau+1}(j)}{\sum_j \sum_\tau \hat{\mathcal{F}}_\tau(i) \hat{P}_{ij} p(X^{\tau+1} | \omega_j, \hat{\theta}_j) \hat{\mathcal{B}}_{\tau+1}(j)} \tag{29}$$

where $p(X^{\tau+1} | \omega_j, \hat{\theta}_j) \sim N(X^{\tau+1}; \hat{\mu}_j, \hat{\Sigma}_j)$ with

$$\hat{\mu}_j = \frac{\sum_\tau \hat{\mathcal{F}}_\tau(j) \hat{\mathcal{B}}_\tau(j) X^\tau}{\sum_\tau \hat{\mathcal{F}}_\tau(j)\hat{\mathcal{B}}_\tau(j)} = \frac{\sum_\tau \hat{P}(\omega^\tau = \omega_j | X^1, \cdots, X^T) X^\tau}{\sum_\tau \hat{P}(\omega^\tau = \omega_j | X^1, \cdots, X^T)} \tag{30}$$

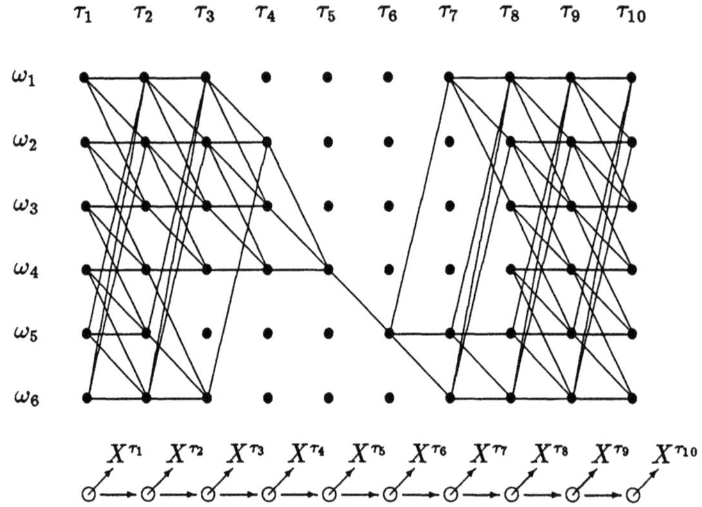

Figure 3: Each term in the numerator of the re-estimation formula for $\hat{P}_{ij}$ is the probability of observing the sequence $X^{\tau_1}, \cdots, X^{\tau_{10}}$ and making the specified transition in a given time interval.

and

$$\hat{\Sigma}_j = \frac{\sum_\tau \hat{\mathcal{F}}_\tau(j)\hat{\mathcal{B}}_\tau(j)(X^\tau - \hat{\mu}_j)(X^\tau - \hat{\mu}_j)'}{\sum_\tau \hat{\mathcal{F}}(j)\hat{\mathcal{B}}_\tau(j)} \tag{31}$$

As with the standard maximum likelihood method for iid data, convergence to the (finite) global maximum of the likelihood function is not guaranteed. A local extremum may be attained as well as a singular solution on the edge of the parameter space. See [38] for further details. Baum *et al.* [6] have investigated the behavior of the algorithm for mixtures of univariate Poisson distributions on the non-negative integers, binomial distributions on the integers, and univariate normal and gamma densities. Liporace [38] extended their results to multivariate normal and Cauchy densities. Experiments by Levinson *et al.* [37] have shown that skewness of the underlying Markov model is detrimental to convergence rate and that the choice of initial values is quite critical. See [42] for an application to speaker-independent, isolated words recognition, and [31] for an investigation of the sparse-data problem.

4.2. A Learning Algorithm for the Pickard Random Field Model

In the preceding section, we have seen how to estimate the parameters of a hidden Markov chain from one sample realization of the chain. In most applications one would be interested in using several sample realizations from the same chain to improve the quality of the learning. We shall develop this idea in the context of Haslett's labeling technique under a Pickard random field assumption. Recall from Section 3.2 that, in this method, any pixel label is assumed to depend only on labels of pixels in the same row and column, and that each row and each column are themselves Markov chains with the same parameters. To simplify matters, we shall first confine the discussion to binary random fields in order the avoid the complications involved by the requirements that these chains should be reversible.

For the sake of simplicity of notation, let Y_k designate the realization of the kth row in a $M \times N$ image. In the notation of Section 3.2, $Y_k = (\overline{\boldsymbol{X}}_{k,1}^{k,N})$. Likewise, let $Z_\ell = (\overline{\boldsymbol{X}}_{1,\ell}^{M,\ell})$, *i.e.*, the realization of the ℓth column of the image. We shall treat each row and column as if they were mutually independent of each other (which of course they are not). Therefore, the *pseudo-likelihood* of the entire image is $[\prod_{k,\ell} P(Y_k)P(Z_\ell)]^{1/2}$. As we intend to determine the parameters which optimize this pseudo-likelihood, it makes no difference if we take the squared pseudo-likelihood as an objective function. Moreover, it will be evident from the derivation that rows Y and columns Z are treated in exactly the same way[6]. Hence, to further simplify the presentation, we shall presently examine the problem of maximizing the objective function

$$\boldsymbol{\Pi} = \prod_{k=1}^{M} P(Y_k)$$

with respect to the transition probability P_{ij} under the constraint $\sum_j P_{ij} = 1$. The optimizations with respect to the other parameters are treated in a similar manner.

We form the dummy objective functions $\boldsymbol{\Pi} + \varrho_i(\sum_j P_{ij} - 1)$, where ϱ_i is a Lagrange multiplier, $i = 1, \cdots, \vartheta$. By equating the partial derivatives to zero and solving for ϱ_i we get

$$P_{ij} = \frac{P_{ij} \dfrac{\partial \boldsymbol{\Pi}}{\partial P_{ij}}}{\sum_j P_{ij} \dfrac{\partial \boldsymbol{\Pi}}{\partial P_{ij}}}. \tag{32}$$

As $\boldsymbol{\Pi}$ is a product of factors, we can write

$$\begin{aligned} \frac{\partial \boldsymbol{\Pi}}{\partial P_{ij}} &= \sum_{k=1}^{M} \prod_{m \neq k} P(Y_m) \frac{\partial P(Y_k)}{\partial P_{ij}} \\ &= \boldsymbol{\Pi} \sum_{k=1}^{M} \frac{\partial P(Y_k)}{\partial P_{ij}} \frac{1}{P(Y_k)} \end{aligned} \tag{33}$$

By substitution from (33)into (32) the factor $\boldsymbol{\Pi}$ which is common to both the numerator and denominator can be factored out and we obtain

$$P_{ij} = \frac{\sum_{k=1}^{M} P_{ij} \dfrac{\partial P(Y_k)}{\partial P_{ij}} \dfrac{1}{P(Y_k)}}{\sum_{k=1}^{M} \sum_j P_{ij} \dfrac{\partial P(Y_k)}{\partial P_{ij}} \dfrac{1}{P(Y_k)}} \tag{34}$$

[6] In actual fact, for square images ($M = N$), the easiest way to implement the technique that we are about to describe is to produce a copy of the image rotated by 90°, to append it at the bottom of the original image and to process row-wise the new $2M \times M$ image so obtained.

At this point, we may capitalize on the results of the preceding section, *viz.*,

$$\begin{aligned} P_{ij}\frac{\partial P(Y_k)}{\partial P_{ij}} &= \sum_{\ell=1}^{N-1} {}_k\tilde{\mathcal{F}}_\ell(i) P_{ij} p_j(X_{k,\ell+1})_k\tilde{\mathcal{B}}_{\ell+1}(j) \\ &= \sum_{\ell=1}^{N-1} P(Y_k, \lambda_{k,\ell} = i, \lambda_{k,\ell+1} = j), \end{aligned} \tag{35}$$

where ${}_k\tilde{\mathcal{F}}_\ell$ and ${}_k\tilde{\mathcal{B}}_\ell$ have to be interpreted as in Section 3.2. From (35), we obtain

$$\sum_j P_{ij}\frac{\partial P(Y_k)}{\partial P_{ij}} = \sum_{\ell=1}^{N-1} P(Y_k, \lambda_{k,\ell} = i) \tag{36}$$

By making the substitution from (35) and (36) into (34), we notice that the division of each term by $P(Y_k)$ has the effect of turning the joint likelihoods in the right hand sides of (35) and (36) into posterior probabilities. In this way, we naturally end up with a computational procedure which is again immune to the underflow problem. (Note that this observation, together with the material in Section 3.1, offer the solution to the normalization problem addressed in Section IV of [37].) Thus, we get

$$P_{ij} = \frac{\sum_k \sum_\ell {}_k\mathcal{F}_\ell(i)_k\mathcal{N}_{\ell+1} P_{ij}\, p_j(X_{k,\ell+1})_k\mathcal{B}_{\ell+1}(j)}{\sum_k \sum_\ell {}_k\mathcal{F}_\ell(i)_k\mathcal{B}_\ell(i)} \tag{37}$$

where $\mathcal{F}$'s and $\mathcal{B}$'s are to be computed by the recurrences (17)-(18) (or, preferably, (21)) and (20) respectively.

At this point, the reader should have little difficulty to guess the form of the re-estimation formulae for the other parameters under the assumption that $p_{\lambda_i}(X) \sim N(X; \mu_i, \Sigma_i)$. For the sake of completeness, they are given hereafter.

$$P_i = \frac{\sum_k {}_k\mathcal{F}_1(i)_k\mathcal{B}_1(i)}{\sum_k \sum_i {}_k\mathcal{F}_1(i)_k\mathcal{B}_1(i)}, \tag{38}$$

$$\mu_i = \frac{\sum_k \sum_\ell {}_k\mathcal{F}_\ell(i)_k\mathcal{B}_\ell(i) X_{k,\ell}}{\sum_k \sum_\ell {}_k\mathcal{F}_\ell(i)_k\mathcal{B}_\ell(i)}, \tag{39}$$

$$\sigma_i^2 = \frac{\sum_k \sum_\ell {}_k\mathcal{F}_\ell(i)_k\mathcal{B}_\ell(i)(X_{k,\ell} - \mu_i)^2}{\sum_k \sum_\ell {}_k\mathcal{F}_\ell(i)_k\mathcal{B}_\ell(i)}. \tag{40}$$

These re-estimation formulae are used in exactly the same way as Eqs. (26)–(28): $\mathcal{F}$'s and $\mathcal{B}$'s are computed using the forward and backward recurrences respectively for the current values of the parameters; they are then used in (37)–(40) to compute updated values of the estimates, and the procedure is iterated until convergence at a maximum of the pseudo-likelihood function. Moreover, it is not too difficult to extend the convergence properties of the procedure to this more general case.

One should recall that the learning algorithm derived from (37)–(40) should be confined to binary random fields, because, as seen is Section 2.2, rows and columns of a Pickard random field are segments of a *reversible* Markov chain and, as pointed out in Section 2.1, binary ergodic Markov chains are automatically reversible. For multivalued random field, the optimization problem must be solved under the additional constraint that the chain be reversible. Probably the easiest way to impose reversibility is to impose instead that the transition matrix be symmetric. Of course, this further restricts the generality of the model. Though, we know of no other functional constraint that results in reversibility of the chain and can be incorporated in our iterative optimization problem.

If we had imposed that $P_{ij} = P_{ji}$, $\forall i, j$, in our constrained optimization problem, the re-estimation formula for P_{ij} would have been

$$P_{ii} = \frac{\sum_k \sum_\ell {}_k\mathcal{F}_\ell(i)\,{}_k\mathcal{N}_{\ell+1} P_{ii}\, p_i(X_{k,\ell+1})\,{}_k\mathcal{B}_{\ell+1}(i)}{\sum_k \sum_\ell \left\{ \begin{array}{l} {}_k\mathcal{F}_\ell(i)\,{}_k\mathcal{B}_\ell(i) \\ \qquad - \sum_{j\neq i} \frac{P_{ij}}{P_{jj}}\,{}_k\mathcal{F}_\ell(j)\,{}_k\mathcal{N}_{\ell+1} P_{jj}\, p_j(X_{k,\ell+1})\,{}_k\mathcal{B}_{\ell+1}(j) \end{array} \right\}}, \tag{41}$$

for the diagonal elements of the transition matrix and

$$P_{ij} = \frac{\sum_k \sum_\ell \left\{ \begin{array}{l} {}_k\mathcal{F}_\ell(i)\,{}_k\mathcal{N}_{\ell+1} P_{ij}\, p_j(X_{k,\ell+1})\,{}_k\mathcal{B}_{\ell+1}(j) \\ \qquad - \frac{P_{ij}}{P_{jj}}\,{}_k\mathcal{F}_\ell(j)\,{}_k\mathcal{N}_{\ell+1} P_{jj}\, p_j(X_{k,\ell+1})\,{}_k\mathcal{B}_{\ell+1}(j) \end{array} \right\}}{\sum_k \sum_\ell \left\{ \begin{array}{l} {}_k\mathcal{F}_\ell(i)\,{}_k\mathcal{B}_\ell(i) \\ \qquad - \sum_{j\neq i} \frac{P_{ij}}{P_{jj}}\,{}_k\mathcal{F}_\ell(j)\,{}_k\mathcal{N}_{\ell+1} P_{jj}\, p_j(X_{k,\ell+1})\,{}_k\mathcal{B}_{\ell+1}(j) \end{array} \right\}} \tag{42}$$

for the off-diagonal elements. (In (41) and (42) one has to adopt the convention that $\frac{0}{0} = 0$.) In the learning algorithm for multivalued random fields, (41) and (42) have to be substituted to (37). As the symmetry constraint for the transition matrix does not affect the other parameters of the model, the re-estimation formulae (38)–(40) remain unchanged.

5. Experiments

The labeling and learning algorithms discussed above were implemented in PASCAL and extensive experimentation was carried out with the aim of assessing both the validity of the assumptions underlying our derivations and the effectiveness of the approach. In accordance with the material of the previous section, the prior information available at the start was limited to the number of desired states and the assumption that observations were drawn from Gaussian distributions (with unknown means and variances).

As already mentioned, the choice of initial values for the parameters to be estimated is quite critical. In our current implementation which is tuned to the segmentation of grey-level images, this choice is specified as follows:

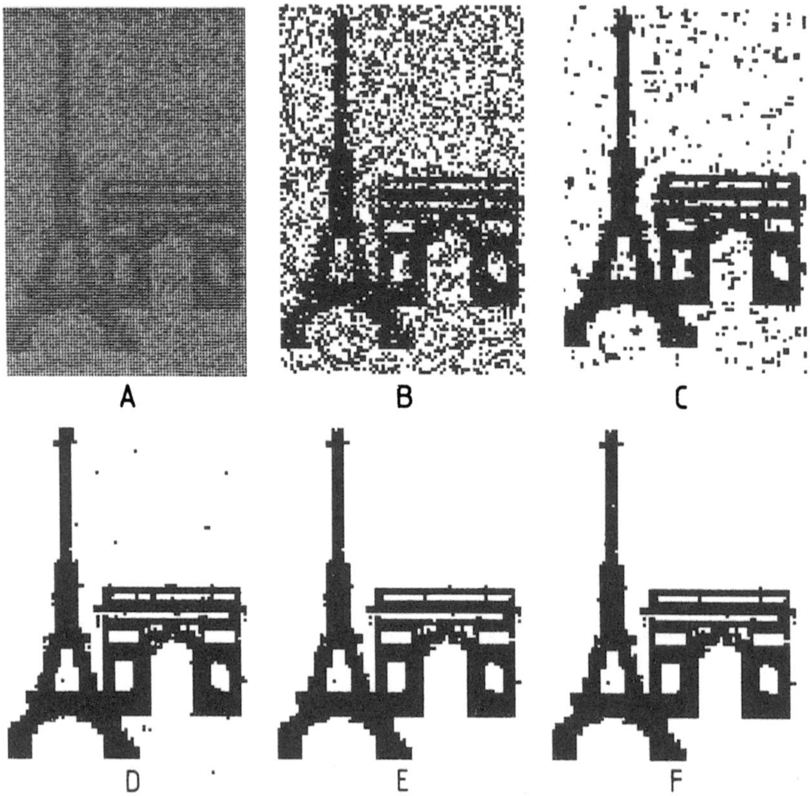

Figure 4: Learning and labeling applied to the "Paris" image. See text for explanation

i) $P_i = 1/\vartheta$, $P_{ii} = 0.5\ \forall i$, $P_{ij} = 1/(\vartheta - 1)\ \forall i, j,\ i \neq j$; (for $\vartheta = 2$, this is a no-information prior distribution, for $\vartheta > 2$, it is somehow assumed that regions are uniform patches of a "certain" extent).

ii) μ_i is set equal to the $(i/(\vartheta+1))$th quantile of the cumulated grey-level histogram of the input image, $i = 1, \cdots, \vartheta$; (this guarantees a rather uniform initial distribution of cluster means over the full dynamic range of the image).

iii) $\sigma_i = (\mu_\vartheta - \mu_1)/3(\vartheta - 1)$, $i = 1, \cdots, \vartheta$; (initial means vectors are assumed to be, on the average, 3σ away from each other).

Our first illustration concerns an artificial 120×80 image which is a degraded version of a poster that was quite popular in pattern recognition circles in 1986. The noiseless, binary image was represented as an 8–bit, two-tone, grey-level image with levels 100 and 140 respectively. (The representation as black and white images in Figure 4 is for mere visual convenience.) The noiseless image was degraded by additive Gaussian noise ($\mu = 0$, $\sigma = 20$) and produced the input picture shown in Figure 4.a.

Figure 4.b—f show the experimental results. Specifically, Figure 4.b is the labeling of the input image obtained by using Eq. (24) with the estimated values of the parameters at the end of the first iteration of the learning algorithm. Likewise, Figure 4.c through

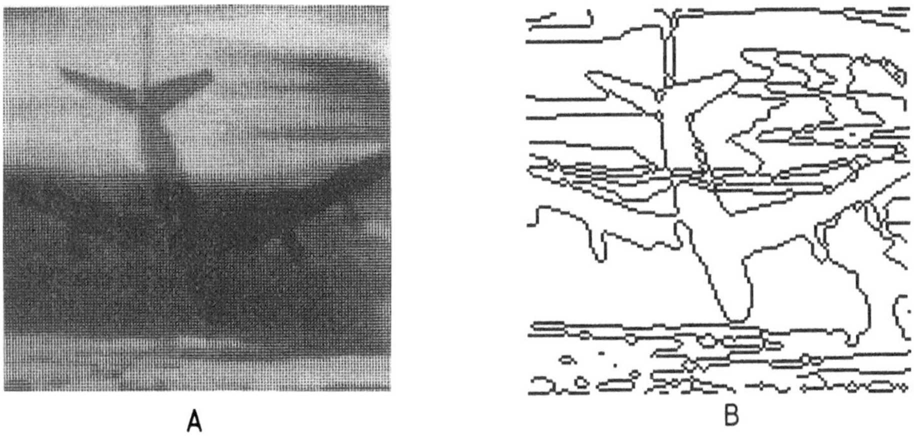

Figure 5: The "Airplane" image : a) input images, b) boundaries of the segmented image.

4.f show the labeling (of the same input image) obtained with the estimated model parameters at the end of the 5th, 9th, 13th, and 17th iteration respectively. Further iterations did not improve the restoration any more.

The gradual improvement of the restoration as the learning proceeds is clearly visible from Figure 4. Unbiased convergence to the true parameter values could also be observed : the estimated mean values and variances were 100.34 and 140.24, 20.51 and 19.82 respectively at the last iteration. It has been our past experience that the labeling error-rate is generally not a suitable figure of merit in image restoration. Nevertheless, in this particular instance, it seems justified to point out that *i)* non-contextual maximum likelihood labeling based on perfect knowledge of the noise parameters would result in about 15% mislabelings, *ii)* the labeling error-rate in Figure 4.b amounts to 28%, which is reasonable for an initial guess, and *iii)* the final labeling error-rate is reduced to a satisfying 1%.

The second illustration is concerned with a real 128×128, 8–bit image of an airplane, see Figure 5. The histogram of this image is a complicated mixture of peaks and flat regions. Parts of the object we are interested in—the plane—is very poorly contrasted against a changing background. The learning algorithm was applied with parameter $\vartheta = 7$. In this instance, convergence to a stable labeling was very fast : Figure 5.b shows the boundaries of regions obtained with the parameters estimated at the end of the third iteration. It is particularly satisfying that the wings and fuselage, and the tail of the plane are extracted as single (connected) regions.

From both these experiments, we can conclude that the labeling and learning algorithms discussed above are subjectively relevant to the picture restoration and segmentation problem.

6. Concluding Remarks

In this paper, we have presented a unified treatment of the labeling and learning problems for the hidden Markov chain model currently used in speech recognition and the hidden Pickard random field image model suggested by Haslett. Experiments exploiting only the statistics of grey-level histograms — in addition to the Markovian nature of the underlying model — have shown gratifying image restoration and segmentation results.

The work reported here can be extended in a number of directions, two of which deserve mentioning. In the first place, the computational complexity of the learning algorithm can be greatly reduced by resorting to *decision directed* re-estimation formulae [22], [19], (instead of (37)–(40)). In spite of the fact that the method is known to give definitely inconsistent and asymptotically biased results quite generally [11], it has been our experience that image restoration and segmentation results are very similar to those presented above : For all practical purposes, it would be impossible to distinguish which of the two learning techniques is being used[7]. The decision directed learning technique will be reported elsewhere.

On the other hand, we emphasized in Section 1 that the feasibility of our approach to the learning problem relied heavily on the crucial assumption of causality for the underlying Markovian model. Besides, we also mentioned in Section 2.2, the class of causal Markov mesh random fields generated by Eq. (8) — of which Pickard random fields form only a subclass — for which various labeling techniques have been proposed recently [15], [17], [20]. Therefore, computational hurdles not accounted for, learning techniques for hidden Markov mesh random fields could be developed in very much the same way as was done above. It is, in fact, a very simple exercise to derive the re-estimation formulae to be used in this more general case. However, at the time of this writing, the approach is marred by problems of a computational nature, and finding ways of circumventing the computational complexity involved is a topic of current research.

References

[1] E. Aarts, and P.J.M. van Laarhoven, "Statistical cooling: Approach to combinatorial optimization problems," *Philips Jl of Research*, **40**, pp. 193–226, 1985.

[2] K. Abend, "Compound decision procedures for unknown distributions and for dependent states of nature," in *Pattern Recognition*, L.N. Kanal ed., Washington D.C. : Thompson Book Cy, 1968, pp. 207–249.

[3] K. Abend, T.J. Harley, and L.N. Kanal, "Classification of binary random patterns," *IEEE Trans. Inform. Theory*, IT–11, pp. 538–544, Oct. 1965.

[4] M. Askar, and H. Derin, "A recursive algorithm for the Bayes solution of the smoothing problem," *IEEE Transactions on Automatic Control*, **AC–26**, pp. 558–560, 1981.

[7] Surprisingly enough, we are not aware that *decision directed* learning was ever used for speech recognition purposes.

[5] L.E. Baum, "An inequality and associated maximization technique in statistical estimation for probabilistic functions of Markov processes," *Inequalities*, **3**, pp. 1–8, 1972.

[6] L.E. Baum, T. Petrie, G. Soules, and N. Weiss, "A maximization technique occurring in the statistical analysis of probabilistic functions of Markov chains," *Ann. Math. Statist.*, **41**, pp. 164–171, 1972.

[7] J. Besag, "Nearest-neighbour systems and the auto-logistic model for binary data," *Jl. Royal Stat. Soc*, **B-34**, pp. 75–83, 1972.

[8] J. Besag, "Spatial interaction and the statistical analysis of lattice systems," *Jl. Royal Stat. Soc.*, **B-36**, pp. 192–236, 1974.

[9] J. Besag, "On the statistical analysis of dirty pictures," paper read at the SERC Research Workshop on Statistics and Pattern Recognition, Edinburgh, July 1985.

[10] H. Bourlard, C. Wellekens, and H. Ney, "Connected digit recognition using vector quantization," *Proc. Intern. Conf. Acoustics, Speech and Signal Processing*, San Diego, 1984.

[11] P. Bryant, and J.W. Williamson, "Asymptotic behavior of classification maximum likelihood estimates," *Biometrika*, **65**, pp. 273–281, 1978.

[12] P. Carnevalli, L. Coletti, and S. Patarnello, "Image processing by simulated annealing," *IBM Jl. of Research and Development*, **29**, pp. 569–579, Nov. 1985.

[13] H. Cerf–Danon, A.-M. Derouault, M. El–Beze, B. Merialdo, and S. Soudoplatoff, "Speech recognition experiment with 10,000 words dictionary," in this volume.

[14] G.R. Cross, and A.K. Jain, "Markov random field texture models," *IEEE Trans. Pattern Anal., Machine Intell.*, **PAMI–5**, pp. 24-39, Jan. 1983.

[15] H. Derin, H. Elliot, R. Christi, and D. Geman, "Bayes smoothing algorithms for segmentation of binary images modeled by Markov random fields," *IEEE Trans. Pattern Anal., Machine Intell.*, **PAMI–6**, pp. 707–720, Nov. 1984.

[16] P.A. Devijver, "Classification in Markov chains for minimum symbol error rate," *Proc. 7th Intern. Conf. Pattern Recognition*, Montreal, 1984, pp. 1334–1336.

[17] P.A. Devijver, "Probabilistic labeling in a hidden second order Markov mesh," in *Pattern Recognition in Practice II*, E. Gelsema and L.N. Kanal Eds., Amsterdam: North Holland, 1985, pp. 113–123.

[18] P.A. Devijver, "Baum's forward-backward algorithm revisited," *Pattern Recognition Letters*, **3**, pp. 369–373, Dec. 1985.

[19] P.A. Devijver, "Cluster analysis by mixture identification," in *Data Analysis in Astronomy*, V. Di Gesù et al. Eds., New York: Plenum, 1985, pp. 29–44.

[20] P.A. Devijver, "Segmentation of binary images using third order Markov mesh image models," to appear in *Proc. 8th Internat. Conf. Pattern Recognition*, Paris, Oct. 1986.

[21] P.A. Devijver, and J. Kittler, *Pattern Recognition: A Statistical Approach*, Englewood-Cliffs: Prentice Hall, 1982.

[22] R.O. Duda, and P.E. Hart, *Pattern Classification and Scene Analysis*, New York: Wiley, 1973.

[23] G.D. Forney, Jr., "The Viterbi algorithm," *Proc. IEEE*, **61**, pp. 268–278, Mar. 1973.

[24] S. Geman, and D. Geman, "Stochastic relaxation, Gibbs distributions, and the Bayesian restoration of images," *IEEE Trans. Pattern Anal., Machine Intell.*, **PAMI–6**, pp. 721–741, Nov. 1984.

[25] D. Geman, S. Geman, and C. Graffigne, "Locating texture and object boundaries," in this volume.

[26] S. Güler, G. Garcia, L. Gülen, and M.N. Toksöz, "The detection of geological fault lines in radar images," in this volume.

[27] A.R. Hanson, E.M. Riseman, and E. Fisher, "Context in word-recognition," *Pattern Recognition*, **8**, pp. 35–46, 1976.

[28] R.M. Haralick, "Decision making in context," *IEEE Trans. Pattern Anal., Machine Intell.*, **PAMI–5**, pp. 417–428, July 1983.

[29] J. Haslett, "Maximum likelihood discriminant analysis on the plane using a Markovian model of spatial context," *Pattern Recognition*, **18**, pp. 287–296, 1985.

[30] M. Hassner, and J. Sklansky, "The use of Markov random fields as models of texture," *CGIP*, **12**, pp. 357–370, 1980.

[31] F. Jelinek, and R.L. Mercer, "Interpolated estimation of Markov source parameters from sparse data," in *Pattern Recognition in Practice*, E. Gelsema and L. Kanal Eds., Amsterdam: North-Holland, 1980, pp. 381–397.

[32] F. Jelinek, R.L. Mercer, and L.R. Bahl, "Continuous speech recognition: Statistical methods," in *Handbook of Statistics 2*, P.R. Krishnaiah and L.N. Kanal Eds., Amsterdam: North-Holland, 1982, pp. 549–573.

[33] L.N. Kanal, "Markov mesh models," *Computer Graphics and Image Processing*, **12**, pp. 371–375, 1980 (also in *Image Modeling*, A. Rosenfeld Ed., New York: Academic Press, 1981, pp. 239–243).

[34] J.G. Kemeni and J.L. Snell, *Finite Markov Chains*, New York: Springer-Verlag, 1976.

[35] R. Kinderman and J.L. Snell, *Markov Random Fields and their Applications*, Providence RI: American Mathematical Society, 1980.

[36] D.S. Lebedev, "Probabilistic characterization of images in filtration and restoration problems," in *Signal Processing: Theories and Applications*, M. Kunt and F. De Coulon Eds., Amsterdam: North-Holland, 1980, pp. 55–64.

[37] S.E. Levinson, L.R. Rabiner, and M.M. Sondhi, "An introduction to the application of the theory of probabilistic functions of a Markov process in automatic speech recognition," *B.S.T.J.*, **62**, pp. 1035–1074, 1983.

[38] L.A. Liporace, "Maximum likelihood estimation for multivariate observations of Markov sources" *IEEE Trans. Inform. Theory*, **IT–28**, 729–734, 1982.

[39] D.L. Neuhof, "The Viterbi algorithm as an aid to text-recognition," *IEEE Trans. Inform. Theory*, **IT–21**, pp. 222–226, Mar. 1975.

[40] D.K. Pickard, "A curious binary lattice process," *Jl. Appl. Prob.*, **14**, pp. 717–731, 1977.

[41] D.K. Pickard, "Unilateral Markov fields," *Adv. Applied Probability*, **12**, pp. 655–671, 1980.

[42] L.R. Rabiner, S.E. Levinson, and M.M. Sondhi, "On the application of vector quantization and hidden Markov models to speaker independent, isolated word recognition," *B.S.T.J.*, **62**, pp. 1075–1105, 1983.

[43] J. Raviv, "Decision making in Markov chains applied to the problem of pattern recognition," *IEEE Trans. Inform. Theory*, **IT–3**, pp. 536–551, 1967.

[44] R.A. Redner, and H.F. Walker, "Mixture densities, maximum likelihood and the EM algorithm," *Siam Review*, **26**, pp. 195–239, 1984.

[45] E. Riseman, and R.W. Ehrich, "Contextual word recognition using binary digrams," *IEEE Trans. Comput.*, **C–20**, pp. 397–403, April 1971.

[46] R. Shinghal, D. Rosenberg, and G.T. Toussaint, "A simplified heuristic version of a recursive Bayes algorithm for using context in text recognition," *IEEE Trans. Syst., Man, Cybern.*, **SMC–8**, pp. 412–414, May 1978.

[47] G.T. Toussaint, "The use of context in pattern recognition," *Pattern Recognition*, **10**, pp. 189–204, 1978.

[48] G. Wolberg and T. Pavlidis, "Restoration of binary images using stochastic relaxation with annealing," *Pattern Recognition Letters*, **3**, pp. 375–388, 1985.

[49] S. Yakovitz, "Unsupervised learning and the identification of finite mixtures," *IEEE Trans. Inform. Theory*, **IT–16**, pp. 330–338, 1970.

[50] S. Yakovitz, and J. Spragins, "On the identifiability of finite mixtures," *Ann. Math. Stat.*, **39**, pp. 209–214, 1968.

LOCATING TEXTURE AND OBJECT BOUNDARIES

Donald Geman[1], Stuart Geman[2] and Christine Graffigne[3]

[1]Department of Mathematics and Statistics
University of Massachusetts
Amherst, Massachusetts 01003 USA

[2,3]Division of Applied Mathematics
Brown University
Providence, Rhode Island 02912 USA

Abstract

Two models are given for the extraction of boundaries in digital images, one for discriminating textures and the other for discriminating objects. In both cases a Markov random field is constructed as a prior distribution over intensities (observed) and labels (unobserved); the labels are either the texture types or boundary indicators. The posterior distribution, *i.e.*, the conditional distribution over the labels given the intensities, is then analyzed by a Monte-Carlo algorithm called stochastic relaxation. The final labeling corresponds to a local maximum of the posterior likelihood.

1. Introduction

A fundamental problem in computer vision (automated perception) is the semantical analysis of a three-dimensional scene based on a two-dimensional intensity image. Most techniques for recognition and labeling are rather ad hoc and often restricted to special domains, for instance industrial automation. A major goal of our past ([9], [10], [11]) and present research has been to develop a unified family of stochastic models and algorithms, which are mathematically coherent and which can be crafted to specific tasks in low and "middle" level image processing, such as filtering and de-convolution, tomographic reconstruction, object identification, and boundary and texture analysis.

It is a general perception that "segmentation", the decomposition of the intensity image into sets of pixels which correspond to the objects and regions in the underlying three-dimensional scene, is an indispensable step in image understanding. In the usual paradigm, segmentation would be followed by the imposition of a relational structure among the segments, and a final description would result from "matching" these data

[1]Research partially supported by Office of Naval Research contract N00014-86-K-0027 and National Science Foundation grant DMS-8401927.

[2]Research partially supported by Office of Naval Research contract N00014-86-0037, Army Research Office contract DAAG29-83-K-0116, and National Science Foundation grant DMS-8352087.

NATO ASI Series, Vol. F30
Pattern Recognition Theory and Applications
Edited by P. A. Devijver and J. Kittler

structures against stored representations of real-world entities. In the future we hope to extend our approach to models which are fully hierarchical, with variables ranging from raw intensity data to stored models in the form of object categories and templates, such as letters. Thus, for example, the extraction of object boundaries might be guided by pending interpretations as well as general expectations about boundary geometry, as in the current work.

We are going to consider two problems which are closely related to segmentation but useful in their own right. One is texture discrimination: the data is a grey-level image consisting of several textured regions, such as grass, wood, plastic, etc., whose maximum number and possible types are known; the goal is to classify the pixels. This problem is more difficult than texture identification, in which we are presented with only one texture from a given list. Discrimination is complicated by the absence of information about the size or shape of the regions. Of course in both cases we assume that models for the possible textures have been previously constructed. There are a number of applications for such algorithms. For example, regions in remotely-sensed images which correspond to ground-cover classes often have a textured quality and cannot be distinguished by methods based solely on shading, such as edge detectors and clustering algorithms. Another application is to wafer inspection: low magnification views of memory arrays appear as highly structured textures, and other geometries have a characteristic, but random, graining.

The second problem is to isolate locations in a digital image which correspond to physical discontinuities in the three-dimensional scene. These discontinuities may correspond to depth (object boundaries), surface gradients (changes in shape), or other macroscopic factors. We refer to these as "boundaries" or "macro-edges" to distinguish them from "edges" or "micro-edges" which refer to basically all significant intensity changes, whether due to noise, digitization, lighting, object boundaries, texture, etc. This crucial distinction will be amplified below. There are many approaches to boundary detection, depending for example on the degree of a priori information that is utilized and the scale of the objects (tumors, windows, houses, lakes). The detection may be "interpretation-guided" or simply the output of a general purpose algorithm based on expectations about boundary behavior, in regard to curvature, connectedness, etc. Digital boundaries tend to be quite noisy, depending on the lighting, resolution, and other factors. It is commonplace for a relatively "sharp" boundary segment in the original scene to be associated in the digital image with a band of pixels over which one object or sub-object slowly gives way to another. In addition, pronounced gradients may appear due to noise or surface irregularities or, conversely, may disappear along actual object boundaries.

Finally, we shall not be concerned here with segmentation per se, which is often superfluous. Further processing may proceed based solely on the detected boundaries, even if the connected components do not produce a "good" segmentation. Applications include stereo-mapping, automated navigation, and the detection of natural and man-made structures (such as roads, rivers, lakes and crop boundaries) in remotely-sensed images.

2. Models for Texture and Texture Discrimination

The data is a grey level image consisting of at most M textures of known type; we wish to label each pixel as $1, 2, \cdots$, or M to indicate its class. We refer the reader to [5] for an overview of approaches to texture modeling. In addition, see the paper of Oja [17] in this volume for an approach based on co-occurrence matrices. More similar to our approach are those of Elliott and Derin [8] and Cohen and Cooper [4]. What follows is a sketch of our model. All the details will appear in a forthcoming paper [12]. (The same remark applies to the boundary model.) As for the stochastic relaxation algorithms, the reader can find a complete discussion in [9]; see also the excellent review of simulated annealing by Aarts and van Laarhoven [1].

Fix a texture type, say ℓ, and let S denote the sites of the $N \times N$ lattice $\{(i,j) : 1 \leq i,j \leq N\}$. Our model is a Gibbs distribution based only on pair interactions, in fact just grey level differences. The parameters are the interaction weights, say $\theta_1, \cdots, \theta_I$, where I denotes the number of pair-bonds under consideration. The sign of θ_i will indicate the promotion of similarity or dissimilarity for bond type i.

The distribution of the grey levels $X = \{X_s,\ s \in S\}$, for the texture type ℓ, is then

$$P(X = x) = \frac{\exp\{-U^{(\ell)}(x)\}}{Z^{(\ell)}}$$

where $Z^{(\ell)}$ is the usual normalizing constant

$$Z^{(\ell)} = \sum_x \exp\{-U^{(\ell)}(x)\}$$

and the "energy function" $U^{(\ell)}$ is given by

$$U^{(\ell)}(x) = -\sum_{i=1}^{I} \sum_{\langle s,t\rangle_i} \theta_i^{(\ell)} \Phi(x_s - x_t), \qquad \Phi(\Delta) \doteq \left(1 + \left(\frac{|\Delta|}{\delta}\right)^2\right)^{-1} \tag{1}$$

The notation $\langle s,t\rangle_i$ indicates a pair of pixels of bond type i; for example, with $I = 6$, the types are shown in Figure 1. They correspond to the first and second nearest neighbors in the vertical and horizontal directions and nearest neighbors in the two diagonal directions. We refer again to [11] for a discussion of the choice of the potential function Φ. The basic idea is to choose a function of $(x_s - x_t)$ that is monotone and bounded in $|x_s - x_t|$. Monotonicity allows us to selectively encourage similarity or dissimilarity, whereas boundedness helps to accommodate the occasional, random, exception to an expected bond relation. Having specified the form of our model, each texture type, ℓ, is identified with an I-tuple of parameters $\theta_1^{(\ell)}, \ldots, \theta_I^{(\ell)}$.

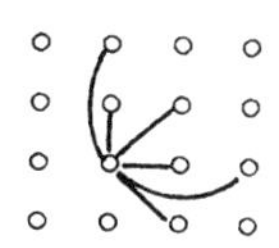

Figure 1: Pair-bonds for texture model.

The parameters are estimated from samples of the textures by the method of maximum pseudo-likelihood ([2], [3]), a powerful estimation technique designed for multiplicative parameters in local Gibbs distributions. It has the advantage over maximum likelihood of circumventing the partition function $Z^{(\ell)}$ which is entirely intractable. The least-squares method proposed recently in [8] and [18] is not feasible in this setting due to large number of possible grey levels: it is unlikely to see any fixed neighbor configuration duplicated in the sample.

Having modeled the M textures, we now construct a composite Markov random field which accounts for both texture labels, say $X^L = \{X_s^L,\ s \in S\}$ and grey levels $X^P = \{X_s^P,\ s \in S\}$. The joint distribution is

$$P(X^P = x^P, X^L = x^L) = \frac{\exp\{-U_1(x^P, x^L) - U_2(x^L)\}}{Z} \tag{2}$$

in which U_2 promotes label bonding (we expect the textures to appear in patches rather than interspersed) and U_1 specifies the interaction between labels and intensities. Specifically, we employ a simple Ising-type potential for the labels:

$$U_2(x^L) = -\beta \sum_{[s,t]} 1_{x_s^L = x_t^L} + \sum_{s \in S} w(x_s^L), \qquad \beta > 0 \tag{3}$$

Here β determines the degree of clustering, $[s,t]$ indicates a pair of nearest horizontal or vertical neighbors, and $w(\cdot)$ is adjusted to eliminate bias in the label probabilities.

To describe the interaction between labels and pixels we introduce the symbols $\tau_1, \tau_2, \ldots, \tau_I$ to represent the lattice vectors associated with the I pair-bonds (Figure 1). Thus s and $s + \tau_i$ are neighbors, constituting a pair with bond type i. The interaction is then given in terms of pixel-based contributions,

$$H(x^P, \ell, s) \doteq -\sum_{i=1}^{I} \theta_i^{(\ell)} \left\{\Phi(x_s^P - x_{s+\tau_i}^P) + \Phi(x_s^P - x_{s-\tau_i}^P)\right\} \tag{4}$$

and local sums of these called block-based contributions,

$$Z(x^P, \ell, s) \doteq \frac{1}{z} \sum_{t \in N_s} H(x^P, \ell, t). \tag{5}$$

Here, N_s is a block of sites centered at s (5 by 5 in all of our experiments), and the constant z is adjusted so that the sum of all block-based contributions reduces to $U^{(\ell)}$ (see(1)):

$$U^{(\ell)}(x^P) = \sum_{s \in S} Z(x^P, \ell, s) \tag{6}$$

This amounts to ensuring that each pair-bond appears exactly once ($z = 50$, for example, when N_s is 5 by 5). More or less obvious adjustments are made at boundaries. In terms of (4) and (5), the "interaction energy", $U_1(x^P, x^L)$, is written

$$U_1(x^P, x^L) = \sum_{s \in S} Z(x^P, x_s^L, s). \tag{7}$$

Because of (6), the model is consistent with (1) for homogeneous textures, $X_s^L = \ell$, $s \in S$. The idea is that each local texture label, X_s^L, is influenced by the pixel grey levels in a neighborhood of s.

Let us briefly examine the local characteristics of the field, specifically the conditional distributions for the labels given all the intensity data and the values of the neighboring labels. The updating mechanism and bias correction will then be more evident. (The actual neighborhoods of the Markov random field corresponding to (2) can be easily inferred from (3) and (7).) The log odds of texture type k to type j is

$$\log\left\{\frac{P(X_r^L = k \mid X_s^L = x_s^L,\ s \neq r;\ X_s^P = x_s^P,\ s \in S)}{P(X_r^L = j \mid X_s^L = x_s^L,\ s \neq r;\ X_s^P = x_s^P,\ s \in S)}\right\}$$

$$= \quad Z(x^P, j, r) - Z(x^P, k, r) + \beta \sum_{t:[t,r]} (1_{x_t^L=k} - 1_{x_t^L=j}) + \omega(j) - \omega(k)$$

$$= \quad \frac{1}{z}\sum_{i=1}^{I} \sum_{s\in N_r} (\theta_i^{(k)} - \theta_i^{(j)}) \left\{\Phi(x_s^P - x_{s+\tau_i}^P) + \Phi(x_s^P - x_{s-\tau_i}^P)\right\}$$

$$+ \beta \sum_{t:[t,r]} (1_{x_t^L=k} - 1_{x_t^L=j}) + \omega(j) - \omega(k)$$

The first term imposes fidelity to the "data" x_s^P, and the second bonds the labels. The efficacy of the model depends on the extent to which the first term separates the two types k and j, which can be assessed by plotting histograms for the values of this quantity both for pure k and pure j data. A clean separation of the histograms signifies a good discriminator. However, since we are looking at log odds, we insist that the histograms straddle the origin, with positive (resp. negative) values associated with type k (resp. j). The function $w(\cdot)$ makes this adjustment.

3. A Model for Object Boundaries

The process consists of grey levels $X^P = \{X_s^P\}$ as above, and boundary variables $X^B = \{X_s^B,\ s \in S^B\}$, which are binary, and indicate the presence or absence of a boundary at site $s \in S^B$. These sites are indicated in Figure 2, together with those of the "micro-edges", which are marked as lines. The boundary variables interact directly with grey level differences and with the micro-edges, which are binary variables determined by the data. We have chosen to model the micro-edges deterministically because, whereas their physical causes may involve many random factors, their placement in the digital image is rather unambiguous. The situation for boundaries is somewhat the opposite: as the images reveal, there may be many equally plausible representations of the same boundary. By the way, it is for this same reason that Bayesian algorithms based on misclassification rate are unsuitable for boundary analysis; the output will generally lack the fine structure we expect of boundary configurations. Placement decisions cannot be based on the data alone; other pending labels must be considered. Consequently we favor the use of MAP estimation for boundary placement.

The literature abounds with papers on edge and boundary detection, and the subject is currently active. A common approach, rather different from ours, is to locate the zero-crossings of a differential operator, e.g. the Laplacian. In regard to the distinction between edges and boundaries, and the placement of the corresponding sites, our outlook is the same as that of Hanson and Riseman [13]; however their approach is rule-based and deterministic, via relaxation labeling. Finally, a special class of Markov fields is o Pixels, | — Edge Sites, + Boundary Sites

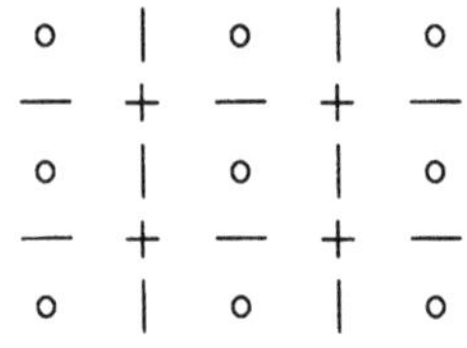

Figure 2: Pixel, "micro-edge", and boundary sites.

utilized in Devijver [7], in which fast algorithms are developed for image segmentation. See [6] and [14] for reviews.

Given the data x_s^P, $s \in S$ and threshold parameters $T_1 < T_2$, we define the edge array as follows: we declare an edge between an adjacent pair of pixels s and t, denoted $e(s,t) = 1$, if either i) the intensity difference $|x_s^P - x_t^P|$ exceeds T_2 , or ii) the difference exceeds T_1 and the difference across one of the six neighboring edge sites (see Figure 3) exceeds T_2; otherwise $e(s,t) = 0$.

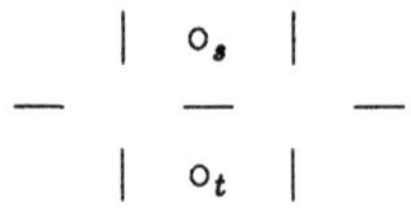

Figure 3: Pixel (o)and edge (|,—) sites that determine the state of edge $\langle a,t\rangle$.

The joint distribution between intensities and boundaries is given by

$$P(X^P = x^P, X^B = x^B) = \frac{\exp\{-U_1(x^P,x^B) - U_2(x^B)\}}{Z} \tag{8}$$

where x^P and x^B indicate grey level and boundary configurations. The first term U_1 provides "boundary seeding" and the second term provides boundary organization in accordance with our geometrical and topological expectations. The seeding is based on contrast and continuation; specifically,

$$U_1 = \theta_1 \sum_{\langle s,t\rangle} (x_s^B x_t^B - 1)\Psi(\Delta_{st}) + \theta_2 \sum_{s \in S^B} (x_s^B - \eta_s)^2, \quad \theta_1 < 0, \quad \theta_2 > 0$$

where $\langle s,t\rangle$ denotes a pair of adjacent horizontal or vertical boundary sites, Δ_{st} is the intensity difference across the edge site associated with s,t and $\Psi(u) = u^4/(C+u^4)$. The second term correlates x_s^B with an index of connectedness η_s which is 1 if there is a "string" of four connected edges with an interior junction at s, and 0 otherwise. The matrix η_s need only be computed once and there is a simple formula.

The second term in (8) is intended to "organize" the boundary "candidates" associated with the low energy states of U_1. Of course these two processes, seeding and organization, are entirely cooperative: low contrast segments may survive if sufficiently well organized and, conversely, many unstructured segments are eliminated by the "smoothing" effect of U_2.

To reduce curvature and inhibit multiple representations we penalize the simultaneous occurrence of boundaries over any of the cliques depicted in Figure 4a, together with their rotations by $\pi/2$. Let $\mathcal{C}_1$ denote this class of cliques; obviously the choice will depend on information about the imagery. Thus

$$U_2 = -\theta_3 \sum_{C \in \mathcal{C}_1} \prod_{s \in C} x_s^B - \theta_4 \sum_{C \in \mathcal{C}_2} \mu(x_s^B,\ s \in C), \quad \theta_3, \theta_4 > 0 \tag{9}$$

The other term in (9) is based on the cliques in Figure 4b. There are 32 possible configurations. The potential function μ down-weights isolated boundaries and endings and favors continuation and other "proper" configurations. One can obtain far better looking boundaries by fitting curves in a post-processing step. We have not done so.

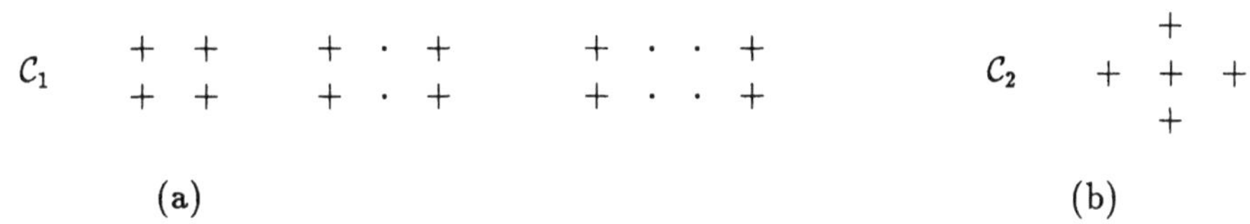

Figure 4: Clique types for boundary potentials.

The parameters $\theta_1, \theta_2, \theta_3, \theta_4$ are not estimated from the data. Rather, they are determined by a method we have called "reparametrization" and which is developed in [12]. Basically the idea is this: We delineate a series of local "situations" in which we can conveniently quantify our a priori expectations about proper boundary behavior. Each situation leads to a constraint, typically of the form

$$a_1\theta_1 + a_2\theta_2 + a_3\theta_3 + a_4\theta_4 \le 0$$

where the constants $a_1, \cdots, a_4$ may depend on "new parameters" such as the minimum contrast between uniform "object" and "background" at which "detection" is preferred. The intersection of the constraints determines a reasonably small subset of the full parameter space. Of course some "fine-tuning" is still necessary.

4. Algorithms

In both models the posterior distribution is simply the conditional distribution of the unobserved variables (texture labels and boundary indicators) given the observed variables, *i.e.*, the grey levels. Thus, in the texture case,

$$P(X^L = x^L \mid X^P = x^P) = \frac{\exp\{-U_1(x^P, x^L) - U_2(x^L)\}}{\sum_{x^L} \exp\{-U_1(x^P, x^L) - U_2(x^L)\}}$$

and similarly for the object-boundary model. The MAP estimator, which is the most likely labeling given the data, is the Bayes rule corresponding to the zero-one loss function $L(x^L, \hat{x}^L) = 1$ if $x^L = \hat{x}^L$ and $= 0$ otherwise. We find this estimator effective in both cases, although any other method which utilizes spatial information could be equally effective. We refer the reader to Ripley [19] for an excellent discussion of the role of spatial context and performance evaluation for statistical image models. There is considerable skepticism about the desirability of a zero-one loss function; see Besag [3], Devijver [7], and Marroquin et al [15]. Two standard criticisms, at least in the context of filtering, de-convolution, and surface reconstruction, are that MAP is too "global", leading to "over-smoothing" or perhaps gross mislabeling, and that it is impractical due to excessive computation. However, pixel-based error measures, as advocated for example in [15] are simply too local for the tasks at hand. As for computational demands, the annealing and other relaxation algorithms are indeed intensive, but too much concern with CPU times can deter progress. Software engineers know that it is often possible to achieve orders-of-magnitude speed-ups by some modest compromises and reworkings when dedicating a general purpose algorithm to a specific task. Besides, advances in hardware are systematically underestimated. Indeed, it was announced at this very conference (Murray et al [16]), that experiments in [9] requiring several hours of VAX time were reproduced in less than a minute on the DAP; the authors even speculate about real-time stochastic relaxation.

In the case of the texture labeling, the processing is along now familiar lines: visit the label sites in a raster-scan fashion, replacing the current values by samples selected from the conditional distribution for the label for that site given the (current) neighboring labels and the data. In addition, a control parameter corresponding to "temperature" is reduced each full sweep (= iteration). The effect is to drive the configurations so generated towards the mode. We refer to this as single-site simulated annealing (SSSA).

The boundary-finding algorithm consists of three distinct steps. First, select threshold values and determine the corresponding location of the micro-edges. (This step is nearly instantaneous.) Next, use SSSA (initialized with $X^B \equiv 0$) to locate a low energy state of the posterior distribution. This requires several hundred sweeps and results in a reasonable, but "flawed" boundary (See the upper right panels in Figures 9, 10, and 11). Finally, we take this state as the starting point of an iterative improvement algorithm. Successively visit each cross-shaped set of five boundary sites and choose the most likely value for these five sites given the remaining sites and the data. Since we are successively maximizing the posterior energy function in five coordinates simultaneously, each such visit can only increase the posterior likelihood. We have referred to this as "0–temperature" reconstruction; Besag [3] calls it ICM, for "iterated conditional modes." This procedure converges in about three or four sweeps and is very sensitive to the starting point, in this case the good one obtained by SSSA. The second and third steps require about equal processing time.

5. Experiments

Three experiments were done on texture discrimination, based on two images with two textures each and one with four. There are four textures involved: wood, plastic, carpet, and cloth. As mentioned above, the parameters were estimated from the pure types using maximum pseudo-likelihood.

Figure 5: Wood on plastic background.

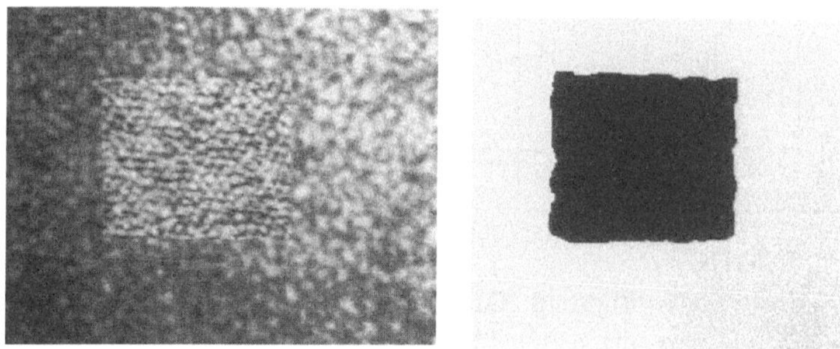

Figure 6: Carpet on plastic backgound.

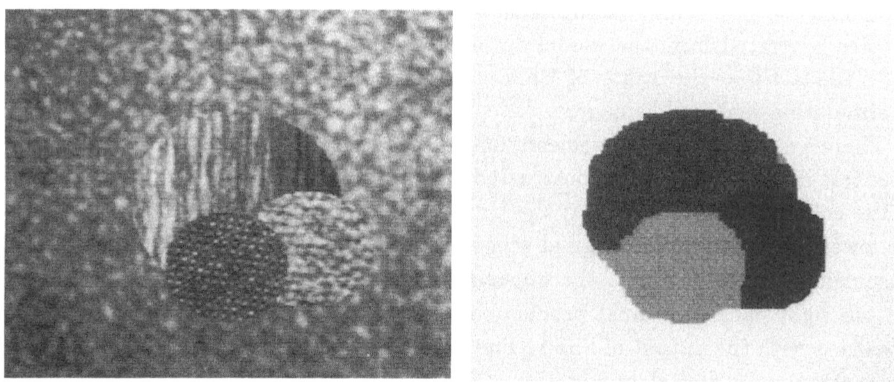

Figure 7: Wood, carpet and cloth on plastic bacground.

The experiments required about 150 iterations of SSSA, initialized by assuming no label-label interactions ($\beta = 0$ in (3)) and then assigning to each label, X_s^P, its most likely value. There was no pre- or post-processing. In particular, no effort was make to "clean-up" the boundaries, expecting smooth transitions. The results are shown in Figures 5, 6, and 7; these correspond to i) wood on plastic, ii) carpet on plastic, and iii) wood, carpet, and cloth on plastic background.

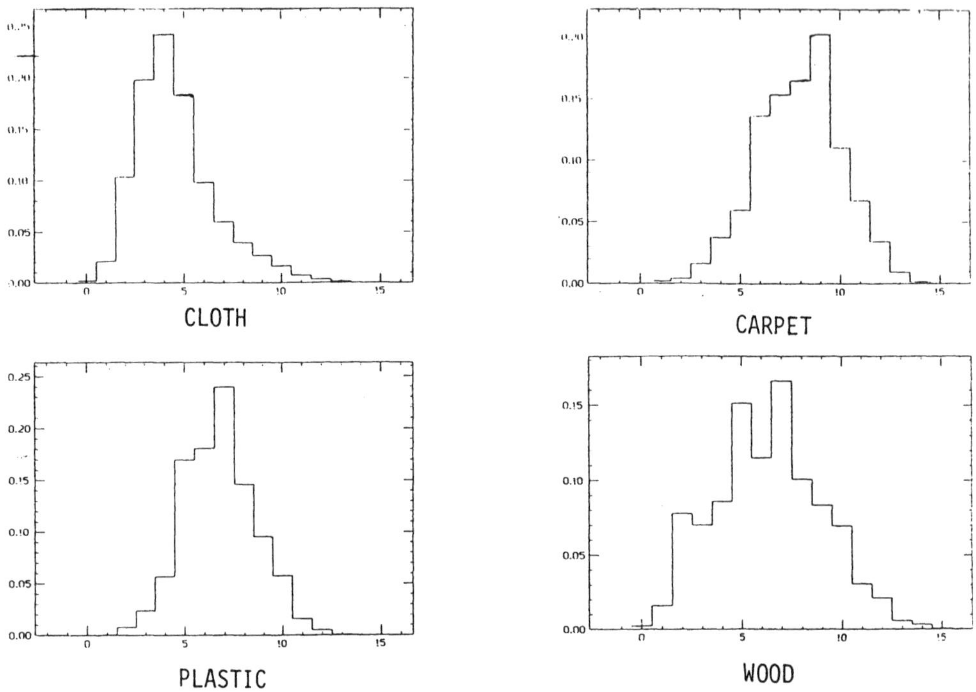

Figure 8: Grey-level histograms.

In each figure, the left panel is the textured scene, and the right panel shows the segmentation, with texture labels coded by grey level. It is interesting to note that the grey level histograms of the four textures are very similar (Figure 8); in particular, discrimination based on shading alone is virtually impossible. We also mention that samples generated from the model do not resemble the textures very well. This illustrates the fact that the utility of Markov field models does not depend on their capacity for simulating real-world imagery.

There are also three experiments on object boundary extraction, corresponding to three test images: two scenes constructed from tinkertoys and an outdoor scene provided by the computer vision group at the University of Massachusetts. In Figures 9 and 10 the lower left panel is the original scene, the upper left panel shows the deterministic placement of "micro-edges", the upper right panel shows the result of SSSA, and the bottom right panel, the final product, is the result of five-site iterative improvement, initialized with the output of SSSA. The stick scene (Figure 9) is 64×64 and illustrates the ambiguity in digital boundaries. The "cart" (Figure 10) is 110×110; we were quite pleased to obtain such straight lines without post-processing. Finally, the house scene (Figure 11) is 256×256 and obviously more varied than the others. The upper left panel is the original scene, the upper right is the result of SSSA, and the bottom panel shows the final placements of boundaries. We re-emphasize that selecting the parameters is arduous and still somewhat ad hoc; we would of course prefer a simple, data-driven method based on solid statistical principles. Apart from the threshold values which depend on the grey level histogram, the same parameters were used in all three experiments.

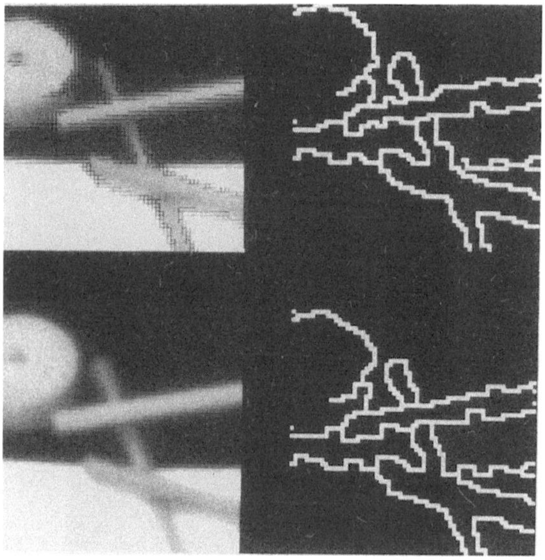

Figure 9: Stick scene.

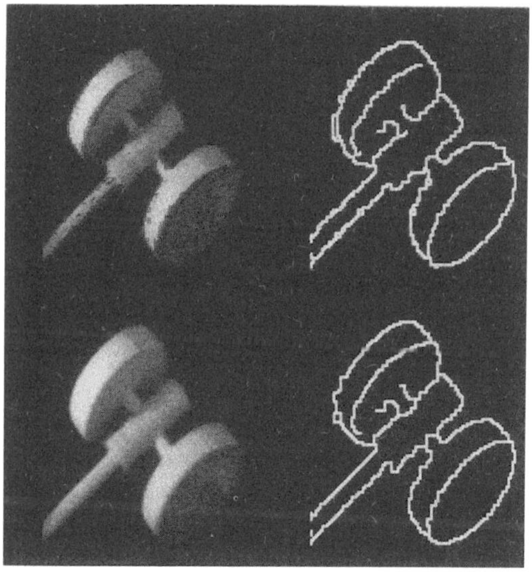

Figure 10: "Cart".

References

[1] E. Aarts and P. van Laarhoven, "Simulated annealing: a pedestrian review of the theory and some applications," NATO Advanced Study Institute on Pattern Recognition: Theory and Applications, Spa, Belgium, June 1986.

Figure 11: House scene.

[2] J. Besag, "Spatial interaction and the statistical analysis of lattice systems" (with discussion), *J. Royal Statist. Soc.*, Series B, 36, 192-236, 1974.

[3] J. Besag, "On the statistical analysis of dirty pictures," *J. Royal Statist. Soc.*, Series B, 1986.

[4] F.S. Cohen and D.B. Cooper, "Simple parallel hierarchical and relaxation algorithms for segmenting noncausal Markovian random fields," *IEEE Trans. Pattern Anal. Machine Intell.*, to appear.

[5] G.R. Cross and A.K. Jain, "Markov random field texture models," *IEEE Trans. Pattern Anal. Machine Intell.*, PAMI-5, 25-40, 1983.

[6] L.S. Davis, "A survey of edge detection techniques," *Comput. Graphics Image Processing*, 4, 248-270, 1975.

[7] P.A. Devijver, "Hidden Markov models for speech and images," Nato Advanced Study Institute on Pattern Recognition: Theory and Applications, Spa, Belgium, June 1986.

[8] H. Elliott and H. Derin, "Modelling and segmentation of noisy and textured images using Gibbs random fields," to appear in *IEEE Trans. Pattern Anal. Machine Intell.*

[9] S. Geman and D. Geman, "Stochastic relaxation, Gibbs distributions, and the Bayesian restoration of images," *IEEE Trans. Pattern Anal. Machine Intell.*, 6, 721-741, 1984.

[10] D. Geman and S. Geman, "Bayesian image analysis," in *Disordered Systems and Biological Organization*, Springer-Verlag, Berlin, 1986.

[11] S. Geman and D.E. McClure, "Bayesian image analysis: an application to single photon emission tomography," 1985.

[12] D. Geman, S. Geman, and D.E. McClure, "Markov random field image models and their applications," invited paper, *Annals of Statistics*, in preparation.

[13] A.R. Hanson and E.M. Riseman, "Segmentation of natural scenes," in *Computer Vision Systems*, Academic Press, New York, 1978.

[14] D. Marr and E. Hildreth, "Theory of edge detectors," *Proc. Royal Soc.* B, 207, 187-207, 1980.

[15] J. Marroquin, S. Mitter, and T. Poggio, "Probabilistic solution of ill-posed problems in computational vision," Artif. Intell. Lab. TECH. REPORT, M.I.T., 1985.

[16] D.W. Murray, A. Kashko, and H. Buxton, "A parallel approach to the picture restoration algorithm of Geman and Geman on an SIMD machine," to appear in *Image and Vision Computing.*

[17] E. Oja, "Texture subspaces," NATO Advanced Study Institute: Theory and Applications, Spa, Belgium, June 1986.

[18] A. Possolo, "Estimation of binary Markov random fields," preprint, 1986.

[19] B.D. Ripley, "Statistics, images, and pattern recognition," *Canadian J. of Statist.*, 14, 83-111, 1986.

SIMULATED ANNEALING: A PEDESTRIAN REVIEW OF THE THEORY AND SOME APPLICATIONS

Emile H.L. Aarts and Peter J.M. van Laarhoven

Philips Research Laboratories
P.O. Box 80000, 5600 JA Eindhoven, the Netherlands

Abstract

Simulated annealing[1] is a combinatorial optimization method based on randomization techniques. The method originates from the analogy between the annealing of solids, as described by the theory of statistical physics, and the optimization of large combinatorial problems. Here we review the basic theory of simulated annealing and recite a number of applications of the method. The theoretical review includes concepts of the theory of homogeneous and inhomogeneous Markov chains, an analysis of the asymptotic convergence of the algorithm, and a discussion of the finite-time behaviour. The list of applications includes combinatorial optimization problems related to VLSI design, image processing, code design and artificial intelligence.

1. Introduction

Many combinatorial optimization (CO) problems belong to the class of NP-hard problems, *i.e.*, no algorithm is known that provides an exact solution to the problem using a computation time that is polynomial in the size of the input of the problem [14] [26] [35]. Consequently, exact solutions require prohibitive computational efforts for the larger problems. Less time-consuming optimization algorithms can be constructed by applying tailored heuristics striving for near-optimal solutions. These tailored algorithms, however, often depend strongly on the structure of the problem to be solved. This is a major drawback of these algorithms since it prohibits fast and flexible implementations, and applications. Furthermore, there is a growing number of combinatorial problems originating from different fields (*e.g.*, the design of computer hard and software) for which no adequate (heuristic) optimization methods are known at all. It is for these reasons that the need is felt for a generally applicable and flexible optimization method. Simulated annealing (SA) can be viewed as such a method: it is a general optimization technique for solving combinatorial problems.

Ever since Kirkpatrick *et al.*, [23] and Černy [11] introduced the concepts of annealing [30] into the field of combinatorial optimization, much attention has been paid to research on the theory and applications of SA [25]. The SA algorithm is based on

[1]Other names to denote the method are Statistical Cooling [1], Monte-Carlo Annealing [22] and Probabilistic Hill Climbing [37]

NATO ASI Series, Vol. F30
Pattern Recognition Theory and Applications
Edited by P. A. Devijver and J. Kittler

randomization techniques. Salient features of the algorithm are its general applicability and its ability to obtain solutions close to an optimum. The quality of the final solution obtained by the algorithm is determined by the convergence of the algorithm which is governed by a set of parameters, *i.e.*, the cooling schedule.

In this monograph we review the basic theory of the SA algorithm based on the asymptotic convergence of homogeneous and inhomogeneous Markov chains. The finite-time behaviour of the SA algorithm is briefly discussed on the basis of some cooling schedules. A number of combinatorial optimization problems is recited related to applications in VLSI design, image processing, code design and neural networks. We merely restrict ourselves in this paper to a summary of the most important results. For a detailed overview the reader is referred to ref. [25].

2. Mathematical model of the algorithm

A CO problem can be characterized by the set $\mathcal{R}$ of all possible *configurations* i, ($\mathcal{R}$ denotes the *configuration space*), each configuration being uniquely determined by a set of values of the variables corresponding with the problem, and a *cost function* $C : \mathcal{R} \to \mathbf{R}$, which assigns a real number $C(i)$ to each configuration i. For convenience sake, we assume that C is defined such that the lower the value of C, the better the corresponding configuration (with respect to the optimization criteria). The objective of the optimization then is to find an optimal configuration i_o for which

$$C(i_o) = \min\{C(i) | i \in \mathcal{R}\}. \tag{1}$$

To apply the SA algorithm a mechanism is introduced to generate a new configuration from a given configuration by a small perturbation. A *neighbourhood* $\mathcal{R}_i$ is defined as the set of configurations that can be reached by a single perturbation of configuration i.

Simulated annealing can be viewed as an optimization algorithm that continuously tries to transform the current configuration into one of its neighbours by repeatedly applying the generation mechanism and an acceptance criterion. The acceptance criterion allows, besides of improvements, also, in a limited way, of deteriorations in the cost function, thus preventing the algorithm from getting stuck at local optima. Initially the algorithm accepts deteriorations with a high probability. In the course of the algorithm the probability is slowly decreased to become zero at the end. This is accounted for by a *control parameter* $c \in \mathbf{R}^+$.

The SA algorithm can mathematically be described by means of a *Markov chain*: a sequence of trials, for which the outcome of each trial depends only on the outcome of the previous one [12]. In the SA algorithm, trials correspond to transitions and it is clear that the outcome of a transition only depends on the outcome of the previous one (*i.e.*, the current configuration).

A Markov chain can be described by means of a set of conditional probabilities $P_{ij}(k-1,k)$ for each pair of outcomes (i,j) [12] [40]; $P_{ij}(k-1,k)$ is the probability that the outcome of the k-th trial is j, given that the outcome of the $(k-1)$-th trial is i. Let $\mathbf{X}(k)$ denote the outcome of the k-th trial, then we have

$$P_{ij}(k-1,k) = Pr\{\mathbf{X}(k) = j \mid \mathbf{X}(k-1) = i\}. \tag{2}$$

If the conditional probabilities do not depend on k, the corresponding Markov chain is called *homogeneous*, otherwise it is called *inhomogeneous*.

In the case of simulated annealing $P_{ij}(c) = P_{ij}(k-1,k)$ denotes the probability that the k-th transition is a transition from configuration i to configuration j at a given value of the control parameter c ($\mathbf{X}(k)$ is the configuration obtained after k transitions). The explicit dependence on k is discussed later. In view of this, $P_{ij}(c)$ is called the *transition probability* and is defined as:

$$P_{ij}(c) = \begin{cases} G_{ij}(c)A_{ij}(c) & j \neq i \\ 1 - \sum_{l=1,l\neq i}^{|\mathcal{R}|} G_{il}(c)A_{il}(c) & j = i, \end{cases} \tag{3}$$

where $G_{ij}(c) \in [0,1]$ denotes the *generation probability* to generate configuration j from configuration i, and $A_{ij}(c) \in (0,1]$ the *acceptance probability* to accept configuration j, given the configurations i and j. $P(c), G(c)$ and $A(c)$ are called the *transition, generation* and *acceptance matrix*, respectively. As a result of Eq. 3, $P(c)$ is a stochastic matrix, *i.e.*, $\sum_j P_{ij}(c) = 1, \ \forall i$.

The convergence of the SA algorithm can be formulated in terms of

- ▷ *a homogeneous algorithm*: the algorithm is described by a sequence of homogeneous Markov chains. Each Markov chain is generated at a fixed value of the control parameter c, which is decreased in between subsequent chains, and
- ▷ *an inhomogeneous algorithm*: the algorithm is described by a single inhomogeneous Markov chain. The value of the control parameter c is decreased in between subsequent transitions.

The SA algorithm finds a global minimum of the optimization problem if, after a (possibly large) number of transitions, say K, the following relation holds

$$Pr\{\mathbf{X}(K) \in \mathcal{R}_{opt}\} = 1, \tag{4}$$

where $\mathcal{R}_{opt}$ is the set of globally minimal configurations, i_o.

In the next section, we briefly discuss the asymptotic convergence of the annealing algorithm to the expression of Eq. 4 for both cases, *i.e.*, the homogeneous and the inhomogeneous algorithm.

2.1. The homogeneous algorithm

Essential to the convergence proof for the homogeneous algorithm is that under certain conditions on the matrices $A(c)$ and $G(c)$, there exists an *equilibrium vector* or *stationary distribution* given by the $|\mathcal{R}|$-vector $\mathbf{q}(c)$, defined as

$$\mathbf{q}^T(c) = \lim_{k\to\infty} \mathbf{a}^T P^k(c), \tag{5}$$

($\mathbf{a}$ denotes the initial probability distribution of the configurations) and that the equilibrium vector converges as $c \downarrow 0$ to a uniform distribution on the set of globally optimal configurations, i.e.

$$\lim_{c\downarrow 0} \mathbf{q}(c) = \pi, \tag{6}$$

where the components of the $|\mathcal{R}|$-vector π are given by

$$\pi_i = \begin{cases} |\mathcal{R}_{opt}|^{-1} & \text{if } i \in \mathcal{R}_{opt} \\ 0 & \text{elsewhere.} \end{cases} \tag{7}$$

The following theorem gives the conditions for the existence of $\mathbf{q}(c)$ in the general case.

Theorem 1 (Feller [12])

If a homogeneous Markov chain is *irreducible, aperiodic* and *recurrent* then there exists an equilibrium vector $\mathbf{q}(c)$ whose components are uniquely determined by

$$\forall i : q_i > 0, \quad \textstyle\sum_i q_i = 1, \tag{8}$$

$$\forall i : q_i = \textstyle\sum_j q_j P_{ji}. \quad \square \tag{9}$$

For irreducibility, aperiodicity and recurrency it suffices to require that [1] [29] [37],

$$(a1) \quad \forall i,j \in \mathcal{R}, \ \exists p \geq 1, \ l_0, l_1, \ldots, l_p \in \mathcal{R} \ (l_0 = i \wedge l_p = j):$$

$$G_{l_k l_{k+1}}(c) > 0, \quad (k = 0, 1, \ldots, p-1), \tag{10}$$

$$(a2) \qquad \forall c > 0, \ \exists i_c, j_c \in \mathcal{R} : A_{i_c j_c} < 1. \tag{11}$$

We now must impose further conditions on the matrices $A(c)$ and $G(c)$ to ensure convergence of $\mathbf{q}(c)$ to the distribution π, as given by Eq. 7. The most general and least restrictive set of conditions is derived by Romeo *et al.*, [37]. A more restrictive set based on a c-independent G-matrix resulting in an explicit expression of the equilibrium vector $\mathbf{q}(c)$ is given by a number of authors [1] [5] [29] [34].

In this case, the equilibrium vector $\mathbf{q}(c)$ is given by

$$q_i(c) = \frac{A_{i_0 i}(c)}{\sum_{j \in \mathcal{R}} A_{i_0 j}(c)} \quad \forall i \in \mathcal{R}, \tag{12}$$

provided the matrices $A(c)$ and G satisfy

$$(b1) \qquad \forall i,j \in \mathcal{R}: \quad G_{ji} = G_{ij}, \tag{13}$$

$$(b2) \quad \forall i,j,k \in \mathcal{R}, \ C(i) \leq C(j) \leq C(k): \quad A_{ik}(c) = A_{ij}(c) A_{jk}(c), \tag{14}$$

$$(b3) \qquad \forall i,j \in \mathcal{R}, \ C(i) \geq C(j): \quad A_{ij}(c) = 1, \tag{15}$$

$$\forall i,j \in \mathcal{R}, \ C(i) < C(j), \ c > 0: \quad 0 < A_{ij}(c) < 1, \tag{16}$$

$$(b4) \qquad \forall i,j \in \mathcal{R}: \quad \lim_{c \to \infty} A_{ij}(c) = 1, \tag{17}$$

$$\forall i,j \in \mathcal{R}, \quad C(i) < C(j): \quad \lim_{c \downarrow 0} A_{ij}(c) = 0. \tag{18}$$

A generalization of condition (b1) is formulated by Anily and Federgrun [5]:

$$\exists \, |\mathcal{R}| \times |\mathcal{R}| - \text{matrix} \ \ Q \ \ \text{for which}$$

$$\forall i \in \mathcal{R}, j \in \mathcal{R}_i: \quad G_{ij} = \frac{Q_{ij}}{\sum_{l \in \mathcal{R}} Q_{il}}; \quad Q_{ij} = Q_{ji}, \tag{19}$$

in which case the equilibrium vector is given by

$$q_i(c) = \frac{(\sum_l Q_{il}) A_{i_0 i}}{\sum_j (\sum_l Q_{jl}) A_{i_0 j}}. \tag{20}$$

Clearly, the $\mathbf{q}(c)$ given by Eq. 12 satisfy Eq. 8. By using conditions (b1), (b2) and (b3) it is straightforward to show that the $\mathbf{q}(c)$ of Eq. 12 satisfy Eq. 9. Conditions (b3) and (b4), finally, guarantee that $\lim_{c \downarrow 0} \mathbf{q}(c) = \pi$.

A frequently used expression for the acceptance probabilities is given by

$$A_{ij}(c) = \min\{1, \exp((C(i) - C(j))/c)\}, \tag{21}$$

which satisfies conditions (a2) and (b2)-(b4). In this case the equilibrium vector takes the form

$$q_i(c_k) = \frac{\exp((C(i_o) - C(i))/c_k)}{\sum_{j=1}^{|\mathcal{R}|} \exp((C(i_o) - C(j))/c_k)}, \tag{22}$$

provided the generation probabilities satisfy conditions (a1) and (b1). The expressions of Eqs. 21 and 22 correspond with the original form of the algorithm introduced by Kirkpatrick *et al.*, [23] and Černy [11].

2.2. The inhomogeneous algorithm

In the previous section it was shown that, under certain conditions on the matrices $A(c)$ and $G(c)$, the simulated annealing algorithm converges to a global minimum with probability 1, if for each value c_k ($k = 0, 1, 2, \ldots$) of the control parameter the corresponding Markov chain is of infinite length and if the c_k eventually converge to 0 for $k \to \infty$. In this section, we discuss conditions to ensure asymptotic convergence for the case, where each Markov chain is of length 1, *i.e.*, after each transition the value of the control parameter is changed. Thus, an inhomogeneous Markov chain is obtained, whose transition probabilities $P_{ij}(c_k)$ are defined by

$$P_{ij}(c_k) = \begin{cases} G_{ij}(c_k)A_{ij}(c_k) & j \neq i \\ 1 - \sum_{l=1, l\neq i}^{|\mathcal{R}|} G_{il}(c_k)A_{il}(c_k) & j = i. \end{cases} \tag{23}$$

Hereinafter, we assume that the sequence $\{c_k\}, k = 0, 1, 2, \ldots$, satisfies the following two conditions:

$$\text{(c1)} \qquad \lim_{k\to\infty} c_k = 0, \tag{24}$$

$$\text{(c2)} \quad c_k \geq c_{k+1}, \; k = 0, 1, \ldots . \tag{25}$$

Thus, we do not exclude the possibility that c_k is kept constant during a number of transitions, in which case we again obtain a homogeneous Markov chain, but of finite length.

Conditions for asymptotic convergence are derived by a number of authors, *i.e.*, by Geman and Geman, [15] Anily and Federgrun [5], Mitra *et al.*, [32], Gidas [16] and Hajek [17]. The results of the first three papers are obtained in a similar way, by using ergodicity theorems for inhomogeneous Markov chains and lead to sufficient conditions on the sequence $\{c_k\}$. The results presented by Gidas and Hajek lead to necessary and sufficient conditions and are obtained by considering the continuous-time analogon of inhomogeneous Markov chains. Here we briefly discuss some of the results obtained by the first set of authors. The results of Gidas and Hajek are reviewed in reference [18].

We need the following two definitions:

Definition 1 (Seneta [40])
An inhomogeneous Markov chain is *weakly ergodic* if for all $m \geq 1, i, j, l \in \mathcal{R}$:

$$\lim_{k \to \infty} (P_{il}(m,k) - P_{jl}(m,k)) = 0, \tag{26}$$

with $P(m,k) = \prod_{l=m+1}^{k} P(l-1,l)$. □

Definition 2 (Seneta [40])

An inhomogeneous Markov chain is *strongly ergodic* if there exists a vector π, satisfying

$$\sum_{i=1}^{|\mathcal{R}|} \pi_i = 1, \quad \forall i, \ \pi_i \geq 0, \tag{27}$$

such that $\forall m \geq 1, i, j \in \mathcal{R}$:

$$\lim_{k \to \infty} P_{ij}(m,k) = \pi_j. \qquad \square \tag{28}$$

Thus, weak ergodicity implies that eventually the dependence of $\mathbf{X}(k)$ with respect to $\mathbf{X}(0)$ vanishes, whereas strong ergodicity implies convergence *in distribution* of the $\mathbf{X}(k)$, *i.e.*, if Eq. 28 holds, we have:

$$\lim_{k \to \infty} Pr\{\mathbf{X}(k) = j\} = \pi_j. \tag{29}$$

For a homogeneous Markov chain, there is no distinction between weak and strong ergodicity.

The following two theorems provide conditions for weak and strong ergodicity of inhomogeneous Markov chains:

Theorem 2 (Seneta [40])

An inhomogeneous Markov chain is weakly ergodic if and only if there is a strictly increasing sequence of positive numbers $\{l_i\}, i = 0, 1, 2, \ldots$, such that

$$\sum_{i=0}^{\infty} (1 - \tau_1(P(l_i, l_{i+1}))) = \infty, \tag{30}$$

where $\tau_1(P)$, the *coefficient of ergodicity* of an $n \times n$-matrix P, is defined as

$$\tau_1(P) = 1 - \min_{m,j} \sum_{k=1}^{n} \min(P_{mk}, P_{jk}). \qquad \square \tag{31}$$

Theorem 3 (Isaacson and Madsen [21])

An inhomogeneous Markov chain is strongly ergodic if it is weakly ergodic and if for all k there exists a vector $\pi(k)$ such that $\pi(k)$ is an eigenvector with eigenvalue 1 of $P(k-1,k)$, $\|\pi(k)\| = 1$ and

$$\sum_{k=0}^{\infty} \|\pi(k) - \pi(k+1)\| < \infty. \tag{32}$$

Moreover, if $\pi = \lim_{k\to\infty} \pi(k)$, then π is the vector in definition 2. □

Under the conditions (a1) and (a2) on the matrices $A(c_k)$ and $G(c_k)$, we know that for each $k \geq 0$, there exists an eigenvector $\mathbf{q}(c_k)$ of $P(c_k)$ (the equilibrium vector of the homogeneous Markov chain). Moreover, under the additional conditions (b1)-(b4) the explicit form for $\mathbf{q}(c_k)$ given by Eq. 12 is obtained satisfying $\lim_{k\to\infty} \mathbf{q}(c_k) = \pi$, where the vector π is given by Eq. 7 provided condition (c1) holds. Using theorem 3 with $\pi(k) = \mathbf{q}(c_k)$, strong ergodicity can be proven by showing that the Markov chain is weakly ergodic and by showing that the $\mathbf{q}(c_k), k = 0, 1, 2, \ldots$, satisfy Eq. 32 (for this proof condition (c2) is required). Using Eqs. 7 and 29, we then have

$$\lim_{k\to\infty} Pr\{\mathbf{X}(k) \in \mathcal{R}_{opt}\} = 1. \tag{33}$$

For simulated annealing, with $\mathbf{q}(c_k)$ given by Eq. 22 the validity of Eq. 32 is shown by Geman and Geman [15] and by Mitra et al. [32]. Furthermore, these authors, as well as Anily and Federgrun [5], use theorem 2 to ensure weak ergodicity and to derive a similar parametric form on the sequence $\{c_k\}, k = 0, 1, 2, \ldots$. Following the lines of Mitra *et al.*, [32] we have

Theorem 4 (Mitra *et al.*, [32])

The inhomogeneous Markov chain associated with generation probabilities satisfying conditions (a1) and (b1) and acceptance probabilities given by Eq. 21, with the following control sequence

$$c_k = \frac{a}{\log(k + k_0 + 1)}, \quad (k = 0, 1, 2, \ldots), \tag{34}$$

for some parameter k_0, $1 \leq k_0 < \infty$, is weakly ergodic if $a \geq r\Delta$ with

$$\Delta = \max_{i,j}\{C(j) - C(i) \mid i \in \mathcal{R},\ j \in \mathcal{R}_i, \quad C(j) > C(i)\}, \tag{35}$$

$$r = \min_{i\in\mathcal{R}/\mathcal{R}_{max}} \max_{j\in\mathcal{R}}\ d(i,j), \tag{36}$$

$$\mathcal{R}_{max} = \{i \in \mathcal{R} \mid C(j) \leq C(i)\ \forall j \in \mathcal{R}_i\}. \quad \square \tag{37}$$

Here $\mathcal{R}_{max}$ denotes the set of all locally maximal configurations and $d(i,j)$ is the minimal number of transitions to reach j from i.

Gidas [16] and Hajek [17] obtain a similar parametric expression as the one given by Eq. 34 using a different derivation. Their condition on the control parameter is conjectured to be necessary and sufficient.

We end this section with some remarks:

- ▷ The asymptotic-convergence proof of the inhomogeneous algorithm is restricted to equilibrium vectors that take the exponential form of Eq. 22. A convergence proof for the more general form of Eq. 12 is not known from the literature.

- ▷ The asymptotic convergence to a global minimum of the homogeneous SA algorithm described above requires a number of transitions that is exponential in the size of the input of the optimization problem [1], resulting in an exponential-time execution of the SA algorithm. For the inhomogeneous algorithm we conjecture a similar complexity result.

▷ An extensive discussion of the convergence properties of the SA algorithm is given by Gidas [16]. He also consideres functional forms of the Markov chains.

▷ There exists a close connection between the SA algorithm and concepts from statistical mechanics. Work in statistical mechanics concerning the calculation of macroscopic quantities, state-space geometry and rate of convergence to equilibrium of many particle systems can be of interest to the analysis of the SA algorithm [1] [8] [20] [24] [31] [45].

▷ A number of quantities determining the convergence of the SA algorithm as described above are difficult to calculate for most CO problems (*e.g.*, r and Δ). Moreover the limits governing the convergence ($c_k \to 0$ and $k \to \infty$) must be approximated in implementations of the SA algorithm. Consequently, heuristic choices have to be introduced to obtain efficient implementations of the algorithm. This subject is addressed in the next section.

3. The Cooling Schedule

In this section we briefly discuss the implementation of the SA algorithm where we restrict ourselves to the acceptance probabilities given by Eq. 21. In the previous section it was shown that the SA algorithm converges to globally optimal configurations. Moreover, analysis of the algorithm shows that asymptotic convergence to globally optimal configurations results in an exponential-time execution of the algorithm. Near-optimal configurations can be obtained by the SA algorithm in polynomial time by choosing appropiate values for the parameters that control the convergence. These parameters are combined in the *cooling schedule* (CS).

Commonly one resorts to an implementation of the SA algorithm in which a sequence of homogeneous Markov chains is generated at descending values of the control parameter c. Individual Markov chains are obtained by repeatedly generating a new configuration from an old one according to some perturbation mechanism satisfying conditions (a1) and (b1) and applying the acceptance criterion of Eq. 21 for a fixed value c. Let L_m be the length and c_m the value of c for the m-th Markov chain. Optimization is performed by starting the chain generation process for a given value of the control parameter, say c_0, ($c_1 = c_0$) and repeating it for decreasing values of c_m until c_m approaches 0. This procedure is governed by the CS. The parameters determining the CS are

1. the *start value* c_0 of the cooling control parameter,

2. the *decrement function* f of the control parameter ($c_{m+1} = f(c_m)$),

3. the *length* L_m of the individual Markov chains, and

4. the *stop criterion* to terminate the algorithm.

Determination of adequate time-efficient CS's has evolved into an important research topic. We briefly discuss some results.

The literature gives a number of conceptually simple CS's that are similar to the original schedule introduced by Kirkpatrick *et al.*, [23]: the algorithms starts off at an experimentally determined value for c_0 for which the *acceptance ratio* $\chi(c_0)$ is close to 1 ($\chi(c_m)$ = the number of accepted transitions / number of proposed transitions at a given c_m). Next a sequence of Markov chains is generated (each chain at a fixed value of c_m) at descending values of c_m where, $c_{m+1} = \alpha c_m$, with α a constant close to 1 (*e.g.*, $\alpha = 0.95$). The length of the individual chains is determined by a minimal number of acceptances and is limited by a total number of proposed transitions.

More elaborate CS's are given by a number of authors [25]. We briefly discuss some results.

Start value c_0

Analytical expressions for c_0 are derived by several authors based on the average difference in cost of subsequent configurations occuring in a Markov chain [1] [6] [27] [45].

Stop criterion

A stop criterion for the SA algorithm can be based on extrapolation ($c \downarrow 0$) of the expected value of the average cost [1] [34] or on the requirement that the probability that the cost of the final configuration obtained by the SA algorithm deviates less than a given finite value from the optimal cost is sufficiently small [29] [45].

Decrement of the control parameter and Markov-chain length

With respect to the decrement of c_m and the Markov-chain length L_m the concept of quasi-equilibrium is of use.

Definition 3

Let L_m be the length of a Markov chain at $c = c_m$ and $\mathbf{p}(c_m)$ be the distribution vector of the configurations after L_m transitions given by

$$\mathbf{p}^T(c_m) = \mathbf{a}^T P^{L_m}(c_m), \tag{38}$$

then we say that the process is in quasi-equilibrium at c_m for some positive value ϵ if

$$\|\mathbf{p}(c_m) - \mathbf{q}(c_m)\| \leq \epsilon. \qquad \square \tag{39}$$

It is intuitively clear that large decrements of c_m require more transitions (longer Markov chains) to restore quasi-equilibrium for a given value of ϵ at the new value c_{m+1}. Thus, there is a trade off between fast decrement of c_m and the length of the Markov chains L_m. In this respect a number of CS's given in the literature can be divided into two classes, i.e.

i) fixed decrement of c_m and variable chain length, and

ii) variable decrement of c_m and fixed Markov-chain length.

ad i) The Markov-chain lengths can be based on escape-time estimates, *i.e.*, for a given fixed decrement rule (not depending on the cost function) the chain length is based on the expected number of transitions required to escape from local minima. In this way the process is assumed to stay in quasi-equilibrium throughout the optimization (at c_0 the process is in quasi-equilibrium by definition) [37].

ad ii) For a fixed Markov-chain length the decrement of c_m can be derived from the requirement that the deviation from quasi-equilibrium introduced by the decrement is sufficiently small such that quasi-equilibrium is restored during execution of the subsequent Markov chain. Using this requirement as a starting point, several authors derive analytical expressions for the decrement function $f(c_m)$ [1] [29] [34].

We end this section with some remarks:

▷ Sofar the literature does not present much material on a performance comparison between the various CS's discussed above. Aarts and van Laarhoven compare their CS with some conceptually simple CS's showing that a reduction in computational effort can be obtained by using more elaborate CS's [2].

▷ Aarts and van Laarhoven [1] and Lundy and Mees [29] show that execution of the SA algorithm using their CS requires a total number of steps of order $R \ln |\mathcal{R}|$, with $R = \max\{|\mathcal{R}_i|, i \epsilon \mathcal{R}\}$, which can be chosen polynomial in the size of the problem, thus resulting in a polynomial-time execution of the SA algorithm.

▷ Moore and de Geus [33] argue that the SA algorithm can be controlled by a rule-based expert system. This may be considered as an interesting alternative approach to the deterministic CS's discussed above.

▷ As a consequence of the asymptotic convergence of the SA algorithm it is intuitively clear that the slower the "cooling" is carried out the larger the probability is that the final configuration is (close to) the optimal configuration. Thus, the *deviation* of the final configuration from the optimal configuration can be as small as desired by investing more computational effort. Sofar the literature does not elaborate on the probabilistic dependency of the deviation from the parameters of the CS. This is considered as an open research topic.

▷ Practical application of the SA algorithm is very simple. The ingredients are a configuration-space description, a cost function, a perturbation mechanism and a CS. This makes the SA algorithm easy to implement and flexible.

4. Applications

The SA algorithm has been applied to many CO problems, both practical and theoretical, in a wide range of disciplines [25]. A number of authors report on investigations of the performance of the SA algorithm using instances of theoretical (CO)-problems [1] [2] [6] [8] [11] [23] [25]. A general conclusion from these studies is that satisfactory solutions can be obtained by the SA algorithm, but some problems require large computational efforts. For randomly generated problem instances the performance of the SA algorithm is found to be excellent. For most of the investigated theoretical CO problems there exist tailored optimization algorithms [26] [35]. Sofar the literature, unfortunately, does not provide much material on a performance comparison between these tailored algorithms and the SA algorithm. In a preleminary paper Aragon *et al.*, [6] present results on such a performance comparison. They argue that for the graph-partitioning problem the SA algorithm performs better that the tailored algorithms. In case of the other CO problems used in the comparative study (the travelling salesman, graph coloring and number partitioning problem) they conclude that the tailored algorithms outperform the SA algorithm. They, furthermore, conclude that the SA algorithm is rather slow, which is also experienced by other authors as mentioned above. We feel that a systematic study of performance comparisons of the SA algorithm with other general and tailored CO algorithms would be of great use to judge the SA algorithm on its merits.

With respect to the application of the SA algorithm to practical CO problems we restrict ourselves here to presenting a list of items (without the pretention of being complete)

▷ **VLSI design**
Floorplanning, placement and routing of circuit components [22] [23] [27] [34] [38] [39] [44].
Test-pattern generation [28].
Logic synthesis [13].

▷ **Image processing**
Image segmentation [43].
Reconstruction of coded or corrupted images [9] [15] [41] [42] [46].
(A general description of the application of the SA algorithm is given in ref. [36]).

▷ **Digital signal processing**
Construction of error-correcting codes [19].
Construction of binary sequences with a maximally flat amplitude spectrum [7].
Design of filter coefficients [10].

▷ **Neural network theory**
A learning algorithm for Boltzmann machines [4].

Other applications of interest are given in ref. [25].

5. Conclusions

The simulated annealing algorithm can be viewed as a general optimization algorithm. The advantages of the algorithm can be formulated as:

▷ near-optimal results can be obtained,

▷ the algorithm is generally applicable,

▷ the algorithm is easy to implement,

▷ the algorithm can be executed in polynomial-time.

The major disadvantage is:

▷ some applications may require large computational efforts.

Researchers believe that the SA algorithm may evolve into a technique that can be applied succesfully to a wide range of CO problems. There is, however, also scepticism especially when the computational effort becomes a critical factor. For some CO problems there exist worthy competing tailored algorithms and it is believed that the strength of the SA algorithm lies in application to problem areas where no such tailored algorithms are available. Further research on large-scale applications and means to speed up the algorithm by parallel execution [3], possibly using dedicated hardware, has to be carried out to provide more insight in the practical use of the algorithm.

References

[1] Aarts, E.H.L and P.J.M. van Laarhoven, Statistical Cooling: A General Approach to Combinatorial Optimization Problems, *Philips Journal of Research*, 40 (1985) 193-226.

[2] Aarts, E.H.L and P.J.M. van Laarhoven, A New Polynomial Time Cooling Schedule, *Proc. Int. Conf. on Computer Aided Design*, Santa Clara, November 1985, pp. 206-208.

[3] Aarts, E.H.L, F.M.J. de Bont, J.H.A. Habers and P.J.M. van Laarhoven, A Parallel Statistical Cooling Algorithm, *Proc. Symposium on Theoretical Aspects of Computer Science, 1986, Springer Lecture Notes in Computer Science* 210(1986)87-97.

[4] Ackley, D.H., G.E. Hinton and T.J. Sejnowski, A Learning Algorithm for Boltzmann Machines, *Cognitive Science*, 9(1985)147-169.

[5] Anily, S. and A. Federgruen, Probabilistic Analysis of Simulated Annealing Methods, preprint, 1985.

[6] Aragon C.R., D.S. Johnson, L.A. McGeoch and C. Schevon, Optimization by Simulated Annealing: an Experimental Evaluation, working paper, 1984.

[7] Beenker G.F.M., T.A.C.M. Claasen and P.W.C. Hermens, Binary Sequences with Maximally Flat Amplitude Spectrum, *Philips J. of Research*, 40(1985)289-304.

[8] Bonomi, E. and J.-L. Lutton, The N-city Travelling Salesman Problem: Statistical Mechanics and the Metropolis Algorithm, *SIAM Rev.*, 26(1984)551-568.

[9] Carnevalli, P., L. Coletti and S. Paternello, Image Processing by Simulated Annealing, *IBM J. Res. Develop.*, 29(1985)569-579.

[10] Catthoor, F., H. DeMan and J. Vanderwalle, SAILPLANE: A Simulated Annealing based CAD-tool for the Analysis of Limit-Cycle Behaviour, *Proc. IEEE Int. Conf. on Computer Design*, Port Chester, October 1985, pp. 244-247.

[11] Černy, V., Thermodynamical Approach to the Traveling Salesman Problem: An Efficient Simulation Algorithm, *J. Opt. Theory Appl.*, 45(1985)41-51.

[12] Feller, W., *An Introduction to Probability Theory and Applications, vol. 1*, (Wiley, New York, 1950).

[13] Fleisher, H., J. Giraldi, D.B. Martin, R.L. Phoenix and M.A. Tavel, Simulated Annealing as a Tool for Logic Optimization in a CAD Environment, *Proc. ICCAD*, Santa Clara, November 1985, pp. 203-205.

[14] Garey, M.R. and D.S. Johnson, *Computers and Intractability: A Guide to the Theory of NP-Completeness*, (W.H. Freeman and Co., San Francisco, 1979).

[15] Geman, S. and D. Geman, Stochastic Relaxation, Gibbs Distributions, and the Bayesian Restoration of Images, *IEEE Proc. Pattern Analysis and Machine Intelligence*, PAMI-6(1984)721-741.

[16] Gidas, B., Nonstationary Markov Chains and Convergence of the Annealing Algorithm, *J. Statis. Phys.*, 39(1985)73-131.

[17] Hajek, B., Cooling Schedules for Optimal Annealing, preprint, 1985.

[18] Hajek, B. A Tutorial Survey of Theory and Applications of Simulated Annealing, *Proc. 24th Conf. on Decision and Control*, Ft. Lauderdale, December 1985, pp. 755-760.

[19] Hemachandra, L.A. and V.K. Wei, Simulated Annealing and Error Correcting Codes, preprint, 1984.

[20] Holley., R, Rapid Convergence to Equilibrium in One Dimensional Stochastic Ising Models, *Annals of Probability*, 13(1985)72-89.

[21] Isaacson, D. and R. Madsen, *Markov Chains*, (Wiley, New York, 1976).

[22] Jepsen, D.W. and C.D. Gelatt Jr., Macro Placement by Monte Carlo Annealing, *Proc. Int. Conf. Computer Design*, Port Chester, November 1983, pp. 495-498.

[23] Kirkpatrick, S., C.D. Gelatt Jr. and M.P. Vecchi, Optimization by Simulated Annealing, *Science*, 220(1983)671-680.

[24] Kirkpatrick, S. and G. Toulouse, Configuration Space Analysis of Travelling Salesman Problems, *J. Physique*, 46(1985)1277-1292.

[25] Laarhoven, P.J.M. van and E.H.L. Aarts, Theory and Applications of Simulated Annealing: An Overview, submitted for publication in *Acta Applicandae Mathematicae*, 1986.

[26] Lawler, E.L., J.K. Lenstra, A.H.G. Rinnooy Kan and D.B. Shmoys, *The Traveling Salesman Problem*, (Wiley, Chichester, 1985).

[27] Leong, H.W., D.F. Wong and C.L. Liu, A Simulated-Annealing Channel Router, *Proc. ICCAD*, Santa Clara, November 1985, pp. 226-229.

[28] Ligthart, M.M., E.H.L. Aarts and F.P.M. Beenker, A Design-fortestability of PLA's using Statistical Cooling, to appear in *Proc. 23rd Des. Automation Conf.*, Las Vegas, June 1986.

[29] Lundy, M. and A. Mees, Convergence of an Annealing Algorithm, *Math. Prog.*, 34(1986)111-124.

[30] M. Metropolis, A. Rosenbluth, M. Rosenbluth, A. Teller and E. Teller, *Equation of State Calculations by Fast Computing Machines,* J. Chem. Phys. 21(1953)1087-1092.

[31] Mezard, M. and G. Parisi, Replicas and Optimization, *J. Physique Lett.*, 46(1985)L-771 - L-778.

[32] Mitra, D., Romeo, F. and A.L. Sangiovanni-Vincentelli, Convergence and Finite-Time Behavior of Simulated Annealing, *Proc. 24th Conf. on Decision and Control*, Ft. Lauderdale, December 1985, pp. 761-767.

[33] Moore, T.P. and A.J. de Geus, Simulated Annealing Controlled by a Rule-Based Expert System, *Proc. Int. Conf. on Computer Aided Design*, Santa Clara, November 1985, pp. 200-202.

[34] Otten, R.H.J.M. and L.P.P.P. van Ginneken, Floorplan Design using Simulated Annealing, *Proc. Int. Conf. on Computer Aided Design*, Santa Clara, November 1984, pp. 96-98.

[35] Papadimitriou, C.H. and K. Steiglitz, *Combinatorial Optimization: Algorithms and Complexity*, (Prentice Hall, New York, 1982).

[36] Ripley, B.D., Statistics, Images and Pattern Recognition, preprint 1985.

[37] Romeo, F. and A.L. Sangiovanni-Vincentelli, Probabilistic Hill Climbing Algorithms: Properties and Applications, *Proc. 1985 Chapel Hill Conf. on VLSI*, May 1985, pp. 393-417.

[38] Rowen, C. and J.L. Hennessy, Logic Minimization, Placement and Routing in SWAMI, *Proc. 1985 Custom IC Conf.*, Portland, May 1985.

[39] Sechen, C. and A.L. Sangiovanni-Vincentelli, TimberWolf3.2: A New Standard Cell Placement and Global Routing Package, to appear in *Proc. 23rd Des. Automation Conf.*, Las Vegas, June 1986.

[40] Seneta, E., *Non-negative Matrices and Markov Chains*, (Springer Verlag, New York, 2nd ed., 1981).

[41] Smith, W.E., H.H. Barrett and R.G. Paxman, Reconstruction of Objects from Coded Images by Simulated Annealing, *Optics Letters*, 8(1983)199-201.

[42] Smith, W.E., R.G. Paxman and H.H. Barrett, Application of Simulated Annealing to Coded-aperture Design and Tomographic Reconstruction, *IEEE Trans. Nuclear Science*, NS-32(1985)758-761.

[43] Sontag, E.D. and H.J. Sussmann, Image Restoration and Segmentation using the Annealing Algorithm, *Proc. 24th Conf. on Decision and Control*, Ft. Lauderdale, December 1985, pp. 768-773.

[44] Vecchi, M.P. and S. Kirkpatrick, Global Wiring by Simulated Annealing, *IEEE Trans. on Computer-Aided Design*, 2(1983)215-222.

[45] White, S.R., Concepts of Scale in Simulated Annealing, *Proc. ICCD*, Port Chester, November 1984, pp. 646-651.

[46] Wolberg, G. and T. Pavlidis, Restoration of Binary Images using Stochastic Relaxation with Annealing, *Pattern Recognition Letters*, 3(1985)375-388.

THE DETECTION OF GEOLOGICAL FAULT LINES IN RADAR IMAGES

S. Güler, G. Garcia, L. Gülen, and M.N. Toksöz

Earth Resources Laboratory
Department of Earth Atmospheric and Planetary Sciences
Massachusetts Institute of Technology
Cambridge, MA 02142 USA

Abstract

A two step approach for delineating geological faults on radar images is developed. The first step is the row-by-row detection of the line elements, or the points at which "gray value" statistics change abruptly. The combination of a Kalman filter and a change detector is used for the line element detection. Connecting these line elements into lines using the a priori geologic information is the second step. Two algorithms are presented for this step: a line following algorithm and line restoration with simulated annealing. Both algorithms are tested on real data and their performances are compared.

1. Introduction

The detection of abrupt changes in image characteristics defining boundaries between regions having slowly varying features is an important problem for various applications, including geological analysis of images of the earth's surface. The investigation of the geological structure of a given region, especially the configuration of active faults, has great importance for earthquake hazards and other geological studies.

In this study, a method to detect candidate fault lines is designed and implemented to provide a framework for the identification of the fault zones. The problem is considered in two steps. In the first step, "line elements" are detected. These are the points which most likely belong to the fault-generated lineaments. In the second step, the fault lines are formed using both the line elements detected in the first step and a set of constraints reflecting the a priori information about the characteristics of the fault zones.

2. Geological Features and Radar Images

Faults are fractures or fracture zones in the earth's crust along which there has been displacement of crustal blocks relative to one another. They are generally long, linear or arcuate features. Delineation of fault lines is traditionally based on three types of data: seismicity, which shows the location and history of earthquakes along active faults; geologic field mapping data, which in remote areas are typically incomplete and of insufficient accuracy; and remote sensing data including Landsat images.

NATO ASI Series, Vol. F30
Pattern Recognition Theory and Applications
Edited by P. A. Devijver and J. Kittler

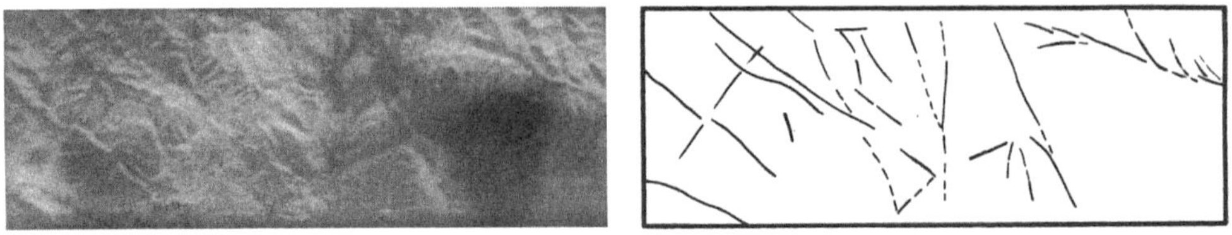

Figure 1: (a) Original SIR photograph. (b) Human interpreted fault map of Figure 1a.

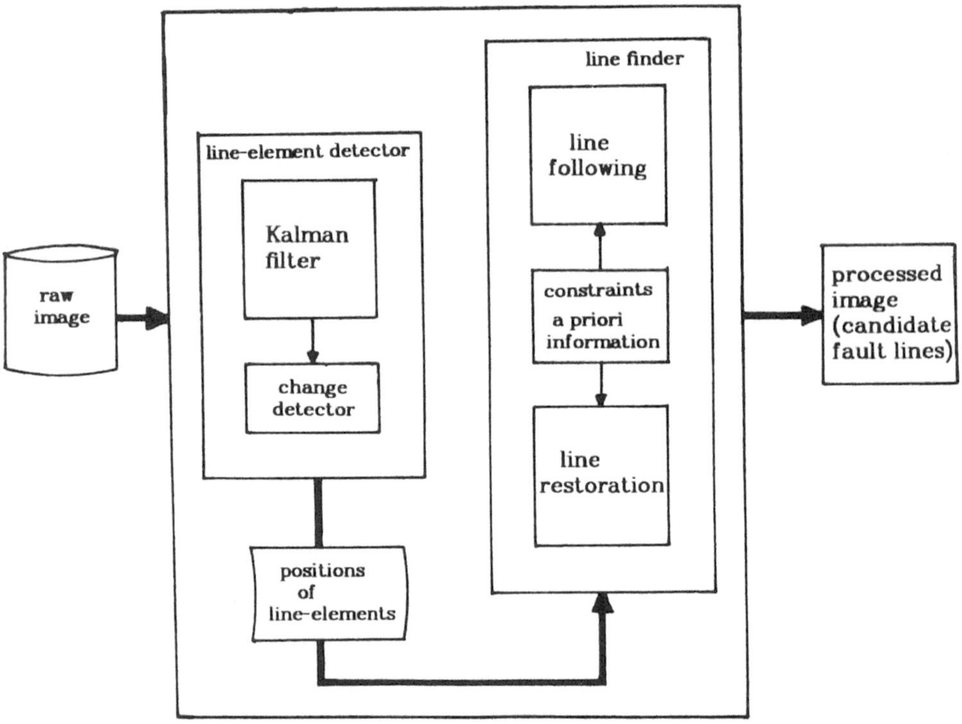

Figure 2: Block diagram of the fault detection system.

Figure 3: Some examples of cell states.

Recently, high resolution images of tectonically active regions have been obtained by Shuttle Imaging Radar (SIR) systems. It has been shown that faults, among other geological features, can be identified on these images (Figure 1).

Geological and physical properties of fault zones relevant to radar imagery with varying importance are (Toksöz *et al.*, 1985):

- They generally have greater moisture;
- They are usually smoother than the surrounding terrain;
- There is usually a scarp or valley parallel to the fault trace;
- Surface characteristics may be different across the fault.

Several features are described in the literature for recognition of faults, but not all features suggestive of faults are caused by faulting, nor do all faults have all or some of those features (Ziony, 1985).

3. The Fault Line Detection Problem

In this study we follow the approach that the detection of fault lines is a general line detection problem and can be decomposed into two subproblems (Martelli, 1972, Basseville *et al.*, 1981). The first one is the detection of changes in local image characteristics, and the second is the construction of the lines by piecing together local changes from a global point of view. A block diagram of the method is given in Figure 2 .

3.1. Detection of Line Elements

Line element detection is realized by the combination of a filter and a change detector, applied to the image in a row-by-row fashion. On each row, abrupt changes in gray value statistics are detected and stored for further processing by the line finder. Among the different approaches we prefer the Kalman filter due to its robustness with respect to modeling errors (Leondes, 1970, Brown, 1983).

For the Kalman filter the following state model is assumed for each row of the image:

$$\begin{aligned} x(k+1) &= \Phi(k)\,x(k) + n(k) \\ y(k) &= H(k)x(k) + v(k) \end{aligned} \tag{1}$$

where $x(k)$ is the state vector of dimension m representing the depth value of pixel vector k, $y(k)$ is the observation vector of dimension p representing the measured intensity value of pixel vector k, $\Phi(k)$ is the state transition matrix, $H(k)$ is the observation matrix, and $n(k)$ and $v(k)$ are independent white Gaussian noise sequences with zero mean and known covariances.

A one dimensional filter using mean-square error minimization criterion is used in the implementation. On each row of the image, the filter estimates the mean gray values at every pixel position following the gradual changes in the mean. Sudden jumps in mean gray value are caught by the change detector by a threshold comparison. The filter is initialized after each detection to improve the quality of the estimations. Besides the mean value estimates, filter estimations for the next data are used to find the one step estimation error for each observation, *i.e.* innovations. The change detector also detects points where the innovations exceed a threshold value. Both mean gray value and innovations jumps are designated as line elements, and a weight is associated with each line element according to the type of the detected change (Figure 3). This one dimensional information obtained for each row is connected over all the rows of the image, in the line construction step, taking the second dimension of the image into account.

3.2. Construction of Candidate Fault Lines

A number of algorithms have been developed in the literature to track the lines from a set of isolated points with constraints or a priori information on the lines to be constructed (Kelly, 1971; Basseville *et al.*, 1981). In this application it is required to find among all lines only those which most likely are fault produced lineaments. At this stage a set of constraints derived from the features of fault zones has to be imposed on the line finding algorithm. Two different approaches, namely a line following algorithm and a stochastic relaxation algorithm (simulated annealing), are used for the formation of global lines.

3.2.1. Line following algorithm

A line following algorithm is developed to link the line elements using a priori information about the direction, length and width of the sought-after lines. While following a line, some possible gaps due to missing line element detections are filled, and some spurious detections are removed.

The algorithm is as follows :

- ▷ Starting from the current line element find the density of line elements in regions of predefined size,
- ▷ Choose a direction to follow.
- ▷ If none of these densities is larger than a certain threshold value ignore this element.
- ▷ Continue the process until a side of the image is reached or there is no continuation:
    - Check predefined regions on the following rows to decide on the line elements to be connected to the current line.
    - Delete a line element from the list of line elements as it is connected to a global line.
- ▷ If the end of a line is reached before a certain length, ignore this line and save previous conditions.

3.2.2. Line restoration with simulated annealing

Simulated Annealing is a stochastic search procedure which seeks the minimum of a deterministic objective function. The algorithm is particularly suited for solving combinatorial optimization problems (Kirkpatrick *et al.*, 1983). Recently it has been shown that this method can be used for Bayesian Restoration of digital images (Geman, 1984).

In this approach, fault lines embedded in the original image are assumed to be a Markov Random Field with the underlying Gibbs Distribution on the two-dimensional image plane S

$$P(f) = \frac{1}{Z}\exp\left\{\frac{-E_f(f)}{T}\right\} \tag{2}$$

where Z is a normalizing constant (the partition function), T is a constant (the "algorithmic temperature" of the system), $E_f(f)$ is an "Energy Function" of the form

$$E_f(f) = \sum_{c\in\eta} V_c(f) \tag{3}$$

where the sum is over η, the second order neighborhood structure, in which a "cell" is defined as a pixel and its eight nearest neighbors (Figure 3). $V(f)$ are the "voltage" values assigned to the different states of a cell, according to the expected geometry of the searched lines.

The detected line elements are then considered as the noisy and incomplete observations of the fault lines. For the restoration of fault lines from the line elements a Maximum a Posteriori estimation scheme is used, which is shown to be appropriate for restoration of piecewise constant images (Geman, 1984).

Geman's model for the degraded image is assumed for the line elements;

$$G = \Psi(H(F), N) \tag{4}$$

where G represents the line elements detected (noisy observations), N is the independent white Gaussian noise, Ψ is the noise addition operation, and $H(F)$ represents the blurred fault lines in the original image, H being a local blurring function. With this model for the line elements, it can be shown that, the posterior distribution for the fault lines is also Gibbsian, in the form

$$P_p(f|g) = \frac{1}{Z_p}\exp\left\{\frac{-E_p(f,g)}{T}\right\} \tag{5}$$

where the lowercase letters are the realizations of the corresponding uppercase processes. For zero-mean white Gaussian noise, $E_p(f,g)$ reduces to;

$$E_p(f,g) = \sum_{c\in\eta} V_c(f) + \alpha\sum_{S}(f-g)^2 \tag{6}$$

where α is a constant reflecting the noise characteristics. The first term in Eq.(6) reflects the a priori information imposed in the restoration process, while the second term measures the quality of the estimate.

At this point, simulated annealing is used to find the optimal Maximum a Posteriori, MAP estimate by minimizing E_p. The idea is to visit every cell infinitely often and update its state, while iterating over the image. The temperature of the system is decreased on each iteration.

Geman and Geman showed that this algorithm converges to the global minima if T is decreased with the rate

$$T_k = C/log(k+1) \tag{7}$$

where k is number of iterations and C is constant.

The algorithm proceeds as follows:

▷ For k=0 to K, iterate while $T > T_0$ with $T_k = C/\log(k+1)$

▷ For $n = 1$ to $n = D/T_k$

▷ Randomly select a cell to visit,

▷ From the set of allowable states randomly choose a state S_{new}

▷ Compute the difference in energy $\Delta\ E_p$ caused by the state change from S_{old} to S_{new}

If $\Delta E_p \leq 0$ set the state to S_{new}

If $\Delta E_p > 0$ generate a random number r between 0 and 1,

If $r \leq \exp(-\Delta E_p/T_k)$ set the state to S_{new}

If $r > \exp(-\Delta E_p/T_k)$ leave the state at S_{old}

D is a constant that controls the time spent on each iteration.

Theoretically the optimum solution is reached at zero temperature, but experiments have shown that reasonable results are obtainable at higher temperatures, depending on the complexity of the image.

4. Experimental Results

The study area of this paper is the tectonically complex region of Southern California, including the San Andreas and Garlock faults around the Mojave plate. The original SIR-B image was obtained from Jet Propulsion Laboratory and consists of 2589 by 7044 pixels, where each pixel covers a 12.5 m. × 12.5 m. area, and is digitized in 256 gray levels. Fault scarps and valleys generally have widths of tens to hundreds of meters. In order to emphasize features of this scale 100 pixels of original image are averaged into one pixel to obtain a new image. This averaged image was used in the experiments (Figure 4).

Line elements detected as described in Section 3.1 are shown in Figure 5. To connect this elements first, the line following algorithm of Section 3.2.1 is used. Based on the a priori geologic information and the orientation of the San Andreas fault, greater weights are assigned to the north-west, south-east direction and to elements having one pixel width. Figure 6 shows the results along with the fault lines identified by experienced geologists.

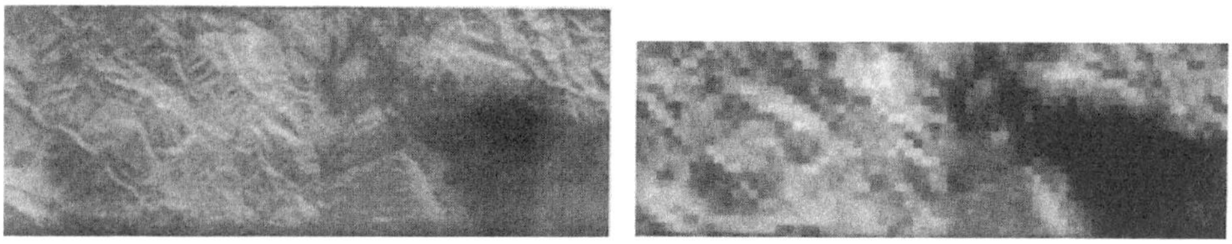

Figure 4: (a) Original SIR photograph. (b) Averaged image for experiments.

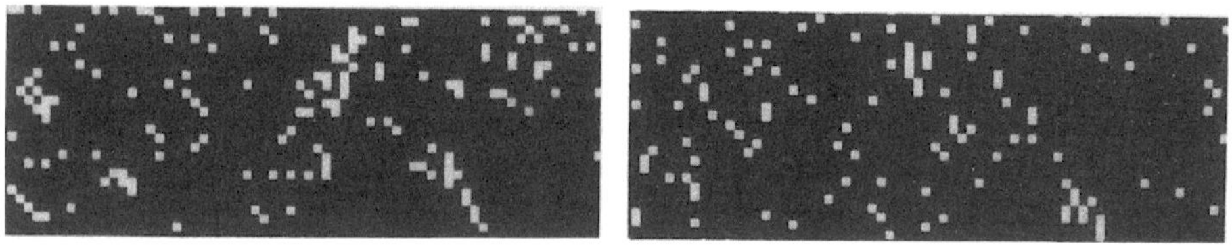

Figure 5: Line elements detected by (a) Mean gray value changes,
(b) Innovation changes.

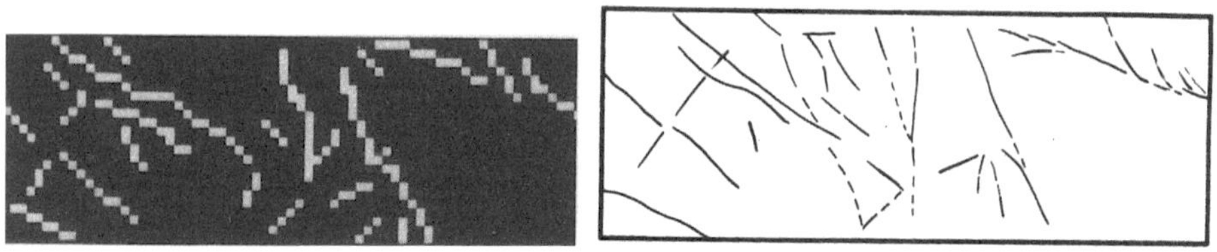

Figure 6: (a) Line following algorithm output. (b) Fault lines identified by geologists.

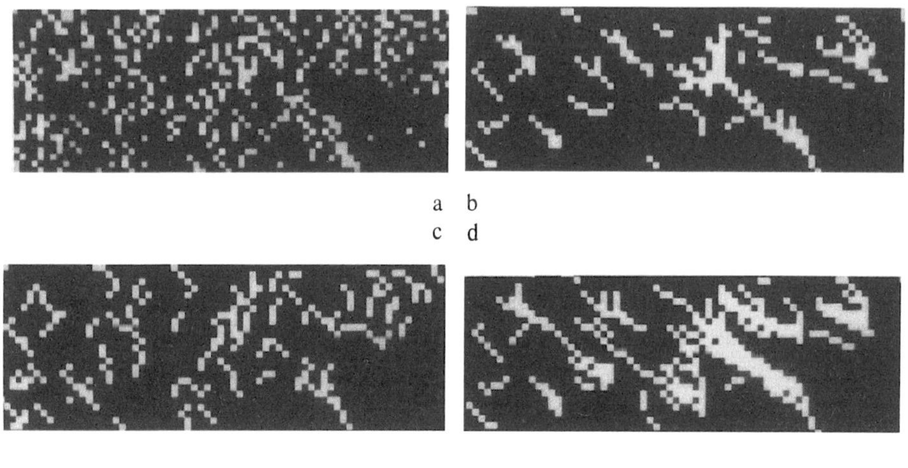

Figure 7: Lines restored with simulated annealing. (a) 25 iterations, T=2.12,
(b) 100 iterations, T=1.49, (c) 150 iterations, T=1.32, (d) 250 iterations, T=1.21.

The algorithm is quite successful in identifying both the major and many of the minor faults.

The application of simulated annealing for the line restoration is illustrated in Figure 7, where four snapshots show the results at different iterations and the associated temperatures. The values of constants in the implementation are $C = 4, D = 500$ and the initial temperature of $T_0 = 5$. When these results are compared with those shown in Figure 6, note that the major faults become identifiable in step c (150 iterations, T=1.32). Continuing the iterations (250, T=1.21) brings out the minor faults, but it also results in "over exposure" of major faults.

5. Conclusions

In this study we investigated different techniques for delineating geologic faults on Shuttle Imaging Radar (SIR-B) data. The two step approach that consists of line element detection followed by the line construction was successful. The best results were obtained by the line following algorithm that included a priori geologic information as constraints. The initial results from simulated annealing are promising. Its advantage is that it does not require very specific constraints, unlike the line following algorithm. Hence it can be applied to areas with little or even no a priori geologic information. It has a disadvantage that it is computationally slow, and the point at which to stop iterations with reasonable results changes from one image to another. We are still investigating this latter point with various images.

6. Acknowledgements

This research was supported by the grant NASA JPL Contract No. 956943. We would like to thank Jet Propulsion Laboratory for making the data available. We benefited greatly from the assistance and suggestions of Aykut Barka, Michael Prange and Joe Matarese.

References

[1] Basseville M., Espiau B., and Gasnier J., "Edge Detection Using Sequential Methods for Change in Level-Part l: A Sequential Edge Detection Algorithm," *IEEE Trans. Acoust., Speech, Signal Processing*, vol. ASSP-29, No.1, pp. 24-31, Feb. 1981.

[2] Brown R. G., *Introduction to Random Signal Analysis and Kalman Filtering*, John Wiley and Sons, 1983.

[3] Geman S. and Geman D., "Stochastic Relaxation, Gibbs Distributions, and The Bayesian Restoration of Images," *IEEE Trans. on Pattern Anal. Machine Intell.*, vol. PAMI-6, No.6, Nov. 1984.

[4] Kelly M., "Edge Detection by Computer Using Planning," *Machine Intell.*, vol. 6, Edinburgh, Scotland: Edinburgh Univ. Press, 1971.

[5] S. Kirkpatrick, C. D. Gellat, and M. P. Vecchi, "Optimization by Simulated Annealing," IBM Thomas J. Watson Res. Center, Yorktown Heights, NY, 1982

[6] Leondes C. T., "Theory and Applications of Kalman Filtering," University of California at Los Angeles, 1970.

[7] Martelli A., "Edge Detection Using Heuristic Search Methods," *Comput.Graphics Image Processing*, vol. 1, 1972.

[8] Toksoz M. N., Gulen L., Prange M., Matesrese J., Pettengil G. H. and Ford P. G., "Delineation of Fault Zones Using Imaging Radar," 1986.

[9] Ziony J. I., "Evaluating Earthquake Hazards in the Los Angeles Region; An Earth Science Perspective," P. 1360, Dept. of the Interior, USGS, Nov. 1985.

SPEECH RECOGNITION EXPERIMENT WITH 10,000 WORDS DICTIONARY

Hélène Cerf–Danon, Anne–Marie Derouault,
Marc El–Beze, Bernard Merialdo,
and Serge Soudoplatoff

IBM France Scientific Center
36 Avenue Raymond Poincaré
75116 Paris FRANCE

Keywords: Speech recognition, automatic dictation, hidden Markov model.

1. Introduction

Important progress has been achieved in Speech Recognition during the last ten years. Some small recognition tasks like vocal commands can now be accomplished, and more fundamental research involves the study and design of large vocabulary recognition. The research on Automatic Dictation is becoming very active, and recent realizations have shown very good performances. A key factor in the development of such Listening Typewriters is the ability to support Large Size Dictionary (LSD, several thousands words), or even Very Large Size Dictionaries (VLSD, several hundred of thousands words), because any restriction on the vocabulary is a restriction on potential users. This is even more important for inflected languages, such as French, because of the number of different forms for each lemma (on the average: 2.2 for English, 5 for German, 7 for French).

A crucial step has been done with the use of probabilistic methods arising from Information Theory, to model the great variability of natural speech. Since the beginning of this work by F. Jelinek in 1975, an increasing number of laboratories have brought their contributions to this mathematical formulation of the speech recognition problem.

In principle, this kind of probabilistic model is built from the statistical observation of the speech phenomenon, and requires little linguistic or phonetic knowledge. One of the greatest advantages is therefore the automatic learning from data.

Moreover, this principle applies to acoustic modeling as well as to linguistic modeling. It provides a unified viewpoint for all the levels of the recognition process.

In this paper, we report some experiments in Large Size Dictionary recognition in French.

NATO ASI Series, Vol. F30
Pattern Recognition Theory and Applications
Edited by P. A. Devijver and J. Kittler

2. Information Theoretic Point Of View

2.1. Communication Through Speech

The communication point of view towards the speech phenomenon leads to the following formulation: the speaker encodes a text string into sound features (source and channel coding); the sound is sent to a microphone, then processed to be compressed (acoustic channel), and at last the original text string is retrieved (linguistic decoding).

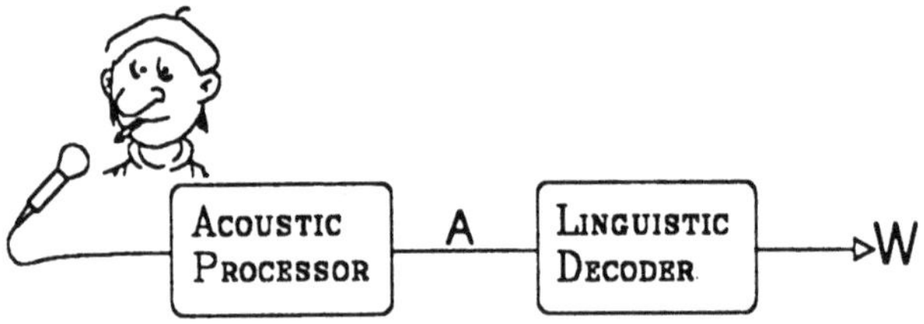

The linguistic decoder has to find the sentence W that has been pronounced, given the acoustic observation. The minimum error probability decoding consists in choosing the word sequence that minimizes the probability of error, which is equivalent to maximize the a-posteriori conditional probability $p(W/A)$. By Bayes' rule, this probability is equal to $p(A/W) \times p(W)/P(A)$. Since A does not depend on W, maximizing $p(W/A)$ over W, is equivalent to maximize the numerator $p(A/W) \times p(W)$. Therefore, a speech recognition system will be built around 4 components:

- ▷ The acoustic processor that converts the speech signal into the acoustic observation. This observation in defined by the various parameters that are chosen to be computed.
- ▷ A model of the acoustic channel that defines the probability $p(A/W)$. Generally, the probability for a sentence is computed from probabilities given by acoustic models of individual words.
- ▷ A language model that defines the probability $p(W)$.
- ▷ A decoding algorithm that finds the most probable sentence, (generally a sub-optimal search is performed, because of the combinatorial complexity of the problem).

The main interest of this probabilistic formulation, besides its strong theoretical background, is its flexibility, in the sense that different models can be used inside this framework.

2.2. Hidden Markov Models

A source producing symbols is frequently modelled by a "Markov Source": more precisely, a Markov Source is defined as follows:

1. A finite set of states, S,
2. A finite set of output symbols, called the alphabet A of the source.
3. A set of transitions, T, which is a subset of the product set $S \times A \times S$. In other words, a transition goes from one state to another while producing a symbol. For each state, there is a probability distribution on the transitions leaving it. These probabilities are the parameters of the source, and will be denoted by $q(s, a, s')$.

Most often, an initial state and a final state are specified among the states.

A Markov Source is also called "Hidden" Markov model, because a sequence of symbols might be produced by different sequences of states, and in general, the symbols are observed, but the state sequence is unseen.

The interest of this formulation is that, once the parameters are known, the probability of any path (transition sequence) can be computed as the product of the transition probabilities, and the probability of a symbol sequence is the sum of the probabilities of the paths that produce it. Moreover, training algorithms are available to automatically compute the parameters, and classical algorithms (Viterbi, Jelinek's Stack decoding) can be used to perform a graph search of the maximum likely path [4].

3. Dictation Experiment With 10,000 French Words

3.1. Conditions

The words in the dictionary are the 10,000 most frequent inflected forms in a large corpus of French texts.

The dictionary contains relevant information for each word, such as standard phonetic form, grammatical parts of speech, and frequency.

The system is single speaker. The sentences are from written letters, and are dictated in a syllable stressed mode, that is, with a slight pause between syllables. This dictating mode, which would be most unnatural for stressed languages like English, is appropriate for French: since the syllables are normally accentuated all the same way, it is very easy for a speaker to cut his sentence into syllables. Sometimes there are different possible split-ups, which are all allowed and taken into account by the system.

3.2. Acoustic Processing

In our system, speech is sampled at 10 kHz, with a 12 bits coding. Then we perform a Fourier transform on vectors corresponding to 12.8 ms speech windows. We keep the energy values in 20 frequency bands on the Mel scale. The vectors are then quantified, with a codebook of size 200. The acoustic observation is then a sequence of codewords (or numbers between 1 and 200), approximately 100 symbols per second.

3.3. Acoustic Modeling

We model the production of acoustic codewords with two embedded levels: each word is represented by a linear string of phonetic symbols, and each phoneme corresponds to a Markov Source. A Markov Source for a word is then a concatenation of phonetic machines. The model for a sentence is taken as the concatenation of the word machines. This allows to compute the acoustic probability $p(A/W)$ for a given observation and a sentence.

3.3.1. Word representation

Each word in the dictionary is represented as a sequence of phonemes (standard pronunciation), from a system of 36 phonemes. This phonetic representation includes the silence phoneme between the syllables. Two symbols are added to mark a vowel end (".v"), and a consonant end (".c"). Some words may have several representations, accounting for variants in the pronunciation, or in the syllable decomposition. With the .v and .c convention, it is easy to mark the French "liaison": When the final consonant is normally silent (like in "sont"), but pronounced if a vowel follows, the word will have two representations, one with .v at the end (no liaison) and one with the consonant at the end (without .c), indicating that since this consonant will be pronounced linked with the following vowel, there is no consonant end.

The apostrophe is treated in an analog way: for example "j' " (I in english) will be represented by "-J", while "je" will be "-JOE.v".

3.3.2. Phonetic sources

Each individual phoneme is represented by a Hidden Markov Model whose output symbols are the codewords from the vector quantizer.

All the phonetic machines have the same number of states (7), except the machine for silence, which has only 2 states. The figure below shows the structure of these sources:

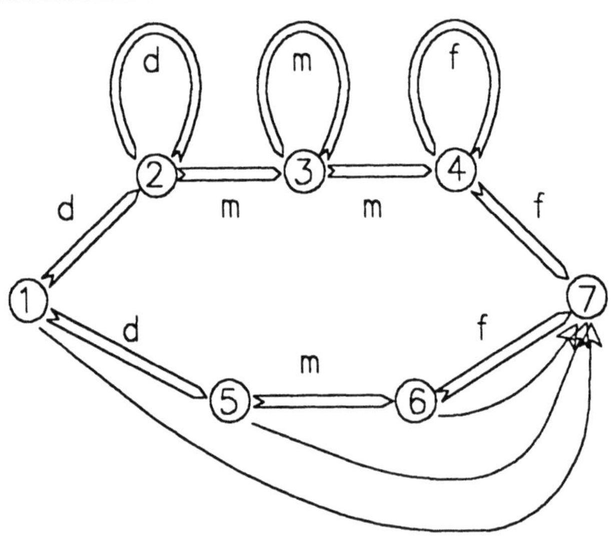

The double arrows represent 200 transitions, each of them emitting one of the 200 codewords. The simple arrows represent null transitions, which emit no symbol. The transitions (1,2), (2,2) and (1,5) are *tied* [4] by a distribution d, (initial part of the phoneme), so that their probabilities are of the form:

$$p(s,a,s') = q(s,s') \times q_d(a)$$

Similarly, the transitions (2,3), (3,3), (3,4), (5,6) are tied with the distribution m (middle of the phoneme), and (4,7), (4,4), (6,7) with the distribution f (final part of the phoneme).

3.3.3. Training

The transition probabilities, and output distributions, for each phonetic machine, are automatically adjusted from recorded data. The training is done on 410 known sentences, using the Forward-Backward (also known as Baum-Welch) algorithm.

We start from equiprobable distributions. The 90 first sentences have been segmented manually into phonemes. During the 5 first iterations, the Forward Backward algorithm is applied on these 90 sentences, with the segmentation constraint. This allows a good boot-strapping of the initial parameter values. Then 5 iterations are run on the whole corpus, without restriction on the segmentation. Deleted interpolation [4] is done to smooth the obtained distributions: the distributions d, m, f are linearly combined with equiprobable distributions. The weights are optimally chosen with the Forward Backward. More precisely, the training corpus is divided into three parts P1, P2, P3. For each part, the weights are computed according to the counts of the distributions in the two remaining parts. The weights are then added for the three parts and renormalized.

3.4. Language Model

As introduced in Section 1, the goal of the language model is to compute a probability for a word string. Of course, the notion of probability for a sentence is not well defined in an abstract way, and it can only be justified when referring to a given mathematical model.

Rigorously, the probability for a word to be produced, should depend conditionnally upon the whole past string. The probability of a word sequence W_1^n would be written as the product of conditional probabilities:

$$P(W_1^n) = P(W_1) \prod_{i=2}^{n} P(W_i/W_1^{i-1})$$

In practice, these probabilities would be difficult to estimate (from a huge corpus), and would require too much storage. As first proposed by F. Jelinek [4], a possible solution is to reduce the number of events, by defining an equivalence relation on the word strings.

In general, if the equivalence class of the past string is noted C_n, the probability of w given C_n will be estimated by the relative frequency $f(w/C_n)$ in a large training corpus of texts. The probabilistic structure of the set (classes, words, frequencies) can be expressed in terms of a Markov source, where the states are the equivalence classes, the output symbols are the words in the vocabulary, the transition probabilities are the frequencies.

The equivalence relation should be chosen to predict correctly the words, for the specific task. For a given corpus size, the coarser the classification is, the more reliable the prediction, but also less precise. If we have several classifications at our disposal, we can combine them, and linearly interpolate the probabilities arising from each of them. This interpolated estimation can be considered as arising from another Markov source, where a fictive state has been added for each classification. The weights are seen as particular parameters of this source, and can be optimized from text with the standard Forward Backward algorithm [1].

For our dictation experiment, we use the "tri-pos" language model which was elaborated to transcribe phonetic to French [2]. We will denote by "tri-POS" (respectively "bi-POS") a triplet (respectively a pair) of parts of speech. The Markov source modeling the production of a word is precisely defined as follows:

- ▷ The states are the pairs of parts of speech,
- ▷ the alphabet of symbols is the set of words in the dictionary,
- ▷ a transition between the states (p_1, p_2) and (p_2, p_3) is given by a word w_3 of part of speech p_3.

We first estimate the probability of such a transition by the product of the relative frequency of p_3 after (p_1, p_2), and the probability of the word w_3 given the POS p_3. This last distribution is stored in the dictionary for each word.

The corpus where the frequencies are collected contains 1.2 million words. In this corpus, 50,000 different triplets did occur, *i.e.*, 5% of all the possible triplets. This means that the frequencies obtained are not fully reliable. For example, if a triplet never occurred in the corpus, any sentence to be transcribed (at the decoding stage), which contains this triplet, will have zero probability. To take care of this problem, we consider another distribution based on a coarser classification given by the last part of speech. The frequencies $f(p_3/p_2)$ are also collected. This time, half of the possible pairs did occur, therefore the prediction based on them will be less precise, but more reliable. We take for final estimate of the probability to produce the part of speech p_3 after (p_1, p_2), a linear interpolation of the two frequency distributions. The final expression of the probability to produce the word w_3 from the state (p_1/p_2) is as follows:

$$p(w_3/p_1,p_2) = (\lambda_1 f(p_3/p_1,p_2) + \lambda_2 f(p_3/p_2)) \times k(w_3/p_3) + \epsilon$$

The ϵ (equal to 10^{-10}), has been added in all cases to prevent the probability from ever being zero, for in such a case all the sentences containing the triplet would also have zero probability. The weights λ are automatically adjusted [3].

3.5. Decoding

The tests were done on 80 new sentences, pronounced by the same speaker in a syllable stressed mode. The phonetic dictionary is organized in a arborescent way.

A Viterbi-like decoding algorithm performs a sub-optimal search of the most probable sentence. The error rate is automatically computed as the number of words incorrectly transcribed. This error rate is presently 12.5%. Here are typical examples of decoded sentences, with the errors in bold face and the solution in parenthesis:

le conseil d'administration se réunit une fois au moins tous les six mois sur convocation du président virgule ou sur la demande du quart de ses membres point **quand un** ("en cas") de partage virgule la voix du président **et** ("est") prépondérante point tout membre du conseil **si** ("qui") virgule sans excuse n' aura pas assisté à trois réunions consécutives **vous en a** ("pourra") être considérée comme démissionnaire

A part of the errors is due to the acoustic probability (like "quand un", "vous en a"), and another part is due to the linguistic probability (like "et"). Currently, the proportion is around 3/4, 1/4. This suggests that the next improvement can be obtained from the refinement of the system of phones, by taking into account some coarticulation effects.

References

[1] L. Baum, "An inequality and association maximization technique in statistical estimation for probabilistic function of Markov processes," *Inequality*, III, 1972.

[2] A.M. Derouault, B. Merialdo, J.L. Stehlé, "Automatic transcription of French stenotypy," *Linguisticae Investigationes*, Tome VII, 1983, Fascicule 2, Publisher John Benjamins B. V., Amsterdam.

[3] A.M. Derouault, B. Merialdo, "Language modeling at the syntactic level," *7th International Conference on Pattern Recognition*, August 1984, Montreal.

[4] F. Jelinek, L. R. Bahl, R. L. Mercer, "Continuous speech recognition: statistical methods," *Handbook of Statistics II*, H. P. Krishnaiah Ed., North Holland, 1982.

ADAPTIVE NETWORKS AND SPEECH PATTERN PROCESSING

John S. Bridle

Speech Research Unit
Royal Signals and Radar Establishment
Malvern England

Abstract
This is an introduction to and interpretation of some techniques which have been developed recently for pattern processing. The first part is concerned with the stochastic modelling approach to pattern recognition, which includes structural and statistical aspects. Various varieties of hidden Markov models, which are the basis of the most successful current automatic speech recognition systems, are viewed as a special case of Markov random fields. The second part is concerned with adaptive networks which "learn" to do jobs such as pattern classification, without necessarily containing explicit models of the data distributions. The main approaches covered are the Boltzmann machine (which is also interpreted as a Markov random field) and a recently invented multi-layer perceptron network.

1. Introduction

We start with some motivational background based on the author's experience in Automatic Speech Recognition (ASR) research, but most of the text is much more general. Indeed, many of the techniques described later were developed for machine vision or perceptual modelling of a general kind.

Three of the important characteristics of a pattern recognition system are: the amount and type of a-priori knowledge incorporated, the amount of automatic "tuning" based on examples, and the method of deciding on the identity (class) of any given unknown input pattern (inference).

Some would say that what we lack most in ASR is the use of speech knowledge. Yet there is a great deal of knowledge about speech available, and ASR is still very difficult. After many years of intense effort to build ASR systems based on available knowledge, the most successful systems today are almost an insult to Speech Science. Current ASR systems use very little a-priori knowledge: all the details are acquired automatically from "training" examples using rather sophisticated statistical estimation methods, and inference (usually Bayesian) is done using mathematical optimization algorithms.

There are several possible reasons for this state of affairs. I suggest that the following lessons can be taken, and can be expected to apply even when we know how to apply a great deal more prior knowledge to ASR.

NATO ASI Series, Vol. F30
Pattern Recognition Theory and Applications
Edited by P. A. Devijver and J. Kittler

Speech patterns are complicated. The relationship between acoustic speech patterns and the linguistic representations that are useful is very complicated. A speech recognition system must contain information about that relationship in general, and use it to infer a linguistic pattern which corresponds to the acoustic pattern. The main mistake made in many ASR attempts was to directly construct a system that performed the transformation directly. Today we use indirect methods for constructing the information about the relationship, and then use indirect methods for performing the transformation.

The lesson is that people cannot be expected to provide sufficiently detailed information about the relationship between sounds and words, and they certainly should not attempt to specify the details of a process to transform acoustic patterns into linguistic interpretations. Unless we have a clean separation between the knowledge and the search, then we will be left with a "program debugging" problem of horrendous proportions: because the behaviour of any non-trivial ASR system when exposed to a few minutes of speech is going to be fantastically complicated. We must be able to stand back from the details.

There will always be discrepancies between real speech patterns and the knowledge in the machine. Modern ASR systems gain much of their power from careful modelling of these discrepancies, and for this reason have been dubbed "ignorance-based systems" [1]. The most important thing to know about is the extent of one's ignorance.

The relationship between acoustic pattern and meaning is very complicated. We suspect that it would be useful to describe the relationship via several intermediate layers such as words. Speech Science provides several other useful-looking intermediate concepts, such as formant and phoneme. Unfortunately, when we come to apply such ideas we find them lacking in the kind of precise definition that we need.

We assume that in order to make progress in ASR we need to find new ways of describing the relationship between measurable and desired representations of speech patterns, which are not only more compatible with the nature of the relationship as we understand it from the results of speech science, but also compatible with powerful techniques for acquiring all the details automatically and for performing the inference. The above attitude is normally taken to be an alternative to the "expert systems" approach to difficult problems.

The methods described below are important because they include automatic procedures for making use of intermediate levels, even when these are provided in a very general form. Current techniques are able to do rather more than simply "tune" the detail of many continuous parameters of a model. They can also "learn" structure from examples. The main trick is to turn a structure learning problem into a parameter learning problem.

In the rest of this chapter we first briefly review various stochastic model based techniques, some of which are currently very popular in ASR. We then look at some other techniques which are worthy of consideration as the basis of ASR and other pattern recognition systems.

2. Stochastic Models

A Model is a representation of information about a class or set of classes of patterns. A Stochastic system is one that evolves in time or space according to probabilistic laws [2]. In a stochastic model the patterns are treated as if they are outputs of a stochastic system. Information about the classes of patterns is encoded as the structure of the "laws" and the probabilities that govern their operation.

The class of stochastic models thus includes, at two extremes, both simple probability distributions (such as discrete and multi-dimensional Gaussian) and structural models such as grammars.

Note that the decision to use a particular type of stochastic model as the basis of an ASR system does not necessarily imply a belief that speech patterns ARE the output of such a stochastic system. Although we may believe that there is a truly random element in the variability of the patterns we have to deal with, the main point is to sweep up all the many remaining un-modelled details in an allegedly random process, so that they will not be forgotten completely.

A SM defines a distribution of patterns for each class. For any given observation and class, the model defines the probability of generating that observation. It is useful to think of the internal structure of the model as encoding some of the higher-order statistics of the distributions.

2.1. Markov Random Fields

The Markov Random Field [3] can be used as a very general formulation of knowledge about the relationship between different levels of description, such as measurable data and desired labels. The dependence of the labels on the data can be expressed via intermediate variables, the agreement of any labelling with the data and the built-in knowledge is well defined, and any suitable search procedure can be used to find the best labelling.

A general search method for MRFs is the Gibbs Sampler, which uses a Metropolis Monte-Carlo method to produce samples from the posterior distribution (*i.e.*, given the data). Note that this algorithm is itself stochastic: not to be confused with the stochastic nature of the model. For special types of MRF there are alternative algorithms for search and for parameter tuning which may be preferred. For instance, for continuous-valued states and Gaussian dependencies the log-likelihood is a quadratic function of the state, and finding the single global optimum is a linear problem [4].

Another simple type of MRF has binary site states and no higher than pairwise dependencies (clique sizes 1 and 2). The Gibbs Sampler can use a direct sampling from the local characteristics of a single site. The resulting special kind of MRF is known as a Boltzmann machine (BM), and is considered in more detail later. There is a learning algorithm (the +/− procedure) for the pairwise dependencies.

If we restrict the topology of a MRF to a one-dimensional "backbone" of connected sites, possibly with other sites hanging off them, then it is possible to use Dynamic Programming and related algorithms. If the 1-D MRF is also homogeneous, then the position along the backbone can be used to represent time in a sequence. The backbone sites then correspond to the values taken at each time by the internal state of a "Hidden

Markov Model", and the dangling sites can represent observations. Such structures have been applied very successfully to speech recognition.

2.2. Hidden Markov Models

For HMMs it is usual to work not with the symmetrical MRF formulation, but an asymmetrical one which emphasizes the dependence of the internal state on the state at the previous time, and the dependence of the observations on the corresponding state, in a state transition matrix and a set of output distributions respectively.

In a Hidden Markov Model the machine is supposed to proceed through a sequence of states which are not directly observed. The state sequence is a first-order Markov Chain. The output of the model at each position in the observed sequence is a probabilistic function of the state sequence. There are two alternative conventions used in Hidden Markov Modelling: each observation depends on the corresponding state in one formulation, and on a transition between two states in the other formulation. We shall use the former convention. The output distributions can be discrete (multinomial) or continuous with parameters (*e.g.*, multi-variate Gaussian). HMMs are currently particularly popular for modelling the relation between words and acoustic data.

In a Hidden Semi Markov Model (or explicit state dwell HMM, or variable duration HMM) [5], each state visit generates not one but a sequence of observations, and this sequence of observations is drawn from a distribution which depends on the state. As an example, consider a HSMM in which each state visit generates an output length, from a distribution characteristic of the state, then chooses each of the symbols in a string of that length independent of one another. If an ordinary (synchronous-output) HMM is allowed transitions from each state to itself, then it is equivalent to such a HSMM in which all the output duration distributions are geometric.

2.3. Stochastic Grammars

The stochastic generalization of a conventional (formal) grammar is called a stochastic grammar [6]. In a stochastic grammar every production rule has a probability associated with it. The probabilities for all the productions with the same left hand side must sum to unity. Associated with any derivation of a string is a probability which is the product of the probabilities of the productions used in the derivation. The probability of the grammar producing a given string is the sum of the probabilities of all the derivations of the string. Formal grammars of the class called regular grammars are equivalent to finite state automata and transition networks. Stochastic regular grammars are equivalent to probabilistic finite state automata and to hidden Markov models.

Context-free grammars are more powerful than regular grammars. Each instance of a non-terminal symbol gives rise to a sub-string of the observations, and these sub-strings form a hierarchy. Stochastic context-free grammars are thus a generalization of HMMs. Using Baker's "nodal span" principle it is possible to generalize the algorithms for tuning and using HMMs so that they can be used for SCFGs [7].

3. Summary of Main Algorithms for Stochastic Models

3.1. Pattern Generation

The most natural way to operate most stochastic models is to synthesize an instance of a pattern of a given class (driven by a random number generator). For HMMs the generator is obvious enough: choose a new state with a probability determined by the old state and the state transition matrix, then generate an "observation" by sampling from the appropriate output distribution. For more general MRFs we can use the Gibbs Sampler.

3.2. Pattern Recognition

In pattern recognition we infer an explanation of the data in terms of the model. Typically we wish to maximize the probability of the explanation given the observations. Dynamic programming can be used to find the best (most likely) explanation of the data in terms of a given model for HMMs and SCFGs. The forward-backward algorithm for HMMs will compute the total likelihood of the data given a model, and also the likelihood of each state at each time. The corresponding algorithm for SCFGs [7] has been called the inside-outside algorithm. For more general MRFs the Gibbs Sampler can be applied to sample from the posterior distribution. The maximum a-posteriori interpretation can be found by sharpening this distribution slowly using the control parameter, T (*i.e.*, Optimization by Simulated Annealing) .

3.3. Parameter Tuning

The other important automatic operation is tuning the model: probabilities or parameters of distributions are adjusted to increase the fit of the model (generated distribution) to the training data (observed distribution). Available algorithms include the Baum-Welch iteration for HMMs, which uses the results of the forward-backward algorithm. The Boltzmann Machine Learning Algorithm will tune the weights of a binary-valued, pairwise-interacting MRF expressed in Gibbs form, and extensions apply to more general MRFs.

3.4. Model Specification

Finally, we must consider what means exist to allow us to set up the structure and initial values of the parameters based on our knowledge, insight, and prejudices. It is usual to specify the bare minimum when using HMMs (number of states, and form of output distributions). If some values of the state transition matrix are initially zero they will remain zero in the Baum-Welch iteration. One common state transition matrix restriction is tri-diagonal: the states are ordered, and each transition is to the same state, next state or next-but-one.

4. Adaptive Networks

As an alternative to explicit models plus algorithms for tuning and recognition, we can attempt to construct a "recognizer" directly. We still leave all the details to a learning algorithm, but instead of learning the parameters of a model, it learns the parameters of a recognition process.

A simple example is the adaptive linear binary discriminator, which adjusts a hyperplane to separate two classes of patterns. This is different from the corresponding "stochastic model" approach, with a separate model for distribution for each class, which would end up with a linear hyperplane decision surface if the two class distributions were taken as multivariate normal with equal covariance matrices[8].

Linear threshold units can be used to compute any boolean logic function. Unfortunately, the only useful learning algorithms are applicable only to a single layer of linear threshold units, (the inputs and the desired outputs of the adapting units have to be specified during training).

The other well-known adaptive network is the adaptive linear filter, which can be deployed on various signal-processing problems, including adaptive equalization and echo cancellation. It is closely related to the Kalman filter and to "linear predictive analysis" which has been in vogue for speech signal analysis. The problem here is that non-linearity is necessary for decision making, and if internal units are to be worth having.

The functions computed by the "building blocks" of both the above are very similar in form. First a weighted sum of input values is formed. This is transformed by a transfer function which is a threshold at zero, or the identity. (A variable threshold is achieved by including an input which always has unit value.)

Since the publication of Minsky and Papert's book "Perceptrons" [9] it has been generally believed that no learning algorithm was possible for multi-layer non-linear classification networks. However, some types have been found recently. The Boltzmann Machine (see below) is really very different from a standard multi-layer perceptron network, in that all connections are bi-directional and operation is stochastic. However, the back-propagation procedure of Rummelhart, Hinton and Williams [10] can now be seen as a natural generalization of the adaptation methods used for the threshold and linear units, and it works (though not infallibly) for multi-layer networks.

Rummelhart Networks: a solution to the multi-layer perceptron training problem

The first trick is to choose a transfer function intermediate between linear and a hard threshold. The output of a "semilinear" unit is a differentiable function of the net input. A suitable simple "soft-threshold" non-linearity is the hyperbolic tangent compression function,

$$L(x) = \frac{1}{2}(1 + \tanh x) = \frac{1}{1 + e^{-x}}$$

Assuming that all the inputs, to the jth unit can be treated as if they are the outputs, O, of other units, we have

$$I_j = \sum_i W_{ij} O_i \quad \text{and} \quad O_j = L(I_j)$$

This is applied to all the units. The learning procedure is simplified in the case of feed-forward layered networks, in which $i < j$.

We shall need the derivative of the non-linearity later:

$$\frac{dO_j}{dI_j} = L'(I_j) = O_j(1 - O_j)$$

in the case of the particular transfer function defined above.

The aim of the learning rule is to find a set of weights that minimizes the discrepancy between the outputs of the complete network and the target outputs supplied with the training patterns. The error to be minimized is

$$E = \frac{1}{2}\sum_c\sum_j(O_{jc} - D_{jc})^2$$

where O_{jc} is the output of unit j and D_{jc} the desired output of unit j for the cth training pattern. The sum is over those units whose outputs we are interested in.

The principle is to compute the derivative of E with respect to each weight, and perform a gradient descent on the error in weight space [10]. The chain rule for differentiation is used repeatedly.

Starting at the output, the back-propagation pass computes

$$e_j = \frac{\partial E}{\partial O_j} = O_j - D_j$$

$$f_j = \frac{\partial E}{\partial I_j} = e_j\frac{\partial O_j}{\partial I_j} = e_jL'(I_j) = e_jO_j(1 - O_j)$$

$$d_{ij} = \frac{\partial E}{\partial W_{ij}} = f_jO_i$$

$$e_i = \frac{\partial E}{\partial O_i} = \sum_j\frac{\partial E}{\partial I_j}\frac{\partial I_j}{\partial O_i} = \sum_j f_jW_{ij}$$

etc.

The weights are changed by an amount proportional to $-\frac{\partial E}{\partial W}$, to decrease the error. In principle, such gradient methods are prone to stick in local minima of E, but in practice this is apparently not a big problem.

As a very simple example of a problem that needs intermediate units, consider the exclusive OR. The back-propagation procedure can learn various solutions if given at least one intermediate unit.

Further examples, such as encoders and shifters, can be found in [10].

The BP method can be extended to "recurrent" networks (no restrictions on connections) and can then learn a structure which has dynamic responses.

5. Boltzmann Machines

The Boltzmann Machine [11]–[14] is a combination of ideas from (or relevant to) several diverse fields, including: combinatorial optimization, statistical mechanics, information theory, neural network modelling, machine vision, parallel computing, and associative memory modelling.

In a Boltzmann Machine, knowledge for perception is stored as the pattern and strengths of connections in a network of simple decision units, each of which can be thought of as dealing with one "elementary hypothesis". The connections encode knowledge about the relationship between these elementary hypotheses, and between the EHs and the input and output. The "perceptual" process then amounts to searching for states of the network (combinations of EHs) which correspond to good (plausible, likely) interpretations of the current input pattern.

The "goodness" is measured in terms of an "energy", E, (lowest energy is best) composed of pairwise interactions between the states of the units.

$$E = \frac{1}{2} \sum_{i,j} s_i s_j W_{ij}$$

where s_i is 1 if the ith unit is ON, and 0 otherwise, and W_{ij}, the i, j "weight", is the strength of the connection between units i and j. E is therefore the sum of the weights joining "active" units. Each unit has a connection to a permanently ON unit to provide a threshold.

Input data is applied by "clamping" the states of some of the units, and the output of the network is the states of some of the other units. The remaining units help to relate the input and output.

As a very simple example of how information might be represented in such a network, consider Figure 1. Connections with arrows have positive weights (reinforcing, excitatory) which tend to make both units come on together. Connections with circles have negative weights (inhibitory) which tend to suppress one unit if the other is ON. The unconnected circles are biases (all negative in this case) which can be treated as weights to a permanently-ON unit.

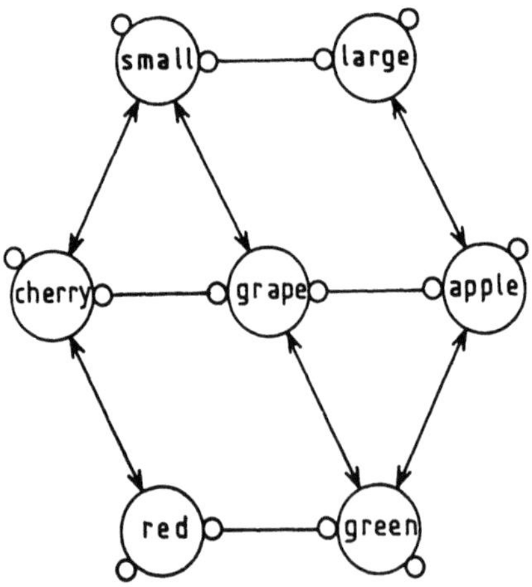

Figure 1: A very simple constraint satisfaction network

The network can be thought of as expressing logical relationships, such as "cherries are red", and "something cannot be both small and large". However, in line with the

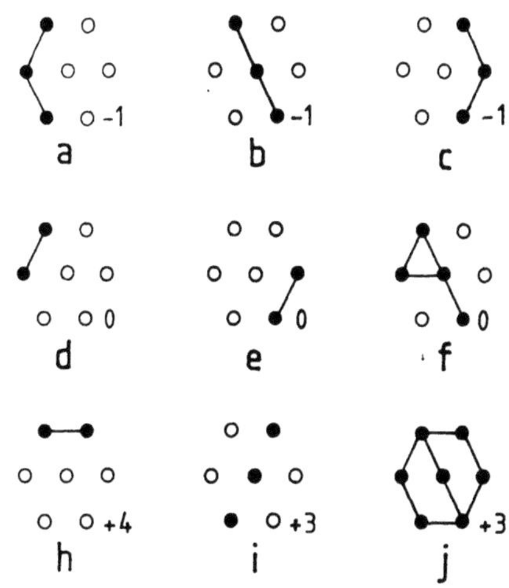

Figure 2: Energies for some global states

fact that not all cherries are red, the global (energy) evaluation principle simple scores any possible configuration as more or less plausible.

Figure 2 shows the energies for some representative global states, for the case that all the weights are plus or minus two and the biases are -1. The minimum energy states correspond to complete statements that are acceptable (2a–c). Slightly higher energy states correspond to partial or somewhat conflicting "interpretations" (2d–f) while the highest-energy states are meaningless.

The "recognition" search is performed by repeatedly doing the following:

▷ pick a unit at random (say i);

▷ compute E_i, the difference between values of E with unit i ON and OFF, (Clearly $E_i = \sum_j s_j W_{ij}$);

▷ set unit i ON with probability $(1 + \exp\{E_i/T\})^{-1}$.

When this process has reached equilibrium at a fixed value of T the distribution of states of the complete network is a Boltzmann (Gibbs) distribution, where:

$$\frac{P(A)}{P(B)} = \exp\{-(E_A - E_B)/T\},$$

where A, B are global states with energies E_A and E_B respectively.

At equilibrium at some fixed temperature (say $T = 1$), the probabilities of the global states can be taken as a model of the co-occurrence of the features coded for by the units, and the network is a stochastic model: in fact it is a Markov random field in Gibbs distribution form.

If $T = 0$, then only "downhill" steps will be chosen. The system then falls into a (local) minimum of E. To improve the chances of ending in a good minimum, we start with a high value of T and reduce it slowly. Depending on the application, we may wish to retain the information contained in the distribution of states of the output units when $T = 1$, or obtain a single interpretation of the data, at $T = 0$, or the output of a set of separate "annealings" to $T = 0$.

The similarity to the Markov Random Field is evident. The difference in the local decision rule may be puzzling at first. It is just that with 1/0 states it is possible to sample exactly from the local characteristics:

$$\frac{P(s_i = 1)}{P(s_i = 0) + P(s_i = 1)} = \frac{\exp\{(-E_0 + E_i)/T\}}{\exp\{-E_0/T\} + \exp\{(E_0 + E_i)/T\}}$$
$$= \frac{\exp\{-E_i/T\}}{1 + \exp\{-E_i/T\}} = \frac{1}{1 + \exp\{E_i/T\}}$$

where E_0 is the global energy with $s_i = 0$, and $E_0 + E_i$ is the global energy with $s_i = 1$.

For an analysis of the BM in terms of Bayesian inference see [15].

There is a "learning algorithm" for adapting the weights so that the responses of the network to given classes of stimuli tend to be correct. The learning rule is derived by differentiating an information-theoretic measure of the agreement of the statistics of the output with the statistics of the desired output [12], but the form of the rule is similar to the perceptron one, and is very reminiscent of proposals for the function of dream sleep.

Define C_{ij}^- as the proportion of the time that $s_i = s_j = 1$ at equilibrium at $T = 1$ while example inputs are being applied, and C_{ij}^+ as the corresponding quantity while in addition the output units are being clamped to the desired states. Then changing W_{ij} in proportion to $(C_{ij}^+ - C_{ij}^-)$ will tend to make the outputs agree with the desired outputs.

To see how this might be so, note that if i and j are not coming on together enough then $C_{ij}^- < C_{ij}^+$, and we need to increase W_{ij}. When the outputs are correct then $C_{ij}^+ = C_{ij}^-$ for all i, j, so no change is needed.

See reference [11] for several cunningly chosen examples in which "intermediate concepts" are "discovered" by the learning algorithm when applied to multi-layer BMs.

The style of computation is very unusual in a technological system: inherently massively parallel, very simple processing units (noisy threshold), dominated by connections. An adaptive network needs only simple computation in the connections. There is no central control, except for the plus/minus state decision. There are suggestive relationships to neurophysiology, psychology, novel processing architectures, and device physics.

There are many problems associated with the practical use of BMs, particularly speed of convergence of the learning algorithm, and scaling properties. Another problem is opacity: it does not seem possible to obtain explanations of decisions, or intelligible descriptions of what has been learnt. However, it has been argued [16] that the best representations of concepts in a learning network are distributed — a concept is coded as a pattern of activity of many individual elementary hypothesis units. In that case we should abandon the desire to understand the system in detail and seek "higher-level" types of understanding. The energy/likelihood notion is an important tool in this respect [17].

Many of the interesting properties of BMs are shared with Rummelhart networks. However, BMs share with MRFs in general the appealing property that they are initially neutral with respect to the direction of information flow: the network encodes information about the joint distribution of patterns of inputs and outputs, and the Gibbs Sampler produces a distribution of inputs and outputs conditioned by whatever patterns we choose to impose: if we specify an input we will get a distribution of class labels at the output, but if we specify an output we will get examples of that class of patterns projected onto the input units. In fact there is no real distinction between inputs and outputs, and the action of the BM is more naturally regarded as completion of a partially-specified pattern.

Perhaps the main lessons that have been learnt from BMs are that there is a great deal more mileage left in the old, almost dead, subject of adaptive networks, and the possibility of much fruitful connection between the two quantities both called entropy, as defined in statistical physics and in information theory.

6. Applications to Speech

The adaptive network techniques described above are very new, and examples of their application to speech and other realistic problems are only just beginning to emerge [18,19,20].

NETtalk [18] is an apparently successful demonstration of the use of the back-propagation method in a significant existing problem, although it is not claimed to produce better results than the established hand-crafting technique. Sejnowski and Rosenberg have demonstrated automatic acquisition of knowledge about the correspondence between letters in sequence in an English text and the phonemes appropriate for speaking the text. About 100 hidden units and nearly 10000 weights were used. The system was demonstrated by passing the output phoneme string to an existing speech synthesis system.

The author has sought to understand the newer methods presented here because of a dissatisfaction with the limitations imposed on the formulation of speech knowledge by the requirements of the Markov property, which is necessary in order to be able to use Dynamic Programming and the related algorithms [14]. We can expect some interesting developments as the new techniques, perhaps in partnership with the old, and guided by knowledge from speech science, allow our systems to discover and use higher-order and non-linear relationships implicit in our data.

References

[1] J.Makhoul and R.Schwartz, "Ignorance modelling," in J.Perkell and D.Klatt eds., *Invariance and Variability in Speech Processes*, Erlbaum, 1986, pp. 344–345.

[2] D.R.Cox and H.D.Millar, *The Theory of Stochastic Processes*, Methuen, 1965.

[3] S.Geman and D.Geman, "Stochastic relaxation, Gibbs distributions, and the Bayesian restoration of images," *IEEE Trans. on Pattern Analysis and Machine Intelligence*, vol. PAMI–6, no.6, November 1984, pp. 721–741.

[4] T.Poggio *et al.*, "Computational vision and regularization theory," *Nature*, Vol. 317, 26, Sept. 1985.

[5] M.R.Russell and R.K.Moore, "Explicit modelling of state occupancy in hidden Markov models for automatic speech recognition," *IEEE ICASSP-85*.

[6] S.E.Levinson, "A Unified theory of composite pattern analysis for automatic speech recognition," in F.Fallside and W.Woods eds., *Computer Speech Processing*, Prentice Hall, 1984.

[7] J.K.Baker, "Trainable grammars for speech recognition," Speech communication papers for the 97th meeting of the Acoust. Soc. Amer., D.H.Klatt & J.J.Wolf eds. 1979, pp. 547–550.

[8] J.S.Bridle, "Pattern recognition techniques for speech recognition," in *Spoken Language Generation and Understanding*, NATO ASI Series, Reidel, pp. 129–145.

[9] M.Minsky and S.Papert, *Perceptrons: An Introduction to Computational Geometry*, M.I.T. Press, 1969.

[10] D.E.Rummelhart, G.E.Hinton and R.J.Williams, "Learning internal representations by error propagation," ICS Report 8506, University of California, San Diego, Sept. 1985.

[11] G.E.Hinton, T.J.Sejnowski and D.H.Ackley, "Boltzmann machines: constraint satisfaction networks that learn," Technical Report CMU-CS-84-119, Carnegie-Mellon University, May 1984.

[12] D.H.Ackley, G.E.Hinton and T.J.Sejnowski, "A learning algorithm for Boltzmann machines," *Cognitive Science*, 9, 1985, pp. 147–168.

[13] G.E.Hinton, "Learning in parallel networks," *BYTE*, April 1985, pp. 265–273.

[14] J.S.Bridle and R.K.Moore, "Boltzman machines for speech pattern processing," *Proc. Inst. Acoust.*, Nov. 1984, pp. 1–8.

[15] G.E.Hinton and T.J.Sejnowski, "Optimal perceptual inference," *Proc. IEEE Computer Soc. Conf. on Computer Vision and Pattern Recognition*, Washington, D.C., June 1983, pp. 448–453.

[16] G.Hinton, "Distributed representations," Dept. Computer Science, Carnegie-Mellon University, Pittsburgh, Oct. 1984.

[17] J.A.Feldman, "Energy and behavior in connectionist models," Rochester U., CS Tech. Rep. TR155, Nov.1985.

[18] T.J.Seinowski, and C.R.Rosenberg, "NETtalk: A parallel network that learns to read aloud," Johns Hopkins U., EE&CS Tech. Rep. JHU/EECS–86/01, 1986.

[19] J.F.Traherne *et al.*, "Speech processing with a Boltzmann machine," *IEEE ICASSP-86*, Tokyo, pp. 725–728.

[20] R.G.Prager *et al.*, "Boltzmann machines for speech recognition," *Computer Speech and Language*, Vol.1, No.1, 1986.

ENERGY METHODS IN CONNECTIONIST MODELLING

Jerome A. Feldman

Computer Science Department
The University of Rochester
Rochester, NY 14627, U.S.A.

Abstract

Massively parallel (connectionist) computational models are playing an increasingly important role in cognitive science. Establishing the behavioral correctness of a connectionist model is exceedingly difficult, as it is with any complex system. For a restricted class of models, one can define an analog to the energy function of physics and this can be used to help prove properties of a network. This paper explores energy and other techniques for establishing that a network meets its specifications. The treatment is elementary, computational, and focuses on specific examples. No free lunch is offered.

1. Introduction

Massive parallel (connectionist) models are playing an increasingly important role in cognitive science and are beginning to be employed more widely. The success of initial exploratory studies has led to efforts to systematize and analyze this style of computation. One important aspect of this effort involves the use of formal techniques to specify the required behavior of a model and to verify that the realization meets the stated requirements.

While the verification of complex computational systems has a long history within computer science, these efforts have not led to significant benefits in the design or performance of computer software. Similarly, verification of computer hardware arose as a topic in artificial intelligence and is not part of the normal design cycle. There is currently a mood of greatly reduced expectations among researchers in formal verification.

It is not realistic to assume that we will be able to provide complete specifications for complex connectionistic models any better than we can for traditional programs such as operating systems on digital computers, or for digital circuits. This is certain to hold for the complex connectionist models needed to study such intelligent behaviors as vision and language.

Granting that formal specification and proof will not be feasible for complex models, there are still several reasons for exploring these ideas. It is feasible to characterize subsystems, and these can then be used with confidence in larger projects. The attempt to specify formally a sub-system is often of considerable heuristic value in itself, and the verification process inevitably leads to insights and often uncovers errors in design.

NATO ASI Series, Vol. F30
Pattern Recognition Theory and Applications
Edited by P. A. Devijver and J. Kittler

In addition, having an explicit goal of formal specification and verification influences the choice of primitive units used in a model, how they are connected, and the rules of timing and data transmission assumed.

This paper explores the "energy" formulations modeled on statistical mechanics. All of the models considered share the notions of a large network of simple computing units joined by links of varying numeric weights. We are beginning to understand the computational basis of the success of connectionist models (CMs) and that this success is fairly robust over a variety of choices in details. The two central ideas are the use of numerical parameters and the simultaneous utilization of all relevant information at points of decision. Numerical values can be looked upon as providing *evidence* for various propositions or states of the system and have proved to be useful on problems that have proved difficult in formalisms based on logic and symbolic parameters. Evidential inference does not require parallel treatment, but there does seem to be a natural fit which is well captured by connectionist models. The network form emphasizes the *interaction* among contributing factors rather than isolating them as rule-based formulations tend to do. The implied computational rule, shared by all CMs, is that *all* of the inputs to a given unit be combined to yield its output value. The following definitions attempt to capture the key ideas shared by CMs while leaving open the precise form of combination and propagation rules.

The general computational form of a *unit* in our models will be comprised of:

▷ $\{Q\}$ – a set of discrete *states* < 10

▷ P – a continuous value in $[-10, 10]$ called *potential*

▷ X – an output *value* $-1 \leq X \leq 10$

▷ D – a vector of data inputs $d_1 \ldots d_n$

and functions from old to new value of these:

$$\begin{aligned} P &\leftarrow f(D, P, Q) \\ Q &\leftarrow g(D, P, Q) \\ X &\leftarrow h(D, P, Q) \end{aligned} \tag{1}$$

The form of the f, g, and h functions and the precise rule for updating them will vary within this paper and can entail probabilistic functions. Some of the notation will be suppressed when it is not needed, e.g., we will sometimes have X identically equal to P and will also sometimes refer to the inputs to a unit by X_j, the output of a predecessor unit.

Most models use only potentials in the range $[-1, 1]$ and outputs in the range $[0, 1]$. Some authors [Smolensky, 1986; Selman & Hirst, 1985] find it technically convenient to use outputs of ± 1 while acknowledging that negative outputs do not map well to biology. Others, particularly at Rochester, emphasize the limited dynamic range of neural signals by restricting outputs to be integers in the range $[0, 10)$ while allowing continuous valued potentials. None of the issues addressed in this paper are effected by such considerations.

More generally, there is (already) a significant range of connectionist models with varying goals and assumptions. The work on CM models overlaps a much broader area of parallel algorithms, particularly for constrained optimization problems. The distinguishing characteristic of connectionistic models is the requirement that all decisions be computable in distributed fashion by simple computing units. The biological or electronic plausibility of a given model is of second-order concern here, but will be given some attention.

The definitions above are essentially the same as those given in [Feldman & Ballard, 1982]. The hope there was that the definitions would be sufficiently general to accommodate all connectionist paradigms and, so far, through a rich variety of subsequent efforts, this has essentially held. The major difference here is that I explicitly allow continuous valued output functions, whereas they were discouraged in the earlier version. Continuous output values are unrealistic for most neural computation, but are harmless if the model does not depend on the fine structure of the values. The question of the exact rule for timing the updates of P, Q, and X is a critical one for formal treatment of behavior. The original definitions specified a strictly synchronous rule, and most energy models rely on a strictly asynchronous rule. What one would like is a methodology which is oblivious to the form of the update rule. This issue is discussed further in Section 3. One additional condition that might be made part of the definition is that the h function specifying the output be a monotonically increasing function of the potential. All models have satisfied this constraint and it is probably time to canonize it. Potential is used to capture an internal level of activity and the external activity should increase with potential for both computational clarity and biological verisimilitude.

In this paper, a number of particularizations will be employed because many results hold only for special choices. All of our examples in Sections 1 and 2 will have only one state so that parameter Q will be supressed for now. The first system to be examined is composed entirely of binary linear threshold units. Each unit has an output equal to its potential of 0 or 1. The potential and output are computed by the rule:

$$\begin{aligned} P_i &= \sum w_{ji} X_j - \theta_i \\ X_i &= \texttt{if } P_i > 0 \texttt{ then } 1 \texttt{ else } 0 \end{aligned} \tag{2}$$

where w_{ji} are *weights* of either sign. This is essentially the standard perceptron [Minsky & Papert, 1969] and has been used as the basis for much current work, e.g., [Ackley *et. al.*, 1985]. A simple illustration of how such units might be employed is given in Figure 1, which is a vastly oversimplified version of the word recognition network of [McClelland & Rumelhart, 1981]. The idea is to have recognizing units for letters in different positions (I_1, T_2) that are linked to units that recognize words ("IT"). One could have, e.g., all the weights be 1 and have the rule for "IT" be

$$X_{IT} = X_{I_1} + X_{T_2} - 1$$

so that "IT" would be recognized just when it should be. The major concern of this chapter is formalizing the notion of a connectionist network "doing what it should," and we will see that this is not usually straightforward.

The Goodness/Energy Paradigm

One promising approach to proving the correctness of networks is based on the notion of a global "goodness" or "energy" measure [Hopfield, 1982; Ackley *et al.*, 1985; Smolensky, 1986]. These notions are usually motivated by analogies from statistical mechanics but do not require such treatment. The basic idea is quite simple—one would like to find a global measure that could be shown to decrease every time an appropriate change was made to the potential and output of a unit in the network. Should we be able to establish such a measure, and if it is bounded in value, then the networks will always converge. A locally monotonic goodness measure can also be used probabilistically to search for solutions of more complex problems. The remarkable fact is that, under a specific set of assumptions, such a measure can be established. We will proceed by pulling a goodness measure out of a hat and then show how and why it works.

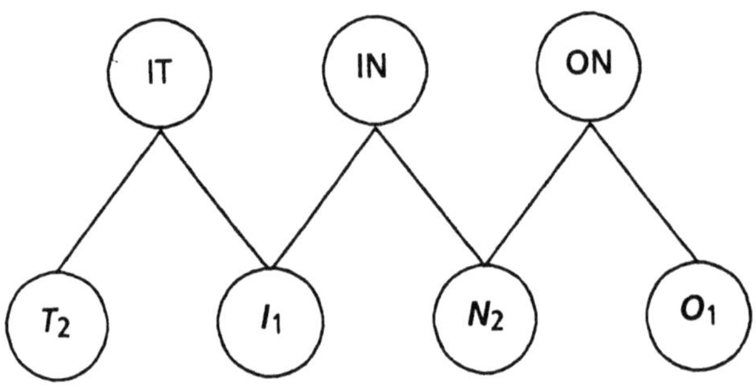

Figure 1: A network fragment for recognizing three 2–letter words

We will first assume the goodness measure G for a network is the sum of contributions G_i from its individual units. For each unit, its contribution will consist of terms describing its interactions with other elements of the network. For convenience we consider the threshold terms and any external inputs to be from extra units whose outputs never change (cf. Figure 2). In this case, the contribution of unit i and the total for the network are given by:

$$G_i = X_i \sum_j w_{ji} X_j \text{ and } G = \sum_i G_i \tag{3}$$

First notice that $G_i = 0$ if $X_i = 0$; a unit that is off makes no positive or negative contribution. If $X_i = 1$, then every unit connected to X_i (i.e. $w_{ji} \neq 0$) and that is also on ($X_j = 1$) makes a positive contribution if $w_{ji} > 0$ and a negative one if $w_{ji} < 0$. Intuitively this goodness measure is higher when units linked by positive weights are simultaneously active. Our goodness measure is essentially the same as the Harmony of [Smolensky, 1986] and its negative is essentially the *energy* of [Hopfield, 1982; Ackley *et al.*, 1985]. We will talk both of increasing goodness or decreasing energy depending on what sounds more natural in context.

Now our purpose in developing the goodness function was to show convergence of network computations by establishing that G can be made to always increase. This will be true if its derivative is always greater than zero. Let us assume that at each time slot exactly one unit, X_i, evaluates whether to change its value. We will look at the effect of *continuous* change of X_i on G which will be needed later anyway. The total energy function G can be rewritten to pull out the role of the variable X_i that is being considered:

$$G = X_i \sum_j w_{ji} X_j + \sum_{j \neq i} (X_j \sum_k w_{kj} X_k) \tag{4}$$

The derivative of G with respect to X_i has two terms — from the first term of (4) comes the term $\sum w_{ji} X_j$. From the remaining sum over $j \neq i$ the derivative is non-zero only where X_i appears in the inner sum (i.e., when $k = i$) and the derivative of each summand is $X_j w_{ij}$, yielding:

$$\frac{\partial G}{\partial X_i} = \sum w_{ji} X_j + \sum_{j \neq i} w_{ij} X_j \tag{5}$$

If we make a further major assumption that $w_{ij} = w_{ji}$ everywhere (symmetric weights) and a minor one that $w_{ii} = 0$ we get the main result:

$$\frac{\partial G}{\partial X_i} = 2 \sum_j w_{ji} X_j \tag{6}$$

In this case, the entire effect on G of changing X_i can be determined from only the incoming weights and values to X_i. The factor of 2 in Equation 6 will be suppressed throughout the paper for simplicity. Now recall that we wanted to guarantee that each choice of X_i makes G increase. This will be assured by rule (2) above.

This is just the original rule for binary linear threshold units—we have provided a rationale for choosing this particular rule [Hopfield, 1982]. That is, our goodness function was chosen so that its derivative with respect to X_i was positive exactly when $X_i = 1$ by Rule 2. The remainder of Section 1 and all of Section 2 explore the goodness/energy formulation and its strengths and weaknesses.

Let us consider how the G function would work for the example of Figure 1. Assume that exactly I_1 and T_2 were on and the unit for "IN" was tested to see whether it should go on.

$$\begin{aligned} X_{IN} &= 1 \cdot X_{I_1} + 1 \cdot X_{N_2} - 1 \\ &= 0 \quad \text{in this case} \end{aligned}$$

and rule (2) says X_{IN} should be zero. We can also compare the value of G with $X_{IN} = 0$ or 1.

$$\begin{aligned} G_{IN} &= X_{IN}(X_{I_1} + X_{N_2} - 1) \\ &= 0 \text{ for } X_{IN} = 1 \text{ or } X_{IN} = 0 \end{aligned}$$

Now if the unit for "IT" is tested, we see that

$$\begin{aligned} G_{IT} &= X_{IT}(X_{I_1} + X_{T_2} - 1) \\ &= X_{IT} \cdot 1 \end{aligned}$$

The value G_{IT} is obviously one where $X_{IT} = 1$ and zero when $X_{IT} = 0$. Thus G is higher when $X_{IT} = 1$ and, of course, equation (2) does specify $X_{IT} = 1$. We will look very soon at more interesting examples.

A number of assumptions were necessary to establish the increasing goodness relation. The units had to be binary and to compute their output by a linear threshold function. The weights linking any two units had to be symmetric. For future reference, we will refer to networks with (binary) linear threshold elements as (B)LTE networks. If symmetric weights are also required, the networks will be denoted SLTE or BSLTE when outputs are binary. Furthermore, a major assumption was made about the timing of the units' actions: only one unit could act at a time, and its output had to reach all other units before they could act. All of these assumptions are considered further below.

Even under all these assumptions, we have not shown that our networks do what they should do, only that they converge. (They converge because goodness never decreases, if we follow rule (2), and goodness clearly has an upper bound for any specific network.) In order to extend the convergence proof to a correctness one, we must show that the right answer is the one to which the network will converge. This turns out to involve three hard sub-problems. The first sub-problem is to specify formally the desired behavior; this is independent of any particular proof technique and constitutes a recurrent theme. The second sub-problem is to show that the desired state (for each input configuration) has the greatest goodness. The third sub-problem is to show that the system actually reaches this state of maximum goodness. It may seem, at first, that we have already solved the third problem by showing convergence. The difficulty here is that while goodness always increases with each change, the system might converge to a value of goodness which is only a regional maximum, not the greatest possible value. This issue of regional (local) optima is ubiquitous in search problems and is another theme of the chapter.

The example in Figure 2 depicts a situation in which the regional optimum problem can arise in a tiny system. The additions to Figure 1 are a unit for the word "I," an explicit θ node for the thresholds, and some specific weights on the connections (all unlabelled connections have weight = 1). The idea here is that the word "I" is in a mutual inhibition relation to longer words starting with "I" such as "IT" and "IN." The threshold for the word "I" is assumed to be .5 and for "IT" to be 1. This should all seem plausible; the network meets our conditions and the various words seem to be activated when the right letters are activated. There is a bug, however, and it shows up as a regional maximum in goodness. Assume that exactly I_1 and T_2 are active (=1), and consider the contributions to G of the units for the words "I" and "IT."

$$\begin{aligned} G_I &= X_I \cdot (X_{I_1} - X_{IT} - .5) \\ G_{IT} &= X_{IT} \cdot (X_{I_1} + X_{T_2} - X_I - 1) \end{aligned}$$

If unit "I" is considered first, $X_{IT} = 0$ and so $\sum w_{ij}x_j = 1 - .5 > 0$ and X_I will be set to 1. This yields a contribution of .5 to G. Now if unit "IT" is considered, its $\sum w_{ij}X_j$ term turns out to be $(1 + 1 - 1 - 1) = 0$ (because $X_I = 1$), and so $X_{IT} = 0$. However, if "IT" were chosen before "I" for consideration, X_I would be 0 and X_{IT} would be set to 1. This would inhibit "I" but, more importantly, would make a contribution of +1 to G. Thus the configuration with $X_{IT} = 1$ is better than the one with $X_I = 1$, but is unreachable from there. This is entirely typical of the general case; an early decision precludes one that would turn out to be better (for G).

In this case, one could fix the bug—for example, by having a negative link from any letter in the second position (e.g., T_2) to the word "I." More generally, it is not at all clear how one could avoid the regional extremum problem, and much effort has been devoted to overcoming it, at least partially.

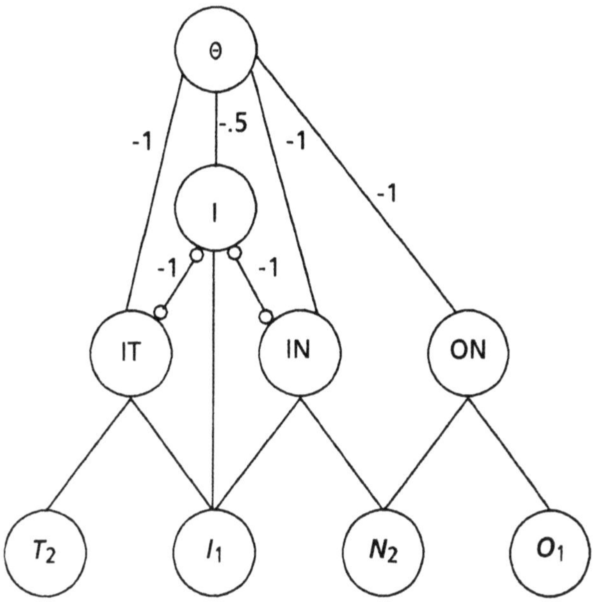

Figure 2: An extended word recognizer. The θ unit represents the threshold of each word recognizer. Circle-tipped links are inhibitory. Unlabelled links have weight = 1.

It is also interesting to consider what happens to the example of Figure 2 under an updating rule that examines all units simultaneously rather than one at a time. Again assume that exactly I_1 and T_2 are on to start. Now at the first simulation step, both "IT" and "I" will be turned on, according to rule (1). At the second step (since each now has a rival), they would both be turned off, and so on, looping forever. This shows how the choice of timing of the updating can have a major effect on the behavior of a network. An important aspect of modeling is to develop models whose behavior is not dependent on such properties of the simulation. Again, we don't currently know how to do this in general.

One proposed way of evading regional optima is to add a controlled element of randomness to the unit updating process. In the binary output case, we can have the output be 0 or 1, depending on the value of a random variable, which is a function of the unit's potential. The analog with physics suggests the function

$$prob(X_k = 1) = \frac{1}{(1 + e^{-\Delta G/T})} \tag{7}$$

where ΔG is the difference in goodness between when $X_k = 1$ and when $X_k = 0$. This formulation is called the Boltzmann machine [Ackley *et al.*, 1985]. The parameter T is analogous to temperature and will be discussed later. For now, we assume $T = 1$, yielding the solid curve in Figure 3. Qualitatively, we note that $prob(X_k = 1)$ is 1/2 when its contribution to energy (goodness) is zero and goes up as ΔG_k increases. In our little example, $\Delta G_I = .5$ and $\Delta G_{IT} = 1$, and the better answer will be chosen more often. That is, even if unit "I" is tried first, there is a smaller chance that it will be set to 1. By changing the value of T, one can make the system closer to a random choice (T large, dashed line in Figure 3) or to a deterministic system like we started with ($T \sim 0$; dotted line). One could arrange to start T at a high value (to avoid regional extrema) and then lower it (to get exact fit locally). This is the idea of "simulated annealing," and will be discussed below. There are a number of other interesting issues that arise even in this simple example.

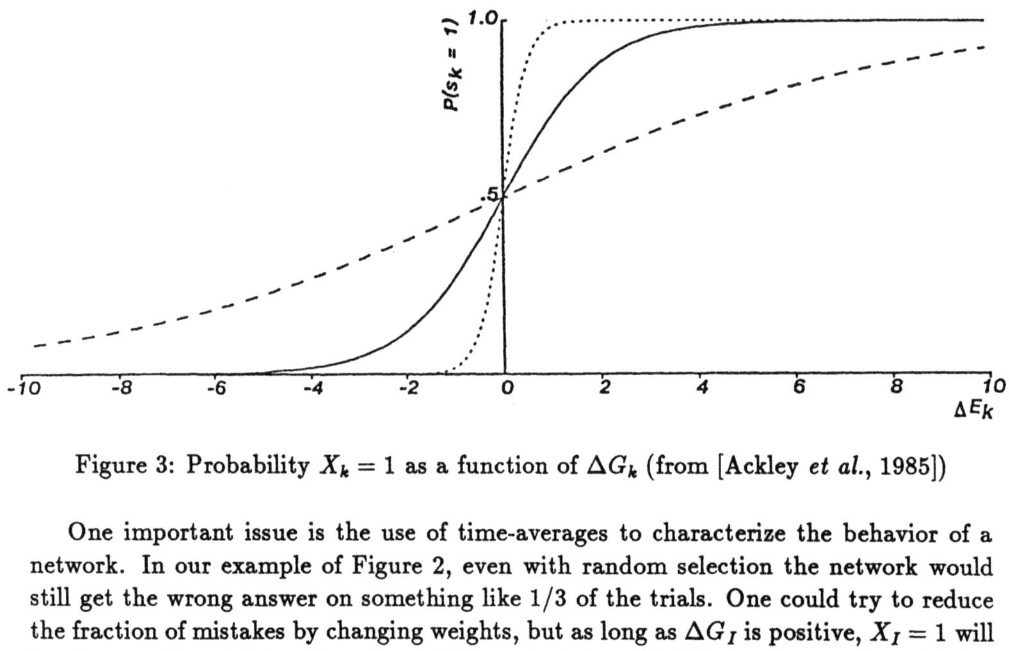

Figure 3: Probability $X_k = 1$ as a function of ΔG_k (from [Ackley *et al.*, 1985])

One important issue is the use of time-averages to characterize the behavior of a network. In our example of Figure 2, even with random selection the network would still get the wrong answer on something like 1/3 of the trials. One could try to reduce the fraction of mistakes by changing weights, but as long as ΔG_I is positive, $X_I = 1$ will be chosen at least 1/4 of the time. (The probability of "I" being tried before "IT" = 1/2, and for $\Delta G_I > 0$, the probability of $X_I = 1$ is $\geq 1/2$). People differ in their taste for the general idea of time-averages as a criterion for behavior. It seems to me to be difficult to have a system make a decision or choose an action based on a time average without a network that essentially computes the averages. Other workers have made a virtue of necessity by claiming that time averages are a good model of reversible figures or ambiguous words [Selman, 1985], but the time course of phenomena appears to be out of scale with the computational model. An extreme view, which we will not pursue here, is that a mental activity is represented by correlations among the firing patterns of neurons [Bienenstock, 1985].

Much of the work based on goodness and energy takes a different approach to the problem of uncertain behavior in networks that depend heavily on stochastic elements. One can show formally [Ackley *et al.*, 1985] that a system that uses the computation rule

(2) with the modification given in (7) will settle into different states with probability related to their energy difference.

$$\frac{P(B)}{P(A)} = e^{-(E_A - E_B)/T} \tag{8}$$

This doesn't help much by itself unless the desired state (correct solution) is much better than all others, in which case the system will almost always be right. In the more general case, people rely on an "annealing schedule" to increase the probability that the system will settle in the lowest energy state (always assuming that it has been shown to be the correct answer). One can see from equation (8) that as $T \to 0$, the probability ratio can get arbitrarily small, even for small energy gaps. The problem is that for very small T, the updating rule in (7) is almost deterministic and thus has only a small chance of escaping a regional optimum (cf. also Figure 3) and the system will take a very long time to reach the state where it is almost always activating the right answer. A typical annealing schedule for a small problem might start with a fairly high value of T (typically ~ 20) and lower it in steps down to 2. The results, roughly speaking, are that a moderate number of temperature changes (~ 10) can lead to a solution that is usually right, but with a significant fraction of error. Again, people differ in their taste for computations that require several successive approximations and have significant error probabilities. In the learning paradigms where the idea has been most widely used, it doesn't matter much because the learning typically involves thousands of runs. We will return to the role and plausibility of annealing later in the paper. A particularly clean presentation of the idea and its relation to physics can be found in [Smolensky, 1986].

An alternative to binary outputs is to model the computation with continuous valued outputs whose value might be taken to represent average firing frequency. There have been some very nice results developed for binary output units, particularly in learning, and we discuss these in Section 2, but we will focus on the continuous output case. In general, the restriction to binary outputs makes it difficult to treat many important phenomena. For example, the McClelland and Rumelhart work that was the basis for Figure 2 was concerned with visual features and how they might contribute to recognizing a letter like I_1 or T_1 (which share many features). To model this, one would seem to need (as was used) a richer output space than (0,1) to capture the notion of how confident a detecting unit might be that it had seen its target. It turns out that the goodness/energy theory extends neatly to this case.

In fact, our treatment of the goodness function and its derivatives was done assuming continuous valued outputs X_i and then specialized to setting X_i to 0 or 1. Now that we allow continuous valued outputs, the question arises as to what value of output should correspond to a given value of potential $P_j = \sum w_{ij} X_j$. Most work uses only non-negative outputs, and in such a system a negative potential should obviously yield an output of zero. But what about positive potentials? Any monotonic function of potential is defensible, and the choice turns out to be a trade-off between speed of convergence and the avoidance of regional extrema. We will look more carefully at a sigmoidal output rule in Section 2b.

Even the simplest continuous output rule

$$X_i = \texttt{if } P_i > 0 \texttt{ then } P_i \texttt{ else } 0$$

will suffice to fix the regional optimum problem we had in connection with Figure 2. Suppose everything is as before and (the worst case) unit "I" is considered first. Now $X_I = P_I = .5$, not 1 as before. The effect of this is that when "IT" is tested, it will have $X_{IT} = (1 + 1 - .5 - 1) = .5$, and at this point both hypotheses will be equally active. However, the next time that unit "I" is tested, X_I will be zero, and this will lead to X_{IT} being 1 on its next test and forevermore. This simple example is illustrative of several general points. A continuous output system can sometimes avoid traps that would catch the binary equivalent. Indeterminate situations are well-modeled by equal potentials. Finally, we see how continuous output systems can settle into a final state with binary outputs. More information and examples on these points can be found in [Hopfield & Tank, 1985; Rumelhart *et al.*, 1986]

2. The Range of Computations Covered by Goodness

2.1. Some Cautionary Tales

In this section, we will attempt to explain some of the strengths and limitations of the SLTE/energy model. The model is clearly not universal—the operative question is whether or not it constitutes an adequate basis for essentially all modeling (with minor adjustments) or rather should be treated as one of several special-purpose techniques available in more general formulations. This first subsection points out some computational restrictions on the use of linear combination rules, goodness functions, symmetric links, and the proof techniques that depend on these assumptions.

The idea of using the goodness/energy formulation to understand the behavior of networks is very attractive and has been used successfully in some important cases (cf. Section 2.2). It has also been apparent from the outset that not all computations are expressible as energy minimizations. Certainly any behavior that requires a loop or cycle cannot be described by a monotonic goodness function. The system cannot be made to return systematically to the same state while continuously (or probabilistically) increasing the goodness measure. In this section we discuss some other limitations on the computation that arise from the goodness paradigm.

Recall the key assumptions underlying the formulation:

1. linear threshold elements (sometimes with stochastic component);

2. symmetric weights; and

3. an instantaneous asynchronous updating rule.

We first show that linear threshold elements not restricted to symmetric weights on connections are universal, i.e., can compute any computable function. This is trivial because one can easily make a complete set of binary logic devices (e.g., OR and NOT) from binary linear threshold devices. An OR unit has its two weights as one and its threshold as .5.

$$X_{\mathrm{OR}} = d_1 + d_2 - .5$$

A negation unit has a weight of -1 and a threshold of -.5.

$$X_{\mathrm{NOT}} = -d + .5$$

This is well known and hardly surprising, but serves as a baseline for further study. Notice that universality does not mean that a particular network of LTE will suffice to realize a behavior. There are both computational and biological reasons for using more general elements. With the symmetry condition added, there are many computations that cannot be done at all.

This is true even for the case of asymmetric links of the same sign which occurs routinely in practice. One obvious instance is when the weights represent evidential links (e.g., conditional probabilities) between nodes. These are normally of the same sign, but of different values. For example, the likelihood (in Figure 1) of T_2 given the word "IT" is much greater than the likelihood of the word given only the letter position. It has been claimed that one can routinely eliminate asymmetric weights in binary networks by changing the thresholds in one of the units. A typical case is the transformation suggested by Figure 4, where $\theta_3 = \theta_2 + (w_1 - w_2)$. This only holds when the unit B has no other inputs; otherwise the changed threshold can obviously effect the behavior of unit B when A is silent. And for the continuous valued model, threshold revision doesn't even work when B has no other inputs. It may be possible in some cases to eliminate an asymmetric weight by substituting more complex symmetric constructions, but this does not seem to be a promising avenue to pursue. Similarly, results showing that isolated boolean functions can be realized with SLTE [Hinton & Sejnowski, 1983b] should not be read to imply that arbitrary boolean networks can be so realized. We will examine below the question of whether there might be a generalization of goodness which would accommodate asymmetric weights of the same sign.

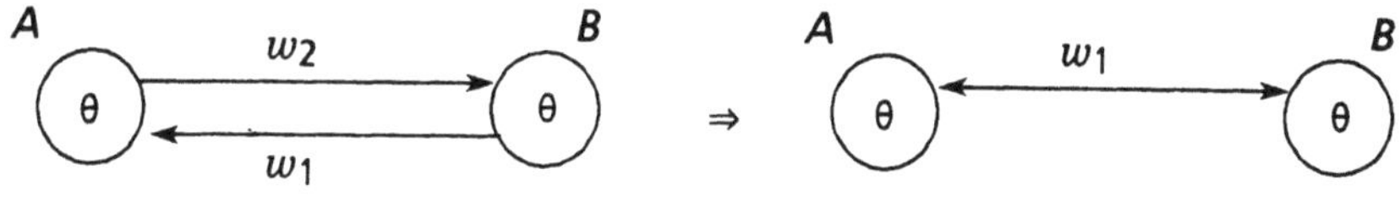

Figure 4: Proposed transform from asymmetric links to symmetric. It works only in special cases.

For subnetworks with weights of opposite sign (Figure 5), the situation is even worse. Suppose the symmetric weight chosen to replace w_1 and w_2 were positive. Then the effect of $B = 1$ on unit A would be the opposite of what it was in the original network. This will only lead to an equivalent computation when the original network had w_2 so small as to have no effect on A. Notice also that the asymmetric situation violates our intuitive notions behind the goodness measure. The idea of mutual consistency doesn't make sense between two nodes with links of opposite sign. This suggests that it might be difficult to find an extension of the goodness/energy paradigm to networks with links of opposite sign. Notice that such a network is the natural way to implement sequencing, unit A activating B and being silenced by it in turn.

Another assumption of the standard SLTE/goodness model is that no unit has a

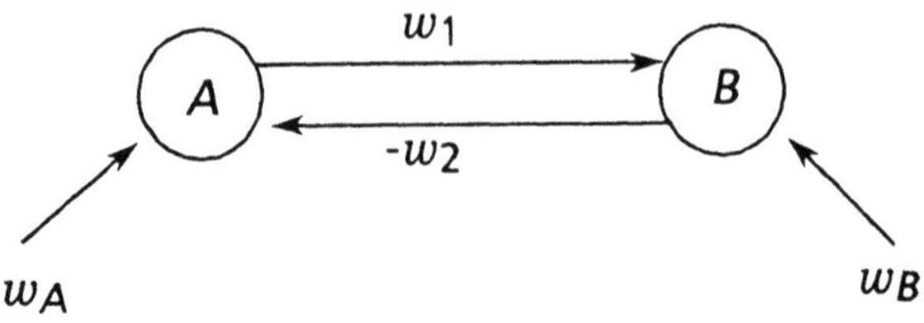

Figure 5: Units linked by weights of opposite sign

link to itself or retains any "memory" of its previous values (hysteresis). This is natural for the thermodynamic situation, but is not appropriate for neurons. There are also a number of computational problems that become easier when memory across firings is permitted. For example, the usual way to prevent regional maxima problems like those of Figure 2 is to have units accumulate evidence internally for some time before outputting values that might short-circuit the computation [Sabbah, 1985]. Another use of unit memory would be to support models that did not require the inputs to be clamped on, i.e., to implement what is called a "latch" in circuit design. Fortunately, there does seem to be a systematic modification of the goodness paradigm that will accommodate unit memory for some versions of the continuous output model. The idea is to augment any unit requiring memory with an auxiliary linked only to it by some positive weight, w.

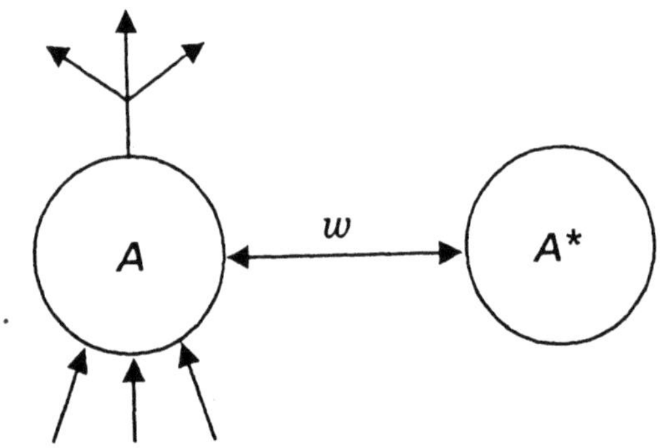

Figure 6: Auxiliary unit A^* can model fairly well memory or self-coupling of unit A.

The conventional goodness model has the output of A^* always available to unit A, so A^* acts as internal memory. If the model being modified has output of units equal to their potential, the value w can be set to 1. If the memory is intended to decay with time, the weight w can be set to less than 1. In the event that output is not equal to potential ($X \neq P$), the memory of P can be approximated by using a value of w and a threshold in A^* to approximate memory. The relation between output and memory input for A is:

$$\text{memory input} = w(w \cdot \text{output} - \text{threshold}).$$

In addition, one would probably want to arrange the simulation so that A^* was evaluated between evaluations of A without exception. To the best of my knowledge, no one has tried this. It may also be possible to use a different goodness function that incorporates self-links, but I have not found a way to do so.

Thus far we have seen that the symmetric weight requirement imposes several computational restrictions, but that asymmetric linear threshold units are universal. The notion of increasing goodness could be extended to networks with unequal weights of the same sign, but not without a heavy price. The crucial step in going from (5) to (6) in the derivation of monotonicity exploited symmetric weights and, without them, the effect on global goodness of a local change cannot be computed at that unit. There are some applications where having the system compute the global effect of a change might be effective, but this takes us out of the range of connectionist models. Even so, one could not extend the goodness paradigm to networks with links of opposite sign.

One can also question the possibility of using symmetric weights but non-linear rules of combination. Many investigators have used non-linear rules such as product, maximum, or logic functions to combine inputs, and there is no biological reason to assume only linear combinations. Now the goodness derivation depends in a crucial way on both the unit combination rule and on summation as the global measure of goodness. There is a natural extension to conjunctive connections that are symmetric in all three directions using an update rule analogous to (2), namely:

$$P_i = \sum_{k,j} w_{kji} x_k x_j - \theta_i \tag{9}$$

and the appropriate energy function [Hinton, personal communication]. It is not at all obvious how to extend the goodness model to more general combination rules while preserving the crucial property that the global effect on goodness be computable at the unit contemplating change. The derivation of local computability depends heavily on the form of the combination function and no direct extension to functions like maximum or logic functions goes through.

In addition to the computational restrictions like those described above, the goodness/SLTE paradigm imposes severe control limitations on models. For example, one scientific goal in the McClelland and Rumelhart work behind our first example (and other models) was to explain why some letter identifications were faster than others. The whole question of computational time becomes problematical in the goodness formulation. The standard version relies upon random asynchronous activation, instantaneous transmission, and potentially unbounded memory at each incoming site for the activation level of its source. Versions that employ simulated annealing add another level of time variation in using several separate settlings of the system. Quite aside from the electronic or biological plausibility of these assumptions, there does not appear to be a mapping to psychological time. A different and promising treatment of time in an energy *cum* annealing paradigm is the bipartite harmony model of Smolensky [1986], as depicted in Figure 7. The current version uses BSLTE, a goodness function, temperature, and annealing, but restricts connectivity to a bipartite graph. The idea is that each unit in the lower layer connects only to units in the upper layer, and vice-versa. The advantage of this is that the system can be shown to have good convergence properties (and can be simulated) with *synchronous* updating. This can be viewed as inserting a layer of synchronization units between levels of a tree of representational units. This and some other possible modifications to the paradigm will be discussed in Section 2.3, after we look at some successes of the methodology.

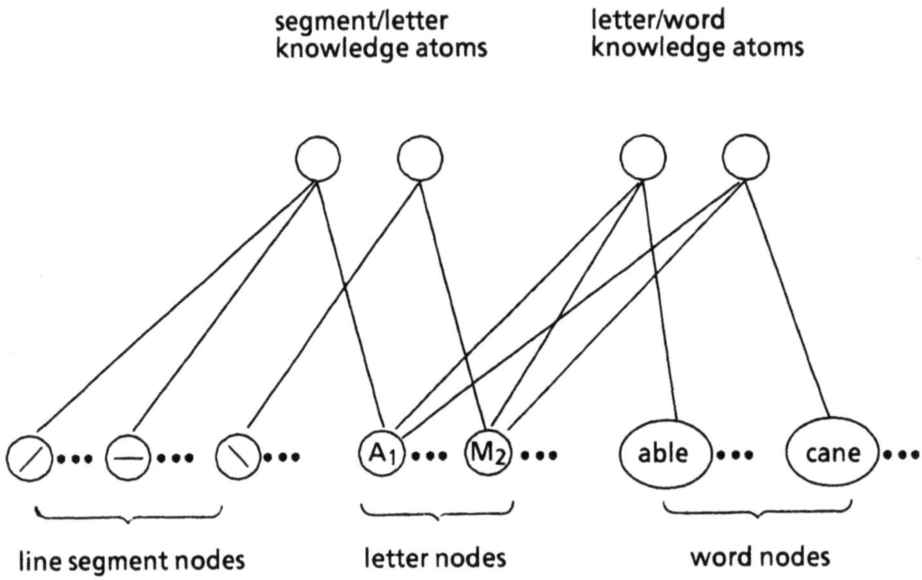

Figure 7: Bipartite harmony networks for words (from [Smolensky, 1986])

One question that arises about all these limitations is: do they matter? Perhaps the SLTE formalism can compute all functions of interest, or a learning mechanism can produce good approximations to any important computation. Computer science has extensive experience with underpowered formalisms, and the prognosis is not good for attempts to get by with one. A particularly clear example arises in the case of formal grammars, where finite-state grammars (FSGs) play a role analogous to SLTE networks. There are all sorts of lovely decidability and optimality theorems for FSGs, and some practical problems where they are clearly the method of choice. However, for problems with a slightly richer structure (e.g., matching parentheses), FSG techniques fall apart. Any attempt to construct or learn an FSG for an inappropriate language leads to ever larger approximate models that (necessarily) fail to incorporate the structure of the domain. It is true that investigators who favor the energy paradigm tend to believe in (although not necessarily to use) massively distributed representations, but I fail to see how this could effect the basic limitations of SLTE networks.

2.2. Some Success Stories

We have seen that many computational problems have no formulation in goodness/ energy terms. The problems that have thus far been handled effectively by goodness techniques all fall into the general category of constrained optimizations. The additive goodness function, uniform combination rule, and symmetric weights comprise a natural vocabulary for expressing problems in which the individual choices have degrees of compatibility and where the best solution maximizes the sum of these individual measures. Several important questions have this character and, for some of these, goodness formulations have provided valuable insights. Smolensky [1986] suggests that mutual compatibility (harmony) is exactly the domain of goodness methods. With this restriction on the domain, Smolensky can present a coherent story covering all of my behavior criteria. The correct answer to a compatibility problem is (by definition) the maximum entropy solution, and this is found (with high probability) by an annealing schedule. Other work has focused on solving problems for which the answer is specified by external criteria.

Both the word recognition discussed earlier and the WTA problem of [Feldman, 1985a] can be at least partially understood in goodness terms. For discrete assignment problems, the fit can be even better. A simple example can be found in [Rumelhart & McClelland, 1986], where the Necker cube is treated as a problem of assigning to each vertex a labeling such as "front lower left." Each vertex has two mutually incompatible labels, and these partition into mutually compatible subsets in the obvious way. However, by plotting the goodness function over the various values for the number of units in the two alternative coalitions, one can get a much better feel for the structure of the computation (Figure 8). The local peaks correspond to interpretations that are not three-dimensional objects.

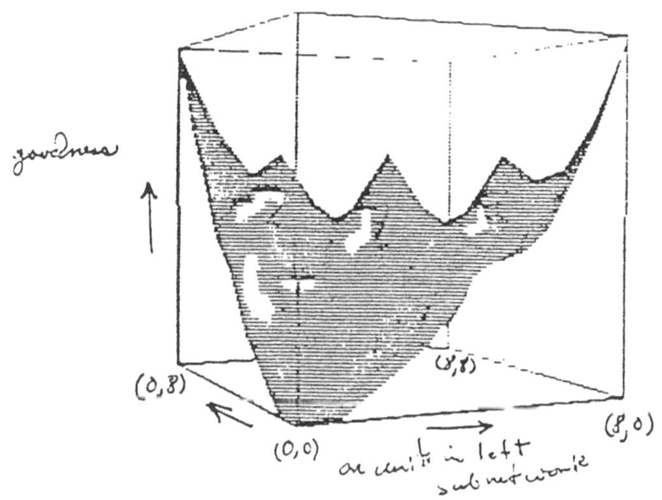

Figure 8: The goodness of fit surface for the Necker cube network (from [Rumelhart *et al.*, 1986]). The low point at the (0,0) corner correspond to the start state. The peaks on the right and left correspond to the standard interpretations of the cube.

The Necker cube example was one where the goodness map functioned as an aid for a problem whose solution was known. There are some other cases in which the goodness/energy formulation is central. Perhaps the most interesting of these is the recent work of Hopfield and Tank [1985] on the Traveling Salesman problem (TSP). The TSP is to find the shortest path through a graph in which each node is visited exactly once. This is clearly a constrained optimization problem, and one of considerable theoretical and practical importance. A key trick in the Hopfield and Tank formulation is to represent the solution as a binary square matrix with a 1 only in the entry corresponding to the sequential position in the tour (column) of a node (row). Thus an acceptable answer is a binary matrix with a single 1 in each row and each column. An energy function is constructed which is much better for such configurations than for other binary matrices. This is done with strong mutual inhibition links in the usual way. Finally another term representing the total distance of a tour is added to the energy function. The problem is now in the form where minimizing energy would probably yield the shortest tour.

Another interesting aspect of this paper is the method used to "search for" the energy minimum. Even though the final answer has only binary entries in the assignment matrix, Hopfield and Tank allow the corresponding units to take on any value between 0 and 1. They view the binary matrix as corners of a phase space and the continuous values as specifying interior points. One can also view the approach as avoiding local minima by moving more cautiously through energy space than strictly binary units would permit. This idea was illustrated in Section 1 and was also used in the Necker cube example above. It is interesting that Hopfield and Tank employ a sigmoid function to map potentials to output values; this tends to push high and low values to the extremes, but is more nearly linear in the middle. With some additional adjustments, like adding small random bias to initial values to break symmetry, the system turns out to do pretty well, and would be very fast on appropriate hardware. The paper discusses performance and a number of heuristics that might improve it. Some of the assumptions of the model are oriented around electronic circuits and are questionable for neurons; we will discuss this further in Section 3.

Another important paper whose success is at least partially due to energy considerations is that of [Geman & Geman, 1984]. They are concerned with the restoration of gray-scale images that have been corrupted by noise of a known statistical character. Given this knowledge and the statistical character of the domain, the best Bayesian restoration is the image which would most likely have led to what we started with. The problem is that this maximum a posteriori (MAP) estimate has been computationally intractable. Geman and Geman exploit the equivalence of Markov Random Fields and the Gibbs distribution in thermodynamics to convert the MAP problem into one of minimizing an energy functional. Using essentially the same ideas as we discussed earlier, they show that local decisions which reduce energy are possible. The results, within the limited domain approached, are quite good.

We briefly discussed simulated annealing in the energy paradigm in Section 1. The general idea of simulated annealing in optimization problems has attained considerable success. Some formulation of problems in vision, such as the Gemans' work (above) and [Poggio *et al.*, 1985], result in constrained maximization problems, and simulated annealing will be one of the solution techniques employed. But most of this work is not concerned with connectionist models. I will briefly discuss the biological plausibility of annealing in Section 3. As a computational construct, annealing has been primarily used to avoid regional optima, and doesn't add any functionality to the models. One potentially interesting exception to this generalization arises in Selman's Master's thesis [Selman, 1985; Selman & Hirst, 1985].

Selman was concerned (like several others) with building a connectionist parser for context-free grammars. One nice aspect of Selman's work is an automatic method of constructing the connectionist parser from a limited context-free grammar. Figure 9 shows a tiny grammar and the resulting network. The construction algorithm also supplies weights and thresholds and is one of several elegant new model builders that will be discussed in Section 3. For our current purposes, the interest centers on the mutually inhibitory "binder" nodes labeled 1-4 in Figure 9. The idea is that only one of the three alternative constructions for VP can be present in a sentence. (The three alternatives are represented by four binders for technical reasons.) One could build a deterministic parsing network using enough nodes and memory or state within the computational units [Cottrell, 1985a; Waltz & Pollack, 1984]. What Selman does instead is to minimize the number of units in his network and employ an annealing schedule to find good matches. The interesting aspect of this is that annealing is playing a role similar to the sequential search and back-tracking of conventional parsers. Unfortunately, the Master's thesis only involved simple examples, and it is not clear how far the analogy will take us. The thesis itself [Selman, 1985] contains interesting discussions of design decisions and other considerations concerning the energy paradigm, and some possible modifications.

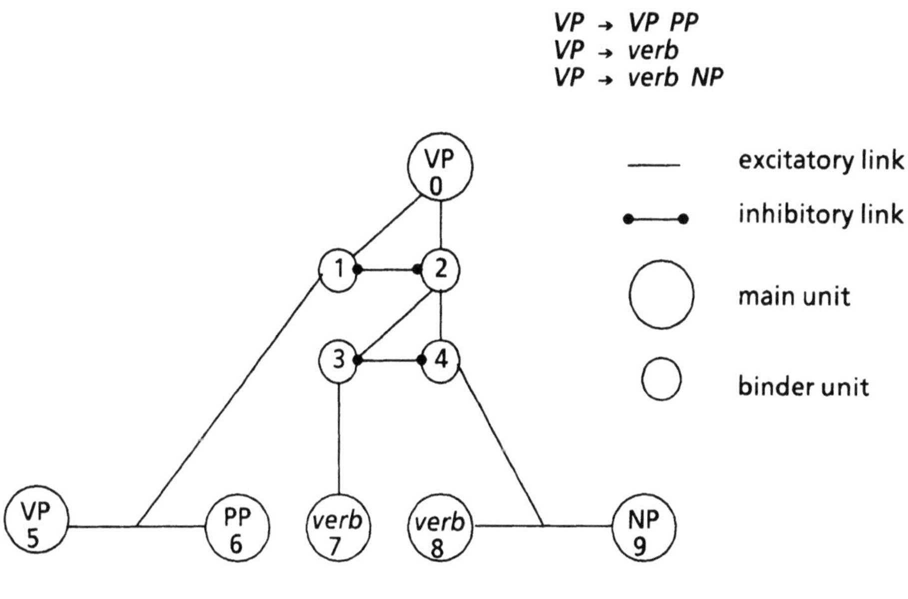

Figure 9: A small grammar and its network (from [Selman, 1985])

Some of the greatest successes with the goodness/energy paradigm have come in studying abstract computational questions, particularly learning. Learning is a central issue of intelligence and is particularly important for connectionist models, which reject the notion of an interpreter and a store of encapsulated knowledge. It turns out that SLTE systems, particularly the binary Boltzmann machine, have remarkable properties of adaptation and learning. These have been explored in a series of papers by Hinton, Sejnowski, and their collaborators [Ackley *et al.*, 1985; Derthick, 1984; Sejnowski *et al.*,

1985].

The learning algorithm for Boltzmann machines again is based on the average occupancy rate of various states when the system has reached equilibrium. Learning is designed to produce a system that will spontaneously produce the same statistics in input/output units as was used in training. If later some partial input is specified, the system will generate maximum entropy estimates of the unspecified inputs. Given that one accepts this model of learning, a very powerful local learning rule obtains. Since relative energy among various states determine their frequency, any errors in frequency must be due to some weights in the network being set sub-optimally. But the energy function is a sum of local energy functions at each unit, which is in turn a sum of contributions by each link. Therefore one can use the following simple update rule. Let p_{ij} be the probability of units i and j both being on in the clamped situation and p'_{ij} be the joint probability when the system is free running. Then the weight-updating rule:

$$\Delta w_{ij} = \epsilon(p_{ij} - p'_{ij})$$

where ϵ is a scale factor, will converge to the correct expected values. The proof of this is given in [Hinton *et al.*, 1984] and uses partial derivative techniques like our treatment in the introduction. A distributed version of this algorithm would require that the system go through successive cycles of stochastically accurate training and free-running simulation. The free-running state has been likened to dreams (cf. also [Crick & Mitchison, 1983; Hopfield *et al.*, 1983]). The value of the learned weight p_{ij} would have to be stored (for each connection) during the simulation runs and recalled for normal activity. Again, reasonable men can differ on the plausibility of all this.

One way of looking at these results is to notice that the Boltzmann learning algorithm will eventually converge (in the appropriate sense) for any function computable by a Boltzmann machine, assuming enough units and connections are available. Of course, the range of learnable functions is limited, but it does provide an excellent vehicle for theoretical study. Very recently some powerful results on learning in more general networks have begun to appear [Rumelhart *et al.*, 1985; Parker, 1985]. Although they do not employ SLTE, energy, or annealing, there is a clear intellectual link with the Boltzmann formulation. The course of true science does not run smooth.

2.3. Some Possible Extensions

The results of the previous section show that there are some modeling problems for which the SLTE goodness/energy formulation can be directly applied to good effect. All of the ones discovered so far are optimal assignment problems with symmetric constraints and an additive quadratic objective function. In this section we will look at the question of regional and global maxima, of classes of problems that might fit directly into the paradigm, and of modifications that might extend its applicability.

The results of the previous sections enable us to provide a clear answer to the primary question raised in the paper. Linear threshold elements, symmetric weights, and asynchronous updating support a powerful paradigm in which termination and sometimes correctness can be established. They do not, however, come close to covering the range of computational problems of interest in connectionist models. The situation is no different than it is with any other mathematical formalism; it requires considerable judgment to decide whether a problem might fit into the energy paradigm and how best to do it. To start a modeling project on the assumption that it must be made to fit the energy model is to court disaster. Of course, one must also consider whether any connectionist model is appropriate for the task at hand.

For those with appropriate background, the analog with statistical mechanics can be quite suggestive. Smolensky [1986] has the best treatment of this. What one must realize is that statistical mechanics is most powerful in systems lacking significant structure. For structured domains, e.g., protein folding, statistical considerations play a minor role. It seems to me that cognition is much more like the interaction of complex structures than an ideal gas. Moreover, the symmetric weight (interaction strength) condition does hold in complex physical situations but not in many cognitive domains. The physics model would have to be expanded greatly to explicate the nature of parallel computation. On the other hand, the general metaphorical notion of a parallel system settling into a stable state could have lasting value.

The principal attraction of the energy paradigm is the property that it is guaranteed to converge. To ensure that a network will deterministically converge to the right answer, one must also show that the right answer has the lowest energy and that the energy surface is convex (uni-modal). We assume for now that the former is accomplished, and examine the latter question. It should be clear from the Necker cube example (Figure 4) that it will not generally be feasible to construct a uni-modal energy or goodness map. This does not mean that networks cannot be proven to converge, only that the simplest methods do not suffice. The most common way of addressing the problem of regional minima has been the use of random perturbation, usually becoming less random as the computation progresses. This idea of "annealing" is taking its place in the general repertoire of combinatorial optimization techniques [Aragon *et al.*, 1985], but does not seem to be a useful idea for connectionist models, for several reasons, some of which were outlined earlier. The annealing process has been much too slow and uncertain to form the computational basis for basic neural perception, action, etc.

Given a problem that will fit the SLTE energy model, there are a variety of other ways to combat the problem of regional optima. One method was discussed in connection with Hopfield and Tank's TSP network, where the amount of descent (in the steepest direction) was varied. Of course, no such deterministic technique will escape an energy valley, but it should work fairly well for neutral (non-perverse) initial conditions.

Another interesting possibility arises from making a virtue of the transmission delay present in neurons but missing from all the models. If, in a real or simulated system, we allow units to be evaluated with information that might be out of date, this will have the effect of adding noise. If one assumes that the probability of outdated information is random (as would occur with random choice of units to activate), then there will be random noise. Moreover, as Francis Crick first pointed out, the noise will be greater in the early stages of computation when things are changing a lot, and will be less later in the computation; thus simulating simulated annealing. Some preliminary experiments by Sejnowski along these lines have had moderate success. It will also be interesting to see how the bipartite synchronous formulation [Smolensky, 1986] extends to more complex problems.

Another way of improving the pure energy method is to develop the analogy to multigrid and resolution hierarchy techniques. The idea there is to first solve a (spatially) crude approximation to the optimum and then refine it. One way to carry this idea over to the SLTE world is to put in extra units that explicitly represent areas of the solution space and establish heavily weighted inhibitions among them. In an ideal case one could even make the solution space uni-modal.

One major problem with the energy method is that (except for noise) it must improve the metric on each and every calculation. One trivial, but powerful, modification would be to allow some fore-play period of time in which energy was ignored. One way to realize this idea is to use the state variable, Q, from our original definition. One could allow enough time for information to spread through the network and then have units switch to a state where the energy minimization became operative. In addition, one could restrict the energy minimization to a selected subset of the units. The early phases and non-energy units could have asymmetric links and would presumably be characterized by different methods, like those of the next section. Recall that the whole idea of the method is to show convergence and, hopefully, correctness. There is no reason why these results can't be established considering part of a network for a restricted part of the computation. In fact, these are some of the kinds of techniques that have been used to construct connectionist models in the past.

3. Related Issues and Conclusions

Computational models involving very large numbers of simple computing units are certain to be the subject of considerable effort for some time. Animal nervous systems clearly have this character, and neuroscience is rapidly advancing to the point where computational models (theories) are a central aspect of the field. People are already building computer hardware designs that allow for a million or more simple processors [Hillis, 1985]. At the abstract level, many investigators have found massively parallel formulations of their problems more effective than descriptions in more traditional computational formalisms. Even on computers without enormous parallelism, algorithms expressed in connectionist language may prove to be efficient to write and run.

With all of this existing and potential achievement, the deep understanding of massively parallel computation takes on increasing importance. No one is satisfied with a large network having ad hoc units, connections, and simulation rules. Progress in all aspects of massively parallel computation will depend on systematic treatment of underlying computational questions. The formal analysis and proof techniques discussed in this paper represent one line of approach to structuring connectionist systems. A few points that transcend these particular methods are pursued in this section.

One major source of confusion (not surprising in this early stage) is that the scientific goals of a particular modeling effort are often not clear. For many of us, the ultimate goal is detailed models of intelligent behavior that are directly testable down to the single neuron level. At present, this perfectly explicit goal provides direct guidance on modeling requirements only for the simplest systems. Essentially all cognitive level models deal at a level of abstraction at which units of the model cannot be identified with neurons or groups of them or parts of them. The question becomes: what should "biologically plausible" mean in this setting? My view of this is that there are basic computational constraints which are sufficient to keep the models reasonable. The foremost of these are the restrictions on the number of units and connections, the processing and information transfer rate limitations, and the absence of an interpreter that can operate above the level of the network. An important additional consideration, which is often ignored, is that the simulation itself be robust over variations in exact values transmitted and timing of updates. Neither the purely synchronous or purely asynchronous model is biologically plausible, and we do not have good tests for the robustness of models over variations. None of the proof techniques discussed in the paper take this question seriously. We have done some simulations using a synchronous rule with random noise added to each output. This appears to be a robust and biologically realistic methodology, but nothing is known on its formal properties. Insightful recent discussions of the biological role of conectionist models can be found in [Ballard, 1986] and [Sejnowski, 1986]. There has been some work in computer science on asynchronous systems with variable timing. The problems encountered have been sufficiently difficult to establish a strong bias towards synchronous computers and to restrict inherently asynchronous systems, such as networks, into very simple modes of processing. Nevertheless, it does seem possible to develop connectionist models that are robust over simulation details.

Consider, for example, a variation on the Winner-Take-All task discussed in [Feldman 1985a]. Suppose each unit in the WTA network got input from all the others and computed the maximum activity level of its rivals. If each unit simply turned itself off when it saw a rival of greater activity, the WTA property would obtain. Moreover, this construction will work for any reasonable simulation method. A variant of this network that does not require N^2 connections was used in [Shastri & Feldman, 1984]. Each rival fed its output to a single MAX unit which fed back to all the rivals. The units computed their new output by subtracting MAX from their previous output; again this is stable over all reasonable simulation strategies. There is no compelling evidence on the biological plausibility of a MAX function, but it will be surprising if nature did not evolve something of this sort to solve computational problems like those suggested by the WTA example.

In addition to biological motivations, several groups studying massive parallelism are interested in hardware realizations. The physical constraints here are quite different. Speed of computation and transmission become less critical and the number and length of connections much more so. The robustness of simulations also takes on a different flavor, getting into the standard problems of synchronous and asynchronous circuits. Another important issue is the physical plausibility of models that assume continuously valued output functions. Such models are biologically realistic for only the restricted range of problems involving non-spiking neural signals. For most neural processing of interest in cognitive science, the limited range of neural firing frequencies limits outputs effectively to a few bits, and this has major consequences in modelling. For electronic circuits, the continuous output assumption is fine, and this may turn out to change our ideas of "digital" computation. It is almost certainly a mistake to take the same model as an engineering proposal and a description of neural functioning.

In addition to the robustness and physical realizability issues discussed above, there are important questions about connectionist networks as expressive formalisms. While it is clear that the connectionist framework is the right kind of formalism for many tasks, the understandability of a particular model is less obvious. For example, the McClelland and Rumelhart model [1981] was helpful in understanding a number of experimentally important effects, but did not incorporate a great many known constraints on the structure and interaction of lexical items. There is a danger that connectionist models can grow so complex that it is difficult or impossible to recognize the governing principles behind the behavior. Notice that if some system learned such a network for itself, we would be in an even worse position to extract the principles of organization. The specification and proof techniques discussed in this paper can only help if the abstract specification itself contains manifest information characterizing the structure of the problem.

This general idea of a higher-level description which captures the structure of a domain is one of the most promising recent developments in connectionist modeling. We saw in Section 2.2 how Selman transformed a restricted context-free grammar into a connectionist parser. The point, of course, is that we can consider the linguistic adequacy of the grammar independent of its realization. Cottrell [1985] has indicated how automated construction could be employed to cover semantic case-roles of words in English. Returning to the current paper, a critical step in this ambitious program would be to prove that some translation realized the given formal specification.

In a simpler domain, this is just what Shastri [Feldman, 1985a] was able to do for his evidence theory. In this case the input to the system is just semantic network knowledge with relative frequency information on properties, values, and sub-types. Given this input, Shastri's constructor builds a connectionist network that produces optimal answers to inheritance and categorization queries, by the maximum entropy criterion. The point, here again, is that the theory of evidence and the knowledge base structure and content can be studied independently of the realization. And again, the connectionist implementation is claimed to be sufficiently realistic to support direct behavioral tests.

Formal specification and proof techniques will become increasingly important as connectionist modeling matures. The current flurry of interest in energy models is motivated by the right goals, but the formalism itself is too weak to carry us very far. Professional theoretical computer scientists are beginning to take a serious interest in some of these problems and are providing valuable insights [Valiant, 1985; Goldschlager, 1984]. Automatic learning is a central issue and can be fruitfully studied independently of domain. For direct modeling of intelligent behavior, the greatest promise appears to lie with methods for automatically translating formal specifications into connectionist networks.

Acknowledgements

This research was supported in part by the Office of Naval Research [Grant N00014-84-K-0655], the Defense Advanced Research Projects Agency [Grant N00014-82-K-0193], and the National Science Foundation (Coordinated Experimental Research [Grant DCR-8320136]).

The connectionist clique communicates continually, and many of the ideas in this paper arose in conversation. Valuable assistance with the current version has come from Gary Cottrell, Gary Dell, Mark Fanty, Steve Small, Mandayam Srinivas, Terry Sejnowski, and Paul Smolensky.

References

[1] Ackley, D.H., G.E. Hinton, and T.J. Sejnowski, "A learning algorithm for Boltzmann machines," Cognitive Science 9, 147-169, 1985.

[2] Aragon, C.R., D.S. Johnson, and L.A. McGeoch, "Optimization by simulated annealing: an experimental evaluation," manuscript in preparation, 1985.

[3] Arbib, M.A., "Artificial intelligence and brain theory: unities and diversities," Annals of Biomedical Engineering 3, 238-274, 1975.

[4] Ballard, D.H., "Cortical connections and parallel processing: structure and function," TR 133, Computer Science Dept., Univ. Rochester, revised January 1985; to appear, Behavioral and Brain Sciences, 1986.

[5] Ballard, D.H. and P.J. Hayes, "Parallel logical inference," Proc., Sixth Annual Conf. of the Cognitive Science Society, 286-292, Boulder, CO, June 1984.

[6] Ballard, D.H., P.C. Gardner, and M.A. Srinivas, "Graph problems and connectionist architectures," TR-167, Computer Science Dept., Univ. Rochester, March 1986.

[7] Barnden, J.A., "On short-term information-processing in connectionist theories," Cognition and Brain Theory 7, 1, 25-59, 1984.

[8] Bienenstock, E., "Dynamics of central nervous system," Proc., Workshop on Dynamics of Macrosystems, Laxenburg, Austria, September 1984; to be published by Springer-Verlag, J.P. Aubin and K. Sigmund (Eds), 1985.

[9] Cohen, M.A. and S. Grossberg, "Absolute stability of global pattern formation and parallel memory storage by competitive neural networks," IEEE Trans. on Systems, Man, and Cybernetics SMC-13, 5, 815-826, September/October 1983.

[10] Collins, A.M. and E.F. Loftus, "A spreading-activation theory of semantic processing," Psychological Review 82, 407-429, November 1975.

[11] Cottrell, G.W., "A connectionist approach to word sense disambiguation," TR154 and Ph.D. thesis, Computer Science Dept., Univ. Rochester, May 1985.

[12] Cottrell, G.W., "A model of lexical access of ambiguous words," Proc., Natl. Conf. on Artificial Intelligence, Austin, TX, August 1984.

[13] Crick, F. and G. Mitchison, "The function of dream sleep," Nature 304 (5922), 111-114, 1983.

[14] Dell, G.S., "Positive feedback in hierarchical connectionist models: applications to language production," Cognitive Science, 3-23, January-March 1985.

[15] Derthick, M., "Variations on the Boltzmann machine learning algorithm," CMU-CS-84-120, Computer Science Dept., Carnegie-Mellon U., August 1984.

[16] Fahlman, S.E., "Three flavors of parallelism," Proc., Fourth Natl. Conf. of the Canadian Society for the Computational Studies of Intelligence, Saskatoon, Saskatchewan, May 1982.

[17] Fanty, M., "Context-free parsing in connectionist networks," TR 174, Computer Science Dept., Univ. Rochester, November 1985.

[18] Feldman, J.A., "Energy and the Behavior of Connectionist Models," TR 155, Computer Science Dept., Univ. Rochester, November 1985a.

[19] Feldman, J.A., "Four frames suffice: a provisional model of vision and space," Behavioral and Brain Sciences 8, 265-289, June 1985b.

[20] Feldman, J.A., "Dynamic connections in neural networks," Biological Cybernetics 46, 27-39, 1982.

[21] Feldman, J.A. and D.H. Ballard, "Connectionist models and their properties," Cognitive Science 6, 205-254, 1982.

[22] Fogelman–Soulie, F., P. Gallinari, Y. LeCun, and S. Thiria, "Automata networks and artificial intelligence," to appear in Automata Networks in Computer Science, Theory and Applications, F. Fogelman–Soulie, Y. Robert and M. Tchuente (Eds.), Manchester Univ. Press, 1986.

[23] Fukushima, K., S. Miyake, and T. Ito, "Neocognitron: a neural network model for a mechanism of visual pattern recognition," IEEE Trans. on Systems, Man, and Cybernetics SMC-13, 5, 826-834, September/October 1983.

[24] Geman, S. and D. Geman, "Stochastic relaxation, Gibbs distributions, and the Bayesian restoration of images," IEEE Trans. on Pattern Analysis and Machine Intelligence 6, 6, 721-741, November 1984.

[25] Goldschlager, L.M., "A computational theory of higher brain function," technical report, Computer Science Dept., Stanford Univ., April 1984.

[26] Hillis, D.W. The Connection Machine. Cambridge, MA: The MIT Press, 1985.

[27] Hinton, G.E. and T.J. Sejnowski, "Analyzing cooperative computation," Proc., Fifth Annual Conf. of the Cognitive Science Society, Rochester, NY, May 1983a.

[28] Hinton, G.E. and T.J. Sejnowski, "Optimal perceptual inference," Proc. IEEE Conf. on Computer Vision and Pattern Recognition, Washington, DC, 1983b.

[29] Hopfield, J.J., "Neural networks and physical systems with emergent collective computational abilities," Proc., Natl. Acad. Sciences USA 79, 2554-2558, 1982.

[30] Hopfield, J.J., "Neurons with graded response have collective computational properties like those of two-state neurons," Proc., Natl. Acad. Sci. 81, 3088-3092, May 1984.

[31] Hopfield, J.J., D. Feinstein, and R.G. Palmer, "Unlearning has a stabilizing effect in collective memories," Nature 304, p. 158, 1983.

[32] Hopfield, J.J. and D.W. Tank, "'Neural' computation of decisions in optimization problems," Biological Cybernetics, 1985.

[33] Kirkpatrick, S., C.D. Gelatt, Jr., and M.P. Vecchi, "Optimization by simulated annealing," Science 220, 4598, 671-680, 1983.

[34] Koch, C., T. Poggio, and V. Torre, "Nonlinear interactions in a dendritic tree: localization, timing, and role in information processing," Proc., Natl. Acad. Sciences USA 80, 2799, 1983.

[35] McClelland, J.L. and D.E. Rumelhart, "An interactive activation model of context effects in letter perception, Part 1: An account of basic findings," Psychological Review 88, 375-407, 1981.

[36] Minsky, M. and S. Papert., Perceptrons. Cambridge, MA: MIT Press, 1969.

[37] Parker, D.B., "Learning-logic," TR 47, Center for Computational Research in Economics and Management Science, MIT, 1985.

[38] Pearl, J., "Fusion, propagation and structuring in Bayesian networks," TR CSD-850022, Cognitive Systems Laboratory, U. California, Los Angeles, April 1985; also presented at the Symposium on Complexity of Approximately Solved Problems, Columbia U., April 1985.

[39] Poggio, T., V. Torre, and C. Koch, "Computational vision and regularization theory," Nature 317, 26 September 1985.

[40] Pollack, J.B. and D.L. Waltz, "Natural language processing using spreading activation and lateral inhibition," Proc., Fourth Annual Conf. of the Cognitive Science Society, 50-53, Ann Arbor, MI, August 1982.

[41] Posner, M.I. Chronometric Explorations of Mind. Hillsdale, NJ: Lawrence Erlbaum Associates, 1978.

[42] Ratliff, K. and F. Hartline, Studies on Excitation and Inhibition in the Retina. New York: The Rockefeller U. Press, 1974.

[43] Rumelhart, D.E., G.E. Hinton, and R.J. Williams, "Learning internal representations by error propagation," ICS Report 8506, Institute for Cognitive Science, U. California, San Diego, September 1985.

[44] Rumelhart, D.E. and J.L. McClelland (Eds). Parallel Distributed Processing: Explorations in the Microstructure of Cognition. Vol. 1: Foundations. Cambridge, MA: Bradford Books/MIT Press, 1986.

[45] Rumelhart, D.E., P. Smolensky, J.L. McClelland, and G.E. Hinton, "PDP models of schemata and sequential thought processes," in D.E. Rumelhart and J.L. McClelland (Eds). Parallel Distributed Processing: Explorations in the Microstructure of Cognition. Vol. 1: Foundations. Cambridge, MA: Bradford Books/MIT Press, 1986.

[46] Sabbah, D., "Computing with connections in visual recognition of Origami objects," Cognitive Science 9, 1985.

[47] Sejnowski, T.J., "Open questions about computation in cerebral cortex," in McClelland, J.L. and D.E. Rumelhart (Eds). Parallel Distributed Processing: Explorations in the Microstructure of Cognition. Vol. 2: Applications. Cambridge, MA: Bradford Books/MIT Press, 1986.

[48] Selman, B., "Rule-based processing in a connectionist system for natural language understanding," TR CSRI-168 and Master's thesis, Computer Systems Research Institute, U. Toronto, April 1985.

[49] Selman, B. and G. Hirst, "A rule-based connectionist parsing system," Proc., 7th Annual Conf. of the Cognitive Science Society, 1985.

[50] Shastri, L. and J.A. Feldman, "Evidential reasoning in semantic networks: a formal theory," Proc., 9th Intl. Joint Conf. on Artificial Intelligence, 465-474, Los Angeles, CA, August 1985.

[51] Shastri, L. and J.A. Feldman, "Semantic networks and neural nets," TR 131, Computer Science Dept., Univ. Rochester, June 1984.

[52] Smolensky, P., "Foundations of harmony theory: cognitive dynamical systems and the subsymbolic theory of information processing," in D.E. Rumelhart and J.L. McClelland (Eds). Parallel Distributed Processing: Explorations in the Microstructure of Cognition. Vol. 1: Foundations. Cambridge, MA: Bradford Books/MIT Press, 1986.

[53] Valiant, L.G., "Learning disjunctions of conjunctions," Proc., 9th Intl. Joint Conf. on Artificial Intelligence, Los Angeles, CA, August 1985.

[54] Waltz, D.L. and J.B. Pollack, "Phenomenologically plausible parsing," Proc., Natl. Conf. on Artificial Intelligence, 335-339, Austin, TX, August 1984.

LEARNING AND ASSOCIATIVE MEMORY

F. Fogelman Soulie[1], P. Gallinari[2] and S. Thiria[2]

[1]Laboratoire de Dynamique des Réseaux
CESTA, 1 rue Descartes, 75005 Paris
and University Paris V
and
[2]Laboratoire de Dynamique des Réseaux
CESTA, 1 rue Descartes, 75005 Paris
and Conservatoire National des Arts et Métiers, Paris
France

1. Introduction

Models for learning have been widely developed in the literature and applied to many problems, such as: classification, pattern recognition, data bases or vision [6, 18, 26] ... . They are based on methods related to those used in other domains: statistical methods, linear classifiers, clustering, relaxation (see Devijver, Jain, Kittler in this volume) ... . Recently, more models have been designed, called "connectionist", which originated in the work on linear classifiers. These models make use of networks of interconnected elements (automata) and provide a general framework for distributed representation of knowledge (in the connections) [7], distributed processing, learning and restoration. Originally designed as models for the brain, these models include today many domains traditionally part of artificial intelligence: vision [3,4], speech and language processing [23], games, semantic networks [13], cognitive science [20] ... . Probabilistic models have also been developed along similar lines to solve problems in pattern recognition: restoration of images [10], figure-ground separation [22], translation invariance [16,17,21] ... .

We will present in this paper a review of some aspects of connectionist models. We will focus on the problem of building a network capable of encoding the knowledge necessary to perform an association: input $\rightarrow$ desired output, *i.e.*, to produce the correspondence

$$\text{input} \rightarrow \text{output} = \text{desired output (see Figure 1)}$$

This building process can be decomposed into three distinct phases:

▷ characterize the network architecture adapted to the problem.

▷ learn the correspondence *i.e.*, find the algorithms that allow to encode the knowledge into the connections.

NATO ASI Series, Vol. F30
Pattern Recognition Theory and Applications
Edited by P. A. Devijver and J. Kittler

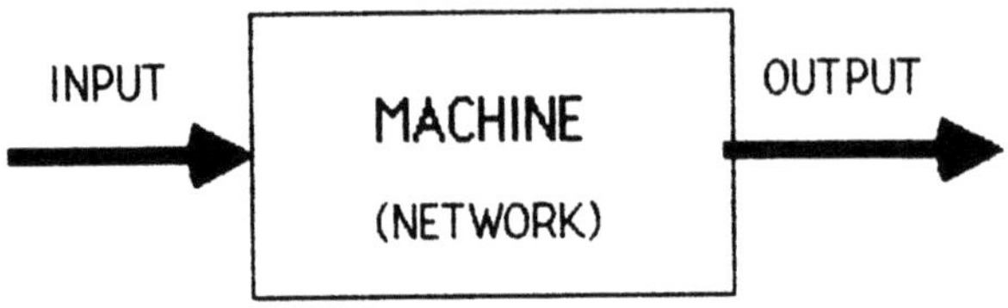

FIGURE 1: Association through a network of an (input, output) pair of patterns.

▷ finally, when the two previous phases have been performed, decide how to realize the retrieval.

In the following, we will successively discuss those three phases: in Section 2, we discuss various network architectures and their incidence on the network abilities; in Section 3, after a general discussion on learning, we present the general model of linear learning, mainly developed by Kohonen [15] and the corresponding algorithms; in Section 4, we review various retrieval processes. In the later part, Section 5, we test on a particular example the different processes and compare their performances and behaviour.

2. Architecture

An automata network can be characterized by its processing elements and its connection structure. For sake of clarity, we will use the three following parameters to describe a network (see Figure 2):

1. the number of automata
2. the number of layers
3. the network connection

These characteristics are related to the "size" and the complexity of the task. They determine the amount of computation necessary to encode the problem into the network. Let us give two examples:

▷ Increasing the number of automata and connections both rises the network capability (capacity storage, complexity of the task that can be handled, ...) and the computational burden. Therefore, a compromise between the size of the network and its required ability must be found.

▷ The information content of the examples is often somewhat redundant. The global task may then be achieved by using only local information of connection, which will reduce the amount of required computation and/or take into account the particular local structure of the problem.

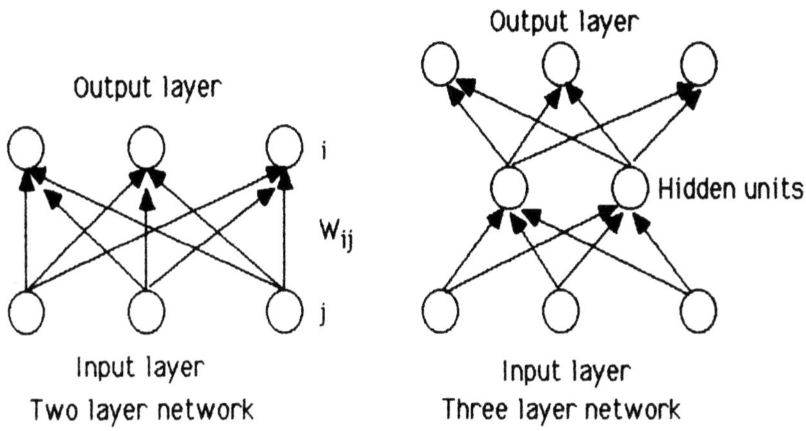

FIGURE 2: Architecture.
Examples of two kinds of networks discussed in the paper. Architecture like the one on the left has been extensively used for linear learning. The one on the right is an example of network for which the GBP algorithm has been proposed as a general learning rule.

There is no general purpose architecture, each network must be adapted to its given task. The design of the architecture is very important, because the results of the learning and retrieval phases heavily depend on it. Furthermore, in our models, there is no learning on the architecture itself, but only on the connection weights. The architecture must thus be designed so as to optimally use what is known a priori about the task: for example, if one works with digitalized images, one would select the features to be used, so as to reduce the network size.

Only partial results are available for the adaptation of a network to a particular task. Just a few architectures have been used and studied. Most authors have proposed two layers networks with full connectivity [2,14,15]. More recently, models of general learning multilayers networks have been proposed [1,16,17,20,23], most studies being restricted to networks for which connections go from one level to the one just above. In fact, networks are usually built "*by hand*" using the general knowledge — or expertise — of the domain and of the behavior of automata networks. In the following, we will present results for networks with many layers: the first layer will usually receive the input to the network, and the last one give the answer or output computed by the network; optional intermediate layers, containing so-called "hidden units", are not directly connected to the outside (see Figure 2.).

3. Learning

3.1. Learning Theory

We study here models where learning is achieved by presenting examples to an automata network whose dynamical evolution will allow the retrieval of stored information. This approach is clearly different from the rule based learning methods [26].

Training of a network can make use of all the items in the data-base or of only part of them. The first case is just learning, in the last case, the network is supposed to find in the "learning set" the relevant features and to generalize its knowledge to samples it has not learned: the "test set".

We formalize the problem as follows: the initial connections of a network are given through an initial weight matrix $W(0)$. These connections are then modified so as to extract the knowledge from the learning set: we give in the following a general algorithm to perform this extraction. Learning is successfully achieved when the network associates the correct answer to each pattern learned.

We call S_{ik} the state (or output) of the ith cell in the output layer corresponding to a particular pattern k presented on the input layer, and Y_{ik} the desired state of this cell. The learning problem has been formalized as the problem of realizing the equality: $S_k = Y_k$. This can be achieved by minimizing a cost function which is an evaluation of a distance between S_k and Y_k. We will use here a quadratic cost function:

$$E = \sum_k \sum_i \| S_{ik} - Y_{ik} \|^2 \tag{1}$$

where i is a cell on the last (output) layer and k indexes the patterns in the learning set. Let us denote x the state of the network, x_i^t will be the state of cell i in layer t. We thus have: $S_{ik} = x_i^N$, where N is the number of the output layer. Minimizing function E gives rise to two problems:

- ▷ how are the states of the network computed?
- ▷ which algorithms are to be used for the minimization?

3.2. General case

3.2.1. The problem

The state of the automaton i in layer t: x_i^t is computed through the weights of the network from the state of the automata in the previous layers. A natural way to do this is to use the weights so as to produce a linear or quadratic combination of the states of all the automata in previous layers. Let us give an example (see Figure 3):

For $t = 0$, we present an input pattern to the network, *i.e.*, we force the state of the automata on the first layer into the state x_i^0. At level $t = h$, the state is computed as a function of the states of previous layers $t < h$. This corresponds to a block-sequential iteration of the network [7]: automata in one layer (block) are updated in parallel, and the layers change state sequentially one after the other. For sake of simplicity, we assume here that connections go from each layer to its follower only. We will deal here with an output function of the general form:

$$x_i^{t+1} = f\left(\sum_j W_{ij} x_j^t\right) \tag{2}$$

where f is a differentiable function, W_{ij} is the weight of the connection from automaton j to automaton i and the summation is taken on all the inputs j to cell i. In the case

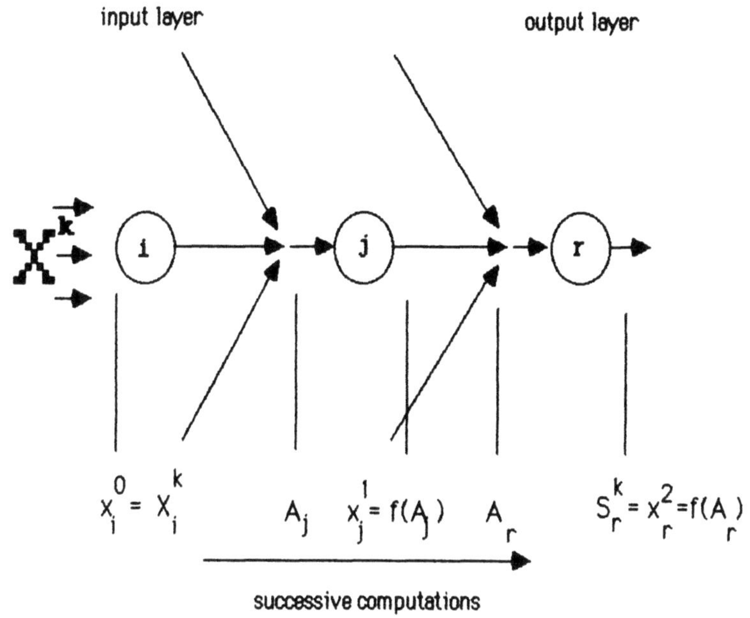

FIGURE 3: State dynamics.
When pattern X^k (the kth pattern presented to the network, whose i^{th} components is $X^k{}_i$) is presented to this network, the three layers are activated sequentially and the units inside a layer compute in parallel. This forward step ends when the last layer is activated and the network outputs a pattern S^k.

where f is a threshold function:

$$f(x) = 1(x - b), \text{where } 1(x) \text{ is } -1 \text{ if } x < 0, \text{ and } +1 \text{ if } x \geq 0$$

b is known as the *threshold* of f. By introducing a cell j_0, constant in state -1, we can write the threshold function f with threshold b in the form of equation (2), where the weight from cell j_0 is b. In the following we will always make this assumption when necessary, whatever the form of f, and thus $\sum_j W_{ij} x_j^t$ will eventually contain a term associated to the threshold of unit i.

The following form $f(x) = a(e^{kx}-1)/(e^{kx}+1)$ has been widely used, where a and k are parameters, problem dependent. Parameter k has been interpreted as a "temperature": allowing its variation during the learning session may help escaping from local minima (this technique is known as "simulated annealing" [5] and Aarts and van Laarhoven in this volume).

The cost function E, computed from the elements of the training set, is a function of all the W_{ij}. Minimizing E is a classical problem. Generally exact solutions cannot be derived, so approximate solutions must be computed, which is classically done using gradient methods [6]. However classical gradient methods are not adapted:

- the amount of computation involved may be very large.

- more important, these methods require, for the global minimization criterion, the knowledge at each step of ALL the associated (input, output) pairs. This is a very undesirable point, since we would like to produce networks that are able to evolve when new data are presented, instead of recomputing the whole structure from scratch. This problem has been extensively studied in the design of adaptive filters, and various algorithms have been proposed to solve it.

In the following, we will use one of the most simple and famous of these adaptive algorithms, namely the Widrow-Hoff rule [25] which is an adaptive gradient method. It allows to minimize at each step the error on one pattern only.

Let X_i be one input pattern and Y_i the corresponding desired output. Patterns $X_1, X_2, \cdots, X_m$ are introduced sequentially and repeatedly, until convergence. To simplify notations, we will denote the temporal sequence

$$(X_1, Y_1), (X_2, Y_2), \cdots, (X_m, Y_m), (X_1, Y_1), (X_2, Y_2), \cdots$$

by

$$(X^1, Y^1), (X^2, Y^2), \cdots, (X^m, Y^m), (X^{m+1}, Y^{m+1}), (X^{m+2}, Y^{m+2}), \cdots$$

The cost function to be minimized at step k is:

$$C(W) = \sum_i (S_i^k - Y_i^k)^2 \tag{3}$$

where the sum is taken on the cells i in the last layer.

The Widrow-Hoff rule used to modify the weights W_{ij} of the network is:

$$W_{ij}(k) = W_{ij}(k-1) - \epsilon(k)\, \partial C / \partial W_{ij} \tag{4}$$

where $\epsilon(k)$ is the iteration step.

As an illustration, this general rule will be applied in the next two sections to different network architectures.

Three problems must be solved in order to apply this formula:

- ▷ how to compute the gradient $[\partial C / \partial W_{ij}]$? Section 3.2.2. provides a general answer to this question.

- ▷ how to choose the initial weights $W(0)$? Initial weights represent the a-priori knowledge about the domain. Usually, when no relevant information is available, those weights are chosen at random. In practice, it has been found that convergence heavily depends on this initial choice and thus incorporating knowledge would help improving performances.

- ▷ in which order present the patterns in the sequence and how can we adjust the $\epsilon(k)$? This is the problem of the "pedagogy": the ordering and individual repetition of the examples may in some cases be crucial for convergence. There is no universal answer to this problem and a solution must be designed in each particular case. In the examples that we present here (Section 5), we have adopted a trivial pedagogy, presenting the examples, one after the other, repeatedly without changing the order. This procedure has been found successful in this case.

It may often be efficient to modify the $\epsilon(k)$, during the learning process, to help force into the network patterns badly memorized. In this paper, we have not used this possibility.

3.2.2. Adaptive gradient computation.

Let A_i be the total input to cell i. Then:

$$A_i = \sum_j W_{ij} x_j \qquad x_i = f(A_i) \tag{5}$$

Chain rule gives:

$$\partial C/\partial W_{ij} = \partial C/\partial A_i \cdot \partial A_i/\partial W_{ij} = \partial C/\partial A_i \cdot x_j$$

For a cell i on the last layer and the kth pattern in the sequence, we have, if we denote $S_i^k = f(A_i)$ the computed output of this cell:

$$\begin{aligned} \partial C/\partial A_i &= 2(S_i^k - Y_i^k)\, \partial S_i^k/\partial A_i \\ &= 2(S_i^k - Y_i^k) \cdot f'(A_i) \end{aligned}$$

Let us now denote $\partial C/\partial A_i = y_i$, we thus have:

$$y_i = 2(S_i^k - Y_i^k) \cdot f'(A_i) \tag{6}$$

For the other layers, *i.e.*, for a hidden cell i :

$$\partial C/\partial A_i = \sum_h \partial C/\partial A_h \cdot \partial A_h/\partial A_i$$

where h indexes the cells which receive their input from i.

$$\partial C/\partial A_i = \sum_h y_h \cdot \partial A_h/\partial x_i \cdot \partial x_i/\partial A_i$$

but from (5):

$$\partial C/\partial A_i = \sum_h y_h \cdot W_{hi} \cdot f'(A_i)$$

i.e.,

$$y_i = \left(\sum_h y_h \cdot W_{hi}\right) \cdot f'(A_i) \tag{7}$$

The general Widrow Hoff rule (4) for weights modification becomes:

$$W_{ij}(k) = W_{ij}(k-1) - \epsilon(k) y_i \cdot x_j \tag{8}$$

Example: Let us illustrate this process on the example of a three layered network (Figure 4). For such a network, the above algorithm corresponds to a general learning rule that has been proposed recently by different authors [16,17,20]. It has come to be known as the *Gradient-Back-Propagation* (GBP) algorithm.

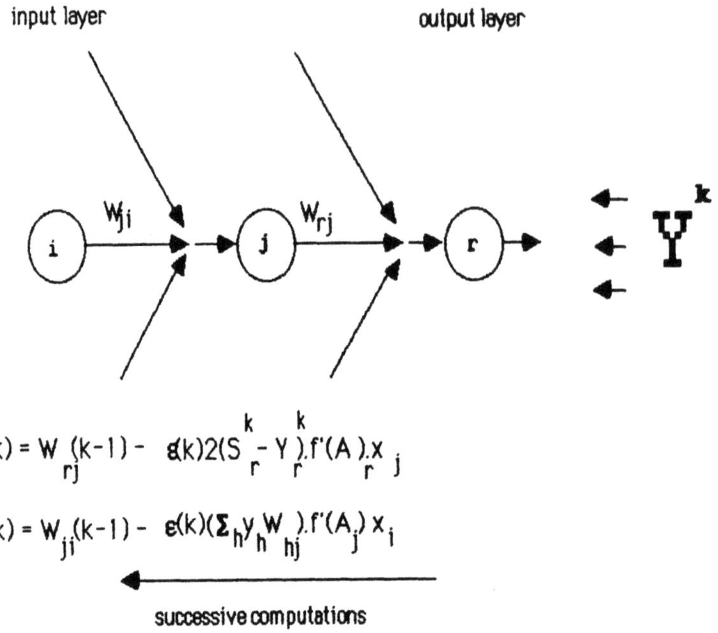

FIGURE 4: Gradient back propagation.
After the forward step, the computed output S^k is compared to the corresponding desired output Y^k. The weights of the network are modified according to the gradient of the cost function, one layer after the other, right to left.

3.3. Linear Learning

3.3.1. General results

As was mentioned previously, most studies have been devoted to two layered networks and linear learning [15]. We now discuss in more detail this case. It can be viewed as a particular case of the general problem presented above. With the same notations, this corresponds to the case where $f = Id, N = 2$ and full connectivity. The previous problem of realizing $S_k = Y_k$ here simply amounts to solving the following equation:

$$WX = Y \tag{9}$$

where X and Y are the matrices with columns the input patterns X_i and the desired output patterns Y_i respectively. If $Y \neq X$ the problem is known as "hetero-association" and if $Y = X$ as "auto-association". This problem is clearly much simpler, which explains why various solutions have been devised, among which exact ones are particularly interesting. We present some of the algorithms below.

A formal solution to system (9) is given through the generalized inverse theory [19].

Definition: X^+ is the pseudo inverse of X iff:

1. $XX^+X = X$

2. $X^+XX^+ = X^+$

3. XX^+ and X^+X are hermitian (*i.e.*, symmetric for a real matrix).

Pseudo inverses can be used to solve matrix equations such as: $WX = Y$ where X and Y are given and W is unknown. Let us give now some results.

Theorem: Equation (9) has an exact solution iff:

$$YX^+X = Y \tag{10}$$

and in this case, there exists an infinite number of solutions given by:

$$W = YX^+ + Z(I - XX^+) \tag{11}$$

where Z is an arbitrary matrix with the same dimensions as W.

Theorem: Among all solutions to equation (9),

$$W = YX^+ \tag{12}$$

(XX^+ in the case of auto-association where $X = Y$) is of minimum quadratic norm.

If condition (10) is not satisfied, then equation (9) has no solution, but it can be shown that matrices W for which the quadratic norm $\| WX - Y \|$ is minimum are just those given by equation (11), and of course, among those, matrix $W = YX^+$ is of minimum quadratic norm. Hence, when (10) is not satisfied, (11) gives the general expression of approximate solutions to (9), and (12) the best approximate solution.

3.3.2. Computational techniques.

Exact methods to compute X^+ have been derived [15]: they usually are very time consuming and need matrices inversions.

A method that is quite reasonable in computational time is a recursive algorithm, due to Greville [12], which does not need to invert matrices and may be implemented by *successively* presenting the examples $X_1, \cdots, X_m$: let us denote $\mathcal{X}_k = (\mathcal{X}_{k-1}X_k)$ a matrix with k columns, where $\mathcal{X}_{k-1}$ is the submatrix of X formed with its $k-1$ first columns and X_k is the k-th column of X. We thus have: $X = \mathcal{X}_m$. Greville's theorem states that X^+ can be computed in m steps (where m is the number of input patterns) by:

$$\mathcal{X}_k^+ = \begin{bmatrix} \mathcal{X}_{k-1}^+(I - X_k p_k^t) \\ p_k^t \end{bmatrix}$$

where

$$\begin{aligned} p_k &= \frac{(I - \mathcal{X}_{k-1}\mathcal{X}_{k-1}^+)X_k}{\| (I - \mathcal{X}_{k-1}\mathcal{X}_{k-1}^+)X_k \|^2} && \text{if the numerator is non zero} \\ &= \frac{(\mathcal{X}_{k-1}^+)^t \mathcal{X}_{k-1}^+ X_k}{1 + \| \mathcal{X}_{k-1}^+ X_k \|^2} && \text{otherwise} \end{aligned}$$

As $\mathcal{X}_1$ is just the first column X_1 of X we have:

$$\begin{aligned} \mathcal{X}_1^+ &= (X_1^t X_1)^{-1} X_1^t && \text{if } X_1 \text{ is non zero} \\ &= 0 && \text{otherwise} \end{aligned}$$

and of course $X^+ = \mathcal{X}_m^+$.

In practice, it is more convenient to compute W directly: we will use an adaptation of Greville [15] which allows a recursive computation. By keeping the same notations for $\mathcal{X}_k$ and evident notations for $\mathcal{Y}_k$ and denoting $W_k = \mathcal{Y}_k \mathcal{X}_k^+$, we have:

$$W_k = W_{k-1} - (W_{k-1} X_k - Y_k)\, p_k^t$$

where p_k is the same vector as in Greville.

At iteration step k, W_k is the solution to equation $W\mathcal{X}_k = \mathcal{Y}_k$ with minimum norm. This matrix thus encodes the associations between input patterns $X_1, \cdots, X_k$ and output patterns $Y_1, \cdots, Y_k$. If the columns of X are independent, the computation of W becomes simpler we then have:

$$\begin{aligned} W_k &= W_{k-1} - (W_{k-1} X_k - Y_k)[\chi_k^t / \parallel \chi_k \parallel^2] && \text{if } \chi_k \neq 0 \\ & W_{k-1} && \text{otherwise} \end{aligned}$$

where the χ_k are computed through the Gram-Schmidt orthogonalization process:

$$\begin{aligned} \chi_1 &= X_1 \\ \chi_k &= X_k - \textstyle\sum_{i=1,\cdots,k-1} \langle X_k, \chi_i \rangle \chi_i / \parallel \chi_i \parallel^2 \quad k = 2, \cdots, m \end{aligned}$$

where the summation runs on all non zero χ_i. More details can be found in Kohonen [15].

3.3.3. Approximated computation

As was mentioned before, matrices W minimizing $\parallel WX - Y \parallel$ are just those given by equation (11). We can thus use the Widrow-Hoff algorithm to find W. It consists here in choosing arbitrarily $W(0)$ and adjusting W by:

$$W(k+1) = W(k) - \epsilon(k)(W(k)X^{k+1} - Y^{k+1})[X^{k+1}]^t \tag{13}$$

This last rule is the corresponding particular case of (8), written with vector notations. As in the general case there is no existing proof of the convergence of this algorithm. However, in practice, it has been observed that with $\lambda_i = \lambda_1 / i$ the algorithm usually converges to a solution. The problem of adding one pattern to the memory is quite easy, it is sufficient to start with $W(0) = W$ and iterate with the new pattern until convergence. As the starting matrix is probably close to the solution, the computing time will usually not be long before convergence.

This algorithm is quite robust with respect to the initial value of W, one can choose for example $W = 0$ or W random.

3.3.4. Other models

We have seen that equation (9) may have an infinite number of solutions given by (11). In some cases, it may be interesting to impose further constraints on the solution so as to choose an "optimal" matrix Z. One possible choice, for example, in the auto-association case, is to impose the condition of 0-diagonal on W, which corresponds obviously to a particular choice of Z [9]. In the following, we will give the results of various simulations which allow to compare the performances for different Z.

A simplified solution of equation (9) is also known under the name of "Hebb law", introduced by D. Hebb in 1949 to fit biological evidence: any two neurons firing at the same time, when "shown" a given pattern, will have their connection strength reinforced. This leads to a modification rule of the weights W_{ij} that, in the auto-association case, is:

$$W_{ij} = W_{ij} + X_{ik}X_{jk}$$

which can be shown [9,17] equivalent to:

$$W = XX^t$$

Note that, when patterns X_k are linearly independent and orthonormal, then $W = XX^t$ is the solution of minimum norm of equation (9). Hence Hebb rule, can be considered as an approximated version of the solution given in Section 3.4. Although not very efficient, this simple rule allows to derive interesting analytical results [8,11,14,24] and has been extensively studied in the literature about neural networks [14].

Remark

It has been known since the book by Minsky-Papert on perceptrons [18] that certain tasks could not be achieved by linear classifiers. Multilayered networks ($n \geq 3$), because of their hidden units, are not submitted to these limitations [9,21]. They can compute more complicated predicates. For example this kind of network is able to learn the XOR function [9]. One can understand these increased capabilities by viewing the layers as performing successive steps in the decomposition of a "hard" problem into elementary tasks. This has been put in evidence for some simple problems [9,20].

4. Retrieval

4.1. Introduction

After the learning phase, connection weights are supposed to encode some desired knowledge. The network can then be used for the specific task it has been designed for; while performing this task, we will assume that this knowledge will not be changed any more, *i.e.*, that the weights are FIXED. Of course, the network could be modified later on (re-learning), so as to take into account a modification of the environment. Depending upon the application, the following performances are expected for the network:

▷ classification (auto-association or hetero-association) of patterns presented to the network.

▷ generalization: the network has encoded some relevant features of the task by learning from examples. It can then perform this task on patterns that it has not learned. For example, it can retrieve memorized items from noisy or incomplete patterns (associative memory), or produce relations between patterns it has not learned.

The recognition process can be decomposed into the successive following phases:

▷ present a pattern to the input layer of the network

▷ let the network evolve *i.e.*, compute the state of the automata, from one layer to the following ones, applying the formula:

$$x_i^{t+1} = g\left(\sum_j W_{ij} x_j^t\right), \tag{14}$$

t corresponding here to the layer number. g can be the same function as during the learning phase (see (2)), but not necessarily as will be seen below.

▷ the answer is obtained on the output layer.

It often appears that it is useful to introduce some additional ingredients, which may drastically improve the performances:

▷ *thresholding*: very often, the output of the network must take its values into a finite set. This is the case for example if the network is an associative memory for retrieving images in r gray levels. The output must then be thresholded so as to be interpreted.

▷ *iterations*: in the case of auto-association, better results are obtained if the output is fed-back to the network and the process iterated. This allows to use dynamic properties of the networks.

We will now review different retrieval processes for two layered networks, see [9,20] for multi-layered network.

4.2. Algorithms

In this paragraph, W denotes the weight matrix computed during the learning phase, whatever the learning algorithm.

Linear retrieval

This process has been widely used for associative memory [15]. In this case, the g function is the identity. The process consists in applying this linear operator to the input patterns. Thus the algorithm simply consists in performing: $Y = WX$. As we mentioned before, this algorithm can often be improved by thresholding the output and, in the case of auto-association, iterating the process. The corresponding algorithm is known as *Threshold Network* [7,8,14].

Brain state in the box

Using biological considerations in perception, Anderson [2] assumes, in a model for auto-association, that the pattern and the feed-back are present at the same time during the retrieval process and that the activities of the neurons are bounded. He proposes the following model, known as "Brain State in the Box" or BSB.

Let $M = \alpha W + \beta I$, and $B = [s, S] \subset \mathbf{R}$ (B is called the "box"), then the retrieval process consists, for an input pattern x, in computing the following sequence:

$$\begin{aligned} Y(0) &= x \\ Y(k+1)_i &= \begin{cases} s & \text{if } MY(k)_i < s \\ MY(k)_i & \text{if } MY(k)_i \text{ is in } B \\ S & \text{if } MY(k)_i > S \end{cases} \end{aligned}$$

This procedure is iterated until either a fixed point or a maximum number of iterations is reached. Generally, this process needs a lot of iterations to converge and then most of the automata are saturated (*i.e.* in state s or S).

Iteration with a smooth function

Let $W = XX^+ + Z(I - XX^+)$ be a solution of (9) in the case of auto-association: $WX = X$. The operator M used in the BSB model can be put into the following form:

$$\begin{aligned} M &= \alpha W + \beta I \\ M &= [\alpha XX^+ + \alpha Z(I - XX^+) + \beta I](XX^+ + I - XX^+) \\ M &= (\alpha + \beta)[XX^+ + ((\alpha Z + \beta I)/(\alpha + \beta))(I - XX^+)] \\ M &= (\alpha + \beta)W' \end{aligned}$$

where W' is a solution of equation (9) (given by (11)), which can be interpreted as a weight matrix obtained during the learning phase. The g function in this case is piecewise linear, and just $(\alpha + \beta)I$ inside the box (see Figure 5).

Let $A_i = \sum_j W'_{ij} X_j$ be the total input to cell i through the weight matrix W'. The BSB process can be seen as a limiting case of the retrieval process by a "smooth" function g: iterate on each cell $y = g(A_i)$, where $g(x) = a(e^{kx} - 1)/(e^{kx} + 1)$. The size of the box and the slope of the function are respectively defined through the a and k coefficients. The two methods will be compared in Figure 8.

When the smooth function is used, one cannot hope to reach a fixed point within a reasonable time (computing a smooth function is of course time consuming). So, for computation convenience, the process is simply iterated a certain number of times, after which the result is thresholded.

5. Examples

The performances of the above algorithms have all been tested on the same simple example of auto-association so as to allow for their comparison. The learning set will be part of a 26 letters alphabet. Each letter is binarily $(-1, 1)$ encoded on an 8×8 grid (Figure 6).

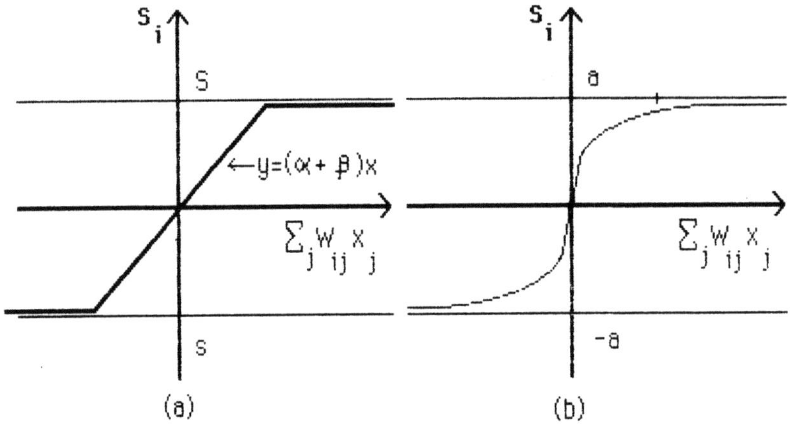

FIGURE 5: examples of g functions.
Both curves represent a g function corresponding to the output cell i of the network (the pattern index has been omitted)
(a) is a piecewise linear function used in the BSB model with a box B = [s,S].
(b) is a smooth function of the form $g(x) = a(e^{kx}-1)/(e^{kx}+1)$.

It is not claimed that this example should be considered as representing an application in pattern recognition: we did not use any trick (coding, ...) to improve performances. The example is simply intended to illustrate the behavior of the algorithms presented so far and to compare their performances.

Architecture

We have used networks with two layers of 8×8 automata each, fully interconnected (Figure 7). Each input unit receives the value of a pixel, the corresponding output unit is expected to be in this same value after computation (auto-association).

Learning

Two algorithms have been tested with memory sizes of 10, 18, 26 letters:

▷ XX^+ computed through Greville's algorithm (Section 3.5). Figure 8 shows the curves $W10$, $W18$, $W26$ for the corresponding memory sizes.

▷ a solution of equation $WX = X$ constrained to have a zero diagonal, computed through a projected gradient method (Section 3.7). Figure 8 gives the curves $W10{,}0$, $W18{,}0$, $W26{,}0$ for the different sizes.

In order to compare the learning algorithms, we have used the linear retrieval process with thresholding (threshold network with threshold 0: Section 4.2.) The complete memorization has been obtained for each learning set. Performances of the $W*{,}0$ memories appear to be always better. Thus, depending on the problem, constraints may be introduced during the learning phase to help retrieval.

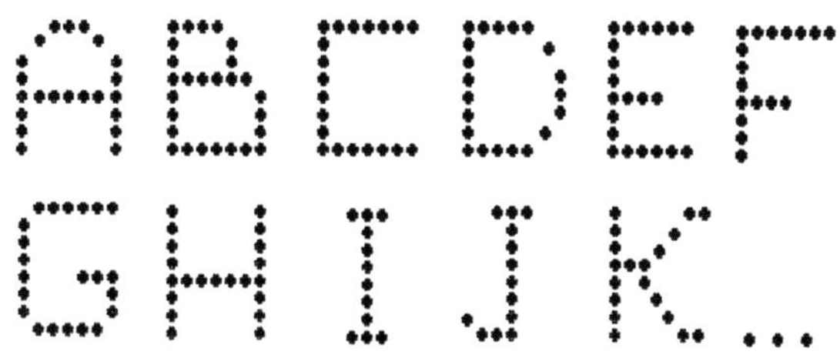

FIGURE 6: Some of the letters that have been used for the tests. Each of them is binarily encoded (with -1,1) on an 8*8 grid.

Retrieval

We compare the performances of three retrieval algorithms and present the results on Figure 9. In the three cases we have used matrix $W18,0$ which corresponds to the memorization of the 18 first letters of the alphabet (see above). Those algorithms are:

- ▷ threshold network: same process as in Figure 8.
- ▷ BSB network: we use $M = 0.2W + 0.9I$, with box $B = [-1.3, +1.3]$ (as in [2]). We allow for a maximum number of 60 iterations and 0–threshold the final result.
- ▷ "smooth" network: we have iterated — with a maximum of 10 iterations — the function: $g(x) = a(1 - e^{-k.x})/(1 + e^{-kx})$. Various choices of the parameters a and k have been tested, we present the results for $a = 1.7$ and $k = 4$.

The performances of the different algorithms appear on Figures 8 and 9. We represent the recognition rate (percentage of correct retrieval of a stored pattern from a noisy input) in terms of the "noise" of this input. The noise corresponds to an exact number of inverted pixels with respect to the memorized pattern.

The retrieval capacity has been tested by presenting for each letter a set of 100 noisy patterns to the network: each point on the curves is thus an average of these 100 results for all the letters in the learning set. Figure 10 gives examples of the retrieval process starting from various noisy patterns, in the case of the threshold and BSB networks.

Note that the retrieval rate differs from one letter to another (Figure 11). In our example the threshold-retrieval needs only a few iterations to reach a fixed point. The other two methods need more iterations, and the number of iterations needed to converge increases with the size of noise: distance from the input pattern to the corresponding memorized one. However allowing for iterations provides better performances.

6. Conclusion

We have presented here some basic techniques of connectionist models, especially for learning and retrieval, and illustrated the behavior of some algorithms on a simple example. This example allows to point out some characteristic features of this approach:

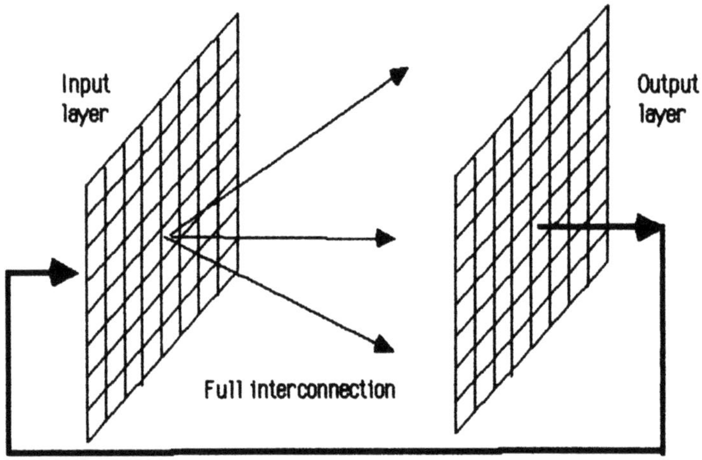

FIGURE 7: Architecture of a 2-layered network fully connected.
The two layers of this network having the same number of cells, when performing auto-association, the ouput can be fed back to the input layer, allowing for iterations during the retrieval.

▷ a general learning algorithm, *domain-independent* can be derived.

▷ knowledge is automatically encoded in the connections, leading to a *distributed representation.*

▷ the retrieval process is a *dynamical* process: allowing for iterations increases performances.

▷ the process is *noise-resistant*: reference patterns can be retrieved from noisy items. This resistance to noise can be used to implement *generalization* in some learning problems.

Various applications have been proposed in the literature. The field of multilayer networks is especially promising: Boltzmann Machines and Gradient Back Propagation algorithms have shown that it was possible to transcend the limitations of previous models (perceptrons, linear classifiers). But still, only very few real-world applications exist, which leaves many open questions about the exact performances of this type of model. Feldman in this volume presents other aspects of the connectionist point of view.

Acknowledgement: We are very grateful to Y. Le Cun for valuable discussions, to Dr. Devijver for inviting us to the ASI in Spa and to NATO for its support.

References

[1] Ackley, D.H., G.E. Hinton, T.J. Sejnowski, "A learning algorithm for Boltzmann Machines," *Cognitive Science*, **9**, 147-169, 1985.

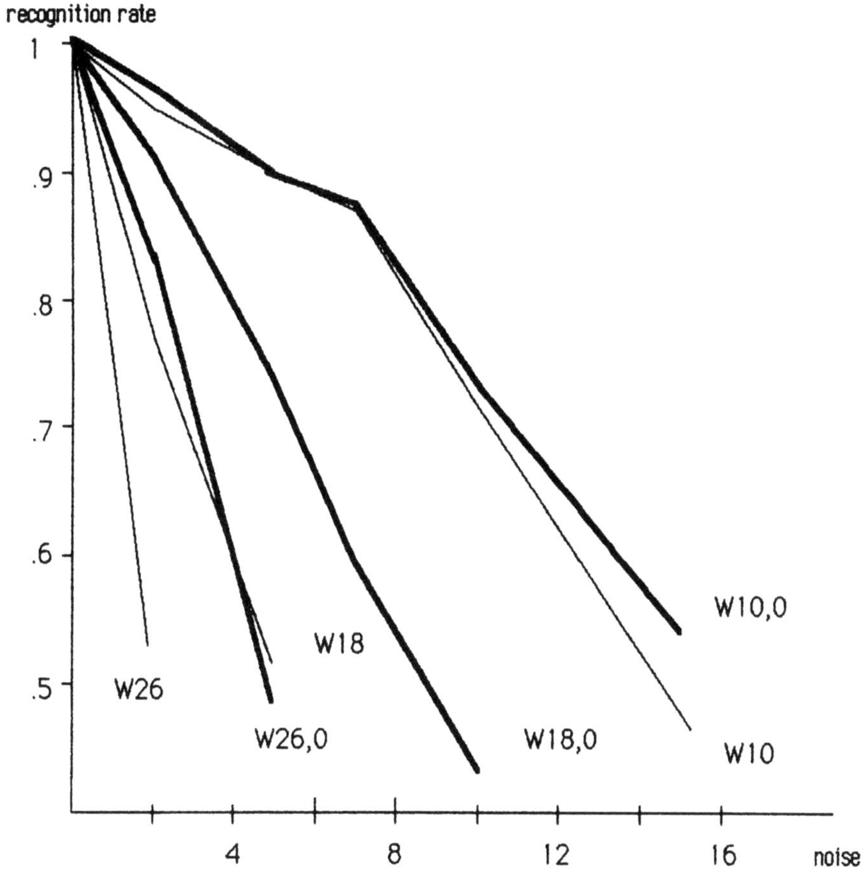

FIGURE 8: comparison of two learning algorithms for different memory sizes.
Curves Wp and Wp,0 have been obtained by learning the p first letters of the alphabet respectively through Greville's algorithm and through a constrained (0-diagonal) gradient method. The threshold network retrieval process (0-threshold) has been used to compare their performances, a pattern was considered to be retrieved when it matched exactly the reference pattern.

[2] Anderson, J.A., "Cognitive capabilities of a parallel system," in [5], 109-226.

[3] Ballard, D.H., G.E. Hinton, T.J. Sejnowski, "Parallel visual computation," *Nature*, **306**, 21-26, 1983.

[4] Ballard, D.H., "Parameter nets," *Artificial Intelligence*, **22**, 235-267, 1984.

[5] Bienenstock, E., F. Fogelman Soulie, G. Weisbuch Eds., *Disordered Systems and Biological Organization*, Springer Verlag, NATO ASI Series in Systems and Computer Science, F20, 1986.

[6] Duda, R.O., P.E. Hart, *Pattern Classification and Scene Analysis*, J. Wiley, 1973.

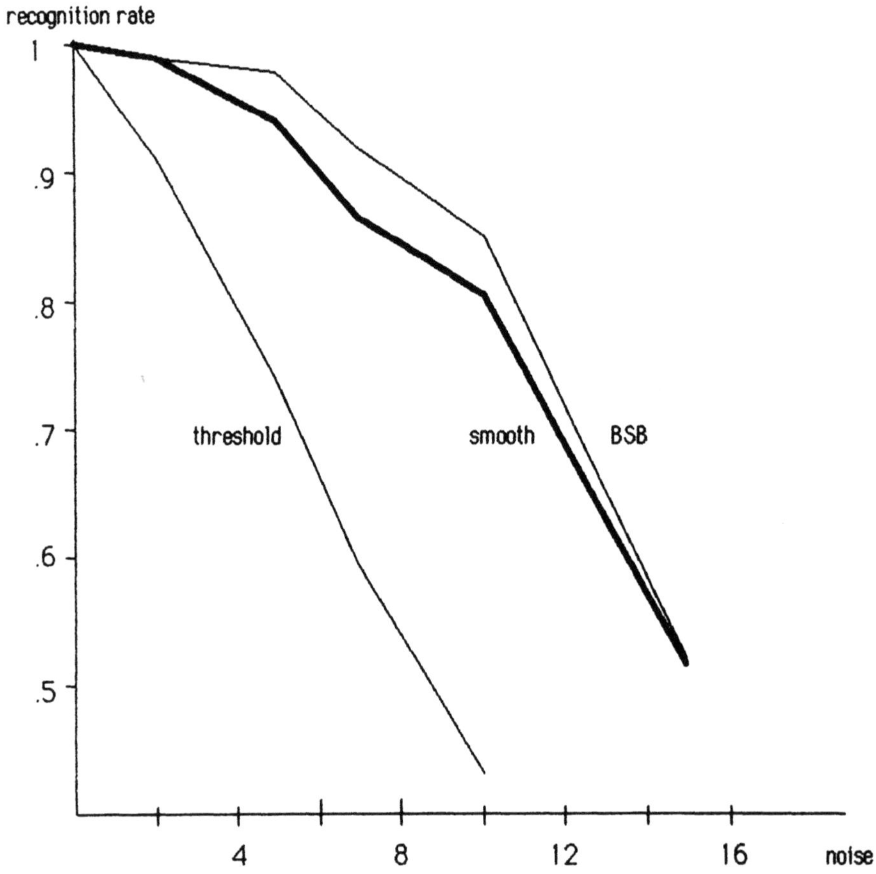

FIGURE 9: comparison of three retrieval algorithms.
The learning matrix being W18,0, retrieval performances corresponding to threshold network, Brain State in the Box and Smooth network are plotted. In all cases, the final result has been thresholded (0-threshold) for the comparison (exact match) with the reference pattern.

[7] Fogelman Soulie F., E. Goles Chacc, "Knowledge representation by automata networks," in *Computer and Computing*, P. Chenin, C. di Crescenzo, F. Robert Eds., Masson-Wiley, 175-180, 1985.

[8] Fogelman Soulie, F., G. Weisbuch, "Random iterations of threshold networks and associative memory," to appear in *Siam J. on Computing*.

[9] Fogelman Soulie, F., P. Gallinari, Y. Le Cun, S. Thiria, "Automata networks and artificial intelligence," in *Computation on Automata Networks*, F. Fogelman Soulie, Y. Robert, M. Tchuente Eds., Manchester Univ. Press, to appear.

[10] Geman, S., D. Geman, "Stochastic relaxation, Gibbs distribution and the Bayesian restoration of images," *IEEE Trans. PAMI*, **6**, 721-741, 1984.

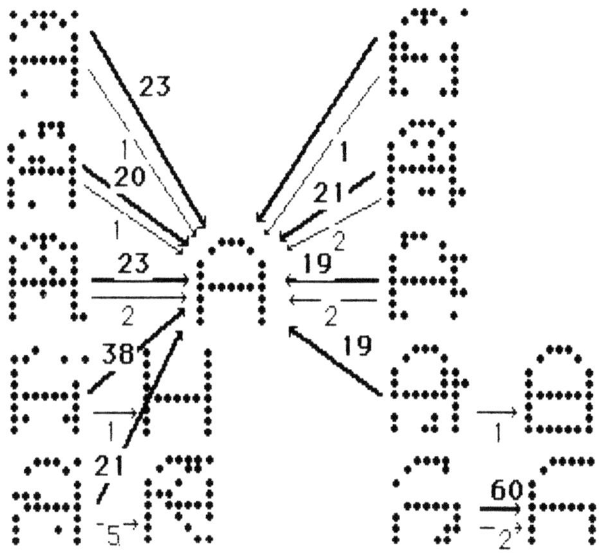

FIGURE 10: Retrieval with threshold and BSB network.
The figure shows examples of associated pairs (input pattern = noisy "A", computed output pattern) with the two networks. Thin lines correspond to the threshold network and bold ones to the BSB network. The number of iterations needed for the retrieval is indicated along the lines. The learning matrix was W18,0, the noisy "A" 's have exactly 7 pixels inverted.

[11] Goles-Chacc, E., F. Fogelman Soulie, D. Pellegrin., "Decreasing energy functions as a tool for studying threshold networks," *Disc. Appl. Math*, **12**, 261-277, 1985.

[12] Greville, T.N.E., "Some applications of the pseudo inverse of a matrix," *Siam Rev.*, **2**, 15-22, 1960.

[13] Hinton, G.E., J.A. Anderson Eds., *Parallel Models of Associative Memory*, L. Erlbaum, 1981.

[14] Hopfield, J.J., "Neural networks and physical systems with emergent collective computional abilities," *Proc. Nat. Acad . Sc.*, USA, 2554-2558, 1982.

[15] Kohonen, T., *Self-Organization and Associative Memory*, Springer Verlag, 1984.

[16] Le Cun, Y., "A learning scheme for asymmetric threshold network," in *Cognitiva 85*, CESTA–AFCET Eds., t.2, 599-604, 1985.

[17] Le Cun, Y., "Learning process in an asymmetric threshold network," in [5], 209-226, 1986.

[18] Minsky, M., Papert, S., *Perceptrons*, MIT Press, 1969.

[19] Rao, C.R., Mitra, S.K., *Generalized Inverses of Matrices and its Applications*, Wiley, 1971.

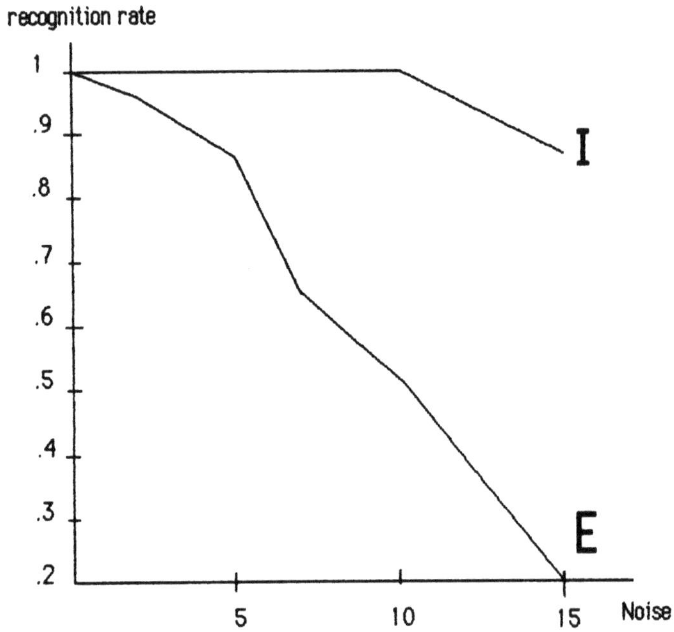

FIGURE 11: Comparison of the retrieval performances in a BSB network (with W18,0) for two different letters.
The retrieval rate can be very different from a letter to an other. The values plotted on fig.8 and fig.9 where averaged on all the letters of the test set.

[20] Rumelhart, D.E., G.E. Hinton, R.J. Williams, "Learning internal representations by error propagation," in *Parallel Distributed Processing, Explorations in the Microstructure of Cognition*, vol. 1, Foundations, D.E. Rumelhart, J.L. McClelland Eds., MIT Press, 1986.

[21] Sejnowski, T.J., Kienker, P.K., G.E. Hinton, "Learning symmetry groups with hidden units: beyond the perceptron". Submitted to *Physica D*.

[22] Sejnowski, T.J., G.E. Hinton, "Separating figures from ground with a Boltzmann machine," in *Vision, Brain and Cooperative Computation*, M.A. Arbib, A.R. Hanson Eds., MIT Press, 1985.

[23] Sejnowski, T.J., C.H. Rosenberg, "NETtalk: a parallel network that learns to read aloud," Johns Hopkins Technical Report JHU/EECS-86-01.

[24] Weisbuch G., F. Fogelman Soulie, "Scaling laws for the attractors of Hopfield networks", *J. Physique Lett.*, **46**, 623-630, 1985.

[25] Widrow, B., H.E. Hoff, "Adaptive switching circuits," *60 IRE Wescon Conv. Record*, Part 4, 96-104, Aug 1960.

[26] Winston, P.H., *Artificial Intelligence*, Addison Wesley, 2nd Ed., 1984.

NETWORK REPRESENTATIONS AND MATCH FILTERS FOR INVARIANT OBJECT RECOGNITION

Harry Wechsler

Department of Electrical Engineering
University of Minnesota
Minneapolis, MN 55455, U.S.A.

1. Introduction

Artificial Intelligence (AI) deals with the types of problem solving and decision making that humans continuously face in dealing with the world. Such activity involves by its very nature complexity, uncertainty, and ambiguity which can "distort" the phenomena (*e.g.*, imagery) under observation. However, following the human example, any artificial vision system should process information such that the results are invariant to the vagaries of the data acquisition process.

Computer Vision (CV) (Ballard and Brown, 1982) represents the computational study of processes which produce useful descriptions from visual input. Computational models, central to the study of all of AI, then describe in a precise (algorithmic) way how a solution to a particular problem can be found.

The challenge of the visual recognition problem stems from the fact that the interpretation of a 3-D scene is confounded by several dimensions of variability. Such dimensions include uncertain perspective, orientation and size (pure geometric variability) along with sensor noise, object occlusion, and non-uniform illumination. Vision systems must not only be able to sense the identity of objects despite this variability, but they must also be able to explicitly characterize such variability. This is so because the variability in the image formation process inherently carries much of the valuable information about the image being analyzed.

It is interesting to note that objects can be recognized when viewed from novel orientations (object transfer) under moderate levels of visual noise and/or occlusion, while novel instances of a category can be rapidly classified. Information which is the basis of recognition should be therefore invariant under linear transformation (LT) and modest image degradation; partial matches should be solved as well. Available machine vision systems fail in the above requirements. They usually assume limited and known noise, even illumination, objects do not touch each other and are learned for a given stable state (position/appearance prespecified) set. Both industrial automation and

Acknowledgement: This work was supported in part by the National Science Foundation under Grant ECS–8310057, and by MEIS (Microelectronics and Information Science) center at the University of Minnesota.

NATO ASI Series, Vol. F30
Pattern Recognition Theory and Applications
Edited by P. A. Devijver and J. Kittler

target tracking and identification are hampered by the restrictions quoted above. An enhanced capability for dealing effectively with noisy and partially occluded objects is needed if solutions to the Bin-Picking Problem are sought.

Most vision research, whether studying biological or computer vision, has a common goal of understanding the general computational nature of visual perception. It is widely acknowledged that synergism of various fields like neuro-physiology, psychophysics, the physics related to image formation, and signal analysis can further the progress toward the above goal. And indeed, it is the very availability of such a synergetic methodology which made computer vision the premier area for both development and success in AI. As one example, the parallel processing streams for motion and form detection and their interactions, as identified by Van Essen (1983) within the visual cortex, are pointing toward the concept of data integration.

Our goal is to solve basic problems in computer vision by looking for general ("deep") rather than particular, goal-oriented ("surface") solutions. From a conceptual development viewpoint we are aiming toward a hypothetico-deductive (HD) theory characteristic of a formal-operational thinker rather than the lower level associations characteristic of a concrete-operational thinker. Specifically, the formal-operational thinker starts by considering possibilities and only subsequently proceeds to reality (for prediction and verification). Possibility is subordinated to reality, which is seen as the realm of a much wider world of possibilities and which happens to exist or hold true in a given problem situation. Such a theory is starting to gain acceptance and it is being used for advanced intelligent (expert) systems dealing with the visual world. One of the crucial concepts for such a theory is the availability of transformations. (As Simon (1984) points out, all mathematical derivation can be viewed simply as change of representation, making evident what was previously true but obscure. This view can be extended to all of problem solving — solving a problem then means representing it (transforming it) so as to make the solution transparent. In other words, knowledge has to be made explicit if and when needed.) As far as the concrete-operational thinker is concerned, the realm of abstract possibility is seen as an uncertain and only occasional extension of the safer and surer realm of palpable reality. The theory is of a non-theoretical and non-speculative (empirico-inductive S-R) reasoning type (Flavell, 1985).

Componential analysis of brain function (Farah, 1985) is just one of the research areas suggesting the following generic process for image recognition.

STM —— Matcher —— LTM

where LTM is long term memory, and STM is short term memory (visual buffer). Intelligent systems for computer vision, based on such a generic process, are implemented as a loop of both bottom-up (image (pre)processing and feature extraction), hypothesis (model) formation and top-down (model instantiation, prediction and verification.) The bottom-up step provides an image representation. The models are stored in memory and there is a match between representation and memory. Based on the result, the identity of an object and its attitude in space can be assessed or the loop is again traversed until enough information and confidence is gained about the identity. Such a model is strongly supported by psychophysical phenomena like that of familiar size. As an example, Granrud *et al.* (1985) show that top-down information mediates perception and that memory has a direct impact on space perception. Recent research also suggests that there are mid-level representations (Mulgaonkar and Shapiro, 1985) which populate the area between low- and high-level. The role of mid-level vision could be defined as being that of searching for regularity in the visual input. Assuming causality and non-accidentalness of properties, this amounts to looking for real world structures (Witkin and Tenenbaum, 1983). The above discussion suggests that variability can be dealt with by specifying a prototypical memory and by matching its different deprojections (parametrized transformations) (Brooks, 1981) against a computed image representation. Memory (LTM) accounts for occlusion and noise by allowing partial key-indexing. Furthermore, memory is reconstructive, *i.e.*, it yields the entire output vector (or a closed approximation of it) even if the input is noisy or only partially present. (representations are object-centered in a 3-D environmental frame. The deprojection can be executed at either the STM or LTM level.) A capability like the one mentioned above is provided by distributed associative memories (DAM) (Kohonen, 1984).

2. Distributed Associative Memories (DAM)

The generic recognition process matches derived image representations (STM) against visual memory (LTM). A particular organization of LTM in terms of DAMs and its implications are discussed next. Conceptually, DAM are related to GMF (generalized match filters) (Caulfield and Weinberg, 1982) and SDF (synthetic discriminant functions) (Hester and Casasent, 1981). Like them, the DAMs attempt to capture a distributed representation which averages over variational representations belonging to the same object class. Such distributed representations are consistent with Gestalt (holistic) recognition, where the holistic organization can be imposed over space and/or time. Furthermore, DAMs allow for the implicit representation of structural relationships and contextual information, helpful constraints for choosing among different interpretations. As such, a relatively automatic process of detection of familiar patterns, characteristic to expert recognition, could be then achieved). One could make the case that DAMs implement procedural memory subsystems which are characteristic of skilled performance. It is the proceduralization of knowledge which leads to expert performance).

The principle of distributed and concurrent computation is embedded in DAM. It is consistent with the modular and parallel architecture suggested by present models of the visual cortex (Hubel and Wiesel, 1979) (Ballard, Hinton and Sejnowski, 1983). The associative nature of the model allows for both extensive indexing and cross-referencing and intra-modal data fusion based on the synchrony of occurrence. The requirement of recognizing noisy and/or partially occluded (STM) objects is well served by an associative high-density net of connections. Specifically, the DAM allows for memory to be "reconstructive," *i.e.*, the matching of incoming (STM) and stored (LTM) representations yields the entire output vector (or a closed approximation of it) even if the input is noisy, partially present or if there is noise in the memory itself (computer components like neurons are not always reliable and they might fail as well).

The DAM is like a "holographic memory" and its basic principle of operation for the autoassociative case is given below

$$M = FF^{+}$$

where M is the optimum DAM, and F^+ is the pseudoinverse of the input matrix F. (A heteroassociative model can be easily developed by assuming a memory of the type $M = F_1 F_2^+$ where $F_1 \neq F_2$). F_1 and F_2 are called the forcing and coupling functions, respectively. If one can assume linear independence between the representations (rasterscanned as vectors) which make up the matrix F then

$$M = F(F^T F)^{-1} F^T$$

The recall operation, *i.e.*, the attempt to recognize a (test) representation t yields a retrieved approximation given by

$$\hat{f} = Mt$$

(The recall operation for the heteroassociative case can retrieve either the forcing (input) function f or the coupling (association) a. Specifically, if the corresponding matrices are F and A, respectively, then

$$i)\ t \in \{a\},\ M = FA^+,\ \hat{f} = Mt;$$
$$ii)\ t \in \{f\},\ M = AF^+,\ \hat{a} = Mt.\ )$$

The memory matrix M defines the space spanned by the input representations in STM. The recall operation is implemented through the use of M as a projection operator. The retrieved data $\hat{f}$ obeys the relationship

$$t = \hat{f} + \tilde{f}$$

where $\hat{f}$ plays the role of an optimal autoassociative recollection/linear regression in terms of M. $\tilde{f}$, the residual, is orthogonal to the space spanned by M, and represents the novelty in t with respect to the stored data in M. It is the decomposition of t in terms of $(\hat{f}, \tilde{f})$ which can be then used to facilitate learning/discovering new things.

The DAMs belong to neural networks, a field of constantly increasing relevance and importance (Ballard *et al.*, 1983). They could be structured both hierarchically and heterarchically for improved performance and through available efferent ($\downarrow$), afferent ($\uparrow$), and lateral ($\leftrightarrow$) connections, the limitations due to local processing and characteristic of early perceptrons (Minsky and Papert, 1968) could be removed. Neural networks would then implement a type of distributed image representation and computation. Network interdependency rather than linear processing could thus facilitate contingency (feedback) object recognition through the implicit evidential reasoning (Garvey and Lowrence, 1983) as required for data fusion. The process of recognition is not necessarily a one-step procedure, and one would be well-advised to design an iterative algorithm. Relaxation (Davis and Rosenfeld, 1981) and/or simulated annealing (Kirpatrick, Gelatt and Vecchi, 1983) (Hopfield, 1982) could be coupled to the recall operation ($\hat{f} = Mt$) in order to improve on the recognition results. (The computational complexity of such iterative procedures is an important research issue on its own (Nahar *et al.*, 1985).)

Neural networks, like the DAMs, can be conceptually thought of as self-modifying systems by their changing the synaptic connections. The issue of recognition/classification is then reflected in some kind of differential amplification, *i.e.*, the alteration of the connection strengths of the synapses of any particular network which happens to fit a particular image representation. The neural model also suggests the possibility of a degenerate set, *i.e.*, a non-isomorphic set of isofunctional structures, such that the recognition is good over the ensemble of possibilities to be encountered in the future. The scheme discussed is then more akin to development than to learning. Specifically, spontaneous (rather than imposed), structural reorganization (rather than mere local change) and reflective abstraction (rather than practice with knowledge of results) are facilitated. (It is interesting to note that recent research by Hopfield (1982) seems to suggest that DAMs when activated in a hierarchical network structure occasionally "construct" new memories out of the locally activated memories. Such a capability is characteristic to both implicit learning and suggesting of new conjectures. It is useful for creating adaptive recognition systems which do not have to be "instructed" (*i.e.*, given a template), for each pattern to be recognized. Furthermore, a "conjecturing" capability will facilitate that advanced stage of development as defined by the hypothetico-deductive level.) Furthermore, the neural models which improve through selective adaptation (perturbation) are philosophically more appealing and natural than instructionist models which improve under the guidance of a teacher ((Kuhn, 1970), (Edelman, 1982), (Searl, 1985)). Finally, an additional advantage of DAMs is that they provide for the recognition of novel (contextual) instances of a category/type. One has to remember that Aristotelian attempts of defining natural concepts in terms of a predetermined set of attributes are not too successful, and that significant philosophical investigations (Wittgenstein, 1953) suggest that only "contextual" definitions are meaningful.

3. Invariance

The specifications, in terms of fidelity and invariance, for both the STM (image representations - visual buffer) and LTM (visual memory) are met through the use of the following modules:

(a) Homomaphic Filtering

The multiplicative law of image formation becomes additive if one takes the logarithm of the image-value function. Spatial filtering in the form of a high-pass filter can then suppress the illumination component and thus recover reflectance as an intrinsic (Barrow and Tenenbaum, 1978) characteristic.

(b) Conformal Mappings

Assume Cartesian plane points given as $(x, y) = (\Re(z), \Im(z))$ where $z = x + jy$. One can write $z = r\exp\{j\theta\}$ where $r = |z| = \sqrt{x^2 + y^2}$ and $\theta = \arg(z) = \arctan(y/x)$. The CL(Complex Logarithmic)-mapping is then the conformal mapping of points z onto points w defined by

$$w = \ln(z) = \ln(r\exp\{j\theta\}) = \ln(r) + j\theta$$

Logarithmically spaced concentric rings and radials of uniform angular spacing are mapped into uniformly straight lines. More generally, after CL-mapping, rotation and scaling about the origin in the Cartesian domain correspond to simple linear shifts in the $\theta(\text{mod } 2\pi)$ and $\ln(r)$ directions, respectively. Correlation techniques can then be used to detect invariance (to scale and rotation) within a linear shift between image representations.

(c) Deprojection
Invariance to perspective distortions – slant and tilt (σ, τ) – can be achieved via deprojection. Either the STM or LTM representation is transformed until it comes in close match with its counterpart, if at all. The deprojection need not be exhaustive over all possible pairs of (slant, tilt). 3-D cues, like shape from shading, texture gradients, motion and/or monocular cues, could filter out unlikely candidate pairs (σ, τ).

(d) Cross-Talk Elimination
The quality of retrieved information following a DAM-recall operation ($\hat{f} = Mt$) depends on the memory structure. Specifically, if the associations are such that the forcing functions are "similar" in appearance then the memory structure is far from approximating an orthogonal system. As a result, if the test image hitting the memory is t then the retrieved representation is a mixture (cross-talk) of all those coupling functions f_i which were originally associated with forcing functions "similar" to t. The way of reducing the cross-talk is that of increasing the orthogonality of the system by making the forcing functions as dissimilar in their appearance as possible. One method aimed at achieving just such a result is that of preprocessing, where techniques like the Laplacian and/or factor analysis can filter out the common structures among the forcing functions.

An experimental system called FOVEA (Jacobson and Wechsler, 1985b) implements high resolution conjoint image representations of space/spatial frequency (Jacobson and Wechsler, 1985a). Invariance to linear transformations (LT) and perspective is provided via CL-mapping, different fixation points and deprojection. We are presently implementing the distributed associative memories (DAM) and plan to integrate them within a multi-resolution pyramid (Tanimoto and Pavlidis, 1975).

4. Conclusions

Our research suggests the following approaches as the most likely to advance the field of invariant object recognition.

(a) A cognitive approach, where an adequate knowledge-base, via deprojection, can account for geometrical distortions and thus both identify the object and its attitude in space. Such an approach, if implemented, represents in fact an expert system (ES) for computational vision (CV).

(b) Neural networks as recently discussed by Edelman (1982) and Fukushima (1984). Such networks allow for self-organization, *i.e.* unsupervised learning. Furthermore, they suggest a *selectionist* rather than *instructionist* approach for modeling the information processing task of any intelligent system.

(c) Finally, it is unlikely that one approach by itself will provide all the answers. It is more likely that a synergetic approach will be more successful. The reasons are twofold: the analogies drawn from different fields and the powerful mix that such methods can provide if and when they are combined together. One example is the matched filter (signal analysis) together with statistical PR yielding synthetic discriminant functions (SDF) for object recognition. We also suggest the mix of neural networks–DAM (distributed associative memories) and statistical analysis.

It appears that the recognition memory has to approximate in a conceptual way the equivalent of a match filter.

References

[1] Ballard, D.H., C.M. Brown (1982), "Computer Vision," Prentice Hall, 1982.

[2] Ballard, D.H., G.E. Hinton, T.J. Sejnowski, (1983), Parallel visual computation, "Nature," 306, 5938, 21-26.

[3] Barrow, H.G., J.M. Tenenbaum (1978), Recovering intrinsic scene characteristics from images, in "Computer Vision Systems," A. Hanson and E. Riseman (Eds.), Academic Press.

[4] Brooks, R. (1981), Symbolic reasoning among 3-D models and 2-D images, "Artificial Intelligence," 17, 1-3.

[5] Caulfield, H.J., M.H. Weinberg (1982), Computer recognition of 2-D pattern using generalized matched filters, "Applied Optics," 21,9.

[6] Davis, L.S., A. Rosenfeld, (1981), Cooperating processes for low-level vision: a survey, "Artificial Intelligence," 17, 1-3, 245-263.

[7] Edelman, G.M. (1982), Group selection and higher brain function, "Bulletin of the American Academy of Arts and Science," vol. XXXVI, 1.

[8] Farah, M.J. (1985), The neurological basis of mental imagery: a componential analysis, in "Visual Cognition," S. Pinker (Ed.), MIT Press.

[9] Flavell, J.H. (1985), "Cognitive Development," (2nd Ed.), Prentice Hall.

[10] Fukushima, K. (1984), A hierarchical neural network model for associative memory, "Biol. Cybernetics," 50, 105-113.

[11] Garvey, T.D., J.D. Lowrance (1983), Evidential reasoning: an implementation for multisensor integration, TN 307, AI Center, SRI, Palo Alto, CA.

[12] Granrud, C., R. Haake, A. Yonas (1985), Sensitivity to familiar size: the effects of memory on spatial perception, "Perception Psychophysics," 37, 459-466.

[13] Hester, C., D. Casasent (1981), Interclass discrimination using synthetic discriminant functions (SDF), "Proc. SPIE on Infrared Technology for Target Detection and Classification," Vol. 302.

[14] Hopfield, J.J. (1982), Neural networks and physical systems with emergent collective computational abilities, "Proc. Natl. Acad. Sci. USA," 79, April 1982.

[15] Hubel, D., T. Wiesel (1979), Brain mechanisms of vision, "Scientific American," October.

[16] Jacobson, L., H. Wechsler (1985a), Joint spatial/spatial frequency representations for image processing, "SPIE/Cambridge Int. Conference on Intelligent Robots and Computer Vision," Boston, MA.

[17] Jacobson, L., H. Wechsler (1985b), FOVEA - A system for invariant visual form recognition, "2nd Int. Symposium on Optical and Electro-Optical Applied Science and Recognition," Cannes, France.

[18] Kirpatrick, S., C.D. Gelatt, M.P. Vecchi (1983), Optimization by simulated annealing, "Science," 220, 671.

[19] Kohonen, T. (1984), "Self-Organization and Associative-Memories," Springer-Verlag.

[20] Kuhn, T. (1970), "The Structure of Scientific Revolution," The University of Chicago Press.

[21] Minsky, M., S. Papert (1968), "Perceptrons," MIT Press.

[22] Mulgaonkar, P.G., L.G. Shapiro (1985), Hypothesis-based geometric reasoning about perspective images, "Proc. of the Third Workshop on Computer Vision, Representation and Control" Bellaire, Michigan.

[23] Nahar, S., S. Sahni, E. Shragowitz (1985), Simulated annealing and combinatorial optimization, TR 85-56, Dept. of Computer Science, University of Minnesota.

[24] Searl, J. (1985), "Mind, Brain and Science," Harvard University Press.

[25] Simon, H.A., (1984), "The Science of the Artificial," (2nd ed.), MIT Press.

[26] Tanimoto, S., T. Pavlidis (1975), A hierarchical data structure for picture processing, "Computer Graphics and Image Processing," 4, 2, 104-119.

[27] Van Essen, D.C., J.H.R. Maunsell (1983), Hierarchical organization and functional streams in the visual cortex, TINS (Trends in Neuro Sciences).

[28] Witkin, A.P., J.M. Tenenbaum (1983), On the role of structure in vision, in "Human and Machine Vision," J. Beck, B. Hope and A. Rosenfeld (Eds.), Academic Press.

[29] Wittgenstein, L. (1953), "Philosophical Investigations," MacMillan.

PROBLEMS AND POSSIBLE SOLUTIONS IN THE ANALYSIS OF SPARSE IMAGES

Vito Di Gesù

Istituto di Matematica, Università di Palermo
Via Archirafi 34, 90100 Palermo, Italy
and
IFCAI/CNR di Palermo
Via Mariano Stabile 172, 90100 Palermo, Italy

Abstract

Images where the "on" pixels are spatially spread are named "sparse images". Their analysis cannot be performed usually in a standard fashion and requires new methodologies. The paper aims at showing some of the techniques used in order to analyze "sparse images". Results of their application on simulated and real data are also given.

Key words: Clustering, Image Analysis, Uniformity Test, Fuzzy Sets

1. INTRODUCTION

The paper deals with the analysis of images, whose "on" pixels are spatially spread and embedded in a noise background. Such kind of images look like a "random graph", the nodes of which are the "on" pixels. In the following they are named "Sparse Images" (SI). Their analysis is often hard and calls for the use of non-standard techniques [1,2,3]. The problem becomes even harder whenever the signal intensities are very low with respect to the background and/or the last one is structured.

Handling of SI is done in several fields as for example in experimental psychology and biomedicine. Analysis of SI is done in the framework of the X and gamma-ray astronomy, where the photons detected generate maps in which extended-faint objects appear as clusters of events embedded in a noise-background.

The definition of "on" pixel depends on the application. For example, "on" pixels may be chosen by thresholding.

From the formal point of view SI's are sets of points on a two-dimensional normed space, X. Alternatively, the image may be considered as a weighted, complete and undirected graph $G = \langle X, W \rangle$, where W is a weight-edge function. In the following the Euclidean distance will be assumed as weight function. We call "cluster-ϕ" of G, with respect to some threshold ϕ, all the subsets C of X such that $\forall x, y \in C$ and $\forall z \in X - C : W(x, y) < \phi$ and $W(z, x) \geq \phi$.

In Figure 1 is shown, as an example of SI, the image of the sky in gamma-energy range as detected by the COS-B satellite [4].

NATO ASI Series, Vol. F30
Pattern Recognition Theory and Applications
Edited by P. A. Devijver and J. Kittler

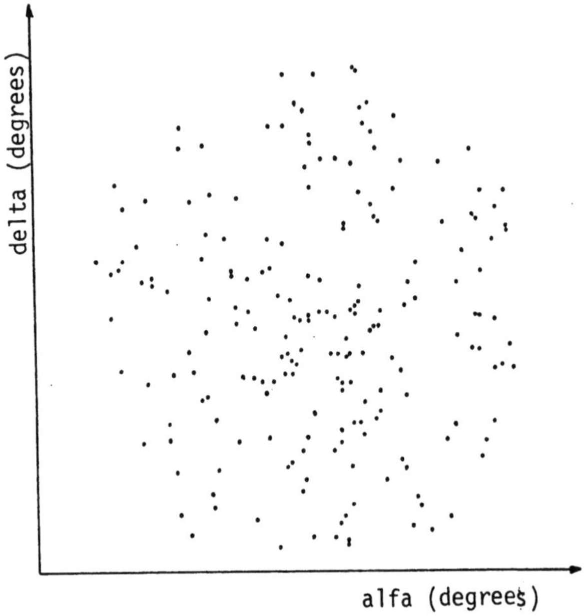

Figure 1: An example of SI in gamma astronomy.

The whole analysis is developed in the following phases:

- Preprocessing
- Features selection
- Segmentation
- Shape classification
- Structural analysis
- Interpretation

There does not exist a complete separation between the phases mentioned above and in a complete analysis system, some feedback mechanism must be included. For example features selection and segmentation levels are very closely related as well structural analysis and interpretation level.

In the analysis of the SI's "features selection" and "segmentation" phases are very crucial because of the nature of the data. Non-parametric techniques seems to be the most promising because "a priori" models for the data are not well known or very complex.

In Section 2, we give an overview of the whole analysis. Some examples of preprocessing techniques in order to establish the presence of signal in the SI, and a clustering technique in order to retrieve relevant "segments" are outlined. A shape-classification method based on the evaluation of the 'belonging degree' of an SI to a fuzzy-set [2,5] and the computation of some quantitative parameters of the classified shapes, based mainly on the properties of the convex hull, are also described. Section 3 shows some applications of the proposed methods on simulated data and real SI from astronomical observations. Section 4 is dedicated to final remarks.

2. Analysis of Sparse Images

The analysis procedure for SI's follows the same conceptual scheme as the classical one. However the meaning of each phase and the techniques adopted may be quite different. For example we operate more on density-points rather than intensities, contiguity between the "on" pixels is replaced by the nearest-neighbour relation. In the following, we describe some of the techniques that have been developed in order to carry out our analysis of SI's.

2.1. Preprocessing

The aim of the preprocessing phase is the selection of SI's in order to perform on them further analysis (from this point of view may be considered as a filter phase) and, in the affirmative case, to provide a list of 'candidate segments' (clusters) in the selected SI's.

Clustering techniques, which take into account the relationship between the points in X, seem to be the most suitable in order to detect "segments" (clusters) and study their validity [6,7,8,9]. In the proposed method the selection of the candidate SI's is performed by means of a Uniformity Test (UT) based on the expected number of components in the Minimum Spanning Forest (MSF) of G [1]. The number of components, $Nc(\phi)$, of the MSF of G, is computed by cutting all the edges of G greater than a given threshold, ϕ.

If the nodes in G are uniformly distributed, the expected number of clusters is:

$$Nc(\phi) = 1 - (N-1)\exp[-\lambda \cdot \pi \cdot \phi^2 \cdot A] \tag{1}$$

where N is the number of points and λ is the point density. The parameter $A = 0.55$ corrects, partially, two factors. The first is related to the effective volume surrounding each points in the sample, the second one is related to the border effect, resulting from the windowing of the data [10].

Figure 2.a shows an example of Nc versus ϕ, for an SI representing a flat and uniform zone of the sky as detected by the gamma-ray COS-B satellite.

Under the zero hypothesis of uniform Poisson distribution the parameter $Nc(\phi)$ follows the binomial distribution and its experimental values $Nc(\phi)$, computed for several thresholds $\phi_1, \phi_2, \cdots, \phi_n$ are compared with the theoretical expected ones. The probability, Q, that the set of values, $\{Nc(\phi_i)\}$, is compatible with the theoretical ones is given by:

$$Q_1 = 1, \quad Q_i = P_i Q_{i-1}(1 - \log(P_i Q_{i-1})) \quad i > 1 \tag{2}$$

where

$$P_i = \binom{N-1}{N_c-1} P(\phi_i)^{N_c-1}(1-P(\phi_i))^{N-N_c} \quad \text{and} \quad P(\phi_i) = \exp[-\lambda \cdot \pi \cdot \phi^2 \cdot a] \tag{3}$$

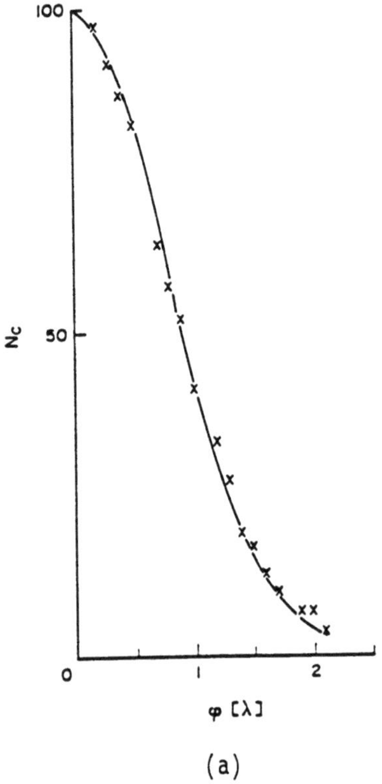

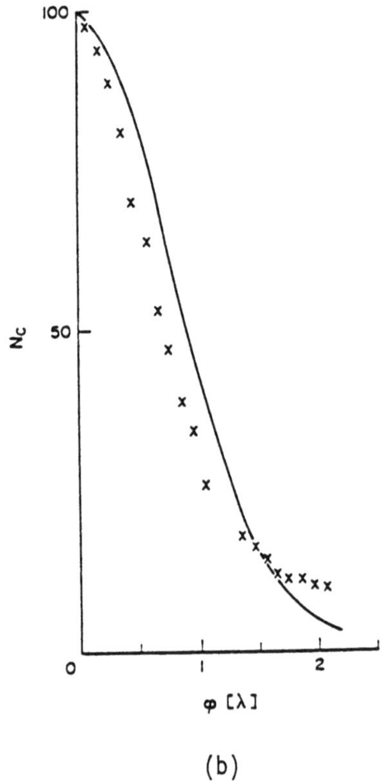

Figure 2: Nc versus ϕ : a) flat sky zone; b) structured sky zone.

Figure 2.b shows Nc versus ϕ for a zone of the sky as detected by the COS-B satellite, in which structured spatial celestial objects are present. If there is a strong a priori evidence of non-uniformity, this step may be omitted.

2.2. Features Selection and Segmentation

In this phase the main feature considered is the number of points in each "candidate-segment", Np, and it has been used to select the relevant segments. The validation problem is hard and an exact solution has been proposed in [11] in order to compute the mean and the variance of the number of points in each candidate-cluster starting from the knowledge of the same parameters for the variable $Nc(\phi)$.

An approximate solution may be used under a gaussian assumption and the threshold value for which this assumption is more accurate is $\phi = \sqrt{\log(2)/\pi A}$. The last threshold value is obtained by maximizing the variance of the law (3). In this case,

$$E[N/Nc(\phi)] = N/\overline{Nc}(\phi) + N \cdot \mathrm{Var}[Nc(\phi)]/\overline{Nc}(\phi)^3 \tag{4}$$

$$\mathrm{Var}[N/Nc(\phi)] = N \cdot \mathrm{Var}[Nc(\phi)]/\overline{Nc}(\phi)^4 \tag{5}$$

In this phase, significant segments are selected for which:

$$Np > E[N/Nc(\phi)] + K\mathrm{Var}[N/Nc(\phi)] \tag{6}$$

with $K > 0$. In the following the selected 'segments' are named 'objects'.

2.3. Shape Classification

Shape classification of the objects is performed by considering them as elements of a "fuzzy set" [12,13]. The belonging degree is evaluated with respect to a preclassified set of shape-prototypes, $\{A_1, A_2, \cdots, A_n\}$. Each shape-prototype is defined from a real or simulated training-set, the nature of which depends upon the application. For example in astronomical applications they may be {CIRCLE, ELLIPSES, SPIRAL, ...}.

The "membership degree" of x to the fuzzy-set A, $M(x, A)$, may be considered as a generalized characteristic function. It must satisfy at least the following properties:

1) $M(x, A) \in [0, 1]$;

2) $M(x, A)$ increases with the belonging of x to A;

3) let A and B be two different fuzzy-sets, then:

$$M(x, A \cup B) = \max\{M(x, A), M(x, B)\}.$$

A measure of symmetry has been considered in order to characterize the shape of the objects. It is computed by means of the normalized axial moments, m_i, computed around the barycenter of the object in r directions. Figure 3 shows an example of objects and related axial moments.

The "membership degree" has been evaluated by using several functions (Camberra, correlation, Minkowsky, ...), and the most promising one seems to be the normalized fuzzy entropy (NFE) [14]:

$$\mathrm{NFE}(x, A_i) = 1 - 1/r \sum_{i,j}^{r} [-\eta_{ij} \log \eta_{ij} - (1 - \eta_{ij}) \log(1 - \eta_{ij})] \tag{7}$$

where $\eta_{ij} = |m_j^x - m_j^{A_i}| < 1$.

The shape of object x is assigned to the "fuzzy-set", A_i, such that:

$$\mathrm{NFE}(x, A_i) = \max_{\ell}\{\mathrm{NFE}(x, A_\ell)\}$$

2.4. Quantitative Analysis

Structural and morphological descriptions can not be made on the basis of classical quantities (contours, edges, skeleton, ...). Thus, the information contained in the convex-hull (CH), [15], has been used to evaluate some classical parameters as the area, the perimeter, the diameter and elongatedness, [16,17].

The convex hull of a finite planar set of points, P, is defined as the minimum convex polygon containing P. If a pair of consecutive vertices $p(i)$, $p(i+1)$ defines an edge of the CH, where $i = 1, 2, \cdots, m$ and $p(m+1) = p(1)$, the following parameters may be

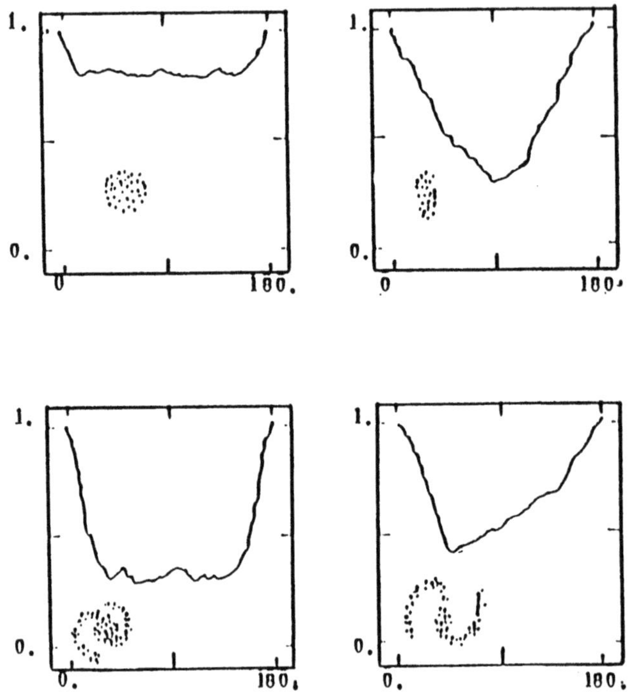

Figure 3: Normalized quadratic moments vs. the axial direction.

easily computed:

- the perimeter as the sum of all edges of CH;
- the diameter as the maximum distance between two vertices;
- the area as the surface enclosed in the CH;
- the elongatedness as the ratio between the minimum and the maximum distances among all the vertices.

The information contained in the edges of the CH may be used to evaluate the concavities in the object. First of all, the number of candidate concavities is set equal to the number of edges in CH greater than some threshold, which depends from the distribution of the edges in the CH. Further analysis on the candidate concavities will start from the endpoints of the related edges. The CH is iteratively computed on all set of points which do not belong to any of the CH's previously computed, starting from the first one. Figure 4 displays an example of the technique used.

3. Experimental Results

Experiments on Monte-Carlo simulated data have been made in order to assess the results and test the performance of the methods. Experiments on real SI's have also been carried out on data from satellite observation of the sky in X and gamma astronomy [4,18].

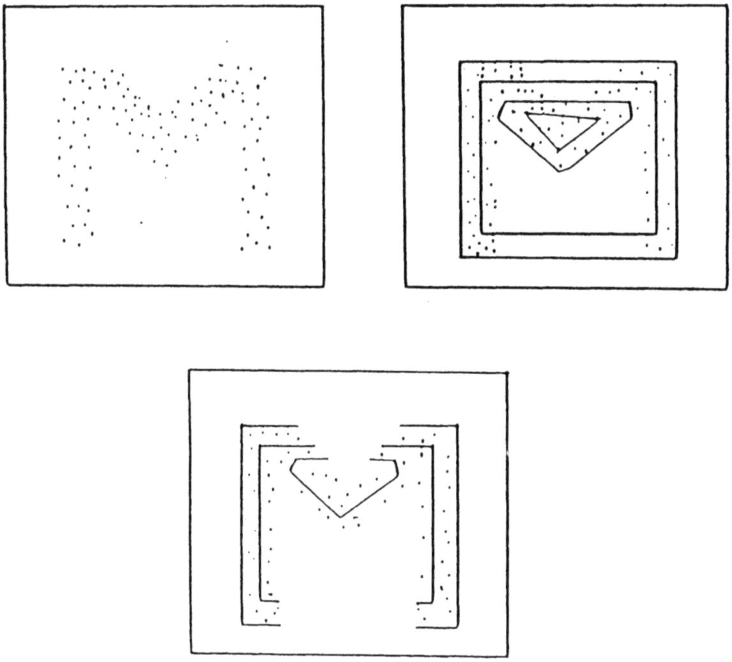

Figure 4: Application of the CH on a simulated M character.

To evaluate the shape-classification performance 600 simulated SI's have been generated. The SI's had variable density, ranging from .03 counts/pixel to .09 counts/pixel. The prototypes selected were CIRCLE, ELLIPSE, TWO-ARMS-SPIRAL, FOUR-ARM-SPIRAL. Figure 5 displays the percentage of correct classification versus the density of the SI's.

A set of experiments aiming at detecting the presence and the position of the end-points of concavities has been made on a sample of 200 SI's with density of about 0.4 counts/pixel. The percentage of correct detection was of 93%.

As an example of the preprocessing phase, Figure 6.b shows the results of the segmentation applied to the X-ray image of the extended object THICO shown in Figure 6.a. After the analysis, the extended structure of THICO is evidenced, as are the toroidal structure of the object and the central line emission.

In Figure 7.a is shown the CENTAURUS-A galaxy in X-energy range, in Figure 7.b are given the results of the quantitative analysis. The main concavity detected is consistent with observations in the optical energy range.

The methods described are part of a hierarchical system for the analysis of SI's. It has been implemented in FORTRAN77 under the MIDAS/ESO environment [19] on a VAX11/750. It has pictorial and graphics facilities. Menu facilities allow the user to operate in interactive fashion (select operation mode, parameters, data, prototypes, belonging degree function, input/output modalities).

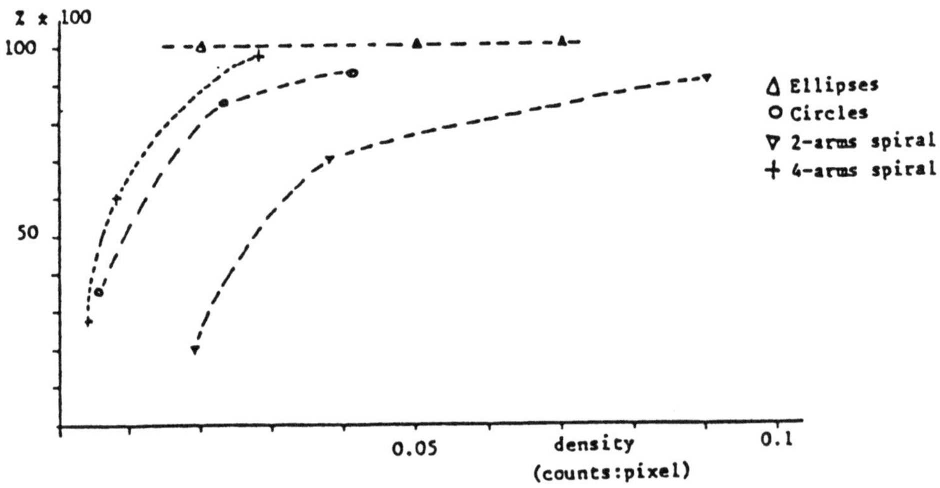

Figure 5: Percentage of correct classification vs. density.

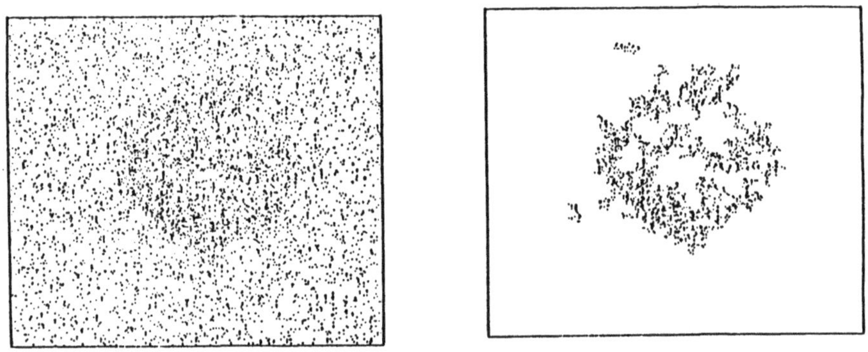

(a) (b)

Figure 6: An example of segmentation of an SI.

4. Concluding Remarks

The analysis of SI's is hard and the general solution is far away. The paper suggests some solutions that have given encouraging results in selected classes of applications. The combination of statistics, fuzzy-set theory and geometry seems to be promising in order to design systems for the analysis of SI's. The introduction of complementary information (included in a knowledge base) and feedback mechanisms (backtrack), in order to re-consider previous decisions, seems to be helpful for a more complete analysis [20].

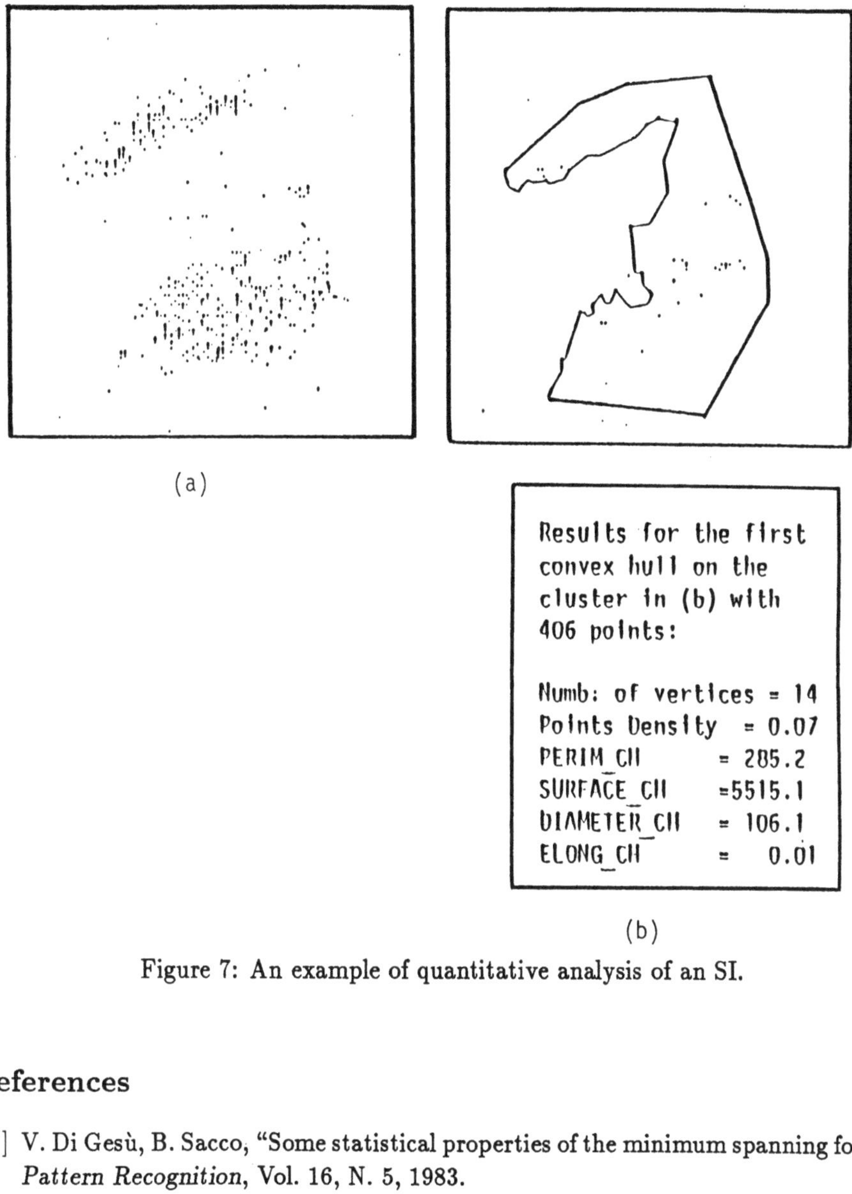

Figure 7: An example of quantitative analysis of an SI.

References

[1] V. Di Gesù, B. Sacco, "Some statistical properties of the minimum spanning forest," *Pattern Recognition*, Vol. 16, N. 5, 1983.

[2] V. Di Gesù, M.C. Maccarone, "A Method to classify spread shapes based on the possibility theory," *Proc. 7th Int. Conf. Pattern Recognition*, Vol. 2, pp. 869–871, Montreal, 1984.

[3] G.A. De Biase, V. Di Gesù, B. Sacco, "Detection of diffuse clusters in noise background," *Pattern Recognition Letters*, Vol. 4, pp. 39–44, 1986.

[4] L. Scarsi *et al.*, "The COS-B experiment and mission," *Proc. 12th ESLAB Symp. Recent Advances in Gamma-Ray Astronomy*, R.D. Wills and B. Battrick, Eds., Frascati, 1977.

[5] V. Di Gesù, M.C. Maccarone, "A hierarchical approach to classify and describe fuzzy objects," *Proc. 1st IFSA Congress*, Palma de Mallorca, Spain, July 1985.

[6]]R. Dubes, A.K. Jain, "Validity studies in clustering methodologies," *Pattern Recognition*, Vol. 11, pp. 235–254, 1979.

[7] J.V. Schultz, L.J. Hubert, "Data analysis and the connectivity of a random graph," *Journal of Mathematical Psychology*, Vol. 10, pp. 421–428, 1973.

[8] R.F. Ling, "An exact probability distribution on the connectivity of random graph," *Journal of Mathematical Psychology*, Vol. 12, pp. 90–98, 1975.

[9] R. Hoffman, A.K. Jain, "A test of randomness based on the minimal spanning tree," *Pattern Recognition Letters*, Vol. 1, pp. 175–180, 1983.

[10] V. Di Gesù, B. Sacco, "Note on the effective hypervolume and the windowing effect," submitted to *Pattern Recognition*, 1986.

[11] P.A. Devijver, personal communication, 1984.

[12] L.A. Zadeh, "Fuzzy sets," *Information and Control*, Vol. 8, pp. 338–348, 1965.

[13] R.R. Yager, "A foundation for a theory of possibility," *Cybernetics Journal*, Vol. 10, pp. 177–204, 1980.

[14] A. De Luca, S. Termini, "A Definition of a nonprobabilistic entropy in the setting of fuzzy set theory," *Information and Control*, Vol. 20, pp. 301–312, 1972.

[15] G.T. Toussaint, "Computational Geometric Problems in Pattern Recognition," in *Pattern Recognition Theory and Applications*, J. Kittler, K.S. Fu, L.F. Pau Eds., D.Reidel Publ. Comp., pp. 73–91, 1982.

[16] A. Rosenfeld, J.S. Weszka, "Picture recognition," in *Digital Pattern Recognition*, K.S. Fu Ed., Springer Verlag, pp. 135–166, 1980.

[17] D.G. Batchelor, "Hierarchical shape description based upon convex hull of concavities," *Journal of Cybernetics*, Vol. 10, pp. 205–210, 1980.

[18] B.G. Taylor, R.D. Andresen, A. Peacock, R. Zobl, "The EXOSAT mission," *Space Science Review*, Vol. 30, p. 513, 1981.

[19] K. Banse, P. Crane, C. Ounnas, D. Ponz, "MIDAS:ESO's interactive image processing system based on VAX/VMS," *Proc. DIGITAL Equipment Computer Users Society*, Zurik, 1983.

[20] M. Thonnat, "Automatic morphological description of galaxies and classification by an expert system", INRIA, Centre Sophia Antipolis, Rapport de Recherche, N.387, March 1985.

STOCHASTIC GEOMETRY AND PERCEPTION

Robert L. Manicke

U.S. Naval Academy
Annapolis, MD 21402, U.S.A.

1. Introduction

Recently the concept of a proximity measure has emerged as a computational cornerstone for modelling human perception. In particular, for visual perception a proximity measure is an index defined over pairs of images that quantifies the degree to which the two objects are alike as perceived by a respondent at the particular time of measurement. Analyses of these proximity measures have been done almost solely under the purview of the multidimensional scaling (MDS) technique.

MDS involves the mapping of percepts or images, the psychophysical equivalents of stimuli as stimulus points into a pre-defined modelling space. The coordinate system of these modelling spaces has been, without exception, the Cartesian co-ordinate system and the putative modelling spaces have been Euclidean or l_p spaces of dimension $p \leq 2$. Generally, the reason for this has been one of mathematical convenience; there does not exist any conclusive theoretical or empirical evidence to justify either.

The works of Beals and Krantz (1967) and Lew (1978) give geometrical and analytical results on how to construct metrics from a priori orders on stimulus space point-pairs. These results do not deal with the problems of modelling empirical relations with metrics.

Manicke (1985) extends the findings of Lew into the purview of topology. This is accomplished by incorporating the following theorem into Lew's point-pair order analysis:

> X is a Hausdorff topological space if and only if when $f, g : Y \to X$ are each continuous, then $\{(y_1, y_2) \in Y \times Y \mid f(y_1) = g(y_2)\}$ is closed.

By defining the map 0 from a pre or partially ordered set X^2 into classes of subsets of X^2 where $0(x_1, x_2) = \{(y_1, y_2) \in X^2 \mid (y_1, y_2) \leq (x_1, x_2)\}$ and

$$0(X^2) = \{0(x_1, x_2) \mid (x_1, x_2) \in X^2\}$$

and classifying these orders on X or X^2 as

(1) total if $x \leq y$ or $y \leq x$ for any $x, y \in X$;

(2) symmetric if $(s, t) \leq (t, u)$ for all elements in X^2;

NATO ASI Series, Vol. F30
Pattern Recognition Theory and Applications
Edited by P. A. Devijver and J. Kittler

(3) diagonal if $(s,s) \leq (t,u)$ for all elements in X^2; Manicke derives the following:

Theorem 1: For any pre-order $\leq$ on X^2, $\leq$ is induced by a metric and X^2 as a topological space is (at least) Hausdorff if, and only if, $\leq$ is diagonal, total, symmetric and $(X^2, \leq)$ contains a countable-dense subset, while Δ is closed and $\Delta \in 0(X^2)$ where $\Delta(X^2) = \{(x_1, x_2) \mid x_1 = x_2\}$.

2. Distributions Over Stimulus Spaces

An implicit assumption in all MDS techniques is that a respondent's response to an instrument used to realize proximity data is without error, true and static. Shepard (1962) shows that subjects may fluctuate in attention and in doing so may in some manner distort their psychophysical attribute space. To develop a probabilistic framework to describe this variability hypothesize that:

(1) a respondent's attribute space changes with time;

(2) in this attribute space the set of points S_i representing any stimulus is measurable (has a σ algebra defined on it but not necessarily a probability measure);

(3) the set of all measurable transformations from S_i to S_j, denoted by S_{ij}, is not empty.

It is necessary to consider orders among stimulus pairs since this is the only way the proximity data can be experimentally realized. As in Theorem 1, let the proximity space be measurable, T_2 as a topological space, and the point–pairs be related by a pre-order. Now consider the notion of a "random procedure for choosing a member of S_{ij}". To accomplish this define a distribution on S_{ij}, *i.e.*, a probability measure on S_{ij} as the pair (ψ, ρ) where ψ is a σ-ring and ρ is a probability measure on ψ.

By assumption 1, the function relating these point pairs could change at each occasion of measurement. To model the uncertainties in choosing both the stimulus point and path, consider the distribution of a point on a path when both path *and* point are chosen *randomly*. Fix distributions (ψ, ρ) on S_{ij} and η on S_i, then define $\Theta(g,p) = g(p)$. Θ can be considered as a random variable which again has a distributon only if it is a measurable transformation. So for any subset A of S_j: $Pr\{f(p) \in A\} = (\rho \times \eta)\{\Theta^{-1}(A)\}$, when A is measurable in S_j, $\Theta^{-1}(A)$ must also be measurable in $S_{ij} \times S_i$. Hence, the structure ψ on S_{ij} must be such that Θ is a measurable transformation.

For the general space S_{ij} without any restrictions it is not possible to define a measurable structure such that Θ is also a measurable structure, Mackey (1957). So restrict attention to a subset G of S_{ij} that gives these reasonable properties for Θ. As above, let G be contained in S_{ij} and define $\Theta_G : G \times S_i \to S_j$ by $\Theta_G(g,p) = g(p)$ such that the measurable structure on G allows Θ_G to be a measurable transformation. Call the set G and its appropriate structure *admissible*. G has been classified by Mackey (1957) and Dugundji *et al.* (1951) for various conditions.

Returning to $*$ it can be concluded that the concept definiton of a distribution over S_{ij} is given by (G, γ, ρ), where γ is an admissible measurable structure on the admissible set G, and ρ is a probability measure on γ.

These minimal considerations will allow a random procedure for picking a member of S_{ij} in which members of S_{ij} can actually occur and are the only members of G.

3. Random Variables Over Stimulus Spaces

Now consider a random variable f with range values in S_{ij}. Symbolically, let $(\Omega, \Lambda, \alpha)$ be its sample space or probability space. These random variables are functions from Ω to S_{ij}. Again consider the distribution of $f(p)$ when both f and p are chosen randomly. To guarantee $f(p)$ has a distribution assume f is measurable and consider the following: For any $f : \Omega \to S_{ij}$ associate the function $F : \Omega \times S_i \to S_j$ given by $F(\omega, p) = f(\omega)(p)$. If $p \in S_i$ is chosen according to a distribution η, then for any B contained in S_j: $Pr\{f(p) \in B\} = (\alpha \times \eta)\{F^{-1}(B)\}$. Hence the minimal foundational condition necessary for the existence of a random variable over S_{ij} with sample space $(\Omega, \Lambda, \alpha)$ is a measurable transformation $F : \Omega \times S_i \to S_j$.

4. Relationship Between Distributions And Random Variables Over Stimulus Spaces

The random variable F has as its range the set of functions S_{ij} of the form $F(\omega, \cdot)$. Indeed, the set of all points (from S_{ij}) that exist or can occur is precisely its range. Hence, the concept of the range of a random variable over S_{ij} corresponds to the concept of an admissible set under the distribution context. This association is made exact by the following:

Theorem 2: Every admissible set G admits a sample space and a random variable such that the range of the random variable is G, and every range is admissible, Manicke (1985).

5. Unique Probability Measure on Stimulus Spaces

As in Theorem 1, assume the topology of any stimulus space is at least T_2. It is both empirically and logically reasonable to assume that at any time t a respondent creates instruments which focus on the local variations of their discrimination or pattern recognition abilities relative to the stimuli. These devices or "psychometric probability measures" (Falmagne, 1982) can be modelled as measures of the likelihood of a respondent choosing a set of points in each stimulus space (point set population), and for each stimulus i will be labelled m_i. The points representing the stimulus i at any time t are elements of S_i and shall be referred to as points of indifference S_i^t. So at time t, $m_i(S_i^t) = 1$ for all i.

It is certainly possible for two stimulus spaces to have points in common. Indeed, suppose at some time t, $S_i^t \cap S_j^t \neq 0$ but

$$m_i|_{S_i^t \cap S_j^t} \neq m_j|_{S_i^t \cap S_j^t} .$$

If for a respondent the ith stimulus was perceptibly indistinguishable to the jth stimulus then $S_i^t = S_j^t$ but $1 = m_i(S_i^t) \neq m_j(S_j^t) = 1$. Hence, assume at any measurement t

$$m_i|_{S_i^t \cap S_j^t} = m_j|_{S_i^t \cap S_j^t} .$$

To establish a single space that models the attributes let $S = \bigcup_{i=1}^n \bigcup_t S_i^t$ describe this space, and be called differentiable attribute space. To derive any technique to locate an unknown S_i^t in a pre-defined embedding space S it is necessary that there exists a unique probability measure on S_i^t, say μ, such that $\mu|_{S_i^t} = m_i$ for any t.

To show the unique existence of a probability measure it is sufficient to assume any S_i^t is compact. To construct a unique μ let $C(S_i^t)$ be the normed vector space of continuous functions on each S_i^t under the supremum norm: $\| g \| = \sup|g(y)|$ for all $y \in S_i^t$ and let $CK(S_i^t)$ denote the space of continuous functions on S_i^t with compact support (closure of $\{y \mid y \in S_i^t,\ g(y) \neq 0\}$). Then a Radon probability measure on a locally compact space S is a linear mapping $\mu : CK(S) \to$ Reals such that for any $g \in CK(S)$, $g \geq 0$ implies $\mu(g) \geq 0$ with total mass equal to one (Dieudonne, 1968).

By utilizing two theorems from Bourbaki (1965, 1974) under the above setting, Manicke (1986) derives the following:

Theorem 3: Let S be the locally compact space as given where each S_i^t is considered an open set of S. If for each i there exists a Radon probability measure m_i such that $m_i|_{S_i^t \cap S_j^t} = m_j|_{S_i^t \cap S_j^t}$, $i \neq j$, then there exists a unique probability distribution μ on S such that $\mu|_{S_i^t} = m_i$ for all i.

6. Metrical Probabilities of Utility Values For Stimuli Differentiation

Many models of multidimensional decision and perception theory consider the utility of any stimulus S^i to be the multivariable function $U(S^i) = F(x_1^i, x_2^i, \cdots, x_k^i) \in (-\infty, \infty)$, where $(x_1^i, x_2^i, \cdots, x_k^i) \in (V_1^i, V_2^i, \cdots, V_k^i)$ and where V_j^i, $j = 1, 2, \cdots, k$, represents an acceptable set of values for the jth dimension of the stimulus (Mattenklott, Sehr, and Mieschke, 1982).

To classify these utility functions for later analysis consider this list of assumptions:

(1) each set V_j^i has a minimum value;

(2) if any V_j^i achieves its minimum value m_j^i, then $U(S^i) = 0$ or the utility of S^i is said to be null;

(3) the domain of F is the Cartesian product of k real intervals, called a k-box.

Suppose B is a k-box whose vertices are all in the domain of F, define the signed F-measure of B to be $\mu_F(B) = \sum_c \mathrm{sgn}_B(c)F(c)$ where the summation is taken over all vertices of B and

$$\mathrm{sgn}_B(c) = \begin{cases} 1 & \text{if } c_j^i = m_j^i \text{ for an even number of } j\text{'s} \\ -1 & \text{if } c_j^i = m_j^i \text{ for an odd number of } j\text{'s} \end{cases}$$

From this define F to be (4) utility preserving if $\mu_F(B) \geq 0$ and (5) utility reversing if $\mu_F(B) \leq 0$ for all k-boxes B whose vertices are in the domain of F. Hereinafter the superscript i will be omitted.

To further classify F say (6) F is nonincreasing in each dimension if $x < y$ and $F(x_1, \cdots, x, \cdots, x_k) \geq F(x_1, \cdots, y, \cdots, x_k)$ and say (7) F is increasing in each dimension if $x < y$ and $F(x_1, \cdots, x, \cdots, x_k) \leq F(x_1, \cdots, y, \cdots, x_k)$. Also (8) if each V_j has a maximal element q_j, then $F_j = F(q_1, \cdots, x, \cdots, q_k)$ will be the jth one dimensional margin of F.

These foundational assumptions give the following theorems.

Theorem 4: If F has properties (2) and (5), then it has property (6).

Proof: Let $B = [(m_1, \cdots, x, \cdots, m_k), (x_1, \cdots, y, \cdots, x_k)]$, by (5) $\mu_F(B) \leq 0$ and by (2) $\mu_F(B) = F(x_1, \cdots, y, \cdots, x_k) - F(x_1, \cdots, x, \cdots, x_k) \leq 0$.

Similarly, we get

Theorem 4': If F has properties (2) and (4), then it has property (7).

Analogously, we get

Theorem 5: If F has properties (2), (5) and (8), then $F_j(x) \leq F(x_1, \cdots, x, \cdots, x_k) \leq 0$ and

Theorem 5': If F has properties (2), (4) and (8) then $0 \leq F(x_1, \cdots, x, \cdots, x_k) \leq F_j(x)$.

Now for the main result of this section:

Theorem 6: If F has properties (2), (4) and (8), then for $x < y$

$$F(x_1, \cdots, y, \cdots, x_k) - F(x_1, \cdots, x, \cdots, x_k) \leq F_j(y) - F_j(x).$$

Proof: For $n = 2$ by (4) for the 2 box $[\vec{m}, \vec{q}]$ we have

$$F(y, q_2) - F(x, q_2) - F(y, x_2) + F(x, x_2) \geq 0$$

and

$$F(q_1, y) - F(q_1, x) - F(x_1, y) + F(x_1, x) \geq 0.$$

Together these give the theorem's conclusion for $n = 2$.

For $n > 2$ define the boxes $A_1, \cdots, A_{k-1}$ by

$$\begin{aligned} A_1 &= [(x_1, m_2, \cdots, x, \cdots, m_k), (q_1, x_2, \cdots, y, \cdots, x_k)] \\ A_2 &= [(m_1, x_2, \cdots, x, \cdots, x_k), (q_1, x_2, \cdots, y, \cdots, x_k)] \\ &\vdots \\ A_{k-1} &= [(m_1, m_2, \cdots, x, \cdots, x_k), (q_1, q_2, \cdots, y, \cdots, q_k)] \end{aligned}$$

By property (4) we get $\sum_{j=1}^{k-1} \mu_F(A_j) \geq 0$ and by property (2) each $\mu_F(A_j)$ reduces to

$$\begin{aligned} &F(q_1, \cdots, q_j, \cdots, y, \cdots, x_k) - F(q_1, \cdots, q_j, \cdots, x, \cdots, x_k) \\ &- F(q_1, \cdots, x_j, \cdots, y, \cdots, x_k) + F(q_1, \cdots, x_j, \cdots, x, \cdots, x_k) \end{aligned}$$

and substituting each of these gives the theorem's conclusion.

And, yet another analogous

Theorem 6': If F has properties (2), (5) and (8), then for $x < y$

$$F(x_1, \cdots, y, \cdots, x_k) - F(x_1, \cdots, x, \cdots, x_k) \geq F_j(y) - F_j(x).$$

From Theorems 6 and 6' we get the following inequalities:

$$|F(x_1, \cdots, x, \cdots, x_k) - F(x_1, \cdots, y, \cdots, x_k)| \leq |F_j(x) - F_j(y)|$$

and

$$|F(x_1, \cdots, x, \cdots, x_k) - F(x_1, \cdots, y, \cdots, x_k)| \geq |F_j(x) - F_j(y)|$$

Suppose that the stimuli are ordered by preference or proximity. In von Neumann and Schoenberg (1941) it is shown that an order does not determine a unique metric. Indeed, they show an order can be isometrically embedded into an infinitude of geometries. Hence any order on the stimuli is associated with an infinitude of metrics of which each could equivalently represent the stimuli.

Furthermore, for an order on the stimuli, assume the probability space S has a metric defined on it that is a member of the class of metrics associated with this order. For any elements p, q in S, let $G_{pq}(x)$ denote the probability that the distance between p and q is less than x. Now, $0 \leq G_{pq}(x) \leq 1$ for every $x \geq 0$, and if $x < y$, $G_{pq}(x) \leq G_{pq}(y)$, this implies G_{pq} is a probability function, hereinafter referred to as a (ddf) distance distribution function (Menger, 1942).

Consistent with the metric space axioms assume (1) $G_{pq} = G_{qp}$ and (2) $G_{pp} = \epsilon_0$ where

$$\epsilon_0(x) = \begin{cases} 0, & x \leq 0 \\ 1, & x > 0 \end{cases}$$

To give a probabilistic context to the metric triangle inequality assume Serstnev's (1962) triangle axiom: for all p, q, r in S there exists a function τ such that the domain of τ is all ordered pairs of ddfs on S and has a range of ddfs on S, such that (3) $G_{pr} \geq \tau(G_{pq}, G_{qr})$

Using this structure where $p \sim q$ if and only if $G_{pq} = \epsilon_0$ and where $G = \{G_{pq} : p, q \in S\}$ we get:

Theorem 7: Let (S, G, τ) satisfy (1), (2), and (3), then $\sim$ is an equivalence relation. For any $p \in S$, let p^* denote the equivalence class containing p and let S^* denote the set of the equivalence classes. Then $G^*_{p^*q^*} = G_{pq}$ for any $p \in p_*$, $q \in q_*$ defines a function G^* from $S^* \times S^*$ into the set of all ddfs on S. (S^*, G^*, τ) satisfies (1), (2), (3).

Proof: If $p_1 \sim p_2$ and $q_1 \sim q_2$, then

$$\begin{aligned} G_{p_1q_2} \geq \tau(G_{p_1q_2}, G_{q_2q_1}) &= G_{p_1q_2} \geq \tau(G_{p_1q_2}, G_{q_2q_1}) = \tau(G_{p_1q_2}, \epsilon_0) \\ &= G_{p_1q_2} \geq \tau(G_{p_1p_2}, G_{p_2q_2}) = \tau(\epsilon_0, G_{p_2q_2}) \\ &= G_{p_2q_2}. \end{aligned}$$

Likewise $G_{p_2q_2} \geq G_{p_1q_1}$ whence $G_{p_1q_1} = G_{p_2q_2}$.

To give each stimulus space a probabilistic context define: stimuli i and j are perceived as identical if and only if each is represented by the same equivalence class of points. That is, if p and q represent imperceptibly different (by a respondent) stimuli then $G_{p^*q^*} = \epsilon_0 = G_{pq}$ Moreover, by this definition if p and q represent perceptibly different stimuli, then $G_{p^*q^*} = G_{pq} \neq \epsilon_0$

If F is the utility function for the ith and jth stimuli and F is utility preserving, has a nullity and margins, and in the nth dimension, $1 \leq n \leq k$, $x < y$, then

$$0 < G_{p_i^* p_j^*}(|F(x_1, \cdots, x, \cdots, x_k) - F(x_1, \cdots, y, \cdots, x_k)|) \leq G_{p_i^* p_j^*}(|F_n(x) - F_n(y)|) \leq 1$$

and with the same conditions except F is utility reversing then

$$0 < G_{p_i^* p_j^*}(|F_n(x) - F_n(y)|) \leq G_{p_i^* p_j^*}(|F(x_1, \cdots, x, \cdots, x_k) - F(x_1, \cdots, y, \cdots, x_k)|) < 1.$$

References

[1] Bourbaki, N., *Integration*, Hermann, Paris, 1965.

[2] Bourbaki, N., *Topologie Generale*, Hermann, Paris, 1974.

[3] Beals, R. and D. Krantz, "Metrics and geodesics induced by order relations," *Mathematische Zeitschrift*, 1012, 258–298, 1967.

[4] Dugundgi, J. and R. Arens, "Topologies for function spaces," *Pacific J. of Math.*, 1, 5–31, 1951.

[5] Falmagne, J., "Psychometric function theory," *J. of Math. Psyc.*, 25, 1–50, 1982.

[6] Lew, J., "Some counterexamples in multidimensional scaling," *J. Math. Psyc.*, 17, 247–254, 1978.

[7] Mackey, G., "Borel structures in groups and their duals," *Trans. Amer. Math. Soc.*, 85, 134–165, 1957.

[8] Manicke, R., "On the stochastic geometrical foundations of metric multidimensional scaling," *J. Math. Soc. Sci.*, 9, 53–62, 1985.

[9] Manicke, R., "The unique existence of a probability measure for human pattern recognition," submitted to the *J. of Math. Psyc.*, 1986.

[10] Mattenklott, A., J. Sehr and K. Miescke, "A stochastic model for paired comparisons of social stimuli," *J. of Math. Pscy.*, 26, 149–168, 1982.

[11] Menger, K., "Statistical metrics," *Proc. Nat Acad Sci U.S.A.*, 28, 535–537.

[12] Serstnev, A., "Random normed spaces," Kazan. Gos. Univ. Ucen. Zap, 122, 3–20.

[13] Shepard, R., "Attention and the metric structure of the stimulus space," *J. of Math. Psyc.*, 1, 54–87, 1964.

COMPUTATIONAL GEOMETRY: RECENT RESULTS RELEVANT TO PATTERN RECOGNITION

Godfried T. Toussaint

McGill University
School of Computer Science
Montréal, Canada H3A 2K6.

Abstract

In this paper we survey recent results in computational geometry relevant to the problem of shape description and recognition by machines. In particular we consider the medial axis of a polygon, shape hulls of sets of points, decomposition of polygons into perceptually meaningful components, smoothing and approximating polygonal curves, and computing geodesic and visibility properties of polygons.

1. Introduction

The term *computational geometry* has been used recently in several different senses [2]-[5]. In this paper we consider computational geometry in the sense of Shamos [5]-[7]. In this sense it has direct relevance to pattern recognition [8]-[10] and to the broader science of morphology [1], [70], [71]. In this paper we survey some key recent results in computational geometry that have direct bearing on pattern recognition problems. To avoid duplication we concentrate on results not covered in [6]-[11] and refer the reader to these references for earlier work as well as basics such as the models of computation used, etc..

2. The Medial Axis of a Polygon

Let $P = (p_1, p_2, \cdots, p_n)$ be a simple polygon with *vertices* $p_i, i = 1, 2, \cdots, n$ specified in terms of cartesian coordinates in order. The *medial axis* of P, denoted by $MA(P)$, is the set of points $\{q\}$ internal to P such that there are at least two points on the boundary of P that are equidistant from $\{q\}$. Figure 1 taken from [24] illustrates a simple polygon and its medial axis. The medial axis of a figure was first proposed by Blum [12] as a descriptor of the shape or form of the figure. It has since evolved into a theory of biological shape and shape change [37]-[39].

Since the introduction of the notion of *medial axis* there has been considerable interest in computing it efficiently under different models of computation [13]-[23]. Most of these algorithms take time proportional to n^2. Recently, Lee and Drysdale [19] and Kirkpatrick [18] have presented a general algorithm for finding continuous medial axes

NATO ASI Series, Vol. F30
Pattern Recognition Theory and Applications
Edited by P. A. Devijver and J. Kittler

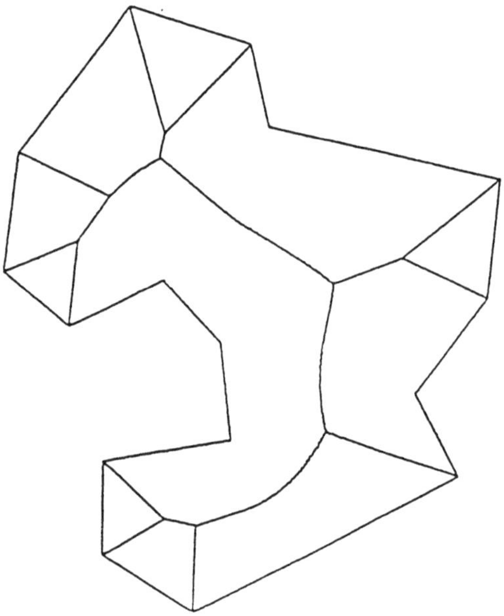

Figure 1: A simple polygon and its median axis.

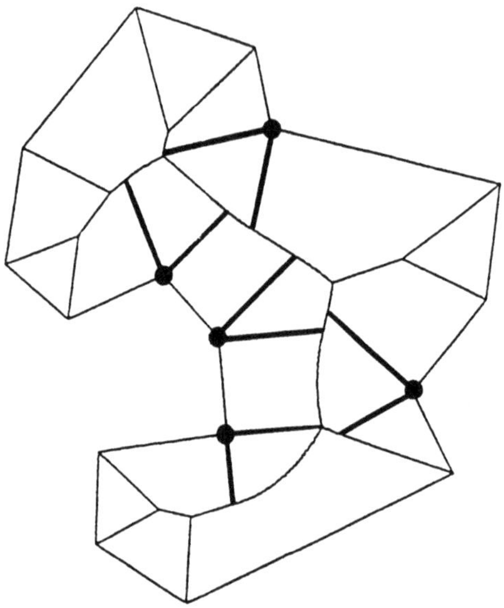

Figure 2: The generalized Voronoi diagram of P.

(or *skeletons*) of a set of *disjoint* objects. Lee & Drysdale's algorithm takes $\mathcal{O}(n \log^2 n)$ time whereas Kirkpatrick's algorithm runs in $\mathcal{O}(n \log n)$ time. Even more recently, a simpler $\mathcal{O}(n \log n)$ algorithm was proposed by D.T. Lee [24]. Lee [24] shows that the *medial axis* is a subgraph of a structure known as the *generalized Voronoi diagram* and his algorithm first computes this diagram and subsequently removes the edges of it that are incident on *concave* vertices of P. Lee describes an $\mathcal{O}(n \log n)$ divide-and-conquer algorithm for computing the *generalized Voronoi* diagram (GVoD(P)) of a polygon P. Since GVoD(P) has $\mathcal{O}(n)$ edges, once it is obtained, the medial axis can actually be obtained in linear time. Figure 2 illustrates the GVoD(P) with its *reflex* vertices along with out-going edges marked.

3. The Shape of a Set of Points

When points in the plane have a finite diameter so that they are visible, and when they are fairly densely and uniformly distributed in some region in the plane then a human observer is quick to perceive the "shape" of such a set. These sets are usually referred to as *dot patterns* of *dot figures*. A polygonal description of the boundary of the shape is referred to as the *shape hull* of a dot pattern, where the vertices are given in terms of the cartesian coordinates of the centers of the dots. There are two versions of the shape hull (SH) problem: in one there are no "holes" in the dot pattern and the dot pattern is "simply connected" and hence the shape hull is a simple polygon, whereas in the more difficult problem both "holes" and "disconnected" components may exist. To add to this difficulty, in some instances illusory contours are perceived between "disconnected"

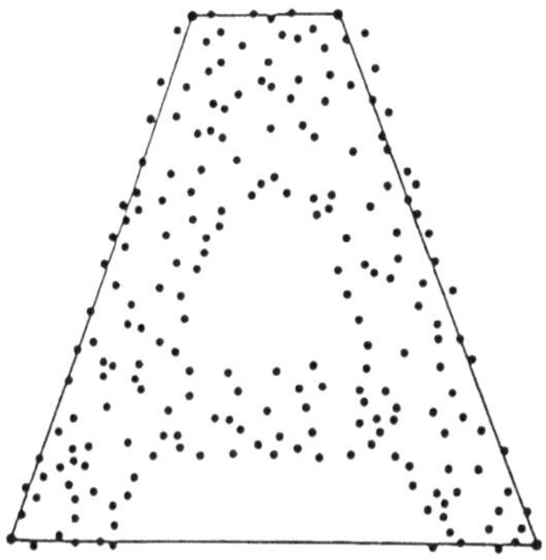

(a)

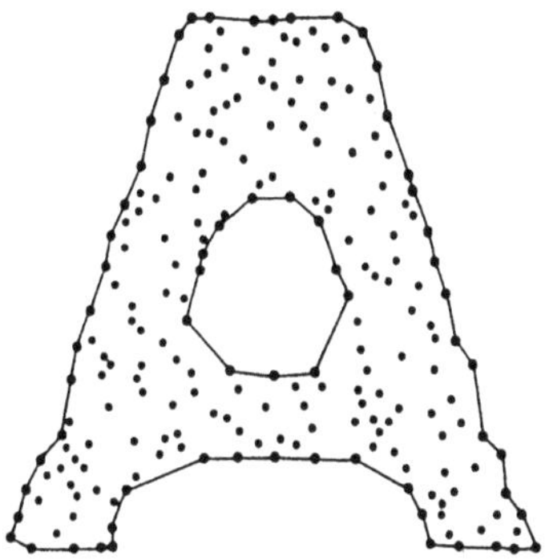

(b)

Positive and negative α-shape.

Figure 3: Two different α-shapes of a common point set.

components as illustrated by Kennedy and Ware [25]. For more details on this problem and early approaches to solving it, see [8]. A more recent paper addressing this problem is that of Medek [26].

In addition to describing the shape or structure of a set of points by its *shape-hull* or *external shape* we may also use the *skeleton* or *internal shape*. An early step in this direction was taken by Zahn [27] with the minimal spanning tree. More recent approaches have used the *relative neighborhood graph* [28]-[33].

A very elegant definition of the external shape of a set of points was put forward recently by Edelsbrunner, Kirkpatrick, and Seidel [34]. They propose a natural generalization of convex hulls that they call α-hulls. The α-hull of a point set is based on the notion of generalized discs in the plane. For arbitrary real valued α, a *generalized disc* of *radius* $1/\alpha$ is defined as follows [34]:

(i) if $\alpha > 0$, it is a (standard) disc of radius $1/\alpha$;

(ii) if $\alpha < 0$, it is the complement of a disc of radius $1/\alpha$; and

(iii) if $\alpha = 0$, it is a half plane.

The *α-hull* of a point set S is defined to be the intersection of all closed generalized discs of radius $1/\alpha$ that contain all the points S. The convex hull of S is precisely the 0-hull of S. The family of α-hulls includes the smallest enclosing circle (when $\alpha = 1/\text{radius}(S)$), the set S itself, (for all α sufficiently small) and an essentially continuous set of enclosing regions in between these extremes.

Edelsbrunner *et al.* [34] also define a combinatorial variant of the α-hull, called the *α-shape* of a point set, which can be viewed without serious misunderstanding as the boundary of the α-hull with curved edges replaced by straight edges. Unlike the family of α-hulls, the family of distinct α-shapes has only finitely many members. These provide a spectrum of progressively more detailed descriptions of the external shape of a given point set. Figure 3 (copied from [34]) illustrates the α-shape of a point set for two different values of α. In [34] efficient algorithms are also presented for computing the α-shapes of dot patterns consisting of n points in $\mathcal{O}(n \log n)$ time. Subsequently, Kirkpatrick and Radke [69] outlined a new methodology for describing the *internal shape* of planar point sets. We should note that the ideas in [34] are closely related to the notions of *opening* and *closing* sets, found in mathematical morphology [35], [36].

We close this section by describing a new graph which I call the *sphere-of-influence* graph which I believe has some very attractive properties from the viewpoint of computer vision [40].

Let S be a finite set of points in the plane. For each point $x \in S$, let r_x be the closest distance to any other point in the set, and let C_x be the circle of radius r_x centered at x. The sphere of influence graph is a graph on S with an edge between points x and y if and only if the circles C_x and C_y intersect in at least two places. It is shown in [41] that:

(i) The sphere of influence graph has at most $29n$ edges ($n = |S|$).

(ii) Every decision tree algorithm for computing the sphere of influence graph requires at least $\mathcal{O}(n \log n)$ steps in the worst case.

As an application of (i), El Gindy observed that an algorithm of Bentley and Ottman [42] can be used to find the sphere of influence graph in $\mathcal{O}(n \log n)$ time. Figure 4 shows a set of points and its sphere-of-influence graph. The resemblance to a *primal-sketch* is astounding.

Motivated by the work in [34] we can also use the *sphere-of-influence* graph to define the *boundary* of a planar set S as either the *contour* of the union of the circles $C_x, x \in S$ (the *sphere-of-influence hull*) or the graph composed of those edges corresponding to pairs of points in S that have adjacent arcs on the *contour* defined above (the *sphere-of-influence shape*). These structures can be computed in $\mathcal{O}(n \log n)$ time *without* computing the sphere of influence graph [40]. For the related problem of finding a perceptually meaningful *simple* polygon through S see [49]. Finally, the problem of drawing a simple polygon through a set of *line segments* is considered in [50].

Given a set of non-intersecting line segments in the plane, we are required to connect the line segments such that they form a simple circuit (a simple polygon). However, not every set of segments can be so connected. This leads to the challenging problem of determining when a set of segments admits a simple circuit, and if it does, then find such a circuit. In [50] an optimal algorithm is presented to determine whether a simple circuit exists, and deliver a simple circuit, on a set of line segments, where each segment has at least one endpoint on the convex hull of the segments (a CH-connected set of segments). Furthermore this technique can be used to determine a simple circuit of minimum length, or a simple circuit that bounds the minimum area, with no increase in computational complexity. For a general set of segments Rappaport [72] has shown that the problem is NP-complete.

4. Decomposition of Polygons into Perceptually Meaningful Components

Since [9] not much progress has been made on the morphological aspect of this problem. However, some new results are available on the geometrical side which are relevant.

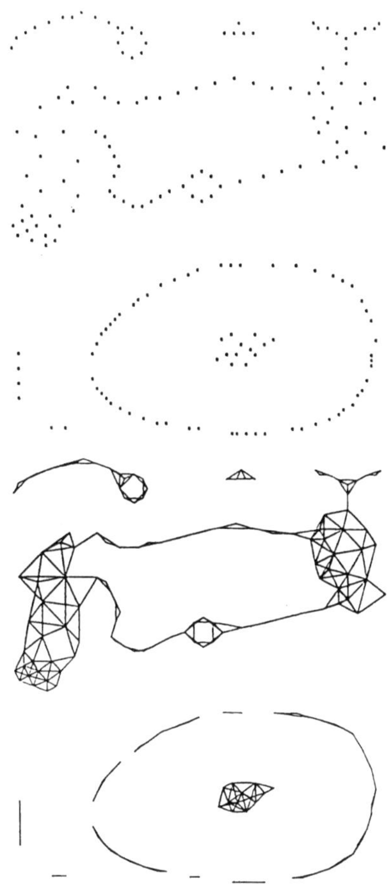

Figure 4: A set of points (above) and its sphere-of-influence graph (below).

Chazelle & Dobkin [43] solve the problem of decomposing a non-convex simple polygon into a minimum number of convex polygons.

They obtain an algorithm that runs in $\mathcal{O}(n + c^3)$ time where n is the total number of vertices and c is the number of concave angles. For a recent survey of this area see [44].

One decomposition which appears to capture well the morphological aspect of the problem is the *relative-neighbour* decomposition [45]. In [45] an $\mathcal{O}(n^3)$ algorithm is given for computing this decomposition. Recently, an $\mathcal{O}(n^2)$ algorithm has been discovered [46].

5. Approximating Polygonal Curves

Let $P = (p_1, p_2, \cdots, p_n)$ be a polygonal planar curve, i.e., P consists of a set of n distinct points (or nodes) $p_1, p_2, \cdots, p_n$ specified by their cartesian coordinates, along with a set of $n-1$ line segments joining pairs p_ip_{i+1}, $i = 1, 2, \cdots, n-1$. Note that in general P may intersect itself. Polygonal curves occur frequently in pattern recognition, image processing, and computer graphics. In order to reduce the complexity of processing polygonal curves it is often necessary to approximate P by a new curve which contains far fewer line segments and yet is a close-enough replica of P for the intended application. Many different approaches to this general problem exist and for a recent paper with 37 references the reader is referred to [47]. Different methods are more-or-less suited to different applications and yield solutions with different properties. In one instance of the problem it is required to determine a new curve $P' = (p'_1, p'_2, \cdots, p'_m)$ such that 1) m is less than n, 2) the p'_i are a subset of the p_i, and 3) any line segment $p'_jp'_{j+1}$ which substitutes the chain corresponding to $p_r, \cdots, p_s$ in P is such that the distance between each $p_k, r \le k \le s$, and the line segment $p'_jp'_{j+1}$ is less than some predetermined error tolerance w. An often used error criterion is the minimum distance between p_k and $p'_jp'_{j+1}$, i.e., $d(p_k, p'_jp'_{j+1}) = \min_x\{d(p_k, x) \mid x \in p'_jp'_{j+1}\}$, where $d(p_k, x)$ is the Euclidean distance. No attempt has been made at minimizing m. Recently, Imai and Iri [48] proposed an $\mathcal{O}(n^3)$ algorithm for determining the approximation that minimizes m subject to the two other constraints. Another criterion, often used, measures the distance between p_k and $p'_jp'_{j+1}$ as the minimum distance between p_k and a line $L(p'_jp'_{j+1})$ colinear with p'_j and p'_{j+1}, i.e,

$$d(p_k, p'_jp'_{j+1}) = \min_x\{d(p_k, x) \mid x \in L(p'_jp'_{j+1})\}.$$

This is termed the "*parallel-strip*" criterion [47] since it is equivalent to finding a strip of width $2w$ such that p'_j and p'_{j+1} lie on the center line of the strip and all points p_k, $r \le k \le s$, lie in the strip. In [47] it is shown that if the *parallel-strip* criterion is used, the complexity of the algorithm of Imai and Iri can be reduced to $\mathcal{O}(n^2 \log n)$. Furthermore, if the polygonal curves are *monotonic*, and a suitable error criterion is used, the complexity can be further reduced to $\mathcal{O}(n^2)$. More recently O'Rourke [73] reduced the complexity of the algorithm of Imai and Iri [48] to $\mathcal{O}(n^2 \log n)$.

6. Computing Geodesic Properties of Polygons

Given a polygon P and two points $a, b \in P$, the shortest path (or *geodesic* path) between a and b is a polygonal path connecting a and b which lies entirely in P such that the sum of its Euclidean edge-lengths is a minimum over all other internal paths. Intuitively, it is the shape an ideal elastic band would take if it were attached to a and b and the boundary of P consisted of barriers. We denote it by $GP(a, b \mid P)$ where the direction is from a to b. Geodesic paths find application in many areas such as image processing [51], operations research [52], visibility problems in graphics [53], and robotics [57]-[58]. Recently, Chazelle [54] and Lee & Preparata [52] independently discovered the same $\mathcal{O}(n \log n)$ algorithm for computing $GP(a, b \mid P)$. Both of these algorithms first triangulate P and then find the shortest path in $\mathcal{O}(n)$ time. An algorithm due to El Gindy [55] computes $GP(a, b \mid P)$ *without* first triangulating P, also in $\mathcal{O}(n \log n)$ time. More recently, it has been discovered that a simple polygon can be triangulated in $\mathcal{O}(n)$ time [59]. This result allows one to compute the geodesic path between two points in $\mathcal{O}(n)$ time [60].

In the context of morphology, shortest paths are used for measuring shape properties of figures [38], [51], [61]. For example, the *length* of a biological object [51] is the length of the *longest* geodesic path (the *geodesic diameter*) between any pair of points in the object. Several algorithms have been proposed for computing the geodesic diameter of a simple polygon; for example, an $\mathcal{O}(n^2)$ time and $\mathcal{O}(n^2)$ space algorithm [54], an $\mathcal{O}(c^2 n)$ time and $\mathcal{O}(n)$ space algorithm [61] where c is the number of convex vertices, and an $\mathcal{O}(n^2)$ time and $\mathcal{O}(n)$ space solution [62]. Most recently, Subhash Suri [74] has shown that the geodesic diameter can be computed in $\mathcal{O}(n \log n)$ time and $\mathcal{O}(n)$ space.

Another very useful geodesic property is the *geodesic center* of a polygon, i.e., that point in P that minimizes the length of the *longest* geodesic path to any point in P. Parallel algorithms for computing both the *geodesic diameter* and *center* of a pattern on a lattice are given in [51]. Asano and Toussaint [63] show that the geodesic center of a polygon can be computed in $\mathcal{O}(n^4 \log n)$ time.

7. Computing Visibility Properties of Polygons

The notion of visibility is one that appears in many applications. In a morphological context visibility relations between vertices and edges of a polygon can be used as shape descriptors [9]. Much attention has been given to the problem of the visibility from a *point*.

A topic which has not been as much investigated as visibility from a *point* concerns the notion of *visibility from an edge*. A polygon P is *weakly visible from an edge* $[p_i p_{i+1}]$ if for every point $x \in P$ there exists a $y \in [p_i p_{i+1}]$ such that $[xy]$ lies inside P. Given a polygon P and a specified edge $[p_i p_{i+1}]$ of P, the *edge visibility polygon of P from an edge*, denoted by $EVP(P, [p_i, p_{i+1}])$ is that region of P that sees at least one point of $[p_i p_{i+1}]$. Intuitively, it is the region of P visible, at one time or another, by a guard patrolling edge $[p_i p_{i+1}]$. Recently, El Gindy [55], Lee & Lin [64], and Chazelle & Guibas [65] all independently proposed three different algorithms for computing $EVP(P, [p_i p_{i+1}])$ in $\mathcal{O}(n \log n)$ time. In the case where the polygon may have n "holes", Suri & O'Rourke [66] present an $\mathcal{O}(n^4)$ algorithm for computing the boundary of the polygonal region *visible from an edge* and prove that it is optimal.

Toussaint [67] has shown that with the result of [59] the *edge visibility polygon* of P from an edge can be computed in $\mathcal{O}(n)$ time. A similar approach to solving visibility problems in [58] and [67] was later independently discovered by Guibas *et al.* [60] who also consider other problems.

A related problem concerns itself with answering queries of the type: are two specified edges in a polygon visible [53]? While this problem can be answered with the algorithms in [67] and [60] in $\mathcal{O}(n)$ time, the machinery used [59] is rather heavy. In [68] it is shown that even without all the heavy machinery of [59] such queries can still be answered in $\mathcal{O}(n)$ time.

Note: It should be pointed out that the triangulation algorithm reported in [59] does not run in $\mathcal{O}(n)$ time as claimed [75]. Therefore, any algorithms in the present paper that claim $\mathcal{O}(n)$ time with triangulation should be taken to do so after triangulation. With triangulation, they run in $\mathcal{O}(n \log \log n)$ time [75].

References

[1] Thompson, W.d'A., *On Growth and Form*, Cambridge University Press, 1917.

[2] Mortenson, M.E., *Geometric Modeling*, John Wiley & Sons, Inc., 1985.

[3] Minsky M., S. Papert, *Perceptrons: An Introduction to Computational Geometry*, M.I.T. Press, 1969.

[4] Bernroider, G. "The foundation of computational geometry: theory and application of the point-lattice-concept within modern structure analysis," in *Geometrical Probability and Biological Structures*, Eds., R.E. Miles & J. Serra, Springer- Verlag, 1978, pp. 153–170.

[5] Shamos, M.I. "Computational Geometry," Ph.D. Thesis, Yale University, May 1978.

[6] Preparata F.P., and M.I. Shamos, *Computational Geometry: An Introduction*, Springer-Verlag, 1985.

[7] Toussaint, G.T., Ed., *Computational Geometry*, North Holland, 1985.

[8] Toussaint,G.T.,"Pattern recognition and geometrical complexity," *Proc. 5th International Conf. on Pattern Recognition*, Miami Beach, December 1980, pp.1324–1347.

[9] Toussaint, G.T., "Computational geometric problems in pattern recognition," in *Pattern Recognition Theory & Application*, NATO Advanced Study Institute, J. Kittler, Ed., Oxford University, 1981, pp. 73–91.

[10] Toussaint, G.T., "New results in computational geometry relevant to pattern recognition in practice," in *Pattern Recognition in Practice II*, E.S. Gelsema & L.N. Kanal, Eds., North-Holland, 1986, pp. 135–146.

[11] Lee, D.T., & F.P. Preparata, "Computational geometry: a survey," Tech. Report 84-05-FC-03, August 1984, Northwestern University.

[12] Blum, H., "A transformation for extracting new descriptors of shape," in *Proc. Symp. Models for Perception of Speech and Visual Form*, W. Whaten-Dunn, Ed. Cambridge, MA: M.I.T. Press, 1967, pp. 362–380.

[13] Badler N.I., & C. Dane, "The medial axis of a coarse binary image using boundary smoothing," in *Proc. Pattern Recognition and Image Processing*, Aug. 1979, pp. 286–291.

[14] Blum H., & R.N. Nagel, "Shape description using weighted symmetric axis features," *Pattern Recognition*, vol. 10, pp. 167–180, 1978.

[15] Bookstein, F.L., "The line-skeleton," *Comput. Graphics Image Processing*, vol. 11, pp. 123–137, 1979.

[16] Calabi, L., & W.E. Hartnett, "Shape recognition, prairie fires, convex deficiencies and skeletons," *Amer. Math. Month.*, vol. 75, pp. 335–342, April 1968.

[17] de Souze, P.V., P. Houghton, "Computer location of medial axis," *Comput. Biomed. Res.*, vol. 10, pp. 333–343, 1977.

[18] Kirkpatrick, D.G. "Efficient computation of continuous skeletons," in *Proc. 20th Annu. Symp. Found. Computer Sci.*, Oct. 1979, pp. 18–27.

[19] Lee, D.T., R.L. Drysdale, "Generalization of Voronoi diagrams in the plane," *SIAM J. Comput.*, vol. 10, pp. 73–87, Feb. 1981.

[20] Montanari, U., "A method for obtaining skeletons using a quasi-Euclidean distance," *J. Ass. Comput. Mach.*, vol. 15, pp. 600–624, Oct. 1968.

[21] Montanari, U., "Continuous skeletons from digitized images," *J. Ass. Comput. Mach.*, vol. 16, pp. 534–549, Oct. 1969.

[22] Pfaltz, J.L., & Rosenfeld, A., "Computer representation of planar regions by their skeletons," *Commun. Ass. Comput. Mach.*, vol. 10, pp. 119–125, Feb. 1967.

[23] Preparata, F.P., "The medial axis of a simple polygon," in *Proc. 6th Symp. Math. Foundations of Comput. Sci.*, Sept. 1977, pp. 443–450.

[24] Lee, D.T., "Medial axis transformation of a planar shape," *IEEE Trans. Pattern Analysis & Machine Intelligence*, vol. PAMI-4, no. 4, July 1982, pp. 363–369.

[25] Kennedy, J.M., & C. Ware, "Illusory contours can arise in dot figures," *Perception*, vol. 7, 1978, pp. 191–194.

[26] Medek, V., "On the boundary of a finite set of points in the plane," *Computer Graphics & Image Processing*, vol. 15, 1981, pp. 93–99.

[27] Zahn, C.T. "Graph-theoretical methods for detecting and describing gestalt clusters," *IEEE Trans. Computers*, vol. C-20, Jan. 1971, pp. 68–86.

[28] Toussaint, G.T., "The relative-neighborhood graph of a finite planar set," *Pattern Recognition*, vol. 12, pp. 261–268.

[29] O'Rourke J., "Computing the relative-neighborhood graph in the L_1 and L_∞ metrics," *Pattern Recognition*, vol. 15, 1982, pp. 189–192.

[30] Urquhart, R.B., "Some properties of the planar Euclidean relative neighborhood graph," *Pattern Recognition Letters*, vol. 1, 1983, pp. 317–322.

[31] Supowit, K.J., "The relative neighborhood graph with an application to minimum spanning trees," *J.A.C.M.*, vol. 30, 1983, pp. 428–448.

[32] Lee, D.T., "Relative neighborhood graphs in the L_1 metric," *Pattern Recognition*, vol.18, 1985, pp. 327–332.

[33] Ichino, M., J. Sklansky, "The relative neighborhood graph for mixed feature variables," *Pattern Recognition*, vol. 18, 1985, pp. 161–167.

[34] Edelsbrunner, E., D.G. Kirkpatrick, & R. Seidel, "On the shape of a set of points in the plane," *IEEE Trans. Information Theory*, vol. 29, July 1983, pp. 551–559.

[35] Matheron, G., *Random Sets and Integral Geometry*, John Wiley, 1975.

[36] Serra, J. *Image Analysis & Mathematical Morphology*, Academic Press, 1982.

[37] Bookstein, F.L., *The Measurement of Biological Shape and Shape Change*, Springer-Verlag, 1978.

[38] Blum, H., "Biological shape and visual science," *Journal of Theoretical Biology*, vol. 38, 1973, pp. 205–387.

[39] Blum, H., "A geometry for biology," *Conference on Mathematical Analysis of Fundamental Biological Phenomena*, Annals New York Academy of Sciences, July 1973.

[40] Toussaint, G.T., "A graph-theoretic primal sketch," manuscript in preparation.

[41] Avis D., J. Horton, "Remarks on the sphere of influence graph," in *Discrete Geometry and Convexity*, Eds., J.E. Goodman et al., New York Academy of Sciences, 1985.

[42] Bentley J., & T. Ottman, "Algorithms for reporting and counting geometric intersections," *IEEE Trans. Computers*, vol. C-28, pp. 643–647.

[43] Chazelle B., & D. Dobkin, "Optimal convex decompositions," in *Computational Geometry*, Ed., G.T. Toussaint, North Holland, 1985, pp. 63–133.

[44] Keil, J.M., & J.R. Sack, "Minimum decompositions of polygonal objects," in *Computational Geometry*, Ed., G.T. Toussaint, North Holland, 1985, pp. 197–216.

[45] Toussaint, G.T., "Decomposing a simple polygon with the relative neighborhood graph," *Proc. Allerton Conference*, October 1980, pp. 20–28.

[46] El Gindy, & H., G.T. Toussaint, "Computing the relative-neighbor decomposition of a simple polygon," manuscript in preparation.

[47] Toussaint, G.T., "The complexity of approximating polygonal curves in the plane," *Proc. IASTED International Symposium on ROBOTICS AND AUTOMATION '85*, Lugano, Switzerland, June 24–26, 1985.

[48] Imai, H., & M. Iri, "Computational geometric methods for polygonal approximations of a curve," Tech. Report, RMI 85-01, Jan. 1985, University of Tokyo.

[49] O'Rourke, J., H. Booth, & R. Washington, "Connect-the-dots: a new heuristic," Tech. Report JHU/EECS-84/11, Johns Hopkins University.

[50] Rappaport D., H. Imai, & G.T. Toussaint, "On computing simple circuits on a set of line sements," *Proc. ACM Symposium on Computational Geometry*, 1986, to appear.

[51] Lantuejoul C., & F. Maisonneuve, "Geodesic methods in quantitative image analysis," *Pattern Recognition*, vol. 17, 1984, pp. 177–187.

[52] Lee, D.T., & F.P. Preparata, "Euclidean shortest paths in the presence of rectilinear barriers," *Networks*, vol. 14, 1984, pp. 393–410.

[53] Toussaint, G.T., "Shortest path solves edge-to-edge visibility in a polygon," School of Computer Science, McGill University, "Technical Report" SOCS-85, 19, September 1985: also to appear in *Pattern Recognition Letters*.

[54] Chazelle, B. "A theorem on polygon cutting with applications," *23rd Annual IEEE Symposium on Foundations of Computer Science*, 1982, pp. 339–349.

[55] El Gindy, H., "Hierarchical decomposition of polygons with applications," Ph.D. Thesis, School of Computer Science, McGill University, May 1985.

[56] Imai, H., Tetsuo Asano , & Takao Asano, "Visibility polygon search and Euclidean shortest paths," Technical Report, University of Tokyo, 1985.

[57] Brady M. et al., Eds., *Robot Motion: Planning and Control*, MIT Press,1983.

[58] Toussaint, G.T. "Shortest path solves translation separability of polygons," Technical Report No. SOCS-85.27, McGill University, October 1985.

[59] Tarjan R.R., & C.J. Van Wyk, "A linear-time algorithm for triangulating simple polygons," *Proc. 18th Annual ACM Symposium on Theory of Computing*, May 1986, pp. 380–388.

[60] Guibas, L., J. Hershberger, D. Leven, M. Sharir, & R. Tarjan, "Linear-time algorithms for visibility and shortest path problems inside simple polygons," *Proc. ACM Symposium on Computational Geometry*, 1986, to appear.

[61] Toussaint, G.T., "Computing geodesic properties of polygons," manuscript in preparation.

[62] Reif J., & J.A. Storer, "Shortest paths in Euclidean space with polyhedral obstacles," Technical Report CS-85-121, Brandeis University, April 1985.

[63] Tetsuo Asano, & G.T. Toussaint, "Computing the geodesic center of a simple polygon," Technical Report No. SOCS-85.32, McGill University, Dec. 1985.

[64] Lee, D.T., & A. Lin, "Computing the visibility polygon from an edge," Technical Report, Northwestern University, 1984.

[65] Chazelle, B., & L.J. Guibas, "Visibility and intersection problems in plane geometry," *Proc. Symposium on Computational Geometry*, Baltimore, June 1985, pp. 135–146.

[66] Suri, S., & J. O'Rourke, "Worst-case optimal algorithms for contructing visibility polygons with holes," Technical Report, JHU/EECS-85/12, Aug. 1985.

[67] Toussaint, G.T., "A linear-time algorithm for solving the strong hidden-line problem in a simple polygon," Technical Report No. SOCS-86.2, Jan. 1986.

[68] Avis, D., T. Gum, & G.T. Toussaint, "Visibility between two edges of a simple polygon," Technical Report SOCS-85.20, McGill University, Oct. 1985.

[69] Kirkpatrick, D.G., & J.D. Radke, "A framework for computational morphology" in *Computational Geometry*, G.T. Toussaint, Ed., Amsterdam: North Holland, 1985, pp. 217–248.

[70] Toussaint, G., "Computational geometry and morphology," *Proc. First International Symposium for Science on Form*, Tsukuba, Japan, November 1985.

[71] Toussaint, G., Ed., *Computational Morphology*, North Holland, to be published.

[72] Rappaport, D., "Computing simple circuits on a set of line segments is NP-complete," Tech. Rept. SOCS-86.6, McGill University.

[73] O'Rourke, J. "Polygonal chain approximation: An improvement to an algorithm of Imai and Iri," manuscript, Johns Hopkins University, June 1985

[74] Suri, S., "Computing the geodesic diameter of a simple polygon," Tech. Rept. JHU/EECS-86/08, Johns Hopkins University, March 1986.

[75] Tarjan, R.E. & C.J. Van Wyk, "An $\mathcal{O}(n \log\log n)$ time algorithm for triangulating simple polygons," *SIAM J. Computing*, in press.

STRUCTURAL METHODS IN PATTERN ANALYSIS

Michael G. Thomason

Department of Computer Science
University of Tennessee
Knoxville, TN 37996 USA

Abstract

This chapter summarizes some of the contemporary work in structural pattern analysis which uses explicit or implicit representations of structure. The two major areas described are formal relational approaches and syntactic/semantic approaches. The techniques are illustrated with examples from the literature.

1. Introduction

The following counts are from an INSPEC keyword/title search of publications dated 1979-1985:

(1) PATTERN or IMAGE or PICTURE	50652
(2) STRUCTURAL or STRUCTURE	143404
(1) and (2)	6191

A reasonable working definition of structural pattern analysis can use typical dictionary [2] definitions:

structural: Of, relating to, having, or characterized by structure.

structure: The configuration of elements, parts, or constituents in a complex entity; the interrelation of parts or the principle of organization in a complex entity.

Typical structures used in pattern analysis are strings of symbols, labeled trees, and labeled graphs. (A higher order structure may be represented by a string, *e.g.*, the representation of a tree as a bracketed string; but we will not consider these kinds of string representations and their semantics in this paper.)

Structural aspects may be defined explicitly as formal mathematical specifications or may be implicit in the models and algorithms used. An illustration of the first mode would be the specification of relations among pattern primitives in a perfect prototype of a class in which each relation is defined by an explicit listing of related primitives [27,30]. An example of the second would be the definition of a pattern class as the

NATO ASI Series, Vol. F30
Pattern Recognition Theory and Applications
Edited by P. A. Devijver and J. Kittler

language generated by a given grammar [5,8,21], in which case the structural relations would be implied by the rewriting rules of the grammar and might be quite difficult to describe concisely for a complex grammar.

For any sort of structural model, areas in which one would like to have practical definitions and tractable algorithms include:

1. inference of a model from a set of samples of a class (automatic or semi-automatic construction of a structural representation, given a subset of items of the class);

2. analysis of structural models (quantitative measures of structural complexity or information content; similarity or distance measures between structural models of classes);

3. flexible matching using measures of inexactness (optimally computed similarity or distance measures from a candidate to a structural model of a class);

4. obtaining structural forms from raw data.

In structural pattern analysis, the complexity of algorithms is a problem for the more complex cases, *i.e.*, the general algorithms for inference, inexact matching, etc., incorporate exhaustive searches that become impractical in their computational requirements as the size of the input problem increases. Thus, often implemented are algorithms that yield approximations and avoid combinational explosions by suboptimal, "best guess" methods.

2. Formal Relational Approaches

2.1. Morphisms

To illustrate the more formal structural approaches, we note that the definitions and results of modern discrete mathematics seem the most relevant and useful. A fundamental concept is a homomorphism (called simply a morphism in some references today) from a set of elements P to a set of elements Q, denoted $h : P \to Q$. $h : P \to Q$ is a function (*i.e.*, a mapping of each item in P to some item in Q) which "carries" an operation in P into an associated operation in Q. For example, if $\otimes$ is a binary operation on elements in P [so that $(p_1 \otimes p_2)$ gives a value in P] and $\oplus$ is a binary operation on elements in Q [so that $(q_1 \oplus q_2)$ gives a value in Q], then we must have

$$h(p_1 \otimes p_2) = h(p_1) \oplus h(p_2)$$

In other words, h not only maps elements in P to elements in Q but also "preserves" the $\otimes$ operation as an operation denoted by the symbol $\oplus$.

We can view the binary functions $\otimes : P \times P \to P$ and $\oplus : Q \times Q \to Q$ as ternary relations: $\otimes$ is a subset of $P \times P \times P$, a cartesian product usually denoted concisely as $P \otimes \otimes 3$; and $\oplus$ is a subset of $Q \times Q \times Q = Q \otimes \otimes 3$. Then $h : P \to Q$ is a homomorphism iff $(h(p_i), h(p_j), h(p_k))$ is found in relation $\oplus$ for each (p_i, p_j, p_k) found in relation $\otimes$. Thus, a general idea of a homomorphism is that it is a way of associating elements in

P with elements in Q such that the structure described by relation(s) in P is preserved in the structure described by relation(s) in Q.

The following terms are commonly used for a homomorphism h:

- ▷ if h is one-to-one (injective), then h is called a monomorphism;
- ▷ if h is onto (surjective), then h is called an epimorphism;
- ▷ if h is both onto and one-to-one (bijective), then h is called an isomorphism.

Intuitively, if $h : P \to Q$ is an isomorphism, then $(P, \otimes)$ and $(Q, \oplus)$ have a totally identical structure insofar as the relations $\otimes$ and $\oplus$ are concerned. If h is a monomorphism, then $(P, \otimes)$ may be identified with a substructure of $(Q, \oplus)$, *i.e.*, $(P, \otimes)$ may be "smaller" than $(Q, \oplus)$ and may be mapped by h into a part of $(Q, \oplus)$. If h is an epimorphism, then $(P, \otimes)$ may be "larger" than $(Q, \oplus)$ and may be compressed as it is mapped by h onto $(Q, \oplus)$. These ideas are illustrated in Figs. 1 and 2. In both figures, P includes edges a, b and "right of" relation R_1 with bR_1a. In Fig. 1, Q includes edges x, y, z and "above" relation R_2 with xR_2y, xR_2z, yR_2z; in Fig. 2, Q includes edge x, surface w, and "above" relation R_3 with xR_3w.

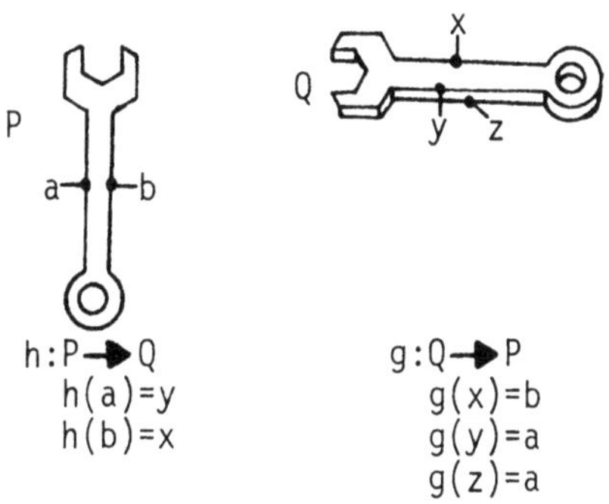

Figure 1: Monomorphism h and epimorphism g

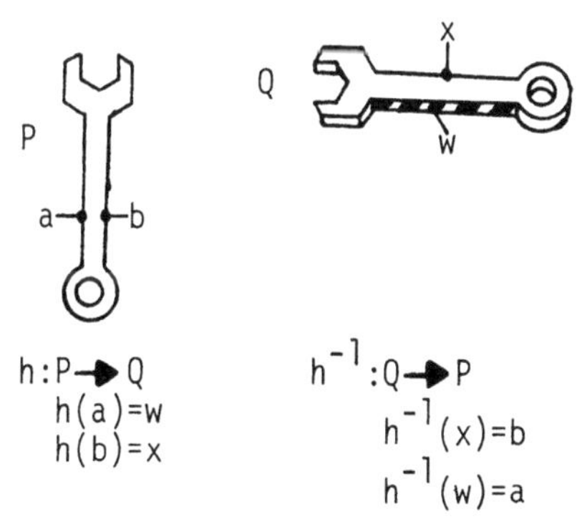

Figure 2: Isomorphisms h and h^{-1}

By using the standard definitions and concepts of discrete mathematics, we acquire the body of results that have been proved about these systems. For example, if h :

$P \to Q$ is an isomorphism, so is its inverse map from Q to P; and if $h : P \to Q$ and $g : Q \to T$ are mono- (or epi- or iso-) morphisms, so is the composite map $hog : P \to T$ in this diagram:

$$\underbrace{P \xrightarrow{h} Q \xrightarrow{g} T}_{hog}$$

2.2. Relational Graphs with Attributes

A specific illustration of the formal relational approach to structural pattern analysis is Shapiro and Haralick's use of graphs with attributes [27]. A pattern description is defined as a pair $D = (P, R)$ where $P = p_1, p_2, \ldots, p_n$ is a set of primitives (subobjects or parts or constituents) and $R = R_1, R_2, \ldots, R_k$ is a set of relations over cartesian products of P. A primitive p_i is defined as a binary relation in $A \times V$ where A is a collection of attributes and V is a collection of attribute-values, so each p_i is a list of attributes and the values assignable to them. A relation R_j is defined as an M_j-ary relation in $P \otimes \otimes M_j$, *i.e.*, as a subset of the product of P with itself M_j times; so each R_j is a list of M_j-tuples giving the primitives that are in relation R_j.

In practice, each primitive in P, each structural relation in R, and each attribute in A is usually given a descriptive name for reference. For example, we might define a "right-side" relation R_1 such that aR_1b means "object a is attached to object b's right side" or an "equal length" relation R_2 such that xR_2y means "edge x has the same length as edge y". R_2 is an example of establishing a relationship by comparing the values of an attribute for two primitives. An important extension is based on ideas of approximate matching because we would often want to define R_2 as "approximately equal in length" and have "approximately" taken into account either *(i)* explicitly by actually including approximately equal pairs (x, y) in R_2, or *(ii)* implicitly by allowing inexact matching of x with y using an algorithm to compute a weight to reflect the inexactness (a similarity measure, a probability, etc.).

To consider a homomorphism for structural relations, suppose we have a relation R in $P \otimes \otimes N$ and a function $h : P \to Q$. The composition Roh is a subset of $Q \otimes \otimes N$,

$$Roh = \{(h(p_1), h(p_2), \ldots, h(p_N)) | (p_1, p_2, \ldots, p_N) \text{ is in } R\}$$

Suppose S is an N-ary relation in Q, so that S is also a subset of $Q \otimes \otimes N$. Then $h : P \to Q$ is a homomorphism for relation R to relation S iff Roh is a subset of S; in this case, we know that the structural relation R among certain primitives in P is carried along by h into relation S among certain primitives in Q.

Suppose that $D_p = (P, R)$ is a prototype structural description representing a perfect item from a pattern class of interest. Then a candidate description $D_c = (Q, S)$ is said to match D_p if there is a homomorphism $h : P \to Q$ such that:

1. $h(p_i) = q_j$ implies that the p_i-list is contained in the q_j-list;

2. if R_i and S_j have the same name, then $(R_i)oh$ is contained in S_j.

The first condition requires that a primitive-to-primitive correspondence $h : P \to Q$ be found such that the attributes and their values listed in the model D_p per primitive are among those observed in D_c per primitive; the second requires that the structural relations imposed by D_p be carried into the same relations among corresponding primitives in D_c.

Note that the above definition of "matching" based on subsets allows some flexibility because, in the prototype $D_p = (P, R)$, the primitives would be listed with only those attributes deemed important in a given application. For example, attribute "shape" may be critical whereas attribute "color" may be irrelevant. Similarly, one would list only the critical structural relations in D_p. In other words, extra attributes and relations in D_c are ignored and do not prevent matches from being found.

To extend matching to allow missing elements from D_c and to allow approximate correspondence of attribute values, costs may be defined for missing items in P or R and thresholds may be introduced for differences between D_p and D_c attribute values [27]. Specifically, each primitive in D_p and each entry in each structural relation in D_p may be assigned a cost proportional to its importance in a match; then one searches for a mapping $h : P \rightarrow (Q \cup NULL)$ such that:

1. the attribute values of corresponding primitives match to within their allowed thresholds;

2. there may be D_p primitives not associated with any D_c primitives (*i.e.*, there may be primitives in P that are mapped by h to $NULL$), but the sum of their costs must be acceptably low; and

3. the sum of the costs of relational entries in R that are not carried by h into entries in D_c must also be acceptably low.

Shapiro and Haralick [27] study various computational methods to search for the "best" mapping $h : P \rightarrow (Q \cup NULL)$ according to various criteria for inexact matching using tree search with look-ahead operations.

Tsai and Fu [30] formally consider error-correcting isomorphisms of attributed relational graphs for pattern analysis. They define a pattern primitive $a = (s, x)$ to have a syntactic symbol s (the name of the item) and a semantic vector x of numerical/logical attribute values. A relation between primitives $e = (u, y)$ has a syntactic symbol u (the name of the structure represented by e) and a vector y of semantic attributes. An attributed relational graph over labels V_N and V_B is a four-tuple (N, B, n, b) where N is a finite set of nodes; B is a finite set of branches, a subset of $N \times N$; V_N is a finite set of node labels, each of the form (s, x) for a primitive; V_B is a finite set of branch labels, each of the form (u, y) for a relation; $n : N \rightarrow V_N$ is a "node interpreter" function; and $b : B \rightarrow V_B$ is a "branch interpreter" function. Thus, there is an underlying graph with nodes N and arcs B in which each node is labeled as a pattern primitive and each branch is labeled as a structural relation.

Suppose that an attributed relational graph P has been constructed as a model of a pure pattern, but that an observed pattern graph P' has been corrupted. If the only changes are in node labels, then P' is said to have local deformations; if changes are also present in branches, then P' has structural deformations. Tsai and Fu [30] consider in detail the case in which the underlying (unlabeled) graphs for P and P' are the same, but the interpreter functions may be different, and describe a state-space search approach to "correcting" P' into P using deformation weights (probabilities when available; assigned values otherwise).

2.3. Additional Illustrations

Isenor and Zaky [10] use a graph matching approach for fingerprint identification. After some preprocessing (ridge thinning, ridge ordering), each ridge is represented by a node with attributes like length, and arcs are used to represent "side neighbor" and "end neighbor" relations. The graph is subjected to a "defect repair" algorithm which fills in broken ridges and tries to remove false joins of ridges due to excess ink or dirt; this amounts to an imposition of known constraints on the graph for error-correction purposes. A heuristic, weighted graph-matching algorithm is then used to compare two fingerprint graphs.

Wong and You [33] use random graphs to incorporate probabilities into structural representations with attributes. The distribution assigned to a graph is estimated as the structural probability distribution of a class, and an entropy-based distance measure between graphs is defined for purposes of comparison and analysis of classes.

The following are two examples of the use of structure in stereo imagery. For stereo vision in robotic assembly, Kak *et al.* [12] use structural descriptions of left and right images of a scene as the basis for searching for the "best" function $h : P \rightarrow Q$ to associate the set of primitives P in the left image with the set of primitives Q in the right image of the same scene. The following assumptions are made:

1. each primitive in the left image has at most one corresponding primitive in the right image, and vice versa;

2. the "best" mapping of primitives in a left image to primitives in a right image, given as a function $h : P \rightarrow Q$, results in the greatest apparent redundancy in the structural descriptions of the two images;

3. the image primitives and structural relations are defined such that an algorithm to find the "best" primitive-to-primitive function h can initially make use of the information content of the primitives themselves.

Suppose that primitive q_j in the right image could correspond to primitive p_i in the left image. In order to employ probabilistic information theory, one must have the conditional probability $P = p(v_r = A(q_j)|v_l = A(p_i))$ of the event that primitive q_j has value $v_r = A(q_j)$ for attribute A in the right image, given that p_i has value $v_l = A(p_i)$ for the attribute A in the left image. The conditional information contributed by A is the information content of this event [1], *i.e.*,

$$I(v_r = A(q_j)|v_l = A(p_i)) = \log(1/P).$$

The primitive-distance between p_i and q_j is defined as the sum of those conditional information terms taken over all attributes. The distance $D(h, P, Q)$ between primitive sets P and Q under a function $h : P \rightarrow Q$ is the sum of these primitive-distances for all pairs (p_i, q_j) such that $h(p_i) = q_j$. Then one searches for a specific function $h : P \rightarrow Q$

minimizing this distance $D(h, P, Q)$ as the "best" primitive-to-primitive matching in the two images.

Kak *et al.* [12] also suggest ordering attributes for evaluation according to expected information gain. Suppose $p(v_j)$ is the a priori probability that attribute A has value v_j; then the entropy of the assignment of a value to A is

$$H[A] = \sum_j p(v_j) \log(1/p(v_j))$$

The conditional entropy of A with value v_i in the right image, given A with value v_j in the left image, is

$$H[A_{rt}|A_{lf}] = \sum_j \left\{ p(v_j) \sum_i [p(v_i|v_j) \log(1/p(v_i|v_j))] \right\}$$

This may be interpreted as the expected uncertainty of A's value in the right image, given knowledge of A's value in the left image. Kak *et al.* use the term $(H[A] - H[A_{rt}|A_{lf}])/H[A]$ as a figure of merit to order attributes according to their expected performance in removing uncertainty in matches of primitives. The representations reported in practice for thinned binary images of objects are attributed graphs for edge-vertex structures, where the edge attributes include edge-length, edge-mass, and various ratios, and the vertex (node) attributes include in-degree, location, and distance to nearest neighboring vertex. In experiments, the process generally worked well for well segmented images even with segmentation noise; poorest performance was on poorly segmented images with only broken pieces on which to attempt the matching [12].

Ohta and Kanada [19] use dynamic programming for stereo matching in left-right images by matching subintervals intra-scanline under constraints on consistency of vertically connected edges imposed inter-scanline. In this edge-based technique, the horizontal scanlines in the registered left and right images are paired top to bottom and are represented as intensity profiles; then a search is conducted to align subintervals intra-scanline that define matching left-right image edges (the edges having been detected and ordered by other methods). This search may be described as computation with a two-dimensional dynamic programming matrix as in Fig. 3(a). The cost function for alignments is based on the subinterval lengths and the variance of intensity values in the subintervals; specifically, if $A = a_1, a_2, \ldots, a_k$ and $B = b_1, b_2, \ldots, b_l$ are intensity value intervals between edges in right and left images on the same scan line, then the cost of matching the two intervals is

$$d = \text{var}(A, B) \times (k^2 + l^2)^{(1/2)}$$

where var(A, B) is the variance of all values in the two intervals on a per symbol basis.

The additional constraints imposed by continuity of vertical edges inter-scanline are needed to resolve ambiguities in the intra-scanline computations; this essentially yields a three-dimensional dynamic programming cube as a top-to-bottom stack of the two-dimensional matrices; the additional constraints are propagated on the third axis as in Fig. 3(b). The intra- and inter-scanline matchings both reflect structural relations that must hold as the left-right image correspondence is established. Experimental results are given for aerial images in which the connected edges for alignment are outlines of the major buildings.

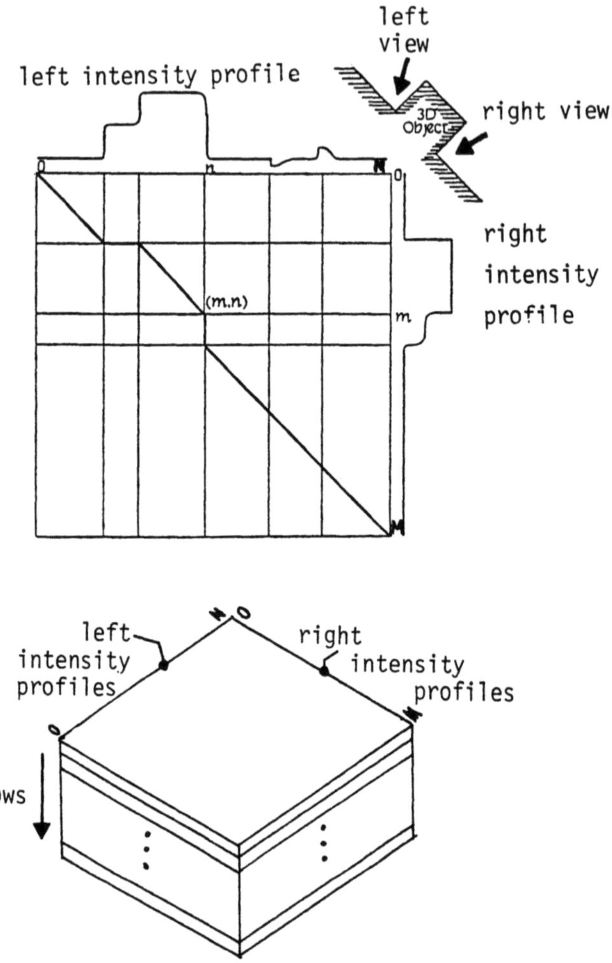

Figure 3: (a) *(top)* 2-D dynamic programming to align registered horizontal scanlines; (b) *(bottom)* 3-D dynamic programming to include intra-scanline edge constraints.

3. Syntactic/Semantic Methods

3.1. General Concepts; String Generators

The structure of some classes of patterns may be efficiently described by the discrete math models of formal language/automata theory [5,8,21]. An advantage of using syntactic/semantic models where possible is that the area has received considerable attention over several years, with especially important results obtained by the research program of the late Prof. K.S. Fu [4,5,6]. Thus, one can find algorithms in the literature which are potentially useful in various applications, *e.g.*, for inference of generators of sets of strings or trees or for error-tolerant parsing that handles imperfectly formed candidates via error-detecting/correcting parsing.

The standard definition of a string-generating grammar $G = (N, T, P, S)$ has its finite sets of nonterminals N, terminals T, productions P, and the unique initial nonterminal S. This model emphasizes the use of productions as rewriting rules by listing them in the form $x \rightarrow y$ ("x may be rewritten as, or replaced by, y"). But the actual use of P is to define the language generated by G via an implicit relation on strings; specifically, the derivation relation $\rightsquigarrow$ is the reflexive-transitive closure of $\rightarrow$ and the language generated by G is

$$L(G) = \{x | x \text{ is a string of terminals}, S \rightsquigarrow x\}.$$

The definition of a grammar may be extended to include attributes assigned to the nonterminals and terminals by attribute-value computation rules, usually called "semantics" and "semantic rules". These rules may interact with the syntactic productions: attribute values may constrain the use of productions, and vice versa. In formal terms, there is a syntax-vs-semantics trade-off in the sense that, to define a specific language by a grammar, one has a choice of less complex syntax with more complex semantics, or vice versa [22]; but semantic rules are often useful in practice because they focus directly on the attributes/features of primitives. A grammar may also be extended to weighted derivations, *e.g.*, by attaching probabilities to the productions to describe stochastic aspects of variations in structure [5,8].

Inference of structure may be deductive or inductive. Using the data for one perfect item from a class to construct a single structural prototype is an example of deductive inference; constructing an iterative description of repetitive substructure by analyzing a set of samples of a class is an example of inductive inference. An objective of many grammatical inference methods is to find substructure(s) common to the samples, generally by searching for repetitive substructures as instances of "pumping" to characterize the language. These instances are then represented by recursion in a grammar. More complex inference methods also estimate weights for options in structure, *e.g.*, by using relative frequencies of occurrence as probabilities [5,8,28]. Methods of inference of attributes simultaneously with syntactic structure are not well developed.

The minimized sum of the local costs of operations to edit a candidate into a target structure is often used as a similarity measure in inexact matching for pattern recognition purposes. The total cost is usually computed as the accumulated costs of operations on substructures of the candidate. For error-tolerant syntactic matching with strings, for example, a standard method for computing the dissimilarity of a candidate string x to a language $L(G)$ is to define the individual costs of the atomic operations of match/substitution/deletion/insertion on the symbols in x, and to compute $d(x, L(G))$ as the total cost of editing x into a string y in $L(G)$ where $d(x, y)$ is minimized. This is the "minimum-cost string-editing problem", the optimal solution of which in general involves exhaustive searching. More subtle models may take the probability of y in $L(G)$ into account in a Bayesian approach [5,8].

If attribute values are attached to symbols, then approximate matching of these values may also be incorporated as computations with weights [4,5]. In string representations for shape, Tsai and Yu [31] give one reference item for each variant of a class instead of using a grammar. They use angle with respect to a standard reference and length as two attributes for line-segment primitives, and they include a "merge" operation along with insert, delete, and substitute as edits for error-correcting matching of candidate string to reference prototype. The merge allows shorter, sequential line seg-

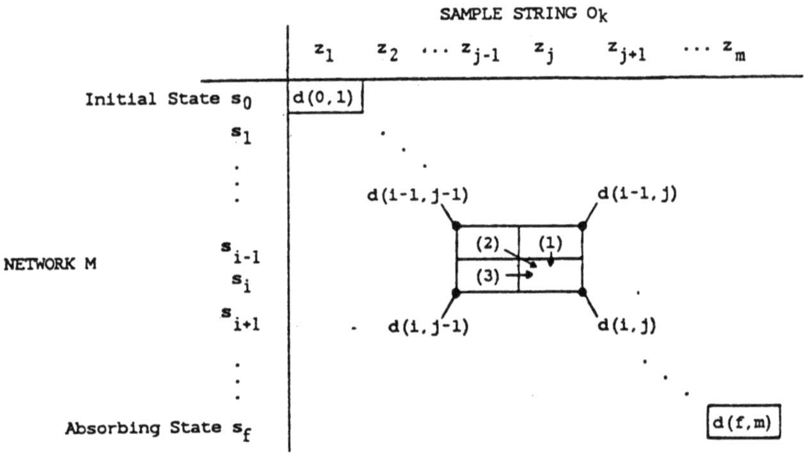

(a) Dynamic programming matrix for string-to-network alignment.
(1) deletion, (2) match or substitution, (3) insertion.

$$d(i,j) \text{ is maximum of } \begin{cases} (1) \quad d(i-1,j) + \log\left(\frac{f_{i-1,i}+1}{f_{i-1}+1}\right) + \log\left(\frac{1}{f_i+1}\right) \\ (2) \quad d(i-1,j-1) + \log\left(\frac{f_{i-1,i}+1}{f_{i-1}+1}\right) + \begin{cases} 0 & \text{if } z_j = s_i \\ \log\left(\frac{1}{f_i+1}\right) & \text{if } z_j \neq s_i \end{cases} \\ (3) \quad d(i,j-1) + \log\left(\frac{1}{f_i+1}\right) \end{cases}$$

(b) Details of additive, relative frequency cost function.
$f_{i-1,i}$ is frequency count on arc from state s_{i-1} to state s_i.
f_i is frequency of state s_i.

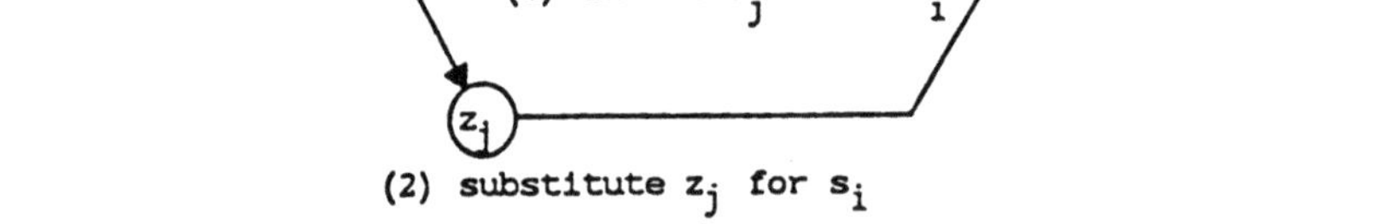

(c) Network modifications in neighborhood of state s_i.
One of these occurs if the neighborhood is on an optimal alignment.

Figure 4: Dynamic programming for string-to-network alignment

ment primitives to be merged into a single longer one for matching purposes, provided that the short segments form an approximately straight line.

Among the areas in which various combinations of these ideas are useful is contemporary automatic speech recognition, in which Levinson [15] identifies stochastic modeling/parsing, along with "template matching", as successful structural methods. He notes further that the common themes of finite data structures and dynamic programming are found in the various approaches, but with different interpretations.

As an illustration of both inference and inexact matching with a stochastic generator of strings, consider the dynamic programming method of Thomason and Granum [28]. This technique infers a Markov network by sequentially processing a set of sample strings using a relative-frequency cost function to seek patterns of "landmarks" as substrings occurring at about the same locations in large percentages of samples. Fig. 4 shows the dynamic programming matrix for string-to-network alignments, the relative-frequency cost function, and the local network adjustments allowed as a new sample is incorporated. Network entropies are valuable analysis measures; computing a candidate string's probability via the above cost function as a similarity measure has proven useful for error-tolerant pattern recognition [28,29].

Minimal cost editing of a string x into a string y is also used at times as a nearest-neighbor calculation for comparing two languages $L(G1)$ and $L(G2)$; *i.e.*, find x in $L(G1)$ and y in $L(G2)$ that minimize a relevant string-to-string measure $d(x, y)$. An interesting class-to-class measure using concepts of cross-entropy for probability distributions has been suggested for comparing hidden Markov chains as stochastic generators of strings [11]. Specifically, if M_1 and M_2 are Markov chains, we use a recurrent version of M_1 to generate an increasingly long string of symbols. Let $S(t)$ be that generated string out to t symbols; then the probabilistic distance from M_1 to M_2 is defined as the limit of

$$\log\left[Prob(S(t)|M_1)\right] - \log\left[Prob(S(t)|M_2)\right]$$

as t approaches infinity. This is not symmetric in M_1 and M_2. A symmetric mathematical metric may be computed as the average of the above added to a similarly computed term for $S(t)$ generated by M_2 [11]. The idea is that $S(t)$ in the limit reflects the probability distribution of M_1 as a model and that the measure above quantifies the difference in M_2 as a model. Some initial results in a variant of the above which uses dynamic programming to match Markov networks are also promising and easily computed [29].

3.2. Tree Grammars

Generative grammars may be defined for trees and graphs as complex structures [3,4,5, 8,9,20,21]. Several methods for inference of tree grammars from sample trees have been described [5,7,8,14]: a search for k-equivalent sublanguages for merging based on depth parameter k, a search for recurrent subtrees as instances of "pumping" in trees, and a computation of order-m tree derivatives as a generalization of derivatives of strings used to construct a tree-recognizing automaton. All three methods look for some kind of repetition in substructure as a basis for generalization.

The idea of error-correction is extended to trees by defining tree-editing operations [4,5], typically, substitution of a node label, insertion of a node between an existing node and its predecessor, insertion of a node to the left of all successors of a node, insertion of a node to the right of an existing node, and deletion of a node of rank 0 or 1. A generalized error-correcting tree automaton is available for minimum cost correcting when costs of the individual edit operations are known [4,5]. Fu [5] has described the use of stochastic tree models for studies of texture.

3.3. Graph Grammars

Pavlidis [20] discusses properties of graph grammars for applications like picture segmentation and global shape analysis. For sequential subgraph replacement, Nagl [18] identifies a graph-production as a triple $p = (g_l, g_r, E)$ where g_l is the lefthandside (the subgraph to be replaced), g_r is the righthandside (the replacing subgraph), and E is the embedding transformation that describes in detail how g_l is replaced by g_r. Nagl [18] surveys several versions of sequential embedding and also discusses parallel graph-rewriting systems (with biology mentioned as the main application field of these systems).

Based on concepts in the algebraic theory of graph grammars, Kreowski [13] proves a pumping lemma for context-free graph grammars that use an arc-replacement embedding rule. A sufficiently large graph in the language can be decomposed into three subgraphs FIRST, LINK, and LAST such that the subgraph LINK may be pumped any finite number of times to create a graph still in the language. The pumping is described in terms of "gluing graphs together" where gluing is interpreted to be a generalization of the operation of string-replacement in string languages. Specifically, a production's righthandside is a nonterminal A (which must appear as the label of a directed arc in a graph in order to use the production) and its lefthandside B is a graph with nonterminal/terminal arc labels and with two unique nodes designated as the gluing points for B (these two are the nodes by which B is embedded when replacing the arc labeled A). The relationship between the pumping lemma for context-free strings (the "uvwxy theorem") and for arc-replacement graphs may be represented as

```
u    - v    - v    -  . . .  - v   -------
                                         |
FIRST-LINK-LINK-  . . .  -LINK-LAST     w
                                         |
y    - x    - x    -  . . .  - x  --------
```

via the correspondences

```
        u                v
FIRST   |        LINK    |        LAST w
        y                x
```

Syntactic error-correction has been extended to graph-to-graph matching for graphs with node and arc labels by defining six edit operations: substitute the label of a branch, delete a branch, insert a branch, substitute the label of a node, merge nodes, and split a node [4].

Bunke [3] defines an attributed graph to consist of a set of labeled nodes, a set of labeled arcs, a set of node attributes, and a set of arc attributes (names of attributes and their assigned values). A production for an attribute-graph grammar is a list of five items $(g_l, g_r, T, pred, F)$ where g_l and g_r are labeled graphs without attributes, respectively, the left- and right-handside graphs; T is an embedding transformation consisting of two relations, L and R, which respectively give the details of how to handle arcs terminating in g_l and leaving g_l as g_l is replaced by g_r; *pred* is an applicability predicate which must be TRUE in order to use the production and may be defined so as to reflect constraints on g_l attributes; and F is a set of node attribute and edge attribute transfer functions used analogously to attribute-computation functions in strings. A control diagram may be used to control the sequencing of productions, and certain error-correcting capability is developed to handle common flaws in circuit diagrams and flow charts (insertions of extra line segments, deletions of line segments, gaps in line segments, etc.).

4. Conclusion

This chapter summarizes some of the contemporary work in structural pattern analysis using explicit and implicit specifications of structure. The approaches are illustrated with a few examples from the literature. Significant areas of research include not only contributions to the theory but also specific applications and the development of practical algorithms, say, as parallel computations or VLSI implementations.

References

[1] Abramson, N., *Information Theory and Coding*, McGraw-Hill: New York, 1963.

[2] *American Heritage Dictionary of the English Language*, Houghton Mifflin: Boston, MA, 1971.

[3] Bunke, H., "Attributed graph grammars and their application to schematic diagram interpretation," *IEEE Trans. PAMI*, vol. PAMI-4, no. 6, pp. 574-582, 1982.

[4] Fu, K.S., "Picture syntax," in *Pictorial Information Systems*, Springer-Verlag: New York, 1980.

[5] Fu, K.S., *Syntactic Pattern Recognition and Applications*, Prentice-Hall: Engelwood Cliffs, NJ, 1982.

[6] Fu, K.S. et. al., Reprinted papers in "Special Memorial Issue for Professor King-Sun Fu," *IEEE Trans. PAMI*, vol. PAMI-8, no. 3, 1986.

[7] Fukada, H. and Kamata, K., "Inference of automata from sample set of trees," *Int'l. Jour. Comput. Info. Sci.*, vol. 13, no. 3, pp. 177-196, 1984.

[8] Gonzalez, R.C. and Thomason, M.G., *Syntactic Pattern Recognition: An Introduction*, Addison Wesley: Reading, MA, 1978.

[9] *Graph-Grammars and their Application to Computer Science*, Lecture Notes in Comp. Sc., Springer-Verlag: New York, 1983.

[10] Isenor, D.K. and Zaky, S.G., "Fingerprint identification using graph matching," *Jour. Pat. Recog.*, vol. 19, no. 2, pp. 113-122, 1986.

[11] Juang, B-H., and Rabiner, L.R., "A probabilistic distance measure for hidden Markov models," *AT & T Tech. Jour.*, vol. 64, no. 2, pp. 391-408, 1985.

[12] Kak, A.C., Boyer, K.L., Chen, C.H., Safranek, R.J., and Yang, H.S., "A knowledge-based robotic assembly cell," *IEEE Expert*, vol. 1, no. 1, pp. 63-83, 1986.

[13] Kreowski, H.J., "A pumping lemma for context-free graph grammars," in *Graph-Grammars and their Application to Computer Science and Biology*, Lecture Notes in Comp. Sc., Springer-Verlag: New York, 1979.

[14] Levine, B., "Derivatives of tree sets with applications to grammatical inference," *IEEE Trans. PAMI*, vol. PAMI-3, no. 3, pp. 285-293, 1981.

[15] Levinson, S.E., "Structural methods in automatic speech recognition," *Proc. of the IEEE*, vol. 73, no. 11, pp. 1625-1650, 1985.

[16] McKeown, D.M., Harvey, W.A., Jr., and McDermott, J., "Rule-based interpretation of aerial imagery," *IEEE Transactions PAMI*, vol. PAMI-7, no. 5, pp. 570-585, 1985.

[17] Merelli, D., Mussio, P. and Padula, M., "An approach to the definition, description, and extraction of structures in binary images," *Comp. Vision, Graphics, and Image Proc.*, vol. 31, pp. 19-49, 1985.

[18] Nagl, M., "A tutorial and bibliographical survey on graph grammars," in *Graph-Grammars and their Application to Computer Science and Biology*, Lecture Notes in Comp. Sc., Springer-Verlag: New York, 1979.

[19] Ohta, Y., and Kanada, T., "Stereo by intra- and inter-scanline search using dynamic programming," Tech. Rept. CMU-CS-83-162, Carnegie-Mellon University, 1983.

[20] Pavlidis, T., "Structural descriptions and graph grammars," in *Pictorial Information Systems*, Springer-Verlag: New York, 1980.

[21] Pavlidis, T., *Structural Pattern Recognition*, Springer-Verlag: New York, 1977.

[22] Pyster, A. and Buttleman, H.W., "Semantic-syntax-directed translation," *Inform. Contr.*, vol. 39, pp. 320-361, 1978.

[23] Richetin, M. and Vernadat, F., "Efficient regular grammatical inference for pattern recognition," *Jour. Pat. Recog.*, vol. 17, no. 2, pp. 245-250, 1984.

[24] Sanfeliu, A. and Fu, K.S., "A distance measure between attributed relational graphs for pattern recognition," *IEEE Transactions SMC*, vol. SMC-13, no. 3, pp. 353-362, 1983.

[25] Shapiro, L.G., "A structural model of shape," *IEEE Trans. PAMI*, vol. PAMI-2, no. 2, pp. 111-126, 1980.

[26] Shapiro, L.G. and Haralick, R.M., "Organization of relational models for scene analysis," *IEEE Trans. PAMI*, vol. PAMI-4, no. 6, pp. 595-602, 1982.

[27] Shapiro, L.G. and Haralick, R.M., "Structural descriptions and inexact matching," *IEEE Trans. PAMI*, vol. PAMI-3, no. 5, pp. 504-519, 1981.

[28] Thomason, M.G. and Granum, E., "Dynamic programming inference of Markov networks from finite sets of sample strings," *IEEE Trans. PAMI*, in press.

[29] Thomason, M.G., Granum, E., and Blake, R.E., "Experiments in dynamic programming inference of Markov networks with strings representing speech data," to appear in *Jour. Pat. Recog.*

[30] Tsai, W.H. and Fu, K.S., "Error-correcting isomorphisms of attributed relational graphs for pattern analysis," *IEEE Trans. SMC*, vol. SMC-9, pp. 757-768, 1979.

[31] Tsai, W.H. and Yu, S.S., "Attributed string matching with merging for shape recognition," *IEEE Trans. PAMI*, vol. PAMI-7, no. 4, pp. 453-462, 1985.

[32] Vilnrotter, F. M., Nevatia, R., and Price, K.E., "Structural analysis of natural textures," *IEEE Trans. PAMI*, vol. PAMI-8, no. 1, pp. 76-89, 1986.

[33] Wong, A.K.C. and You, M., "Entropy and distance of random graphs with application to structural pattern recognition," *IEEE Trans. PAMI*, vol. PAMI-7, no. 5, pp. 599-609, 1985.

STRUCTURAL PATTERN RECOGNITION: A RANDOM GRAPH APPROACH

Andrew K.C. Wong

Department of Systems Design Engineering
University of Waterloo
Waterloo, Ontario
Canada N2L 3G1

Abstract

This paper presents the notion of random graphs and their associated probability distributions. It addresses both the structural and probabilistic aspects of structural pattern recognition. A structural pattern can be explicitly represented in the form of attributed graphs and an ensemble of such representations can be considered as outcomes of a mapping, called random graph mapping. To account for the variation of structural patterns in the ensemble, a lower order probability distribution is used to approximate the high order joint probability. To synthesize an ensemble of attributed graphs into a probability distribution (or a set of distributions) of a random graph, we introduce a distance measure together with a hierarchical clustering algorithm. The distance measure is defined as the minimum change of a specially defined Shannon's entropy before and after the merging of the distributions. With this new formulation, both supervised and unsupervised classification of structural patterns can be achieved.

1. Introduction

In structural pattern recognition a pattern can be represented by a set of primitives and the relations among them. Such a pattern can be modelled by an attributed graph [1]-[3]. Some proposed graph representations of patterns are the picture description language (PDL) and picture languages developed by Shaw [4],[5], the primary graphs and region adjacency graphs (RAG) proposed by Pavlidis [6],[7], and the attributed relational graphs (ARG) introduced by Tsai and Fu [2],[8]. To account for the variations of structural patterns in an ensemble, a probabilistic description of the ensemble is desirable. This paper presents the random graph approach [3],[9] for such a description. By random graph, we mean a mapping (analogous to random variable) from a sample space onto a range space consisting of all possible attributed graphs as outcomes of the random graph. We call the union attributed graph of all attributed graphs in the range space together with its associated probability distribution a random graph representation of the ensemble.

In order to estimate a low order approximation of high order probability distribution from an ensemble of attributed graphs, a random graph representation synthesis

NATO ASI Series, Vol. F30
Pattern Recognition Theory and Applications
Edited by P.A. Devijver and J. Kittler

process is proposed [3]. First a special Shannon entropy measure defined for probability distribution of a random graph is used to reflect the variation of the attributed graphs in the ensemble. Since an attributed graph itself can be treated as an unique outcome of a random graph, it can be considered also as a random graph representation. The synthesis process can be realized by merging random graph representation using an optimal graph monomorphism algorithm [3],[10]-[13] that minimizes the change of entropy for the distributions before and after the merging process. A hierarchical graph synthesis algorithm [3] is used for the synthesis of a random graph representation from an ensemble of attributed graphs.

The increment of entropy in the synthesis of two random graph representations possesses properties that render it a distance measure between random graph representations [3]. Since an attributed graph can be treated as a special case of a random graph representation, the above distance can be defined for 1) two attributed graphs, 2) an attributed graph and a random graph distribution and 3) two random graph distributions. These distance measures are then used to formulate various tasks for structural pattern recognition.

In general, a random graph representation is the synthesis of a cluster of individual attributed graphs. If the class memberships for a given set of graphs are not known priorly, the synthesis which generates more than one random graph representations is considered as an unsupervised learning (or clustering). Since corresponding to each random graph representation is a cluster of attributed graphs, the probability distribution associated with each random graph can then be referred to as the structural probability distribution of the cluster (or pattern class). If all the graphs in the input set belong to a single pattern class, then only one random graph representation would be obtained. This synthesis process can then be considered as a supervised learning. Thus, to classify an attributed graph representing a structural pattern to one of the several given random graph representations characterizing different classes of patterns, the nearest neighbor rule or the maximum likelihood rule can be used. By nearest neighbor rule, an unknown pattern is placed in a given class if the distance between the attributed graph of that pattern and the random graph distribution of the class is minimized. By Baye's decision rule, an unknown pattern is assigned to a class when the likelihood of the attributed graph of the pattern being an outcome of the random graph of that class is the maximum.

2. Attributed Graphs and Random Graphs

In the attributed graph representation of a structural pat- tern, a vertex with attribute values is used to represent a primitive and an attributed arc is used to represent the rela- tion between them.

Let $Z = \{z_i \mid i = 1,2,\cdots,I\}$ be a nonempty and finite set of possible attributes for describing pattern primitives and $Si = \{s_{ij} \mid j = 1,2,\cdots,J\}$ be the set of possible attribute values associated with z_i for each i.[1] Let $L_v = \{(z_i, s_{ij}) \mid i = 1,\cdots,I; j = 1,\cdots,J_i\}$ be the set of legal attribute-value pairs. A pattern primitive π is simply a

[1]These values could be nominal, ordinal, continuous, logical, etc.

specification of (unique) values for attributes. Thus, π is a subset of L_v having at most one ordered pair for any particular z_i. Let Π be the set of all possible pattern primitives.

Similarly, let $F = \{fi \mid i = 1, 2, \cdots, I'\}$ be a nonempty finite set of possible relational attributes between primitives and $T_i = \{tij\}$ be a set of possible values of f_i. Let $L_a = \{(f_i, t_{ij}) \mid i = 1, \cdots, I'; j = 1, \cdots, |Ti|\}$. A relation w is a specification of a set of (unique) values for some relational attributes. It is a subset of L_a. Let Θ be the set of all relations.

Definition 1. An *attributed graph* G over $L = (L_v, L_a)$, with an underlying graph structure $H = (N, E)$, is defined to be a pair (V, A), where $V = (N, \nu)$ is called an *attributed vertex set* and $A = (E, \delta)$ is called an *attributed arc set*. The mappings $\nu : N \to \Pi$ and $\delta : E \to \Theta$ are called *vertex interpreter* and *arc interpreter* respectively.

For comparison of attributed graphs, the concept of graph morphism is introduced. In general, a graph morphism is considered as an incidence preserving vertex to vertex mapping. It is referred to as monomorphism if the mapping is one-to-one; an epimorphism if it is onto and an isomorphism if it is one-to-one and onto. These definitions can be extended to attributed graph.

Definition 2. Two attributed graphs $G_1 = (V_1, A_1)$ and $G_2 = (V_2, A_2)$ are said to be *structurally isomorphic* if there exists an isomorphism $\eta : H_1 \to H_2$ where $H_1 = (N_1, E_1)$ and $H_2 = (N_2, E_2)$ represent the structural aspects of G_1 and G_2 respectively. G_1 and G_2 are said to be *completely isomorphic*, written $G_1 = G_2$, if there exists an attribute value preserving structural isomorphism μ between G_1 and G_2.

For matching graphs of the same order, the concept of the extension of a graph is introduced.

Definition 3. A graph $G = (V, A)$ of order n can be extended to form a complete graph $G' = (V', A')$ of order k, $k \geq n$, by adding vertices and arcs with null attribute values. We call G' the *k-extension* of G, and G the *n-reduction* of G'.

We next proceed to the definition of random graphs. This definition is adopted from [3],[10].

Definition 4. A random graph is a pair of tuples $R = (W, B)$ such that

1. W, representing the random vertex set, is an n-tuple $(\alpha_1, \alpha_2, \cdots, \alpha_n)$ where each α_i, called a random vertex, is a random variable;

2. B, called the random arc family is an m-tuple $(\beta_1, \beta_2, \cdots, \beta_m)$ where each β_j, called a random arc, is also a random variable; and

3. associated with each possible outcome graph G of R and a graph monomorphism (or subgraph isomorphism) $\mu : G \to R$, there is a probability $p(G, \mu) = Pr(R = G,\ Q = m)$, Q being the family of graph morphisms, which satisfies:

$$p(G, \mu) \geq 0 \text{ for all } G \in \Gamma \tag{1}$$

$$\sum_{\Gamma} p(G, \mu) = 1 \tag{2}$$

where Γ is the range of R.

To simplify the definition of probability and entropy of random graphs we introduce the term *random element*, denoted by γ, which is referred to as either a random vertex or a random arc, or both, wherever a distinction between them is unnecessary. Hence, a random graph with n vertices and m arcs can also be expressed as an $(n+m)$-tuple with $n+m$ random elements, *i.e.*,

$$R = (\gamma_1, \gamma_2, \cdots, \gamma_n, \gamma_{n+1}, \cdots, \gamma_{n+m}). \tag{3}$$

The range of each element consists of a set of attribute values including the *null attribute value* ϕ that corresponds to a null outcome of γ. Therefore, if either endpoint of an random arc β has a null outcome, the outcome of the arc must also be null, *i.e.*,

$$Pr\{\beta = \phi \mid \sigma(\beta) = \phi \text{ or } \tau(\beta) = \phi\} = 1 \tag{4}$$

where $\sigma(\beta)$ and $\tau(\beta)$ are the initial and terminal endpoints of β respectively.

In the definition of attributed graph, if z_i in Z are considered as random variables taking values s_{ij} with probabilities p_{ij}, and similarly, f_i in F are random variables taking values t_{ij} with probabilities q_{ij}, then the attributed graph just becomes a random graph in the obvious way.

With graph extension defined, we can slightly modify our representation of a random graph. Let $R = (W, B)$ be of order n. We represent the *n-extension* of R by $R' = (W, B')$, such that for each random arc $\beta' \in B'$, $Pr\{\beta' = \phi\} = 1$ if $\beta' \in B$. Furthermore, for each outcome graph $G = (V, A)$ of R with a monomorphism $\mu : G \to R$, we can consider its *n-extension* $G' = (V', A')$ as an outcome of R' with a monomorphism $\mu'' : G' \to R'$ such that μ is a restriction of μ'', and G' is structurally isomorphic to R'. It is obvious that the modification of R by R' does not affect either the probability of the outcome graph G or the monomorphism of G into R.

Figure 1 gives an example of a random graph R and its outcomes. R consists of random vertices (A, B, C, D) and random arcs (U, V, W, X, Y). The range of A, B, C, D are $\{a, b, \phi\}$, $\{f, \phi\}$, $\{c, e\}$, $\{b, \phi\}$ respectively, and those for U, V, W, X, Y are $\{\phi\}$, $\{v\}$, $\{\phi\}$, $\{u, \phi\}$, $\{y, z\}$, $\{x\}$ respectively. Figure 1(b) is an extension of a graph of order 3 to one of order 4 by adding the null elements. Figure 1(c) is an outcome of order 4 whereas Figure 1(d) is an infeasible outcome since non-null arcs cannot be incident to a null vertex.

Extending the concept of attributed isomorphism to random graph we arrive at the following definition.

Definition 5. Two random graphs $R_1 = (W_1, B_1)$ and $R_2 = (W_2, B_2)$ are *completely isomorphic* iff there exists a structural isomorphism $\eta : R_1 \to R_2$, such that the probability distributions of their random vertices and random arcs are identical. R_1 and R_2 are said to be *equivalent*, denoted by $R_1 = R_2$, iff they are completely isomorphic.

3. Probability and Entropy of Random Graphs

Let $\mu : G \to R\}$ be the underlying monomorphism which is a restriction of an isomorphism $\mu' : G' \to R$ where $G' = (V', A')$ is an extension of G to the order of R. Then μ' can be denoted by two sets of mappings (ζ, ξ) where $\zeta : V' \to W$ and $\xi : A' \to B$. Then we can write the probability of G with respect to R as below.

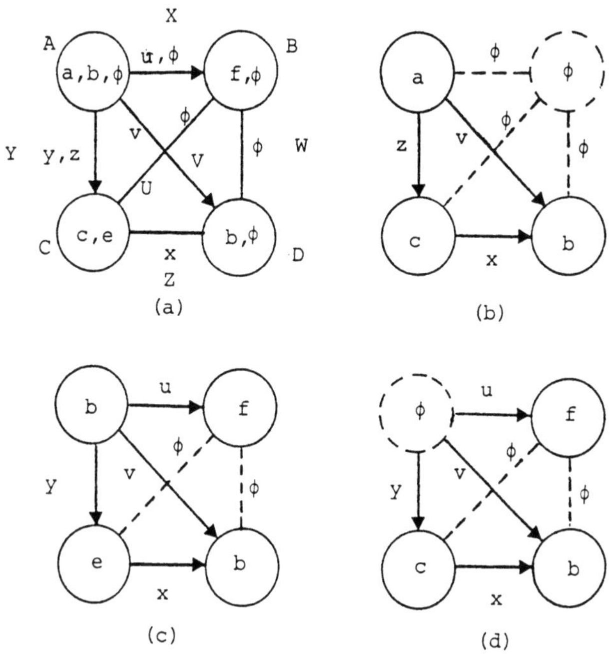

Figure 1: An example of a random graph and its outcomes. (a) A random graph R of order 4. (b) An outcome graph of order 3 and its extension to order 4. (c) An outcome graph of order 4. (d) An infeasible outcome of R.

Definition 6. Let x and b (possibly null) be the outcomes of the random vertex α and random arc β. We define the probability of G with respect to R under μ as:

$$p(G,\mu) = p(G',\mu') = Pr\{(\alpha = x \cup \alpha \in W), (\beta = b \cup \beta \in B)\}. \tag{5}$$

In random graph application, since the consideration of high order joint probability is impractical, a lower order approximation is introduced. However, if we assume that all random elements are mutually independent, we would preclude significant structural information from the graphs. Here, we present a probability estimation which takes into consideration some structural (relational) and contextual information in the random graph representation.

We first introduce the following assumptions:

1. The random vertices α are mutually independent.
2. A random arc β is independent of any random vertex other than its endpoints $\sigma(\beta)$ and $\tau(\beta)$.
3. The conditional distributions $\{\beta|\alpha = x\}$ are mutually independent.

Based on the above assumption, (5) becomes

$$p(G,\mu) = \prod_{\alpha\in W} Pr\{\alpha = x\} \prod_{\beta\in B} Pr\{\beta = b \mid \sigma(\beta) = x,\ \tau(\beta) = y\} \tag{6}$$

By putting $p(x) = Pr\{\alpha = x\}$ and $p(b \mid x,y) = Pr\{\beta = b \mid \sigma(\beta) = x,\ \tau(\beta) = y\}$ we write (6) as:

$$p(G,\mu) = \prod_{\substack{\alpha\in W \\ \zeta^{-1}(\alpha)=v' \\ \nu(v')=x}} p(x) \prod_{\substack{\beta\in B \\ \xi^{-1}(\beta)=a' \\ \delta(a')=b}} p(b \mid x,y) \tag{7}$$

where v' and a' are vertices and arcs in G' respectively.

In order to reflect the variability of the outcomes of a random graph, Shannon's entropy is adopted.

Definition 7. The *entropy* $H(R)$ of a random graph $R = (W,B)$ is defined by

$$H(R) = -\sum_{(G\mu)} p(G,\mu)\log p(G,\mu) \tag{8}$$

where the summation is over all outcome graphs of R. Using (7), we can express

$$\begin{aligned} H(R) &= -\sum_{x} p(x)\log p(x) \\ &\quad -\sum_{x,y} p(x)p(y)\sum_{b} p(b \mid x,y)\log p(b \mid x,y). \end{aligned} \tag{9}$$

Example 1. Figure 2 is a random graph with its vertex distributions listed inside the vertices and conditional probability distributions of the random arcs given in Figure 2(b). Figure 2(c) and Figure 2(d) are two outcome graphs, G_1 and G_2. Based on (9), the probability of G_1 and G_2 can be estimated as below.

$$\begin{aligned} p(G_1,\mu_1) &= [p(a)p(c)p(e)][p(u \mid a,c)p(x \mid a,e)p(z \mid c,e)] \\ &= 0.104. \\ p(G_2,\mu_2) &= [p(a)p(d)p(f)][p(v \mid a,d)p(w \mid a,f)p(y \mid d,f)] \\ &= 0.022. \end{aligned}$$

The entropy of R can then be obtained as

$$H(R) = [H(A)+H(B)+H(C)] + [H(X)+H(Y)+H(Z)] = 4.271.$$

4. Synthesis of Random Graphs With Known Morphism

Let $C = \{G_1, G_2, \cdots, G_m\}$ be a class of attributed graphs. Suppose that associated with each $G_i = (V_i, A_i)$ there exists a vertex mapping $\psi_i : V_i \to L$ which assigns each vertex $v \in V_i$ a distinct label from a vertex label set. We say that two graphs G_i and G_j are equivalent under L if $\psi_i \circ (\psi_j)^{-1}$ is a complete isomorphism of G_i onto G_j. Hence, we can partition C into equivalence classes $\{C_1, C_2, \cdots, C_n\}$ under L, where $n \leq m$. Thus, each equivalence class C_i can be represented by a graph $G_i \in C_i$. Hence, we can represent C by a set of distinct graphs $D = \{G_1, G_2, \cdots, G_n\}$. For each G_i in D, we associate a frequency f_i indicating the size of C_i.

From D and its associated frequencies, we can derive a random graph R satisfying the following conditions:

1. There exists a vertex labeling $\phi : R \to L$;

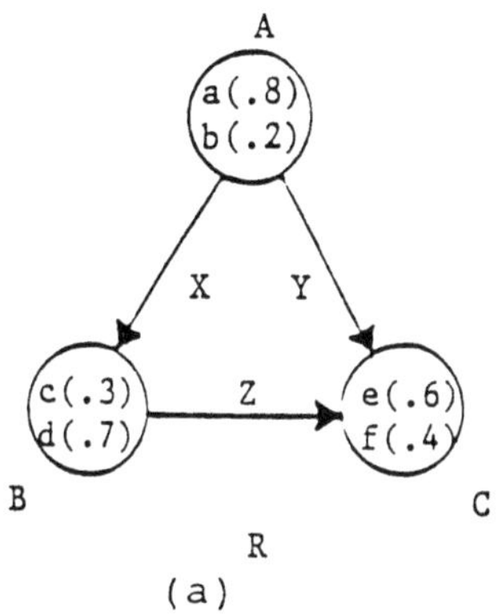

X	p	Y	p	Z	p
u|a,c	0.8	w|a,e	0.1	y|c,e	0
v|a,c	0.2	x|a,e	0.9	z|c,e	1.0
u|a,d	0.7	w|a,f	0.8	y|c,f	0.1
v|a,d	0.3	x|a,f	0.2	z|c,f	0.9
u|b,c	0.1	w|b,e	0.4	y|d,e	0
v|b,c	0.9	x|b,e	0.6	z|d,e	1.0
u|b,d	0.2	w|b,f	0	y|d,f	0.4
v|b,d	0.8	x|b,f	1.0	z|d,f	0.6

(b)

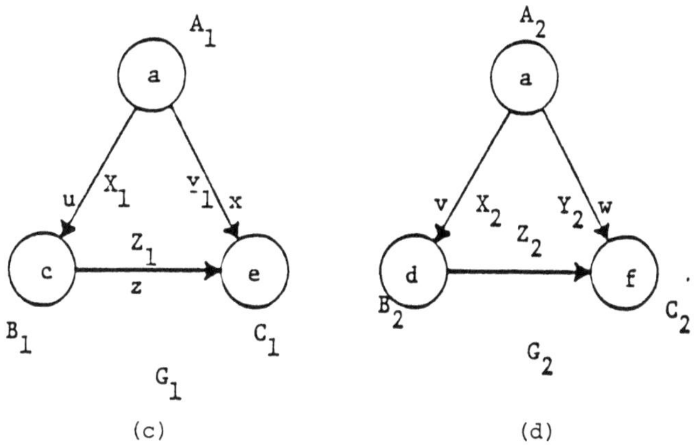

Figure 2: A random graph and two of its outcomes. (a) The random graph R. (b) The probability distribution of random arcs in R. (c)–(d) Two outcomes G_1 and G_2.

2. There is a monomorphism $\mu_i : G_i \rightarrow R$ such that $\psi_i = \mu_i \circ \phi$.

3. The probability of each G_i can be estimated as the relative frequency of G_i in D, i.e.,

$$p(G_i, \mu_i) = Pr\{R = G_i,\ Q = \mu_i\} = \frac{f_i}{\sum_{i=1}^{n} f_i}. \tag{10}$$

Let the vertex set corresponding with label k among G_i's in D be $U_k = \{v_{k_1}, v_{k_2}, \cdots, v_{k_n}\}$, where $v_{k_i} \in V_i$. Let α_k be the random vertex and let x be an arbitrary outcome associated with α_k. Then, $p_k(x)$ can be estimated by:

$$p_k(x) = Pr\{\alpha_k = x\} = \sum_{\substack{i=1 \\ \zeta(v_{k_i})=x}}^{n} f_i \Big/ \sum_{i=1}^{n} f_i. \tag{11}$$

Similarly, we denote the set of the corresponding arcs among G_i's in D by $S_j = \{a_{j_1}, a_{j_2}, \cdots, a_{j_n}\}$, such that for $i = 1, 2, \cdots, n$, both the initial and terminal endpoints of a_{j_i} have respectively identical labels. Let β_j be the random arc with outcomes being the values of a_{j_i} in S_j. Then, the conditional probability that β_j assumes a value b given the endpoints values x and y can be estimated by:

$$\begin{aligned} p_j(b \mid x, y) &= Pr\{\beta_j = b \mid \sigma(\beta_j) = x, \tau(\beta_j) = y\} \\ &= \sum_{\substack{i=1 \\ \nu(\sigma(a_{j_i}))=x \\ \nu(\tau(a_{j_i}))=y \\ \delta(a_{j_i})=b}}^{n} f_i \Big/ \sum_{\substack{i=1 \\ \nu(\sigma(a_{j_i}))=x \\ \nu(\tau(a_{j_i}))=y}}^{n} f_i \end{aligned} \tag{12}$$

Therefore, a random graph R consisting of the random vertices and random arcs with probability distributions defined in the form of (11) and (12) is more general than the one given in (10). We call a random graph R obtained from D using (11) and (12) a *synthesis* of D.

Synthesis of Random Graphs

Suppose that a set of random graphs $F = \{R_1, R_2, \cdots, R_m\}$ can be independently obtained from subgroups of a class of pattern graphs. Let n_i be the number of graphs in the ith subgroup. Suppose further that a set of morphisms $\{\phi_i \mid \phi_i : R_i \to L\}$ exists which maps each R_i into a common label set L. Then, we can obtain for F a synthesis which is a "super" random graph to encompass all R_i's in F.

Assume that $\{\alpha_{k_1}, \alpha_{k_2}, \cdots, \alpha_{k_m}\}$ and $\{\beta_{j_1}, \beta_{j_2}, \cdots, \beta_{j_m}\}$ are the sets of the kth random vertices and jth random arcs among $\{R_i\}$ according to $\{\phi_i\}$. Let $\{p_{k_i}(x)\}$ and $\{p_{j_i}(b \mid x, y)\}$ denote the probability distributions of α_{k_i} and β_{j_i} respectively. We can define the synthesis of the set of random vertices and random arcs as follows.

Definition 8. The *synthesis* α_k of a set of random vertices $\{\alpha_{k_1}, \alpha_{k_2}, \cdots, \alpha_{k_m}\}$ is defined to be a random vertex having the probability distribution:

$$p_k(x) = Pr\left\{\alpha_k = x \,\middle|\, \cup_{i=1}^{m} \alpha_{k_i}\right\} = \sum_{i=1}^{m} q_i\, p_{k_i}(x) \tag{13}$$

where

$$q_i = n_i \Big/ \sum_{i=1}^{m} n_i \tag{14}$$

is the relative frequency (or a *priori* probability) of R_i in the combined sample after the merging of all R_i's, and $p_{k_i}(x) = Pr\{\alpha_{k_i} = x\}$ is the probability of the random vertex α_{k_i} having outcome x.

Definition 9. Let k and *ell* be indices of the random vertices incident to a set of random arcs β_j. The synthesis β_j of a set of random arcs $\{\beta_{j_1}, \beta_{j_2}, \cdots, \beta_{j_m}\}$ is defined to be a random arc having the following conditional probability distribution $\{p_j(b \mid x, y)\}$:

$$\begin{aligned} p_j(b \mid x, y) &= Pr\Big\{\beta_j = b \Big/ \bigcup_{\substack{i=1 \\ \sigma(\beta_{j_i})=x \\ \tau(\beta_{j_i})=y}}^{m} \beta_{j_i}\Big\} \\ &= \left[\sum_{i=1}^{m} q_i r_{j_i} p_{j_i}(b \mid x, y)\right] \Big/ [p_k(x) p_\ell(y)] \end{aligned} \tag{15}$$

where

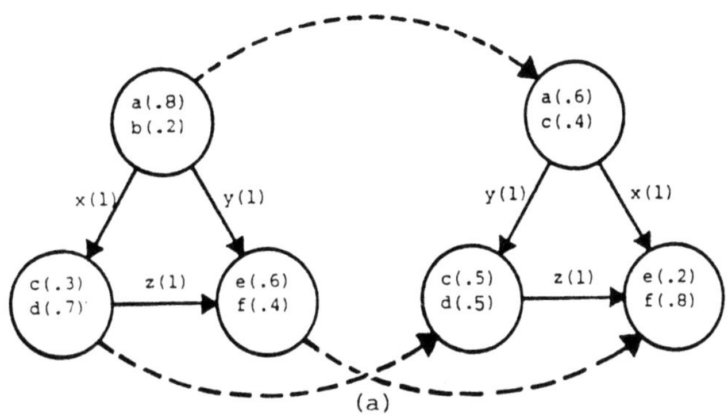

(a)

X_1	p	Y_1	p	Z_1	p
x|a,c	1.0	y|a,e	1.0	z|c,e	1.0
x|a,d	1.0	y|a,f	1.0	z|c,f	1.0
x|b,c	1.0	y|b,e	1.0	z|d,e	1.0
x|b,d	1.0	y|b,f	1.0	z|d,f	1.0

X_2	p	Y_2	p	Z_2	p
x|a,c	1.0	y|a,e	1.0	z|c,e	1.0
x|a,d	1.0	y|a,f	1.0	z|c,f	1.0
y|c,c	1.0	x|c,e	1.0	z|d,e	1.0
y|c,d	1.0	x|c,f	1.0	z|d,f	1.0

(b)

Figure 3: Example of random graph synthesis. (a) $\mu : R_1 \rightarrow R_2$. (b) The probability distributions of random arcs in R_1 and R_2.

1. $r_{j_i} = Pr\{\sigma(\beta_{j_i}) = x,\ \tau(\beta_{j_i}) = y\} = p_{k_i}(x)p_{\ell_i}(y)$

2. $p_{j_i}(b \mid x, y) = Pr\{\beta_{j_i} = b \mid \sigma(\beta_{j_i}) = x, \tau(\beta_{j_i}) = y\}$

3. $p_k(x)p_\ell(y) = Pr\{\sigma(\beta_j) = x\} \times Pr\{\tau(\beta_j) = y\} = Pr\{\sigma(\beta_j) = x, \tau(\beta_j) = y\}$ (the probability of the synthesis random arc β_j with endpoints x and y obtained using (13)).

The random graph R composed of random vertices and random arcs defined above is called a synthesis of F according to the given morphism. Two random graphs R_1 and R_2, as shown in Figure 3, are synthesized under a given morphism μ. Here, R_1 and R_2 are supposed to have equal *a priori* probabilities $q_1 = q_2$. Figure 4 shows the result of the synthesis.

So far, morphism between graphs is assumed known in the synthesis. When morphism is not known a priori, an optimal isomorphism between random graphs will be used. This leads to the introduction of increment of entropy in the synthesis of random

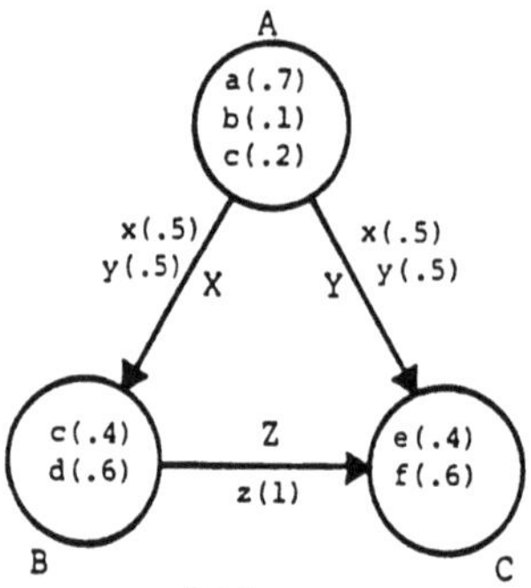

(a)

X	p	Y	p	Z	p
x|a,c	1.0	y|a,e	1.0	z|c,e	1.0
x|a,d	1.0	y|a,f	1.0	z|c,f	1.0
x|b,c	0.5	y|b,e	0.5	z|d,e	1.0
x|b,d	0.5	y|b,f	0.5	z|d,f	1.0
y|c,c	0.5	x|c,e	0.5		
y|c,d	0.5	x|c,f	0.5		

(b)

Figure 4: The synthesis of the graphs in Figure 3. (a) $R = +(R_1, R_2, \mu)$. (b) The probability distribution of randoms arcs in R.

graphs. Such increment of entropy will later be used in the definition of distance and similarity measures between attributed graphs and random graphs.

5. Distance Measure Between Random Graphs

Let $R = +(R_1, R_2, \mu)$ denote that $R = (W, B)$ is the synthesis of the random graphs R_1 and R_2 under a given morphism μ, and $\gamma = +(\gamma_1, \gamma_2, \mu)$ denote that γ is the synthesis of the corresponding random elements γ_1 and γ_2 in R_1 and R_2 respectively according to μ. Then we have the following definition.

Definition 10. Let q_1 and q_2 be the relative frequencies of the samples associated with R_1 and R_2 respectively. The *increment of entropy* in γ after R_1 and R_2 are synthesized is defined as:

$$H'(\gamma) = H(\gamma) - [q_1 H(\gamma_1) + q_2 H(\gamma_2)]. \tag{16}$$

Analogously, the *increment of entropy* in R is defined as

$$H'(R) = H(R) - [q_1 H(R_1) + q_2 H(R_2)]. \tag{17}$$

Property 1. The increment of entropy in $\gamma = +(\gamma_1, \gamma_2, \mu)$ is bounded:

$$0 \leq H'(\gamma) \leq 1. \tag{18}$$

Property 2. If R is of order N, then

$$0 \leq H'(R) \leq N. \tag{19}$$

The proofs of these properties can be found in [17].

Distance and optimal isomorphism

If a random graph is used to represent the structural probability distribution of an ensemble of attributed graphs, then the synthesis of two random graphs should produce a resultant random graph whose probability distribution should be one closest to both of the random graphs before the synthesis. Thus, the increment of the entropy of the distribution after the synthesis with respect to those before the synthesis should be minimum. To achieve this, the synthesis process should consist of two phases: 1) the determination of the best correspondence between the two sets of random elements and 2) the combination of their probability distributions accordingly. Hence, the increment of the entropy of the synthesis, denoted by $H"(R)$ based on a random graph isomorphism μ between R_1 and R_2 can be used to determine their optimal graph isomorphism, denoted by μ^*. We can further use this increment of entropy as a distance measure between the random graphs R_1 and R_2.

Definition 11. The *distance* between two random graphs R_1 and R_2 is defined to be:

$$d(R_1, R_2) = \min_{\mu}\{H"(R) \mid R = +(R_1, R_2, \mu)\} \qquad (20)$$

or

$$= H(R) \text{ where } R = +(R_1, R_1, \mu^*).$$

Property 3. Let the order of the synthesis of R_1 and R_2 be N. The distance measure $d(R_1, R_2)$ has the following properties:

1. $0 \leq d(R_1, R_2) \leq N^2$;
2. $d(R_1, R_2) = 0$ iff $R_1 = R_2$ (complete isomorphism); and
3. $d(R_1, R_2) = d(R_2, R_1)$.

Unfortunately, this distance measure generally does not satisfy the triangular inequality of a metric due to the averaging effect weighted by the a *priori* probabilities.

In order to compare random graphs of different orders, it is desirable to normalize the absolute distance, making it a measure of relative similarity. Since the increment of entropy in a synthesis of two random graphs is bounded by 0 and N^2, we arrive at the following definition.

Definition 12. Let $d(R_1, R_2)$ be the distance defined by an optimal isomorphism between R_1 and R_2 of order N. We define the *similarity* $s(R_1, R_2)$ between R_1 and R_2 to be:

$$s(R_1, R_2) = 1 - d(R_1, R_2)/N^2. \qquad (21)$$

Property 4. The similarity measure defined above has the following properties:

1. $0 \leq s(R_1, R_2) \leq 1$;
2. $s(R_1, R_2) = 1$ iff $R_1 = R_2$ (completely isomorphic); and
3. $s(R_1, R_2) = s(R_2, R_1)$.

Since an attributed graph can be treated as a special case of a random graph, the above distance (or similarity) can be defined for 1) two attributed graphs, 2) an attributed graph and the probability distribution of an random graph and 3) the probability distributions of two random graphs.

6. Synthesis of Random Graphs With Morphism Unknown

Since $H(R)$ is a measure of the variability of its outcomes, a low entropy value indicates greater similarity among its outcome graphs. Furthermore, $H(R)$ depends on the interpretation of each graph in the ensemble as outcomes of R, *i.e.* on the choice of the morphism μ among them. Assuming that graphs given in an ensemble retain considerable similarity, we can use entropy as an objective function to direct the labeling and estimation process. Hence, it is possible to obtain a minimum entropy in synthesizing R by solving the optimization problem [3]:

$$\min_{\mu} H(R). \tag{22}$$

However, when the ensemble size is large and the order of the graphs is high, we need a hierarchical method for approximating the optimization process. At each stage, a local optimum is obtained. And eventually, a final result is selected among the local optima. The synthesis obtained is then adopted as the approximation of the random graph which represents the class pattern of the entire ensemble.

Besides simplicity in computation, the hierarchical approximation has another advantage. It is capable of detecting sub-classes in the ensemble. Without such capability, the synthesis process may lead to unnatural and misleading results.

6.1. A Hierarchical Synthesis Process

Let $D = \{G_1, G_2, \cdots, G_n\}$ be the observed graphs in an ensemble. Without loss of generality, each G_i in D can be treated as a random graph R_i. We can thus equate D to a set $F = \{R_1, R_2, \cdots, R_n\}$, where each R_i in F is a random graph representation of the attributed graph G_i in D. Let R_{ij} denote the synthesis of R_i and R_j under the optimal isomorphism μ_{ij}. Then, the distance d_{ij} between them is $H"(R_{ij})$. We use two $n \times n$ matrices[2] $L = [\mu_{ij}]$ and $M = [d_{ij}]$, to direct the synthesis of F. Obviously, M is a symmetric matrix with diagonal elements $d_{ii} = 0$ for all i.

In the iterative process, those pairs of distinct graphs in F with a minimum distance in M are synthesized and replaced by their synthesis. After re-indexing, F is reduced to $F = \{R_1, R_2, \cdots, R_m\}$, $m \leq n$. This procedure is repeated until one random graph, the synthesis of the set, remains, or until it is terminated by a thresholding criterion. The final remaining random graph(s) represent(s) the class pattern (or sub-class patterns), encompassing all possible variations among its members in D.

The pseudo-code of the hierarchical random graph synthesis algorithm can be found in [3]. Its complexity is of order $\mathcal{O}(n^2)$ times the order of the average optimal graph isomorphism algorithm.

6.2. Thresholding

When a class of patterns is composed of several subclasses, we can introduce a threshold to determine the splitting condition. If the threshold criterion between two random

[2]The term "matrix" here is used in a general sense. For example, in stead of scalar values, the entries may contain pointers to lists.

graphs exceeds the threshold, instead of synthesizing them, we allow them to coexist as tentative representations of separate sub-class patterns of the same class.

A readily usable criterion for thresholding is the similarity measure s_{ij} between graphs R_i and R_j. It is a normalized measure ranging from 0 to 1. An appropriate point t in this range can be prescribed so that only random graph pairs with $s_{ij} \geq t$ will be synthesized.

At the beginning of the process, it is difficult to prescribe the value t. To overcome this a dynamic thresholding criterion is proposed. Let S_i and S_j be lists of all previous similarity measures that lead to the synthesis of R_i and R_j, respectively. We define the *average similarity measure* of R_i and R_j to be

$$s^* = \left(\sum_{s \in S_i} s + \sum_{s \in S_j} s \right) \Big/ (|S_i| + |S_j|) \tag{23}$$

Now, the dynamic threshold t^* can be defined to be

$$t^* = r \times s^* \tag{24}$$

where r again is a prescribed rate with a value in [0,1].

In applications, R_i and R_j will be synthesized only if $sij \geq t^*$. Apparently, t^* becomes tighter when the set of graphs sustain higher similarity. This variability characteristic of t^* makes it flexible and useful when no *a priori* knowledge of the class of graphs is available, even though the determination of r in (24) depends on the informed knowledge of the problem domain.

7. Applications of Random Graph in Pattern Recognition

The application of random graph in structural pattern recognition can be illustrated by two simple examples. First, we use an English character recognition problem to illustrate both the unsupervised and supervised classification. Next, we use a string mutation and alignment problem to show how random the graph approach can be used to synthesize a class of strings and detect their underlying probability pattern.

7.1. Characterization of Structural Pattern Classes

A random graph, synthesized from a cluster of attributed graphs, reflects the probabilistic configuration of the cluster. If the graphs are designated as pertaining to the same pattern class, the synthesis process is referred to as *supervised* construction of class pattern. If the class memberships for a given set of graphs are not known, the synthesis which generates more than one random graph is considered as *unsupervised* classification or clustering.

The probability distribution of a random graph can be considered as the *structural probability distribution* of a pattern class. One of the advantages of using such a distribution is that it can also be used as a base graph in graph matching for classification purposes [3]. Other major advantages are:

1. The distribution encompasses both the structural and the statistical information of the entire class of graphs. It is a better representation of the class than, say, the cluster prototypes.

2. The random graph allows varied or deformed patterns as members of the class even though they were not included in the training set.

3. The classification of a pattern can be achieved by comparing the pattern to each random graph in a class.

7.2. Classification of Structural Patterns

Suppose that $R_1, R_2, \cdots, R_n$ represent n different classes (or subclasses) of structural patterns. Let G be an attributed graph representing an unknown pattern. To classify G, we can use either the nearest neighbor rule or the maximum likelihood rule. For either rule, we first find a graph optimal isomorphism $\mu_i : G \rightarrow R_i$, $i = 1, \cdots, n$. Depending on the criterion used in finding μ_i, the distances $d(G, R_i)$ between G and R_i or the probabilities $p(G, \mu_i)$ of G being an outcome of R_i can be obtained. If for some R_k, μ_k does not exist (*e.g.*, the matching cost (distance) is infinity or the probability is 0), then class k can be excluded. Using the nearest neighbor rule, we classify G to class i, iff

$$d(G, R_i) < d(G, R_j), \quad i \neq j, \quad \forall j \tag{25}$$

Using the maximum likelihood rule, we classify G to class i iff

$$p(R_i)p(G, \mu_i) > p(R_j)p(G, \mu_j), \quad i \neq j, \quad \forall j \tag{26}$$

where $p(R_j)$ is the a *priori* probability of class j characterized by R_j, and $p(G, \mu_j)$, based on (11), is the estimated probability of G being an outcome of R_j.

7.3. An Illustrative Example in Character Recognition

Here an English character recognition problem is used to illustrate the application of random graph to structural pattern recognition. A pseudo random number generator is used to generate strokes with various orientations in the handwritten English letters F, H, and E. Among the 60 characters generated, 20 for each letter, all 47 distinct variations are taken and listed in Figure 5, where the numbers to the left and right of ':' denote the character index and its frequency of occurrence respectively. The attribute codes for character primitives and primitive relations are defined in Figure 6.

With the graph synthesis procedure, pairwise distances among the attributed graphs are first computed and tabulated. The pair(s) with the shortest distance are then merged. Next, new distances between the merged graphs and the remaining graphs are computed. The closest pair(s) are merged again. The process continues as indicated in the hierarchical tree (Figure 7(a)) from which we observe that all 47 distinct characters are successfully clustered into their respective letter classes.

Using the three estimated distributions representing variations of letters F, H, and E Figure 7(b), we can classify the attributed graph of an unknown sample to one of the pattern classes. For the three unknown patterns (Figure 8), not contained in the ensemble for the clustering process and not used in the training process, we classify each of them into its correct class using both rules.

Figure 5: Variations of handwritten English letters F, H, and E.

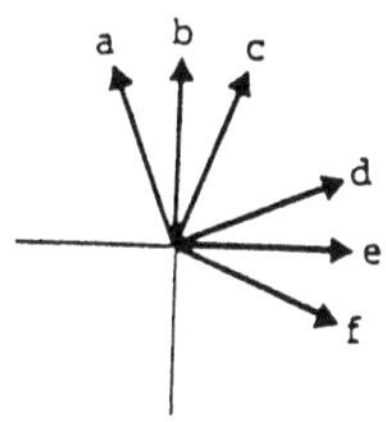

(a)

Code	Description	Diagram
u	above	
v	bending	or
w	branching	or
x	crossing	
y	near (gap)	or or
z	left of	

(b)

Figure 6: Attribute codes for primitives and relations. (a) Primitive codes. (b) Relation codes.

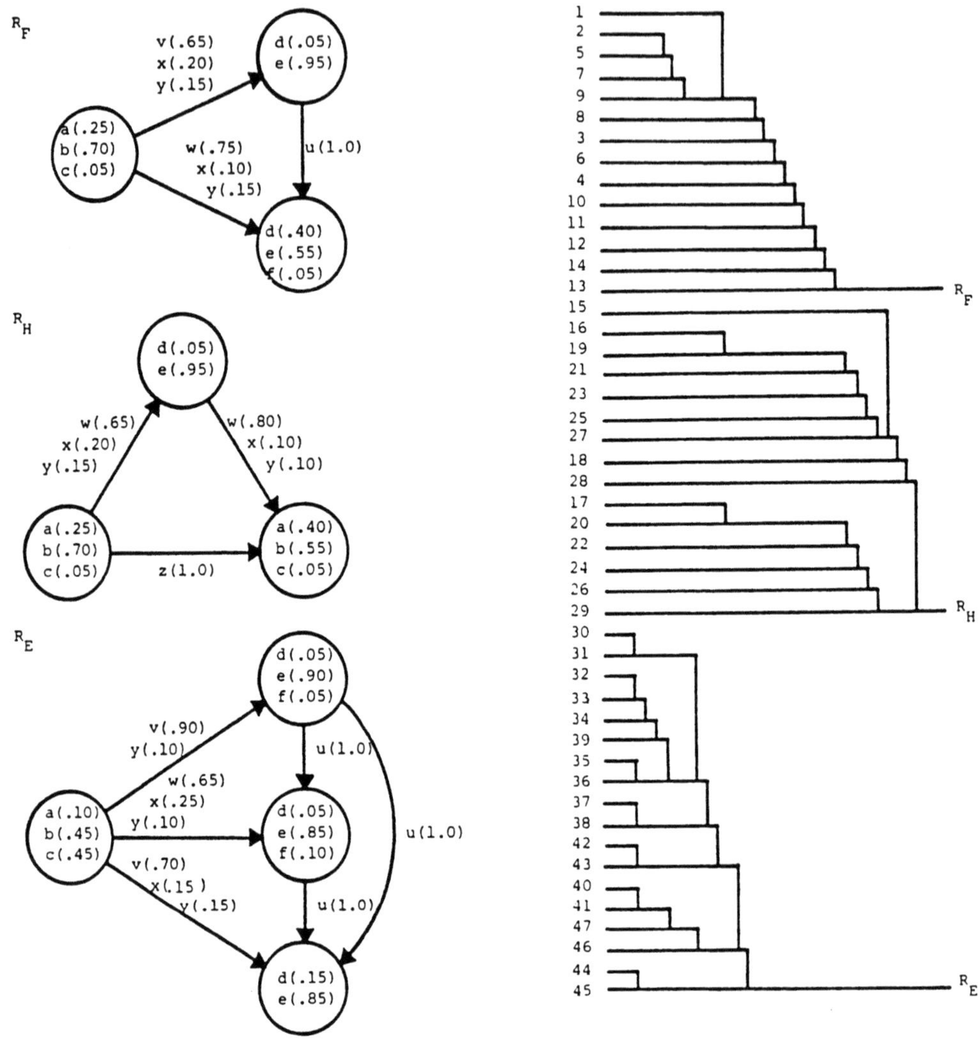

Figure 7: The hierarchical clustering process. Random graphs representing F's, H's and E's.

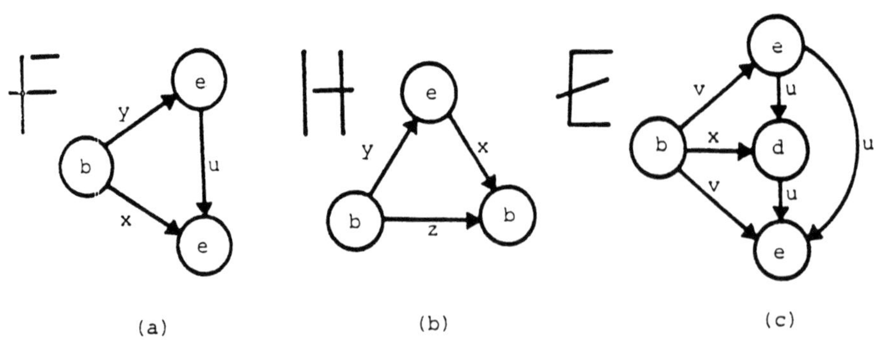

Figure 8: Three unknown patterns and their attributed graphs

7.4. The String Mutation and Alignment Problem

The string mutation and alignment problem is of great importance in the study of mutation of biomolecules [18],[19] as well as in syntactic pattern recognition [20]–[22]. Up-to-date, most of the distance or similarity measures used for comparing or aligning strings are based on certain criterion function defined for the two strings under comparison. In other words, the characteristics of the ensemble or subensembles of strings are not taken into consideration in the comparison process. As a result, it is extremely difficult to resolve ambiguity when only two strings are compared or to reveal the characteristics of the ensemble or subensembles. By treating a string as a special case of an attributed graph, we can use random graph synthesis to synthesize an ensemble of strings and thus reveal explicitly their probabilistic pattern [17]. Such pattern, in terms of probability distributions, can enable us to recover the common label scheme (a common alignment) from which individual strings can be compared with the distribution of the random strings or with each other.

A string is an ordered sequence of symbols. Let $\{x_i\}$ be a set of strings generated from the same source (or belonging to the same class). Let us suppose that due to variations, mutations or deformations, the individual x_i may be different in their corresponding symbols, or even in length. Given $\{x_i\}$, we are interested in the synthesis of a random string R such that the individual symbols in all x_i are aligned accordingly and characterized by a sequence of random elements. The random elements describe the probabilistic aspect of the variation of the corresponding symbols in the string. Therefore, each symbol in x_i can be described as an outcome, associated with a probability, of its corresponding random element in R. This can be considered as a supervised learning process.

To study the variation of strings in an ensemble, we consider that a string could be mutated or deformed into another through certain local changes of symbols, including deletion, insertion and replacement of a symbol by another. Suppose that the strings are made up of an alphabet $A = \{a_1, a_2, \cdots, a_n\}$ of n symbols. Let $s = s_1 s_2 \cdots s_m$ $(s_i \in A)$ be a source string composed of m symbols from A. Suppose that $p(j|i) = Prob\{a_i \rightarrow a_j\}$ denotes the substitution probability that a symbol s_i is deformed into another symbol a_j $(a_i, a_j \in A)$, and $q(\phi|i) = Prob\{a_i \rightarrow \phi\}$ denotes the deletion probability that a_i is deformed into a null symbol ϕ. Furthermore, suppose that $r(j|i) = Prob\{a_i$ inserted next to $s_i\}$ denotes the insertion probability that the symbol a_j is inserted right after s_i in the string s.

In this illustration, we let $A = \{a_1, a_2, \cdots, a_8\} = \{$a,b,$\cdots$,h$\}$ and $s = s_1 s_2 \cdots s_8 =$ gahcagba. Assume that the substitution and deletion probabilities are as shown in Table 1 and the insertion probabilities following s_4 and s_8 are listed in Table 2. The other insertion probabilities not listed in Table 2 are 0. Based upon the mutation or deformation probabilities tabulated in Tables 1 and 2, we can use the source string $s =$ gahcagba to generate a set of strings which are mutations or variations of s. In this example, 150 strings were generated and then sorted, first according to their lengths and then the alphabetic order, yielding a total of 112 distinct strings with their corresponding frequency, f, as listed in Table 3.

The set of 112 strings is then used as input to our hierarchical graph synthesis algorithm. For each pair of the input strings, the similarity is computed. Though

Table 1: Substitution and deletion probabilities of symbols.

p,q	a	b	c	d	e	f	g	h	ϕ
a	0.8	0.1	0	0	0	0	0	0	0.1
b	0	0.8	0.1	0	0	0	0	0	0.1
c	0	0	0.8	0.1	0	0	0	0	0.1
d	0	0	0	0.8	0.1	0	0	0	0.1
e	0	0	0	0	0.8	0.1	0	0	0.1
f	0	0	0	0	0	0.8	0.1	0	0.1
g	0	0	0	0	0	0	0.8	0.1	0.1
h	0.1	0	0	0	0	0	0	0.8	0.1

Table 2: Insertion probabilities next to s_4 and s_8.

r	a	b	c	d	e	f	g	h	ϕ
s_4	0.1	0.1	0	0	0	0	0	0	0.8
s_8	0	0.1	0.1	0	0	0	0	0	0.8

various definitions of distance between strings have been available [20],[21], the one adopted here is based on (21). The most similar pairs of strings are first synthesized into random strings in the early phase. The process repeated as described before untill the synthesized random string for the entire ensemble is obtained. This random string then characterizes the ensemble.

Table 4 shows the probability distributions of the 10 random elements in the final random string. For instance, the first random element has a probability distribution $p(g) = 0.787$, $p(h) = 0.087$, and $p(\phi) = 0.126$, where ϕ represents the null outcome. We note that the probabilities of the outcome symbols in the random elements are slightly different from the variation probabilities of symbols defined in Tables 1 and 2. This can be attributed mainly to the effect of the small sample size (150) generated by the pseudo random number generator. We would expect a closer matching in the corresponding probabilities if a larger sample size were adopted.

Table 5 illustrates the alignment of the individual strings according to the common labelling scheme (or the optimal matching between the input string and the random string) resulted from the synthesis. Here a null symbol is represented by '*'. Since the hierarchical synthesis algorithm merges the most similar pairs of strings iteratively, we note that the ordering of the strings in Table 5 is no longer in the ascending order of their ID numbers as in Table 3.

Table 3: Variations of the given source string s = gahcagba.

ID	f	String	ID	f	String	ID	f	String
1	1	ahcab	39	1	gahcagb	77	4	gahcbgba
2	1	ahcba	40	1	gahcahb	78	1	gahcbgbb
3	1	ahchb	41	1	gahcgba	79	1	gahcbgca
4	1	gaagb	42	1	gahdbab	80	1	gahcbhba
5	1	gagba	43	1	gahdbga	81	1	gahdaagb
6	1	gcagb	44	1	gahdbgb	82	3	gahdagba
7	1	ghcab	45	1	gahgbab	83	1	gbacagba
8	1	hahba	46	1	gbcagba	84	1	gbacahba
9	1	aacgba	47	1	gbhaaca	85	1	gbhbagba
10	1	acbgba	48	2	gbhagba	86	2	gbhcagba
11	1	gahaga	49	1	gbhcaha	87	1	gbhcagca
12	1	gahcaa	50	4	ghcagba	88	1	gbhcahcb
13	1	gahcab	51	1	haacgbb	89	1	ghcagcab
14	1	gahcga	52	1	hadagba	90	1	ghcbgcab
15	1	gahdba	53	1	hahcaba	91	5	hahcagba
16	1	gbagba	54	1	hcbgbab	92	1	hahcagca
17	1	gbcabb	55	1	acbagbac	93	1	hahcbgba
18	1	hcagba	56	1	ahcagbab	94	1	hbacagbc
19	1	aacaaha	57	1	ahcagbac	95	1	hbhdagbb
20	1	ahcagba	58	1	ahcbagba	96	1	bacaahbbb
21	1	ahcbgca	59	1	gaacabab	97	1	gaacagbac
22	1	ahcbhba	60	1	gaacagba	98	1	gaadaagba
23	1	bhcagba	61	1	gaacagbb	99	1	gahcaagba
24	1	bhcbgba	62	1	gaacbaga	100	1	gahcaagca
25	1	gaaagbb	63	1	gaacbgbb	101	1	gahcaahbb
26	1	gaacaga	64	1	gacaagba	102	2	gahcagbab
27	1	gabhcac	65	1	gacbagba	103	1	gahcahbac
28	1	gacagba	66	1	gacbbgbb	104	1	gahcbahba
29	1	gacagca	67	1	gahaagbb	105	1	gahcbgbab
30	1	gacahba	68	1	gahagbab	106	1	gahdaagba
31	2	gacbgba	69	2	gahcaaba	107	1	gahdagbab
32	1	gacbhba	70	1	gahcabab	108	1	gbcbahbab
33	1	gadagba	71	19	gahcagba	109	1	gbhcaagba
34	2	gahagba	72	1	gahcagbb	110	1	gbhcahbab
35	1	gahagbb	73	2	gahcagca	111	1	hahbbgbac
36	1	gahagcb	74	1	gahcahac	112	1	gahcaagbab
37	1	gahcaba	75	1	gahcahba			
38	2	gahcaga	76	1	gahcbaba			

8. Conclusion

In this paper, we have shown that structural patterns can be explicitly and effectively represented by attributed graphs and random graphs. We first introduced the basic concepts and notations. We then provided formal definitions of attributed graphs, random graphs and various classes of graph morphisms. We have also described the estimation of probability distributions and entropy of random graphs.

Table 4: Probability distributions with the random elements.

R.E.	Prob. Dist'n.		R.E.	Prob. Dist'n.		R.E.	Prob. Dist'n.	
	g	0.787		a	0.133		a	0.827
1	h	0.087	5	b	0.140	9	b	0.087
	ϕ	0.126		ϕ	0.727		ϕ	0.086
	a	0.767		a	0.747		b	0.140
2	b	0.147	6	b	0.093	10	c	0.053
	ϕ	0.086		ϕ	0.160		ϕ	0.807
	a	0.113		g	0.760			
3	h	0.753	7	h	0.132			
	ϕ	0.134		ϕ	0.108			
	c	0.780		b	0.813			
4	d	0.093	8	c	0.093			
	ϕ	0.127		ϕ	0.094			

Remark: R.E. denotes "Random Element".

By considering attributed graphs as special cases of random graphs, an entropy increment measure has been introduced as a distance measure between random graphs. From such distance measure, a normalized similarity measure between attributed graphs and random graphs is derived. With this, we have shown that unsupervised classification of structural patterns can be realized by a hierarchical random graph synthesis procedure. Using an appropriate threshold, a set of attributed graphs can be synthesized into several random graph representations each of which corresponds to a cluster. The resulted probability distribution of the respective random graph then reflect the probabilistic pattern of the contextual and structural characteristics of each cluster. We have also shown that when classes of structural patterns are given, the random graph synthesis process can be used to estimate the probability distribution for each class. Unknown pattern graphs can then be classified by using the proposed distance or by applying the maximum likelihood rule.

The random graph synthesis process relies heavily on optimal graph isomorphism or monomorphism algorithms. To provide good algorithms, various techniques have been developed for matching attributed graphs [2],[11]–[13]. Recently, based on a branch-and-bound tree searching technique, we have developed a more efficient algorithm for finding optimal graph isomorphisms and monomorphism [14] using a heuristic function for a consistent lower bound cost estimation.

Finally, the proposed method can be extended to include more complex structural patterns by including n-ary relations known as hyperedges under the definition of hypergraphs. It is also desirable to include the notion of hierarchical graphs [1],[17]. Both attributed hypergraphs and hierarchical graphs can be generalized to random hypergraphs and hierarchical graphs for solving more complex structural pattern recognition problems.

Table 5: The alignment of strings after synthesis.

ID	f	String	ID	f	String	ID	f	String
96	1	*bacaahbbb	110	1	gbhc*ahbab	11	1	gah**ag*a*
19	1	*aacaah*a*	3	1	*ahc**hb**	45	1	gah***gbab
47	1	gbh*aa*ca*	32	1	ga*c*bhba*	68	1	gah**agbab
101	1	gahcaahbb*	22	1	*ahc*bhba*	107	1	gahd*agbab
98	1	gaadaagba*	80	1	gahc*bhba*	65	1	ga*cbagba*
27	1	ga***bhcac	30	1	g*ac*ahba*	58	1	*ahcbagba*
111	1	hah*bbgbac	84	1	gbac*ahba*	14	1	gahc**g*a*
52	1	ha*da*gba*	24	1	*bhc*bgba*	10	1	*a*cb*gba*
43	1	gahd*bg*a*	6	1	g**c*agb**	41	1	gahc**gba*
44	1	gahd*bgb**	46	1	gb*c*agba*	31	2	ga*cb*gba*
33	1	ga*da*gba*	83	1	gbac*agba*	77	4	gahcb*gba*
82	3	gahda*gba*	5	1	g****agba*	105	1	gahcb*gbab
81	1	gahdaagb**	16	1	gb***agba*	13	1	gahc*a*b**
106	1	gahdaagba*	48	2	gbh**agba*	40	1	gahc*ahb**
90	1	g*hc*bgcab	85	1	gbh*bagba*	76	1	gahcba*ba*
94	1	hbac*agb*c	23	1	*bhc*agba*	75	1	gahc*ahba*
54	1	**hc*bgbab	86	2	gbhc*agba*	104	1	gahcbahba*
95	1	hbhd*agbb*	109	1	gbhcaagba*	12	1	gahc*a**a*
66	1	ga*cbbgbb*	78	1	gahc*bgbb*	18	1	**hc*agba*
51	1	haac**gbb*	74	1	gahc*ah*ac	37	1	gahc*a*ba*
35	1	gah**agbb*	103	1	gahc*ahbac	69	2	gahcaa*ba*
67	1	gah*aagbb*	2	1	*ahcb***a*	28	1	ga*c*agba*
55	1	*a*cbagbac	21	1	*ahcb*gca*	64	1	ga*caagba*
63	1	gaac*bgbb*	79	1	gahcb*gca*	20	1	*ahc*agba*
4	1	ga***ag*b*	9	1	*aac**gba*	57	1	*ahc*agbac
36	1	gah**agcb*	1	1	*ahc*a*b**	39	1	gahc*agb**
15	1	gahd***ba*	93	1	hahc*bgba*	72	1	gahc*agb*b
42	1	gahd***bab	53	1	hahc*a*ba*	70	1	gahc*a*bab
89	1	g*hc*agcab	91	5	hahc*agba*	56	1	*ahc*agbab
17	1	gb*c*a*b*b	87	1	gbhc*agca*	102	2	gahc*agbab
108	1	gb*cbahbab	92	1	hahc*agca*	50	4	g*hc*agba*
59	1	gaac*a*bab	26	1	gaac*ag*a*	38	2	gahc*ag*a*
25	1	gaa**agbb*	62	1	gaacbag*a*	34	1	gah**agba*
61	1	gaac*agbb*	29	1	ga*c*agca*	71	19	gahc*agba*
8	1	**h**ahba*	73	2	gahc*agca*	99	1	gahcaagba*
7	1	g*hc*a***b	100	1	gahcaagca*	112	1	gahcaagbab
88	1	gbhc*ahc*b	60	1	gaac*agba*			
49	1	gbhc*ah*a*	97	1	gaac*agbac			

Remark: * denotes a null symbol.

References

[1] Wong, A.K.C. and Goldfarb, L., 1978, "Modeling Systems and Multilevel Hierarchical Relational Structures," in Savage, G.J. and Roe, P.H., ed., *Large Engineering Systems 2*, Sanford Educational Press, Waterloo, Ontario, pp. 37-44.

[2] Tsai, W.H. and Fu, K.S., 1979, "Error-Correcting Isomorphism of Attributed Relational Graphs for Pattern Analysis", *IEEE Trans. on Systems, Man and Cybernetics*, vol. SMC-13, pp. 353-362.

[3] Wong, A.K.C. and You, M.L., 1986, "Entropy and Distance of Random Graphs with Application to Structural Pattern Recognition," *IEEE Trans. on Pattern Analysis and Machine Intelligence*, vol. PAMI-7, pp. 599-609.

[4] Shaw, A.C., 1969, "A Formal Picture Description Scheme as a Basis for Picture Processing Systems," *Information and Control*, vol. 14, pp. 9-52.

[5] Shaw, A.C., 1970, "Parsing of Graph-Representable Pictures," Journal of ACM, vol. 17, pp. 453-481.

[6] Pavlidis, T., 1977, *Structural Pattern Recognition*, Springer-Verlag.

[7] Pavlidis, T., 1980, "Structural Description and Graph Grammars," in Chang, S.K. and Fu, K.S., ed., *Pictorial Information Systems*, Springer-Verlag, pp. 86-103.

[8] Sanfeliu, A. and Fu, K.S., 1983, "A Distance Measure Between Attributed Relational Graphs for Pattern Recognition," *IEEE Trans. on Systems, Man, and Cybernetics*, vol. SMC-13, pp. 353-362.

[9] Wong, A.K.C. and Ghahraman, D.E., 1980, "Random Graphs: Structural-Contextual Dichotomy," *IEEE Trans. Pattern Analysis and Machine Intelligence*, vol. PAMI-2, pp. 341-348.

[10] Ghahraman, D.E., Wong, A.K.C. and AU, T., 1980, "Graph Optimal Monomorphism Algorithms," *IEEE Trans. on Systems, Man and Cybernetics*, vol. SMC-10, pp. 189-196.

[11] Shapiro, L.G. and Haralick, R.M., 1981, "Structural Descriptions and Inexact Matching," *IEEE Trans. on Pattern Analysis and Machine Intelligence*, vol. PAMI-3, pp. 504-519.

[12] Ghahraman, D.E., Wong, A.K.C. and Au, T., 1980, "Graph Monomorphism Algorithm," *IEEE Trans. on Syst., Man Cybern.*, vol. SMC-10, pp. 181-196.

[13] You, M.L. and Wong, A.K.C., 1984, "An Algorithm for Graph Optimal Isomorphsim," *Proc. of the Seventh International Conference on Pattern Recognition*, pp. 316-319.

[14] Masumi, A.E., 1973, Picture Analysis of Graph Transformation, Ph.D. Thesis, Dept. of Computer Science, University of Illinois at Urbana-Champaign.

[15] Fu, K.S., 1980, "Picture Syntax," in Chang, S.K. and Fu, K.S., ed., *Pictorial Information Systems*, Springer-Verlag, pp. 104-127.

[16] Niemann, H., 1980, "Hierarchical Graphs in Pattern Analysis," *Proc. 1980 Int. Conf. on Pattern Recognition*, pp. 213-216.

[17] You, M., 1983, A Random Graph Approach to Pattern Recognition, Ph. D. Thesis, Dept. of Systems Design Engineering, University of Waterloo, Waterloo, Ontario, pp. 37-44.

[18] Wong, A.K.C., Reichert, T.A., Cohen, D.N., and Aygun, B.O., 1974, "A Generalized Method for Matching Informational Macromolecular Code Sequences," *Comput. Biol. Med.*, vol. 4, pp. 43-57.

[19] Cohen, D.N., Reichert, T.A., and Wong, A.K.C., 1975, "Matching Code Sequences Utilizing Context Free Quality Measures," *Mathematical Biosciences*, vol. 24, pp. 25-30.

[20] Fu, K.S., 1983, "A Step Towards Unification of Syntactic and Statistic Pattern Recognition," *IEEE Trans. on Pattern Analysis and Machine Intelligence*, vol PAMI-5, pp. 200-205.

[21] Abe, K. and Sugita, N., 1982, "Distance between Strings of Symbols - Review and Remarks," *Proc. 1982 Int. Conf. on Pattern Recognition*, vol. 1, pp. 172-174.

[22] Fu, K.S., 1982, *Syntactic Pattern Recognition and Applications*, Prentice-Hall.

INEXACT GRAPH MATCHING USED IN MACHINE VISION

Eric Backer and Jan J. Gerbrands

Delft University of Technology
Department of Electrical Engineering
Delft, The Netherlands.

Abstract

The recognition of three-dimensional solid objects is a well known problem from the field of machine vision for industrial applications. In the stereo vision approach two two-dimensional images are obtained from calibrated camera positions. In the method discussed here, a graph is constructed for each of the two images with the nodes corresponding to the object vertices. For both the correspondence problem and the recognition stage, the inexact graph matching is used. In order to reduce the computational complexity, several search and pruning strategies are investigated in connection with both A* and Branch and Bound aiming at speeding up the inexact matching procedure. The discussion is restricted to trihedral objects.

1. Stereo Vision

It is well understood that machine vision will play an important role in flexible automation and computer-aided manufacturing. Most robot vision systems functioning to date are essentially two-dimensional (2-D) in nature. In the emerging field of robot vision and sensory control, much research is devoted to the problem of actually obtaining three-dimensional (3-D) information about the robot's environment. This includes the recognition of 3-D objects as well as the determination of object position and orientation in 3-D world coordinates. There are a number of ways in which this problem can be attacked. One distinguishes active and passive imaging techniques. In the active technique some sort of active source (ultrasound, laser) is used, while the passive techniques employ overall scene illumination. A second dichotomy is to distinguish methods which use triangulation and methods which use the perspective transform.

The stereo vision approach to be discussed here is a passive triangulation method. In stereo vision two 2-D images of the 3-D scene are acquired from two distinct camera positions, as shown in Fig. 1.

The point V in 3-D space is projected on the 2-D coordinates v1' and v2' in the 2-D images I1 and I2, respectively. The 3-D coordinates of the point V can now be computed from the 2-D coordinates v1' and v2' if the positions and orientations of the cameras are known [1].

NATO ASI Series, Vol. F30
Pattern Recognition Theory and Applications
Edited by P. A. Devijver and J. Kittler

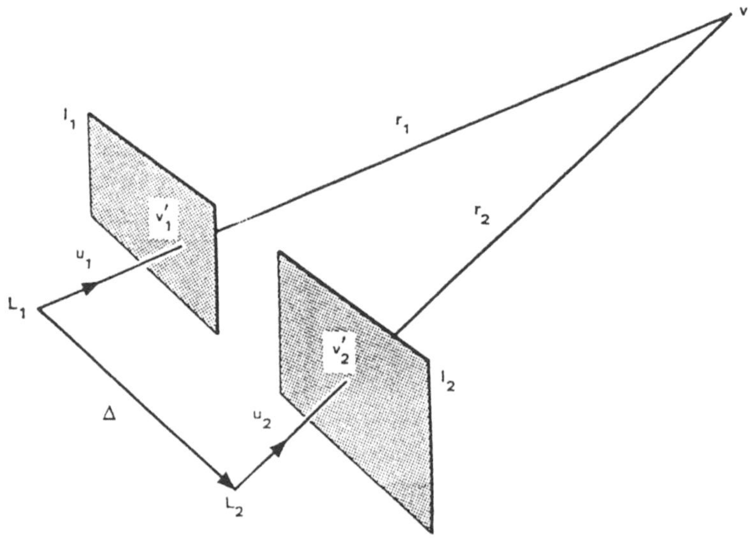

Figure 1: The principle of triangulation

2. The Correspondence Problem

In order to apply the method of triangulation, one has to find pairs of corresponding points v1' and v2' in the two images. This correspondence problem is greatly facilitated if we restrict the complexity of the scene. In a first attempt we consider isolated trihedral objects. A trihedral object is an object from the blocks world with not more than three edges at every vertex [2]. As trihedral objects are completely described in terms of vertices and edges, it is most natural to consider the vertices, as observed in the 2-D images, as characteristic points in the correspondence problem.

Returning to Fig. 1, it is obvious that a point in one of the 2-D images, say point v1', may be the projection of any point on the projection ray r1. The projection of r1 onto the second image I2 is called the matchline of v1', and all points on the matchline are candidates to be corresponding point of v1'. So, if we consider a projected object vertex in I1, we search on or close to its matchline in I2 for its corresponding projection. Frequently, this is done by computing the cross correlation between greyvalue subimages. This is extremely time consuming. Instead, we use a minimum cost graph matching technique.

3. Finding the Vertices

In order to detect the vertices in the 2-D greyvalue images we construct a line drawing of the object [3,4]. First the greyvalue image is convolved with linear discrete difference operators to obtain the components of the Sobel-gradient.

As we have used a 3×3 convolution, the linear operators are defined by:

$$\text{row}: \begin{matrix} -1 & -2 & -1 \\ 0 & 0 & 0 \\ 1 & 2 & 1 \end{matrix} \qquad \text{col}: \begin{matrix} -1 & 0 & 1 \\ -2 & 0 & 2 \\ -1 & 0 & 1 \end{matrix}$$

For each 3×3 pixel-neighborhood $\begin{matrix} a & b & c \\ d & p & e \\ f & g & h \end{matrix}$

we obtain one-directional Sobel-gradient magnitudes

$$S_{row} = (a + 2b + c) - (f + 2g + h) \quad \text{and} \quad S_{col} = (c + 2e + h) - (a + 2d + f).$$

Then, the Sobel-gradient magnitude is given by

$$S(p) = S_{col} + S_{row}$$

whereas the orientation of the edge-element is given by

$$\theta(p) = \arctan(S_{row}/S_{col}).$$

Next, a spatial clustering scheme is applied to find clusters of pixels with high gradient values and similar gradient directions. Such clustering procedure is schematized by the following steps:

▷ Select a start edge-pixel

▷ define a $n \times n$ pixel-neighborhood

▷ sort pixels in decreasing order of $S(p)$ as long as their gradient value exceeds a certain threshold

▷ select the pixel for which the maximum value of $S(p)$ is found setting the reference orientation $\theta_r(p)$

▷ label the pixels according $\theta_r(p)$ and count the number of pixels having the same orientation θ_r

▷ select from the set of pixels which are not labelled yet that pixel having the maximum value of $S(p)$

▷ repeat the θ-labelling.

If the number of counted pixels in a given direction is larger than a certain threshold, move the $n \times n$ neighborhood in that direction and repeat the above procedure.

Finally, the projected object edges are found by fitting a straight line through the pixels of each cluster. If the line to fit is represented by

$$row(col) = rc.col + c$$

and the squared error to minimize is given by

$$e^2 = \sum\{row(i) - (rc.col(i) + c)\}^2$$

then determine

$$\frac{d\,e^2}{d\,c} = 0 \quad \text{and} \quad \frac{d\,e^2}{d\,rc} = 0$$

yielding the best fitting-coefficients c and rc, respectively.

The projected vertices are then detected at the intersection points of the fitted lines. Obviously, the same procedure is applied to the second image.

4. Structural Matching

In the structural matching approach the line drawings of the projected objects are used as graphs, the nodes of the graphs being the projected object vertices. Consider two nodes: node N1 of graph G1 representing vertex v1' in image I1, and node N2 of graph G2 representing vertex v2' in image I2. Let L1 denote the matchline of v1' in I2 and L2 the matchline of v2' in I1. Those matchlines are used to define appropriate costs for matching pairs of vertices. The euclidean distance between a vertex v' (represented by node N) and a matchline L is denoted as d(v',L). Now we define the costs of matching N1 and N2 as

$$\mathrm{C(N1,N2) = d(v1',L2) + d(v2',L1)}$$

and compute these cost coefficients for all pairs of nodes of the graphs G1 and G2. As an example, consider the line drawings in Fig. 2 being the graph representations G1 and G2.

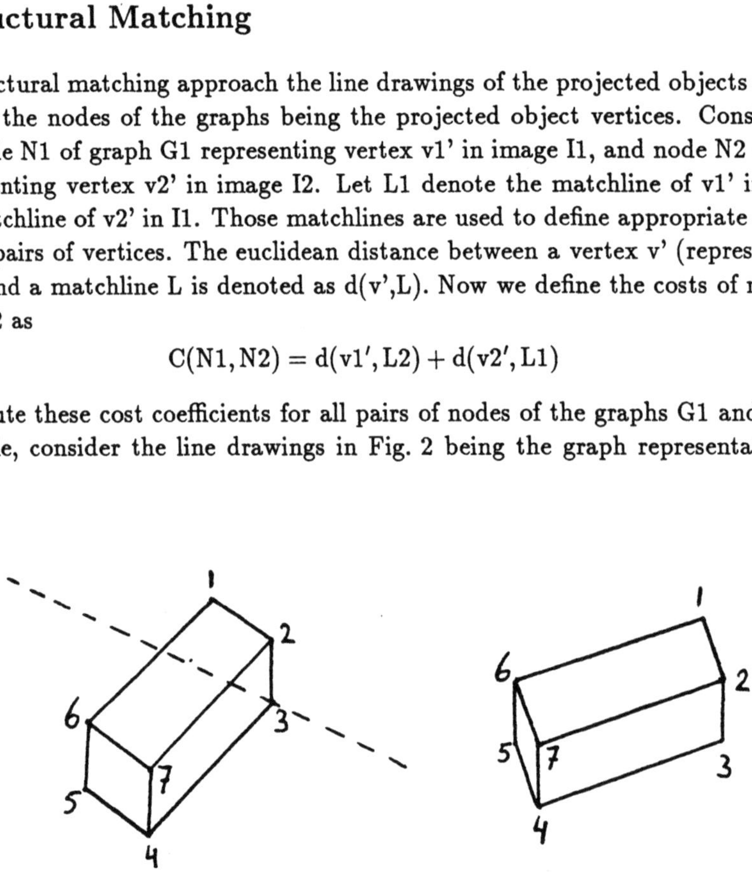

Figure 2: Projected line drawings as they are used in the structural match

Here the cost-assignment may be the following:

$$\begin{array}{ll} Cost_{RL}(3,1) = 10 & Cost_{LR}(1,3) = 12 \\ Cost_{RL}(3,2) = 8 & Cost_{LR}(2,3) = 10 \\ Cost_{RL}(3,3) = 1 & Cost_{LR}(3,3) = 2 \end{array}$$

Clearly, the cost-assignment from the Right image (R) to the Left image (L) will not be identical perse compared to the costs from left image to right image as the cost-assignments are based on different matchlines. Following the definition above, the ultimate symmetric cost matrix yields:

$$\begin{aligned} Cost_{TOT}(1,3) &= Cost_{LR}(1,3) + Cost_{RL}(3,1) &= 22 \\ Cost_{TOT}(2,3) &= &= 18 \\ Cost_{TOT}(3,3) &= &= 3 \end{aligned}$$

and so on.

The cost of matching two graphs is defined as the sum of the cost coefficients of all pairs of nodes in the match. The pairs of nodes in the optimal match define the corresponding projected object vertices. A branch-and-bound algorithm is used to find the minimum cost match between G1 and G2.

5. Object Recognition: Inexact Graph Matching

Having solved the correspondence problem, the 3-D coordinates of the object vertices can be computed. It is then possible to compute the lengths of the object edges in 3-D space as well as the angles between edges at the vertices. These values are used as attributes in a 3-D graph representation of the object. Each object class is represented by a prototype graph. Again the inexact graph matching technique is applied to find the optimal match between the vertices in the observed object and those in the prototype. In principle, this is repeated for all prototypes and the observed object is assigned the label of the model with the minimum matching costs. The matching costs are defined as the absolute difference of edge lengths and the absolute difference of angles between the observed object and the model. The speed of the recognition stage is greatly improved by performing a preselection with respect to the prototypes to be considered in detail. This preselection implies that for each node pair the cost of the best match of edges is computed. This is repeated for all node pairs independently and summed. If these costs exceed a certain threshold, the prototype model is discarded.

6. Search and Pruning Strategies

As known, those matching procedures can be based on a state space search [5,6]. Search strategies like A* [7] and Branch-and-Bound [8] can be used to search the state space for the optimal inexact match. The costs for the substitution, deletion and insertion of nodes and branches during the matching process are used to guide the search. Finding the optimal inexact match requires exponential time with respect to the number of nodes in the graphs. A considerable saving in time and memory requirement can be achieved if we accept a sub-optimal match instead of the optimal inexact match.

The A* algorithm is a breadth-first strategy which expands the state with the minimal costs until a final state has the minimal costs. The algorithm uses the actual costs of the partial inexact match plus a conservative estimate of future costs to reach the final state. Such a strategy is characterized by the advantage of finding the optimal inexact match, and the disadvantage of having to be kept the entire state space in memory. Moreover, A* does not yield a near-optimal match and is very sensitive to cost estimation.

The Branch-and-Bound algorithm is a depth-first strategy which finds also the optimal match, requires less memory and —most important— gives a best-match-until-now. The main disadvantages are the number of expanded states and the fact that B&B makes less efficient use of heuristic information [9]

Pruning is used in combination with A* to delete systematically states from the search space to save time and free memory. Specific a priori knowledge about the search problem can be used to determine what states should be deleted. Especially, if we delete the states at lower levels we can prevent A* from returning to the lower levels too frequently. In the following, $PRUNE(m,n)$ stands for a pruning of the state space every m expansions in which all the states n levels below the maximum level are deleted. Generally, the best choice of m and n in a given search problem is not trivial and will have to be determined experimentally.

Diverting A* to lower levels can also be obtained by using the maximum increase in costs as an estimate of the total costs (Least Maximum Cost), or dividing the cost of a state by the level in the search tree (Cost/Search-level estimate). The latter strategy can also be used in connection with B&B.

As B&B is a depth-first method that finds a final state and uses its costs as a bound in the search process until another final state is found with lower costs, we can accept the nth final state as a sub-optimal solution to save time.

Random graph experiments

The above search strategies have been implemented in Pascal on a 68000 microprocessor system. The programs keep track of the time and memory needed for the inexact matching. The described search strategies have been tested by matching 100 randomly constructed connected graphs against their randomly distorted versions. The N nodes of the graphs used in the testing have 1 attribute; the B branches have no attributes. N is fixed, the attribute is a random value between 0 and 100, and B is fixed or random between $N-1$ and N^2. The deformed version of the graph is constructed by taking a deform-value D (fixed or random between 0 and 100). A random number between 0 and $100/D$ is added to the node attributes, and $B.D/100$ elements in the adjacency matrix are inverted.

The following costs were used:

▷ the absolute difference in node attributes

▷ cost for deletion or insertion of a node = 100

▷ cost for deletion or insertion of a branch = 30

▷ cost for deletion or insertion of a branch if the connecting node is also deleted or inserted = 10.

As a result, Fig. 3 shows the results of the random graph experiments with 5 nodes and a random number of branches and a random deform-value. The number of expansions required and the number of states show a similar behaviour. Fig. 4 shows the results for 8-node graphs with 32 branches and a deform value of 20. A* used 17 seconds and is not plotted, [10].

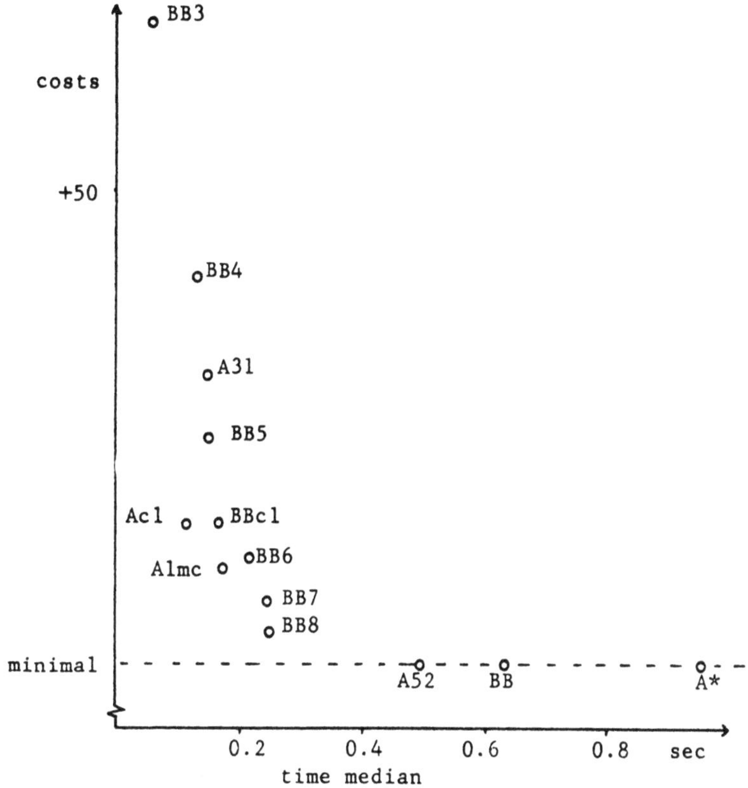

Figure 3: Random graph matching: $N = 5$, B and D random

We conclude that a considerable amount of pruning can be applied without serious draw-backs. It should be noted that instead of systematic pruning as applied here, the pruning mechanism may very well be controlled by using a priori knowledge such as geometrical constraints and symmetry.

7. Trihedral Object Recognition: Results

In the machine vision application as described the models are represented by attributed graphs where the attributes for lines and vertices were lengths and angles, respectively. As shown, the attributed graphs representing the observed object do have attributes computed from 3-D positions of vertices. Originally, a branch-and-bound algorithm yielded a typical recognition time of 150 msec (all implementations in Pascal on a 68000). A $PRUNE(2,1)$ strategy reduces the match time to a typical match time of 15 milliseconds and about 14 expansions. The single object recognition rate was 100%.

For partial objects, one vertex and two edges, out of 29 experiments, 10 objects were recognized and the remaining objects were rejected. For partial objects, having one vertex and three edges, the result was 15 objects recognized and all others rejected.

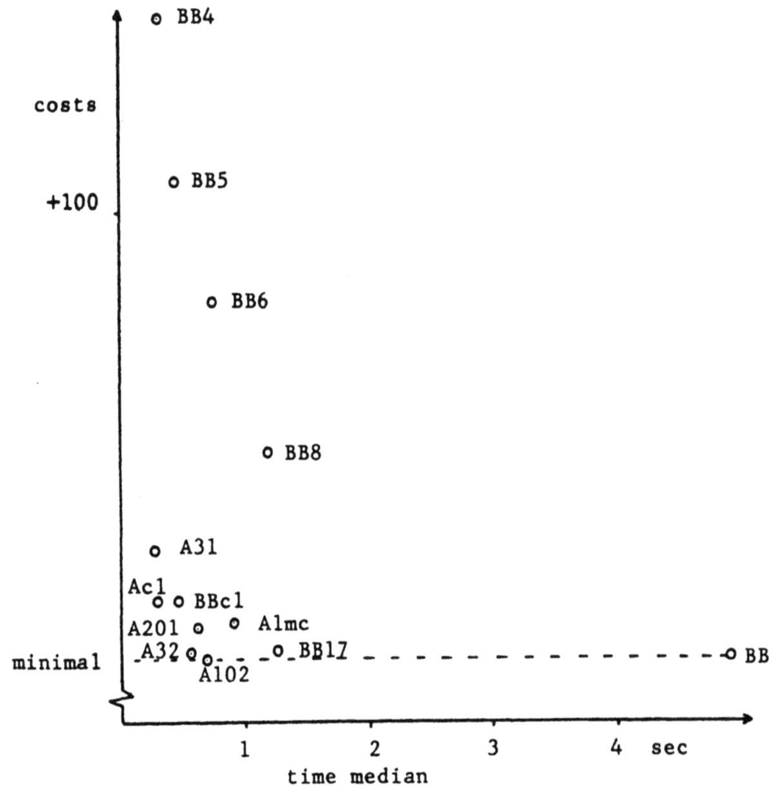

Figure 4: Random graph matching: N=8, B=32, D=20

8. Concluding Remarks

The structural matching in the correspondence problem performs extremely well. Also the recognition of the trihedral objects is very good even if considerable pruning or nth final state in B&B is used. The computational burden of matching plus recognition can be kept within very reasonable limits, and is still an order of magnitude less than the image processing part. The method is restricted to highly structured objects. Decomposition of more complex scenes is necessary but seems to be feasible [11].

Acknowledgements

The contributions of ir. P. Hofland, ir. J.N.M. Kuijpers and ir. E. van Mieghem in this project are gratefully acknowledged.

References

[1] Y. Yakimovsky and R. Cunningham, "A system for extracting three dimensional measurements from a stereo pair of TV cameras," *Computer Graphics and Image Processing*, 7 (1978) 195-210.

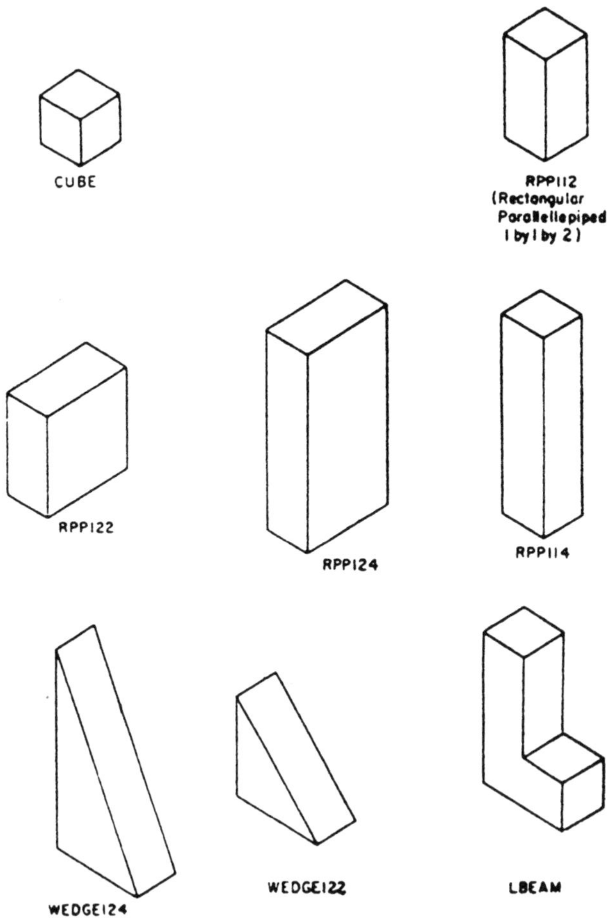

Figure 5: Trihedral objects used in the recognition experiment

[2] A. Barr and E.A. Feigenbaum, *Thc Handbook of Artificial Intelligence*, Ditman, London, 1982.

[3] M. Akkermans and M. van Thillo, "An algorithm for the extraction of line drawings for polyhedral scenes and their use in stereo vision," *Proceedings SPIE*, 449 (1984) 534-540.

[4] P. Hofland, "De bepaling van een lijntekening van een scene t.b.v. robot vision," M.Sc. Thesis Delft University of Technology, 1985.

[5] W.H. Tsai and K.S. Fu, "Error-correcting isomorphisms of attributed relational graphs for pattern analysis," *IEEE Trans. SMC*, 9 (12), 1979.

[6] H. Bunke and G. Allermann, "Inexact graph matching for structural pattern recognition," *Pattern Recognition Letters*, (1) 4, 1983, 245-253.

[7] N.J. Nilsson, *Principles of Artificial Intelligence*, Springer, 1982.

[8] C.H. Papadimitrou and K. Steiglitz, *Combinatorial Optimization: Algorithms and Complexity*, Prentice Hall, 1982.

[9] J. Pearl, "Knowledge versus search: A quantitative analysis using A^*," *Artificial Intelligence*, (20), 1983, 1–13.

[10] J.N.M. Kuipers, "Inexact graph matching," M.Sc. Thesis Delft University of Technology, 1984.

[11] E.F.P. van Mieghem, "De herkenning van 3-D voorwerpen met behulp van stereo-vision," M.Sc. Thesis Delft University of Technology, 1985.

DEVELOPMENT OF AN INCREMENTAL GRAPH MATCHING DEVICE

Richard E. Blake

Computer Science Department,
University of Tennessee,
Knoxville, TN 37996, USA.

Abstract

The paper introduces a multi-process graph matching device. The behavior of the device is demonstrated as it matches a reference graph to an image sequence with elements that exhibit a changing scale and level of resolvable detail. The device uses analysis by synthesis to consume the graphs to be matched. For the present work these are formed by skeletal line segments, but it is pointed out that relational matching will be investigated in future work. The responsibilities of the 8 cooperating processes are described and a cycle in the matching is stepped through. The theoretical dangers of taking suboptimal matches are contrasted with the practical advantages of greatly reducing the search space. The need for recovery after accepting associations that later prove to be wrong is pointed out. Comments on the description of the convergence to a labeling in terms of Scott's lattice theory are given.

1. Introduction

There are many applications where an object to be observed and recognized approaches a sensor. As the range changes there will be a change in the apparent size of the object. There is a second effect that arises because of the fundamental properties of the sensor and the preprocessing. For each detailed feature of the object, there will be a range beyond which the feature cannot be resolved. It follows that, as the range decreases, successively greater amounts of detail can be resolved and are passed to the pattern recognition stage.

Practical examples of a change of scale and a change in resolution include the approach to a work station of an object on a conveyor belt and the approach of a robot's gripper mounted camera to an object on the work-table.

The problem of missing features has been investigated before, [1], [2], [3]. The work reported here is an attempt to treat the case of an image sequence. A pilot version of a system that incrementally labels the features of an object will be described. Successive elements of the sequence contain images from decreasing ranges and with successively more features resolvable.

The incremental labeling is controlled by a graph matching device and so graph-like features have to be chosen to represent the objects to be labeled. The method used in this paper is to obtain the skeleton of a thresholded image and attempt to recognize the

NATO ASI Series, Vol. F30
Pattern Recognition Theory and Applications
Edited by P. A. Devijver and J. Kittler

skeleton as a graph. This is a very unreliable method of characterizing shape because of the irregular information destroying operations of thresholding and thinning. However, careful choice of the object, the background, and the conditions of view have allowed the method to be usable for exploratory work.

The image sequence used in the paper was obtained in this way. The parameter values for the pre-processing were chosen interactively to promote the behavior that this paper is designed to demonstrate. Some minor pixel editing was also needed.

Section 2 presents an example of the incremental labeling of an image sequence. Section 3 describes the philosophy for the labeling and the system's architecture. Section 4 gives some comments on the theoretical background that is also being developed. Section 5 concludes the paper with some comments on the direction of further work.

Fig. 1.1

```
Nodes on the unknown.          Node equivalence table.
*A at  <59  59>                     REF   UNK
*B at  <70  59>                      K  =  C
 C at  <58  53>                      L  =  D
  D at  <71  53>

              ( * nodes are not associated )
```

Fig. 4.1

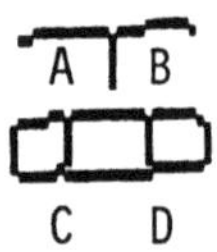

Fig. 2.1

```
  C at  <58  52>
  D at  <71  52>
```

Fig. 1.2

```
Nodes on the unknown.          Node equivalence table.
 A at  <65  70>                     REF   UNK
*B at  <65  59>                      A  =  A
 C at  <62  52>                      B  =  F
 D at  <68  54>                      F  =  E
 E at  <79  58>                      K  =  C
 F at  <51  56>                      L  =  D
```

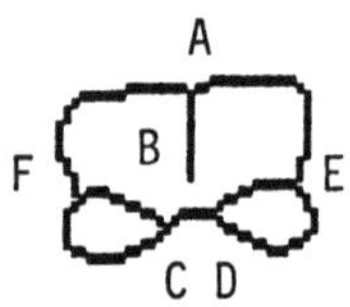

Fig. 2.2

Fig. 4.2

Fig. 1.3

```
Nodes on the unknown.          Node equivalence table.
 A at  <64  76>                     REF   UNK
*B at  <64  66>                      A  =  A
 C at  <53  50>                      B  =  F
 D at  <76  51>                      F  =  E
 E at  <82  62>                      K  =  C
 F at  <47  59>                      L  =  D
*G at  <76  61>
*H at  <52  59>
```

Fig. 4.3

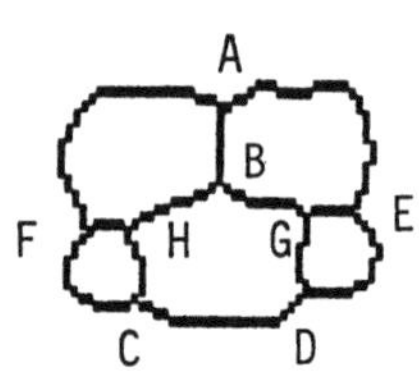

Fig. 2.3

2. An Example

This section describes the incremental labeling of a sequence of five graphs extracted from an image sequence. The sequence was generated by bringing a toy truck steadily closer to a TV camera. The earlier images tend to contain less detail than the later ones, and are smaller. The sequence of Figures 1.1 to 1.5 shows the output of the adaptive thresholding. Figures 2.1 to 2.5 show the skeletons that are extracted by thinning the elements of Figure 1.

It can be seen that in Figure 2.1 the representation is fragmented. In fact, only the lower portion of the image will be processed. In Figure 2.2, the outline is fully formed, but an internal line, though present, is not properly connected. Some other internal lines are missing. In Figure 2.3 the outline is complete and all lines that are present are properly connected. Some internal lines are still missing. In Figures 2.4 and 2.5 the skeletons are complete but Figure 2.5 is larger than Figure 2.4. The growth of detail in the sequence is not smooth.

The skeletons of Figure 2 have "interesting points", branch points or free ends, that are marked with identification letters. These identifications are allocated in a top to bottom, left to right sequence by the system as it is analyzing the pattern. The identification letters are re-allocated until the interesting point that they label is associated with an interesting point on the reference, at which time the name of this point is fixed.

The image working board is a 128 square array of pixels. The images have been positioned so that the point $\langle 64,64 \rangle$ is the focus of expansion.

The reference graph, depicting the ideal skeletonized version of the toy truck, is shown in Figure 3 with the identification letters of its interesting points. Identification letters on the reference are fixed.

The interesting points can be considered as nodes in a graph. The nodes are related by having lines in the skeletons joining them. The progress of the labeling is shown in the node equivalence table which associates nodes of the unknown with nodes of the reference.

Figure 4 shows the sequence of states of the node equivalence table. The steps in the sequence represented by Figure 2.1 to 2.5 are aligned with the node equivalences, Figures 4.1 to 4.5, which were reported at the end of a matching attempt for the corresponding skeleton.

The steady growth in the number of associated nodes represents increasing knowledge about the identity of the features that can be resolved on the unknown, and which can be associated with features on the reference.

Figure 4.1 shows that of the four nodes, A, B, C, D, found on the unknown, nodes C and D are associated respectively with K and L of the reference. Nodes A and B of the unknown are not associated with any nodes of the reference. Thus the names A and B are not fixed to particular features of the unknown, and will be tentatively given to other features of the unknown when a new image of the sequence is to be processed.

Figure 2.2 shows the second skeleton of the sequence. The nodes C and D were associated with features of the reference and have been preserved. Nodes A, B, E and F have been allocated to the other nodes and are candidates for association.

Fig. 1.4

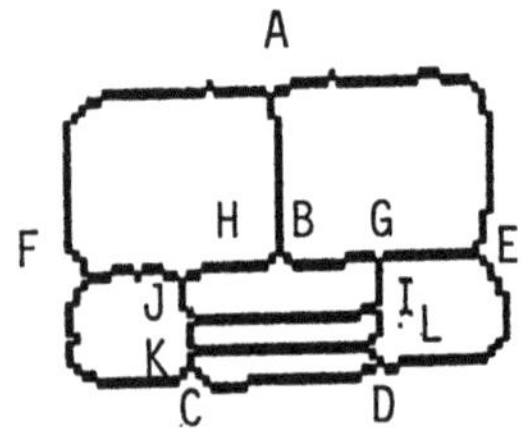

Fig. 2.4

Nodes on the unknown.

A at	<63	84>
*B at	<64	64>
C at	<52	49>
D at	<77	49>
E at	<90	63>
F at	<39	61>
*G at	<77	62>
*H at	<51	60>
*I at	<76	56>
*J at	<53	55>
*K at	<53	51>
*L at	<75	51>

Node equivalence table.

REF		UNK
A	=	A
B	=	F
F	=	E
K	=	C
L	=	D

Fig. 4.4

Fig. 1.5

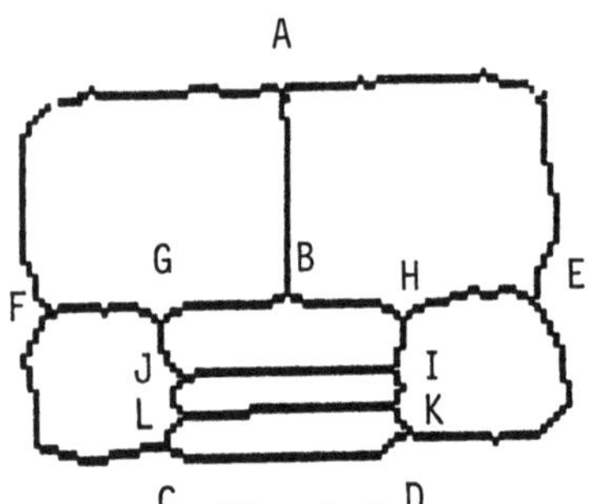

Fig. 2.5

Nodes on the unknown.

A at	<62	96>
B at	<63	63>
C at	<43	38>
D at	<86	38>
E at	<103	61>
F at	<24	60>
G at	<42	58>
H at	<82	58>
I at	<80	50>
J at	<46	49>
K at	<80	44>
L at	<46	43>

Node equivalence table.

REF		UNK
A	=	A
B	=	F
C	=	G
D	=	B
E	=	H
F	=	E
G	=	J
H	=	I
I	=	L
J	=	K
K	=	C
L	=	D

Fig. 4.5

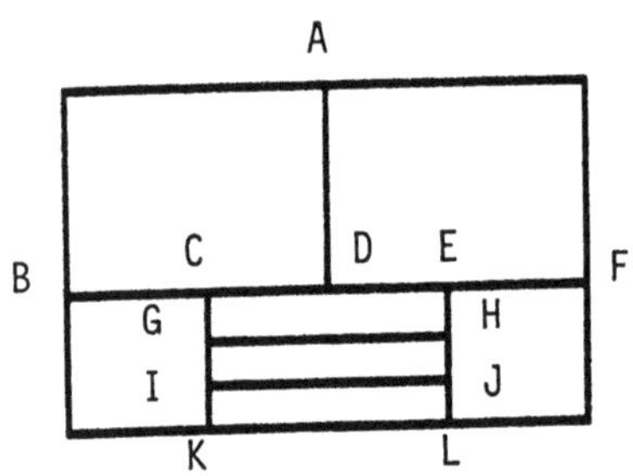

Fig. 3

Figure 4.2 shows a further extension of the node equivalence table. The prediction from the known scale change was that the nodes C and D would be found respectively at ⟨58,52⟩ and ⟨71,52⟩. A search was invoked to locate the nearest nodes and they were found at ⟨62,52⟩ and ⟨68,54⟩. Position errors such as this arise because of instabilities in the image processing and because the image may not be centred on the focus of expansion. The only node of Figure 2.2 that remains unassociated is B wrongly detected as a free end.

Figures 4.3 and 4.4 show no additions to the node equivalence table. Although Figures 2.3 and 2.4 show that further nodes could be added, the sequence of trials is unfavourable and the system times-out before its recursive search strategy has found consistent pairings.

Figure 4.5 shows that all the nodes are finally paired. It happens that at the higher resolution of this final member of the sequence, the provisional associations of arcs for matching by shape, leads to an order of tests that finds a consistent association within the allowed time frame

This example shows acceptable operation of the system. For this sequence it happens that none of the labelings needs to be modified in the light of further evidence. This should be regarded as unusual. The absence of any backtracking on the association between nodes implies that the cost and constraint mechanism guided the system to make reasonable initial guesses.

3. Method

Figure 5 shows a block diagram of the system as it is currently implemented. The 8 cooperating processes can pass synchronizing messages through the channels. They also share access to some data structures that show the state of the match. These are updated as the system expends effort in developing the match.

The processes and their responsibilities are:

SUPERVISOR: Direct system's attention to the most promising line of inquiry based on the current state of the match, and cost criteria measuring the similarity of the shapes of the fragments of the graphs. Monitor a matching attempt and terminate it if it appears to be be making unacceptable progress in the time consumed.

MATCHER: Obtain matches, and their costs, between two graphs provided by other parts of the system. Report the state of the match at various milestones, or when required.

REFERENCE SUBGRAPH PROPOSER: Provide candidate subgraphs for matching based on the interest defined by the *SUPERVISOR*, taking into account the current conditions of view, for example scale and orientation, and including the composition of arcs (or relations) to span detail that may be expected to be unobservable.

KNOWN SUBGRAPH INTERPRETER: Provide details on subgraphs currently believed to be matched, taking into account the current conditions of view. It is important to note that the current conditions, and thus the interpretation of the arcs or relations, may differ significantly from that at the time of original matching.

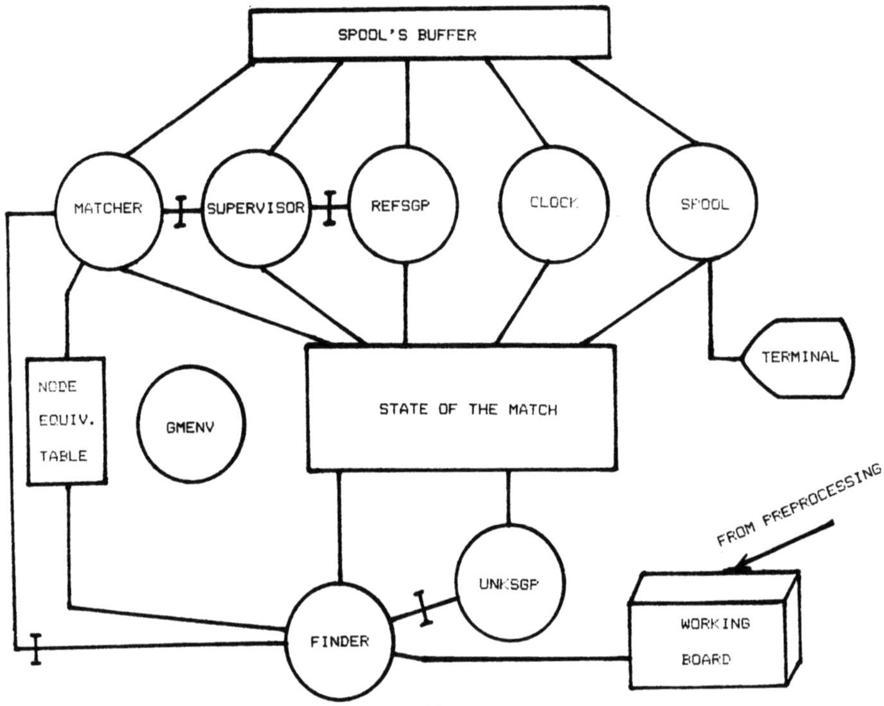

Fig. 5

FINDER: Perform certain image processing operations on the line drawing. Identify the interesting points in the drawing and trace the lines, representing them with a chain code. Call the two subroutines *CONSUME* and *EXTRACT* defined below. (In the next version of *FINDER* these two routines will become processes to better exploit parallel operations on the working board.)

1. CONSUME: Erase from the working board those subgraphs that are believed to be identified.

2. EXTRACT: Identify subgraphs, from the residue on the working board that are candidates for matching, given the current interests defined by the supervisor.

GMENV: Simulate the closing of the target and the sensors. Sequence the graphs of Figure 2 in being presented to the system.

SPOOL: Present summaries of system activities to an observer.

CLOCK: Mark the passing of real time for the system.

Some scraps of information, for example, whether an arc is on the perimeter of the graph, are carried as attributes to the arcs to be matched. "Cost" calculations include terms for the agreement between the expected attributes and those actually found. "Interest" is defined in terms of current class hypothesis, attributes of arcs that are preferred, and current node considered as a starting point for explorations in the working board.

The following paragraphs explain the steps that occur in a matching iteration. For sake of a simple introduction, the very first step is examined. It is assumed that the system knows approximate scale and orientation values. The differences that will occur in later steps are pointed out separately.

Suppose that the pre-processing has just completed the latest skeleton and that this has been passed to the system as an array of pixel values. The *FINDER* process begins work to encode the shape of the lines and determine the junction points in the skeleton. Various attributes of the lines may be deduced from the pixel values. For the example in this paper there are two possible attributes, nothing special known and line known to be on the perimeter of the drawing. This is the first mention of the "perimeter" attribute. It is an example of the mechanism by which scraps of information can be brought to bear to help with the matching.

The *SUPERVISOR* chooses an interest for the system to focus on, including, in general, a reference class to match against. Lines attributed as being on the perimeter are the most tightly constrained, these attributes are prefered first for matching. The *EXTRACT* routine, in *FINDER*, identifies subgraphs of the unknown that the preprocessing marked with this attribute. The selected lines are passed to the *MATCHER*.

Meanwhile, the *REFERENCE SUBGRAPH PROPOSER* also received a message from the *SUPERVISOR* defining the system's current interest. It has been constructing the system's expectation of the subgraphs that should be visible for the class that is being tested, bearing in mind the current conditions of view. These subgraphs are passed to the *MATCHER*.

The *MATCHER* attempts to find a consistent association between the subgraphs from the reference and the unknown. Assuming that it succeeds, the *FINDER* uses the *KNOWN SUBGRAPH PROPOSER* to predict how the lines that have just been matched should appear under the latest conditions of view. A new snapshot of the incoming data is obtained from the pre-processing, and the routine *CONSUME* erases the latest form of the matched arcs from the working board.

Meanwhile, the *SUPERVISOR* has chosen another interest for the system. *FINDER* calls *EXTRACT* to obtain a candidate subgraph for matching from the residue on the working board.

The cycle then repeats. The whole match is completed when the residue on the working board is reduced to nothing, or, when the *MATCHER* decides that some criterion of success has been reached in fitting arcs.

The matching strategy can be seen to be classical "analysis by synthesis". The problem is divided into sub-problems by using the attributes to the lines. The solutions to successive sub-problems are communicated to later attempts through the states of the data structures. As the system expends effort, the state of knowledge summarized by the data structures grows.

The steps above avoided discussion of the many additional complications that are present. A helpful way to view the matching system is as a computer operating system specialised to perform the matching task. As with any operating system, computing resources must be allocated and exception conditions must be handled.

The scheduling of the system's activities is essentially based on cost functions. The *MATCHER* assigns a cost to the potential matching of each pair of lines. In calculating this cost the attributes and shape of the line are considered. It then makes trial associations of lines of the reference with lines from the unknown in order of increasing cost. At worst, it is still possible for the matcher to try all possible line associations. In practice it has been found that the sequencing by cost is a powerful guide to obtaining the correct association.

The *MATCHER* stops trying to match when it has paired enough lines from the reference and unknown propositions and the pairings that have been made are not inconsistent.

When the *MATCHER* is trying to match two subgraphs that are essentially unmatchable, perhaps because the class of current interest is wrong, it may not be able to terminate with any consistent labelling at all. Such a trap for the *MATCHER* would be disastrous for the whole system. The solution adopted here is for the *SUPERVISOR* to monitor the reports given by the matcher. If no success is reported within some allowed time interval, the supervisor orders the matcher to abandon its current attempt and a new interest is then chosen.

When the unknown drawing is at a great distance from the sensor, the system expects that some details may not be resolvable. For example, none of the internal lines of the unknown in Figure 1.1 can be resolved.

In this case, the *REFERENCE SUBGRAPH PROPOSER* makes predictions that step over the fine features of the class being tested and so omit unobservable detail from the predicted appearance. The lines composing the predicted subgraph are passed to the MATCHER.

4. Background

Relational matching has been widely considered, [4], for similar problems. Although the graph used in this case is not relational, the literature on relational matching has been a major influence on the system design. The case where the relational graphs from the reference and the unknown do not exactly match, and some form of approximation must be accepted is of particular interest, [5].

Matching which accommodates missing detail involves the subgraph matching problem, and this is known to be NP-complete, [6]. The risk of exponential growth in the number of matching steps has to be reduced. A divide and conquer strategy that uses carefully selected matching moves is appropriate. The main emphasis in developing the pilot system has been to engineer it to take as much advantage as possible from intuitively reasonable divisions of the problem. It has been shown that very significant reductions in run time can be achieved if the problem has the formal property of separability as defined by Shapiro in [7].

Backtracking will always occur to some extent because if the problem is "divided" then not every inconsistent association can be detected at the time it is made. These inconsistent associations must be resolved by corrective attention at some later stage in the matching. This same corrective attention can also be used to resolve conflicts in incoming data and the deductions that have been made from it. Of course, the more reliable the "dividing" the less the risk of backtracking.

Algorithms for matching have been given, for example [8], [9] and [10]. A constructive approach is in use here. The initial labeling is empty, and, based on the evidence available, the system finds reasons to build sets of consistent labels.

There appears to be no guarantee that the system can escape the deadly embrace of the exponential explosion in the matching steps. Thus it is important that the system should be able to monitor its performance to avoid unpromising approaches.

5. Concluding Remarks

The algorithms used to obtain a match are discrete. The notion of convergence, familiar from numerical computing, is still important because the steps followed as the data structures are updated to reach their final values determine the algorithm's performance.

There exists a lattice based theory of computable functions, [11], originally designed to support a theory of semantics of programming languages. This can describe the convergence of the matching system. Essentially, every data type in use in the system has a partial ordering defined for it. The processes must be designed to have a monotonic behavior, meaning that the ordering is preserved between comparable points in the n-tuples that correspond to the input and output.

The monotonic behavior persists while no unacceptable clashes are detected in forming the labeling. Resolution of these clashes, which may arise from conflicts of evidence as well as from inappropriate associations, will be modelled by having a non-monotonic demon selectively delete associations before allowing the processes to resume. This demon is not yet implemented.

Recent work, [12], shows a way of integrating this with the system described formally as a communicating sequential processes.

References

[1] Sanfeliu, A., "A Distance Measure Based on Tree-graph-grammars: A Way of Recognizing Hidden and Deformed 3–D Complex Objects," *Proceedings of Seventh International Conference on Pattern Recognition*, Montreal, 1984, pp. 739-741.

[2] Sanfeliu, A. and Fu K-S., "A Distance Measure Between Attributed Relational Graphs for Pattern Recognition," *IEEE Transactions on Systems, Man and Cybernetics*, May-June, 1983.

[3] Eshera, M.A. and Fu K-S, "An Image Understanding System Using Attributed Symbolic Representation and Inexact Graph Matching," to be published in *IEEE Transactions on Pattern Analysis and Machine Intelligence.*

[4] Cheng, J.K. and Huang, T.S., "Image Recognition by Matching Relational Structures," *Proceedings of PRIP 81*, pp. 542-547, August 1981.

[5] Shapiro, L.G. and Haralick, R.M., "Structural Description and Inexact Matching," *IEEE Transactions on Pattern Analysis and Machine Intelligence*, Vol. PAMI-3, No 5, pp. 504-519, September 1981.

[6] Garey, M.R. and Johnson, D.S., *Computers and Intractability — a Guide to the Theory of NP-completeness*, Freeman, 1979.

[7] Shapiro, L.G.; "Solving Consistent Labeling Problems Having the Separation Property," *Proceedings of Seventh International Conference on Pattern Recognition*, Montreal, 1984, pp. 313-315.

[8] Mcgregor, J.J., "Relational Consistency Algorithms and Their Application in Finding Subgraph and Graph Isomorphisms," *Inf. Sciences*, 19, pp. 229-250, 1979.

[9] Mackworth, A.K. "Consistency in Networks of Relations," *Artificial Intelligence*, Vol 8, No 1, pp. 99-118, 1977.

[10] Nudel, B., "Consistent-Labeling Problems and their Algorithms: Expected-Complexities and Theory-Based Heuristics," *Artificial Intelligence*, Vol 21, No 1 and 2, pp. 135-178, March 1983.

[11] Scott, D., *Lectures on a Mathematical Theory of Computation, Theoretical Foundations of Programming Methodology*, Reidel, 1982.

[12] Hoare, C.A.R.; *Communicating Sequential Processes*, Prentice Hall, 1984.

HYBRID METHODS IN PATTERN RECOGNITION

Horst Bunke

Universität Bern
Institut für Informatik und angewandte Mathematik
Länggassstrasse 51, CH–3012 Bern, Switzerland

1. Introduction

The field of pattern recognition has grown enormously in recent years and a wide variety of techniques have been developed for various applications. Traditionally, these techniques can be categorized into statistical, or decision theoretic, and structural methods. Additionally, artificial intelligence based approaches have become very important recently. Each of the different methods has its strength and its limitations. For overcoming these limitations, statistical, structural, and artificial intelligence based methods are mixed sometimes. This results in a hybrid approach.

This paper discusses various pattern recognition methods with a particular emphasis on the question how different methods are related with each other and how they can be combined into a single hybrid approach. The organization of the paper follows the diagram shown in Fig. 1. Among the conventional approaches to pattern recognition, we will consider decision theoretic methods, syntactic methods, structural prototypes, and relaxation in Section 2.

In Section 3, three important approaches to knowledge representation will be discussed, namely formal logic, production systems, and semantic nets. Again, we are interested how these techniques are connected among each other and how they are related with the conventional approaches to pattern recognition discussed in Section 2.

2. Hybrid Approaches Based on Conventional Pattern Recognition Methods

2.1. A Short Review of Basic Methods

Decision theoretic methods are applied primarily for the purpose of classification. The task in pattern classification is to assign an unknown input pattern to a class out of M classes, where $M \geq 2$. An individual pattern is represented by a N-dimensional vector of features. Depending on the way the classes are represented, we distinguish between nonparametric and parametric statistical classification. The most important subclasses of nonparametric and parametric statistical classification are nearest neighbor, or NN, classification, and Bayes-classification, respectively. For more details on statistical classification see [Fukunaga 1972, Duda-Hart 1973, Devijver-Kittler 1982].

NATO ASI Series, Vol. F30
Pattern Recognition Theory and Applications
Edited by P. A. Devijver and J. Kittler

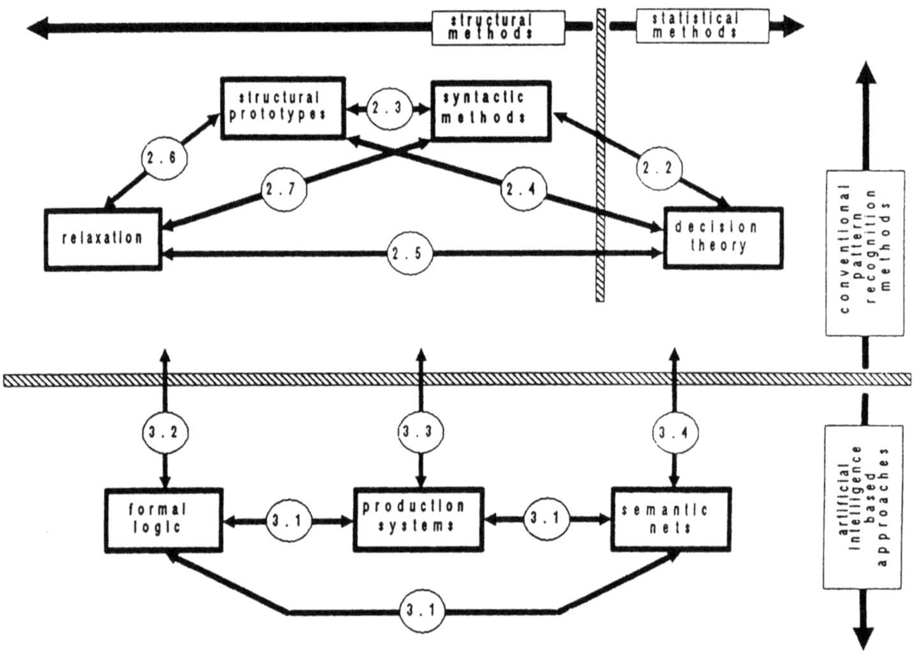

Figure 1: A categorization of different approaches to pattern recognition and relationships among them

Decision theoretic methods have a long tradition in pattern recognition and are based on a well founded mathematical theory. They have been proven useful in numerous applications. The algorithms are usually computationally inexpensive as compared to structural or artificial intelligence based methods. However, there are also several disadvantages and limitations of the statistical approach. Although a great deal of effort has been undertaken in deriving optimal algorithms with respect to classifying the extracted features, the features themselves are often chosen arbitrarily. Statistical methods provide only a class description of a pattern. They do not describe a pattern so as to allow its generation given its class, nor do they describe aspects of a pattern which make it ineligible for assignment to another class. Moreover, the various relations which may exist between the chosen features are completely neglected in the statistical approach.

The fundamental idea in *structural pattern recognition* is the explicit utilization of structural information in pattern representation. Structural information is used for modelling two important aspects, namely the hierarchical composition of a complex pattern based on simpler subpatterns, and the various relations which may exist between different subpatterns and/or characteristic features.

Syntactic methods are an important subclass of the structural approach. They are characterized by using formal grammars for pattern class representation. The terminals of the grammar correspond to primitive subpatterns which can directly be extracted from an input pattern by means of suitable preprocessing and segmentation methods. The set of grammar nonterminals corresponds to subpatterns of greater complexity which are successively built up from primitive elements. The process of building up complex (sub)patterns from simpler constituents is modelled by the grammar productions. Finally, the recognition process is based on a parser which analyzes an unknown input pattern according to the given grammar. Various types of grammars for a wide variety of applications have been proposed within this framework. For a detailed treatment, the reader is referred to [Gonzalez-Thomason 1978, Fu 1982].

Syntactic methods are advantageous for many tasks since they allow, as recognition result, not only pattern classification but also the inference of a structural description of an unknown input pattern. Furthermore, these methods are based on the well founded theory of formal languages [Hopcroft-Ullman 1979] which provides many useful results about power, limitations, and computational complexity of certain recognition procedures. On the other hand, the recognition of noisy patterns by means of syntactic methods has not yet been completely solved.

Structural prototypes can be considered as a viable alternative to formal grammars for pattern class representation. The idea is to store, in an explicit way, a finite number of pattern prototypes. In contrast with statistical NN classification, patterns are not stored as N-dimensional feature vectors. Instead, structural representations based on strings, trees, or graphs are preferred. For the recognition of an unknown input pattern x it is necessary to match x with the prototypes in order to detect that prototype pattern which is most similar to x. Inevitably, inexact or error-correcting matching procedures are required for this purpose. A number of algorithms have been proposed in the literature. For an introduction see [Fu 1982]. Further details on string matching can be found in [Hall-Dowling 1980]. For tree matching see [Lu 1979, Cheng-Lu 1985]. Two classical papers on graph matching are [Tsai-Fu 1979, Shapiro-Haralick 1981].

The use of structural prototypes is advantageous if pattern structure is important and if there are too few sample patterns available for deriving a grammar. A disadvantage is that these methods lack a well founded mathematical theory at present, and that their computational complexity — at least for graph matching — is high.

Relaxation is another class of structural methods. It is an iterative procedure which starts with an initial ambiguous labelling of primitive pattern components. Relaxation aims at deriving an unique interpretation of components, which is globally consistent under a given set of constraints. The relaxation procedures reported in the literature can be classified into discrete and continuous, or probabilistic, relaxation [Waltz 1975, Rosenfeld-Hummel-Zucker 1976]. Many different schemes within the latter category have been proposed [Peleg 1980, Faugeras-Berthod 1981, Hummel-Zucker 1983].

Relaxation is suitable for reducing local ambiguities. It has been successfully applied to many pattern recognition problems. The method is appealing particularly for those applications where the available a priori knowledge is in the form of local constraints, as they are required for relaxation. On the other hand there are some problems with relaxation. From a theoretical point of view, there are still open questions, although interesting results have been reported recently [Haralick 1983, Henderson 1984]. From an application oriented point of view, relaxation is limited since only local interpretations of pattern constituents are derived and no interpretation of a pattern as a whole can be achieved.

2.2. Syntactic Methods — Decision Theoretic methods

There are two major ways of combining statistical and syntactic pattern recognition methods, namely probabilistic grammars and attributed grammars. First, we will discuss probabilistic grammars.

Probabilistic grammars can favorably be applied when different pattern classes overlap, due to noise and distortion. The basic idea in probabilistic grammars is the attachment of a probability $p(r)$ to each production $r : X \rightarrow A_1 \cdots A_n$. Given an element $x \in L(G)$ (where $L(G)$ denotes the language generated by G, *i.e.* the set of terminal strings which can be derived), we can determine the probability $p(x/G)$ of x under grammar G by multiplying all probabilities of the productions which are used in the derivation $S \rightarrow x$ (where S denotes the grammar start symbol). For ambiguous strings, we have to sum over all possible derivations of x. If a particular pattern x is generated by different grammars $G_i, i = 1, \cdots, M$, each representing a different pattern class, then we parse x according to each G_i, determining the probability $p(x/G_i)$, and decide for pattern class j if $p(x/G_j) = \max\{p(x/G_i)/i = 1, \cdots, M\}$. So probabilistic grammars are a hybrid method based on techniques from statistical decision theory and syntactic pattern recognition.

Problems with probabilistic grammars are consistency, *i.e.* the condition $\sum p(x/G) = 1$ (where the sum is over all $x \in L(G)$) and the assessment of the production probabilities $p(r)$. For these topics, the reader is referred to [Gonzalez-Thomason 1978, Fu 1982]. Not only probabilistic string grammars, but also probabilistic tree grammars have been proposed in the literature [Fu 1982]. The idea of error correcting parsing can be combined with probabilistic grammars. Here probabilities for elementary pattern deformations like substitution, insertion, and deletion are provided. The original grammar is augmented by error productions, the probabilities of which are derived from the elementary pattern deformation probabilities. Using this augmented grammar, a modified Earley error-correcting parser can be applied which determines the most likely correction of a given distorted pattern [Fu 1982].

Attributed grammars are the second major approach to combining syntactic and statistical pattern recognition methods. A classical paper on this subject is [Tsai-Fu 1980]. Further applications can be found in [Fu 1977, Pavlidis-Ali 1979, Tang 1979, Bunke 1982].

The rules of a grammar are a suitable tool for modelling structural properties of patterns. However, there are deficiencies in adequately representing numerical aspects, such as length and orientation of lines, textural parameters of regions, or 3-D surface orientation. In attributed grammars, each grammar symbol A is augmented by a vector of attributes $\alpha(A) = (a_1(A), a_2(A), \cdots, \alpha_N(A))$. Such a vector can be interpreted as a N-dimensional feature vector as used in statistical classification. Remark that the symbol A can denote a subpattern as well as a relation. Considering a context free production $X \rightarrow A_1 \cdots A_n$, we need an additional rule for expressing the relations between the attributes of the left-hand side X and the right-hand side $A_1 \cdots A_n$. Two cases can be distinguished. First, the attributes of X can be dependent on those of $A_1 \cdots A_n$, *i.e.* $\alpha(X) = f(\alpha(A_1), \cdots, \alpha(A_n))$. Secondly, the attributes of A_i can be dependent on X, *i.e.* $\alpha(A_i) = g_i(\alpha(X))$, $i = 1, \cdots, n$. The first case (synthesized attributes) is most suitable for bottom-up analysis, while the second case (inherited attributes) is most suitable for top-down processing. In the extreme case, a context-free grammar results when all attributes are deleted from an attributed grammar. In the other extreme case, a statistical classifier is obtained from an attributed grammar when each pattern is treated as a single entity and not decomposed into subpatterns. A deeper discussion of this subject can be found in [Fu 1983].

2.3. Syntactic Methods — Structural Prototypes

Pattern recognition by means of prototype matching has several aspects in common with syntactic methods. First, both methods emphasize structural properties of patterns, *i.e.* the composition of patterns from subpatterns including relations between subpatterns. Secondly, both approaches rely on the same data structures, namely strings, trees, and graphs. Finally, in both cases capabilities for error-correction are required in order to cope with noisy and distorted data.

Obviously, each finite set of prototype pattern $x_1 \cdots, x_n$ can be described by a grammar. In their simplest form, the grammar productions are $S_i \rightarrow x_i$, $i = 1, \cdots, n$. Conversely, if the language of a grammar is finite, it can directly be represented in such a way that each element is interpreted as a prototype pattern. Despite of this theoretical equivalence, one method can be superior to the other for a specific application. Generally speaking, if the number of sample patterns is small, there is often no need for a grammar and a "direct" representation by means of prototypes is eventually preferable. On the other hand, if a large number of sample patterns is involved, pattern recognition and pattern class representation is eventually more efficient if a grammar is used.

Formal grammars are more powerful than structural prototypes in the sense they can generate an infinite number of elements. Furthermore, the derivation tree mirrors, as a result of parsing, the aggregation of subpatterns into a pattern along a potentially unbounded number of hierarchical levels. This is in contrast with structural prototypes, where the hierarchical composition of a pattern is limited to only two levels. For example, a prototype graph representing a pattern x consists of a number of nodes and arcs where the nodes represent subpatterns of x. These subpatterns are not further decomposed. An exception to this limitation are substructures with priorities, like in PDL [Fu 1982], or hierarchical graphs. The latter subject will further be discussed in Section 3.4.

A hybrid approach combining structural prototypes and formal grammars has been proposed in [Gernert 1981]. For the purpose of classification, an unknown pattern, which is represented by means of a graph, is compared with a number of prototype graphs. More precisely, its distance from each of the prototypes is determined and it is assigned to the same class as the closests prototype belongs to. (Notice that this is a particular kind of NN-classification, as discussed in Section 2.1) In this hybrid approach, the distance between a graph g and a prototype p is defined as the number of derivation steps of a graph grammar which are required in order to transform p into g. So inexact graph matching is accomplished by means of a transformation which is based on a grammar. A similar idea for string matching has been proposed in [Tai-Fu 1982]. However, no practical experience demonstrating the utility of these hybrid approaches has been reported so far.

2.4. Structural Prototypes — Decision Theoretic Methods

There are many interesting relationships between pattern recognition based on structural prototype matching and decision theoretic methods. First, one notices that determining that prototype which is most similar to the input pattern is conceptually closely related with NN classification as discussed in Section 2.1. from this observation it follows that the structural similarity measure should be a metric since then it is possible to employ clustering techniques for efficient prototype, *i.e.* sample pattern, organization [Lu 1979, Shapiro-Haralick 1982].

The inexact graph matching technique proposed in [Tsai-Fu 1979] can be considered from a decision theoretic point of view. If probabilities for elementary graph deformations are provided, graph distance, or similarity, can be interpreted as deformation probability. Consequently, finding the most similar prototype is equivalent to detecting the most probable deformation. Thus, prototype matching in the sense of [Tsai-Fu 1980] can be interpreted as a special decision theoretic approach. Since deformation probabilities are often unknown in practical applications, deformation costs are used instead as an approximation [Bunke-Allermann 1983].

Another hybrid approach combining structural prototypes and decision theoretic methods is the use of stochastic prototypes. In what follows, we will restrict our discussion to prototype graphs. In contrast with [Tsai-Fu 1979], where any node and any edge in a graph is present with a probability equal to 1 and where probabilities indicate only the likelihood of graph deformations, the nodes and edges themselves are stochastic in a stochastic graph. Intuitively, any node and edge is present only with a probability $0 \leq p \leq 1$ in a stochastic graph. This concept has been proposed in [Shapiro-Haralick 1982] for defining the "average" or the "median" graph of a cluster of similar prototypes. In another paper, probability distributions of node and edge attributes have been proposed, in addition to probabilities of node and edge occurrence [Groen-Sanderson-Schlag 1985]. Thus object recognition is based on matching a non-stochastic graph representing the unknown object to each of the stochastic model graphs in order to find the most probable model. For another approach based on a similar idea see [Wong 1983].

Another very interesting relationship between NN-classification and matching of unknown patterns against structural prototypes is established in [Goldfarb-Chan 1984]. The authors consider a set of structural prototypes from different classes together with a pseudometric (*i.e.*, a "distance" function not necessarily fulfilling the triangle inequality) and show how the prototypes can be mapped into a n-dimensional numerical vector representation in such a way that the distance between the prototypes is preserved. In a further step this representation is mapped into another vector representation of low dimensionality (dimensionality one in the example given in [Goldfarb-Chan 1984]). It is claimed that it should be possible by analysis of this low dimensional training set representation to select few characteristic sample patterns for each class, for example the element closest to the mean, or the elements corresponding to the piecewise linear boundaries. So by mapping structural prototypes into a vector representation, a reduction of the sample set size can be achieved. This is similar in its spirit to sample set condensation or sample set editing for numerical NN-classification as described in [Devijver-Kittler 1982].

Another link between structural prototypes and statistical methods can be concluded from [Kasif-Kitchen-Rosenfeld 1983] where subgraph isomorphism detection is accomplished by cluster detection in a parameter space.

2.5. Relaxation — Decision Theoretic Methods

In a number of papers, primarily addressed to the field of pictorial pattern recognition, the combination of statistical classification and relaxation has been proposed. The idea common to all these approaches is to make a classification of each pixel, using a statistical method, and to subsequently refine this initial classification by means of relaxation.

The initial classification can be based on a Bayes-classifier [Kubichek-Quincy 1985], on a particular distance function [Davis-Wang-Xie 1983], on thresholding [Bhanu - Faugeras 1982], or on other histogram based features [Nagin-Hanson-Riseman 1982]. Notice that no contextual information is exploited in this first classification stage, *i.e.*, the classification of a pixel is made without reference to the class of the neighboring pixels. Notice also that the statistical classification may yield ties or near ties between different classes. Relaxation following the initial classification is a suitable tool for making use of contextual knowledge and for breaking ties. In order to facilitate relaxation, it is required that the statistical classifier yields not only a class-name w_j for each pixel i but a vector $[p_i(w_1), \cdots, p_i(w_m)]$ where $p_i(w_j)$ is the probability that w_j is the correct class of pixel i. The principal idea for the exploitation of contextual constraints is to define compatibility coefficients in such a way that identical labels at neighboring pixels reinforce each other while different labels suppress each other. (This principle may be further refined if particular knowledge about the shape of the objects under consideration is available.) An extension to using also temporal context in image sequences has been reported in [Davis-Wang-Xie 1983].

An interesting relationship between probabilistic relaxation and Bayes-classification is derived in [Haralick 1983]. It is shown that under some general conditional independence assumptions probabilistic relaxation can be interpreted as a process which computes conditional probabilities. Assigning finally the class with the highest probability to an object can thus be considered as a special Bayes decision rule.

2.6. Relaxation — Structural Prototypes

Relaxation is based on constraint exploitation for the purpose of reducing local ambiguities. In their most general form, constraints are given by expressions $R(x_1, \cdots, x_n)$, which indicate the likelihood that $x_1, \cdots, x_n$ is a correct interpretation of objects $0_1, \cdots$, 0_n, if there is a relation R between $0_1, \cdots, 0_n$. From this point of view, a structural prototype, *e.g.* a graph, can be considered as an aggregation of several unary and binary constraints. So matching an object with a prototype is nothing else but finding an interpretation of the components of the object which is maximally consistent with the constraints represented by the prototype.

On the other hand, relaxation can be used as a special technique for finding a match between a model and an unknown object. This idea has been applied in a system for aerial image understanding [Faugeras-Price 1981]. The nodes in the model and the object graph correspond to lines and regions in an image. Node attributes represent features like color, texture, size, etc. Spatial relations between lines and regions, like adjacency, nearby, above, etc., are represented by graph edges. Initially, only a fixed number of best matching image nodes are assigned to each model node. For updating of probabilities, the relations between pairs of model nodes are systematically compared with those of corresponding image nodes. Good experimental results have been reported by the authors. Similar approaches to matching relational structures by means of relaxation have been proposed in [Kitchen 1980, Cheng-Huang 1981].

In conclusion, structural matching can be considered as a particular constraint satisfaction paradigm, while on the other hand constraint satisfaction, *i.e.* relaxation, can be used as a special technique for accomplishing structural matching.

2.7. Relaxation — Syntactic Methods

Relaxation follows the principle of least commitment, *i.e.* a maximum number of labels, or interpretations, for an object is considered initially. This idea can be adopted in syntactic pattern recognition in such a way that not a fixed symbol x_i, but a vector $(x_1, \cdots, x_m)$ of possible symbols is considered at each position in an input string. (We restrict our discussion to string grammars in this section.) Eventually, a measure of confidence, or a probability is assigned to each possible symbol at each position. Assume an input string of length n with m alternative symbols at each position, representing an unknown pattern. The "brute force" approach to syntactic recognition is the application of a parser to all possible nm strings which can be formed thus and the determination of that sequence of n symbols which is compatible with the given grammar and has maximum probability among all compatible strings. If n and m are large, this becomes prohibitive. In order to reduce the effort required for parsing, discrete relaxation can be applied beforehand, eliminating successively the symbols in the input string which are incompatible with the given grammar. Using alternatively a probabilistic relaxation scheme, those strings among all possible nm strings which are compatible with the given grammar will be enhanced while all other strings will be suppressed.

This combination of probabilistic relaxation and syntactic pattern recognition was called "syntax-directed probabilistic relaxation" in a recent article [Don-Fu 1985]. A direct solution to the problem of finding the string with maximum probability among the strings compatible with a given grammar, under the condition that the constraints are given by regular expressions, has been proposed in [Bunke-Grebner-Sagerer 1984]. The solution is based on dynamic programming, and is very efficient with respect to time and space, and implementation effort, as well.

The application of grammatical constraints for reduction of ambiguities is limited to terminal symbols in [Don-Fu 1985]. A more general approach taking into regard also constraints between higher-level nonterminals is hierarchical relaxation [Davis-Henderson 1981]. It is basically a bottom-up parsing procedure where, during the whole recognition process, reduction of symbols according to the rules of the given grammar and exploitation of contextual constraints for elimination of inconsistent symbols is intertwined.

3. Hybrid Approaches Based on Artificial Intelligence

Artificial intelligence based methods are characterized by considering pattern classes as abstract concepts and individual patterns as instances thereof. Pattern classes are represented by explicitly storing knowledge describing them. Applying this knowledge to the measurements made on an unknown pattern, recognition is accomplished by drawing domain specific inferences, or logical conclusions. So artificial intelligence based pattern recognition emphasizes the issues of knowledge representation and control of problem solving. A very important category of tasks where these ideas have been applied is diagnostic classification [Shortliffe 1976, Barr-Feigenbaum 1982, Chandrasekaran 1986].

In Section 3.1 we will briefly review the most important techniques for knowledge representation and discuss how they are related with each other. Relationships with conventional pattern recognition methods will be studied in Sections 3.2–3.4.

3.1. Basic Knowledge Representation Methods

Formal logic is a classical artificial intelligence approach to knowledge representation and inference. In what follows, we will consider only first order predicate calculus. For other logics see [Turner 1984]. The basic constituents of first order predicate calculus are well-formed formulas which are built up from predicates, functions, variables and constants according to particular syntactic and semantic rules.

Recently the logic programming language PROLOG has attracted much attention. PROLOG covers a major part of first order predicate calculus (with almost no real restrictions with respect to practical applications) and seems to be well suited for pattern recognition applications. For an introduction to PROLOG see [Clocksin-Mellish 1984]. General introductions to predicate calculus and its applications are [Chang-Lee 1973, Wos *et al.* 1984].

Production systems are a well known tool for knowledge representation in expert systems and they have been used in many pattern recognition applications. Basically, a production system consists of productions, or rules, of the form `IF CONDITION THEN CONCLUSION`. Given an initial set of data stored in a database — the so-called short-term knowledge base — conclusions can be derived by successive application of rules. Control procedures include forward- and backward-chaining as well as mixed-mode chaining of productions.

There are several advantages of production systems, for example perspicuity and modularity. Shortcomings of production systems include particularly the lack of expressive power for certain applications. A general introduction to, and overview of, the field of production systems is given in [Davis-King 1977, Barr-Feigenbaum 1981]. Further applications in pattern recognition are reported in [Ohta 1980, Nagao-Matsuyama 1980, Nazif-Levine 1984, Duane *et al.* 1985] among many others.

A *semantic net* can be considered as a graph. In contrast with "traditional" graphs, however, where the nodes and edges are atomic units, the nodes and edges in a semantic net (which are also called concepts and relations, respectively) are complex data structures consisting of a number of subunits, each. For example, a concept may have a name, a number of attributes, a number of conditions, a default value etc. With respect to edges, three standard relations are most common in semantic nets, namely "part", "specialization", and "instance". By means of the part–relation, an aggregation of a number of basic entities into a more complex object can be modelled. An important feature of the specialization and the instance relation is the inheritance property, which facilitates compact representation of knowledge. Other relations are problem dependent and may include relations of spatial, temporal, causal, etc. nature.

Inference procedure for semantic nets are mainly based on matching or on search (see also Section 4). More details on semantic nets can be found in [Barr-Feigenbaum 1981]. Examples of applications in pattern recognition are [Hanson-Riseman 1978, Tsotsos *et al.* 1980, Ballard-Brown-Feldman 1978, Niemann *et al.* 1985].

There are various relationships between predicate calculus, production systems, and semantic nets and these approaches can be integrated into a hybrid approach in a variety of ways. First, both production systems and semantic nets can be considered as particular instances of predicate logic. For a detailed treatment the reader is referred to [Nilsson 1982, Chapters 6 and 9]. Semantic nets can be used as an aid for structuring or partitioning the rules in a production system. This results in more efficiency with respect to rule application [Duda-Gaschnig-Hart 1979]. On the other hand, productions can be attached to the concepts in a semantic net as procedural knowledge sources (*i.e.* as slot-fillers). An example is [Niemann *et al.* 1985]. Recent work on the integration of predicate calculus, productions, and semantic nets into one single knowledge representation tool has been reported in [Di Primio-Brewka 1985].

3.2. Formal Logic — Conventional Pattern Recognition

There is a close relationship between formal logic, at the one hand side, and formal grammars and structural prototypes, at the other hand side, insofar as parsing and structural matching can be implemented using logic programming. Details are described, for example, in [Kowalski 1979]. The key idea is to formally describe *what* the problem is instead of specifying *how* it is to be algorithmically solved step by step. However, most PROLOG implementations of today are still slow in execution.

Another close relationship between formal logic and grammars may be concluded from the STRIPS–system [Nilsson 1982, Chapter 7]. There are predicate calculus rules for manipulating other predicate calculus formulas. These rules are very similar to the rules in a grammar. In a sense, STRIPS–rules are more general since they may contain variables that can be matched with other variables or constants. However, these variables can be simulated, in many cases, by means of grammar attributes. Originally, the work on STRIPS was motivated by robot action planning. But the idea may be used in pattern recognition in a similar way for inferring conclusions about patterns.

Fuzzy logic can be considered as a link between predicate calculus and decision theory. For more details about this topic, including applications, the reader is referred to [Zimmermann 1985].

3.3. Production Systems — Conventional Pattern Recognition

From a theoretical point of view, production systems are closely related with formal grammars. A rule in a production system may be interpreted as a grammar rule with the if-part (condition) corresponding to the left-hand and the then-part (conclusion) corresponding to the right-hand side of a grammar rule. Now consider a special type of a production system where the database is a linear string of facts. Each time a rule is applied, its if-part is removed from the database while its then-part is inserted at the place of the if-part. Assume furthermore, that the facts are divided into terminal and nonterminal facts. Initially, there is only one nonterminal fact in the database. The termination condition is that there are only terminal facts in the database. Control is by forward-chaining. Obviously, such a production system is identical with a formal grammar. Conversely, any grammar can be considered as a production system of the type described above. Because of this close relationship, all comments made in Section 2.3 hold also for the relation between production systems and structural prototypes.

Despite of this theoretical equivalence, one notices quite obvious differences between production systems and grammars in practical applications. For example, the database of a production system is usually not organized as a string; a rule may contain variables; there is often a more advanced control procedure than just forward chaining, etc.

Finally, it is to be noted that most production systems include means for coping with uncertainty, *i.e.* uncertain data and knowledge. Examples are certainty factors [Shortliffe 1976], concepts from Dempster-Shafer's theory [Ishizuka *et al.* 1982], or Bayesian uncertainties [Duda-Gaschnig-Hart 1979]. This can be considered as a link with statistical classification methods.

3.4. Semantic Nets — Conventional Pattern Recognition

Semantic nets, at the one hand side, and structural prototypes and grammars, at the other hand side, have much in common. First, we will discuss relations between semantic nets and structural prototypes. Any structural prototype represented by a graph can be considered as a simple semantic net, without part-, specialization-, and instance-relations. In this case, inference is restricted to error correcting graph or subgraph isomorphism detection. A hierarchical graph is a structural prototype for modelling the aggregation of simpler constituents into more complex objects on several levels. Such a prototype can also be considered as a special type of a semantic net, including part-relations but excluding specialization- and instance-relations. Inference in a hierarchical graph needs means for inheriting problem dependent relations (for example, spatial relations like above, right, etc.) up and down the part-hierarchy, in addition to graph or subgraph isomorphism detection. A semantic net in its full generality includes, besides the features of a hierarchical graph, means that can be used for making non-geometrical problem dependent inferences. An example is [Niemann *et al.* 1985].

A grammar rule $X \rightarrow X_1 \cdots X_n$ has a direct analogy in a semantic net, namely a concept X with parts $X_1 \cdots X_n$, and vice versa. Notice that a symbol X_i may not only represent an object but also a relation between objects. In [Hall 1973] the equivalence between grammars and AND/OR graphs is discussed and it is shown that parsing is equivalent to searching for a solution graph. An AND/OR-graph can be considered as a particular type of a semantic net. So the derivation tree of a string can be interpreted as a partial instantiation of the semantic net which corresponds to the grammar. Attributes, procedures for attribute calculation, application conditions, etc. are directly related with the corresponding components of a concept in a semantic net. An application example where a grammar operates on the slots (*i.e.*, attributes) of a semantic net is [Bonamini *et al.* 1982].

4. Further Discussion

The emphasis in Section 3 was on knowledge representation. There are other issues from artificial intelligence which are very important in pattern recognition. One of them is search and control. The task of a pattern recognition system is the transformation of sensory input data into a pattern description, *e.g.* a class-name. Such a transformation is accomplished in a series of processing steps with a number of intermediate results. In a complex system, those intermediate results are ambiguous and the overall sequence of processing steps cannot be uniquely determined beforehand. So a control procedure for optimal selection of processing steps is required. For achieving such an optimal selection, search methods from artificial intelligence can be applied [Nilsson 1982]. For an example, see [Niemann *et al.* 1985]. A deeper discussion of the use of search strategies in pattern recognition can be found in [Kanal 1979].

Another important question is concerned with overall system organization. The blackboard model according to [Erman *et al.* 1980] seems particularly useful for complex systems. It seems ideally suited for organizing large hybrid systems since the blackboard is the only shared global data structure and all the expert modules can be completely independent from each other, from a conceptual and methodological point of view. Further examples of systems which are organized according to the blackboard model are [Nagao-Matsuyama 1980, Levine-Shaheen 1981].

The idea of using hybrid approaches in solving pattern recognition problems is not new [Fu 1982]. The rapid growth of pattern recognition and artificial intelligence will certainly stimulate further research on hybrid methods.

References

[1] Ballard, D.H., C.M. Brown, J.A. Feldman, "An approach to knowledge directed image analysis," in [Hanson-Riseman 1978a], 664–670.

[2] Barr, A., E.A. Feigenbaum (eds.), *The Handbook of Artificial Intelligence* vol. 1, Pitman Books, London, 1981.

[3] Barr, A., E.A. Feigenbaum (eds.), *The Handbook of Artificial Intelligence* vol. 2, Pitman Books, London, 1982.

[4] Faugeras, O.D., "Segmentation of images having unimodal distributions," IEEE Trans. PAMI-4, 1982, 408–419.

[5] Bonamini, R., R. de Mori, A. Lettera, E. Sandretto, "An electrocardiographic signal understanding system" in [Kittler-Fu-Pau 1982], 443–464.

[6] Bunke, H., "Attributed programmed graph grammars and their application to schematic diagram interpretation," IEEE Trans. PAMI-4, 574–582, 1982.

[7] Bunke, H., G. Allermann, "Inexact graph matching for structural pattern recognition," Pattern Recognition Letters 1, 1983, 245–253.

[8] Bunke, H., K. Grebner, G. Sagerer, "Syntactic analysis of noisy input strings with an application to the analysis of heart-volume curves," Proc. 7th ICPR, Montreal, 1984, 1145–1147.

[9] Chang, C., R.C. Lee., *Symbolic Logic and Mechanical Theorem Proving*, Academic Press, New York, 1973.

[10] Chandrasekaran, B., "From numbers to symbols to knowledge structures: Pattern recognition and artificial intelligence perspectives on the classification task," in Gelsema, E.S., L.N. Kanal, (Eds.) *Pattern Recognition in Practice II*, Elsevier Science Publ. B.V., 1986, 547–559.

[11] Cheng, J.K., T.S. Huang, "Image recognition by matching relational structures," IEEE Proc. PRIP, Dallas, 1981, 542–547.

[12] Cheng, Y.C., S.Y. Lu, "Waveform correlation by tree matching," IEEE Trans. PAMI-7, 1985, 199–305.

[13] Clocksin, W.F., C.S. Mellish, *Programming in Prolog*, Springer-Verlag, 1984.

[14] Davis, L.S., T.C. Henderson, "Hierarchical constraint processes for shape analysis," IEEE Trans. PAMI-3, 1981, 265–277.

[15] Davis, L.S., C.Y. Wang, H.C. Xie, "An experiment in multi-spectral, multitemporal crop classification using relaxation techniques," Comp. Vision, Graphics, and Image Proc. 23, 1983, 227–235.

[16] Davis, R., J. King, "An overview of production systems," in Elock, E.W., D. Michie, (Eds.) *Machine Intelligence 8*, Ellis Horwood, Chichester, 1977, 300–332.

[17] Devijver, P., J. Kittler, *Pattern Recognition: A Statistical Approach*, Prentice Hall Int., 1982.

[18] Di Primio, F., G. Brewka, "Babylon, kernel system of an integrated environment for expert system development and operation," Proc. 5th Int. Workshop on Exp. Systems and their Applications, Avignon, 1985, 573–583.

[19] Don, H.S., K.S. Fu, "A syntactic method for image segmentation and object recognition," Pattern Recognition 18, 1985, 73–87.

[20] Duda, R.D., J. Gaschnig, P. Hart, "Model design in the prospector consultant system for mineral exploration" in Michie, D. (Ed.), *Expert Systems in the Micro-Electric Age*, Edinburgh Univ. Press, 1979, 153–167.

[21] Duda, R.O., P.E. Hart, *Pattern Classification and Scene Analysis*, John Wiley & Sons, 1973.

[22] Duane, G.S., S. F. Venable, D.J. Richter, A.M. Wiedemann, "A production system for scene analysis and semantically guided segmentation," SPIE Vol. 548, Applications of Art. Intell. II, 1985, 35–45.

[23] Erman, L.D., F. Hayes-Roth, V.R. Lesser, R. Reddy, "The Hearsay-II speech-understanding system," Comp. Surveys 12, 1980, 213–253.

[24] Faugeras, O., M. Berthod, "Improving consistency and reducing ambiguities in stochastic labeling: An optimization approach," IEEE Trans. PAMI-3, 1981, 412–424.

[25] Faugeras, O.D., K.E. Price, "Semantic description of aerial images using stochastic labeling," IEEE Trans. PAMI-3, 1981, 633–642.

[26] Fu, K.S., *Syntactic Pattern Recognition, Applications*, Springer Verlag, 1977.

[27] Fu, K.S., *Syntactic Pattern Recognition and Applications*, Prentice Hall, 1982.

[28] Fu, K.S., "Hybrid approaches to pattern recognition" in [Kittler-Fu-Pau 1982], 139–155.

[29] Fu, K.S., "A step towards unification of syntactic and statistical pattern recognition," IEEE Trans. PAMI-5, 1983, 200–205.

[30] Fukunaga, K., *Introduction to Statistical Pattern Recognition*, Academic Press 1972.

[31] Gernert, D., "Distance or similarity measures which respect the internal structure of the objects," Methods of Operations Research 43, 1981, 329–335.

[32] Goldfarb, L., T.Y.T. Chan, "On a new unified approach to pattern recognition," Proc. 7th ICPR, Montreal, 1984, 705–708.

[33] Gonzalez, R.C., M.G. Thomason, *Syntactic Pattern Recognition*, Addison-Wesley, 1978.

[34] Groen, F.C.A., A.C. Sanderson, J.F. Schlag, "Symbol recognition in electrical diagrams using probabilistic graph matching," Pattern Recognition Letters 3, 1985, 343–350.

[35] Hall, P.A.N., "Equivalence between AND/OR graphs and context-free grammars," CACM 16, 1973, 444–445.

[36] Hall, P.A.V., G.R. Dowling, "Approximate string matching," Comp. Surveys 12, 1980, 381–402.

[37] Hanson, A.R., R.M. Riseman, "Visions; a computer system for interpreting scenes," in [Hanson, Riseman 1978a], 303–333.

[38] Hanson, A.R., E.M. Riseman (Eds.), *Computer Vision Systems*, Academic Press, New York, 1978(a).

[39] Haralick, R.M. "An interpretation for probabilistic relaxation," Comp. Vision, Graphics, and Image Processing 22, 1983, 388–395.

[40] Haralick, R.M., "Decision making in context," IEEE Trans. PAMI-5, 1983, 417–428.

[41] Henderson, T.C., "A note on discrete relaxation," Comp. Vision, Graphics, and Image Proc. 28, 1984, 384–388.

[42] Hopcroft, J.E., J.D. Ullman, *Introduction to Automata Theory, Languages and Computation*, Addison Wesley, 1979.

[43] Hummel, R., S. Zucker, "On the foundations of relaxation labeling processes," IEEE Trans. PAMI-5, 1983, 267–287.

[44] Ishizuka, M., K.S. Fu, T.P. Yao, "SPERIL: an expert system for damage assessment of existing structures," Proc. 6th ICPR 1982, Munich, 932–937.

[45] Kanal, L.N., "Problem-solving models and search strategies for pattern recognition," IEEE Trans. PAMI-1, 1979, 193–201.

[46] Kasif, S., L. Kitchen, A. Rosenfeld, "A Hough transform technique for subgraph isomorphism," Pattern Recognition Letters 2, 1983, 83–88.

[47] Kitchen, L., "Relaxation applied to matching quantitative relational structures," IEEE Trans. SMC-10, 1980, 96–101.

[48] Kittler, J., K.S. Fu, L.F. Pau (Eds.), *Pattern Recognition Theory and Applications*, D. Reidel Publ. Co., Dodrecht etc., 1982.

[49] Kowalski, R., *Logic for Problem Solving*, North-Holland, 1979.

[50] Kubichek, R.F., E.A. Quincy., "Identification of seismic stratigraphic traps using statistical pattern recognition," Pattern Recognition 18, 1985, 440–458.

[51] Levine, M.D., S.I. Shaheen, "A modular computer vision system for picture segmentation and interpretation," IEEE Trans. PAMI-3, 1981, 540–556.

[52] Lu, S.Y., "A tree-to-tree distance and its application to cluster analysis," IEEE Trans. PAMI-1, 1979, 219–224.

[53] Nagao, M., T. Matsuyama, *A Structural Analysis of Complex Aerial Photographs*, Plenum Press, New York, 1980.

[54] Nagin, P.A., Hanson, A.R., Riseman, E.M., "Studies in global and local histogram guided relaxation algorithms," IEEE Trans. PAMI-4, 1982, 263–277.

[55] Nazif, A.M., M.D. Levine, "Low level image segmentation an expert system," IEEE Trans. PAMI-6, 1984, 555–577.

[56] Niemann, H., H. Bunke, I. Hofmann, G. Sagerer, F. Wolf, H. Feistel, "A knowledge based system for analysis of gated blood pool studies," IEEE Trans. PAMI-7, 1985, 246–259.

[57] Nilsson, N.J., *Principles of Artificial Intelligence*, Springer verlag, 1982.

[58] Ohta, Y., "A region oriented image-analysis system by computer," Ph. D. diss., Dept. of Inform. Sciences, Kyoto Univ., Japan, 1980.

[59] Pavlidis, T., F. Ali, "A hierarchical shape analyzer," IEEE Trans. PAMI-1, 1979, 2–9.

[60] Peleg, S., "A new probabilistic relaxation scheme," IEEE Trans. PAMI-2, 1980, 362–369.

[61] Rosenfeld, A., R.A. Hummel, S.W. Zucker, "Scene labelling by relaxation operations," IEEE Trans. SMC-6, 1976, 420–443.

[62] Shapiro, L.G., R.M. Haralick, "Structural descriptions and inexact matching," IEEE Trans. PAMI-3, 1981, 501–519.

[63] Shapiro, L.G., R.M. Haralick, "Organization of Relational Models for Scene Analysis," IEEE Trans. PAMI-4, 1982, 595–602.

[64] Shortliffe, E.A., *Computer-Based Medical Consultations: Mycin*, American Elsevier, New York, 1976.

[65] Tai, J.W., K.S. Fu, "Semantic syntax-directed translation for pictorial pattern recognition," Proc. 6th ICPR, Munich, 1982, 169–171.

[66] Tang, G.Y., "A syntactic-semantic approach to image understanding and creation," IEEE Trans. PAMI-1, 1979, 135–144.

[67] Tsai, W.H., K.S. Fu, "Error-correcting isomorphisms of attributed relational graphs for pattern analysis," IEEE Trans. SMC-9, 1979, 757–768.

[68] Tsai, W.H., K.S. Fu, "Attributed grammar-a tool for combining syntactic and statistical approaches to pattern recognition," IEEE Trans. SMC-10, 1980, 873–885.

[69] Tsotsos, J.K., J. Mylopoulos, H.D. Covvey, S.W. Zucker, "A framework for visual motion understanding," IEEE Trans. PAMI-2, 1980, 563–573.

[70] Turner, R., *Logics for Artificial Intelligence*, Ellis Horwood Ltd., Chichester, 1984.

[71] Waltz, D., "Understanding line drawings of scenes with shadows," in Winston, P.H. (Ed.): *The Psychology of Computer Vision*, Mc Graw Hill, 1975, 19–91.

[72] Wong, A.K.C., M. You, "Entropy and distance measures of random graphs," IEEE Comp. Soc. Conf. on PRIP, 1983, 371–376.

[73] Wos, L., R. Overbeek, E. Lusk, J. Boyle, *Automated Reasoning Introduction and Applications*, Prentice Hall, Englewood Cliffs, 1984.

[74] Zimmermann, H.J., *Fuzzy Set Theory and its Applications*, Kluwer-Nijhoff Publishing, Boston etc., 1985.

FUZZY SETS IN PATTERN RECOGNITION

Hans-Jürgen Zimmermann

RWTH Aachen
Tempergraben 55
D-5100 Aachen, F.R.G.

1. Uncertainty, Vagueness, Fuzziness

Fuzzy Set Theory is concerned with non-dichotomous structures, *i.e.*, with situations which are not of the either-or-structure, which cannot be characterized by black-or-white, by true-or-false, by certain-or-impossible. These situations are generally considered as containing uncertainty, even though the term "uncertainty" is not defined unequivocally. Often uncertainty is considered to refer to the occurrence of events while vagueness refers to the description of events. Let us consider uncertainty with respect to occurrence first: The statement "The probability of hitting the target is .6" is certainly probabilistic in nature and could well be modelled using classical probability theory. "The chances of winning are good" will already pose some problems, because "good chances" are not well (*i.e.*, crisply) defined. In a phrase like "It is likely that we will make a good profit" the event itself nor its occurrence are well defined. In these situations classical probabilistic models will not even be appropriate for the expression of uncertain occurrences.

Let us now turn to uncertainties of the description of events. Here we can distinguish between intrinsic vagueness and informational vagueness. Intrinsic vagueness refers to a vagueness of the definability of a subject itself. In order to decide whether at a certain location there is a light grey, a dark grey, or a black point, we have to be able to distinguish clearly between a light grey and a dark grey point. The same is true if we want to identify long sticks, short strokes, young men, high pressures, etc. Informational vagueness is an uncertainty of the description of a phenomenon or category due to the large number of descriptors which would be needed to define it properly and of which in a certain context only few can be used. Such notions may, for instance, be "credit-worthy customer", "pleasant company", "mature economy", etc. Eventually relationships may also be vague: "Not much", "larger than", "approximately equal to" etc. are of that type. All these types of vagueness or uncertainties may be relevant when deciding whether a certain element belongs to a certain cluster or not, and it might sometimes be more appropriate to find out to which degrees an element belongs to which clusters. Fuzzy Set Theory is primarily concerned with uncertainties of the non probabilistic type and can serve as a valuable tool to model those situations properly.

NATO ASI Series, Vol. F30
Pattern Recognition Theory and Applications
Edited by P.A. Devijver and J. Kittler

2. Basic Notions of Fuzzy Set Theory

In order to limit the number of different symbols used in this paper we shall denote crisp (non-fuzzy) sets by X, Y, Z and fuzzy sets by A, B, C.
Definition: If X is a collection of objects denoted generically by x then a fuzzy set A in x is a set of ordered pairs: $A = \{(x, \mu_A(x)) \mid x \in X\}$.
Example: A realtor wants to classify the houses he offers to his clients. One indicator of comfort of these houses is the number of bedrooms in it. Let $X = \{1, 2, 3, 4, ..., 10\}$ be the set of available types of houses described by x = number of bedrooms in a house. Then the fuzzy set "comfortable type of houses for a 4-person family" may be described as

$$A = \{(1, .2), (2, .5), (3, .8), (4, 1), (5, .7), (6, .3)\}$$

Definition: A fuzzy number M is a convex normalized fuzzy set M of the real line such that

1. It exists exactly one $x' \in R \mid \mu'(x') = 1$ (x' is called the mean value of M).
2. $\mu'(x)$ is piecewise continuous.

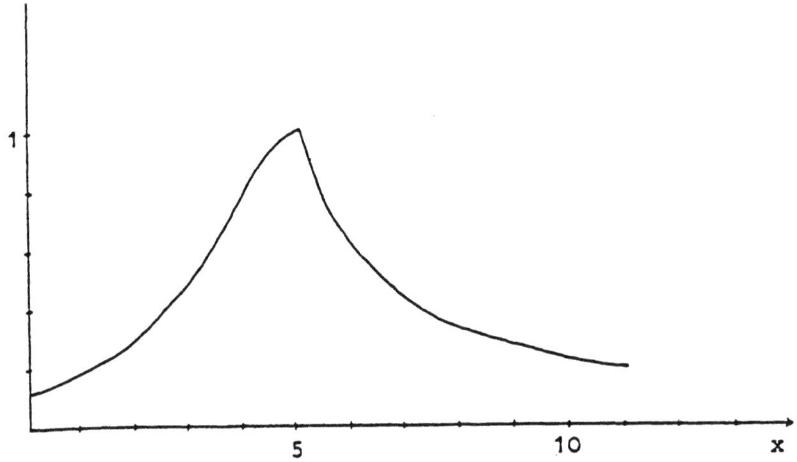

Figure 1: Fuzzy number: "Approximately 5"

Definition: A linguistic variable is characterized by a quintuple $(x, T(x), U, G, M)$ in which x is the name of the variable; $T(x)$ (or simply T) denotes the term-set of x, that is, the set of names of linguistic values of x, with each value being a fuzzy variable denoted generically by x and ranging over a universe of discourse U which is associated with the base variable μ; G is a syntactic rule (which usually has the form of a grammar) for generating the name, X, of values of x; and M is a semantic rule for associating U. A particular X, that is a name generated by G, is called U. It should be noted that the base variable μ can also be vector-valued.

2.1. Basic Operations with Fuzzy Sets

Operations on and with fuzzy sets are defined via their membership functions. In this context it should be realized that the set-theoretic intersection corresponds to the

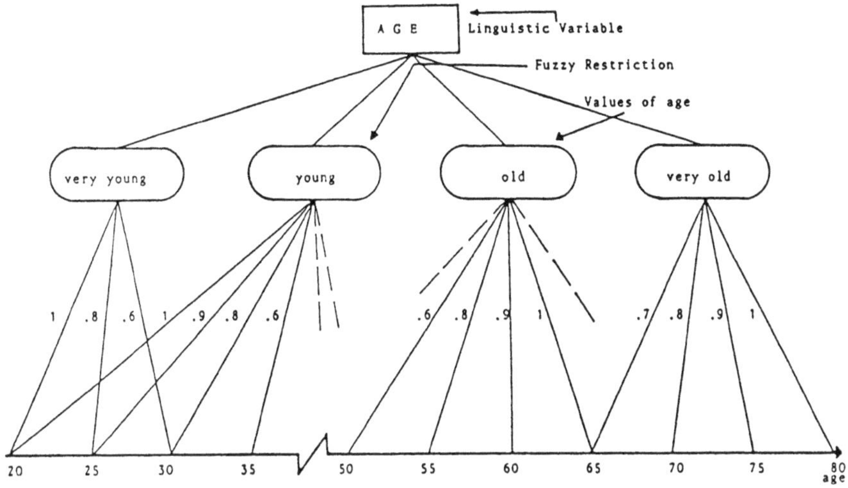

Figure 2: Linguistic variable "Age"

"logical and" and the union to the "inclusive or" in logic, respectively. For the sake of space efficiency we only show definitions for the intersection (and-connective) and general connectives including the logical "and" and "or". The union (or-connective) are defined accordingly.

Let us denote the degrees of membership of fuzzy set A by x and that of B by y. Then the alternative definitions of the membership functions of the intersection of A and B, μ', for binary operations are:

$$\begin{aligned}
\mu' &= \min(x,y) \quad \text{(Zadeh)} \\
&= x \cdot y \quad \text{(Zadeh)} \\
&= \max(0, x+y-1) \quad \text{(Giles)} \\
&= 1 - \min_{p \geq 0}(1, [(1-x)^p + (1-y)^p]^{1/p}) \quad \text{(Yager)} \\
&= \gamma \min(x,y) + (1-\gamma)\tfrac{1}{2}(x+y), \quad \gamma \in [0,1] \quad \text{(Werners)} \\
&= \frac{xy}{\gamma + (1-\gamma)(x+y-xy)} \quad \text{(Hamacher)}
\end{aligned}$$

General connectives: (compensatory and)

$$\begin{aligned}
\mu' &= (xy)^{(1-\gamma)}(1 - [(1-x)(1-y)])^{\gamma}, \quad \gamma \in [0,1] \quad \text{(Zimmerman, Zysno)} \\
&= \gamma \min(x,y) + (1-\gamma)\max(x,y)
\end{aligned}$$

This (non-exhaustive) enumeration already indicates that probability theory, possibility theory, evidence theory in a sense are subsets of fuzzy set theory.
Definition: A fuzzy relation R in the product space $X \times X$ is a fuzzy set $R = \{(x,y), \mu\}$ whose membership function μ associates with each ordered pair (x,y) a grade of membership $\mu \in R$. An n-ary relation in the respective product space is then
Definition: A fuzzy similarity relation is a fuzzy relation which is
reflexive: $\mu(x,x) = 1, \mu(x,y) < 1, x \neq y$

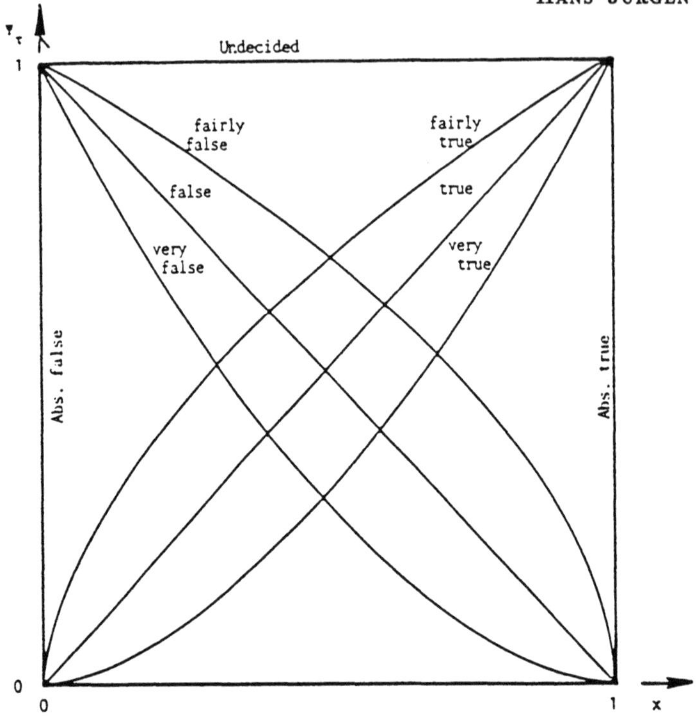

Figure 3: Linguistic variable "Truth"

symmetric: $\mu(x, y) = \mu(y, x)\ \forall\, x, y \in Y$.
max-min transitive: $\mu(x, z) \geq \max\ \min(\mu(x, y), \mu(z, x))$.
Definition: If the membership function of the fuzzy set $B(x) \in Y$, μ', depends on x as a parameter this is denoted by $\mu'(y|x)$. If x ranges over a space X then $\mu'(y|x)$ defines a mapping from X to the space of fuzzy sets defined on Y. In this case a fuzzy set A in X induces a fuzzy set B in Y. The membership function is defined by $\mu' = \sup \min\,(\mu'(x), \mu'(y|x))$.
Definition: An alpha-level set which is a crisp set is defined as

$$R(a) = \{x \in X \mid \mu(x) \geq a\}.$$

3. Fuzzy Set Theory and Clustering

Fuzzy Set Theory has been applied to different kinds of clustering methods. Graph theoretic approaches normally work via alpha-level sets and their results correspond largely to dendrograms.

Here we shall only present models of objective function clustering. These methods work as usual: They first generate crisp partitions, then they assign objects to clusters. For doing that they use degrees of similarity or dissimilarity as objective function. One of the best known of these methods is the fuzzy-c-means algorithm. It uses fuzzy-c-partitions.
Definition: Let X be any finite set. $V(c, n)$ is the set of all real $c \times n$ matrices, $2 \leq c < n$ is integer. The matrix $U(i, k)$ which is contained in $V(c, n)$ is called a fuzzy-c-partition

if it satisfies the following conditions:

1. $\mu(i,k) \in [0,1] : 1 \leq i \leq c, 1 \leq k \leq n$.
2. $\sum_{k=1}^{n} \mu(i,k) < n : 1 \leq i \leq c$.
3. $0 < \sum_{k=1}^{n} \mu(i,k) < n : 1 \leq i \leq c$.

The fuzzy version of the variance criterion used as objective function is then

$$\begin{aligned} \min z(\tilde{U}, v) &= \sum_{i=1}^{c} \sum_{k=1}^{n} (\mu_{ik})^m \|x_k - v_i\|^2 \\ v_i &= [\sum_{k=1}^{n} \mu_{ik}]^{-1} \sum_{k=1}^{n} (\mu_{ik})^m x_k, \quad m > 1 \end{aligned}$$

Here v_i is the mean of the x_k-weighted by their degrees of membership.

One of the differences between classical clustering methods and fuzzy clustering is that objects can be assigned to different clusters to different degrees, thereby often improving the model of the data structure. This shall be illustrated by the following example from [Bezdek 1981]:

Example: The following objects shall be clustered:

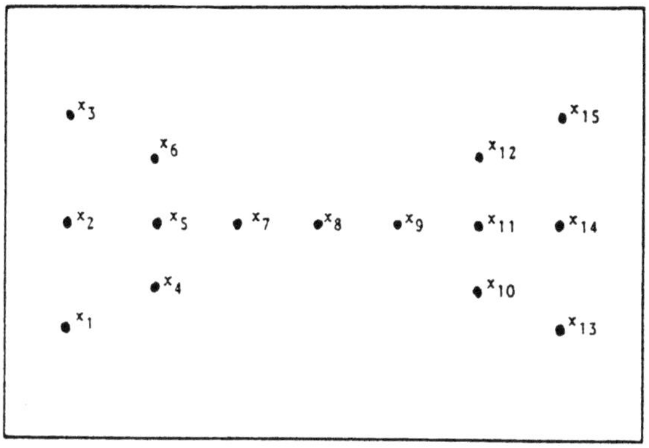

Figure 4: For explanation see text

Two crisp clusters can, for instance, look as in Figure 5.

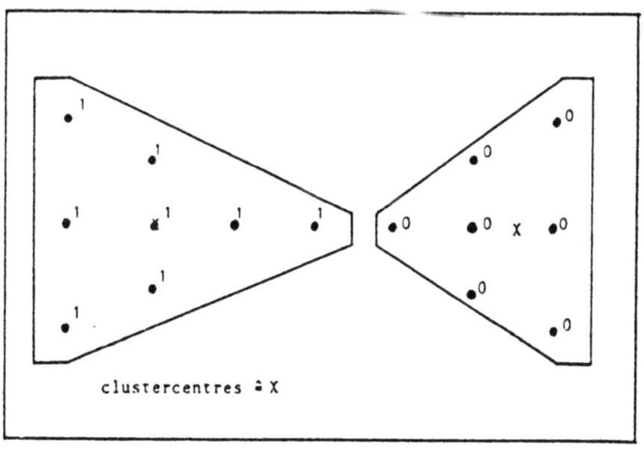

Figure 5: For explanation see text

The two clusters for the Euclidean norm and $m = 2$ in model (1) are shown in Figures 6 and 7.

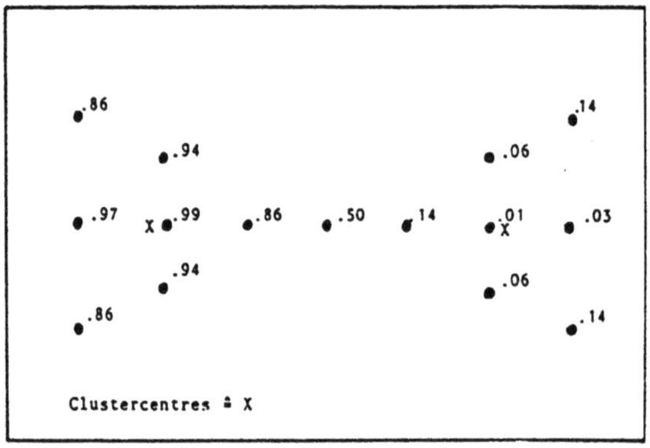

Figure 6: For explanation see text

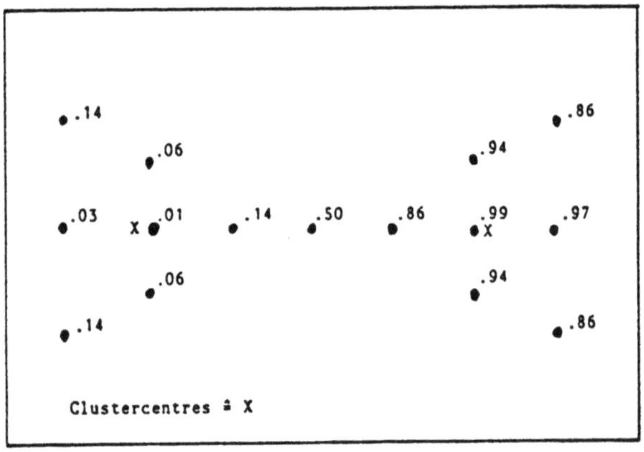

Figure 7: For explanation see text

If $m = 1.25$ is used in model (1) cluster 1 would look slightly different as Figure 8 shows.

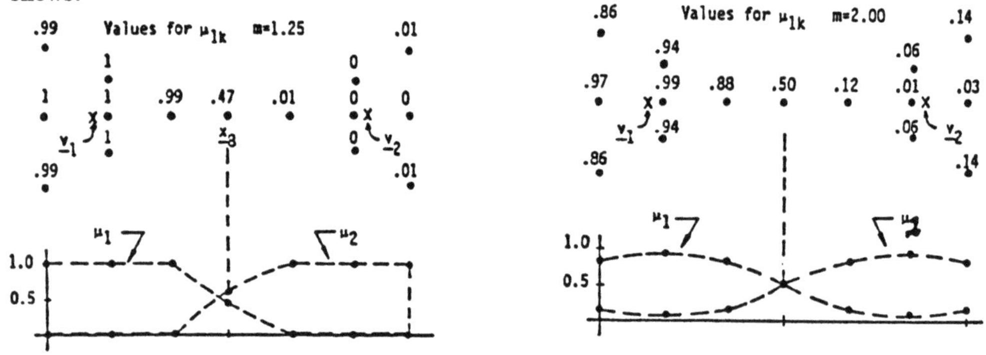

Figure 8: For explanation see text

4. Fuzzy Set Theory and Character Recognition

It was already mentioned that fuzzy set theory has also been applied to a number of other problems in pattern recognition than clustering. The bibliography at the end of this contribution indicates some of those applications. Most of these approaches use either linguistic variables, fuzzy conditional statements or fuzzy algorithms. One of the central components are almost always fuzzy similarity relations. Here we shall just show one example from [Chatterji 1982], which illustrates well the basic approach:

The problem is to recognize handwritten characters.

Each character of the English alphabet is defined by a feature vector which measures the distance from 8 different points in a 20 × 20 binary matrix:

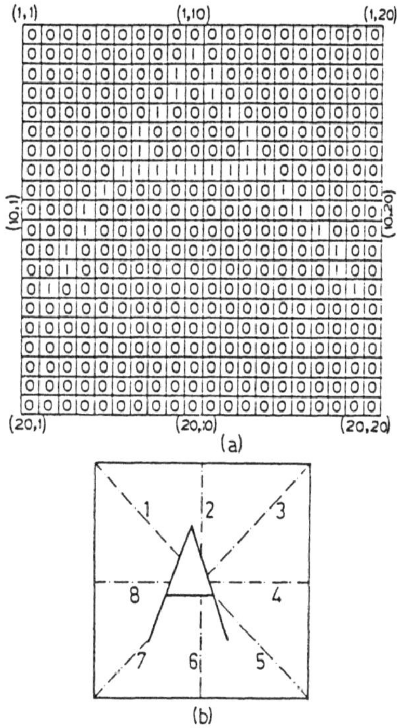

Figure 9: For explanations see text

Standard characters are generated by using the following 8 basic features:

1. Horizontal stroke
2. Vertical stroke
3. Right slant stroke
4. Left slant stroke
5. A curve
6. U curve
7. C curve
8. D curve.

Then the (uppercase English) characters can be described as follows:

English Character	Linguistic Definition	Code
A	Two left slant+two right slant+one horizontal stroke	10220000
B	Two D curves+two vertical stroke	02000002
C	One C curve	00000010
D	One vertical stroke+one D curve	01000001
E	Three horizontal strokes+two vertical strokes	32000000
F	Two horizontal strokes+two vertical strokes	22000000
G	One C curve+one D curve	00000011
H	One horizontal stroke+four vertical strokes	14000000
I	One vertical stroke	01000000
J	Two horizontal stroke+one vertical stroke+one U curve	21000100
K	Two vertical strokes+one left slant+right slant	02110000
L	One horizontal stroke+one vertical stroke	11000000
M	Two vertical strokes+one left slant+one right slant	02110000
N	Two vertical strokes+one left slant	02010000
O	One A curve+one U curve	00001100
P	Two vertical strokes+one D curve	02000001
Q	Two left slants+one C curve+one D curve	00020011
R	Two vertical strokes+one left slant+one D curve	02010001
S	One C curve+one D curve	00000011
T	Two horizontal strokes+one vertical stroke	21000000
U	One U curve	00000100
V	One right slant+one left slant	00110000
W	Two right slants+two left slants	00220000
X	Two right slants+two left slants	00220000

The classification bases on a fuzzy similarity relation with $R = \{(x(i), x(j)), \mu(R)\}$ with

$$\tilde{R} = \{(x_i, x_j), \mu_{\tilde{R}}(x_i, x_j)\} \quad \text{with} \quad \mu_{\tilde{R}}(x_i, x_j) = 1 - [\sum_{k=1}^{8}(a_i^k - a_j^k)^2]^{1/2}$$

This relation is reflexive, symmetric and transitive.

The identification process comprises 8 steps which are described in detail in [Chatterji 1982].

For identification of an unknown character the feature vector is determined first and the similarity relations computed for the standard characters. The pattern with maximum similarity is then determined: here the introduction of a threshold for minimum similarity is possible.

Chatterji reports that the recognition accuracy is approximately 96% and that the recognition time for one character is approximately 1 msec. As primary advantage is considered that no thresholds and only very few restrictions on shape are needed.

References

[1] Bezdek, J.C., Pattern Recognition with Fuzzy Objective Function Algorithms, New York, London 1981.

[2] Bezdek, J.C., Harris, J.D., Fuzzy partitions and relations: An axiomatic basis for clustering, Fuzzy Sets and Systems 1(1978), pp. 111-127.

[3] Cartucci, D., Donati, F., Fuzzy cluster of demand within a regional service system, in: Gupta et al. (edtrs.) 1977, pp. 379-386.

[4] Chatterji, B.N., Character recognition using fuzzy similarity relations, in: Gupta, Sanchez (edtrs.) 1982, pp. 131-138.

[5] De Mori, R., Computer Models of Speech Using Fuzzy Algorithms, New York, London 1983.

[6] Dunn, J.C., Indices of partition fuzziness and the deduction of clusters in large data sets, in: Gupta et al. (edtrs.) 1977, pp. 271-284.

[7] Gupta, M.M., Sanchez, E. (edtrs.), Approximate Reasoning in Decision Analyses, Amsterdam, New York, Oxford 1982.

[8] Gupta, M.M., Saridis, G.N., Gaines, B.R. (edtrs.), Fuzzy Automata and Decision Processes, New York, Amsterdam, Oxford 1977.

[9] Gupta, M.M., Ragade, R.K., Yager, R.R., Advances in Fuzzy Set Theory and Applications, Amsterdam, New York, Oxford 1979.

[10] Gustafson, D.E., Kessel, W.C., Fuzzy clustering with a fuzzy covariance matrix, in: Gupta, M.M. et al. (edtrs.) 1979, pp. 605-620.

[11] Hajnol, M., Koczy, L.T., Classification of textures by vectorial fuzzy sets, in: Gupta, Sanchez (edtrs.) 1982, pp. 157-164.

[12] Kandel, A., Fuzzy Techniques in Pattern Recognition, New York, Chichester, Brisbane, Toronto 1982.

[13] Libert, G., Roubens, M., Non metric fuzzy clustering algorithms and their cluster validity, in: Gupta, Sanchez (edtrs.) 1982 pp. 417-426.

[14] Ovchinnikov, S.V., Riera T., On fuzzy classifications in: Yager, R.R. (edtr.) 1982, pp. 119-132.

[15] Pedrycz, W., An identification algorithm in fuzzy relational systems, in: Fuzzy Sets and Systems, 13 (1984) pp. 153-167.

[16] Roubens, M., Pattern classification problems and fuzzy sets, in: Fuzzy Sets and Systems, 1 (1978), pp. 239-253.

[17] Ruspini, E.H., Recent developments in fuzzy clustering, in: Yager, R.R. (edtr.) 1982, pp. 133-143.

[18] Windham, M.P., Cluster validity for fuzzy clustering algorithms, in: Fuzzy Sets and Systems 10 (1983), pp. 177-185.

[19] Windham, M.P., Geometric fuzzy clustering algorithms, in: Fuzzy Sets and Systems 10 (1983), pp. 271-279.

[20] Yager, R.R. (edtr.), Fuzzy Sets and Possibility Theory, New York, Oxford, Toronto, Sidney 1982.

[21] Zimmermann, H.-J, Fuzzy Set Theory and its Applications, Boston, Dordrecht, Lancaster 1985.

CLASSIFICATION PROBLEM SOLVING: A TUTORIAL FROM AN AI PERSPECTIVE

Bruce Chandrasekaran and Anne Keuneke

Laboratory for Artificial Intelligence Research
Department of Computer & Information Science
The Ohio State University
Columbus, OH 43210, USA

Abstract

This paper is a tutorial discussion on classification problem solving, especially hierarchical classification. First we compare how pattern recognition and AI approaches to classification differ by pointing out how knowledge provides leverage against complexity, and thus point to the rationale behind knowledge-based systems. But we critique much of the work in knowledge-based systems, showing that important distinctions between various generic problem solving activities are often obscured by concentration on the implementation level of abstraction, such as "rules", "logic", or "frames". We then argue that a generic task approach facilitates problem analysis, system design, knowledge acquisition and explanation of problem solving. We describe MDX, a medical diagnosis system that performs knowledge-based hierarchical classification, and motivate a number of issues in classification from that perspective. We also describe a high-level language called CSRL that is specially designed for hierarchical classification problem solving and show its power and utility.

1. Introduction

In this paper, we present a tutorial describing issues involved in classification problem solving. Most of these ideas have been introduced in earlier papers from our laboratory:[6], [8], [9], [10], [3]. The purpose of this paper is to guide the reader through a progression of approaches to classification problem solving to illustrate how knowledge of the *domain* and of the *task* reduces the computational complexity and aids in system building. The flow of the argument is as follows:

1. We trace the evolution of pattern recognition techniques to complex knowledge-based operations.

2. We describe knowledge-based systems as envisioned through the rule-based approach and include a brief overview of the widely known rule-based system, MYCIN, as it performs classification.

3. We motivate a need for a higher level understanding of classification as a problem solving task, and then describe MDX, a medical diagnostic system that explicitly performs knowledge-based classification.

NATO ASI Series, Vol. F30
Pattern Recognition Theory and Applications
Edited by P. A. Devijver and J. Kittler

4. We describe CSRL, a high level language which facilitates the development of classification systems by supporting constructs which represent classification knowledge at appropriate levels of abstraction.

5. We discuss the power and utility of approaching problem solving from this perspective of matching techniques to tasks.

1.1. The Classification Task

Classification is a useful and powerful method of knowledge organization for comprehension and problem solving. In the sciences examples of its use are common. Taxonomic or hierarchical classification has long been a significant methodology in biology. Linnaeus' classification scheme is very well known, and more recently mathematical taxonomy has been used for providing better classifications in this area [25]. The periodic table of elements in chemistry is a masterful example of how man has classified patterns in nature to great advantage.

With the advent of computers, new sciences solved new problems, but the use of classification remained. In fact, in the early days of Pattern Recognition, the problem of recognition was formulated as a problem of classification, in particular one of *statistical classification*. Even when newer techniques, such as *syntactic approaches*, came into the field the problem was still often formulated as a classification problem, this time into grammatical categories.

In Expert Systems, a subarea of Artificial Intelligence, the objective is to capture in computer programs, explicitly and in symbolic form, the *knowledge and problem solving methods* of human experts in selected domains and tasks. If one were to examine the nature of the tasks of the current generation of expert systems, a fact emerges: most of them solve variants of problems which are intrinsically classificatory in nature.

Let us take some examples:

1. MYCIN [24], in its diagnostic phase, has the task of classifying patient data in an infectious agent hierarchy.

2. PROSPECTOR [14] classifies a geological description as corresponding to one or more mineral formation classes.

3. MDX [6,7] explicitly views a significant portion of the diagnostic task as classifying a complex description (the patient data) as an element in a disease classification hierarchy (e.g., liver disease, in particular hepatitis).

4. SACON [1] classifies structural analysis problems into classes for each of which a particular family of analysis methods will be appropriate.

This is by no means to imply that all problems are classification problems, or that all can be usefully converted into such problems. Rather it is important to note that classification seems to be a rather ubiquitous problem solving process, and a number of real world problems can be thought of as having a large classification component. Further, classification has been one of the more *tractable* problems for knowledge-based system technology to handle at this point in its development.

1.2. Why this Ubiquity? The Computational Power of Classification

Why is classification so powerful? A simple computational explanation can be given for the importance of classification as an *information processing strategy.* One can think of the task of an intelligent agent as performing actions on the world in order to accomplish certain goals. Typically the correct action is a function of the state of the world. For example, one can think of the general problem facing the physician as having the following formal character: for each subset of possible symptoms (each *state of the patient*), find an appropriate therapeutic action. But in general the cardinality of the relevant states of the world will be too large to permit each state to be stored explicitly. A table relating all subsets of state variables to actions is bound to be too large for construction, looking up, and modification. This problem is made more tractable, however, if action knowledge can be indexed, not by the states of the world, but by *equivalence classes of states of the world.* Thus a physician's therapeutic knowledge is not indexed directly by the detailed values of the patient state variables, but by diseases each of which can be thought of as defining an equivalence class of patient state variables. The medical problem solving can then be organized, first as mapping from symptoms to disease classes (diagnosis as classification), and then from disease classes to therapeutic actions. Since the number of equivalence classes is much smaller than the number of states, the complexity of the mapping is now considerably reduced.

Thus classification into categories provides a great computational advantage. Much of human thinking is organized around classification, both in creating useful classifications (concept learning) and in using existing categories to perform classifications of particular situations or objects. In this paper our concern is with the latter. By tracing an evolution of problem solving techniques for this process, we hope to give the reader a better grasp of the complexity issues involved, and also show how information processing strategies can be used to circumvent these complexity problems.

2. Pattern Recognition : Knowledge versus Complexity

2.1. The Statistical Classification Paradigm

The typical model in this domain is one where the aim is to arrive at a classification of a multidimensional vector, representing an object of unknown classification, into one of a finite number of classes. Each dimension typically represents an attribute of the object that the system designer has had reason to believe carries useful information about class membership. Intuitively, one would try to choose attributes such that they have the potential to distinguish between classes. Indeed, Kanal and Chandrasekaran [17] pointed out that despite the enormous intrinsic interest of the mathematical problem of designing and improving classification algorithms, the real power often comes from the careful choice of the variables themselves, based on a good knowledge of the domain.

In this model, when the number of dimensions is small it is possible to design classification systems that outperform human experts in that task domain. But what happens when the dimensionality of the vector gets to be very large, or the number of classes gets to be large? In general, when the number of classes increases, in order to make more and more distinctions the number of measurements on the object (*i.e.*, the dimensionality of the pattern vector) will also need to grow rapidly. The complexity of the algorithm to make the discrimination grows much more rapidly, and correspondingly the average performance (*i.e.*, correct classification rate) deteriorates quite rapidly. Sensitivity problems begin to become severe; the required precision of the parameters in the classification algorithm becomes impractically high. Opacity problems result; it becomes increasingly hard to make any kind of statement about what attributes are playing what role in the recognition process. These problems exist whether statistical classification algorithms are used, or perceptron-like linear threshold devices are used. Szolovits and Pauker [26] discuss some of the problems with the Bayesian approaches, and Minsky and Papert [18] the problems with the latter.

2.2. Abstraction by Intermediate Concepts

What is to be done when the number of classes is very large? It is possible to reduce the complexity by a two-fold strategy of *symbolization* and *hierarchicalization*. Instead of doing the classification by a direct discriminant function mapping, intermediate symbols can be constructed, which are then used as attributes to a higher-level classification process. Symbols at each level are produced by a classificatory process using the symbols from the previous level as attributes. Each such computational process is much more tractable.

2.2.1. Signature tables

Consider an example: evaluation functions in chess. These functions usually yield a number which is a measure of the "goodness" of the board. For most purposes, effective use of this information can be made if the goodness is classified into one of a small number of categories. One of the first forms for the evaluation functions was a linear polynomial of attributes of the board; both the attributes and their weights were chosen in consultation with domain experts. Then in order to take into account interactions between the variables in the evaluation function, higher order polynomials were later proposed. This of course resulted in a fairly rapid increase in the complexity of the function. Samuel's *signature tables* [23] provided a solution which exemplifies the symbolization and hierarchicalization ideas mentioned earlier. For the purposes of our discussion, Samuel's method can be described as follows.

1. Identify groups of attributes such that on the basis of domain knowledge there is reason to believe that they contribute to an intermediate abstraction that can be used to construct the final abstraction, in this case, a measure of the "goodness" of the board. In chess, "defensibility of king" and "material advantage" may be such intermediate concepts, each of which can be estimated by a subset of board attributes, while the final decision about the goodness of a board configuration may be made in terms of these intermediate abstractions.

2. Find a method of *classifying* the desirability of these intermediate concepts into a small number of categories from the values of the attributes in each group.

3. The outputs of the classifiers for each group can themselves be thought of as qualitative attributes at the next level of abstraction. These can be grouped and

abstracted into higher level concepts as necessary until the top-level concept is a classification of the "goodness" of the board in a qualitative way.

By trading off the precision of numbers for the simplicity and robustness of a small number of symbolic states, and combining it with hierarchical abstractions, significant computational advantage is being gained. This also points to the fact that often *numbers are too precise* for the task at hand. Robust symbolic abstractions of the appropriate kind can capture almost all of the relevant information.

2.3. Syntactic or Structural Approaches

After about a decade of work within the statistical classification paradigm Narasimhan [20] proposed what he called a *syntactic approach* to pattern recognition. The idea was to describe classes of patterns, not in terms of probability distributions in multidimensional spaces, nor in terms of hierarchic symbolic abstractions, but in terms of *relations between symbols*, much as grammatical categories are described in linguistic analysis. We will not describe the principles of syntactic methods here, but for our purposes the following point should be made: *The ability to describe a class in terms of relations is a move towards descriptions as the basis for class characterization.*

Note that the idea of syntactic pattern recognition is really a special case of the more general notion of *structural relations* as the basis of class characterization. Thus, even when the idea of *syntax* is not appropriate — it is very doubtful that the notion of a picture grammar is as general for the domain of visual objects as seems from a purely formal perspective — the notion of structural relations as the basis for characterizing concepts and classes is a somewhat more general one.

With the introduction of *syntactic/structural models* for pattern recognition, the progression becomes:

$$\text{numbers} \rightarrow \text{symbols} \rightarrow \text{relations.}$$

The major research directions in pattern recognition for capturing structural relations in general were *formal*, *i.e.*, some sort of a mathematical system within which theorems about relationships may be provable regarding the classification performance. In fact, this was the major reason for the original emphasis on syntactic methods, since there was a well-developed theory of formal grammars already available. In any case, the emphasis on formalisms led to two constraints: one, often an attempt was made to force-fit available formalisms to the pattern recognition problem, generally with unsatisfactory results; and two, because human classification performance was more heuristic in nature, restricted formalisms could capture the quality of human performance only fleetingly.

If one is to use relations between symbolic attributes as the basis of class characterization, why restrict oneself to *syntactic* relations? Why not bring to bear the full power, to the extent possible or necessary, the *semantics* of the classes in forming class descriptions? Asking this question prepares the way for the next step in the progression, the AI/Knowledge-Based paradigm:

$$\text{numbers} \rightarrow \text{symbols} \rightarrow \text{relations} \rightarrow \text{complex symbolic descriptions.}$$

These complex descriptions characterizing the classes are the aspects of the domain knowledge relevant for the task.

3. AI/Knowledge-Based Reasoning

3.1. A New Paradigm

It is not an exaggeration to say that the knowledge-based approach in general, and to classification in particular, is a *new paradigm* in the sense that it emphasizes different issues, and poses them in a different language. Instead of issues such as "optimality" and "error rate," which figure in the classical pattern recognition approach, the AI paradigm emphasizes the issues of "knowledge representation" and "control of problem solving". These relate to how the domain knowledge in explicit symbolic form is *represented* (i.e, what language is used to encode the knowledge), *organized*, *accessed*, and *used* to arrive at classificatory conclusions.

As is typical of a science in its infancy, there does not yet exist a single universally accepted paradigm for AI. The basic issues of knowledge representations and control are the same, but approaches vary widely. Since the early success of GPS [21] many researchers have concentrated on developing *uniform mechanisms* to explain and produce knowledge. This has led some to believe that all knowledge can be represented as sentences in a logical calculus, others to adhere to a language of rules, and still others that believe a language of frames is appropriate. Since systems built on these primitives offer the desired trait of computational universality, *i.e.*, *any* computer program can be built in these languages, these constructs are often accepted as the proper level on which to approach problem solving. Unfortunately, use of these constructs often cause a loss of perspicuity of representation at the task level. That is, such knowledge representations and control regimes rarely capture distinctions regarding *what* problems are being solved. Let us look closely at one of these methodologies to see exactly how problem solving is accomplished and what knowledge is used.

3.2. The Rule-Based Approach

The Production System (or equivalently Rule-Based System) is a problem solving methodology that is modeled after a system described by Post [22] in 1943. The model has three main parts: a *rule base* consisting of a set of rules, an *inference engine* to control the system's activity, and a *data base* of working memory which holds specific case data (either given to or deduced by the system).

Rules are a particular kind of knowledge representation. Typically they are a set of condition-action pairs of the form:

```
IF    (   condition 1
          & condition 2
              ⋮
          & condition n  )
THEN  (   action 1
          action 2
              ⋮          )
```

In a standard system, conditions of rules are matched against facts in the data base (working memory), and the action portions write facts into the data base. The rules contain the domain knowledge or *expertise* of the system.

The flow of control is a select-execute (situation-action) cycle. Within each cycle the inference engine goes through three phases:

1. Rule Interpreter — Picks *all* the rules that apply to the current system state
2. Conflict Resolution — From the list of rules chosen by the Rule Interpreter as applicable, choose the rule(s) to fire.
3. Execution — Performs the action indicated by the selected rule(s).

There are two basic mechanisms for matching rules in Production Systems. If the interpreter matches against the *conditions* of rules (commonly called the left-hand side), the approach is *data-driven* and the method of inference is called *forward chaining*. This process is *deductive* and adds facts which are believed to be true to the knowledge base. The system is finished when there are no more rules that have condition parts that match the data. If one desires a *goal-driven* approach, the system should use *backward chaining*. Here the interpreter matches the *action* portion and when a match is found the system tries to establish conditions of the matched rule (the conditions thus become subgoals). The reasoning is *hypothesis-match* and the process is complete when either the goal is established or a subgoal cannot be established.

We have already used medical diagnosis as an example to illustrate some of the ideas in this paper. In discussing the AI approach, the medical diagnosis example is particularly useful, since a number of AI systems have been built in this domain, and also the computational advantages of such an approach can be well motivated. To illustrate the use of rule-based systems we will briefly describe the MYCIN [24] system which was designed to provide consultative advise on diagnosis and therapy for infectious diseases.

3.2.1. MYCIN

As is prescribed by rule-based systems, MYCIN's knowledge is encoded in the form of rules and the system uses a separate inference engine for control of reasoning. A sample rule is given to illustrate the knowledge MYCIN possess:

```
PREMISE (AND (SAME CNTXT INFECT PRIMARY-BACTEREMIA)
             (MEMBER CNTXT SITE STERILESITES)
             (SAME CNTXT PORTAL GI) )
ACTION  (CONCLUDE CNTXT IDENT BACTEROIDES TALLY .7)
```

MYCIN's English translation:

IF 1) the infection is primary-bacteremia, and
2) the site of the culture is one of the sterile sites, and
3) the suspected portal of entry of the organism is the gastrointestinal tract,

THEN there is suggestive evidence (.7) that the identity of the organism is bacteroides

A rule premise (the set of conditions in a rule) is always a conjunction of clauses but it may contain arbitrarily complex conjunctions or disjunctions nested within a clause.

For the diagnostic stage of processing, MYCIN's "goal" is to determine significant infections. MYCIN's basic control strategy is thus goal-driven *backward chaining* in an *exhaustive depth-first* search of an AND/OR goal tree. That is, it retrieves all rules that make a conclusion about the identity in question and invokes each in turn, evaluating each premise clause to determine if the condition specified has been met. The search is depth-first since each premise condition is thoroughly explored in turn, and the tree is AND/OR since the rules can have disjunctions in a clause.

For a measurement of the association between a premise and action clause of a rule, MYCIN uses a certainty factor. These factors indicate how strongly the clause should be believed. A value of 1 indicates complete confidence that the proposition is true, while -1 indicates complete confidence that it is false. During the backward chaining process, if after trying all relevant rules to resolve a subgoal, the total weight (MYCIN has a rule for combining certainty factors) of the evidence about a hypothesis falls between $-.2$ and $.2$, the answer is regarded as still unknown. In this situation the system asks the user for the value of the subgoal in order to continue processing. The diagnostic portion of MYCIN is complete when it concludes what bacterial infection(s) might be present.

What is the nature of the *problem solving task* accomplished by MYCIN? In medical terms, MYCIN uses clinical findings and decides what bacterial infection might be present. In domain-independent terms, the system is *classifying* a set of observables to a plausible hypothesis. Where is the knowledge of how this classificatory task was performed? The only explicit control mechanisms in rule-based systems are the variants of *hypothesis and match* (forward or backward chaining). The knowledge-level of rule systems is exhausted by condition-action pairs; there are no constructs for knowledge structures such as goal structures or plans. The task-specific *classification* control structure is thus hidden, either in inference engine additions or cleverly formulated rules within the knowledge-base. In systems designed in this manner, it often becomes unclear which portions of the system represent domain knowledge and which are programming devices.[1]

3.3. Classification as a Generic Task

Ideally one would like to represent knowledge in a domain by using the vocabulary that is appropriate for the task. For example, in diagnostic reasoning, one might wish to speak in terms of malfunction hierarchies, rule-out strategies, setting up a differential, etc., while for design, the generic terms might be device/component hierarchies, design plans, ordering of subtasks, etc. To do so, however, requires an understanding of the generic information processing tasks that underlie knowledge-based reasoning.

[1]These comments need not be restricted to the rule-based framework. One could represent knowledge as sentences in a logical calculus and use logical inference mechanisms to solve problems, or one could represent it as a frame hierarchy with procedural attachments in the slots. In the former, the control issues would deal with choice of predicates and clauses, and in the latter, they will be at the level of which links to pursue for inheritance, etc. None of these have any natural connection with the control issues natural to the task.

Knowledge should be directly encoded at the appropriate level by using primitives that naturally describe the domain knowledge for a given task. Problem solving behavior for the task ought to be controlled by regimes that are appropriate for the task. If done correctly, this would simultaneously facilitate knowledge representation, problem solving, and explanation.

We will show an application of such a methodology by describing the medical diagnosis system MDX [6,7] which has been developed in our Laboratory over the past several years for classification problems.

3.3.1. The MDX system

The MDX system performs medical diagnosis essentially by viewing the task as one of *classifying* a complex case description as a node in a disease classification hierarchy.[2] The *control problem* here can be stated as one that deals with which classificatory hypothesis to consider at what point in problem solving. In general, for problem solving efficiency, we would like to use domain knowledge to consider only a subset of all the hypotheses or we would like to consider some hypotheses which are more promising ahead of others.

The MDX system is organized as a hierarchical collection of "diagnostic concepts" or "specialists", each of which has diagnostic knowledge that helps it make a determination about the relevance of that hypothesis (at that level of abstraction) to the case at hand. This hierarchy of specialists mirrors the diagnostic classification hierarchy. The total diagnostic knowledge is then *distributed* through the conceptual nodes of the hierarchy.

The problem-solving regime that is implicit in the structure is that of *establish-refine*. That is, each concept first tries to establish or reject. When a concept establishes it means that the concept is relevant and should be considered in further detail. If a concept succeeds in establishing then it refines by passing control to its successors, each of which will try to establish or reject. This technique is performed top down, *i.e.*, the top-most concept first gets control of the case, then control passes to successor concepts, and so on. Large portions of the diagnostic knowledge structure never get exercised, since when a concept rules itself out from relevance to a case, all its successors also get ruled out. On the other hand, when a concept is properly invoked, a small, highly relevant body of knowledge comes into play.

In the medical example, a fragment of such a hierarchy might be as shown in Figure 1.

More general classificatory concepts are higher in the structure, while more particular ones are lower in the hierarchy. It is as if INTERNIST first establishes that there is in fact a disease, then LIVER establishes that the case at hand is a liver disease, while say HEART, etc., reject the case as being not in their domain. After this level, JAUNDICE may establish itself and so on.

Each of the concepts in the classification hierarchy has "how-to" knowledge (criteria for establishment). It is the task of each concept to compare case-specific data with its compiled prototypical knowledge in order to indicate if the hypothesis it represents is worth considering. Notice that *how* such a decision is made within a specialist is

[2] Although MDX performs in the medical domain, it should be noted that the techniques described are domain-independent. That is, the methodology is extendable to other domains (e.g., mechanical diagnosis). This, indeed, is the point of *generic* tasks.

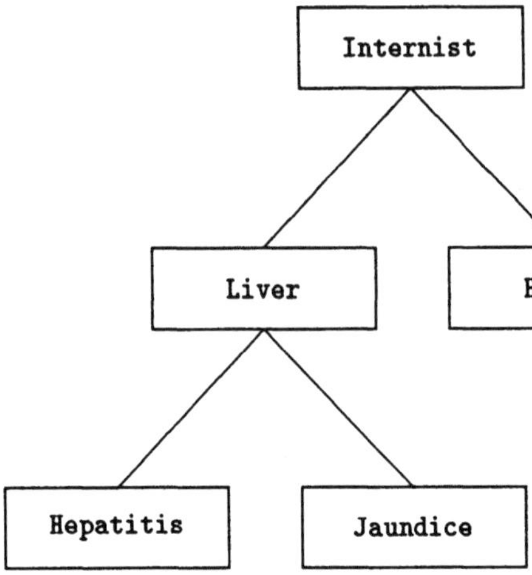

Figure 1: Fragment of a hierarchy

irrelevant to the classifier (qua classifier). Thus each specialist can use a method of problem solving which best fits the task specification and knowledge available.[3]

In MDX, knowledge of the hypothesis is represented as a collection of *diagnostic rules* of the form: ⟨symptoms⟩ → ⟨concept in hierarchy⟩, e.g., "If high SGOT, add n units of evidence in favor of cholestasis." Within each concept these rules are partitioned into several clusters: confirmatory rules, exclusionary rules, and perhaps some recommendation rules. The evidence for confirmation and exclusion can be suitably weighted and combined to arrive at a conclusion to establish, reject or suspend it. Suspension may arise if there is not sufficient data to make a decision. Recommendation rules are further optimization devices to reduce the work of the subconcepts. Further discussion of this type of rules is not necessary for our current purpose.

The concepts in the hierarchy are clearly not a static collection of knowledge. They are active in problem-solving. They also have knowledge only about establishing or rejecting the relevance of that conceptual entity. Thus they may be termed "specialists", in particular, "diagnostic specialists". The entire collection of specialists engages in distributed problem-solving. Classification in MDX is complete when all specialists who are able to establish themselves have done so.

What is the nature of the *problem solving task* accomplished by MDX? Clearly MDX is performing classification. Through the high level control abstraction of *establish-refine* and the knowledge representation and organization of *diagnostic specialists*, knowledge of classification problem solving is *explicitly* available.

It is obvious that classification is not the only problem solving task involved in diagnosis. As a classification problem solver MDX may output a list of disease hy-

[3]In simple cases, statistical classification algorithms can be used. In DART [15] the decision about the fit of hypothesis to data is done by using theorem-proving techniques. In [19] we show how the concepts can make their decisions based on a causal knowledge of the domain. The point is that *how* the hypotheses are evaluated is somewhat independent of the flow of control for the classificatory task as such, even though for complex problems, a rich knowledge structure will be called for to make the decision about how well the hypothesis matches the case at hand.

potheses which are considered likely, *i.e.*, more than one specialist may establish. To complete diagnosis, it may be desirable to make a decision concerning which group of these hypotheses are required and/or necessary. An extension to MDX which generates a composite hypotheses that best explains the data is realized through the generic task *abductive assembly* [16].

3.4. A High Level Tool for Classification Problem Solving

The MDX system is a complex system that has been tested on a number of real-world cases with a high match between its conclusions and that of specialists. In order to facilitate the building of expert systems which use classification we have designed and implemented a representation language for the classification task. Just as EMYCIN [27] is a domain-independent system with the basic control structure of MYCIN, our CSRL [3] is a domain-independent system with the basic control structure for classification problem solving.

3.4.1. CSRL

CSRL (Conceptual Structures Representation Language) is a language for representing the specialists of a classification hierarchy and the knowledge within them. Since this tool was implemented prior to the development of a specific tool for hypothesis matching, CSRL was designed to handle both the problem solving for the classification task and for establishment of hypothesis within the classification hierarchy. It is assumed that a user has performed an analysis of the domain and is confident that the task requires classification. In addition, since CSRL is specifically for *hierarchical classification* the implementor must choose between different ways to classify the domain so that the following criteria are met:[4]

1. For each specialist there must be evidence to confidently establish or reject the hypothesis, especially for general specialists.

2. Evidence to determine confidence is normally available, *i.e.*, accessible.

3. General specialists provide good differential contexts, *i.e.*, there is evidence to differentiate specialists from siblings.

4. Specialists are subtypes of superspecialists

5. Classification can make desired statements, *i.e.*, identify the objects required.

Since the control strategy for classification is explicitly defined and accomplished by the tool, the user need only supply the proper primitives: in this case, define the specialists. Each specialist must be individually defined. An example definition for a "BadFuel" specialist for an automobile diagnostic system is:

[4]For a more detailed specification of the criteria for building a classification hierarchy, the reader is directed to Bylander and Smith [5].

```
(Specialist BadFuel
      (declare (superspecialist FuelSystem)
               (subspecialists LowOctane WaterInFuel DirtInFuel))
      (kgs ...)
      (messages ...))
```

The declaration specifies its relation to other specialists. By thus defining the specialists, the hierarchy is established and CSRL's control strategy of *establish/refine* can be used to accomplish the classification.

Each specialists' definition also specifies knowledge groups (kgs) and messages. Possible messages include "Establish", "Refine", "Establish-Refine", and "Suggest". The meaning of these messages are predefined in CSRL; additional messages may be defined by the user. An establish message for the above defined BadFuel is illustrated as follows:

```
(Establish (if (GE relevant 0)
            then (SetConfidence self summary)
            else (SetConfidence self relevant)))
```

Here "relevant" and "summary" refer to kgs defined within BadFuel. "Self" refers to the specialist itself. Confidence values are integers from −3 to 3. In CSRL, confidence values are used locally (within specialists) to measure the relevance of the specific specialist to the given case. The reader is referred to Chandrasekaran and Tanner [11] for explanation and justification of this local confidence schema.

The above message is interpreted as, "Check to see if BadFuel is a relevant hypothesis (the relevant kg has a value of 0 or greater). If so, determine the summary kg. and set the confidence to that value." Confidence values must be +2 or +3 for a specialist to establish. If a subspecialist establishes itself (+? tests confidence values), then it is sent a Refine message:

```
(Refine (for specialists in subspecialist
      do (Call Specialist with Establish)
         (if (+? Specialist)
            then (Call Specialist with Refine))))
```

Knowledge groups are used to evaluate how the case specific data compares with the prototypical knowledge of the specialist. The default reasoning available through CSRL for this reasoning is hypothesis matching. Capabilities are also present for the user to define other methodologies.

Knowledge groups are helpful in forming hierarchical representations of evidence abstractions to be used for hypothesis matching. More specifically, in the knowledge group formalism, low level data are combined to evaluate higher level abstractions. The resulting certainty about the abstractions is then combined to evaluate still higher abstractions. This hierarchical evaluation produces an evaluation of the overall certainty of the hypothesis.[5] Data that the domain expert uses to evaluate a hypothesis is encoded as expressions in the kgs. During a diagnosis, in order to obtain case-specific data for a kg match the specialist can make queries either to a separate database or to the user of the system. Consider a possible "relevant" kg of our BadFuel Specialist:

[5] as in Samuel's signature tables

```
(relevant Table
   (match
      (AskYNU? "Is the car slow to respond?")
      (AskYNU? "Does the car start hard?")
      (And (AskYNU? "Do you hear knocking or pinging sounds?")
           (AskYNU? "Does the problem occur while accelerating?"))
      with (if T ? ? then -3
           elseif ? T ? then -3
           elseif ? ? T then 3
           else 1 )))
```

The relevant kg determines the values of queries (AskYNU = Ask_Yes_No_Unknown). The first set of tests in the if-then section that matches the queries ("?" means "doesn't matter") determines the value of the kg. This table thus indicates that if the user hears pinging and has problems with accelerating then the problem may very likely be in BadFuel. Otherwise this hypothesis is not valid. The summary kg will combine information gained from the relevant and gas knowledge groups of BadFuel to determine a composite hypothesis confidence value for the specialist.

```
(summary Table
   (match relevant gas
      with (If 3 (GE 0) then 3
         elseIf 1 (GE 0) then 2
         elseIf ? (LT 0) then -3)))
```

The task of a builder of a CSRL classification system thus can be summarized as: (1) determine the hierarchy and (2) define the specialists. Since the knowledge of specialists is localized, the problem solving and implementation becomes quite tractable. Through the explicit structure of the system we gain the advantages of system predictability, ease of debugging, and system extensibility. For more information on this tool the reader is referred to Bylander, *et al.*[3].

3.5. Generic Tasks in the Design of Expert Systems

If expert systems are to be used for consultation or advice, they will need to *explain* their knowledge and problem solving in order to be acceptable and useful. This explanation is difficult to obtain in many current expert systems because of the paucity of "knowledge-level" primitives recognized by the languages in which they have been implemented. More specifically, the epistemology of rule systems is exhausted by data patterns (antecedents or subgoals) and partial decisions (consequents or goals), that of logic is similarly by predicates, functions, and related primitives. If one wishes to talk about types of goals or predicates in such a way that control behavior can be indexed over this typology, such a behavior can often be programmed in these systems, but there is no explicit encoding of them that is possible. An illustration of this is found in Clancey's [12] work using MYCIN to teach students. Here he found it was necessary to attach to each rule in the knowledge base an explanatory skeleton which could encode the role of the rule in problem solving. Explanation of system behavior could thus be couched in terms of this encoding rather than only in terms of "Because $\langle \cdots \rangle$ was a subgoal of $\langle \cdots \rangle$."

We have seen how the use of abstractions at a *classification task level* can facilitate problem solving of that type. Because of the power that is available in the control abstractions that are indexed by the generic task, explanation in these systems can arise directly from the control behavior in the problem solving process.[8]

In general, information processing systems which are analyzed and implemented using a framework of generic tasks with associated types of knowledge and a family of control regimes benefit through the following advantages: (i) Since typically the generic tasks are at a much higher level of abstraction than those associated with first generation expert system languages, knowledge can be represented directly at the level appropriate to the information processing task. (ii) Since each of the generic tasks has an appropriate control regime, problem solving behavior may be more perspicuously encoded. (iii) Because of a richer generic vocabulary in terms of which knowledge and control are represented, explanation of problem solving is also more perspicuous.

3.5.1. Related work

In [13], Clancey also clearly identifies "heuristic classification" as an explicit reasoning activity. Similar to our analysis, he shows how a number of expert systems can be thought of as performing classification. There are a number of points of contact, as well as important differences, between his and our perspectives on the problem. While Clancey identifies heuristic classification as an identifiable information processing phenomenon, for him it is not an information processing "building block" in the sense of having a clear and simple control structure and knowledge primitives associated with it. More explicitly, Clancey's model of classification problem solving is illustrated as:

		HEURISTIC MATCH		
	data abstraction	$\Longrightarrow$	solution abstraction	
DATA ABSTRACTION	$\Downarrow$		$\Downarrow$	REFINEMENT
	data		solution	

From our perspective, the left side of the figure, *i.e.*, the data abstraction part of heuristic classification, is not a part of *classification*, but rather a separate problem solving activity which we call *knowledge-directed data retriever/abstractor*. This reasoning process is not unique to classification. Instead it is an identifiable task, with its own knowledge and control structure, whose functionality is available for other problem solving methods as well.

Thus "heuristic classification", in our view, consists of a classification component which interacts with a knowledge-directed data retriever. On the other hand, our classification is really "hierarchical classification" and more general classification problems may require a more complex mixture of different problem solving types. See [4] for further discussion on this topic.

4. Concluding Remarks

We have taken the reader through a progression of approaches for classification: numerical measures, symbolic abstractions, structural relations, and various knowledge structures. At each stage, more power was gained for controlling the computational complexity by matching the structure of the classifier to the complex structure of the task.

Many of the points made in this paper transcend the particular task of classification. A system is enhanced with extra knowledge, whether it is knowledge of the domain *or* knowledge of problem solving capabilities. Our approach is to utilize the form and organization of knowledge and control structures which are specific to a task as a means of providing explicit knowledge of problem solving. This paper proposes an appropriate level of abstraction at which to discuss the issues in the design of knowledge-based problem solving.

We have designed and implemented representation languages for simple versions of two generic tasks: classification (CSRL) [3], and object synthesis by plan selection and refinement (DSPL) [2]. Work is near completion on our tools for hypothesis matching (HYPER), abductive assembly (PIERCE), and an intelligent database (IDABLE). Future research involves expanding our repertoire of elementary generic tasks and implementing respective representation languages.

References

[1] Bennett, J., Creary, L., Englemore, R., and Melosh, R. SACON: A Knowledge-Based Consultant for Structural Analysis. Sept 1978, STAN-CS-78-699 and HPP Memo 78-23, Stanford University.

[2] Brown, D.C. *Expert Systems for Design Problem-Solving Using Design Refinement with Plan Selection and Redesign.* Ph. D. Th., The Ohio State University, 1984.

[3] Bylander, T., Mittal, S., and Chandrasekaran, B. CSRL: A Language for Expert Systems for Diagnosis. Proc. of the International Joint Conference on Artificial Intelligence, August, 1983, pp. 218-221. An extended version appears in *Computers and Mathematics with Applications*, vol 11, no.5, May 1985, pp. 449-456.

[4] Bylander, T. and Mittal, S. CSRL: A Language for Classificatory Problem Solving and Uncertainty Handling. To appear in *AI Magazine.*

[5] Bylander, T. and Smith, J.W. Mapping Medical Knowledge into Conceptual Structures. Proc. Expert System in Government Symposium, IEEE Computer Society", McLean, Virginia, 1985, pp. 503-511.

[6] Chandrasekaran, B., Mittal, S., Gomez, F., and Smith M.D., J. "An Approach to Medical Diagnosis Based on Conceptual Structures". *Proceedings of the 6th International Joint Conference on Artificial Intelligence*, (August 1979), 134-142. IJCAI79.

[7] Chandrasekaran, B. and Mittal, S. Conceptual Representation of Medical Knowledge for Diagnosis by Computer: MDX and Related Systems. In *Advances in Computers*, M. Yovits, Ed., Academic Press, 1983, pp 217-293.

[8] Chandrasekaran, B. Generic Tasks in Expert System Design and Their Role in Explanation of Problem Solving. Invited presentation at the National Academy of Sciences Office of Naval Research Workshop on AI and Distributed Problem Solving, May 16-17, 1985. To appear in the Proceedings of the Workshop.

[9] Chandrasekaran, B. From Numbers to Symbols to Knowledge Structures: Pattern Recognition and Artificial Intelligence Perspectives on the Classification Task. Invited paper presented at the Workshop on Pattern Recognition in Practice-II, Free University, Amsterdam, June 19-21, 1985. To appear in the book, *Pattern Recognition in Practice-II*, E.S. Gelsema and L.N. Kanal, editors, North-Holland Publishing Company.

[10] Chandrasekaran, B. Generic Tasks in Knowledge-Based Reasoning: Characterizing and Designing Expert Systems at the "Right" Level of Abstraction. Keynote lecture delivered December 13, 1985 at the IEEE Computer Society Second International Conference on Artificial Intelligence Applications, Miami, Florida. Appears in the Proceedings of the Conference.

[11] Chandrasekaran, B. and Tanner, M. Uncertainty Handling in Expert Systems: Uniform vs. Task-Specific Formalisms. To appear in *Uncertainty in Artificial Intelligence*, L.N. Kanal and J. Lemmer, editors, North Holland Publishing Company, 1986.

[12] Clancey, William J. "The Epistemology of a Rule-Based Expert System–a Framework for Explanation". *Artificial Intelligence 20, 3* (May 1983) 215-251.

[13] Clancey, William J. "Heuristic Classification". *Artificial Intelligence 27* (December 85), 289-350.

[14] Duda, R.O., Hart, P.E., Nilsson, N.J., Reboh, R., Slocum, J., and Sutherland, G.L. Development of a Computer-Based Consultant for Mineral Exploration. Annual Report, SRI Projects 5821 and 6415, SRI International, Menlo Park, California.

[15] Genesereth, M.R. "Diagnosis Using Hierarchical Design Models". *Proc. National Conf. on AI* (1982).

[16] Josephson, John R., Chandrasekaran, B. and Smith, J.W. Assembling the Best Explanation. Proceedings of the IEEE Workshop on Principles of Knowledge-Based Systems, IEEE Computer Society, Denver, Colorado, December 3-4, 1984.

[17] Kanal, L. and Chandrasekaran, B. Recognition, Machine 'Recognition' and Statistical Approaches. In Satosi Watanabe, Ed., *Methodologies of Pattern Recognition*, Academic Press, 1969, pp. 317-332.

[18] Minsky, M., and Papert, S. *Perceptrons*. The MIT Press, 1969.

[19] Sembugamoorthy, V. and Chandrasekaran, B. Functional Representation of Devices and Compilation of Diagnostic Problem Solving Systems. In J.L. Kolodner and C.K. Riesbeck, Ed. *Experience, Memory, and Reasoning*, Lawrence Erlbaum, 1986.

[20] Narasimhan, R. "Labeling Schemata and Syntactic Description of Pictures". *Information and Control*, *7* (June 1964), 151-179.

[21] Newell, A., Shaw, J.C., and Simon, H.A. *A variety of intelligent learning in a general problem-solver*. New York: Pergamon Press, 1960.

[22] Post, E. "Formal reductions of the general combinatorial problem". *American Journal of Mathematics 65*, (1943), 197-268.

[23] Samuel, Arthur L. "Some Studies in Machine Learning Using the Game of Checkers II. Recent Progress". *IBM Journal of Research and Development 11*, 6 (1967).

[24] Shortliffe, E.H. *Computer-based Medical Consultations: MYCIN*. Elsevier/North-Holland Inc. 1976.

[25] Sokal, R.R. and Sneath, P.H.A. *Principles of Numerical Taxonomy*. Freeman, W.M., San Francisco, 1963.

[26] Szolovits, P. and Pauker, S. G. "Categorical and Probabilistic Reasoning in Medical Diagnosis". *Artificial Intelligence 11*, 1/2 (August 1978), 115-144.

[27] vanMelle, W. *A domain independent system that aids in constructing consultative programs*. Ph. D. Th., Stanford University, 1980.

ON THE STRUCTURE OF PARALLEL ADAPTIVE SEARCH [1]

Laveen Kanal and Thomas Tsao

The Machine Intelligence and Pattern Analysis Laboratory
Department of Computer Science
University of Maryland
College Park, MD 20742, USA

Abstract

Introducing parallelism into an artificial intelligence (AI) system is a challenge. Within the discipline of logic programming, this can be addressed as exploring AND parallelism and OR parallelism. The simplicity of this approach is due to the separation of control from logic. However, the most *intelligent part* of an AI system is in the control; specifically, control through the utilization of task related information. Almost without exception, current AI systems contain such an "intelligent" part as heuristic rules, or focus of attention rules, etc. The structure and behavior of an AI system with intelligent control, *i.e.* control through the utilization of task related information, is different from one without such a control component. The issues arising from introducing parallelism into such an AI system are also very different from those when introducing AND parallelism and OR parallelism in logic programming.

An AI system may involve many low level computations which can be executed in parallel. However, the real challenge is to explore parallelism at the top level of the problem solving, at the level of searching, decision making and reasoning.

Although game tree search is a class room example, it is a prototype for many sophisticated problem solving situations. Examples are, the problem reduction representation (PRR) in waveform analysis (Stockman and Kanal [83]), and recently, the evidence accumulation approach in high level image understanding expert system designed to explore contextual information for identifying objects, in which the knowledge part is essentially an attributed grammar (Hwang et al [85]).

Our research on parallel game tree search has been motivated by the desire to understand the nature of parallel search and adaptive search, and to explore some fundamental issues of parallel adaptive search. In designing parallel algorithms for game tree search, we set the following goals: (1) exploit full parallelism in a multiprocessor environment, (2) exploit the full utility of *parallel* accumulated information.

We use *dynamic algorithms* to achieve these goals. Using a net based model of parallel computation, we are able to specify the control structure of dynamic algorithms. A dynamic algorithm is a parallel algorithm with its control structure consisting of (1) an adaptive task structure, and (2) an "eager" computation firing

[1]This research has been supported in part by U.S. National Science Foundation Grants to the Machine Intelligence and Pattern Analysis Lab.

NATO ASI Series, Vol. F30
Pattern Recognition Theory and Applications
Edited by P. A. Devijver and J. Kittler

mechanism. The adaptive task structure is defined as a special kind of communication pattern. The eager *computation* is a firing mechanism for parallel computations, governed by processor availabilities.

1. Introduction

Several AI systems for solving perceptual problems are currently being designed and tested (*e.g.*, Hwang *et al.* [85], Levine *et al.* [85], McKeown *et al.* [85], Stockman and Kanal [83]).

In the domain of perceptual problem solving many AI systems use accumulated information in an adaptive manner. The question which then arises is how to conduct such an adaptive search in parallel.

The role of parallelism in perceptual problem solving is unlike that in query answering. In logic programming, the structure of a parallel AI system can be simply expressed by the formula: *logic (of first order calculus) + AND/OR parallelism* (Kasif and Minker [85]). This simplicity derives from the separation of logic from control. In contrast, the feasibility of AI approaches in perceptual problem domains depends on efficiently incorporating intelligent control as an integral part of the system. Thus unlike the logic programming formulation, we use *logic (lambda-definable functions) embedded in a net* to express the structure of our parallel AI system.

Our objective for parallel adaptive algorithm design is to achieve, as much as possible, the result of "never waiting and no wasting" of computations. Both the best use of available processors and best use of accumulated information are desired.

In this paper we explore the structural issues related to parallel adaptive algorithms. We present the concept of a λ-net, study the adaptive behavior exhibited in parallel algorithms in terms of λ-net structures, describe a class of parallel algorithms with the desired features, *i.e.*, they are dynamic algorithms, and give a net representation of a parallel AND/OR tree search algorithm. As is well known, AND/OR trees and graphs are very useful representations for many practical applications (*e.g.*, Stockman and Kanal [83], Hopp [86])

2. The Structure of Parallel Adaptive Algorithms

2.1. The Structure of Parallel Algorithms

A parallel computation involves three aspects: (1) a collection of independent task modules; (2) communication among these task modules; and (3) an enable mechanism for these task modules. A task module may be a primitive operation of a von Neumann processor, or some other direct transformation of information in other computation models, *e.g.*, connectionist computation model (see Anderson [81], Feldman [81]), or may be a sequential process containing many primitive operations or other direct transformations of information. A task module in a parallel computation model is only recognized as a transition from *input* to *output*. It is a functional unit and only has a behavioral description; it does not have a structural description. As an atomic object, a task module has no communication with the outside world during its execution. We call the behavioral description for a task module a *micro logic*.

There are basically two different formulations for parallel problem solving. One is through the execution of a parallel algorithm which is defined as a collection of communicating independent sequential processes. A parallel algorithm in this formulation is a natural extension of a sequential algorithm; it is a collection of cooperating sequential algorithms. This formulation continues to focus on constructing sequential processes. The second formulation of parallel computations, is through the coordination of a set of task modules.

This second formulation, basically focuses on choosing and coordinating functional units. *Coordinating* and *programming* provide two different types of controls: *concurrent control* and *sequential control.* While it is true that sequential control could be at a higher level than concurrent control, *e.g.*, programming the coordinated machine operations, it is also true that when sequential programming is to generate functional units, the concurrent control over these functional units is at a higher level. In parallel computation, we regard *concurrent control* as the *top level control.* Although, as the result of coordinating, the term *net* is a more appropriate descriptor for a parallel computation scheme, most of the time we still use *parallel algorithm* as a general term to include either the parallel algorithm formulation or the net formulation.

Note that in this paper, when we use the term logic we do not refer to the first order predicate calculus. We call a mapping or derivation from one piece of information to another piece of information a logic. A (computable) problem implicitly specifies a logic which is realized by solving the problem.

Thus the concept of a parallel algorithm includes: (1) a global logic; (2) a set of micro logics; (3) a communication pattern among these micro logics; (4) an (physical) enable mechanism over these micro logics. While (1) provides a functional description (specification) of an algorithm, (2), (3), and (4) provide a structural description of a parallel algorithm; (2) specifies the set of functional modules of this structure, and (3), and (4) specify control flow.

The term control means conditions for a functional unit to be fired. The firing of a micro logic depends on two kinds of conditions: (1) the necessary input (information), and (2) (physical) enable conditions for certain computations (e.g., processor conditions).

In this paper we present a net-based model called a λ-net. In a λ-net, the communication pattern specifies channels of the flow of task related information, *i.e.*, the logical conditions for the task modules. We call it *the logical part of the control.* A λ-net also has channels for the flow of (physical) enabling conditions. In the λ-net model, the firing control (later we will simply call it control) mechanism consists of the integration of the logical part and the physical part.

The processor driven firing control implements the "never waiting" principle (for never waiting, see Kung [76]), while the data driven firing control only explores inherent concurrency, and corresponds to a "no hurry" principle in informed search, which says that it is better to have processors idle than to do work which may be unnecessary (see e.g., Akl *et al.* [80]). Neither method of firing control alone provides sufficient control features for parallel adaptive search. And the combination is possible only when both parts of the control can be explicitly specified.

2.2. The λ-net Model

In this section we present a net-based model for expressing patterns of information flow and physical condition flow.

The general concept of a net is described through a definition of the form $N = (S, T; F)$ (Genrich *et al.* [79]).

Definition 2.2.1: Let S and T be two sets and F a binary relation in $S \cup T$. The triple $N = (S, T; F)$ is called a (directed) net in STF-form iff

(1) $S \cap T = 0$

(2) $S \cup T \neq 0$

(3) $F \subseteq S \times T \cup T \times S$

(4) $dom(F) \cup cod(F) = S \cup T$

Definition 2.2.2: A λ-net consists of the following constituents:

(1) a directed net $(S, T; F)$ where

- S is the set of places ○,
- T is the set of transitions |,
- $F \subseteq S \times T \cup T \times S$ is the set of arcs $\rightarrow$.

(2) a labelling of transitions assigning to each element of T a micro logic.

(3) a labelling of places assigning to each element of S a condition set.

(4) a labelling of arcs assigning to each element of F some terms.

We use tokens to represent the presence of certain conditions. A marking is to put tokens into places. Each token in a place is an instance of the labelled condition. In a λ-net, tokens are distinguishable objects. A marked net is called a system.

A piece of information can be a condition for a transition only when it is accessible and acceptable by the corresponding logic. The arcs indicate the information is accessible. In a relation net (for relation net, see Reisig [85]) the terms assigned to the arcs indicate relations among the conditions for a transition. For example, when a micro logic is an operation, and its precondition places are data queues, if only the data with the same index are allowed to be combined for the operation, then the terms (with the same index variable) attached to arcs will serve to indicate such a relationship among tokens from different places. When necessary, the (abstract) micro logic may have predicates for checking if the accessible information is acceptable for use as input for a transition (see checking inscriptions of a transition in a Predicate/Transition-net, Genrich *et al.* [79]). Only the accessible and acceptable information can be a condition for a transition.

2.3. The Structure of an Adaptive Algorithm

The definition of adaptive information given by Traub *et al.* [83] contains a description of the main feature of adaptive algorithms in terms of communication patterns.

Let f be a problem description. The process of problem solving was formulated by Traub *et al.* as a sequence, $U_i, \quad i = 1, \cdots, n$, of information operations:

$$N(f) = [U_1(f), U_2(f), \cdots, U_n(f)],$$

and the adaptive information can be defined as follows:

$$N^a(f) = [U_1(f), U_2(f; y_1), \cdots, U_n(f; y_1, \cdots, y_{n-1})],$$

where

$$y_i = U_i(f; y_1, \cdots, y_{i-1}), \quad i = 1, 2, \cdots, n-1,$$

The above equations indicate that in the adaptive information formulation of problem solving, the later information operations should count on the results of previous information operations. The essence of adaptive information is in the utilization of accumulated information.

We make the following distinction between an argument (f, in the above definition) and parameters (y_is, in the above definition) of a task: Parameters of a task carry optional information while arguments carry necessary information. A task still can be fired if some parameters are absent although the result may be different. But a task can not be fired if an argument is absent.

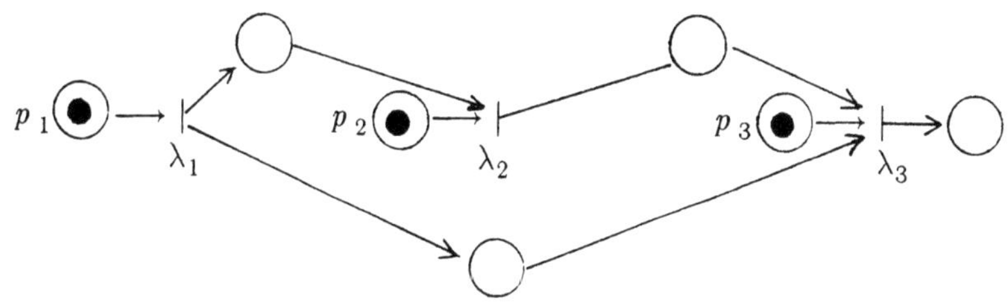

p_1, p_2, p_3 — places for task tokens.
$\lambda_1, \lambda_2, \lambda_3$ — task logics.

Figure 2.3.1: A sequential logic

Taking parameters as direct conditions of a task, we have two distinct choices: keep parameters as direct conditions and accept the sequential nature of the logic, e.g., in Figure 2.3.1, λ_2 can not fire before the completion of λ_1, and λ_3 can not fire before the completion of λ_2, as in the case of those who believe in the "no hurry" philosophy; Or, we can drop parameters as direct conditions and get an eager computation scheme which is parallel, as is done by the "never waiting" school. In Figure 2.3.2, in which λ_1, λ_2, λ_3 are all independent of each other, there is no need for the processes to wait for each other; however, neither can they be of help to each other.

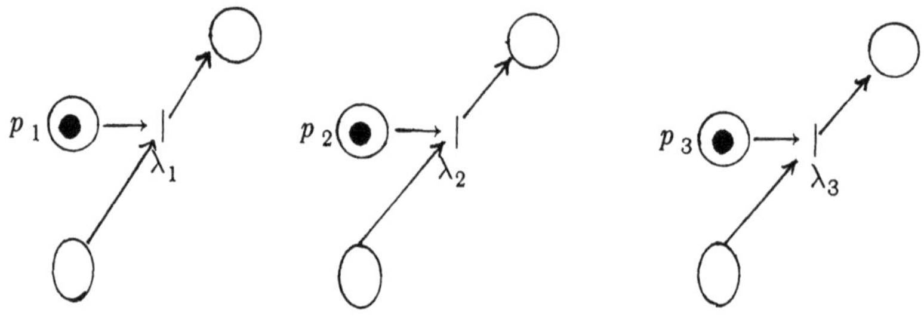

○ ___places for token of processor availabilities.
p_1, p_2, p_3___places for task tokens.
$\lambda_1, \lambda_2, \lambda_3$___task logics.

Figure 2.3.2: An eager computation scheme

Many parallel implementations for AND/OR tree search algorithms seem to fall into one of the above two categories (see a survey in Tsao [85]). The algorithms resulting from either one of the above two approaches are unsatisfactory.

A parallel adaptive scheme is made possible by an indirect entry of parameter data into a task. This technique provides an effective approach to parallelism in AI systems in which the use of accumulated information is crucial to the efficiency and effectiveness of the systems. It addresses both interests: the maximum use of accumulated information, and the maximum use of available processors.

2.4. Adaptive Task Structure and Adaptive Logic

Indirect conditions can be formulated either as an *adaptive task structure*, or as an *adaptive logic*.

Definition 2.4.1: A task structure is a λ-net. A designated set of places of the net is called the task place set, each place in this set is called a task place. A token in a task place is called a task token.

Definition 2.4.2: In a task structure, a transition which removes a task token from a place without replacing one is called an execution; a transition which replace a task token by another task token (possibly) with different identity, is called a modify action.

Definition 2.4.3: A task structure with transitions of the modify action type, is called an interacting task structure.

Definition 2.4.4: A task structure in which the result of an execution can cause firings of modify actions, is an adaptive task structure.

An adaptive task structure is a special kind of interacting task structure in which modify actions are data driven.

Figure 2.4.1 is an example of an adaptive task structure. In this example, the modify actions are "data driven", that is, any available information will immediately be used in modifying the remaining tasks. However, the firing of each task is independent of accumulated information, *i.e.*, they are "processor driven".

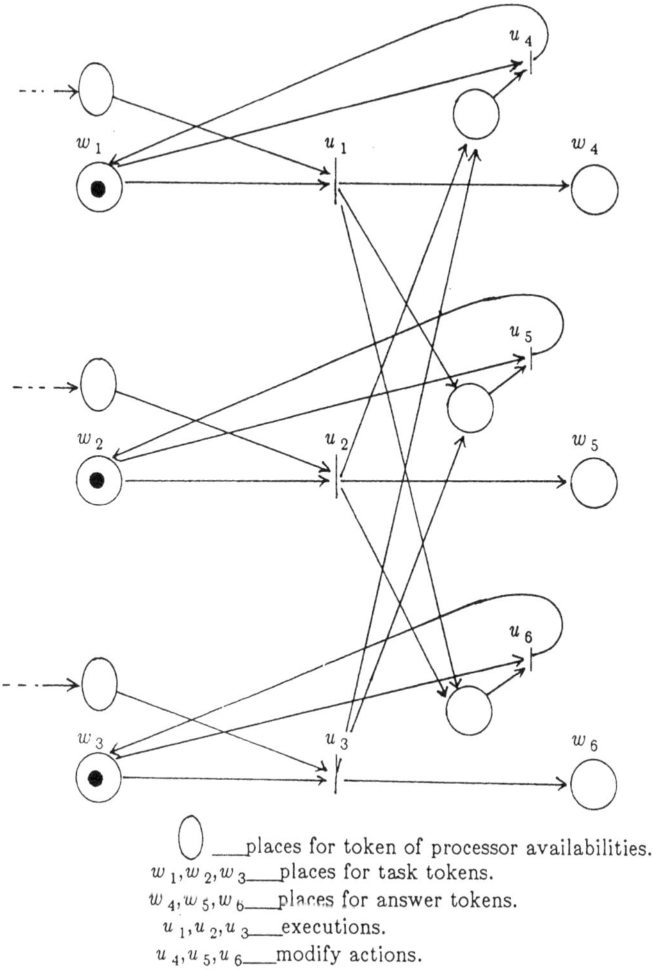

Figure 2.4.1: An adaptive task structure with eager computation control mechanism

Both the adaptive task structure and the adaptive information of Traub *et al.* are essentially communication patterns set for the utilization of accumulated information during the process of problem solving.

In an adaptive task structure, each micro logic stays the same, and the adaptive behavior is formulated through a mechanism for modifying task tokens. This approach to parallel adaptive algorithms has been studied in Tsao [85]. Another approach to parallel adaptive algorithms is to formulate the adaptive behavior through a modification mechanism of some logics. In the following we will present the concept of adaptive logic.

This kind of logic is described as follows: (1) it is executed during a finite period of time; *i.e.*, it is not considered an atomic event; (2) during the period of the execution the logic can accept some optional input information, and the optional inputs may affect the execution of the logic and its output. The above behavioral description indicates that an adaptive logic has a layer of structure above the micro logic level. In the following we first define macro logic, and then define adaptive logic.

Definition 2.4.5: A Net $(S_1, T_1; F_1)$ is called a subnet of net $(S, T; F)$ if

(1) $S_1 \subseteq S$,

(2) $T_1 \subseteq T$,

(3) $F_1 = (S_1 \times T_1 \cup T_1 \times S_1) \cap F$.

Definition 2.4.6: A net is a connected net if it is a connected graph.

Definition 2.4.7: A connected subnet $(S_1, T_1; F_1)$ of net $(S, T; F)$ is called a macro logic if for any $a \epsilon F$, either $a \epsilon F_1$ or $a \epsilon ((S - S_1) \times T) \cup (T \times (S - S_1))$. The arcs in the set $F \cap (S - S_1) \times T_1$ are called input channels, and the arcs in the set $F \cap T_1 \times (S - S_1)$ are called output channels. Places in $S - S_1$ which are attached to an input (output) channel are called preconditions (postconditions) of the macro logic.

The meaning of a macro logic is that all links from a (connected) piece of the net to the rest of the net are through the subnet's transition elements (see Figure 2.4.2 and Figure 2.4.3). Therefore, the subnet appears to the outside world just as a logic.

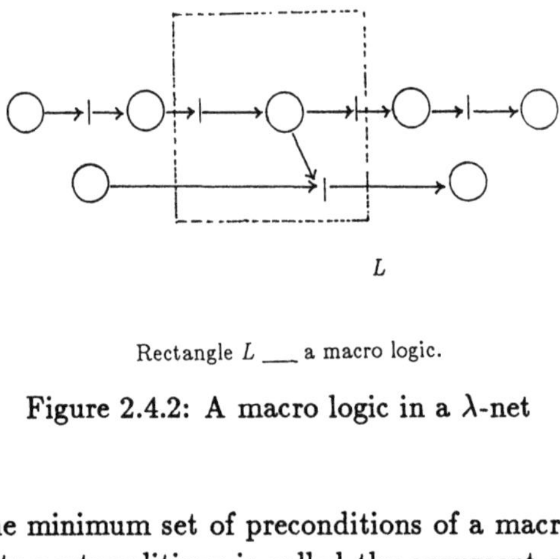

Rectangle L ___ a macro logic.

Figure 2.4.2: A macro logic in a λ-net

Definition 2.4.8: The minimum set of preconditions of a macro logic which can lead to the changes of all its postconditions is called the argument set. Each place in this set is called an argument of this macro logic. The other conditions for this macro logic are called parameters. The set of parameters is called the parameter set for the macro logic.

Definition 2.4.9: An adaptive logic is a macro logic with a nonempty parameter set.

2.5. The Structure of Dynamic Algorithms

Many who emphasize the importance of parallelism adopt the "never waiting" philosophy, and use an eager computation control structure to implement their philosophy.

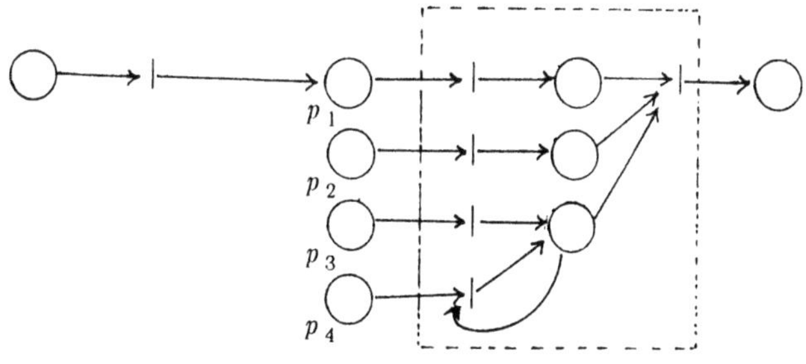

p_1, p_2, p_3 ___ places for arguments.
p_4 ___ a place for parameter.
Rectangle L ___ an adaptive logic.

Figure 2.4.3: An adaptive logic

Those who emphasize the importance of accumulated information adopt the "no hurry" philosophy, and tend to explore only the inherent concurrencies within some well known sequential algorithm.

In Tsao [85] the principle of *never waiting and no wasting* or *useful eagerness*, is addressed. This means the algorithm should have such behavior that each processor is eager to work; the task to be assigned is always updated to be the most necessary one in the sense of adaptive search, *i.e.*, does not contain a part which can be determined to be redundant by using the accumulated information of the parallel search process. An algorithm in which the "never waiting and no wasting" principle is implemented is called a dynamic algorithm.

In this subsection we make the concepts of *data driven* and *eager computation* precise, and show how these mechanisms can be combined in one algorithm.

Following Petri's point of view (see Petri [79]), control is through the flow of "resource type" conditions. The "resource" means those entities which can, by being scarce in a given situation, impede the reaching of a goal. Resources represent items which are subject to depletion. Similarly, control conditions are those conditions which are not always present; *e.g.*, a government controls its departments through its budget, not through the air supply. Although data driven and processor driven can be defined as structural features, more often, and practically, we regard them as behavioral features. The structural and behavioral aspects are defined as follows.

Definition 2.5.1: The structural control of a micro logic consists of all its preconditions. The structural data driven control is a control structure in which all conditions, except data, are always present. Therefore these other conditions, as they are not control conditions, are ignored in the control structure. A similar definition can be given for the structural aspects of processor driven control.

More often it is the case that while one condition is more in control, the others also can not be ignored. In this case the "driven" concept, although it cannot be defined as a pure structural feature, can still be defined as a time related behavioral feature.

Definition 2.5.2: A (pre)condition for a micro logic is a behavioral control feature if it is absent most of the time, and whenever it exists, the micro logic will fire or soon will fire. Behavioral data driven and behavioral processor driven are defined accordingly.
Definition 2.5.3: A dynamic algorithm is a parallel algorithm whose control structure consists of: (1) an adaptive task structure, in which the task modify actions are data driven, and (2) an eager computation control mechanism for task executions.

3. Parallel Adaptive Algorithm for AND/OR Tree Search

We formulate parallel computation as the activity of a λ-net, where each micro logic is a lambda definable function embedded in this net. The λ-net is used to specify concurrent control structures.

The following example presents a coordinated system of parallel AND/OR tree search. It consists of (1) definitions of micro logics, (2) definitions of conditions, and (3) a λ-net with an initial marking.

In this net, by the assumptions made in the previous discussion, L_1 and L_2 behave as data driven logics, and all other logics are processor driven. The system has the desired dynamic behavior.

A Coordinated system of Parallel AND/OR Tree Search

Micro Logics

(1) L_1: Upper-tree Evaluation, a procedure which evaluates the upper portion of a game tree.

(2) L_2: Decompose & Grow & Task-Assignment, a procedure which grows the upper tree and assigns subtrees for searching.

(3) L_3: $\alpha - \beta$ procedure.

(4) L_4: $\alpha - \beta$ procedure.

(5) L_5: $\alpha - \beta$ procedure.

(6) L_6: $\alpha - \beta$ procedure.

(7) L_7: $\alpha - \beta$ procedure.

Conditions

(1) P_1: Global Data Structure (Upper-tree and Task Pool)

(2) P_2: Availability of Processor

(3) P_3: Availability of Processor

(4) P_4: Task Specification

(5) P_5: Availability of Processor

(6) P_6: Availability of Processor

(7) P_7: Availability of Processor

(8) P_8: Availability of Processor

(9) P_9: Availability of Processor

(10) P_{10}: Parameter Space (Imaginary Tokens or Results from Procedures)

The λ-net with Initial Marking

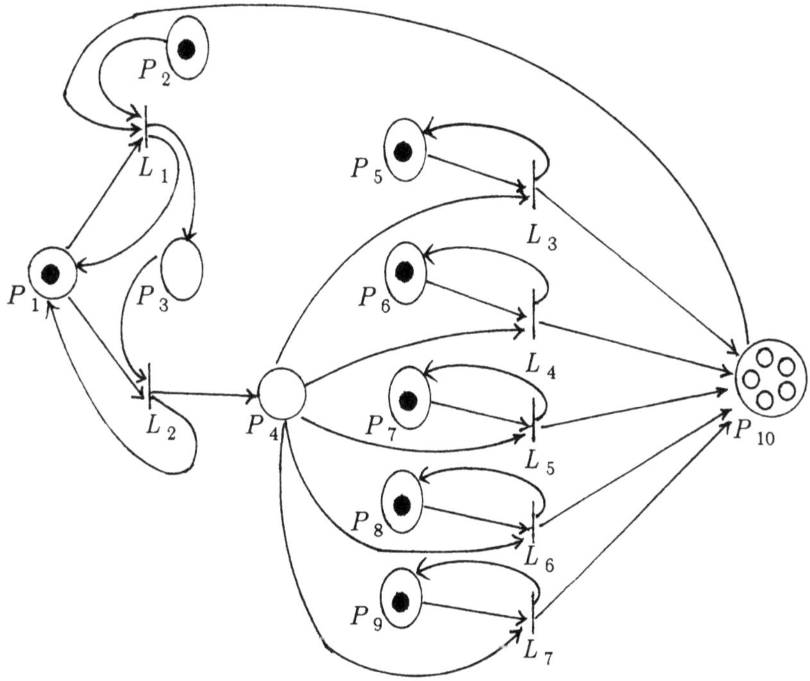

○ ___ **imaginary tokens for some initial conditions**
● ___ **real tokens represent existence of conditions**

/* At the very beginning k (number of worker processors) imaginary tokens (which carry no task related information) are set to enable the first k task assignments. Then each time a subtree $\alpha-\beta$ search (in L_3, L_4, L_5, L_6, L_7) is finished, the result (a token in P_{10}) will trigger L_1, then L_2, so that the remaining tasks can have modified $\alpha-\beta$ windows, and new task will soon be assigned to where a processor is available. The subtree $\alpha-\beta$ searches are very time consuming. The L_1 and L_2 are tasks of management which do not need much time, but need to be done as soon as the new information (token in P_{10}) is available. To guarantee that the management has a data driven control, a token exist in P_2 most of the time. The quick response of the management also guarantees that the subtree search tasks are processor driven. */

4. Conclusion

In perceptual problem domains, AI approaches are characterized by the extensive use of accumulated information during problem solving. Thus such AI systems are adaptive in nature.

In an adaptive algorithm, in general, information to be processed in a task can be divided into arguments and parameters, *viz.*, the information which makes a task possible and the information which can modify the task respectively. The distinction of parameters and arguments of the tasks is crucial to the understanding of adaptive algorithms.

Through setting parameters as indirect conditions for tasks, which are formulated either as conditions for the modify actions in an adaptive task structure, or as parameters for an adaptive logic, we provide a methodology for parallel adaptive algorithm design, *i.e.*, a technique for introducing parallelism into this type of seemingly sequential algorithm.

The λ-net formulation of a parallel adaptive system fits the nature of human perceptual processes, processes performed by many interacting and independent functional modules, in which the accumulated information from one process module can affect the others and *vice versa*. This character has been noticed by many scientists. It has also been noticed that the determinate sequential computation model can not be used to describe such cognitive processes. Feldman suggested a generalized relaxation scheme and a network computation model for perceptual problem solving (see Feldman [81]).

The λ-net computation model is distinguished from network computation models (*e.g.*, Feldman's connectionist model) in the following: a network is a pattern of connections of functional units; a λ-net is a pattern of connections of conditions. In a λ-net, the functional units are totally specified by their preconditions and postconditions, *i.e.* by the information flow. The λ-net computation model is a specification level model and the network computation models are functional level models. The λ-net model is more abstract and more independent of actual implementations than the network models. Cognitive processes are parallel, flexible, and distributed processes, and also highly structured. Compared with network models, the λ-net model is more flexible and powerful for the representation of the structure of cognitive processes. The network models always have to start from some sort of simple functional units (e.g., neurons).

The λ-net formulation has the advantage of providing both a structural analysis as well as behavioral analysis of a parallel algorithm. It is easy to show that the data driven behavior and processor driven behavior of our AND/OR tree search depends on time related statistics of each of the micro logics. The λ-net formulation provides a structural framework which makes statistical research on the performance of such algorithms possible.

References

[1] Akl, S.G., Barnard, D.T. and Doran, R.J., "Simulation and Analysis in Deriving Time and Storage Requirements for a Parallel Alpha-beta Algorithm," *Proc. 1980 International Conference on Parallel Processing*, 231-234.

[2] Anderson, J.A. and Hinton, G.E., "Models of Information Processing in the Brain," in: G.E. Hinton *et al.* (eds.) 1981 *Parallel Models of Associative Memory*, Lawrence Erlbaum Associates, Inc., Publishers.

[3] Feldman, J.A., "A Connectionist Model of Visual Memory," in: G.E. Hinton *et al.* (eds.) 1981 *Parallel Models of Associative Memory*, Lawrence Erlbaum Associates, Inc., Publishers, 49-78.

[4] Genrich, H.J., Lautenbach, K. and Thiagarajan, P.S., "Elements of General Net Theory," in: Wilfried Brauer (ed.) *Net Theory and Applications*, Proceedings of the Advanced Course on General Net Theory of Processes and Systems, Hamburg, Springer-Verlag, 1980, 42.

[5] Hwang, V., Davis, L. and Matsuyama, T., "Hypothesis Integration in Image Understanding System," Report CAR-TR-130, Center for Automation Research, University of Maryland, June. 1985

[6] Hopp, T.H., "Generalized AND/OR Graphs as a Modeling Tool for Diagnostic Problem Solving," Ph.D. Dissertation, Computer Science Department, Univ. of Maryland, May, 1986.

[7] Kasif, S., Minker, J., "The Intelligent Channel: A Scheme for Result Sharing in Logic Programs," *Proceedings of the Ninth Joint Conference on Artificial Intelligence*, Aug. 1985, Vol. 1, 29.

[8] Kung, H.T., "Synchronized and Asynchronous Algorithms," in: J.F.Traub (ed.), *Algorithms and Complexity – New Directions and Recent Results*, Academic Press, New York, 1976, 153-200.

[9] Levine, M.D., Nazif, A.M., "Rule-based Image Segmentation: a Dynamic Control Strategy Approach," *Computer Vision, Graphics, and Image Processing*, 32, 1985, 104-126.

[10] McKeown, D.M., JR., Harvey, W.A., JR. and McDermott, J., "Rule-Based Interpretation of Aerial Imagery," *IEEE Transactions on Pattern Analysis and Machine Intelligence* Vol. PAMI-7, No.5 September 1985.

[11] Petri, C.A., "Introduction to General Net Theory," in: Wilfried Brauer (ed.) *Net Theory and Applications*, Proceedings of the Advanced Course on General Net Theory of Processes and Systems, Hamburg, Springer-Verlag, 1980, 8-19.

[12] Reisig, W., *Petri Nets*, Springer-Verlag Berlin Heidelberg, 1985 124-138.

[13] Stockman, G. and Kanal, L., "Problem Reduction Representation for the Linguistic Analysis of Waveforms," *IEEE Transactions on Pattern Analysis and Machine Intelligence*, Vol. PAMI-5, No.3, May 1983, 287-298.

[14] Traub, J.F., Wasilkowski, G.W. and Woz'niakowski, H., *Information, Uncertainty, Complexity*, Addison-Wisley Publishing Company, 1983.

[15] Tsao, T., "Design and Analysis of Parallel Adaptive Algorithms for Composite Decision Process," Ph.D. Dissertation, Mathematics Department, Univ. of Maryland, Dec. 1985.

THREE DIMENSIONAL ORGAN RECOGNITION BY TOMOGRAPHIC IMAGE ANALYSIS

S. Dellepiane, S.B. Serpico, and G. Vernazza

Department of Biophysical and Electronic Engineering
University of Genova
via Opera Pia 11a, 16145 GENOVA- ITALY

1. Introduction

Biomedical images exhibit some interesting peculiarities; in fact, by using suitable techniques (e.g. Computed Tomography, Nuclear Magnetic Resonance (NMR) and Proton Emission Tomography) it is possible to visualize the internal morphological structures of 3-D organs by means of different 2-D slices (tomographic planes).

In order to attain this goal, various approaches can be followed; we have applied organ recognition to each 2-D slice, on the basis of adequate three-dimensional anatomical knowledge; 3-D organs can be reconstructed by collecting the results obtained from successive slices.

An integrated approach derived from classical Pattern Recognition (PR) and Artificial Intelligence (AI) techniques has been adopted [1], in fact, for our research work, it is of major importance to recognize predefined objects through the description of their structures and relationships, rather than to perform a classification, which may be regarded as a secondary goal. The generation of a model capable of representing parts of the human body is a crucial point in the area of biomedical image understanding. In fact, complex relations and 3-D shapes of anatomic organs have to be represented, and such features often exhibit marked differences between patients.

The purpose of this paper is to present a knowledge-based system (under development in our department) for the recognition of NMR images. A feasible model is proposed which describes the morphology of the main organs in the human head, using both 3-D and 2-D primitives for the representation of intrinsic and relational organ properties.

The system works on images corresponding to 2-D slices of the head; the output is represented by an anatomical map displaying the recognized organs of the slice considered.

At present, the 3-D aspect is only considered at the knowledge representation level; 3-D reconstruction and display is still under development.

2. System Design

The system [Fig.1] is based on a heterarchical control structure merging together top-down and bottom-up strategies. It uses a blackboard model for the global data base

NATO ASI Series, Vol. F30
Pattern Recognition Theory and Applications
Edited by P.A. Devijver and J. Kittler

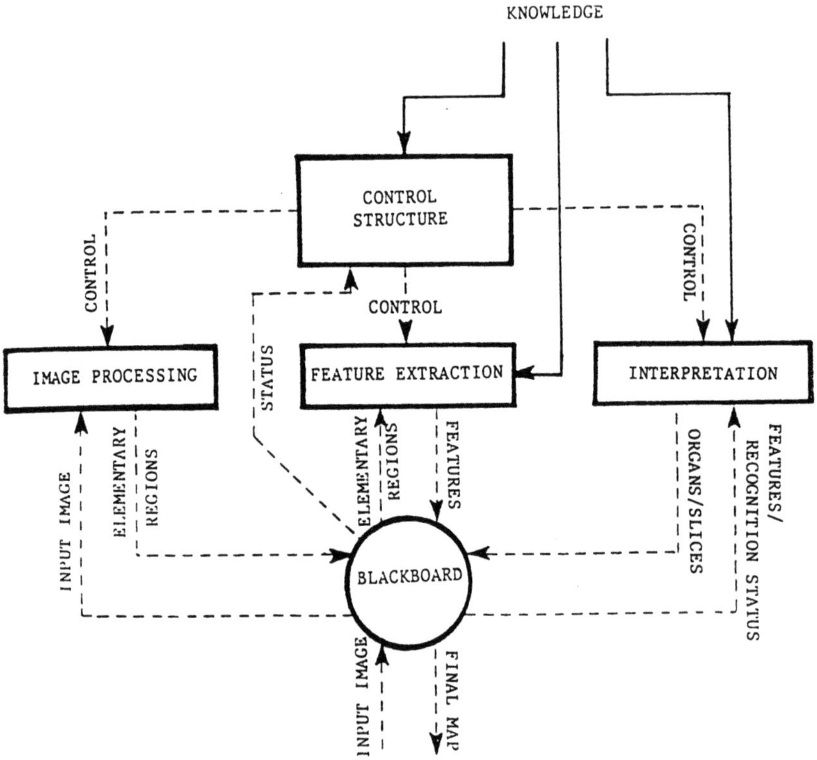

Figure 1: Heterarchical control structure in a system using a blackboard model data base

and a semantic net for the structured knowledge through which production rules are applied. The system executes symbolic processing and uses logical description for the model, without prefixed targets.

The system's architecture can be divided into four parts:

a) The LOW-LEVEL SUBSYSTEM (LLS), characterized by image preprocessing (calibration, smoothing, etc.) and segmentation of each image into many elementary regions. (*i.e.*, the primitives to which the recognition process is applied.)

b) The MIDDLE-LEVEL SUBSYSTEM (MLS), devoted to feature extraction. On the basis of feature values, symbolic processing on elementary regions can be performed.

c) The HIGH-LEVEL SUBSYSTEM (HLS), which consists of two parts: the control structure and the structured knowledge. At this level, the recognition process is performed by the inferential engine, which deduces the production rules from the domain knowledge.

d) The GLOBAL DATA BASE (GDB), which contains the progressive results of the recognition process and is the area where interactions among the various recognition subsystems occur.

Both heuristic and anatomical knowledge has been introduced into the system. Heuristic knowledge suggests the kind and the number of features to be extracted from every elementary region, and the strategy for hypothesis generation and test. Besides, a focusing mechanism is applied by which firstly the regions with salient features are identified (global investigation), and then such regions only are analyzed in greater detail. Heuristic knowledge is also employed to choose the "distinctive organs" in order to select the slice that most likely corresponds to the input image.

The model used to insert and consult anatomical knowledge includes the following three levels:

a) A general 3-D description of the anatomical part (in the present case, the head);

b) A detailed description of the slices related to this part (on different tomographic planes);

c) a detailed description of the organs.

The first level contains a 3-D global description of the organs present in the anatomical part under analysis, together with their relationships; in particular, information is provided about the densitometric, geometric, relational, and 3-D properties of each organ.

The second level contains information about different types and properties of NMR slices; in particular, transversal, coronal, and sagittal slices have been introduced into the system. Such anatomical knowledge is stored in the so-called Slice Detection Subsystems (SDS), which are independent modules describing relationships among organs in a slice. Each SDS also contains a list of the organs usually present in a specific slice and in the neighbouring ones.

The third level is represented by the Organ Detection Subsystems (ODS), which contain part of the expertise used by the production rules, that is, the information about every organ, without any specific knowledge about the relational properties among the various organs (such knowledge is available at the first and second levels).

Different ODS's for the same organ are contemporarily present in the system: usually, there is one for each SDS, corresponding to a particular tomographic plane.

An organ may look very different in shape, area and localization, depending on the different planes used for its acquisition. The various pictorial appearances assumed by the image of an organ in a specific slice define what we call the "A-Slice-Of" (ASO) object for that organ. Our system is characterized by a general 3-D and a particular 2-D knowledge about some prefixed slices of each organ;such knowledge is provided by the ODS's, which also contain specialized features (in particular, shape and texture descriptors) for a detailed description of the model of the organ.

A certain degree of tolerance for the tomographic plane must be introduced to take into account both the differences in the anatomical properties of human beings and the difficulties with identifying exactly the geometric localization of the plane, or with detecting typical small changes in the source parameters. In the present system, which can be regarded as an evolution step towards a 3-D approach, as compared with the previous model described in [2], the global information about the human head, as introduced at the first knowledge level, can be accessed by each SDS and ODS so that it must not be repeated for each slice.

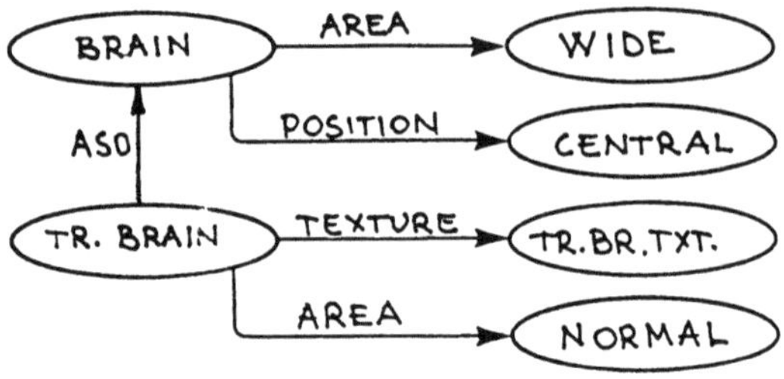

Figure 2: A - Slice - Of link

During the recognition process, the inferential engine is able to select and activate the most appropriate production rules, and to start further investigations when needed, depending on the problem state contained in the GDB.

Different kinds of errors may be incurred at each level during the recognition process; some errors are detected at the SDS level and can be recovered by using relational knowledge; others require a complete backtracking procedure up to the segmentation level (error recovery task).

By introducing a new segmentation threshold into some localized areas only, additional elementary regions can be obtained which also must be submitted to the ODS's for recognition.

Before stopping the recognition process and displaying the final map, the termination task checks if all the organs have been recognized correctly and if all the elementary regions have been identified.

3. Knowledge Representation

Knowledge representation plays a key role in facilitating the solution of complex problems for which expertise is required. A suitable kind of representation should be selected which allows the use of a set of syntactic and semantic conventions to describe things belonging to a problem's domain.

Every knowledge-based system needs the representation of both its domain knowledge and the knowledge contained in its data base, which includes all the facts and assertions related to the problem state.

3.1. Domain (Anatomical) Knowledge

In our case, the representation used is based on a complex semantic network using inheritance mechanisms, default values and demons. The rule interpreter (*i.e.*, the part of the inference engine that applies the domain knowledge) can derive and apply the production rules by using the knowledge contained in the semantic net of the system.

As is well known [3], a semantic net is made up of nodes representing concepts or objects, and of arcs describing the nodes' attributes or relations with the other nodes in the net. In our system, the objects are the organs and their slices; the attributes are the features characterizing each organ or slice; the relations describe structural relationships among organs, or semantic links between objects. In the latter case, we use a particular

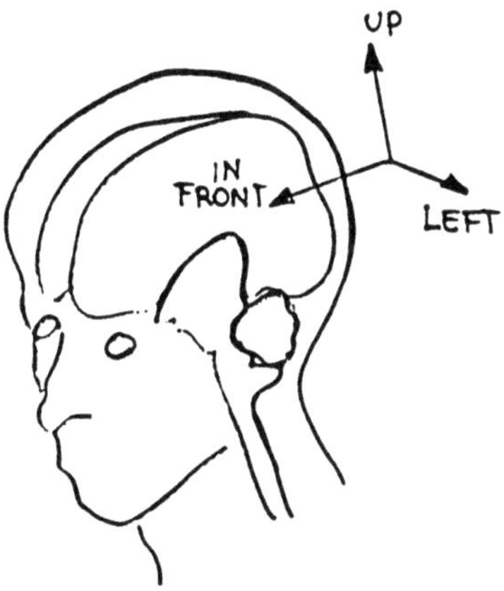

Figure 3: "Only 3-D" properties

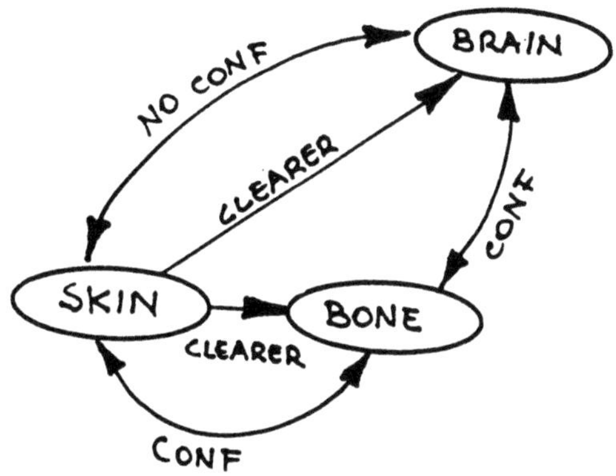

Figure 4: Semantic net containing relations among 3-D organs

kind of links, each allowing us to fix a particular inheritance hierarchy. In fact, we can start from nodes representing real 3-D organs, from which a node representing a typical slice of an organ in 2-D space can be derived.

This new link ASO [Fig.2] represents a 2-D tomographic projection of a 3-D organ and requires a new set of rules for the inheritance process. The description of the father node (describing a 3-D organ) is based on a set of intrinsic properties which are divided into two classes: invariant properties (e.g., densitometric or dimensional features) and "only 3-D" properties (e.g., geometrical or positional descriptions).

The child node (ASO) inherits all the father's properties as default values, unless otherwise specified, and also has its own peculiar properties, which are related to the particular tomographic plane selected for the slice.

Invariant properties can easily be transferred from the 3-D level to the 2-D one, while "only 3-D" properties [Fig.3] need a "translation" into 2-D terms before being used, since some 3-D features change their meaning according to different perspectives.

For example, UP and DOWN keep their respective meaning in coronal and sagittal slices, while they become insignificant in transversal ones; on the contrary, LEFT and RIGHT are suitable for transversal and coronal slices but not for sagittal planes. Analogously, IN FRONT of is translated into UP, and BEHIND into DOWN for transversal slices, in accordance with the convention that transversal slices are always acquired in the same direction.

Relational knowledge is represented at both the 3-D and 2-D levels by means of relational arcs connecting organs and slices, respectively [Figs. 4-5]. These semantic networks represent the knowledge of the system about the structural organ arrangement for each slice. Relational information can be transmitted from the 3-D to the 2-D level by the same inheritance mechanism as used for intrinsic properties and through the default and perspective processes described before. As in the previous case,it is necessary to describe the 2-D relations among different organs in a slice if the 3-D general relations have not been verified in the slice. For example, the 3-D relation: "the BRAIN is above

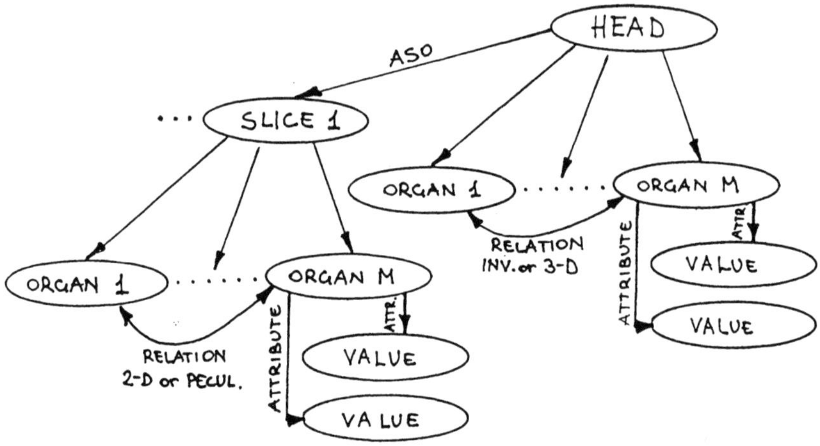

Figure 5: The global semantic net of the system

the eyes" is not true in the case of a sagittal plane where one can also see the back part of the brain that is below the eyes.

3.2. Knowledge Representation Used for the Data Base

The knowledge representation used to describe the facts contained in the data base is similar to the one used for the domain knowledge, for it is necessary to make a comparison between the state of the problem and the goals that should be attained.

To obtain a higher level symbolic representation, we have to pass from elementary regions (*e.g*, the manipulation primitives, like syllables in natural languages) to arrangements of such regions with a particular meaning.

The first step is performed on the basis of intrinsic organ properties, to identify an organ with an elementary region or a group of regions.

A set of "detected organs" is sent to the semantic analyzer. Each newly recognized organ is considered by the control structure for the coherence test based on the structural relations with the already recognized organs. Only allowed arrangements can be maintained and identified as a specific slice.

The conventions used to represent the organs and their relations are exactly the same as used for domain knowledge representation.

As regards intrinsic properties, elementary regions are described by using the same structure of organ slices as in domain-knowledge representation, except for those arcs, called "demons", which are linked with specialized features that are extracted only if required for the recognition process.

4. Results

At present, our system can recognize about 10 organs (brain, skull-bone, skin, eyes, mesencephalon, nose, vein, liquor, cerebellum, corpus callosum, etc.) and is made up of

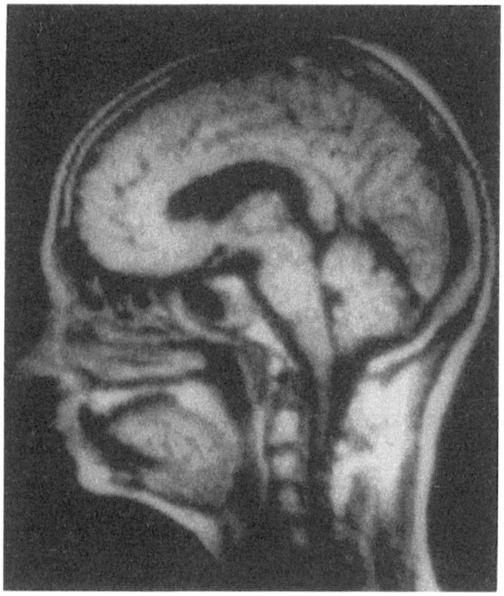

Photo 1: Sagittal slice

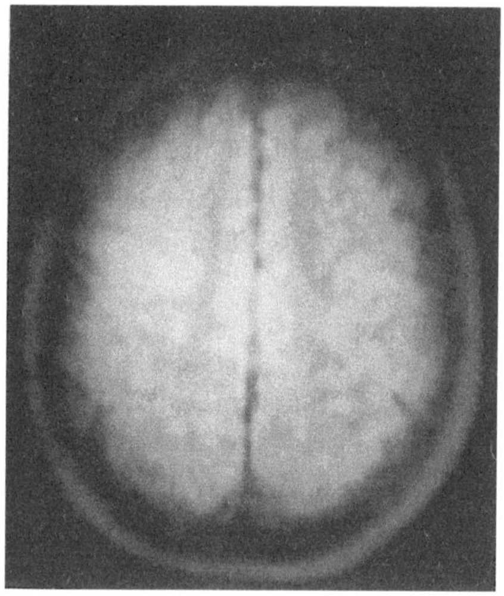

Photo 2: High transversal slice

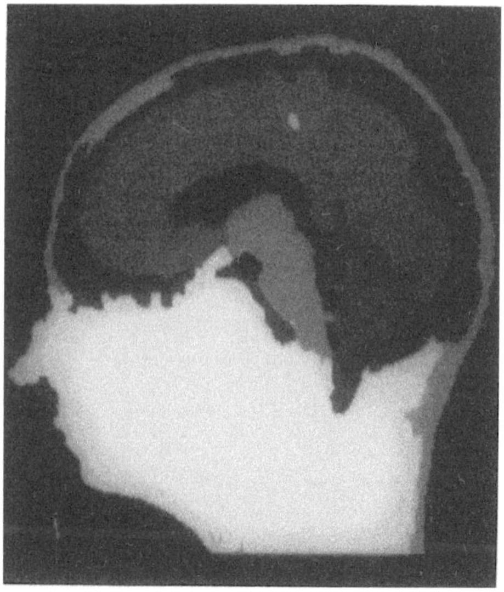

Photo 3: Sagittal final map

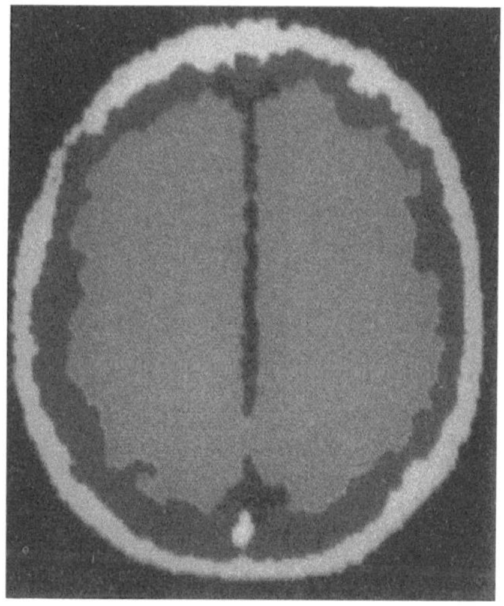

Photo 4: Transversal high final map

50 ODS's and 3 SDS's.

The LLS and a first part of the MLS are implemented in FORTRAN77, while the HLS and a second part of MLS run in LISP (PEARL).

The images ($256 \times 256 \times 8$ bits) regarding sagittal (Photo 1), transversal at the eyes' level and high transversal (Photo 2) slices were considered.

By applying segmentation we found 165, 131 and 84 elementary regions respectively. The backtracking process for all was required for all the images, due to some segmentation errors. In the final map generated for the transversal high level (Photo 4), all the organs were recognized correctly, while in the other map (Photo 3), some unrecognized regions, displayed in white, remained. This was due to the lack of some ODS not yet inserted in the system, such as the one regarding the "chiasma" place, difficult to understand also to human experts. The results so far obtained are very promising; however, many problems (e.g., new organs and slices, unclassified areas, 3-D displaying, etc.) remain to be solved.

References

[1] Nagao M., Matsuyama T., *A Structural Analysis of Complex Aerial Photographs*, Plenum Press, N.Y., 1980.

[2] Dellepiane S., Serpico S.B., Vernazza G., "Structural Analysis in Medical Imaging," EUROCON'86, Parigi, 1986.

[3] Winston P.H., *Artificial Intelligence*, Addison-Wesley, 1984.

KNOWLEDGE-BASED COMPUTER RECOGNITION OF SPEECH

Renato De Mori

School of Computer Science
McGill University
Montréal, Québec, Canada

1. Introduction

At present, a number of scientists and engineers seem to be quite interested in doing research in the area of speech recognition by computer. Different workers in the field have different approaches, and might even describe their motivations for doing speech recognition research somewhat differently. A very common position, for example, is that the main goal of speech recognition research is to develop techniques and systems for speech input to machines. If we consider machines which are real computers, rather than mere automatic dictation devices, this makes speech recognition an instance of the general problem of designing a convenient and pleasant human-computer interface, the ultimate goal being the ability to talk to computers in much the same way we now talk to fellow human beings. Indeed, if both speech recognition and general machine intelligence make sufficient progress in our lifetimes, we could conceivably encounter computers that not only listen but also reply sensibly.

Figure 1 shows the essential transformations of information involved in speech communication. Initially, a sentence generator produces an abstract representation S of the sentence to be transmitted. This abstract representation S is then converted by the speaker into a sequence of sets of discrete articulatory commands which drive the vocal tract actuators, producing a continuously time-varying pressure signal $x_1(t)$.

The signal $x_1(t)$ is transmitted through a noisy acoustic channel, resulting in a different signal $x(t)$ which is perceived by the listener.

The listener transforms the signal $x(t)$ into an acoustic pattern Ω.

The purpose of this transformation is to have a representation of the spoken message which better exhibits the linguistic features than does the signal itself. Furthermore, an attractive hypothesis about the usefulness of this transformation is that it could allow the application to speech patterns of the same interpretation strategies that are used for vision.

The acoustic pattern is then interpreted by a recognition/understanding system which first transforms the acoustic information in Ω into an abstract, linguistic representation Λ.

Unfortunately, Λ is not S. Rather, it may be a continuous string or a lattice of characters or of word hypotheses which has to be interpreted in order to produce $\hat{\mathrm{S}}$, the recognition system's final interpretation of $x(t)$. In a satisfactory recognition system,

NATO ASI Series, Vol. F30
Pattern Recognition Theory and Applications
Edited by P. A. Devijver and J. Kittler

the self-correcting mechanisms of perception function well enough to produce an $\hat{S}$ which is S most of the time.

Some speech recognition workers have chosen to apply the discipline of information theory to the construction of recognizers. That theory as originally conceive is a mathematical theory designed to measure the amount of information necessary to reduce the receiver's doubt concerning given alternatives. The contrasting approach taken here is to model both the source and the sentence interpreter as rule-based systems, where the rules encode the a priori knowledge we have about human speech generation and understanding.

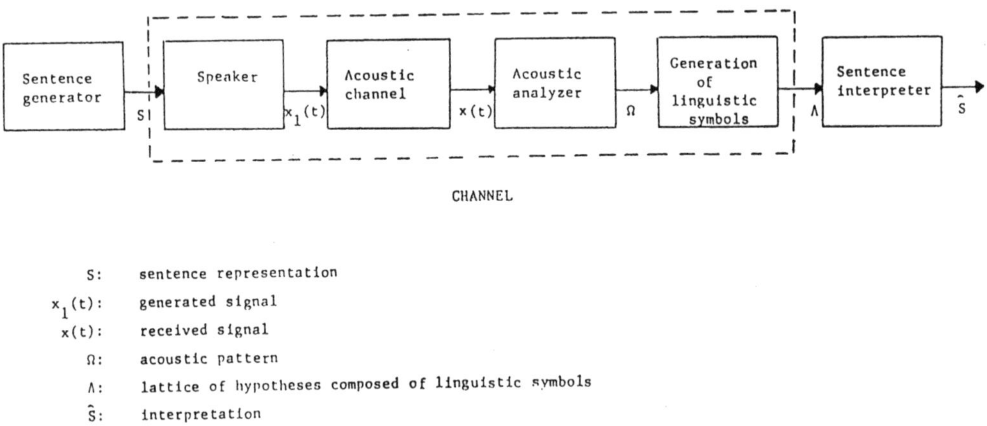

Figure 1: The Speech Communication Channel

There are many dimensions affecting the feasibility and performance of a speech recognition system.

One of the main features affecting the complexity of a speech recognition task is whether the speech is connected or is spoken one word at a time. In the latter case, the system complexity mainly depends on the range of vocabulary. Even the recognition of isolated words is a difficult task because some acoustic ambiguity may be present in the spoken word to be recognized. This ambiguity may depend on the speaker, his personality, his dialect or his speaking rate.

Some of the difficulties may be removed by asking the speaker to be cooperative, pronouncing the words carefully, with sufficiently long pauses between them. But even when speakers are cooperative, there may be ambiguities in the recognition system due to the limitations of the acoustic analyzer and to our imperfect knowledge of the features to be used and the way they have to be extracted. Fortunately, contextual (inter- and intra-syllabic) information can be used to resolve such ambiguities.

The reasons for the inherent difficulty of computer recognition of continuous speech are, at present, well understood. In continuous speech it is difficult to determine where one word ends and another begins. Moreover, co-articulation and other effects lead to a far greater context-dependent variability in the acoustic characteristics of sounds and words. For these reasons continuous speech recognition systems do not achieve the very high performance of isolated word recognition systems. We suggest that very high performance continuous speech recognition could conceivably come, in the long run, as rule-based computer recognition systems mature into deep knowledge-based systems.

Knowledge-based speech recognition systems require mechanisms to pay attention to distinctive acoustic information, detailed phonetic features, and the like. These mechanisms can perhaps be justified by considering alternate recognizers which use little or no speech knowledge.

For example, many workers use a recognition model based on feature extraction and classification. With such an approach, the same set of features are extracted at fixed time intervals (typically every 10 msecs.) and classification is based on distances between feature patterns and prototypes [12] or likelihoods computed from a Markov model of a source of symbols generated by matching centisecond speech patterns and prototypes [2].

These methods are usually speaker dependent and are made speaker independent by clustering prototypes obtained from many speakers. The classifier is not capable of making reliable decisions about phonemes of phonetic features; rather, it generates scored competing hypotheses that are combined together to form scored word and sentence candidates.

If the protocol exhibits enough redundancy it is likely that the cumulative score of the right candidate is significantly higher than the scores of competing candidates. If, however, there is little redundancy in the protocols, as in the case of connected letters or digits or in the case of a large lexicon, then it is important that ambiguities at the phonetic level are resolved before hypotheses are generated. Examples of these difficulties have been reported in the recent literature [2, 18]. For example, in the case of connected letters, in order to distinguish between |p| and |t| the place of articulation is the only distinctive feature, and its detection may require the execution of special sensory procedures on a limited portion of the signal with the time resolution finer than 10 msec.

Some people have argued that speech recognition will require fundamental progress in machine intelligence to deal with problems of context-dependence and disambiguation; we make the more modest claim that knowledge-based recognition systems need only increase their speech competence to improve their recognition performance.

We have referred to the fact that most of the systems proposed so far take advantage of the *redundancy* of the protocols they use. The most difficult and unsolved problems arise when tasks have little redundancy or when speaker independence is required for complex tasks. Examples of such complex tasks are the recognition of letters and digits (isolated or connected) and the recognition of large vocabularies. For such problems, it seems reasonable to extract a large variety of acoustic properties.

2. A Model for Computer Perception

Drawing on important computer science and machine intelligence motivations, a system has been implemented in which both the extraction of acoustic properties and the generation of syllabic hypotheses result from the collaboration of several distinct processes. This cooperation of computational activities has been conceived using the paradigm of an *Expert System Society* [15, 10].

Each expert is associated with a *Long Term Memory* (LTM) containing the specific expert's knowledge and a *Short Term Memory* (STM) where data interpretations are written.

Experts are computing agents which execute reasoning programs using structural and procedural knowledge. The knowledge of each expert is expressed by a set of *plans*, some of which can be executed in parallel. Communication between cooperating tasks is performed by message passing.

Interpretations of the speech waveform are generated by an Expert System Society. Its structure is shown in Figure 2.

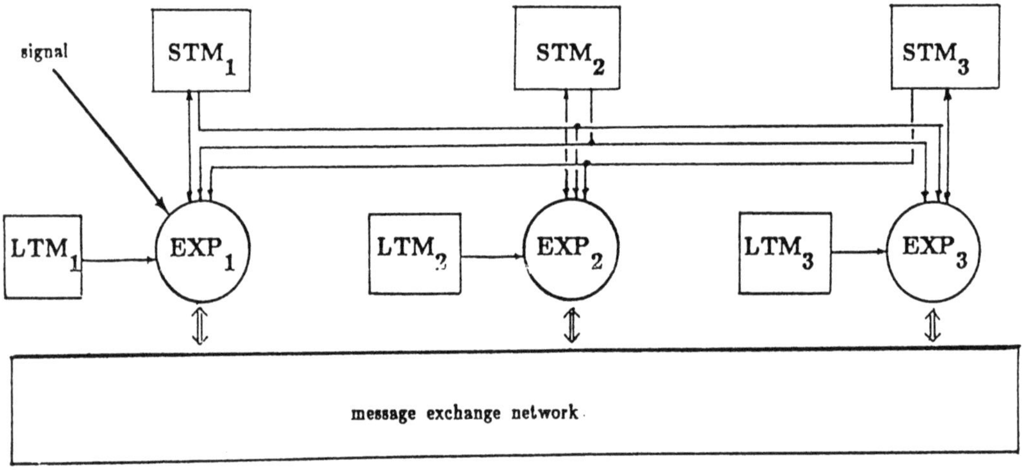

Figure 2: Expert System Society

EXP_1 is the Acoustic Expert (AE). It has the task of sampling and quantizing the signal, performing various types of signal transformations, and extracting and describing acoustic cues. The term *acoustic cues* will be used for indicating spectral or signal properties describing aspects that are relevant for hypothesizing phonetic features. Examples of acoustic cues are formant loci, characteristics of burst spectra like compactness, and peaks and valleys of signal energy.

EXP_1 can perform, for example, an analysis based on Linear Prediction Coefficients (LPC) for segments labelled with vocalic hypotheses in order to find formant loci capable of describing the place and manner of articulation. EXP_1 can also perform a broad-band spectral analysis based on the Fast Fourier Transformation (FFT) when hypotheses of nonsonorant continuant sounds have been made. Like other experts, EXP_1 may carry out both spontaneous *data-driven* activities and *expectation-driven* activities arising out of requests issued by other experts.

Requests and control messages are exchanged among experts through the message exchange network shown in Figure 2. Data, cues, descriptions and hypotheses are written by an expert into its own Short Term Memory (STM). Only the expert which owns the STM can write into it, but any expert can read any STM.

EXP_2 is the Phonetic and Syllabic Expert (PSE). It translates descriptions of acoustic cues into *phonetic feature hypotheses.* These features describe the *manner* and the *place* of articulation of each segment of the spoken utterance. This translation may involve the extraction of new acoustic cues by asking EXP_{1k} to execute sensory procedures.

There are some acoustic cues, like peaks and valleys of time evolutions of energies in fixed bands of the signal, that can be extracted by context-independent algorithms. These acoustic cues will be called *Primary Acoustic Cues* (PAC) and the phonetic features related to them will be called *Primary Phonetic Features* (PPT). A definition of the primary cues and features used in the system described here is given in Tables I, II and III. These algorithms for extracting PACs generate descriptions of a time interval of the signal without being constrainted by contextual information extracted from adjacent segments.

Examples of various types of PACs are shown in Figure 3. The two curves in Figure 3a represent the time evolution of the signal energy (—) and the zero-crossing counts (---) in successive 10 msec intervals of the first derivative of the signal. The phrase is the sequence of letters and digits K3VPCB. Figure 3b shows the corresponding PAC description. The time unit is 0.01 sec. LONG and SHORT refer to the dip duration. DEEP, MEDIUM and HIGH refer to the height of the minimum energy in the dip with respect to the background noise energy.

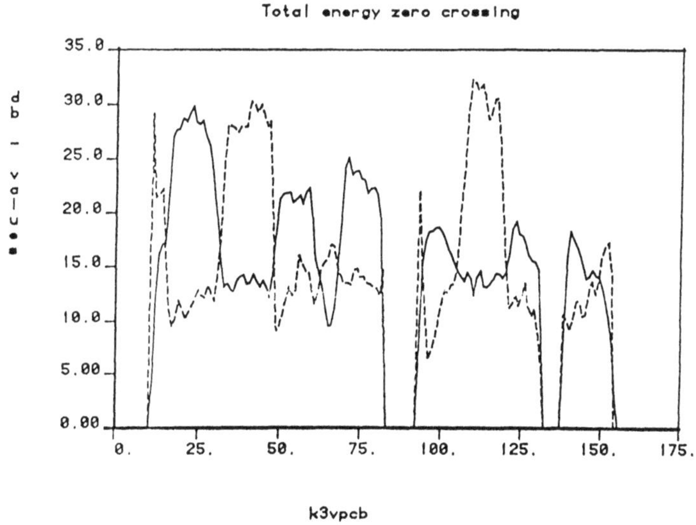

Figure 3: A Concatenation of letters and digits

Other functions of EXP_2 include those of segmenting the speech signal into Pseudo Syllabic Segments (PSS) and of checking or evaluating phonetic hypotheses. How exactly hypotheses are formulated and then tested, whether the hypotheses are highly specific or more open and less specific, and how central the asymmetry between positive evidence and negative evidence is to perception, are all deep questions both for the psychology and philosophy of perception and for the design of computer perception systems; we have identified these questions as subjects for research but do not claim to possess definitive answers to any of them. The current system implementation implicitly models some of these aspects in a tentative fashion.

In EXP_2, the activity of generating PPFs is *data-driven*, while the activities of extracting other phonetic features *expectation-driven*. Expectations may arise from a strategy inside EXP_2 or they can be requests transmitted by EXP_3. This distribution of expectation sources in the computer recognition system has a direct analogy to the fact that, in humans, perception is distributed throughout large regions of the brain; we see again the distinction between distributed sensors and distributed intelligence.

EXP_3 is the Lexical Expert (LE) that generates lexical hypotheses based on prosodic features, phonetic hypotheses, and syntactic and semantic constraints.

3. Acoustic Properties, Phonetic Features, and Plans

This section describes how relations of phonetic features to acoustic properties are embedded in *plans* which are executed by the expert system.

with this approach a phoneme PH_i is expressed by a set of phonetic features, i.e.

$$PH_i = (pf_{i1}, pf_{i2}, \ldots, pf_{ij}, \ldots, pf_{iJ}) \tag{1}$$

Each phonetic feature ph_x is represented by a relation R_x to a set properties ap_x, *i.e.*,

$$pf_x = R_x(ap_{x1}, ap_{x2}, \ldots, ap_{xk}, \ldots, ap_{xK}) \tag{2}$$

For example, the phoneme |p| is represented as follows:

Table I
Primary Acoustic Cues

Symbol	Attributes	Description
LPK	tb,te,ml,zx,	long peak of total energy (TE)
SPK	"	short peak of TE
MPK	"	peak of TE of medium duration
LOWP	"	low energy peak of TE
LNS	tb,te,zx	long nonsonorant tract
MNS	"	medium nonsonorant tract
LVI	tb,te,ml,zx	long vocalic tract adjacent to a LNS or a MNS in a TE peak
MVI	tb,te,ml,zx	medium vocalic tract adjacent to a LNS or a MNS in a TE peak
LDD	emin,tb,te,zx	short deep dip of total energy
LMD	"	long dip of total energy with medium depth
SMD	"	short dip of total energy with medium depth
LHD	"	long non-deep dip of total energy
SHD	"	short non-deep dip of total energy

Table I (continued)

Attribute	**Description**
tb	time of beginning
te	time of end
ml	maximum signal energy in the peak
emin	minimum total energy in a dip
zx	maximum zero-crossing density of the signal derivative in the tract

|p| = (nonsonorant-interrupted-consonant,tense,labial) = (nit,labial).

The phonetic feature 'labial' in the context of 'nit' features is represented by the following relation R_k:

(**relation** R_k)
(**left-side**
(**feature** (labial))
(**feature context** (nit))
(**temporal context** (**followed-by** font vowel)))
(**Bright-side**
(suprasegmental and time-domain properties)
(formant-transition properties)
(burst-spectra properties)))

The rule for 'labial' takes into account different types of *contextual dependencies*. One contextual dependency is represented by the other features that appear with 'labial' in a plosive phoneme. The other contextual dependencies are represented by the class of phonemes that can follow or precede the plosive phoneme under consideration. Relations are used by plans executed by the expert system.

In many cases, acoustic property extraction is context dependent; for example, we may be forced to impose precedence relations on the extraction processes. For more on the latter, we refer to [4] and [11].

A *plan* is a sequence of items. Each item may contain a *precondition expression* for applying rules of the type R_k, *operators* containing sensory procedures for extracting the properties used by R_k, and an *algorithm* for evaluating the evidence of the hypothesis generated by R_k. An example of a plan applying rules like R_k will be given later in this section. In practice, a plan is a sequence of operators. Each operator is associated with a precondition and an action.

The Acoustic Expert is capable of extracting acoustic cues based on the requests it receives from the Phonetic and Syllabic Expert.

An example of such a request is the following:

$$\text{RQ} := \text{plosive-place-of-articulation}\ (t_1, t_2, t_3, \text{ctx})$$

where t_1 is the time of the beginning of the plosive silence or buzz-bar, t_2 is the time of the beginning of the burst, t_3 is the time of the beginning of the voice onset, and ctx is the context in which the plosive sound is hypothesized. For example ctx can be (front-vowel, F1, F2, F3). The time instants t_1, t_2 and t_3 are attributes of the primary acoustic cues which generated a plosive hypothesis.

When the Acoustic Expert receives a request for the extraction of the cues which generated a plosive hypothesis.

When the Acoustic Expert receives a request for the extraction of the cues for the place of articulation of plosive sounds it creates a process "plosive-place-of-articulation $(t_1, t_2, t_3, \text{ctx})$" which executes a plan whose details are given in the following:

Algorithm for process : plosive-place-of-articulation $(t_1, t_2, t_3, \text{ctx})$

```
begin
   find-burst-spectra (t2, t3, bs);
   burst-evidence := f1(bs);
   compact-evidence := f2(bs);
   diffuse-falling-ev := f3(bs);
   diffuse-rising-ev := f4(bs);
   track-formants-in-the-plosive-transitions (for,ctx,t3);
   compute-pseudo-loci (for,pl);
   for-labial-evidence := R_lp (pl,ctx);
   for-alveolar-evidence := R_lp (pl,ctx);
   ev(labial) := R_lp (for-labial-evidence, diffuse-falling-ev, burst-evidence, ctx);
   ev(alveolar:) := R_lp (for-alveolar-evidence, diffuse-rising-ev, burst-evidence, ctx);
   ev(palatal) := R_lp (for-palatal-evidence, burst-evidence,compact-evidence, ctx);
   send (PSE(ev(labial, ev(alveolar), ev(palatal), plosive(t1, t2, t3)))
end
```

PSE collects all the evidences about syllabic hypotheses in a time interval (t_a, t_b) and compares them according to the following algorithm.

"PSE evaluator of hypotheses (t_a, t_b)"

```
begin
   repeat
      receive (evidences,ta, tb);
      compose (evidences,ctx,ta, tb)
   until all-requests-satisfied;
   decide-hypotheses-to-be-kept (evidences,ta, tb, syll-hyp)
end
```

4. Detailed Description of a Plan

The speech signal is first analyzed on the basis of loudness, zero-crossing rates and broad-band energies as described in [8]. The result of this analysis is a string of symbols and attributes. Symbols belong to an alphabet of Primary Acoustic Cues (PAC).

The use of coarse acoustic properties (PAC) for segmenting continuous speech into acoustic segments has been described in a previous paper [8]. The segmentation algorithm based on an attributed grammar has been simplified, in such a way that a preliminary segmentation is performed first based only on signal energy deep dips and friction intervals. Each *acoustic segment* obtained in this way may contain one or more syllables but it never contains less than one vowel. Each acoustic segment could be further described following the scheme shown in Figure 4.

Figure 4 shows the general scheme of an action hierarchy and the planning system that generates its compiled version. Each expansion of an action represents a plan refinement. Each refinement is a sub-plan consisting of a sequence of operators. Preconditions for refinement are generated and updated by a Learning System [7].

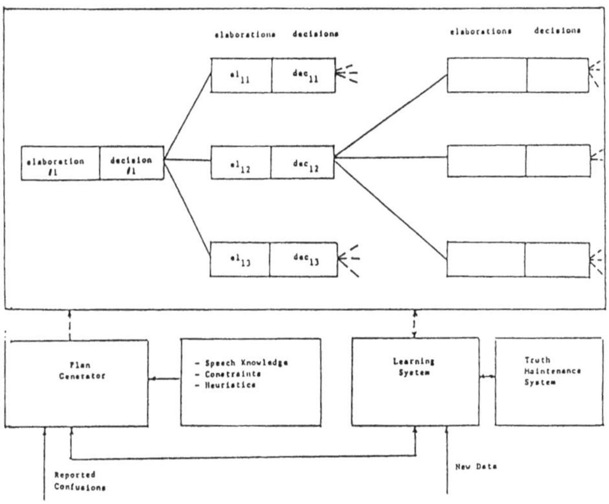

Figure 4: Scheme for Generating Network of Actions in Compiled Form

An action hierarchy is applied for interpreting the consonantal segment of every syllable.

Figure 5 shows the more abstract part of the action hierarchy. PAC extraction and segmentation is a preliminary spontaneous activity that is followed by a decision phase where rule-set(1) is applied. Rule-set(1) is made of preconditions and actions. Preconditions are sequences of PACs. Actions describe what acoustic properties are worth to be extracted given the suprasegmental morphology described by the PAC expression. Rule set (1) is represented in Table II.

For the sake of simplicity only the action corresponding to rule (1.45.1) is shown in Figure 5. The precondition for this rule is (LDD) (LPK + LVI). The symbol + represents here logical disjunction. This PAC morphology may correspond to a vowel after a pause, to the consonants |v| or |g| or to plosive consonants for which burst is not evident in the loudness curve. This precondition represents a speaking mode that is rather frequent for |b| and is one of the most difficult to analyze. The action to be executed in this case is the analysis of the (deep dip) | (peak) transition. Useful operators are those that detect voicing, the existence of burst and some temporal relations among

Table II

Rule–set (1)

No.		Precondition			Confusion set
1	LNS	MVI	SHD	LPK	3
2	MNS	MVI	SHD	LPK	3
		...			
		...			
		...			
8	SDD	LOWP	SMD	LPK	v
		...			
		...			
		...			
11	LDD	SPK	LHD	LPK	k
		...			
		...			
		...			
		...			
41	SDD	LPK			b, d, v
		...			
		...			
		...			
45	LDD	(LPK+LVI)		p, e, b, d, k, 3 v	
		...			
		...			
		...			
74	LDD	MNS	MVI		k, g, t
		...			
		...			
		...			
90	SHD	MPK	LPK		v

the onset of the energies in various bands because delays in these onset time are cues for the presence of plosive sounds.

The approach is that of extracting a *redundant set* of cues so that the final decision about the acoustic properties that describes them is reliable.

According to Figure 5, the activity "dip peak analysis" is refined by a more detailed sub-plan which is produced by the planning system introduced in the previous Section. As broad-band energies have to be analyzed at the end of the buzz-bar and when the signal envelope starts rising, the chaining order shown in Figure 5 is obtained.

If there is enough evidence for burst and if there is still a need of discriminating among classes, then a rule of rule-set (1.45) will invoke the execution of a burst analysis action

Op11 in Figure 5 produces an envelope description by analyzing the signal amplitude before and after preemphasis. Envelope samples are obtained every msec by taking

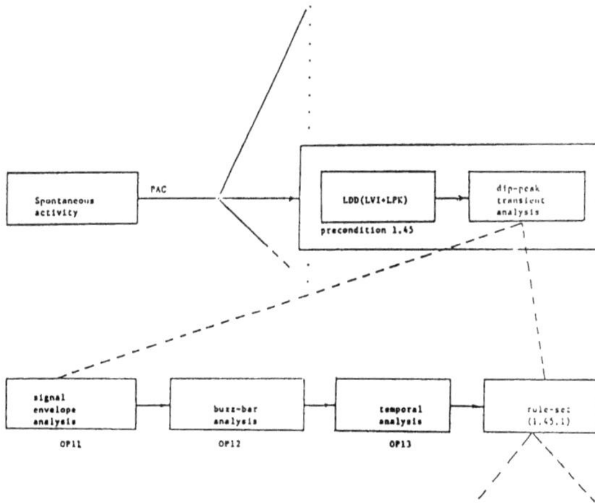

Figure 5: Example of Network of Actions

the absolute value of the difference between the absolute maximum and the absolute minimum of the signal in a 3 msec interval. The envelope description is based on the following alphabets:

A111 = {SHORT–STEP(ST1),
LONG–STEP(ST2),
NOSTEP(STO)}

A112 = {HIGH LOW FREQUENCY ENERGY(BZ1),
ABSENCE OF BUZZ INDICATOR IN THE ENVELOPE (BZ0)}

A113 = {POSSIBLE BURST (PB1),
ABSENCE OF BURST EVIDENCE (PB0)}

A114 = {STRONG BURST EVIDENCE (BU1),
NO STRONG BURST EVIDENCE (BU0)}.

The description produced by Op11 as well as those produced by Op12 and Op13 are attached to the DDN describing the segment under analysis.

Because of the shape of the signal envelope, a description (ST0, BZ1, PB1, BU0) is obtained.

Op12 describes the buzz-bar by analyzing the shape of the time waveform and of the spectra before the voice onset. The alphabets of the description it produces are:

$$BZA1 = \{BI1, BI2, BI3, BI4, BI5\}$$

for the time waveform and

$$BZA2 = \{BR1, BR2, BR3, BR4, BR5\}$$

for the spectra.

Figure 6 shows the LPC (continuous line) and the FFT (dashed line) spectra computed before the TE peak onset. The consistent low frequency peak in the FFT spectrum

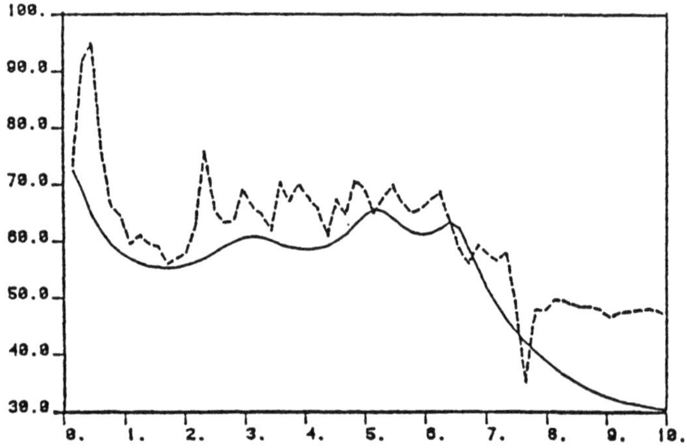

Figure 6:

is the cue for buzz-bar. The low frequency oscillations in the waveform are other buzz cues.

BI1 and BR1 mean no buzz and the other symbols describe degrees of buzz-bar evidence: (BI1,BR2: little evidence; BI5,BR5: strong evidence).

Based on the waveform of Figure 6 and the spectra shown in Figure 6 the segment is described as (BI3,BR5).

Op13 analyzes temporal events of the energy in some frequency bands at the voice onset. These events are related to voice onset time. They are:

- NP : number of short peaks in the time evolution of the energy in the 2–4 kHz band,
- RE : a bar of energy at low frequency before the peak
- DL : the delay between the onset of low and high frequency energies,
- ZQ : the duration of the largest zero-crossing interval of the signal at the onset,
- ZR : the number of zero-crossing counts in the largest sequence of successive zero-crossing intervals with duration less than 0.5 msecs.
- DR : minimum value in a dip of ratio between low and high frequency energies.

The first two cues represent morphologies described by the alphabets: {NP0,..., NP5}, {RE0,RE1}. Intervals of parameters are coded with symbols {DL1,...,DL5}, {ZQ1,..., ZQ5}, {DR1,...,DR5}. From a dip-peak transition, a vector of values of (NP, RE, DL, ZQ, ZR, DR) is extracted and represented by a conjunction of symbols according to the intervals the parameters fall into. Intervals are determined after clustering vectors corresponding to the same letter and intersecting clusters of different letters.

The description obtained by OP11, OP12 and OP13 for the |b| is the following:
Descr. 1.45 : PB1 STO BZ1 BU0 RE0 NP1 DR4 DL2 B13 BR5

This description is compared with the premises of the rule set given in Table III.

The letter candidate with the highest SM with Descr. 1.45 is considered along with the letter candidates with SM close to this maximum. All these letters constitute an *active confusion set.* If the active confusion sets are found containing more than one element, then an action has to be introduced by the planning system. If a refinement already exists, then a detailed subplan will be executed.

Table III

Rule #		Precondition	Letter
1	BZ0 ST0 RE0 NP0 NP1	DR3 DR4 DL1 DL2 ZQ2 ZQ4 BI1 BI2 BR2 BR2	p
2	PB0 ST1 BZ1 BU0 NP0 NP1	DR3 DR4 DL1 DL2 ZQ3 ZQ4 BI3 BI4 BR3 BR5	d
3	BI0 STBI1 BZ1 BU0 NP0 NP1	DR3 DR4 DL1 DL2 ZQ3 ZQ4 BI3 BI4 BR3 BR5	b
4	PB0 ST1 BZ0 BU0 BU1 RE0 RE1 NP0 NP1	DR4 DR4 DL1 DL2 ZQ4 ZQ5 BI1 BI4 BR3 BR3	p
5	PB0 ST0 BU0 RE0 NP0 NP1	DR3 DR4 DL1 DL2 ZQ3 ZQ5 BI1 BI1 BR2 BR4	b
6	PB0 ST0 BI1 BZ0 NP0 NP1	DR3 DR4 DL1 DL2 ZQ2 ZQ4 BI1 BI2 BR2 BR3	e
7	PB1 ST0 BI1 BZ0 RE0 NP0 NP1	DR2 DR4 DL1 DL2 ZQ2 BI2 BI2 BR4 BR4	p
8	PB1 ST0 BZ0 BU0 RE0 NP1	DR2 DR3 DL2 DL2 ZQ5 ZQ5 BI4 BI4 BR4 BR5	p
9	BP0 ST0 BZ1 BU RE0 NP0	DR4 DR4 DL1 DL1 ZQ1 ZQ1 BI1 BI1 BR2 BR2	e
10	PB0 ST0 BZ1 BU0 RE0 NP1	DR2 DR2 DL4 DL4 ZQ4 ZQ4 BI2 BI2 BR3 BR3	3
11	PB0 ST1 BZ1 BU0 RE0 NP0	DR3 DR4 DL4 DL4 ZQ1 ZQ3 BI4 BI4 BR3 BR3	v
12	PB1 ST0 BZ0 BU0 RE0 NP1	DR2 DR3 DL2 DL2 ZQ1 ZQ3 BI1 BI1 BR1 BR2	k
13	PB1 ST0 BZ0 BU0 RE0 NP1 NP2	DR2 DR2 DL2 DL2 ZQ1 ZQ3 BI1 BI1 BR1 BR3	d
14	PB1 ST0 BZ1 BU0 RE0 NP1	DR3 DR3 DL1 DL1 ZQ4 ZQ4 BI1 BI1 BR2 BR2	p
15	PB0 ST0 BU0 RE0 NP0 NP1	DR3 DR4 DL1 ZQ2 ZQ4 BI1 BI1 BR2 BR2	v
16	PB0 ST0 RZ1 RE0 NP0	DR4 DR4 DL1 DL1 ZQ1 ZQ1 BI1 BI1 BR2 BR2	e

For our example the following similarity measures were found:

Letter	SM	Rule component
d	1.000	(2)
b	1.000	(3)
p	0.888	(7)
p	0.824	(8)
p	0.812	(1)
p	0.771	(14)
k	0.757	(12)
e	0.729	(6)
b	0.669	(4)
3	0.656	(10)
d	0.556	(13)

In our example the active confusion set contains two letters [b, d] and the refinement is based on a more detailed analysis of the burst and transition of spectral lines. The refined action contains the calculation of burst spectra and the description of spectral profiles as well as other properties like, center of gravity, frequency above which there is 70% of the spectral energy and other parameters whose details are omitted for the sake of brevity.

In particular example under analysis, the system has tracked the time evolution of the major energy concentration in the frequency band of the second formant. Based on a rule on the curve slope it has decided that the letter was |b|.

Notice that the same hypotheses, *i.e.*, a letter of the E1 set can be hypothesized following different paths in the network of actions. The path followed in generating the hypotheses is remembered by adding a suffix to the hypothesized letter. In the way, the hypothesization of B through the n-th possible path to B will be described a B_n.

5. Experimental Results

The proposed approach has been tested in a multi-speaker environment. An initial learning phase was performed on a corpus of 1000 connected pronounciations of symbols of the E1 set in strings EGP3V and KCBTD of five symbols each. The strings were pronounced by five male speakers, and five female speakers. Each speaker pronounced them ten times.

Knowledge acquisition consisted in plan refinement as well as in precondition learning.

After the first 10 speakers were analyzed and knowledge was determined and updated, an overall error rate of 3% was achieved in the learning set consisting of 1000 samples.

The rules of the planning system do not necessarily produce a single hypothesis, although a-priori probabilities can be collected in the case of multiple hypotheses and used for forcing the system to generate the most plausible hypothesis according to some decision criterion.

This possibility was not used in the experiment described in this Section.

Failure to generate the expected hypothesis is considered an *error*, while the generation of the expected hypothesis together with other candidates is considered an *ambiguity*.

In the learning set, 9% of the cases resulted in ambiguities. The average number of ambiguous hypotheses generated in this 9% was 2.2.

The experiments continued by presenting to the system data collected from successive sets containing always new speakers. Each set was made of 10 speakers randomly chosen among a large group of students with predominance of Francophones and Anglophones. Each speaker in each set was asked to pronounce two sequences of elements of the E1 set. Sequences were generated at random by a computer program with the only constraint that |e| could appear only at the beginning of the sequence. This fact as well as the number of letters of each sequence were not known to the recognition program.

Performances were computed *before* refinement so that the system knowledge was used for recognizing phrases of speakers that were not previously analyzed by the system. Nevertheless, after the analysis of each set of speakers, plan and precondition refinements were performed.

After 5 sets were analyzed containing 100 data from 10 speakers each, all the 1500 utterances corresponding to the first 15 sets were processed again for recognition and statistics of rule application were collected in order to prepare a stochastic model.

Inductive learning of rules is supposed to characterize different speaking modes through chains of property descriptions for short time intervals whose duration typically varies between 10 and 50 msecs. Some properties may have a larger scope both backwards and forwards.

Variations of parameter values and minor distortions of the inferred rules can be characterized by stochastic networks.

A-priori probabilities of rule application have been inferred using data from the first 60 speakers.

For each PAC precondition, other parameters and morphologies are extracted and expressions are derived. If there is enough data available for a given precondition, then statistics of the rules applied at the second level of the action hierarchy can be collected.

Having captured a model of the *structure* of speaking modes, it is possible now to perform a *stochastic generalization* by using the knowledge obtained with inductive learning for setting *initial conditions*.

Initial conditions can be set as follows.
If a transition is associated with a single symbol, then a probability distribution on the symbols of the same alphabet is set with a high value assigned only to the single symbol. For example, ST1 will generate the distribution

$$\{(\mathrm{ST0}, .01); (\mathrm{ST1}, .98); (\mathrm{ST2}, .01)\}$$

If a transition is associated with n symbols of a vocabulary of N symbols, then a probability equal to .01 is assigned to the $(N-n)$ symbols not appearing in the transition and a probability of $(1 - 0.01(N - n))/n$ is associated to the others.

For example, NP0,1 will enerate the distribution:

$$\{(\mathrm{NP0}, .48); (\mathrm{NP1}, .48); (\mathrm{NP2}, .01); (\mathrm{NP3}, .01); (\mathrm{NP4}, .01); (\mathrm{NP5}, .01)\}$$

If a transition is associated to a "don't care" symbol x, then all the symbols of the alphabet will appear with equal probability.

For example, x on RE will generate the distribution

$$\{(\mathrm{RE0}, .5); (\mathrm{RE1}, .5)\}$$

Parameter intervals can be seen as 3σ values of gaussian distributions with mean just in the middle of the interval.

Forward-backward algorithms can be applied for refining the statistics of these stochastic automata.

Stochastic generalizations were performed only for those subnetworks for which there were enough data available. In the other cases, a-priori probabilities of rule application were used for disambiguating multiple generation of letter hypotheses.

The confusions reported in the following refer to a test set containing 500 data from 50 new speakers.

Errors are now due to two causes, namely fault in generating the right hypothesis or fault of selecting the right hypothesis when disambiguation is performed using stochastic networks.

A total of 23 errors due to segmentation and 58 errors due to misclassification have been found making the overall performance of the system in a multispeaker environment equal to 84%.

6. Conclusions

The idea of using a number of phonetically significant properties in a recognition system based on the planning paradigm appears very promising. The analysis of the behavior of each plan and of the errors generated by their application suggests the actions that have to be taken in order to improve recognition accuracy.

Rule 45 is the most frequently used and the one responsible for most of the errors. In particular, in 14 confusions of |b|, |d|, |p| and |3| with |e| are due to the fact that the system has not been able to correctly detect and process the transient at the vowel onset. Transients in such a case are difficult to analyze and the system tends to see the cues of |e| rather than those of the consonant that is supposed to preceed it.

Planning and inductive learning are still interactive and involve human activities, but they are aimed towards characterization of speaking modes and speech styles.

Different speaking modes and styles can be well characterized using descriptions of acoustic properties that represent different phonetic events.

Finer variations of characteristic descriptions of acoustic properties can be represented and learned using stochastic methods. Letters exhibit little redundancy because they are very short sounds. This justifies the introduction of a relatively large number of acoustic properties for characterizing a short time segment. Redundancy helps in reducing ambiguities.

Using different descriptions for the same letter allows one to recognize pronounciations of rare speaking modes provided that descriptions do not interfere with similar descriptions of other letters in other speaking modes.

Criticial problems, are the distinction |d| vs |b| due to the fact that when the burst cues for |d| are not very evident, the system tends to apply the rule that a weak burst is more likely for |b| than for |d|. Other errors are due to misrecognition of voicing (confusion |d|, |t|) and to the incorrect classification of frication noise (confusion |3|, |c|). A few errors may be due to a wrong pronounciation of the speakers. In fact, perceptual tests were not performed in order to assess if the speakers really pronounced what they saw on the screen.

The use of suprasegmental features described by PACs is very effective for locating signal segments where properties have to be extracted even if a few problems remain to be fixed. The research will continue with the analysis of letters and digits including dipthongs and also towards the characterization of rare speaking modes of speakers with different mother tongue.

Acknowledgements

This research was supported by the Natural Sciences and Engineering Research Council of Canada with grant no. A2439.

References

[1] Bahl, L.R., Jelinek, F., Mercer, R.L., "A Maximum Likelihood Approach to Continuous Speech Recognition," IEEE Trans. on Pattern Analysis and Machine Intelligence, Vol. PAMI-5, No. 2, pp. 179-190, March 1983.

[2] Bahl, L.R., Das, S.K., de Souza, P.V., Jelinek, F., Katz, S., Mercer, R.L., Picheny, M.A., "Some Experiments with Large-Vocabulary Isolated Word Sentence Recognition," Proc. of the IEEE Conference on Acoustics, Speech, and Signal Processing, San Diego, CA, pp. 2651-2653, March 1984.

[3] Church, K.W., "Phrase-Structure Parsing: A Method for Taking Advantage of Allophonic Constraints," MIT/LCS/TR-296, Cambridge, MA, January 13, 1983. (MIT Ph.D. thesis)

[4] Demichelis, P., De Mori, R., Laface, P. and O'Kane, M., "Computer Recognition of Plosive Sounds Using Contextual Information," IEEE Trans. on Acoustics, Speech, and Signal Processing, Vol. ASSP-31, No. 2, pp. 359-377, April 1983.

[5] De Mori, R., Giordana, A., Laface, P., Saitta, L., "An Expert System for Interpreting Speech Patterns," Proc. of the AAAI-82, pp. 107-110, 1982.

[6] De Mori, R., Computer Models of Speech Using Fuzzy Algorithms, Plenum Press, New York, NY, 1983.

[7] De Mori, R. and Gilloux, M., "Inductive Learning of Phonetic Rules for Automatic Speech Recognition," Proc. of the CSCSI-84, London, Ontario, pp. 103-106, May 1984.

[8] De Mori, R., Laface, P., and Mong, Y., "Parallel Algorithms for Syllable Recognition in Continuous Speech," IEEE Trans. on Pattern Analysis and Machine Intelligence, Vol. PAMI-6, pp. 56-69, January 1985.

[9] Doyle, J., "A Truth Maintenance System," Artificial Intelligence, Vol. 12, No. 3, pp. 231-272, 1979.

[10] Erman, L.D., Hayes-Roth, F., Lesser, V.R., Reddy, D.R., "The HEARSAY-II Speech-Understanding System: Integrating Knowledge to Resolve Uncertainty," Computing Surveys, Vol. 12, No. 2, pp. 213-253, June 1980.

[11] Kopec, G.E., "Voiceless Stop Consonant Identification Using LPC Spectra," Proc. of the IEEE Conference on Acoustics, Speech, and Signal Processing, San Diego, CA, pp. 4211-4214, March 1984.

[12] Levinson, S., Rabiner, L.R., "Isolated and Connected Word Recognition: Theory and Selected Applications," IEEE Trans. on Communications, Vol. COM-29, No. 5, pp. 621-659, May 1981.

[13] McCarthy, J., "Some Expert Systems Need Common Sense," in The Computer Culture, H. Pagels, ed., Annals of the New York Academy of Sciences, Vol. 426, (1984).

[14] Michalski, R.S., "A Theory and Methodology of Inductive Learning," in Machine Learning: An Artificial Intelligence Approach, Tioga Publishing Company, Palo Alto, CA, pp. 83-134, 1983.

[15] Minsky, M., "A Framework for Representing Knowledge," in The Psychology of Computer Vision, P. Winston, ed., McGraw-Hill, New York, NY, 1975.

[16] Moses, J., "Computer Science as the Science of Discrete Man-Made Systems," Knowledge: Creation, Diffusion, Utilization, Vol. 4, No. 2, pp. 219-226, December 1982, reprinted in The Study of Information: Interdisciplinary Messages, F. Machlup and U. Mansfield, eds., John Wiley and Sons, New York, NY, 1983.

[17] Neisser, U., Cognition and Reality: Principles and Implications of Cognitive Psychology, W.H. Freeman and Co., San Francisco, CA, 1976.

[18] Rabiner, L.R., Wilpon, J.G., Terrace, S.G., "A Directory Listing Retrieval System Based on Connected Letter Recognition," Proc. IEEE Conference on Acoustics, Speech, and Signal Processing, San Diego, CA, pp. 3541-3544, March 1984.

[19] Whitehill, S.B., "Self Correcting Generalization," Proc. of the AAAI-80, pp. 240-242, 1980.

MODELLING (SUB)STRING-LENGTH BASED CONSTRAINTS THROUGH A GRAMMATICAL INFERENCE METHOD

Héctor Rulot and Enrique Vidal

Centro de Informática de la Universidad de Valencia
Burjasot, Valencia, Spain

Abstract

In this paper a new Grammatical Inference method is proposed. In this method, a finite-state automaton is constructed by means of an incremental procedure which performs both Inference and Recognition in an integrated and simultaneous way. The (incremental) growth of the inferred automaton is controlled by explicitly minimizing (by Dynamic Programming Methods) the number of states added when each new sample is presented. This procedure has been shown to achieve an "abstraction" process which tends to capture all the relevant variability present in the local (sub)structures of the patterns being considered, and their concatenation, as well as in the lengths (extents) of these structures. The results of the application of this method to a (simple) Automatic Speech Recognition task are presented, showing its capability of achieving recognition rates which are higher than those obtained with the automata constructed by hand by experienced speech researchers.

1. Introduction

Grammatical Inference (*GI*) is, within the syntactic approach to Pattern Recognition, the "learning" or "model estimation" process which is essential to any proper approach to Pattern Recognition (*PR*). Given an appropriate sample R^+ of patterns taken among those to be recognized, and possibly other sample R^- from those to be rejected, the *GI* procedure must find the Structural Model (grammar) which best accounts for all these patterns. Despite its great importance, and its rather well posed formulation, limitations, and scope [2] [6], this problem has been considered by only a limited number of researchers in the past few years [1] [4] [7] [10] [11] [13].

Because of the difficulties involved with unrestricted, context-sensitive, and context-free grammars, most of the referred works have dealt with the inference of a limited class of structural models; *i.e.* the class of Regular Grammars and/or Finite State Automata. Since a trivial (canonical) regular grammar G_c which strictly generates the given positive sample R^+ ($L(G_c) = R^+$) can be straightforwardly synthesized, the

NATO ASI Series, Vol. F30
Pattern Recognition Theory and Applications
Edited by P. A. Devijver and J. Kittler

central problem raised by GI is to find a "more abstract or general" grammar G such that $R^+ \subset L(G)$, and $L(G) - R^+$ (the "extralanguage") contain only patterns of "similar characteristics" to those of R^+. If the negative sample R^- is not to be taken into account (which is often the case), the specification of the term "similar characteristics" can only be assumed to depend upon the PR problem being considered and, in fact, all the GI methods proposed recently are aimed at accounting for specific PR problems. The properties of the extralanguages generated by the inferred grammars are thus "tailored" to the corresponding applications, but a common characteristic shared by nearly all the methods proposed so far is that this extralanguage is *infinite*; more specifically, it is composed of structures (strings) which derive from those of $R^+$by *arbitrarily repeating* certain substructures (substrings) of its patterns. Although this characteristic is often assumed to represent a "natural" abstraction ability, in many PR problems this leads to a grammar which is "too permissive". In particular, these grammars are completely unable to represent any (sub)string-length-based discriminative features of the patterns to be recognized.

(Sub)string-length-based features are, however, fairly important in many PR areas. Perhaps the most widely considered is Automatic Speech Recognition. In this area, the durations of the different acoustic (sub)structures constitute important features upon which the recognition of the different speech units (phonemes, syllables, words, etc.) must rely. In other areas, like Image or Picture Recognition, the lengths (extents) of some substructures like lines, angles, etc., can also be of great interest for recognizing the corresponding structures. A typical example is the recognition of different classes of chromosomes, in which the lengths of some of their parts are robust discriminating features. Also, in Optical Character Recognition, the lengths of the strokes upon which the characters are made, are often used as relevant information.

To overcome the (inferred) syntactic models lack of this kind of discriminating ability, other complementary information must be incorporated. This can be done through what is often called "hybrid approaches", in which some *numerical attributes* are attached to the structural models in order to handle the complementary information. The best known of these approaches is Stochastic Syntactic Pattern Recognition, as well as its closely related Hidden Markov Modelling. Within this framework, length modelling is accomplished through the use of probabilities to represent the likelihoods of different left(right)-recursive grammar-rules (and/or the corresponding automata loops) repetition. However, it has been widely claimed that, in most cases, this length modelling is quite inappropriate, because it leads to *geometric* (exponential) length probability distributions [8] [12] and, consequently, other ad-hoc refinements must be introduced. Also, other ad-hoc methods, like the introduction of "counters" and "length thresholds" in the states of automata, have been thoroughly utilized. In fact, all these methods can be seen as particular instances of using *Attributed Grammars*. It has been shown [5] that, in this case, arbitrary tradeoffs between *structural* (grammar-rules) and *semantical* (rule-attributes) complexities can be achieved for any given PR problem. Therefore, the obvious alternative to using attributes to represent length constraints, is to represent them by syntax. Since this involves the use of non left(right)-recursive grammars or "circuit"-free automata, this alternative renders inapplicable most previous approaches to GI.

2. The proposed GI algorithm

The algorithm to be presented below builds up a *regular* grammar $G = (N, V, P, S)$ (or its corresponding finite-state automaton), which is *circuit-free* (in that $\nexists A \overset{+}{\rightarrow} \alpha A,\ A \in N,\ \alpha \in V^*$). The grammar is generaly *non deterministic*, *ambiguous*, and always has the property:

$$\forall A, B, C \in N,\ \ \forall x, a \in V,\ \ \text{if } (B \rightarrow aA) \in P \text{ and } (C \rightarrow xA) \in P \text{ then } x = a$$

i.e., the same terminal is associated with all the rules which have the same non-terminal on the right-hand side. This allows us to label the *states* (instead of the arcs) of the equivalent automaton with terminal symbols. This property is not essential, but merely convenient for the implementation of the proposed algorithm.

For the description of the algorithm, we will make use of some error-correcting definitions. These definitions are similar to the usual ones [4], though adapted to our purposes:

Definition 2.1. Error-rules: The following "error rules" are associated to the rules in P (ε is the symbol of the empty string):

$$\left.\begin{array}{rll} \text{Insertion (of } x): & A \rightarrow xA & \forall (A \rightarrow bB) \in P \\ \text{Substitution(of } x \text{ for } b): & A \rightarrow xB & \forall (A \rightarrow bB) \in P;\ A \rightarrow x\, \forall (A \rightarrow b) \in P \\ \text{Deletion (of } b): & A \rightarrow B & \forall (A \rightarrow bB) \in P;\ A \rightarrow \varepsilon\, \forall (A \rightarrow b) \in P \end{array}\right\} \forall x \in V.$$

Definition 2.2. Expanded grammar of G: Is the (non regular) grammar $G' = (N', V, P', S)$ obtained by adding to P the corresponding error-rules.

Definition 2.3. Optimal error-correcting derivation of $\beta \in V^*$: Is the derivation of β that uses a minimum number of error-rules of P'.

Algorithm ECGIA (Error-correcting *GI* Algorithm).

Input: Set of training string samples ($R^+ \subset V^*$).

Initialization: **if** $a_1 \dots a_i \dots a_n \in R^+$ is the first string sample, **then** the **initial** grammar $G_0 = (N, V, P, S)$ is $N = \{A_0, A_1, \dots, A_{n-1}\}$; $V = \{a_1, a_2, \dots, a_n\}$; $P = \{A_{i-1} \rightarrow a_i A_i,\ i = 1, \dots, n-1\} \cup \{A_{n-1} \rightarrow a_n\}$; $S = a_0$.

Inference: for all training string samples $\beta = b_1 \dots b_i \dots b_l \in R^+$ do:

1. Parse: with the current grammar, obtain the optimal error-correcting derivation D of β, $D = p_1 \dots p_i \dots p_k$, $p_i \in P'$, $i = 1 \dots k$.
2. Build: **for every** $p_i = (C_{i-1} \rightarrow c_i C_i)$ and $p_j = (C_{j-1} \rightarrow c_i C_j)$, $i < j$, which are two **non-error** rules of D between which there are (in D) **only** error-rules, **do if** $\beta = b_1 \dots c_i \alpha c_j \dots b_l$, ($\alpha = x_1 \dots x_m$) **then** add to the current grammar the following $m + 1$ rules (and the corresponding terminals and non-terminals): $C_i \rightarrow x_1 X_1; \dots; X_{m-1} \rightarrow x_m X_m;\ X_m \rightarrow c_j C_j$.
   if $\alpha = \varepsilon$ **then** only the rule $C_i \rightarrow c_j C_j$ is added.

Result: The inferred grammar G is the current grammar.

End of ECGIA

To obtain the optimal derivation, and due to the fact that the expanded grammar is non-deterministic and ambiguous, we use a Viterbi-like (Dynamic Programming) algorithm [3], which minimizes in each step the number of error-rules required for the parse. With the above definition of optimal derivation, this is equivalent to obtaining the *Levenstein distance* between the sample string and the "closer" string which can be generated by the current grammar. In a *PR* multiclass framework, in which a *set* of grammars (one of them corresponding to each class) are being inferred, the obtained distance can be utilized for classification purposes in the usual way [4]. Therefore, the algorithm can perform recognition and inference in a simultaneous and integrated way, which is an essential characteristic of any proper learning methodology. If needed for the specific application, it is also possible to specify other than one-zero insertion, deletion and/or substitution error-costs (weights). Nevertheless, if this is used during inference, the resulting grammar will then be correspondingly different.

Two more remarks must be made. First, at each step in the optimization algorithm, the minimized (weighted) number of error-rules used is *normalized* by the (current) path length: *i.e.*, the total number of rules applied to reach the current point of the corresponding trellis. This is also true for the final "distance" utilized for classification, and is equivalent to take into account only the *relative* number of errors, and not the absolute (Levenstein) distance. Making a mistake in a 20-symbol string is not so important as a mistake in a 3-symbol string ! Second, from the inference procedure, it is obvious both that the inferred grammar contains the *canonical* grammar (the grammar generates all the positive samples in R^+), and that the average number of rules added for each training sample is directly related to the *variability* of R^+. The size of the language $L(G)$ generated by the inferred grammar is *finite*, although it can grow exponentially with the number of rules (see examples in Figure 3). On the other hand, it can be empirically proved that most of the strings in $L(G)$ are "near" (in the sense of the normalized Levenstein distance) to the "median" string of R^+, as it has been defined by Kohonen [9].

Although the size (number of rules and non-terminals) of the inferred grammar is not limited a priori, in practice, due to the fact that the variability of any reasonable positive sample R^+ is not unlimited, the grammar grows more and more slowly with each new training sample, because less and less corrections are needed to make these samples fit the current grammar. Figure 1 shows an example of this behavior, where 10 groups of 5 samples of the word [oco] (eight) (average length = 13 symbols), processed as explained below, were successively used for learning the corresponding grammar. The figure shows the evolution of the number of non-terminals (or states) $|N|$, and the total number of input symbols NS given to the algorithm (the sum of all training sample lengths), as well as the ratio $|N|/NS$.

3. Experimental Results

The performance of the proposed *GI* method has been evaluated through its application to an automatic isolated word recognition task. Ten grammars (corresponding to the ten Spanish digits) were inferred, and afterwards used to classify a test set.

First, 58 utterances of each of the ten classes were spoken by a single male speaker

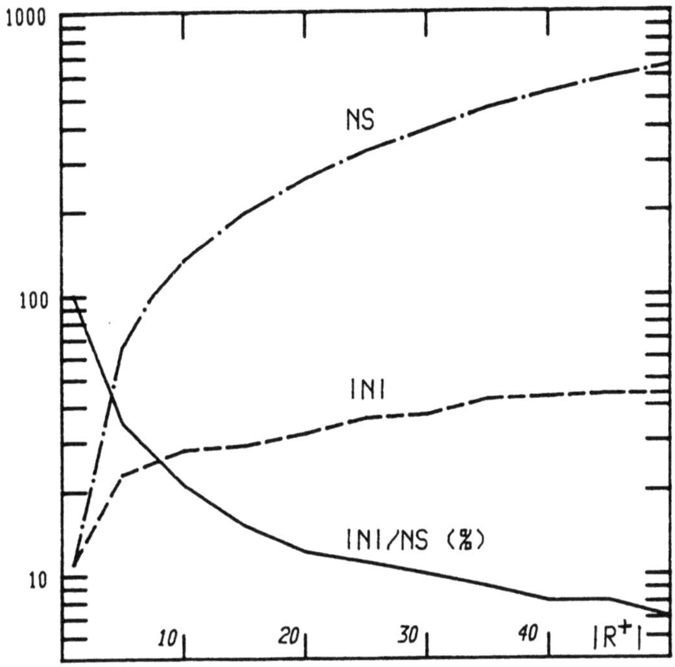

Fig. 1. Evolution of a grammar (automaton) complexity |N| (number of non terminals), as a function of the training-set size $|R^{+}|$. The sum of all training samples length NS, and the ratio |N|/NS are also shown.

(a)

/dos/ (two)

```
ZIIIUUIUUUIISSSSSSSSSSZ
?IIIIUUUUUUINSSSSSSSSSSZ
ZNIUUUUUUUIINSSSSSSSSSSZ
ZTIUIUUUUUUUNSSSSSSSSSSSSSSZ
NIUIUUUUUUUISSSSSSSSSSS
NUUUUUUUIIINNSSSSSSSSSSSSZZ
?IUUUUUUUUUINSSSSSSSSSSSSSZ
?ZZ?IIUUUIUIIINNSSSSSSSSSSSZ
IUUIUUUUUUINSSSSSSSSSSSZ
NIIIIUUIIIINSSSSSSSSSSSSSS
```

/tres/ (three)

```
NIINIIIIIIIIIIUINSSSSSSSSSSSSSZ
ZNINNNIIIIIIIIINSSSSSSSSSSSSSZ
?INTNIIIIIIIIIIINSSSSSSSSSSSSSSZZ
ZIITSIIIIIIIUIINNSSSSSSSSSSSSS
Z?IINIIIIIIIUIIINSSSSSSSSSSSSSZZ
?IITTNUIUUUIIIIIN?SSSSSSSSSSSSSZZ
ZI?TNIIIIIIIIIINSSSSSSSSSSSZ
ZIINSIIUUIIIIINNSSSSSSSSSSSSS
NINTNIIIIIIIIII?SSSSSSSSSSSSZ
Z?INT?IIIIIIIIIIINNSSSSSSSSSSSSSS?Z
```

(b)

/dos/ (two)

```
ZIUIUISZ
?IUINSZ
ZNIUINSZ
ZTIUIUNSZ
NIUIUIS
NUINSZ
?IUINSZ
?Z?IUIUINSZ
IUIUINSZ
NIUINS
```

/tres/ (three)

```
NINIUINSZ
ZNININSZ
?INTNINSZ
ZITSIUINS
Z?INIUINSZ
?ITNUIUIN?SZ
ZI?TNINSZ
ZINSIUINS
NINTNI?SZ
Z?INT?INS?Z
```

Fig. 2. (a): A subsample of the training set used for the inference of the automata of the Spanish words /dos/ and /tres/; (b): the same with all the durational information dropped.

in a quiet room. Sampled at 8533 Hz, each utterance was subsampled at a rate of 66.6 Hz., and parametrized into three very elemental voice parameters (amplitude and two zero-crossing rates); each frame (subsampling segment) was then "fuzzy-labelled" by means of the procedure described in [14]. Later, a crisp string was obtained by selecting the most evident symbol of each fuzzy-label, or the symbol "?" if none was sufficiently evident. The set of (broad-phonetic) symbols are: I=front-vowel, U=back-vowel, N=weak-sonorant, S=strong-fricative, Z=weak-fricative, T=occlusive. A total of 38 utterances of each class were used for learning the corresponding grammars, the remainder 20 × 10 utterances were used as the test set.

TABLE 1

Experiment Number:	1	1a	2	2a
Av.Autom.size/Av.str.length	31/12=2.6		105/43=2.4	
Error rate (%)	11.5	12	3	1
Undecision rate (%)	7.5	14	0	1
Total Recognition rate (%)	81	74	97	98

Performance of the ECGIA in a Spanish digits speech recognition task. Experiments 1-1a correspond to speech samples with all their durational information deleted, and Experiments 2-2a with this information made available to the ECGIA.

Two main experiments were performed. For experiment 1, all the substring-length (durational) information was eliminated from both the training and test set by deleting all adjacent repetitions of any given symbol (see examples in Figure 2). Then, the ten grammars were inferred using the *ECGIA*, and all 200 strings in the test-set were submitted for recognition. Experiment 2 was carried out in a similar way, but keeping the durational information. Two other recognition experiments (1a and 2a) were performed using the grammars inferred in experiments 1 and 2 but, in this case, *only substitution errors* were allowed for recognition (the corresponding insertion and deletion rules were dropped). The recognition and error rates obtained in each case are shown in Table 1. The average length of the strings in the training set and the average number of non-terminals (states) of the inferred grammars are also shown in this table.

Two main conclusions can be drawn from these results: First, as it has been widely claimed, the durational information is very relevant for the proposed task; the relevance is emphasized in this case because of the use of voice parameters with very low spectral descriptive power, which strictly demands the use of temporal features to reach reasonable recognition rates. Second, the proposed algorithm effectively takes advantage of the durational information, leading to a 17% improvement or more (98% recognition rate) when it is made available to the inference procedure.

The 1% improvement achieved in experiment 2, when the insertion and deletion rules are not allowed for recognition, is easily explicable since the inferred grammar itself already accounts for the most likely insertion-deletion errors: allowing only substitutions, penalizes those test samples whose substring-lengths have not been learned and modelized in the grammar. On the other hand, as no durational information is involved in experiment 1, all errors are equally significant and, in this case, the results are improved by applying the full error-correcting scheme.

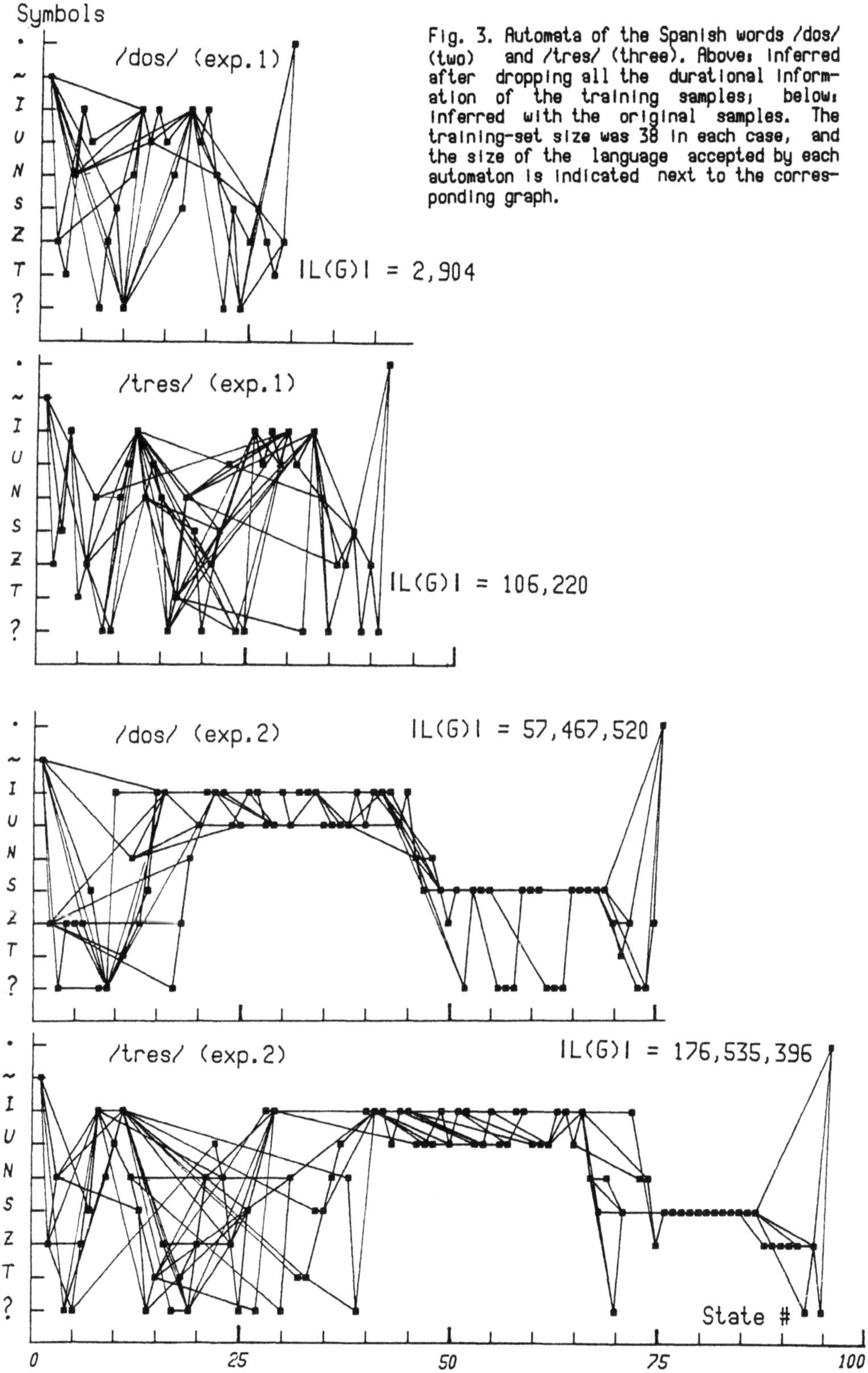

Fig. 3. Automata of the Spanish words /dos/ (two) and /tres/ (three). Above: inferred after dropping all the durational information of the training samples; below: inferred with the original samples. The training-set size was 38 in each case, and the size of the language accepted by each automaton is indicated next to the corresponding graph.

In Figure 3 the automata of the words [dos] (two) and [tres] (three), inferred in experiments 1 and 2, are shown. The horizontal axis represents the numbering of the states, while each point of the vertical axis represents the symbol labelling all the transitions leading to the corresponding states. The symbols $\sim$ and $\cdot$ are, respectively, the initial and the final symbols, added to the strings for implementation purposes.

4. Conclusions

A new *GI* method (*ECGIA*) has been proposed which is specially suited to take advantage of those discriminating features based on the lengths (extends) of the (sub)-structures of the patterns being considered. Also, the "abstraction" process achieved by this procedure has proved that it can capture all the relevant variability in the local substructures and in their concatenation. The performance of this method has been verified through its application to the inference of the automata corresponding to a (simple) Automatic Speech Recognition task. The results have shown the inferred automata to perform consistently better than those constructed by hand by experienced speech researchers [14]. The 98% recognition rate achieved, must be considered quite high given the very coarse speech representation utilized, as well as the very simple recognition procedure applied. Furthermore, these results can be easily improved by taking into account other directly available information sources: first, it is straightforward to extend the recognition procedure to allow the acceptance of (the more information conveying) "fuzzy-symbol" strings as in [14]; second, the frequencies of use of the arcs of the inferred automaton can be easily computed during the inference procedure, and used as estimates of the probabilities required for stochastic recognition. Also, the inferred structural model can be seen as a (very detailed) Markov chain, and consequently, specific Hidden Markov Model probability estimation methods could be applied. Another (no so direct) extension is to implement both inference and recognition directly from vector-string (as opposed to symbol-string) representations of the samples. Finally, although the inference procedure has been explicitly restricted to generate circuit-free automata, if required, it is very simple to modify it to allow single-state loops when (great enough) repetitions of terminal symbols are to be modelled.

References

[1] C.Chirathamjaree, M.H.Acroyd, "A method for the inference of non-recursive context-free grammars," *Int. J. Man-Machine Studies*, Vol. 12, pp. 379-387, 1980.

[2] J.Feldman, "Some decidability results on grammatical inference and complexity," *Information and Control*, Vol. 20, pp. 244-262, 1972.

[3] G.D.Forney, "The Viterbi Algorithm," *IEEE Proc.*, 3, pp. 268-278, 1973.

[4] K.S.Fu, *Syntactic Pattern Recognition and Applications*, Ed. Prentice-Hall, 1982.

[5] K.S.Fu, "A Step Towards Unification on Syntactic and Statistical Pattern Recognition," *IEEE Trans. Pattern Analysis and Machine Intelligence*, Vol.PAMI-5, N.2, pp.200-205, 1983.

[6] E.B.Hunt, *Artificial Intelligence*, Academic Press, New York, 1975.

[7] S.Y.Itoga, "A new heuristic for inferring regular grammars," *IEEE Trans. on Pattern Analysis and Machine Intelligence*, Vol. PAMI-3, N.2, 1981.

[8] B.H.Juang, L.R.Rabiner, S.E.Levinson, M.M.Sondhi, "Recent developments in the application of hidden Markov models to speaker-independent isolated word recognition," *IEEE-ICASSP*, pp. 9-12, 1985.

[9] T.Kohonen, "Median strings," *Patt. Recogn. Letters*, 3, pp.309-313, 1985.

[10] L.Miclet, "Regular inference with a tail-clustering method," *IEEE Trans. on Syst. Man and Cybernetics*, SMC-10, pp. 737-747, 1980.

[11] M.Richetin, F.Vernadad, "Efficient regular grammatical inference for pattern recognition," *Patt. Recognition*, Vol. 17, N.2, pp.245-250, 1984.

[12] M.J.Rusell, R.K.Moore, "Explicit modelling of state occupancy in hidden Markov models for automatic speech recognition," *IEEE-ICASSP*, pp. 5-8, 1985.

[13] F.Vernadat, M.Richetin, "Regular inference for syntactic pattern recognition: a case study," *IEEE-ICPR*, pp. 1370-1372, 1984.

[14] E.Vidal, F.Casacuberta, E.Sanchís, J.Benedí, "A general fuzzy-parsing scheme for speech recognition," *NATO-ASI New Systems and Architectures for Automatic Speech Recognition and Synthesis*, R. De Mori, C.Y. Suen (eds.), Springer-Verlag, pp. 427-446, 1985.

INTRINSIC CHARACTERISTICS AS THE INTERFACE BETWEEN CAD AND MACHINE VISION SYSTEMS[1]

Thomas C. Henderson, Chuck Hansen and Bir Bhanu

Department of Computer Science
The University of Utah
Salt Lake City, Utah 84112, USA

Abstract

Computer Aided Design systems are currently being used to drive machine vision analysis. Such an approach makes it possible to produce recognition and analysis procedures without having to scan a physical example of the object. Typically, these proposed techniques either directly use whatever the CAD model produces or derive information (*e.g.*, points sampled on the surface of the object) to drive a particular recognition scheme. In this regard, there has been some discussion as to an appropriate set of interface data (*e.g.*, points, surface patches, features, etc.). We propose that a coherent general solution to this problem is to characterize a CAD system by the set of intrinsic 3-D shape characteristics (*e.g.*, surface normals, texture, reflectance properties, curvature, etc.) that the CAD system is able to provide. Such a characterization makes it possible to compare CAD systems irrespective of recognition paradigms, and actually makes it possible to determine which recognition strategies can be used with a given CAD-based machine vision system.

Given a set of intrinsic characteristics, techniques and algorithms can be developed which allow the generation of computer representations and geometric models of complicated realizable 3-D objects in a systematic manner. Utilizing the shape information characterized by these intrinsic features and knowledge of existing recognition paradigms, scene analysis strategies (and executable code) can be directly generated.

Keywords: CAD models, shape representation, intrinsic characteristics.

1. Introduction

The representation and analysis of 3-D shape is a strong common concern of researchers in both Computer Aided Design (CAD) and machine vision. Unfortunately, the functional requirements of the two user groups led to the development of representations and

[1]This work was supported in part by NSF Grants ECS-83-07483, MCS-82-21750, DCR-83-41796, MCS-81-21750, MCS-8221750, DCR-8506393, and DMC-8502115, DARPA Grant DAAK11-84-K-0017, and ONR Grant N00014-82-K-0351. Chuck Hansen is an ARO Fellow. All opinions, findings,conclusions or recommendations expressed in this document are those of the authors and do not necessarily reflect the views of the sponsoring agencies.

NATO ASI Series, Vol. F30
Pattern Recognition Theory and Applications
Edited by P. A. Devijver and J. Kittler

models which facilitated the achievement of different kinds of processing. CAD systems typically emphasize such capabilities as rendering, set operations, etc., while machine vision models must provide information which makes possible the automatic analysis of camera data. Moreover, CAD systems are used to design new shapes, whereas machine vision systems are used to analyze objects already in existence. Thus, many machine vision systems require a "presentation" step in which an example of the object to be modeled is shown to the system, and the corresponding internal representation of the object is generated. Recently, it has become possible to merge these different aspects and requirements to obtain an integrated facility in which an object may be designed and which can support vision analysis. Several proposals for systems along these lines have been made [6, 13].

We believe that this approach (*i.e*, CAD-based machine vision) offers many advantages and makes it possible to have a systematic approach to the analysis of shape across a wide spectrum of requirements. Current CAD systems offer an interactive design environment and provide facilities to create images of the designed parts, perform analysis functions on them (*e.g.*, finite element analysis), and produce numerically-controlled machining information for manufacturing. Figure 1 shows the system we envision.

```
Interactive Design  -------    CAGD System     -------  NC Manufacturing
                             Representation
     Graphics       -------    and Models      -------     Analysis
                                   |
                             Computer Vision
                             Representation
                               and Models
                                   |
                             Vision Analysis
```

Figure 1: CAGD-Based Vision Analysis System

In the remainder of the paper, we discuss the nature of CAD and machine vision representations and describe an appropriate interface between them. In particular, Section 2 reviews CAD representations and models; Section 3 gives an overview of machine vision representations. In Section 4, we argue that intrinsic 3-D shape characteristics provide a convenient interface between CAD and vision analysis. In Section 5 we present an example. Finally, in Section 6 a summary is given.

2. Representation in CAGD

Constructive solid geometry (CSG) and boundary representations are the best understood and currently most important representation schemes in computer aided design. Present day 3-D wireframe models used in CAD and model-based vision have many deficiencies including ambiguity — it is easy to build a wireframe model that can be surfaced in several ways [24]. In CSG, the basic idea is that complicated solids can be represented as various ordered "additions" and "substractions" of simpler solids by means of modified versions of Boolean set operators — union, difference and intersection [23]. For inherent boundary representations a number of different approaches are used. These include Coons patches, bicubic surface patches, Bezier methods and B-splines [3].

Current Geometrical Modeling Systems (GMS) use a limited class of primitives such as rectilinear blocks and conic surfaces (cylinders, cones and spheres). Although these are sufficient to cover a large number of conventional unsculptured parts, a GMS which includes sculptured solids is highly desirable. Also since the sculptured design is surface oriented, it is easier to incorporate it in a boundary based system. In general, boundary modelers tend to support stepwise construction of the models more easily than CSG modelers but require greater data storage. CSG modelers are inadequate for modeling sculptured parts: they have no capability at all for constructing and using sculptured surfaces as part of the boundary of the solid model. Some advantages of boundary representation are: there are many known surface models available from which to choose [3]; the mathematics of surface representation is well developed and complex shapes can often be represented with a single primitive [14, 27]; and it results in an intuitive model. A minor disadvantage is that it may be difficult to ensure the validity of a boundary representation of a set. On the other hand, CSG representations are not unique in general, since a solid may be constructed in many ways; the final result may not be easily visualized by looking at the primitives. However, the CSG representation is concise, validity is guaranteed and such a representation can be easily converted to a boundary representation. The comparison of CSG and boundary representation methods can be found in [24, 25].

There have been several attempts to use a set of manipulative operations for boundary models for solid objects to construct a solid modeling system [21, 27]. These are designed for CAD/CAM environments, rather than for computer vision applications. In [21], a set of Euler operators is used on the topology of a boundary model, that is on the relative arrangement of its faces, edges and vertices. The operations allow the system to perform arbitrary modifications necessary for boundary representation models, the faces of which are planar polygons.

Until recently it was not possible to carry out Boolean operations on sculptured surfaces. Thomas [27] has shown how to combine the best attributes of CSG and surface-based representation systems by using subdivision techniques developed by Cohen et al. [16]. He uses a uniform boundary representation. The "primitives" are solids bounded by B-spline surfaces. As compared to the other work in solid modeling, his method does not require that the objects being combined have closed boundaries; they must only satisfy a weak completion criterion. Thus this method results in a powerful shape description system which allows the combination of primitives using set operations into arbitrarily-complex objects bounded by curved surfaces and the production of a model which represents such objects. Adjacency information about surface points and the intersection curve between two surfaces as a polyline can be obtained. Although he has used B-spline surfaces, his techniques are applicable to any surface representation scheme [14]. All this work has been incorporated in the Alpha_1 system [15]. (More details about Alpha_1 are presented below.) Thus, the advantages of both CSG and sculptured surface representation can be obtained in the shape representation of objects and the combination of objects via set operations. As a result of these significant advances in CAGD, we decided to use the Alpha_1 system for exploring the computer vision application.

Alpha_1 is an experimental CAGD based solid modeler system incorporating sculptured surfaces [15]. It allows in a single system both high quality computer graphics and freeform surface representation and design. It uses a rational polynomial spline representation of arbitrary degree to represent the basic shapes of the models. The rational spline includes all spline polynomial representations for which the denominator is trivial. Nontrivial denominators lead to all conic curves. Alpha_1 uses the Oslo algorithm [16] for computing discrete B-splines. Subdivision, effected by the Oslo algorithm, supports various capabilities including the computation associated with Boolean operations, such as the intersection of two arbitrary surfaces [27]. B-splines are an ideal design tool, they are simple yet powerful; many common shapes can be represented exactly using rational B-splines. For example, all of the common primitive shapes used in CSG systems fall into this category. Other advantages include good computational and representational properties of the spline approximation: the variation diminishing property, the convex hull property and the local interpolation property. There are techniques for matching a spline-represented boundary curve against raw data. Although the final result may be an approximation, it can be computed to any desired precision (which permits nonuniform sampling). At present, tolerancing information is not included in the object specification in Alpha_1 system. It is planned to be incorporated in the future. Once it is available, we can make our models in terms of classes of objects (rather than a single object) which are functionally equivalent and interchangeable in assembly operations.

Given the CAGD model (perhaps by combining several modeling paradigms), a corresponding set of vision models (with some control structure) is generated. Once these models are available, they provide the basis for standard 2-D and 3-D scene analysis. An early example of such an interactive system is the ACRONYM system [10, 11] designed for applications in computer vision and manipulation. The world is described to ACRONYM as volume elements and their spatial relationships and as classes of objects and their subclass relationships. It uses a hybrid CSG and general sweep scheme for the representation of rigid solids. The representations are CSG-like trees whose leaves are generalized cylinders. Like PADL (a geometric modeling system [12]) it allows variation in size, limited variation in structure and variation in structural relationships of the modeled objects. However, in ACRONYM, it may be difficult to design algorithms for computing properties of objects.

3. Representation in Machine Vision

Geometric modeling is one of the key components of a domain-independent model-based 3-D industrial machine vision system. Here our interest is in the representation, modeling and recognition of rigid, opaque 3-D solid objects. Three general classes for the representation of 3-D solid objects are (a) surface or boundary, (b) volume, and (c) sweep [2, 23]. In the boundary representation schemes, a 3-D solid object is represented by segmenting its boundary into a finite number of bounded "faces" and describing the structural relationships between the faces. Another approach to surface representation is to express the surfaces as functions on the "Gaussian Sphere"

[18, 26]. Volumetric representations include spatial occupancy, cell decomposition and constructive solid geometry [24, 25]. Sweep representations consist of translational sweep, rotational sweep, 3-D sweep and general sweep.

Since a direct model of a 3-D object in terms of its volume (*e.g.*, as a 3-D array) may easily exhaust the memory capacity of a system, representation by oct-trees has been considered [19]. These may make space array operations more economical in terms of memory space. A simple approach to analyzing 3-D objects is to model them as polyhedra. This requires a description of the objects in terms of vertices, edges and faces. Baumgart [5] developed a 3-D geometric modeling system ("Geomed") for application to computer vision. He used a face-based representation for planar polyhedral objects, called the "winged-edge" representation. The Euler primitives are used for polyhedron construction and shape operators include union, intersection and difference. Geomed provides many capabilities; for example, arbitrary polyhedra may be constructed, altered or viewed in perspective with hidden lines eliminated. Bolles *et al.* [8] have used a CAD model that contains a standard volume-surface, edge-vertex description as well as pointers linking topologically connected features. Their preliminary model uses a pointer structure similar to Baumgart's "winged-edge" representation. Wesley *et al.* [28] have used polyhedral models for automated mechanical assembly in their geometrical modeling system GDP. Their Automated Parts Assembly System (AUTOPASS) [20] language has never been implemented. Before automated assembly can be successful, it is essential to have robust representations, models, and general purpose techniques for determining the orientation and position of 3-D objects for a large class of industrial parts.

For curved and more complex objects, other representations and models have been used, such as generalized cylinders (or cones). Generalized cylinders or cones are a quite popular representation in computer vision [1, 10, 22]. However, there are some problems with this representation. There are infinitely many possible generalized cones representing a single object. More constraints are needed to get a unique description. Although it is possible to represent arbitrary shapes with generalized cones by making them arbitrarily complex, their computation is difficult. They are also not well suited to descriptions of non-elongated objects and objects of arbitrarily deformed surfaces enclosing little volume.

Although sweep representations, such as generalized cylinders, and volume representations, such as constructive solid geometry, imply surface description, they fail to describe the junction or surface peculiarities. In the recognition of 3-D objects from partial views, we detect surfaces first, and only after seeing several different views of the object do we have enough data to obtain volume properties. For objects constructed from thin sheet-like material, surfaces are natural candidates for representation. Further, surfaces are seen first. As such, they are important for computer vision. Hence the need for surface or boundary based representations.

York *et al.* [29] have used a structured collection of Coons surface patches for representing 3-D objects whose boundary curves are approximated by cubic B-splines. Their design of Coons patches is cumbersome, since it requires that a simple surface patch be designed on paper before it may be entered into the data base. Brady [9] proposes a symbolic representation of visible surface based on "curvature patches."

They are computed locally by determining the tangent vectors that indicate directions in which the surface changes. Example directions include the principal curvature directions and the directions in which the normal curvature is zero. Smooth changes in curvature patch descriptions are obtained to determine the larger scale structure of a surface. It is not clear that curvature patch surfaces are perceptually "fairer" than surfaces developed in CAD.

4. Intrinsic Characteristics as the Interface

In order to bridge the gap between shape modeling and shape analysis, it is necessary to give a detailed account of how the machine vision analysis can be performed in terms of the CAD shape model. Bhanu and Henderson [6] have proposed a variety of information that can be produced and used to drive the vision analysis (see Figure 2).

```
                              CAD Model

                       /      |       |     \
                     /        |       |       \
                   /          |       |         \
 ---------------------------------------------------------------------
/                                                                     \
Surface   Surface  Curvature    Holes     Surface    Region Adjacency
Normals   Points                Corners   Patches          Graph
\_____________________________________________________________________/

                   \          |       |         /
                     \        |       |       /
                       \      |       |     /

                         Machine Vision System
```

Figure 2: Typical CAD/Vision Interface

In particular, a CAD system can return a set of points sampled from the surface of the shape (*i.e.*, a range finder can be simulated), or a set of surface features or patches can be generated, or even better, a set of surface patches and their connectivity relation can be produced. Which of these is actually produced would depend on the recognition paradigm being used and on the class of shapes to be recognized.

However, in this paper, we propose that intrinsic characteristics of the 3-D shape be used as the interface between the CAD system and the machine vision model. There are several motivations for choosing intrinsic characteristics as the organizing notion:

1. The intrinsic characteristic approach has been quite successful as a machine vision paradigm for 3-D object analysis. Although originally proposed by Barrow and Tenenbaum [4] as a set of registered images, the method applies equally well to 3-D data structures. Moreover, intrinsic characteristics are just those that

are viewpoint independent and which are inherent in the particular shape being modeled.

2. Many shape analysis algorithms are based on the use of one or more intrinsic characteristics; thus, once it is known what intrinsic characteristics can be easily produced by a particular CAD system, then the possible set of recognition techniques is known.

3. Finally, different CAD systems can be compared on the basis of the set of intrinsic characteristics which they can provide. Thus, the relative tradeoffs in choosing a CAD system can be known more easily with respect to the set of recognition tasks that the system will have to perform.

5. Example

We can demonstrate the ideas presented above with a simple polyhedron. To exemplify the concepts,

1. We have designed a piece using Alpha_1
2. Generated a set of intrinsic features from the CAGD model
3. Built a vision model based on these intrinsic features
4. Sensed the object with a 3-D laser range finder
5. Matched the object with the model.

We design the piece by utilizing the CSG features incorporated in the Alpha_1 system. We start with a primitive box of the desired dimensions. By applying set difference of two planes in the correct orientation, we can realize the object. This polyhedron is composed of 7 convex faces (see Figure 3).

The next step is to generate a set of intrinsic features from this CAGD model. We can obtain the surface normals at uniformly sampled surface points on the object. Currently, we use this same set of points to obtain surface curvature but we anticipate that the Alpha_1 system will provide surface curvature in the future. We find the area for the planar faces. This combined with the surface normals and curvature forms our set of intrinsic features. It should be noted that this is not a complete set in the sense that we could also obtain holes, corners, texture, etc. The additional intrinsic features would aid in the use of other recognition paradigms. Since we have chosen a planar face matcher, these other intrinsic features will not be required. However, for a complete system, one would like a richer set of features.

We used our Technical Arts 3-D laser range finder to scan the object. This system returns Cartesian data for the scanned scene. Using this 3-D data, we obtain surface information at the pixel level (curvature, surface normals, etc.). Once we have the surface normals, we fit planes to these normals, deriving planar faces. From these faces, we compute the area and the average normal (due to sensor noise, the normals vary within some threshold).

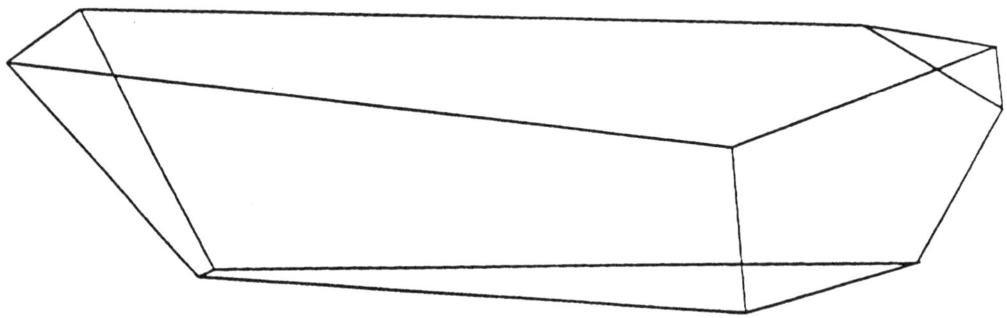

Figure 3: An example polyhedron

The matching paradigm we chose was the planar face matcher introduced by Faugeras [17]. The method uses a combination of matching planar faces and hypothesis testing to locate objects using models. The model is the set of planar patches derived from the CAGD model. Using the segmented scene, a set of candidate patches from an object in the scene is assigned to each model primitives (planar patches). The criterion for assignment is surface area. After two model-object pairs of patches match with similar transformations, occluded patches are eliminated from the search and other model-object pairs are tested using the same transformation. The set with the maximal match defines the located object and the position and orientation of the object.

It should be noted that for non-polyhedral objects, a different matching paradigm would be used and a different model would be built from the intrinsic features. For example, if the CAGD model was primarily cylindrical, a generalized cylinder matching scheme such as that used by Binford or Agin could be utilized [1, 7]. Rather than build a vision model of planar faces, the set of intrinsic features derived from the CAGD model could be used to compute the sweep axis and swept curve.

6. Discussion

We have been studying techniques and algorithms which allow the generation of computer representations and geometric models of complicated realizable 3-D objects in a systematic manner. In order to produce recognition strategies for a machine vision system, it is necessary to specify the interface between the CAD system and the machine vision analysis system. We suggest that this interface be characterized by the set of intrinsic 3-D shape characteristics which can be produced by the particular CAD system under consideration. Notice that the existence of the CAD model may preclude the necessity of a separate machine vision model, and that by providing intrinsic features, the scene analysis strategies (and executable code) can be directly generated.

The simple example demonstrated that intrinsic features generated from a CAD model can be used effectively to drive the recognition process in computer vision. Given a library of recognition schemes and the set of intrinsic features, a future system will automatically generate recognition strategies based on shape information.

References

[1] Agin, G, "Representation and Description of Curved Objects," Memo-AIM 173, Stanford, October, 1972.

[2] N. Badler and R. Bajcsy, "Three-Dimensional Representations for Computer Graphics and Computer Vision," *ACM Computer Graphics*, 12:153-160, August, 1978.

[3] R.E. Barnhill and R.F. Riesenfeld (eds.), *Computer Aided Geometric Design*, Academic Press, New York, 1974.

[4] Barrow, H. and J. Tenenbaum, "MSYS: A System for Reasoning about Scenes," Artificial Intelligence Center 121, SRI, International, April, 1976.

[5] B.G. Baumgart, "Geometric Modeling for Computer Vision," Technical Report AIM-249, STAN-CS-74-463, Computer Science Department, Stanford University, October, 1974.

[6] Bhanu, Bir and Thomas C. Henderson, "CAGD-Based 3-D Vision," in *IEEE Robotics Conference*, pages 411-417, St. Louis, March, 1985.

[7] Binford, T.O., "Inferring Surfaces from Images," *Artificial Intelligence*, 17:205-244, 1981.

[8] R.C. Bolles, P. Horaud and M. J. Hannah, "3DPO: A Three-Dimensional Part Orientation System," in *Proc. 8th IJCAI*, pages 1116-1120, Karlsruhe, August, 1983.

[9] M. Brady, "Representing Shape," in *Proc. International Conference on Robotics*, pages 256-265, March, 1984.

[10] R.A. Brooks, "Symbolic Reasoning Among 3-D Models and 2-D Images," *Artificial Intelligence*, 17:285-348, 1981.

[11] R. Brooks, R. Greiner and T.O. Binford, "The ACRONYM Model Based Vision System," in *Proc. 6th IJCAI*, pages 105-113, Tokyo, 1979.

[12] C.M. Brown, "PADL-2: A Technical Summary," *IEEE Computer Graphics & Applications*, pp. 69-84, March, 1982.

[13] Castore, G. and C. Crawford, "From Solid Model to Robot Vision," in *Proceddings of the IEEE Conference on Robotics and Automation*, pages 90-93, Atlanta, Georgia, March, 1984.

[14] Cobb, Elizabeth, "Design of Sculptured Surfaces Using the B-Spline Representation," PhD thesis, University of Utah, June, 1984.

[15] E. Cohen, "Some Mathematical Tools for a Modeler's Workbench," *IEEE Computer Graphics & Applications*, pp. 63-66, October, 1983.

[16] E. Cohen, T. Lyche and R.F. Riesenfeld, "Discrete B-splines and Subdivision Techniques in Computer-Aided Geometric Design and Computer Graphics," *Computer Graphics and Image Processing*, 14(2):87-111, October, 1980.

[17] Faugeras, O.D., F. Germain, G.Kryze, J.D. Boissonnat, M. Hebert, and J. Ponce, "Toward a Flexible Vision System," in *Proceedings of the 12th International Symposium on Industrial Robotics*, pages 67-78, June, 1982.

[18] B.K.P. Horn, R.J. Woodham and W.M. Silver, "Determining Shape and Reflectance Using Multiple Images," Technical Report A.I. Memo 490, Mass. Inst. of Technology, August, 1978.

[19] C.L. Jackins and S.L. Tanimoto, "Oct-Trees and Their Use in Representing 3D Objects," *Computer Graphics and Image Processing*, 14(3):249-270, 1980.

[20] L.I. Lieberman and M.A. Wesley, "AUTOPASS: An Automatic Programming System for Computer Controlled Mechanical Assembly," *IBM Journal of Research and Development*, pp. 321-333, July, 1977.

[21] M. Mantyla and R. Sulonen, "GWB: A Solid Modeler with Euler Operators," *IEEE Computer Graphics and Applications*, 2:17-31, September, 1982.

[22] R. Nevatia and T.O. Binford, "Description and Recognition of Curved Objects," *Artificial Intelligence*, 8:77-98, 1977.

[23] Requicha, A, "Representations for Rigid Solids: Theory, Methods, and Systems," *Comp. Surv.*, 12(4):437-464, December, 1980.

[24] A.A.G. Requicha and H.B. Voelcker, "Solid Modeling: A Historical Summary and Contemporary Assessment," *IEEE Computer Graphics & Applications*, pp. 9-24, March, 1982.

[25] A.A.G. Requicha and H.B. Voelcker, "Solid Modeling: Current Status and Research Directions," *IEEE Computer Graphics & Applications*, pp. pp. 25-37, October, 1983.

[26] D.A. Smith, "Using Enhanced Spherical Images for Object Representation," Technical Report A.I. Memo 530, Mass. Inst. of Technology, May, 1979.

[27] Thomas, Spencer, "Modelling Volumes Bounded by B-Spline Surfaces," PhD thesis, University of Utah, June, 1984.

[28] M.A. Wesley *et al.*, "A Geometric Modeling System for Automated Mechanical Assembly," *IBM Journal of Research and Development*, Vol 24 (1): 64-74, January, 1980.

[29] B.W. York, A.R. Hanson and E.M. Riseman, "3D Object Representation and Matching with B-Splines and Surface Patches," in *Proc. 8th IJCAI*, pages 648-651, Karlsruhe, August, 1981.

THE TENSOR DIFFERENTIAL SCALE SPACE REPRESENTATION

David Cyganski and John A. Orr

Electrical Engineering Department
Worcester Polytechnic Institute
Worcester, Massachusetts 01609

Abstract

The characteristics and uses of the scale space representation of planar curves is summarized, and new forms of parameterization and curvature definition are developed which extend the applicability of scale space methods. Previously, the scale space approach to image registration and identification has been unable to deal with images skewed by such operations as change in angle between object plane and camera line of sight. The new approach, based on tensor constructions of curve differentials, eliminates this restriction, and is applicable to image pairs related by any affine transformation. Examples of the operation of the method are presented.

1. Introduction

Recently, considerable effort has been devoted by researchers to the investigation of scale space methods for the shape analysis of curves. The scale space representation has the desirable feature of segregating coarse and fine curve information so that image identification and registration may take place despite differences in details of the curves. While naturally invariant to image shift, scale and rotation, the standard scale space representation is not invariant to image skewing. Thus its utility is compromised in such typical applications as satellite reconnaissance where the view is not from directly above the site of interest. In this paper we introduce a new scale space representation which preserves the original invariance properties and is, in addition, invariant to any image skew. This method extends the applicability of scale space methods to more general scene/map registration problems and robot vision problems in which curves must be identified despite a general affine transformation.

The concept of the distribution of information in an image across a continuum of scales is an important one. There are in general identifiable features of an image which are highly localized, such as corners, and others which are associated with global behavior, such as eccentricity. Many physiological experiments suggest that human vision exploits the analysis of images at many resolution levels to take advantage of the information to be found across many levels of scale. For these reasons, a great deal of machine vision work has been devoted to separating the information to be found at different scale levels [1-3].

NATO ASI Series, Vol. F30
Pattern Recognition Theory and Applications
Edited by P. A. Devijver and J. Kittler

New and attractive means were introduced by Witkin [4] in 1983 for the representation of one dimensional signals such that the information at various scales was in some sense separated. In the so-called scale space method, the zero-crossings of the signal subsequent to smoothing by a continuum of Gaussian filters of increasing width are plotted. The resulting zero-crossing contours possess a simple morphology which is highly amenable to computer representation and comparison.

Recently, Mokhtarian and Mackworth [5] showed how the Witkin scale space method could be used to represent planar contours. A contour is completely described by its curvature function versus arc length. This one dimensional representation of the contour may then be processed via Witkin's scale space method. In this paper examples were shown of the registration of Landsat images and maps of the same regions. Because of the inherent separation of detail and coarse information in scale space, a simple Uniform Cost Algorithm was sufficient to match similar but different contours representing the same regions. The goal of this matching procedure is to find the best pairing of some or all of the contours in two scale space representations which may differ by a circular shift of the contours.

While the contour scale space images introduced above are invariant to image scaling, rotation and shift, any image skew causes nonlinear distortion and often a complete change in the morphology of the zero-crossing contours. In the previous work, skew had to be removed manually by finding corresponding pairs of points in the Landsat image. This intolerance to skew compromises the usefulness of this otherwise attractive technique.

The change in the scale space transformation due to general linear transformation of the original image is not very tractable because it arises from an essentially nonlinear transformation of the contour curvature function, $\kappa(t)$, both in the curvature amplitude, κ, and argument, t. That is, considering the curvature function in arc length as a one dimensional time function, it undergoes both a memoryless time varying distortion and a time warping, both of which are functions of both the image transformation and the derivatives of the old contour at that point.

Rather than attempt to invert this distortion of the standard curvature function, we have introduced a new contour parameterization τ, and a new curvature function, K. Both of these new quantities are invariant with respect to general affine transformation. Hence the function $K(\tau)$ is likewise invariant and so the scale space contours of any two curves related by a general linear transformation and shift are identical.

The new parameterization and curvature are developed as the naturally invariant results of contraction of tensor differentials. There is in fact a family of infinite size of such contractions. We describe the derivation of these quantities in this paper.

The new method is amenable to highly parallel processing just as are the original scale space methods. In the paper we show examples of scale space representations of curves under both the original and the new parameterizations.

2. Review of Previous Curvature Based Scale Space Method

The method of Mokhtarian and Mackworth [5] relies upon the representation of a contour as a single one-dimensional function using the curvature function of the curve. If

$\psi(t)$ is the slope angle of the tangent to a curve given by the parametric equations $C = (x(t), y(t))$ where t is defined as the natural arc length along the curve, that is, by the differential

$$dt = \sqrt{dx^2 + dy^2}$$

then the curvature is defined by

$$\kappa(t) = \frac{d\psi(t)}{dt}.$$

The inverse of the curvature describes the radius of a circle whose curvature agrees with that of the contour at the tangent point specified.

The curvature function may be expressed completely in terms of the derivatives of the parametric equations of the curve given as functions of the natural arc length,

$$\kappa(t) = \frac{\dot{x}\ddot{y} - \dot{y}\ddot{x}}{(\dot{x}^2 + \dot{y}^2)^{3/2}} .$$

The curvature function describes identically all curves which are congruent to within any spatial shift and rotation. Using elementary techniques of differential geometry [6] the curve may be reconstructed from the curvature function given an initial origin and tangent specification.

For simplicity, suppose that all given curves are closed. Aspects of the problem for partial or broken curves are discussed at length in [5]. Then, all curves may be first scaled so as to have a unit arc length. In this case, the curvature descriptions of all given curves will match regardless of translation, scaling and rotation. Hence the basic transformational invariances displayed by the curvature based scale space method all result from the choice of the curvature description for contour representation.

Now, the scale space representation may be found from the curvature function by applying a continuum of Gaussian filters and noting the zero crossings of the resulting functions. That is, define

$$\kappa(t,\sigma) = \int_{-\infty}^{\infty} \kappa(u) \frac{1}{\sigma\sqrt{2\pi}} e^{\frac{-(t-u)^2}{2\sigma^2}} du.$$

Then, the locus of points in the (t, σ) plane of the zero crossings of the function $\kappa(t, \sigma)$ is called the scale space representation of the contour C.

The representation above differs from that given by Mokhtarian and Mackworth. In their work, the Gaussian filters are applied to the parametric equations $x(t)$ and $y(t)$ and then the curvature function is found. This approach results in a better behaved curvature function for noisy data, but one can no longer call the result a true scale space representation and assign to it the same meanings and properties derived by others for the Gaussian kernel scale space representation such as found in [7]. More importantly, their formulation cannot be extended to the skew invariant form as we will with the true scale space description above.

3. A Skew Invariant Scale Space Representation

An extension of the Fourier descriptor or ellipse decomposition method for finding the affine transformations relating contours was presented in [8]. The Fourier descriptor method makes use of the Fourier series decomposition of the parametric equations of a contour with respect to the natural arc length parameter. The pairs of parametric harmonics of a given order transform in a simple fashion under scale and rotation of the original curve while translation effects are confined to the zero order harmonic terms. However, these simple transformational properties break down under general image skew. That is, the Fourier descriptor method suffers from the same inability as the curvature based scale space method to deal with general affine transformation of any image.

In [8] means were found to generalize the Fourier method. The fundamental problem with the original method was that an arc of fixed length on the curve undergoes a transformation which is not independent of the location of that segment on the curve. Let $(\bar{x}(\bar{t}), \bar{y}(\bar{t}))$ denote the parametric equations of our curve after general affine transformation. Also, let $\bar{t}$ be the value of arc length on the new curve so that the feature on the curve to which it refers is identical to that indicated by arc length value t on the original curve. Assuming no translation (without loss of generality) then the relationship between the curves can be expressed in terms of a general linear transformation, A, as in the following expression:

$$\begin{bmatrix} \bar{x}(\bar{t}) \\ \bar{y}(\bar{t}) \end{bmatrix} = \begin{bmatrix} A_1^1 & A_2^1 \\ A_1^2 & A_2^2 \end{bmatrix} \begin{bmatrix} x(t) \\ y(t) \end{bmatrix}.$$

But if the differential dt separates two infinitesimally close features on C and if $d\bar{t}$ separates the same features in $\bar{C}$ then obviously

$$d\bar{t} = \sqrt{(A_1^1 dx + A_2^1 dy)^2 + (A_1^2 dx + A_2^2 dy)^2} \neq dt.$$

That is, in general, $\bar{t}$ is a nonlinear function of t. The relationship between these parameters is in fact linear only when the transformation matrix A is orthogonal; that is, when the curves differ only by a scaling and rotation.

To extend the applicability of the Fourier descriptor method to the case of general affine transformations of curves, a new parameterization was introduced called the canonical differential. This differential has the property of remaining invariant over general affine transformation of a curve, hence eliminating the need for a nonlinear adjustment of curve parameters between skewed images.

The existence of a family of such transformation invariant parameters is most easily demonstrated by making use of the notation and properties of tensors. The necessary background for this development can be found in [9]. To begin, let the parametric equations of the curve be denoted by the indexed construct x^i where i ranges from 1 to 2, replacing the functions $x(t)$ and $y(t)$ used before. Furthermore let

$$x^{i(k)} = \frac{d^k x^i}{dt^k}$$

where t is any parameterization of the curve. Then with values of t and $\bar{t}$ chosen as before to match curve features, we find that the positional functions and derivatives behave as tensors. That is, if $\bar{x}(\bar{t})$ refers to the general linear transformation of $x(t)$ then we have

$$\bar{x}^{i(k)} = A_j^i x^{j(k)}$$

where the Einstein summation convention is assumed over all like pairs of indices in an expression.

Now we introduce the relative covariant permutation tensor of weight -1. This numerical tensor is defined by

$$\varepsilon_{ij} = \begin{cases} 1 & \text{if } i = 1 \text{ and } j = 2 \\ -1 & \text{if } i = 2 \text{ and } j = 1 \\ 0 & \text{if } i = j \end{cases}$$

We may use the permutation tensor to contract the positional function and derivative tensors defined above. Hence

$$x^{i(k)}\varepsilon_{ij}x^{j(m)}$$

is a zero rank tensor of weight -1, that is, a scalar density with respect to linear transformation. So that

$$\bar{x}^{i(k)}\varepsilon_{ij}\bar{x}^{j(m)} = x^{i(k)}\varepsilon_{ij}x^{j(m)}|J|^{-1}$$

where the Jacobian factor J is given its usual definition:

$$J = \left[\det\left(A^i_j\right)\right]^{-1}.$$

In general this scalar density will be zero if $k = m$ because of the anti-symmetry of the permutation tensor.

Using this scalar density we see that we can define a new tensor differential

$$d\tau = |x^{i(k)}\varepsilon_{ij}x^{j(m)}|^{\frac{1}{k+m}}dt$$

which has weight $-1/(k+m)$ and is invariant but for the weight scaling to general linear transformation. The $(k+m)$ root permits cancellation of the dt differentials, which is necessary to remove the dependence on the initial parameterization. Then, in general

$$d\bar{\tau} = |J|^{-1/(k+m)}d\tau.$$

For closed curves we may define a completely invariant differential by simply normalizing the above differential by the the total arc length of the contour as measured in terms of the above differential. That is, if T represents the arc length in the differential τ above, then $d\tau/T$ is totally invariant to any linear transformation of the curve. In this case this normalization is not important as it is typical that the total scale space representations are normalized to agree in the spatial parameter extent before comparison. That is, the differential arc length is implicitly normalized on scale space representation.

Now, the curvature based scale space method fails to be skew invariant because it lacks two invariances. The arc length parameter, t, is not invariant to general linear transformation causing here the same problems seen in the Fourier descriptor method. But, even if one of the invariant tensor differentials found above were used in its place, the curvature function while being fundamentally changed (its meaning would no longer be connected with the construction of an osculating circle of the contour) it would still not be invariant to general linear transformation of the curve. However, we need not use the curvature, but instead we may choose another tensor differential from the family of invariants previously derived normalized by the arc length differential or any other invariant differential. The normalization is necessary to cancel the differential nature of the tensor differential. So, we may choose any ratio of invariant differentials from the family derived above as a new pseudo-curvature function, such as

$$K = |x^{i(k)}\varepsilon_{ij}x^{j(m)}|^{\frac{1}{k+m}} dt/d\tau.$$

Any functional expression in the differential invariants that permits the cancellation of the dt differentials is a suitable pseudo-curvature. In fact, any function of such an expression is also a suitable pseudo-curvature.

In the examples to be examined in the next section, we chose the invariant arc length function

$$d\tau = |x^{i(1)}\varepsilon_{ij}x^{j(2)}|^{\frac{1}{3}} dt$$

and as a replacement for the curvature function

$$K = \left(|x^{i(2)}\varepsilon_{ij}x^{j(3)}|^{\frac{1}{5}} dt/d\tau\right)^5$$

where the fifth power of a ratio of differentials is used to eliminate the fifth order rooting operation which would be otherwise necessary if the ratio itself were used.

By applying the scale space representation method with this new function, we obtain a representation which is invariant to any linear transformation of the original curve. That is, the representation is not altered by any scaling, rotation or skewing of the original contour. By choosing differentials of the first order and higher, we also eliminate any variation of the representation due to translation of the contours.

4. Examples

The operation of the method using both the original and the new curvature definitions is illustrated in Figures 1-3. The failure to maintain similar scale space features with image skewing is evident with the original method (Fig. 2). Using the new scale space method, Fig. 3 illustrates the desired behavior, where only minor variations between the scale space representations are noticeable under close inspection.

In these examples, the curve derivatives were obtained from functions fit to the local curve data. It is this fit and its lack of invariance to general linear transformation that results in any small variations in the final scale space representations of image pairs. We are currently investigating the optimization and behavior of the derivative operations.

5. Conclusions

In this paper we have derived a new scale space contour representation and demonstrated its application with respect to invariant representation of image contours that are related by a general affine transformation. This approach maintains the advantages of the previously proposed curvature based scale space contour representation of admitting simple graph matching techniques for the matching of contours. Unlike the previous method however it is skew invariant. Hence surface images taken from positions other than on the zenith can be matched using the new scale space method.

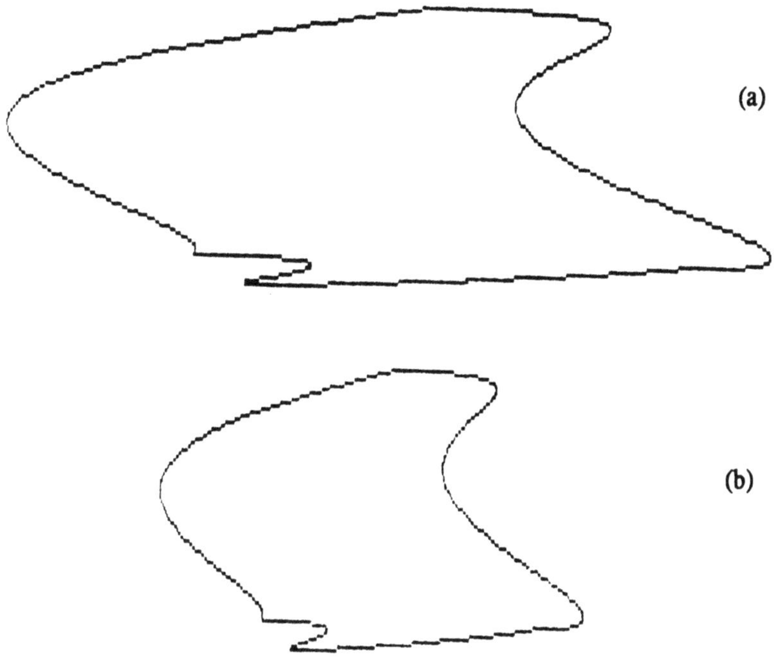

Figure 1: Synthetically-generated image contours to demonstrate the operation of the scale space method. Fig. 1(a): original image; Fig. 1(b): Image after skewing on horizontal axis by factor of 0.556, simulating an off-axis camera view.

This technique should have application in such areas as satellite image registration, map directed automatic navigation and robot vision.

Because of the sparsity of data and the one dimensional nature of the processing, finding the K function of a given set of contour data is a fast operation. Subsequent processing for the scale space information is a highly parallel operation (as the locus of zero crossings for any given scale parameter can be found independently of all the others) involving only FFT operations and zero crossing detection. Hence it should be possible to construct machines that could execute the reduction of image frames to scale space representation in real time.

Because the new scale space representation and the extended Fourier descriptor method [8] both are based on the use of invariant tensor differentials, some comparison of the two methods is desirable. The Fourier descriptor method has two readily apparent advantages. Because it uses lower order differentials in its construction, since only one differential invariant is needed, it will perform with greater robustness in the case of certain kinds of local data corruption. The Fourier descriptor method provides as a result sets of feature vectors that may be used for object identification as well as allows for the direct solution of the affine transformation relating two curves.

The new scale space method, while requiring higher order derivatives for its operation, and not permitting direct solution for all of the affine transformation parameters,

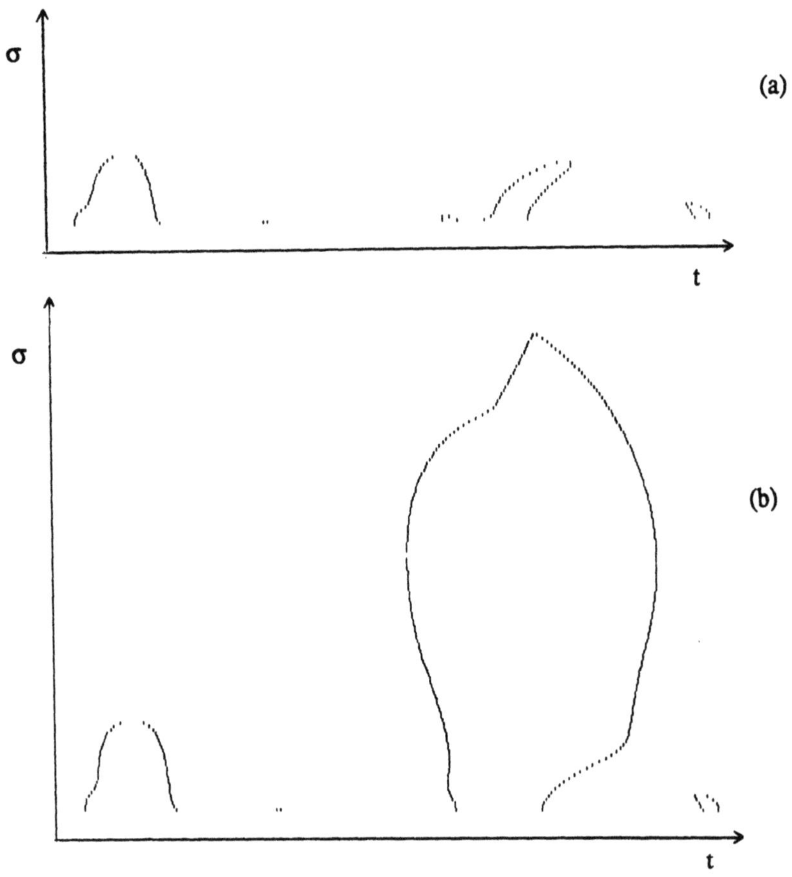

Figure 2: Scale space representations using natural curvature. Fig. 2(a): original image contour; Fig. 2(b): skewed image contour. Note lack of agreement.

does have an advantage. Because the original object is represented in a multi-scale format, large scale image distortions, such as partial occlusion and non-linear image warping may permit the matching of the tree graphs generated from the zero-crossing contours. Hence, it may be possible to identify images that have undergone distortions that would not be admissible in the Fourier descriptor case.

References

[1] A. Rosenfeld and M. Thurston, "Edge and curve detection for visual scene analysis," IEEE Trans. Comput. Vol. C-20, pp. 562-569, 1971.

[2] D. Marr, "Early processing of visual information," Trans. Roy. Soc. London, Vol. 275, pp. 483-519, 1976.

[3] D. Marr, Vision, "A Computational investigation into the human representation & processing of visual information." San Francisco, CA, Freeman Press, 1982.

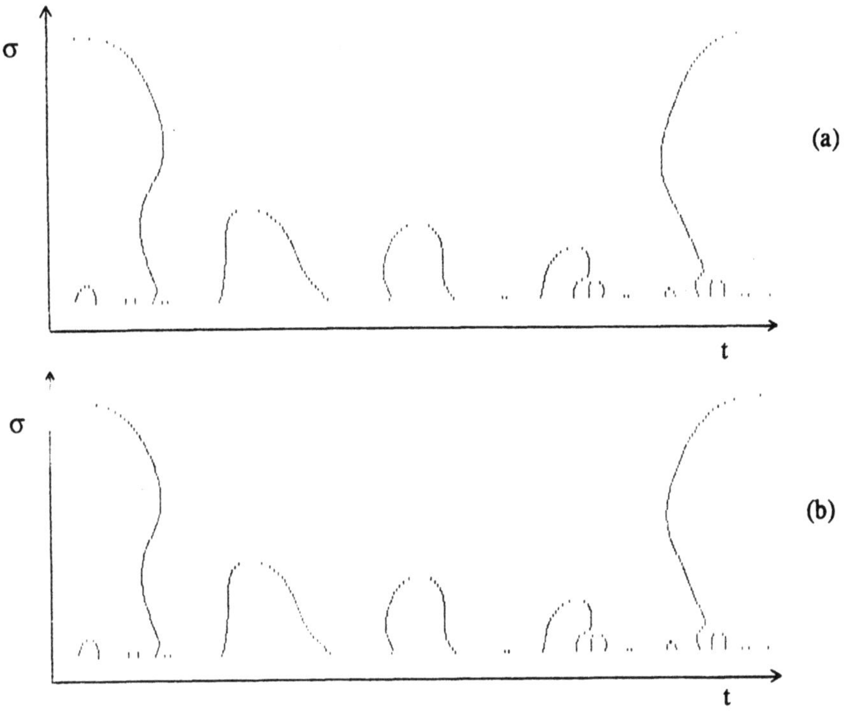

Figure 3: Scale space representations using new curvature definition. Fig. 3(a): original image contour; Fig. 3(b): skewed image contour. Note good agreement.

[4] A. P. Witkin, "Scale space filtering," Proc. 8th Int. Joint Conf. Artificial Intelligence, Karlsruhe, West Germany, pp. 1019-1022, 1983.

[5] F. Mokhtarian, A. Mackworth, "Scale-Based Description and Recognition of Planar Curves and Two-Dimensional Shapes," IEEE Trans. Pattern Analysis and Machine Intelligence, Vol. PAMI-8, No. 1, pp. 34 43, January 1986.

[6] H. W. Guggenheimer, "Differential geometry," New York, N.Y., Dover Publications, 1977.

[7] J. Babaud, A. P. Witkin, M. Baudin and R. O. Duda, "Uniqueness of the Gaussian Kernel for Scale-Space Filtering," IEEE Trans. Pattern Analysis and Machine Intelligence, Vol PAMI-8, No. 1, pp. 26-33, January 1986.

[8] D. Cyganski, J. A. Orr, "3D motion parameters from contours using a canonic differential," IEEE Int. Conf. on Acoustics Speech and Signal Processing, Tampa, Fla., pp. 917-920, March 26-29, 1985.

[9] D. Cyganski, J. A. Orr, "Applications of tensor theory to object recognition and orientation estimation," IEEE Trans. Pattern Analysis and Machine Intelligence, Vol PAMI-7, No. 6, pp. 662-673, November 1985, pp. 662-673.

THE APPLICATION OF IMAGE TENSORS AND A NEW DECOMPOSITION

David Cyganski and John A. Orr

Electrical Engineering Department
Worcester Polytechnic Institute
Worcester, Massachusetts, 01609 USA

Abstract

The tensor method for calculation of the affine transform relating two views of a rigid, planar object is briefly reviewed, and methods for accomplishing the reduction in rank of image tensors which enable affine transform solution via a simple system of linear equations are summarized. A new tensor decomposition is then presented which lends itself to a similar solution technique but provides greater geometrical insight into the process. This technique for accomplishing the needed tensor decomposition is based on Prony's method for solution of a set of non-linear equations. The operation of a complete orientation estimation algorithm based on this decomposition is demonstrated on a camera acquired image.

1. Introduction

An important step in object recognition and robot vision problems often involves identification of the affine transform which relates two views (which may result from camera or object motion) of an object. This information may be used, for example, to calculate robot motion to grasp and properly orient a part or to synthetically re-orient an image to a "standard" view as an initial step in the recognition process. For the case studied here, that of rigid, planar-patch objects, the affine transformation which relates images of the objects in two orientations contains all necessary information to identify the re-orientations in three-space undergone by the object between the two images. These motions are often defined in terms of translations of the centers of mass of the object and the Euler angles of rotation.

The problems of identification of the affine transform relating two images, and of matching two images in different orientations, have been the subjects of considerable previous investigation [1-4]. Methods for identification of the affine transform without requiring knowledge of any point correspondences in the two images have been previously presented [5-8]. These methods rely on calculation of image moments and make use of tensor notation to simplify representation of image information and to derive a straightforward linear solution method for the affine transform. The approach has also been extended to the problem of object identification by allowing standardization of object orientation before application of the identification algorithm. This standardization commonly allows a significant reduction in the complexity and computation time of the identification algorithm.

NATO ASI Series, Vol. F30
Pattern Recognition Theory and Applications
Edited by P. A. Devijver and J. Kittler

The theoretical basis of the tensor approach to affine transform identification is briefly summarized here, and previous methods based on tensor contraction are reviewed. A new method is then presented for the decomposition of high rank tensors into several of unit rank, this being necessary for the generation of the set of linear equations which may be solved for the affine transform coefficients. The technique applies Prony's method and leads to a geometrically-motivated model which should assist in such areas as: determination of the independence of tensors resulting from tensor decomposition and reduction techniques; identification of the existence of singular images which do not permit solution for the affine transform; and development of means for dealing with symmetries and other singularities. It should be noted that in all implementations of the tensor approach, the affine transform is calculated from the image intensity functions without requiring knowledge of any point correspondences.

2. Summary of Tensor Method

The overall method for affine transform identification in the case of images resulting from orthogonal projection of rigid, planar-patch objects is briefly summarized here. More details are provided in the references [5-7]. First, it is necessary to define the tensor notation to be used. With $\underline{e}_1$ and $\underline{e}_2$ representing the basis vectors of a two-dimensional image plane, any point $\underline{x}$ on that plane may be represented by:

$$\underline{x} = \sum_{i=1}^{2} x^i \underline{e}_i = x^i \underline{e}_i,$$

where superscript notation is used to identify coordinate variables, and in the rightmost expression the Einstein summation convention is applied wherein summation over any repeated index is assumed to occur. A new basis set $\underline{\bar{e}}$ may now be related to the original by:

$$\underline{e}_i = A_i^j \underline{\bar{e}}_j \quad \text{or} \quad \underline{\bar{e}}_i = a_i^j \underline{e}_j.$$

It should be noted that the A or "point" transformation is related to the corresponding basis set transformation, a, by:

$$a_j^i A_k^j = \delta_k^i$$

where δ represents the matrix identity.

Given the above notation, it is desired to identify the transformation which maps points in one image (referred to as the "standard image") into points in the other ("reoriented") image where x^i identifies points in the standard image and $\bar{x}^i$ identifies points in the reoriented image. This transformation is represented by:

$$\bar{x}^i = A_j^i (x^j - g^j) + \bar{g}^i$$

where A represents the linear portion of the desired affine transform and g and $\bar{g}$ represent the original and new optical center of gravity locations, respectively. Conventional zero and first-order moments may be used to find g and $\bar{g}$. Centering of the images with respect to their centers of gravity results in a simpler form involving only the linear part of the transformation:

$$\bar{x}^i = A_j^i x^j \tag{1}$$

which is the form assumed in the following.

Moments may be formed from the standard image:

$$T^{ij\cdots} = \int x^i x^j \cdots f(x^1, x^2) dx^1 dx^2$$

where $f(x^1, x^2)$ represents the image intensity function. Similarly for the reoriented image:

$$\bar{T}^{ij\cdots} = \int \bar{x}^i \bar{x}^j \cdots \bar{f}(\bar{x}^1, \bar{x}^2) d\bar{x}^1 d\bar{x}^2 \quad (2)$$

Applying the change of variables in (1) yields:

$$\bar{T}^{ij\cdots} = \int A^i_k x^k A^j_l x^l \cdots f(x^1, x^2)|J|^{-1} dx^1 dx^2 \quad (3)$$

where J is the Jacobian:

$$J = \det(a^i_j) = [\det(A^i_j)]^{-1}.$$

From (2) and (3) the relation between the moments of the standard and reoriented images becomes:

$$\bar{T}^{kl\cdots} = |J|^{-1} A^k_i A^l_j \cdots T^{ij\cdots} \quad (4)$$

which describes an oriented relative tensor of weight -1.

It is desired to solve (4) for the four unknown coefficients in A. Specifically, it is desired to find a sufficient number of unit-rank moment tensors so that equations linear in A may be solved. The first order moments may not be used directly because they are zero as a result of the removal of center of gravity information referred to above.

The following section of this paper presents first a summary of tensor reduction techniques using tensor contraction, and then develops a new method for decomposition of higher order tensors into several of unit rank. This new method provides more geometric insight into the tensor operations than do the previous approaches. The distinction between the terms "reduction" and "decomposition" is that the former implies generation of a lower-order tensor by contraction of two or more higher-order tensors, while the latter implies generation of the lower-order tensor directly from a single higher-order tensor.

3. Generation of Unit-Rank Tensors

It is necessary to produce a set of equations in the form of (4) where a sufficient number of independent values of T and $\bar{T}$ are known so that the four coefficients in A may be found. Eq. (4) is linear in the A coefficients only for first-order moments, which have been noted as having values of zero. It is tempting to use third-order moments (of the form T^{ijk}) which possess four independent components. However, it can be shown that the product form of the affine transform relation in that case $(A^k_i A^l_j A^m_n)$ possesses 20 unknown composite variables. The use of more equations involving moment tensors of other orders is not directly helpful since these involve transform products of correspondingly different orders and hence introduce new composite variables.

Another approach would involve searching for a solution to a nonlinear system of equations in the four unknowns of A^i_j. The problems inherent in iterative solutions to problems of this kind motivate the search for a method to generate a system of equations linear in the A coefficients from moment tensors of different orders.

3.1. Review of Previous Tensor Reduction Methods

The initial approach to generation of the needed unit-rank tensors was developed by the authors by expressing the solution of a simple linear system of equations in tensor form and then proceeding to express and finally extend the related matrix inverse in tensor form. This development made use of the permutation tensor ε_{ij} which permits tensor expression of the linear algebraic operations of the adjoint and determinant. A somewhat more direct derivation is presented here.

The permutation tensor mentioned above is defined as:

$$\varepsilon_{ij} = \begin{cases} 1 & \text{if } i = 1 \text{ and } j = 2 \\ -1 & \text{if } i = 2 \text{ and } j = 1 \\ 0 & \text{if } i = j \end{cases}$$

It is a covariant relative tensor of weight -1. In the search for unit-rank tensors, the contraction $S^k = T^{ijk}\varepsilon_{ij}$ where T is a third-order tensor, could be performed. Unfortunately, the symmetry of the moment tensors contracted in this way via the permutation tensor (which is referred to as antisymmetric) results in tensors whose components are always zero. Moment tensors are inherently symmetric, where symmetry is defined as invariance to exchange of a pair of index values. However, the method of inner products may be used to reduce tensors of different orders by means of the permutation tensor, with only occasional singular instances resulting.

The following equation involving a second-order moment tensor (s^{ij}) and a third-order moment tensor (t^{ijk}) tensor may be constructed:

$$\zeta^m = s^{ij}\varepsilon_{ik}\,\varepsilon_{jl}t^{klm}$$

where ζ^m is a unit-rank relative tensor of weight -4. Similarly, another unit-rank tensor (with weight -11) may be formed:

$$\eta^i = t^{ijk}\varepsilon_{jl}\,\varepsilon_{km}\,\zeta^l\zeta^m.$$

These are of the proper rank, but must be reduced in weight to zero. This may easily be accomplished by use of the zero-order moment tensor z (which has no indices) of weight -1. This weight arises from the relation $\bar{z} = z|J|^{-1}$. Taking the appropriate power of z and dividing, we obtain:

$$u^i = \zeta^i/(z)^4$$

and

$$v^i = \eta^i/(z)^{11}$$

which are examples of the desired unit-rank tensors with a sufficient number (four) of nonzero, independent components to enable solution of the equations:

$$\bar{u}^i = A^i_j u^j$$

$$\bar{v}^i = A^i_j v^j.$$

The above equations define four equations in four unknowns, but may be decoupled into two sets of equations in two unknowns each. These may be solved for the four coefficients in A, and using the old and new center of gravity values obtained from the zero and first order (non-central) moment tensors, the complete image affine transform is given by:

$$\bar{x}^i = A^i_j(x^j - g^j) + \bar{g}^i.$$

Only second and third order moments were used above, but tensors of other, higher, order could also be used. However, high order tensors are more subject to the effects of image distortion, as is introduced by the spatial quantization process. Higher order tensors would obviously be useful in instances in which the systems formed as above are accidently singular. Also, a least-squares method could be formed to combine the information from several tensors of different orders.

3.2. New Decomposition

We will now develop a new decomposition of symmetric odd order tensors from a quite different point of view than that summarized above. We wish to associate a set of unit rank tensors (vectors) ${}_m\bar{v}^i$ with a tensor $\bar{T}^{i_1 i_2 \cdots}$ such that if

$$\bar{T}^{i_1 i_2 \cdots} = A^{i_1}_{j_1} A^{i_1}_{j_1} \cdots T^{j_1 j_2 \cdots} |J|^{-W}$$

then

$$_m\bar{v}^i = A^i_j\, {}_m v^j |J|^{-w}. \tag{5}$$

Such a set of vectors would allow us to simply solve for the transformation A^i_j which underlies the transformation which T undergoes.

Consider the consistency of the following tensor constructed from some set of tensors ${}_m v^i$ with the symmetry of the moment tensor T:

$$V^{i_1 i_2 \cdots i_N} = \sum_{m=1}^{M} \prod_{n=1}^{N} {}_m v^{i_n}$$

Here V is constructed by summing rank N tensors, each of which is the outer product of N identical vectors. Obviously each of the tensor terms is a symmetric tensor since

$$_m v^{i_1}\, {}_m v^{i_2} \cdots {}_m v^{i_N} = {}_m v^{j_1}\, {}_m v^{j_2} \cdots {}_m v^{j_N}$$

where $(i_1, i_2, ..., i_N)$ is any permutation of $(j_1, j_2, ..., j_N)$. A direct and obvious consequence is that the composite tensor V is also symmetric. Hence we can attempt to model the symmetric tensor T with the construct V.

Now say we can associate constructs V and $\bar{V}$ uniquely with symmetric tensors T and $\bar{T}$, creating decompositions into 2-forms ${}_m v^i$ and ${}_m\bar{v}^i$. Are the ${}_m v^i$ and ${}_m\bar{v}^i$ related as tensors? By the properties of multilinear transformations we know that

$$\bar{T}^{i_1 i_2 \cdots i_N} = \sum_{m=1}^{M} \prod_{n=1}^{N} A^{i_n}_{j_n}\, {}_m v^{j_n} |J|^{-w}, \quad W = w^N.$$

But the decompositions of T and $\bar{T}$ were unique. Hence it must be true that

$$_m\bar{v}^i = A^i_j\, {}_m v^j |J|^{-w}.$$

Thus the 2-forms resulting from a unique decomposition do in fact represent tensors.

The number of independent elements in a 2-D symmetric tensor is $N+1$. The number of independent components comprising our model is $2M$. Hence with $M = (N+1)/2$ and with N odd, we know that the possibility exists for a unique solution. We will assume uniqueness and existence of this solution and attempt to solve for it. The equations in this non-linear system are as follows:

$$\begin{aligned} T^{111,\cdots,1} &= {}_1v^1\,{}_1v^1\cdots{}_1v^1 + {}_2v^1\,{}_2v^1\cdots{}_2v^1 + \cdots \\ T^{211,\cdots,1} &= {}_1v^2\,{}_1v^1\cdots{}_1v^1 + {}_2v^2\,{}_2v^1\cdots{}_2v^1 + \cdots \\ &\vdots \\ T^{222,\cdots,2} &= {}_1v^2\,{}_1v^2\cdots{}_1v^2 + {}_2v^2\,{}_2v^2\cdots{}_2v^2 + \cdots \end{aligned}$$

Let

$$\gamma = \frac{{}_nv^1}{{}_nv^2}.$$

We will not use tensor notation with respect to γ so as to make the later equations more readable. We see that our system can be expressed as

$$\begin{aligned} T^{111,\cdots,1} &= ({}_1v^2)^N\gamma_1^N + ({}_2v^2)^N\gamma_2^N + \cdots \\ T^{211,\cdots,1} &= ({}_1v^2)^N\gamma_1^{N-1} + ({}_2v^2)^N\gamma_2^{N-1} + \cdots \\ &\vdots \\ T^{222,\cdots,2} &= ({}_1v^2)^N\gamma_1^0 + ({}_2v^2)^N\gamma_2^0 + \cdots \end{aligned}$$

But this is of the form amenable to solution by Prony's method. Prony's method permits solution of the system of equations

$$c_k = \sum_{n=1}^{N} a_n\gamma_n^k \qquad k = 0, 1, \cdots, 2N-1.$$

for the values a_n and γ_n, $n = 1, \cdots, N$.

Let $P(\gamma)$ be a polynomial such that

$$P(\gamma) = \prod_{n=1}^{N}(\gamma - \gamma_n) = \sum_{i=0}^{N}\beta_i\gamma^i.$$

That is, the roots of $P(\gamma)$ are the solution set for γ_n from our original problem and the β_i are the coefficients of this polynomial.

Now, multiply the system of equations by the coefficients β_i and sum as shown here

$$\begin{aligned} q_j = \sum_{k=0}^{N}\beta_k c_{j+k} &= \sum_{k=0}^{N}\beta_k\sum_{n=1}^{N}a_n\gamma_n^{j+k} \\ &= \sum_{n=1}^{N}a_n\gamma_n^j\sum_{k=0}^{N}\beta_k\gamma_n^k = 0. \end{aligned}$$

Because of the form of the rightmost factor we have that the q_j are zero by definition of the polynomial $P(\gamma)$.

Letting j range from 0 to $N-1$ we have a system of equations

$$\begin{bmatrix} c_0 & c_1 & \cdot & c_N \\ c_1 & c_2 & \cdot & c_{N+1} \\ \cdot & \cdot & \cdot & \cdot \\ \cdot & \cdot & \cdot & \cdot \\ \cdot & \cdot & \cdot & \cdot \\ c_{N-1} & c_N & \cdot & c_{2N-1} \end{bmatrix} \begin{bmatrix} \beta_0 \\ \beta_1 \\ \cdot \\ \cdot \\ \cdot \\ \beta_N \end{bmatrix} = 0.$$

This is a set of autoregressive equations of Hankel form and can be solved for all the β_k in terms of one of the β_k. But from the construction of $P(\gamma)$ we know that $\beta_N=1$; hence we may solve for all the β_k uniquely. Now solving for the roots of $P(\gamma)$ yields the values for γ_n.

Finally, having found the γ_n, we may substitute these known values into our first equation yielding the linear system of equations in the a_n given by

$$\begin{bmatrix} 1 & 1 & \cdot & 1 \\ \gamma_1 & \gamma_2 & \cdot & \gamma_N \\ \cdot & \cdot & \cdot & \cdot \\ \cdot & \cdot & \cdot & \cdot \\ \cdot & \cdot & \cdot & \cdot \\ \gamma_1^{2N-1} & \gamma_2^{2N-1} & \cdot & \gamma_N^{2N-1} \end{bmatrix} \begin{bmatrix} a_1 \\ a_2 \\ \cdot \\ \cdot \\ \cdot \\ a_N \end{bmatrix} = \begin{bmatrix} c_0 \\ c_1 \\ \cdot \\ \cdot \\ \cdot \\ c_{2N-1} \end{bmatrix}$$

which is over determined and may be solved by least squares techniques, or a subset may be solved directly.

Recalling our original system of equations, we see that

$$a_n = ({}_nv^2)^N \tag{6}$$

and

$$\gamma_n = \frac{{}_nv^1}{{}_nv^2} \tag{7}$$

from which all the ${}_nv^i$ may be found directly.

Before we can apply this decomposition of T towards solving our original image matching problem, we must confront two complications. First, the solutions γ_n of the polynomial equation need not be real. That is, a real tensor decomposition may not exist. Second, the solutions are "unlabeled"; hence we do not know how to pair them with the decomposition of $\bar{T}$ for solution of the linear transformation A^i_j.

Complex solutions for γ_n have been observed for typical image data sets. While the derivation of the solution for unit rank tensors above and previously developed solutions for the tensor transformation problem assumed real tensors, we can show that they need not be changed to accommodate complex tensors.

A motivation for the tensor decomposition proposed above was that given real unit rank tensors, we could match the numbers of independent parameters in the original tensor and the model given $M=(N+1)/2$. Introducing complex solutions would seem, at first glance, to double the parameters in the model. But consider the construction of the polynomial $P(\gamma)$. Since this polynomial has real coefficients, the roots must occur in complex conjugate pairs. Thus each such pair of solutions represents only two independent parameters, a radius and an angle. Thus there are no more parameters involved in the model than before. Furthermore, since the tensor transformation rules may be applied to complex tensor components without modification, all the previously developed reasoning holds with respect to the tensor decomposition model. One complication arises in the construction of the decomposition, however. With the possibility that γ_n is complex, we must now deal with the fact that there are N roots of Eq. (6). The correct selection from among these solutions can be made by substituting the solutions into Eq. (5) and using the condition that A must be real.

Because the solutions are "unlabeled", we do not know how to pair the solutions of the decomposition of T with those of $\bar{T}$ to find A^i_j. Yet we know that some such association is possible since the method of tensor reduction (described above) results in labeled unit rank tensors. The key to solving this problem is to realize that we don't need the tensors of decomposition themselves to solve our transformation problem, but rather any labeled set of linear combinations of these tensors. Thus if we can find two unit rank tensor functions $u^i(\ )$ and $v^i(\ )$ which are invariant under permutation of their tensor arguments,

$$u^i({}_{k_1}v^i, {}_{k_2}v^i, \cdots, {}_{k_M}v^i) = u^i({}_{l_1}v^i, {}_{l_2}v^i, \cdots, {}_{l_M}v^i)$$

where $k_1, k_2, \cdots, k_m$ are distinct integers taken from $1, \cdots, M$ and $l_1, l_2, \cdots, l_M$ is some permutation of $k_1, k_2, ..., k_M$, then u^i and v^i for tensor arguments would be two labeled unit rank tensors. For example, decomposing a rank 3 moment tensor, we get two component tensors ${}_1r^i, {}_2r^j$ and likewise some ${}_1s^i$ and ${}_2s^j$ from the decomposition of the transformed moment tensor. While we cannot pair the r and s tensors, we do know that

$$({}_1s^i + {}_2s^i) = \bar{u}^i = A^i_j u^j |J|^{-w} = A^i_j({}_1r^j + {}_2r^j)|J|^{-w}.$$

This relation will be used below in the example implementation.

4. Testing the Decomposition

As an experimental verification of the method, we used the third order moment tensors associated with some images to resolve the transformation relating them. A rank 3 tensor gives rise to two vectors, r^i and s^i, under decomposition. There is only one independent unit rank tensor function symmetric in two tensors, the sum, as given above. However, the difference of two tensors is skew-symmetric under permutation. By assuming $\det(A) > 0$, a sign correction may be chosen for solution of A. This restriction (which is equivalent to the assumption that the transformation does not represent a reflection about any axis) is not essential to the decomposition method but rather serves us in this most simple demonstration of the technique where only two unlabeled tensors are used. Hence we make use of

$$u^i = {}_1r^i + {}_2r^i$$

and

$$v^i = \pm({}_1s^i - {}_2s^i)$$

to solve for A. But with rank three moment tensors we have that

$$\bar{u}^i = A^i_j u^j |J|^{-1/3}.$$

To simplify the solution technique we can use the fact that the rank zero moment tensor, z, is a tensor density with

$$\bar{z} = z|J|^{-1}.$$

Hence

$$\bar{u}^i/(\bar{z})^{1/3} = A^i_j u^j/(z)^{1/3}$$

and likewise for v^i. Given these equations we can proceed as with the tensor reduction method to solve for the affine transformation relating pairs of images.

Operation of the affine transform identification technique with the newly-developed method for tensor decomposition is demonstrated here. Fig. 1(a) shows an image of a planar object which is assumed to be in standard orientation. This resulted from camera acquisition of the image of a real object, spatial quantization on a grid of 128 picture elements, and thresholding to yield a binary-valued image function. Numerical application of the affine transform given in Table 1 yielded the image in Fig. 1(b). This transformation represents a rotated oblique view of the planar object. The camera line of sight is tilted 60 degrees from the perpendicular and the object is rotated 45 degrees about the line of sight.

The result of estimation of this transform by the algorithm of this paper is also shown in Table 1. Transformation of the image in Fig. 1(b) by the inverse of the estimated transform results in a standardized image (Fig. 1(c)). The agreement between the original (Fig. 1(a)) and standardized images is illustrated by the result of an exclusive OR operation shown in Fig. 1(d). The small inaccuracies in this example result from spatial quantization noise inherent in transforming and resampling the image, approximation of the continuous moment integrals by summations, and numerical round-off errors.

TABLE 1

AFFINE TRANSFORMATIONS

ACTUAL	CALCULATED
$\begin{bmatrix} 0.354 & -0.354 \\ 0.707 & 0.707 \end{bmatrix}$	$\begin{bmatrix} 0.359 & -0.347 \\ 0.701 & 0.701 \end{bmatrix}$

5. Conclusions

We have demonstrated a technique for the decomposition of odd rank moment tensors into a sum of outer products of related unit rank tensors. A means of producing labeled unit rank tensors from these has also been presented. From the labeled tensors, the linear transformation relating two images may be found as in the case with unit rank tensors resulting from tensor reduction methods previously introduced. This

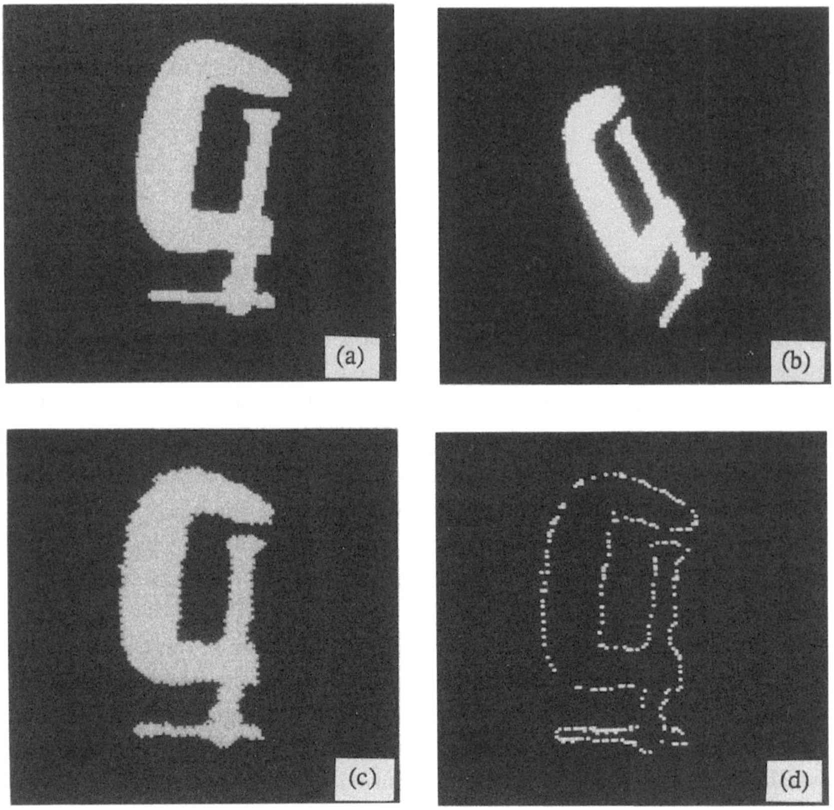

Figure 1: Illustration of the application of the affine transform estimation technique using the algorithm of this paper. Fig. 1(a): object in a "standard" orientation; Fig. 1(b): result of application of the affine transform in Table 1 to the image in Fig. 1(a); Fig. 1(c): the result of application of the inverse of the calculated transform in Table 1 on Fig. 1(b); Fig. 1(d): result of an exclusive OR of Fig. 1(a) with Fig. 1(c).

decomposition should prove useful in the the theoretical developments regarding the existence and sensitivity of solutions to the image transformation problem from image moments. Considerable insight into the geometrical principles underlying the tensor reduction method arise when the reduction is applied to the image tensors expressed in terms of the expansion resulting from the tensor decomposition. We see here the role of the tensor function, symmetric in arguments, in the labeling of the moment based information.

References

[1] T. S. Huang, *Image Sequence Analysis*, Springer-Verlag, 1981.

[2] D. Casasent and D. Psaltis "New Optical Transforms for Pattern Recognition," Proc. IEEE, Vol. 65, pp. 77-84, January, 1977.

[3] H. Dirilten and T. G. Newman, "Pattern Matching Under Affine Transformations," IEEE Trans. Computers, Vol. C-26, pp. 314- 317, March, 1977.

[4] M. K. Hu, "Visual Pattern Recognition by Moment Invariants," IEEE Trans. Inform. Theory, pp 179-187, February, 1962.

[5] D. Cyganski and J. A. Orr, "Applications of Tensor Theory to Object Recognition and Orientation Determination," IEEE Transactions on Pattern Analysis and Machine Intelligence, Vol. PAMI-7, No. 6, pp. 662-673, November, 1985.

[6] D. Cyganski and J. A. Orr, "Object Identification and Orientation Determination in 3-Space with no Point Correspondence Information," Proc. IEEE Conf. ASSP, San Diego, CA, 1984.

[7] D. Cyganski and J. A. Orr, "Object Identification and Orientation Estimation from Point Set Tensors," Seventh Int. Conf. Pattern Recognition, Montreal, Canada, 1984.

[8] B. Bamieh and R. J. P. De Figueiredo, "Efficient New Techniques for Identification and 3D Attitude Determination of Space Objects from a Single Image," Proc. IEEE Intl. Conf. Robotics and Automation, St. Louis, March 1985.

IMAGE UNDERSTANDING STRATEGIES : APPLICATION TO ELECTRON MICROSCOPY

Jean-Michel Jolion and Patrick Prevot

Laboratoire d'Informatique Appliquée
INSA – 502 INFORMATIQUE
69621 VILLEURBANNE CEDEX
FRANCE

Abstract

This paper examine the problems of designing image analysis systems capable of providing morphological and geometrical measurements on a specific phenomenon. Several strategies for designing such a system are presented. One of these is applied to the design of a system for physicist users which allows access to some quantitative information. This information is already present in the image but, in the past, it could not be used due to a lack of suitable tools. These data are important for research on material mechanical property optimization. Finally, we present a prototyping tool which facilitates the design stage of analysis system.

1. Image Analysis System Design

1.1. Context

Imagine that someone calls on an image processing specialist (IPS) to design and build a data processing system. Suppose further that his intention is to automatize a difficult task consisting of extracting multiple measurements. To this end, he first defines objectives and provides data—images—and external information for image understanding (general rules about the application domain, information about image acquisition, ...).

1.2. First Strategy

The IPS builds a procedure link which defines the image analysis algorithm based on his own experience and knowledge. Each component is split into elementary entities by a top down analysis. The user interacts only in the system checking step.

1.3. Second Strategy

Here, the user plays a more important part in system design. In the system class we are concerned about, the image processing part breaks down into three steps :

A : Preliminary processing

NATO ASI Series, Vol. F30
Pattern Recognition Theory and Applications
Edited by P. A. Devijver and J. Kittler

B : Pattern Recognition

C : Measurement on the detected forms

More often, the second step is not a problem for the user who has past experience with this kind of images. On the other hand, the length or difficulty of the third step presses him to call on the IPS. Unfortunately, the second step can not be easily solved by the IPS because of the non existence of theoretical rules (*i.e.*, rules to understand the image content).

The second strategy we present here is based on the mean and knowledge exchange between the computer and the user. One brings his knowledge on the image content analysis, the other its processing power. This approach assumes that the user knows a way of analyzing the images. That is to say that he is able to explain his analysis method. The IPS interviews him on his method and tries to answer two questions :

- what are the rules ?

- how are these rules used ?

Thus, the IPS is the link between user and computer. He must translate the user's intuitive method into a data processing language. This strategy is different from the artificial intelligence approach because we suppose that the user and the IPS can answer the second question completely. This is not always the case in vision, especially in robotics.

1.4. Formalism Choice

The user interview step is made with the intention of extracting a set of rules. Afterwards, these rules are split into elementary procedures which will form the final data processing system. During the interview, the user and the IPS define the rules using a common language. This language must be natural in order to be used by a non IPS user and technical in order to translate the rules more easily.

The use of Artificial Intelligence techniques as a way of communication seems to be a good idea. Now, this is only used for the initial steps of the analysis [Nazif-84], [Haton-85], [Stansfield-86]. We propose a more technical formalism based on three concepts :

⇒ Predicate calculus : a pattern will be characterized by a property set. This principle is applied in Artificial Intelligence techniques.

⇒ Set theory : this formalism is the basis of mathematical morphology [Serra-82].

These two notions have already been used in order to build models in other domains like natural language study [Saint-Dizier-85].

⇒ Basic notions of image processing : pixel, segment, object, ...

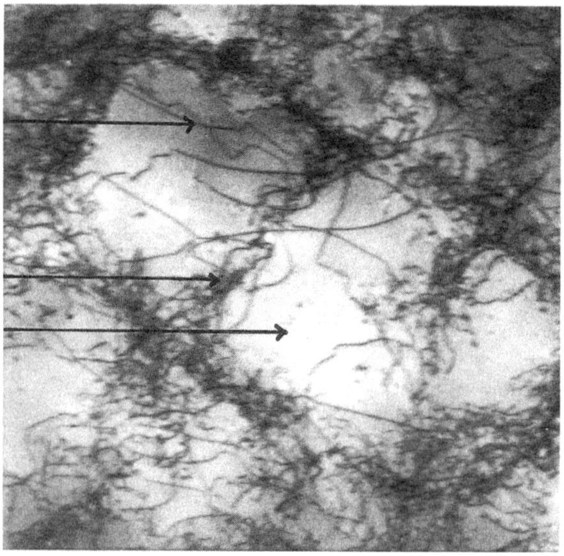

Figure 1: Cellular structure image obtained using an transmission electron microscope.

2. Application to Electron Microscopy

2.1. Problem

Physicists wish to extract quantitative information about the evolution of material microscopic structure during damaging phenomena in order to link microscopic and macroscopic behaviour of metallurgical materials. We are interested in the appearance of cellular structure during such phenomena (see Figure 1); this case is considered as very important by physicists.

The physicist wants to extract from these images geometrical and morphological data which characterize the cellular structure. A lot of images are needed for statistical processing. Thus, the physicist can not do this work by hand.

The system's objective is to obtain a set of parameters that describes the cellular structure. The cells recognition is the most important problem and becomes difficult because of two inconveniences:

- the quality of images varies because of an inability to control the context. Moreover, the experiment complexity (time, cost, sampling difficulties) makes the selection of better images impossible.

- there are situations where we must know if a cell exists. An image is an instantaneous state of the material. So, it can be a creation stage of one or more new cells by cell-wall limbs joining. Moreover, the variation of mixed up dislocation (defect) quantity is the cause of dissimilar cell-wall segments.

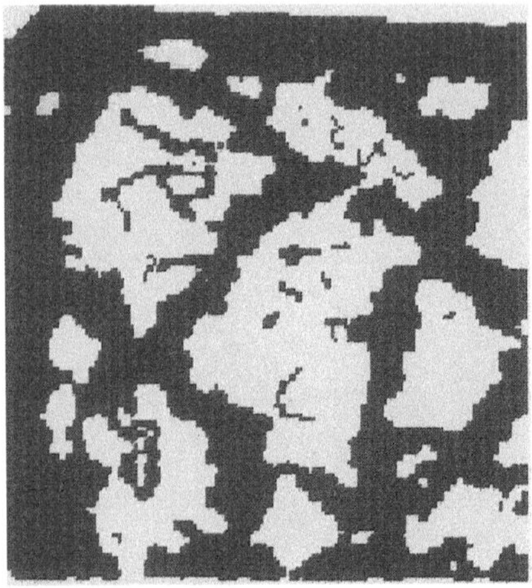

Figure 2: Binary image example (before processing)

Thus, the analysis system needs decision criteria. Like in the second strategy, we choose to use the physicist experience to define these criteria.

2.2. Binary Image Building

The presence of two entities, cells and dislocations, leads us to transform the original image (256 gray-levels) into a binary one [Jolion-86a] (see Figure 2).

2.3. Image Content Analysis

We model the reasoning the physicist uses to analyze an image, thanks to his interview. It is in this way that we build the main processing algorithm which consists of four ordered rules :

1) Reconstruction of badly defined cell-walls

2) Removal of dislocations which are isolated in a cell-heart

3) Split-up of cell clumps

4) Removal of cell-wall limbs which do not divide cells.

2.4. Rule Translation Example

Each rule is divided into elementary procedures using the formalism presented in Section 1.4 [Jolion-85]. Here, we present details on the second rule only.

The isolated dislocations reveal a new cell creation stage. But, the physicist is only interested in the cell size and shape, and takes into account two patterns : intact cells and cell-walls. Therefore, the isolated dislocations have to be eliminated.

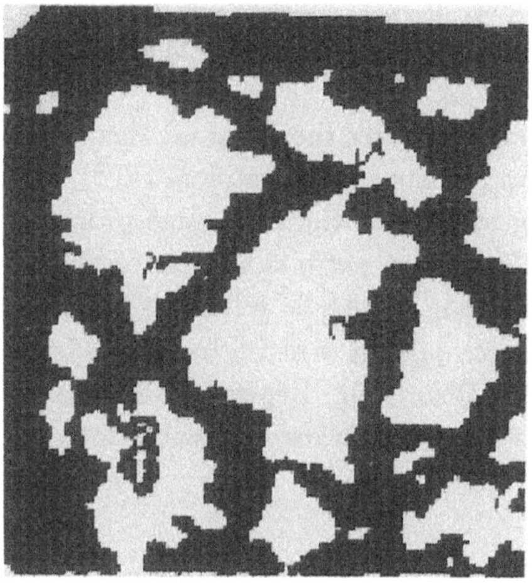

Figure 3: Binary image after processing

The binary image can be split into two entities : shape (dislocations) and background (cells). The image is divided into objects by the method proposed by Veillon (1979). We extract three criteria from the physicist's interview which characterize the dislocations we have to eliminate.

Let D be an object of an image I. Then our criteria are :

C1 : D is in the shape;

C2 : D is a finite object (i.e. D is not tangent to the image side); and

C3 : all the background pixels of the k-neighbourhood(D) are included in the same object.

The neighbourhood notion is linked to distance by :

$$\text{A is k-neighbour of B} \iff d(\text{A}, \text{B}) \leq \text{k}$$

The parameter k must be fixed by the IPS and the physicist, taking into account the image particularities.

Processing then becomes very easy :

$$\forall \text{D} \subset \text{I, if C1(D) and C2(D) and C3(D) then D} \rightarrow \text{background.}$$

An example is shown in Figure 3.

3. Rule Writing Language

Directly translating detailed rules into classical programming language is difficult and time consuming. We have defined PASCAL extensions in order to make this step easier.

The set of these extensions forms a new language: ESSAI, Ecriture Simplifiée pour Système d'Analyse d'Images. It is a prototyping tool which permits the manipulation of two concepts: predicate calculus, intensive sets. This notion is already included in SETL [Schonberg-81], [Kruchten-84].

Specifically, our language provides the usual set theoretical operations (union, intersection, etc.), universal and existential quantifiers ($\forall, \exists$). Moreover, it contains predefined types corresponding to usual notions of image processing : pixel, segment, objet, image [Jolion-86b]. Its library also permits the use of mathematical morphology operators [Lay-85], [Jolion-86c]. So, ESSAI, is well suited to binary image manipulation.

The ESSAI/PASCAL compiler is written in a high-level language LET (compiler writing oriented language) [Beney-80], [Beney-86]. The use of PASCAL and especially LET as programming environment makes it possible to translate ESSAI under several systems.

4. Conclusion

The image analysis system design requires a strategy. The one we have presented is based on the modelling of the understanding method the user applies during his own image analysis. The system we have built along this strategy, allows physicists the access to quantitative data about cellular structures in damaged materials. We consider other developments for the future. We mention three of them :

i) The concepts we use to model the user's rules, are very efficient on binary images. We would like to develop and apply these concepts to grey-level or 3-D images.

ii) ESSAI is a prototyping tool. We need to optimize the generated code so that systems written in this language can be used in a real-time environment. That can be made thanks to the ESSAI implementation within an image processing oriented system like SAPIN [Belaid-85].

iii) The second strategy we propose, requires an image processing and/or data processing specialist. Moreover, the user must know a method to analyze the image content. Artificial Intelligence can then be a way of eliminating this requirement as well as reducing the IPS's part in the system design. We think that this is possible in the low-level of image analysis. But, in the high-level portion, this is now limited by the efficiency of :

- the natural language understanding techniques, for the communication part [Vilnat-85], [Bosc-85]
- the knowledge based vision system performance, for the image content analysis [Riseman-84].

Acknowledgments : The authors would like to thank the GEMPPM Laboratory, INSA Lyon, France and particularly A. Hamel.

References

[1] A. Belaid, "SAPIN : Système d'aide à la programmation du traitement d'images numérisées," (in French) Tech. Rep. No. 83-R-32, Crin, Université de Nancy I, France, June 1983.

[2] J. Beney, L. Frecon, "Langage et système d'écriture de traducteurs," (in French) *RAIRO Informatique*, Vol. 14, No.4, 1980, pp. 379-384

[3] J. Beney, "Langage LET : manuel de référence," (in French) Tech. Rep., LIA INSA Lyon, France, 1980, revised 1986.

[4] P. Bosc, "Spécification de connaissances pour une inter-face en langage à grande liberté syntaxique," (in French), *5ème Congrès RFIA*, AFCET-ADI Grenoble, France, Nov. 1985.

[5] J.-P. Haton, "Intelligence artificielle en compréhension automatique de la parole : Etat des recherches et comparaison avec la vision par ordinateur," (in French), *TSI*, No.3, Vol. 4, 1985, pp. 265-287.

[6] J.M. Jolion, P. Prevot, "Analyse d'image de structures cellulaires dans les matériaux fatigués," (in French) *5ème Congrès RFIA*, AFCET-ADI Grenoble, France, Nov. 1985.

[7] J.M. Jolion, P. Prevot, "Binarisation automatique d'images en microscopie electronique," (in French) to be published in *Traitement du Signal*, 1986.

[8] J.M. Jolion, "ESSAI : Un outil pour l'analyse d'images," (in French) *Bullet*, No.1, May 1986.

[9] J.M. Jolion, "ESSAI : manuel de référence," (in French) Tech. Rep., LIA INSA Lyon, France, April 1986

[10] P. Kruchten, E. Schonberg, "Le système Ada/Ed : Une expérience de prototype utilisant le langage SETL," (in French); *TSI*, No.3, Vol. 3, 1984, pp. 193-200.

[11] B. Lay, M. Gauthier, "Morpholog," (in French) Journées SM-90, Paris, 1985.

[12] A.M. Nazif, M.D. Levine, "Low level image segmentation : An expert system," *IEEE Trans. PAMI*, Vol. PAMI-6, No.5, Sept. 84, pp. 555-577.

A DIFFUSION-BASED DESCRIPTION OF SHAPE

Murray H. Loew

Department of Electrical Engineering and Computer Science
George Washington University
Washington, D.C. 20052 U.S.A

Abstract

A method is presented that uses a diffusion-like process to describe the shape of a region. Convexity is not required, the descriptor is invariant under several common transformations, is applicable in the n-dimensional case, and is easy to compute.

1. Introduction

Shape description is an essential component of any image-understanding system. Many approaches to description of shape have been proposed and used in the fields of image processing and computer vision. Pavlidis (1978) suggested a taxonomy of shape descriptors based on: (1) whether just the boundary, or the entire interior of the object was examined (the techniques were called external and internal, respectively); (2) whether the characterization was made on the basis of a scalar transform (in which a picture is transformed into an array of scalar features), or a space transform (a picture is transformed into another picture); and (3) whether the procedure is or is not information preserving in the sense that the original image can be reconstructed from the shape descriptors.

Existing methods include the Ψ - **s** *curve*, in which Ψ is computed as the angle made between a fixed line and a tangent to the boundary of the region; it is plotted against s, the arc length of the boundary traversed. For a closed boundary, the function is periodic, and may be associated with segmentation of the boundary in terms of straight lines and circular arcs (Ballard and Brown, 1982). Other methods evaluate *eccentricity* (or elongatedness) in a variety of ways, including length-to-width ratio and ratio of the principal axes of inertia; *compactness* (*e.g.*, perimeter^2/area, and Danielsson's method (Danielsson, 1979)); the *slope-density function*, which is a histogram of Ψ collected over the boundary; *curvature*, the derivative of Ψ as a function of **s**; projections of the figure onto an axis (the *signatures*); *concavity*, with a tree of regions that will create the convex

NATO ASI Series, Vol. F30
Pattern Recognition Theory and Applications
Edited by P. A. Devijver and J. Kittler

hull of the original object; *shape numbers* based on chain-coding of the boundary; and the *medial-axis transform*, which transforms the original object to a stick figure that approximates the skeleton of the figure.

We present here a new shape measure that allows rapid assignment of labels that are both intuitively appealing and rigorously based. The descriptor can be computed easily on existing hardware and may be implemented immediately on future parallel-processing systems. Regions need not be convex (although the modest requirement is imposed that each region be simply-connected; *i.e.*, have a single inside and a single outside). This is a significant advantage in light of the comment by Pavlidis (1978) that there exist a number of shape description techniques applicable *only* to convex objects, while some of the general ones perform much better if restricted to that class. The method described below works equally well for convex and non-convex regions. Further, the approach can be extended immediately to three-dimensional objects. With respect to the taxonomy noted above, it is internal, scalar, and non- information preserving.

2. Method

The diffusion-type procedure simulates the release at an initial time of a given number of particles from each pixel along the boundary of a region to be studied. At each instant of discrete time thereafter, new values of pixel contents are computed based on an assumed diffusion constant and the isotropic assumption (*i.e.*, that the diffusion law applies equally in all directions for all parts of the region under study). The process consists of an initial transient and a subsequent steady-state condition. In steady-state all pixels contain the same number of particles. During the transient, however, the number of particles in each boundary pixel depends upon the shape of the boundary. The concentration is greater in concavities than in convexities, with straight or nearly-straight regions having intermediate concentrations. It is necessary therefore to stop the diffusion process during the transient to detect these characteristics of the boundary. When the simulated diffusion process is stopped, the sequence of numbers of particles in the boundary pixels can be used to generate a shape-related code.

This approach is implemented easily on digital computers so that the effects of changes in the following relevant process parameters can be studied: constant of diffusion, stopping-time, and initial number of particles per pixel.

Let $N_{i,j}(t)$ be the number of particles contained in the pixel at coordinates (i, j) at time t. Then the fundamental algorithm to be utilized is:

$$N_{i,j}(t+1) = N_{i,j}(t) - 4KN_{i,j}(t) + K(N_{i-1,j}(t) + N_{i+1,j}(t) + N_{i,j+1}(t) + N_{i,j-1}(t)) \quad (1)$$

Equation (1) expresses the requirement that the number of particles in a given pixel of the image at time $t+1$ equals the number of particles that were there at t, minus the number of particles that were transferred by the assumed diffusion process to the 4 – neighboring pixels, plus the number of incoming particles from those same neighbors, based on their respective contents at t. Neighbors that lie outside the boundary do not participate in the process of Equation (1).

Though in this preliminary communication we will consider only the two-dimensional case, the approach can be generalized easily to any number of dimensions. In the three-dimensional case the basic algorithmic equation is:

$$\begin{aligned} N_{i,j,k}(t+1) &= N_{i,j,k}(t) - 6KN_{i,j,k}(t) \\ &+K\left(N_{i-1,j,k}(t) + N_{i+1,j,k}(t) + N_{i,j-1,k}(t) + N_{i,j+1,k}(t)\right. \\ &\left.+N_{i,j,k-1}(t) + N_{i,j,k+1}(t)\right) \end{aligned} \quad (2)$$

For the problem that we are considering we do not need to adjust the parameter K to experimental data - as should be done in the case of simulation of a real diffusion process of matter or heat. So, for purposes of computation we can assign to K any value in the range $0 < K < 1$. The smaller K is, the higher will be the degree of detail of the results of the diffusion-type process, but of course at the expense of additional computer time.

3. Preliminary Results

The algorithm was tested with two shapes: a square, and an irregular region. The corresponding results are presented. At the initial time (t=0), 10,000 particles were assigned to each boundary pixel for each of the two cases. In the case of the square, the number of particles for each pixel of the image has been computed for times 10, 50, and 100 (See Figures 1a, b, and c, respectively.) For the three cases a value of K=0.01 was used.

Let us assume that we establish an order on the boundary of those squares by labeling the pixels with consecutive natural numbers following a clockwise direction, starting at the left uppermost. In Figures 2a, b, and c the number of particles on the boundary pixels has been expressed as a function of the number utilized as labels for the pixels, for each of the corresponding cases of Figure 1.

In the case of the irregular shape, only the number of particles of each pixel on the boundary has been shown for t = 10 in Figure 3.

For such irregular shapes the boundary pixels are labeled with consecutive integers, again proceeding clockwise from the left uppermost pixel. Graphics of the same kind as Figure 2 appear as Figure 4 for the irregular shape.

Both for the case of the regular shape (the square) and the irregular one, it can be seen immediately that the number of particles per pixel - the concentration - is higher in concavities than in convexities.

If human shape perception does rely heavily on detection of curvature maxima (Attneave, 1954; Biederman, 1985), then the (positive- and negative-going) peaks in a plot of pixel content-vs-boundary location (corresponding, respectively, to segments of high concavity and convexity) are likely to be useful in identifying those important regions.

4. Effect of Rotation

The shape descriptor is invariant under rotations that are multiples of 90°, but what about non-multiples? Several rotations were computed using an incremental algorithm (Braccini and Marino, 1980) and the diffusion process applied to each resulting image. The stopping rule terminated the process when the difference between maximum and

9923	9158	9090	9158	9923
9158	1682	949	1682	9158
9090	949	157	949	9090
9158	1682	949	1682	9158
9923	9158	9090	9158	9923

8940	7605	7106	7605	8940
7605	4654	3541	4654	7605
7106	3541	2197	3541	7106
7605	4654	3541	4654	7605
8940	7605	7106	7605	8940

6406	6402	6399	6402	6406
6402	6398	6395	6398	6402
6399	6395	6393	6395	6399
6402	6398	6395	6398	6402
6406	6402	6399	6402	6406

Figure 1. Number of particles in each pixel for the square region, with k=0.01. (a) t=10; (b) t=50; (c) t=500.

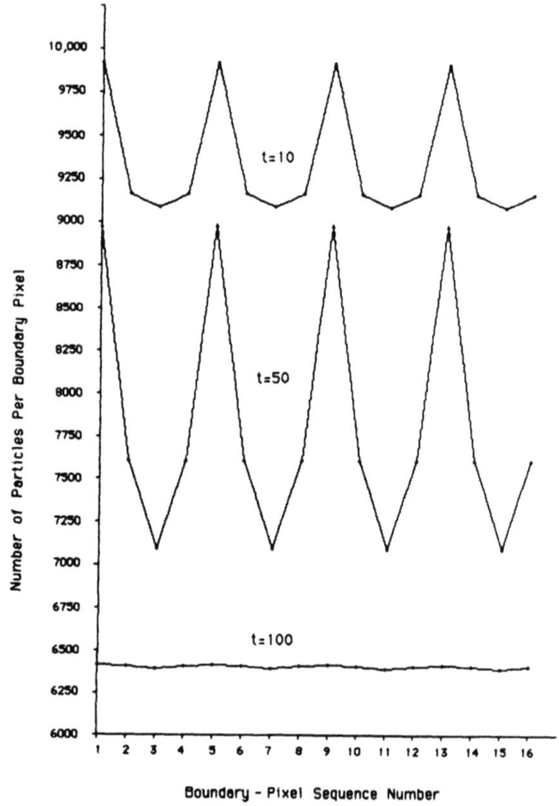

Figure 2. Number of particles for consequence boundary pixels of the three cases of Figure 3, beginning at the left uppermost. (a) t=10; (b) t=50; (c) t=500.

	6006	5235	5116	5114	5113	5114	5113	5114	5116	5126	5171	5326	5782	6711	7682	
6019															6780	
5610															6130	
5494															6148	
5660												3775	4982	5849		
	4099										2406					
		3571										3550				
			2423										4045	4996		
	5284	4039													4664	
6083																6156
6100								3863	4083	3898						6333
6776					4138	4843	5410				5619	5421	5395	5684	6167	
7684	6721	5843	5549	5652												

Figure 3. Number of particles in each boundary for the irregular region (interior pixels' values omitted for clarity, with k=0.01.

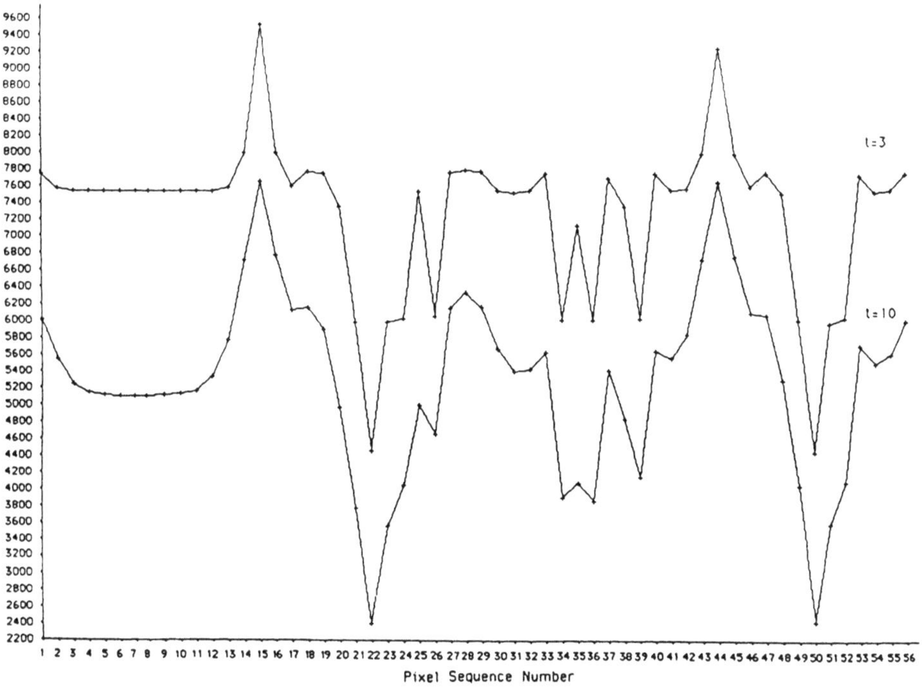

Figure 4. Number of particles for consecutive boundary pixels of the two cases of Figure 3, beginning at the left uppermost.

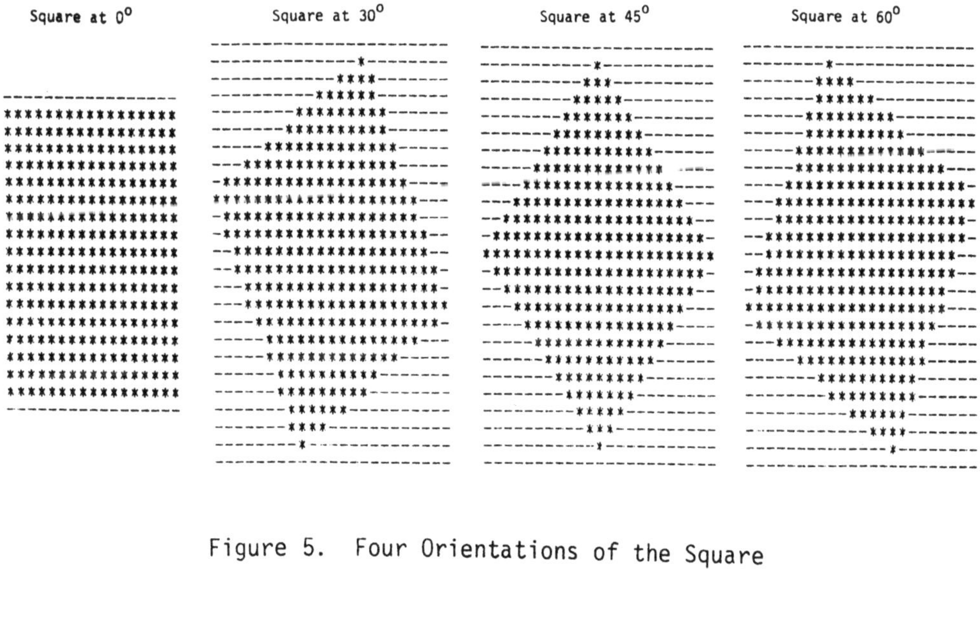

Figure 5. Four Orientations of the Square

minimum values along the boundary was maximized. The cell counts were then normalized by subtraction of the boundary mean and division by the standard deviation. Such cell counts were determined for the two shapes and several values of K each. Invariance was measured as follows:

1. Curves of the types shown in Figures 2 and 4 were plotted.

2. (Duda and Hart, 1973) Pairs of successive points on a given curve were used to compute slopes, which were then represented by their arctangents.

3. Curves representing shape numbers of two orientations were compared by computing the average over the entire boundary of the cosines of the difference angles, point by point. (Where one boundary was longer due to rotation-induced scaling, points were deleted uniformly along the curve to make it conform to the shorter one). Identical shape measures would yield an average of 1.

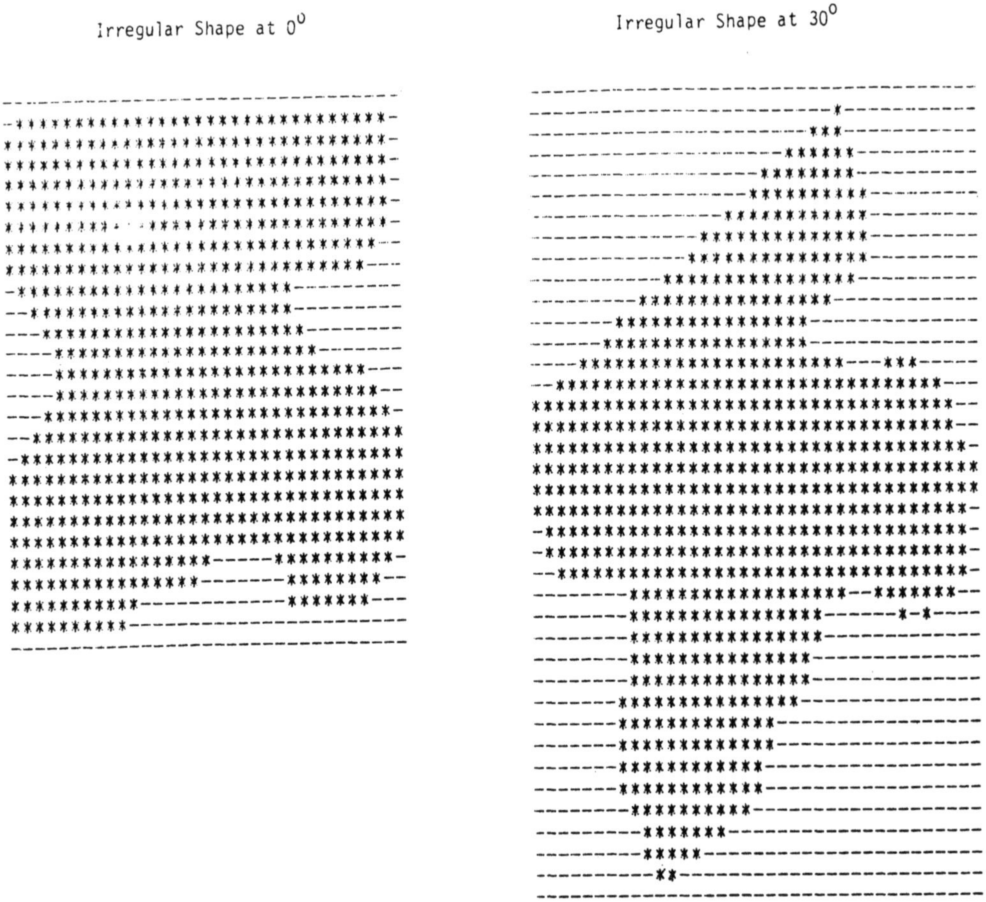

Figure 6: Two orientations of the irregular shape

The square was examined at three rotations for a given K, and the irregular shape at one rotation for three values of K. Figures 5 and 6 show the rotated images, and Table 1 lists the averages of the cosines.

TABLE 1

Object	Rotation Angle	Average of Cosines for Rotated Object vs. Original
Square	30°	0.8747
K = 0.05	45°	0.9888
	60°	0.8578
Irregular		
K = 0.01	30°	0.6008
K = 0.05	30°	0.5999
K = 0.10	30°	0.5996

Clearly, objects are not equally invariant under rotation. Many questions remain, including:

a. What is the minimum detectable rotation?

b. Can absolute thresholds be set for detecting concavities and convexities?

c. What is the effect of object size on invariance under rotation?

5. Conclusions and Perspectives

We have presented a new method for describing the shape of a region. The region must be simply-connected, but need not be convex. The descriptor is invariant under translation, rotations by multiples of 90°, and, it appears, under scale changes. It is almost invariant under rotations of non-multiples of 90°. It can be implemented easily in hardware (especially on future parallel processors), is as effective in higher dimensions as in two, and will lend itself easily to image-processing and pattern-recognition applications. The method appears to be relatively insensitive to noise (*cf.* the medial-axis transform, in which very large changes in the axis are produced by very small changes in the boundary (Nevatia, 1982)), does not pose problems with the definition of slope (Rosenfeld and Johnston, 1973) as occurs in the Ψ - s curve computation, and appears to be capable of dealing with the matching of partially-occluded shapes (*e.g.*, in the robot vision case), since the diffusion-produced boundary descriptors are likely to be less affected far from the occluding boundary and thus can provide the basis for a partial match to a pre-stored description of a complete boundary.

The effect of changes in the diffusion constant, K, and the time at which the process is stopped will be examined in detail in future papers. The present stopping criterion has great intuitive appeal, since we are interested in distinguishing concavities from convexities and can think of this as a sensitivity measure.

Acknowledgements:
We appreciate the computer simulation work of Ms. Mary Mizrahi and Mr. Sotirios Ziavras, and financial support provided by the U.S. Office of Naval Research under Contract No. N00014-83-K-0578 and by the Naval Research Laboratory under Contract No. N00173-86-M-3365.

References

[1] Attneave, F., (1985), "Some Informational Aspects of Visual Perception," *Psychol. Rev.* 61, 183-193.

[2] Ballard, D. and C. Brown, (1982), *Computer Vision*, Prentice-Hall Englewood Cliffs, N.J.

[3] Biederman, I., (1985), "Human Image Understanding: Recent Research and a Theory," *Computer Vision, Graphics and Image Processing*, 32, 29-73.

[4] Braccini, C. and G. Marino, (1980), "Fast Geometrical Manipulations of Digital Images," *Computer Graphics and Image Processing*, 13, 127-141.

[5] Danielsson, P-E., (1978), "A New Shape Factor," *Computer Graphics and Image Processing* 7, 292-299.

[6] Duda, R.O., and P. Hart, (1973), *Pattern Recognition and Scene Analysis*, Wiley, New York; Chapter 9.

[7] Nevatia, R., (1982), *Machine Perception*, Prentice-Hall, Englewood Cliffs, N.J.

[8] Pavlidis, T., (1978), "A Review of Algorithm for Shape Analysis," *Computer Graphics and Image Processing*, 7, 1978, 243-258.

[9] Rosenfeld, A., and E. Johnston, (1973), "Angle Detection on Digital Curves," *IEEE Trans. Computers*, C-22, 1973, pp. 875-878.

STATISTICAL EVALUATION OF COMPUTER EXTRACTED BLOOD CELL FEATURES FOR SCREENING POPULATIONS TO DETECT LEUKEMIAS

H.M. Aus[1], H. Harms[1], V. ter Meulen[2], and U. Gunzer[3].

[1]Image Processing Laboratory,
Institute of Virology,
Versbacher Strasse 7, 8700 Würzburg.
[2]Institute of Virology.
[3]Department of Hematology,
University of Würzburg,
Federal Republic of Germany.

Abstract

This paper outlines image segmentation, feature extraction and classification methods which screen and diagnose blood malignancies. New algorithms had to be developed because analyzing blood malignancies requires higher scanning densities and higher optical magnification than used in screening normal blood cells. The cell image segmentation method combines color differences, equidistance isograms, geometric operations, and a cell model. The algorithm always starts with the largest color differences and successively detects less certain areas. This eliminates the need for contour following algorithms. The feature extraction combines geometric parameters with texture and color. "Classification And Regression Tree" statistical software test the classification power of the cell markers extracted by the image processing. The feature distributions from the tested blood cell population correlate directly to the specific blood malignancies.

1. Introduction

Everyone who has had a medical check-up knows that blood and urine are the two body fluids which are almost always taken as samples for routine laboratory examination. Besides the standard chemical tests run on the serum and plasma, blood samples can also be smeared on a glass slide, dried, and stained with Pappenheim's or Wright's staining agents. The various white blood cell types (leukocytes) can then be viewed in a light microscope, identified according to their morphology, and counted. Many of a cells morphological features, are obvious and distinct; others are quite subtle. The normally occurring cells have, for example, very definite sizes, shapes, and colors of both the nucleus and the cytoplasm. These cell types include: neutrophils, lymphocytes, monocytes, eosinophils, and basophils. Commercial differential white blood cell counting (WBC) systems have been designed to screen for these normal cells. But blood samples can also contain other types of cells. Because these cells occur so infrequently in

NATO ASI Series, Vol. F30
Pattern Recognition Theory and Applications
Edited by P. A. Devijver and J. Kittler

a routinely screened population, the WBC system designers conveniently define them as "rare cells" and ignore their clinical importance; but precisely these "rare cells" are key indicators of hematological disorders. The rare cells are usually not so easily identified and typically appear only in conjunction with some disorder; moreover, the sizes of the discriminating features are often not much larger than the maximum resolution limits of the microscope optics [13]. Nonetheless, health care delivery requires a system which not only screens normal cells but also reliably diagnoses and correctly classifies rare cells from blood disorders in the same blood smears routinely used to screen all patients.

A recent review article on "High Resolution Image Analysis" confronts the reader with the dismal state of imaging cytometry [15]. After more than 30 years of research and commercial development, not a single system can be considered to be even a qualified success. Although the author summarizes the past correctly, his analysis of the present situation is not accurate. Contrary to the title of the paper and the subsection "High-Resolution Microscopy in Hematology", none of the systems he describes can be categorized as "high spatial resolution". All the microscope image acquisition systems reviewed in his paper scan with a scanning density considerably lower than 10 pixels per micron. This choice of low resolution scanning is based, among other things, on reducing the amount of data to be processed; but this often contradicts the requirements posed by the clinical applications. Earlier work by Rzeszotarski [16] showed that the scanning density used in imaging cytometry is too small. As documented in our publication, high resolution scanning and image acquisition starts above 10-12 pixels per micron [1,10,12]. Below this limit, a substantial amount of indispensable information content in a microscope's image is lost. Anything less is simply not high resolution.

In hematology the automation efforts have all concentrated on saving manpower and on screening the normal cells faster than the best trained laboratory personnel [6,14]. But the more important problem is to provide reliable information about blood cells which indicate specific disorders. Commercial systems have not taken this approach. Table 1 in the review article [15] demonstrates the problem using early results from Geometric Data's Hematrak WBC system. The normal white blood cells can typically be classified with a 3% false-alarm rate. The rare cell types (in this case: myelocytes, promyelocytes, nucleated red cells, blasts, and plasmacytes) are, however, seldom classified correctly and usually as the catch-all-cell type "OTHER". The false identification of a blast as either an eosinophil or basophil is particularly distressing to the hematologist. Both of the latter cell types have distinct cytoplasm granulation and color which set them clearly apart from the blasts. Moreover, the monocyte/neutrophil confusion rate (3%) is also unacceptable in the clinical routine. These cell types are morphologically so distinct that no laboratory technologist would confuse them. Underscanning is one reason for such errors [9]. Aside from the financial aspects, the poor clinical acceptance of the white blood cell machines can be contributed largely to the lack of solid diagnostic data. But image processing and "true" high-resolution microscopy can do more than asserted in the review article ! This paper summarizes just one possible application of "true" high spatial resolution microscopy in hematology [1,2,3,7,8].

The goal was to investigate and develop new methods for extracting clinically relevant diagnostic information about leukemias from Pappenheim stained blood smears.

For years the hematologists have contended that there exist small differences in the fine structured texture of so-called blast cells, according to each leukemia. But there has been no direct way to reliably measure the blasts. A blast cell is a generally round, mononuclear cell whose nucleus appears more or less dark magenta after being stained with Pappenheim's or Wright's staining agents; the corresponding cytoplasm is usually stained less in saturation than the nucleus. The occurrence of a single blast cell in the patient's peripheral blood is a first, important warning that a leukemia is present. In health care delivery, it is mandatory to detect this blast cell as early as possible. This simple statement takes on new meaning in the aftermath of Chernobyl. Our hospital is located 30 kilometers from Grafenrheinfeld, currently the most efficient nuclear power plant in the western world. Large metropolitan areas, including Frankfurt am Main and Nürnberg, are within 150 kilometers of a potential nuclear meltdown accident. With high respect for the western nuclear power plant technology, it is never possible to completely exclude an accident at Grafenrheinfeld, or anywhere else. The likelihood of a nuclear accident may be small, but as Chernobyl has shown, the improbable is not impossible. Millions of people would be directly exposed to high radiation contamination which, under the best of circumstances, would be hazardous to their health. The most common short term consequences will be different types of radiation induced leukemias. Screening for these disorders in a population of 3 million people in short intervals, would require more medical personnel than available in the entire Federal Republic of Germany. The treatment of nuclear accident patients depends, obviously, on first diagnosing the disorder as early as possible. With respect to leukemia, the diagnosis is strongly related to exactly identifying each white blood cell occurring in the peripheral blood. This paper outlines the cell image measurement, segmentation, texture and classification methods which have been developed in our leukemia project. The other paper in this volume demonstrates the application of related high-resolution methods to segment images of tissue sections.

2. Cell Data and Cytophotometric Equipment

Over 120 Pappenheim stained blood smears from 80 patients were scanned interactively with the hematologist, automatically segmented and classified in this study, Table 1. Only routine laboratory specimens, prepared without special techniques for cytophotometry, were analyzed. The data set consisted of the 31 nuclear and 31 cytoplasm features listed in Table 2. Most of these features were developed specifically for this project and are based on cell-related quantifiable features. The final set of 62 features was selected from several 100 features which have been empirically tested during the study. Eleven blast-cell classes were analyzed with the statistical software program "Classification And Regression Trees" (CART,5). The VAX-VMS random generator selected a maximum of 300 cells from each leukemia for equally weighted statistical analysis.

Pappenheim stained blood smears can be scanned in an Axiomat microscope (Zeiss, Oberkochen, W. Germany) with a 1.4 aperture condenser, a 100X, 1.3 Planapochromat oil objective, and a 100 Watt Halogen lamp source.

Table 1 Abbreviations of the leukemias in this study

OMSBC	=	Osteomyelosclerosis blast crisis
TALL	=	Acute Lymphoblastic Leukaemia, T-cell type
OMS	=	Osteomyelosclerosis
ALL	=	Acute Lymphoblastic Leukaemia
LBL	=	Malignant non-Hodgkin's Lymphoma, lymphoblastic type (LBL(ALL))
IBL	=	Malignant non-Hodgkin's Lymphoma, immunoblastic type
AUL	=	Acute Undifferentiated Leukemia (Stemcells)
AML	=	Acute Myeloblastic Leukemia
AMOL	=	Acute Monocytic Leukemia
AMMOL	=	Acute Myelomonocytic Leukemia
CML	=	Chronic Myeloid Leukemia

The three channels in the color TV camera (Sony, DXC 600, Japan) are digitized in an Eyecom III unit (Spatial Data, Goleta, Ca.), which is controlled by a LSI 11/23 (DEC). The mean wavelength of the cameras color filters are 460, 540 and 600 nm. The ADC samples at a rate of 12.4 MHz with 8 bits. The maximum image size is 512 $\times$ 640 pixels. The cell images are scanned at a density of 12.5 pixels per micron. The black and white level calibrations in the Sony camera assure the stability of the measured colors. The color calibration itself can be checked with a Tektronix 1421 vectorscope.

3. Description of the Method

3.1. Cell Scene Segmentation

The goal is to use image processing methods to segment images of white blood cells, particularly blast cells which contain leukemia-related morphological differences and, subsequently, to classify subpopulations of blast cells based on these differences. Such blast cells are also referred to as immature mononuclear cells. All commercial systems identify this class of cells using common morphological criteria such as size, shape, optical density and nucleus/cytoplasm (N/C) ratio. But there also exist visually apparent textural differences in both the nucleus and cytoplasm, including vacuoles, and granulation, etc., (Figure 1). Up till now, these variations have not been used in cytophotometry to define subclasses among the blast cells. Contrary to the usually, relatively simple morphological criteria such as size, shape and optical density, the objective identification of blast cells requires a more detailed color and texture analysis of the subtle differences in the nucleus and cytoplasm [2,3,4,7,8,12].

The segmentation algorithm is directed by a cell model. The blood cell model in our segmentation method assumes that cytoplasm usually surrounds nuclei and that a single nucleus cannot belong to two or more different cells. But several areas of nuclear material can be found in one cytoplasm. Normally, the Pappenheim stained nucleus exhibits a different and darker color than the cytoplasm. The cytoplasm of so called mononuclear blood cells is generally stained blue and sometimes includes different colored granulation. Calibration measurements determine the maximum and minimum allowable sizes of both the cytoplasm and the nucleus, relative to the magnification of the TV-microscope system. Harms *et al.* describe the cell model directed segmentation

Table 2 : Computed cell features extracted by the image analysis program system and used in this classification.

	Nucleus	: short feature description	: Cytoplasm
1	SIZE	: nucleus and cytoplasm area, respectively	: 25 CSSIZE
2	PIXCNT	: number of texture points	: 26 CPIXCNT
3	CONTOUR	: number of pixels in the contour of the nucleus	
4	TEXNODS	: number of crossing points in texture lines (TL)	: 27 CTEXNODS
5	TEXENDS	: number of endpoints in TL	: 28 CTEXENDS
6	FORM	: nuclear form factor	
7	TEXMAX	: maximum of the TL density function	: 29 CTEXMAX
8	TEXDIST	: maximum of the equalized texture line (ETL) distance distribution function	: 30 CTEXDIST
9	AVRDIST	: average distance between TL	: 31 CAVRDIST
10	TEX09FC	: 0.9 value of ETL distribution function	: 32 CTEX09FC
11	VDD	: variance of the ETL distribution function	: 33 CVDD
12	VDDXI	: special variance of ETL distribution function	: 34 CVDDXI
13	DISTVAR	: variance of distances between the TL	: 58 CDISTVAR
14	DISTSD	: standard deviation of distances between the TL	: 59 CDISTSD
15	VARFACT2	: special variance of TL function (TLF)	: 35 CVARFAC2
16	FF209	: 0.9 value of the twice equalized TLF	: 61 CFF209
17	VDDXII	: special variance of the twice equalized TLF	: 62 CVDDXII
		color features :	
18	XCOLOR	: average x-coordinate in DIN color diagram	: 36 CXCOLOR
19	YCOLOR	: average y-coordinate in DIN color diagram	: 37 CYCOLOR
20	INTEN	: intensity, Y-coordinate in DIN color diagram	: 38 CINTEN
21	INTVAR	: variance of intensity Y	: 39 CINTVAR
22	AMPCOLR	: amplitude of color coordinates	: 40 CAMPCOLR
23	XNCOLOR	: first digit of coded color coordinates	: 41 CXNCOLR
24	YNCOLOR	: second digit of coded color coordinates	: 42 CYNCOLOR
43	NCRATIO	: ratio of the nucleus / cytoplasm areas (No. 1 / No. 25)	
44	TOTSIZE	: total area = nucleus + cytoplasm (No.1 + No. 25)	
45	INDMAX	: index code for features (7 nuc) (29 cyt)	: 52 CINDMAX
46	INDIST	: index code for features (8 nuc) (30 cyt)	: 53 CINDIST
47	DIST09	: 0.9 value TL distribution function	: 54 CDIST09
48	IMAX	: maximum for TL distance	: 55 CIMAX
49	NORM	: normalized factor	: 56 CNORM
50	MEANFR	: mean frequency	: 57 CMEANFR
51	VARFACT1	: special variance of TL function (diff to 15, 35)	: 60 CVARFAC1

[11]. In the first image segmentation step, the regions with the largest color differences in the nuclei are located and marked. Color differences and geometric properties help optimize nuclear mask. The second step identifies the cytoplasm areas step-by-step using characteristic color differences combined with the knowledge of the cell model. A global mask for the cytoplasm is calculated from a color difference threshold obtained near the border of each nucleus. The method incorporates color features, geometric operations and probability functions. In the third part, the whole calculated cell mask is compared with the cell model and either accepted or rejected. The final scene segmentation masks of the cell images in Figure 1 are shown in Figure 2.

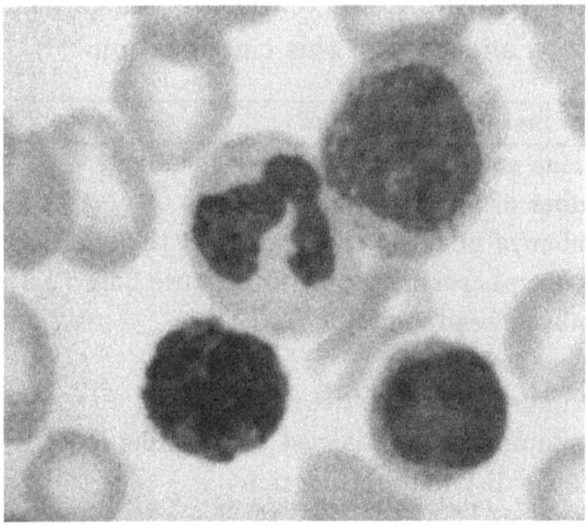

Figure 1: Photograph of a white blood cell scene scanned in a light microscope. Note the various sizes and shapes of the nuclei, the sizes of the cells, and the texture of both the nuclei and the cytoplasm.

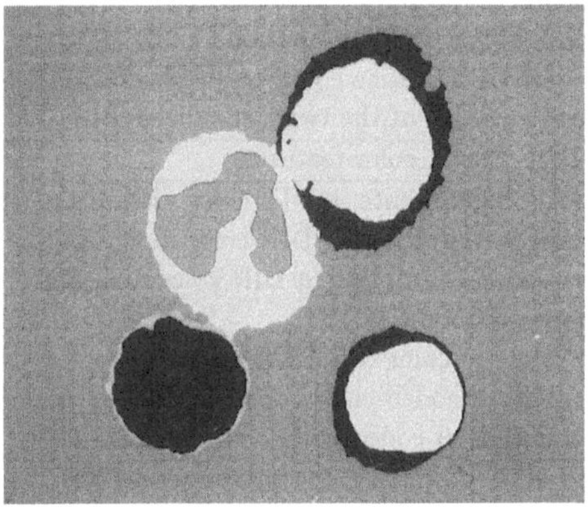

Figure 2: Final segmentation mask of the white blood cells in Figure 1

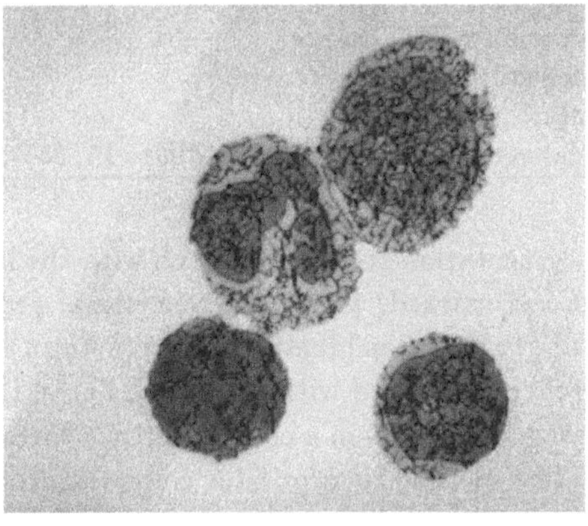

Figure 3: Calculated texture lines superimposed on the blood cell scene in Figure 1.

3.2. Feature Extraction

New cell morphology-related texture and color features were developed for this investigation and tested against the more common cytophotometric features. Gradient and contour following algorithms generate the texture lines. The distances between these texture lines, the number of texture lines and other features are used for the classification. Our texture analysis is independent of the cell's shape [12]. The color feature algorithms process the measured RGB images in both the CIE-color coordinate space (x,y,Y) and in a coded color space, designed specifically for the blood cell application [12]. The texture lines from the cells in Figure 1 are shown in Figure 3. The common cytophotometric features size, shape, optical density and N/C ratio were also included in the feature set, Table 2.

4. Classification Results

CART [5] output includes classification matrices for both the learning set and the cross validation. The predicted leukemia-related class distributions from the CART learning set classification probability matrix, are shown in Figures 4 and 5 as bargraphs. A maximum number of blast cells in each leukemia exhibit specific leukemia-related quantifiable features. Each leukemia also contains smaller amounts of blast cells which are mathematically similar to the blast cells found in the other malignancies. As documented in Figure 4, a majority of the blasts measured in a T-ALL have been classified as being specific for T-ALL; whereas, a substantially smaller amount are mathematically similar to the features found in blast cells from OMS patients. In OMS, on the other hand, the opposite situation is clearly evident. Blast cells from OMS and long lasting OMS in blast crisis (OMSBC) do not overlap in the classification matrix. Small amounts of AML, AMOL, AMMOL and CML blast cell types were also found in the OMSBC and ALL specimens.

Similar distributions can be observed for all the tested leukemias in Figures 4 and 5. The method also found leukemia-specific blast cell feature distributions in the LBL, IBL, and AUL malignancies. In each case over 65% of the malignant cells occurring in the peripheral blood smears were typical of their respective leukemia. Regardless of the percent incidence of occurrence in the other leukemia-blast classes, the maximum always corresponds to the diagnosed malignancy. AML, AMOL, AMMOL and CML are all related by the involvement in the hemopoietic maturation sequence. Nonetheless, the analysis found a dominant class of blasts which corresponds to the specific leukemia, plus a distribution of blast cells from the other subpopulations (Figure 5). AML exhibits the broadest leukemia blast cell distribution of all the leukemias tested. CART also calculates a binary classification tree with complete feature splitting at each node.

5. Comments

This paper summarizes the segmentation, feature extraction and statistical evaluation of blood cell images which directly measure and analyze the cell-related quantifiable differences found in the various blast cells.

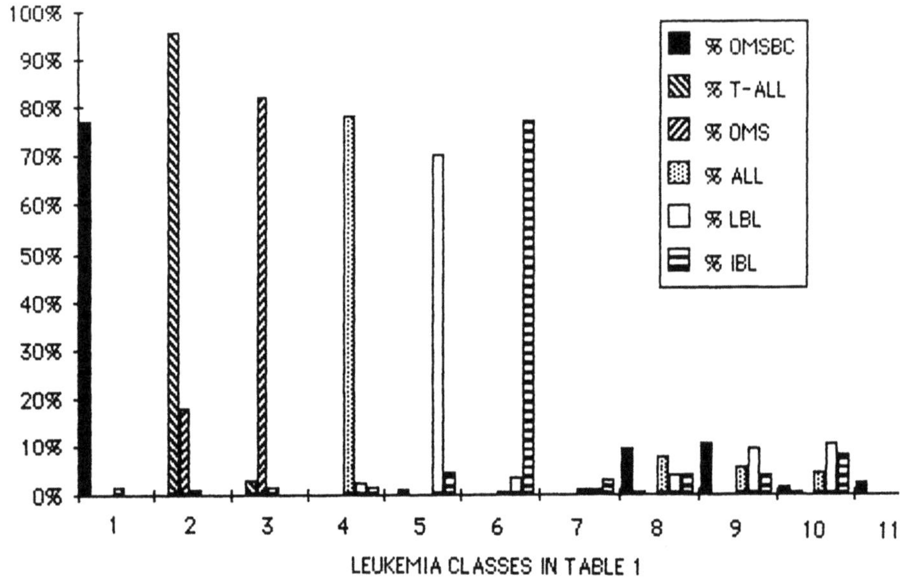

Figure 4 Bargraphs of the learning set probability classification distribution for the first 6 leukemias in table 1.

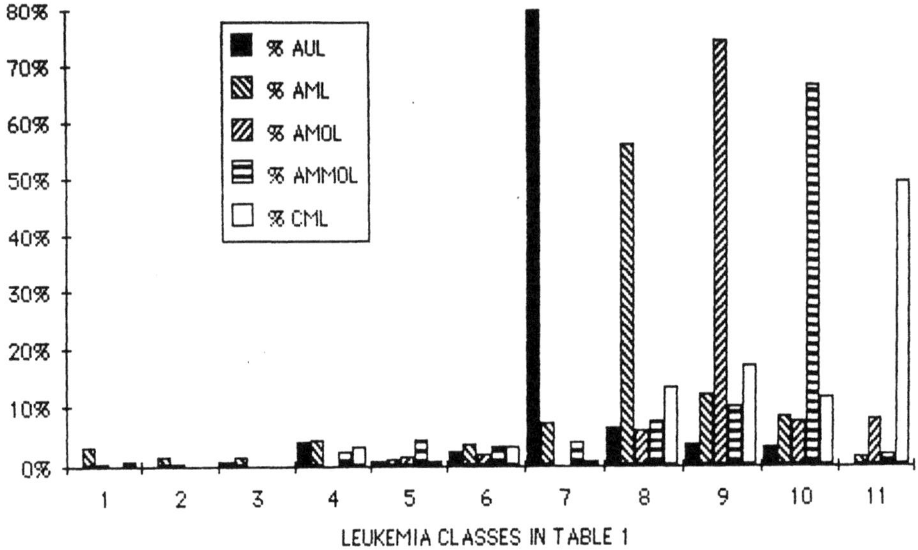

Figure 5 Bargraphs of the learning set probability classification distribution for the last 5 leukemias in table 1.

The data demonstrates the potential of using the detected differences to identify and classify the various blast cell populations occurring in leukemias. In order to achieve this, the spatial scanning requirements had to be refined; new segmentation and texture algorithms had to be developed; and the color cell image acquisition and processing system had to be improved. The routine clinical diagnosis of the leukemia took place independently of this study.

One could argue that the whole concept presented here will be outdated after specific histochemical or immunochemical stains have been developed to exactly and reliably identify each blast cell type. Up to now, this hasn't happened. Only morphology, which has been developed and clinically tested over the last 90 years, enjoys an international acceptance in routine hematological diagnosis. In contrast to the unsuccessful commercial systems which ignore the rare cells, it is indispensable that clinical systems not only screen the blood for normal cells but also correctly diagnose all cells which may occur in the peripheral blood. Anything less is useless.

The challenge is clear ! In the aftergrowth of Chernobyl, the need will be urgent.

Acknowledgement

This project is partially supported by the German Science Foundation and the German Federal Ministry for Research and Technology, Bonn, West Germany. The technical assistance of M. Haucke, J. Beritova and I.Baumann is greatly acknowledged.

References

[1] Aus HM, Harms H, Gunzer G, Haucke M, Baumann I, Hinterberger J, ter Meulen V: Validierung von Zellparametern zur computergestützten Diagnostik leukämischer Blutbildveränderungen. Project report to the German Federal Ministery of Research and Technology (1986).

[2] Aus HM, Harms H, Haucke M, Beritova J, ter Meulen V, Gunzer U, Baumann I: Leukemia Related Morphological Features in Blast Cells. Cytometry, in press (1986).

[3] Aus HM, Harms H, Haucke M, Beritova J, ter Meulen V, Gunzer U, Baumann I: Statistical Evaluation of Computer Markers to Detect Leukemias. Pattern Recognition Letters, in press (1986).

[4] Bins M, van Montfort LH, Timmers T, Landeweerd GH, Gelsema ES, Halie MR: Classification of Immature and Mature Cells of the Neutrophil Series using Morphometrical Parameters. Cytometry 3: 435-438, California (1983).

[5] Breiman L, Friedman JH, Olshen RA, Stone CJ: Classification and Regression Trees. Wadworth International, Belmont, California, and California Statistical Software, Inc., 961 Yorkshire Court, Lafayette, California (1984).

[6] Green JE: A practical application of computer pattern recognition research: The Abbott ADC-500 differential classifier. J. Histochem Cytochem 827: 160-165 (1979).

[7] Gunzer U, Harms H, Haucke M, Gerlach B, Thieme S, Aus HM, ter Meulen V: Computeranalysen in der Hämatologie: Ein Beitrag zur Früherkennung von bösartigen hämatologischen Systemerkrankungen. In: Schwabe HW, Unz F: Automation der zytologischen Diagnostik. DFVLR NT-1 84/3, 115-136 (1984).

[8] Gunzer U, Harms H, Haucke M, Aus HM, ter Meulen V: Computer-Aided Image Analysis for the Differentiation of Mononuclear Cells in Peripheral Blood Smears from Leukemic Patients. Analytical and Quantitative Cytology, 3:26-32 (1981).

[9] Harms H., Gunzer U., Aus H.M. (1982): Ein Verfahren zur Segmentierung und quantitativen Farbdifferenzbestimmung von peripheren Blutzellen. Optik 61:1, 29 - 44.

[10] Harms H, Aus HM (1984): Estimation of Sampling Errors in a High- Resolution TV Microscope Image-Processing System. Cytometry 5:228-235.

[11] Harms H, Haucke M, Aus HM (1986): Segmentation of Stained Blood Cell Images Measured at High Scanning Density with High Magnification and High Numerical Aperture Optics, Cytometry, in press.

[12] Harms H, Gunzer U, Aus HM (1986): Combined Local Color and Texture Analysis of Stained Cells. Computer Vision, Graphics and Image Processing, in press.

[13] Lessin L.S., Bessis M, Douglas S.D. (1977): Morphology of Monocytes and Macrophages. Hematology, Williams W.J., Beutler E., Erslev A.J., Rundles R.W. (eds.), Mc Graw Hill, 251 - 860.

[14] Preston K (1979): Automation of the Analysis of Cell Images. Analytical and Quantitative Cytology.

[15] Preston Jr. K. (1986): High Resolution Image Analysis. J. Histochem. Cytochem 34:1, 67 - 74.

[16] Rzeszotarski M.S., Thomas C.W., Martin A.O. (1978): Sampling Considerations in Human Chromosome Images. San Diego Biomed Conference 17: 413 - 417.

TISSUE IMAGE SEGMENTATION WITH MULTICOLOR, MULTIFOCAL ALGORITHMS

Harry Harms and Hans–Magnus Aus [1]

Biomedical Image Processing Research Laboratory
Institute of Virology,
Versbacher Strasse 7, 8700 Würzburg,
Federal Republic of Germany.

Abstract

A new strategy for image segmentation of different biological tissue sections is presented. Color differences, geometric operations and an object model are the major components of the segmentation process. In a light microscope the depth of focus is so small that only a part of a 1.5 – 10 micron thick section is visible; more than one measurement is necessary for image acquisition, segmentation and analysis of the whole section. The image segmentation process is generally the same for different biological tissue sections, regardless of how they have been prepared and stained. Only some factors depend on the optical magnification and the biological material. The basic underlying idea of this segmentation has been developed and tested on more than 20,000 stained white blood cells.
Keywords : Model directed image segmentation, multifocus, color differences, geometric operations, probability functions.

1. Introduction

Segmentation is the first, important step in image analysis. Since the objects are all very different, the segmentation methods are also inherently different [2,3]. Image segmentation must always be done relative to the subsequent analysis which may be either simple cell counting, feature measurement or subtle cell classification. The regions of an image which contain an object of interest must be separated from those of no interest or background. Although almost an unlimited number of image segmentation and analysis algorithms are known from the literature [3], only a few methods have been developed to segment images from stained tissue sections [4,6] measured in a light microscope. The complexity of such scenes is one of the major reasons for this. Image analysis of the morphology from tissue sections is more complicated than cytophotometry on single layer cells in blood smears or tissue imprints; in tissue sections the complete optical information of any object of interest requires more than one focus setting. Segmentation of tissue section images must process information from a 3-D image space.

[1] In collaboration with: R.Schäffer, Institute of Pathology, Würzburg; A.Schauer, R.Brehler, Institute of Pathology, Göttingen; K.Hempel, P.Jacobi, H.Bloß, Institute of Medical Research, Würzburg; and U.Gunzer, Department of Hematology, University Würzburg.

NATO ASI Series, Vol. F30
Pattern Recognition Theory and Applications
Edited by P. A. Devijver and J. Kittler

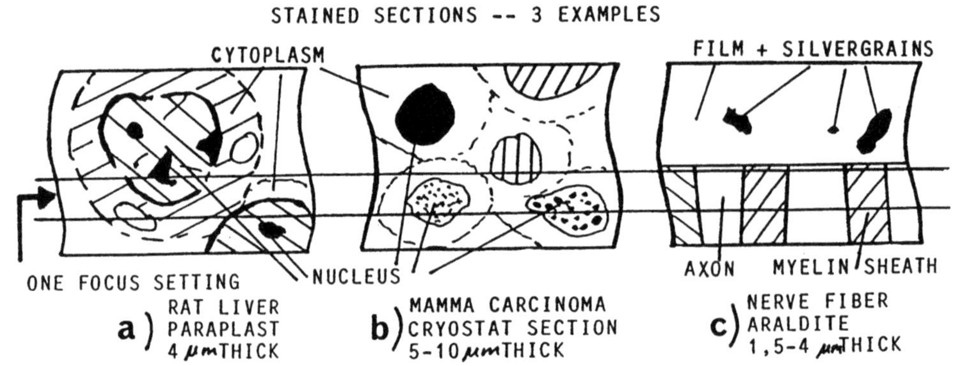

Fig. 1. Three schematical examples of various tissue sections.

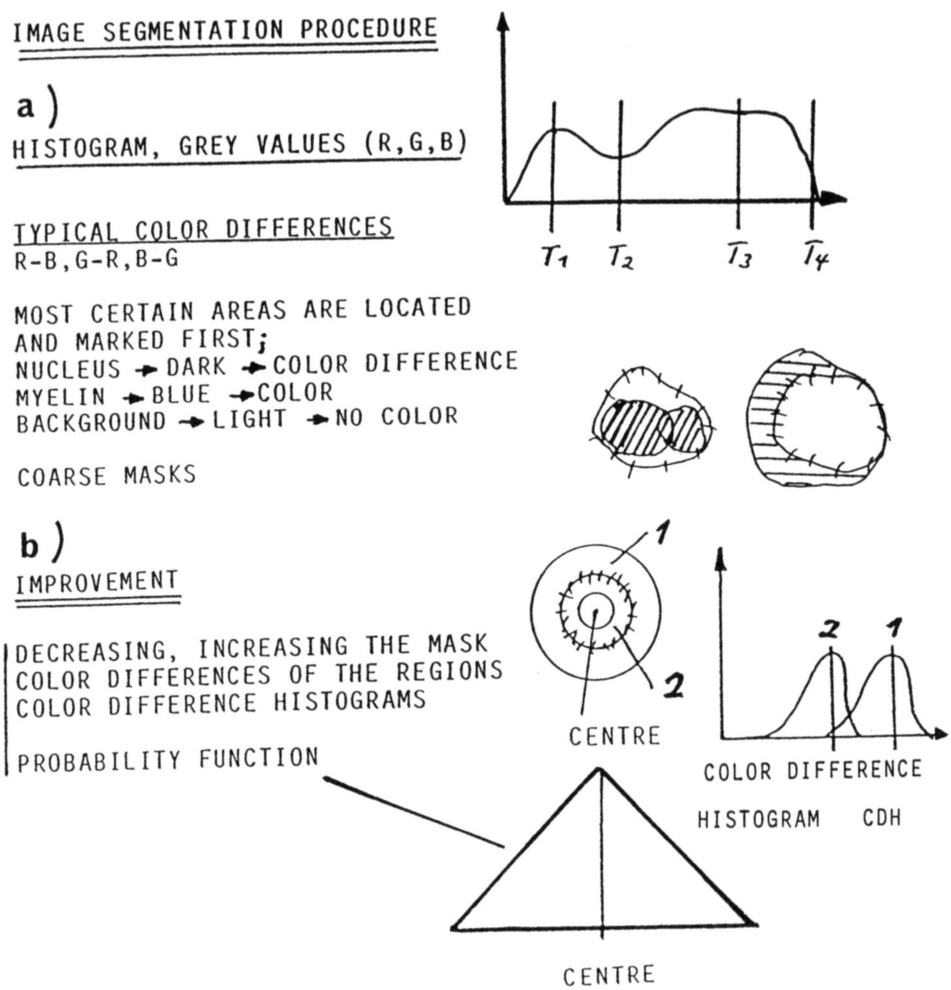

FIG. 2. Segmentation strategy in symbolically figures (a-f).

In this paper an image segmentation procedure for tissue sections is presented and demonstrated on three different clinical applications. The general strategy must be applicable to various types of biological material differing in thickness, preparation and staining. Microscopic magnification and the information content of the scanned images might also be different. The basic idea was developed for routinely Pappenheim stained blood smears scanned in 2-D space [5]. In that study, more than 20,000 leukcoyte images of 120 specimens were segmented and analyzed [1].

2. The Image Processing System

The image acquisition and processing system consists of three major logical components: A) The microscope (Zeiss, Axiomat), and the color TV-camera with controller (Sony) for image acquisition. A microscope digital focus control, with a 0.1 micron resolution is mandatory for reproducibly measuring tissue sections in different focus settings. B) The color TV camera's signals (RGB) are digitized in an EYECOM III system with an ADC at 12.4 MHz and 8-bit resolution. The EYECOM-system is controlled by a LSI 11/23, linked by DMA to the host computer VAX 11/750. All the image processing algorithms are implemented in FORTRAN 77 on the VAX 11/750. C) Several color TV-monitors are used for visually checking the camera output images, the segmentation masks and other analyzed images. Classification and analysis results are also available.

3. Schematic Description of the Segmentation Challenge

Representations of three different tissue sections, from various biological material with different thicknesses and staining, are shown schematically in Figure 1. The image segmentation algorithm is outlined in Figure 2. The first example (Figure 1.a) is a 4 micron rat liver section embedded in paraplast and stained with Mayers Iron Haematoxilin. The membranes of the nuclei are seldom closed contours and the cytoplasm is barely visible. A paradigmatic scene, in one of the five focus settings photographed from the TV-screen, is shown in Figure 3. The second example (Figures 1.b and 4) demonstrates the challenge from a breast carcinoma embedded in a cryostat 5-10 micron thick section. The monoclonal antibodies in some dark nuclei mark the oestrogen receptor's content, an indicator of the malignancy. Such sections are measured at lower microscopic magnification than used in the measurement of the rat liver sections. Consequently, only three focus settings are necessary because the depth of the focus is inversely related to the optical magnification. The number of marked nuclei and both their color and intensity indicate the degree of malignancy. Homogeneous dark brown nuclei are supposedly malignant, and the heterogeneous light blue ones are supposedly benign. Between benign and malignant there are, however, many different degrees of malignancy which lead to pathomorphological grading. Consequently, all cell nuclei must be correctly identified regardless of their color. In the third example (Figures 1.c and 5), nerve fiber sections are shown which require only two focus settings for complete measurement; one setting for the stained nerve fibers and one for the superimposed silvergrains in the autoradiographic film. The myelin sheaths of the fibers are blue and both the axons and the background areas are light and uncolored.

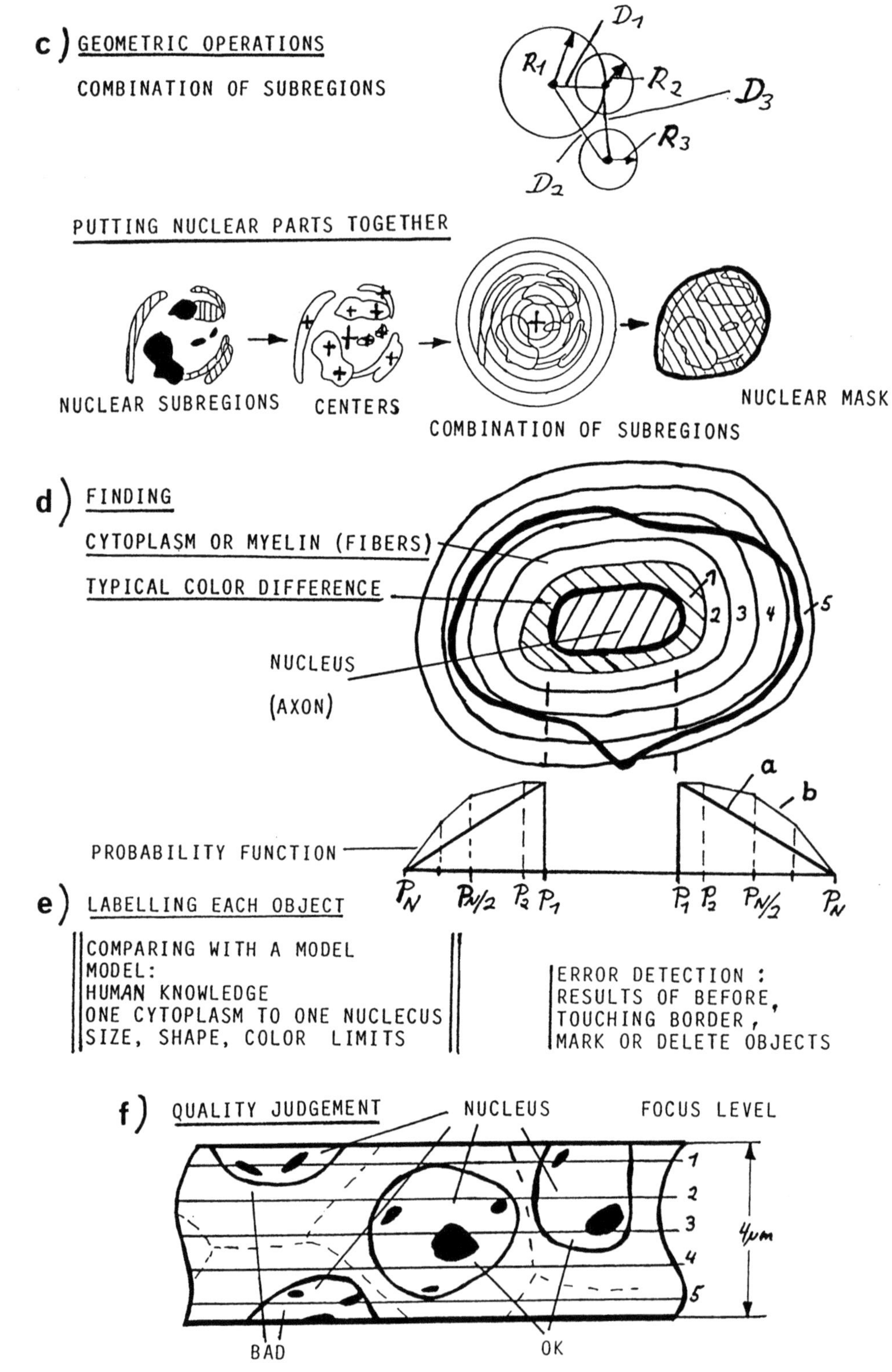
c) GEOMETRIC OPERATIONS
COMBINATION OF SUBREGIONS
D1
R1
R2
D3
R3
D2
PUTTING NUCLEAR PARTS TOGETHER
NUCLEAR SUBREGIONS
CENTERS
COMBINATION OF SUBREGIONS
NUCLEAR MASK
d) FINDING
CYTOPLASM OR MYELIN (FIBERS)
TYPICAL COLOR DIFFERENCE
NUCLEUS
(AXON)
1
2
3
4
5
a
b
PROBABILITY FUNCTION
PN PN/2 P2 P1
P1 P2 PN/2 PN
e) LABELLING EACH OBJECT
COMPARING WITH A MODEL
MODEL:
HUMAN KNOWLEDGE
ONE CYTOPLASM TO ONE NUCLECUS
SIZE, SHAPE, COLOR LIMITS
ERROR DETECTION :
RESULTS OF BEFORE,
TOUCHING BORDER,
MARK OR DELETE OBJECTS
f) QUALITY JUDGEMENT
NUCLEUS
FOCUS LEVEL
1
2
3
4
5
4µm
BAD
OK

The autoradiographic analysis must be done in a second focus level where the silvergrains are located. The silvergrains exhibit grey to black color and are sometimes very difficult to distinguish from the dark blue myelin sheaths, as shown in Figure 5.

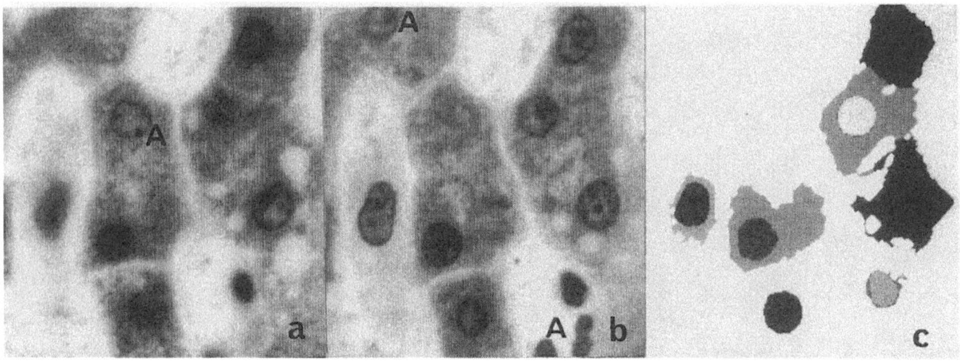

Fig. 3a,b) Black and white images of two focus settings out of the measured five focus levels from a rat liver section. c) Calculated cell mask image.

4. Image Segmentation Strategy

For better understanding, the entire segmentation algorithm is demonstrated schematically in Figure 2. The segmentation process consists of seven major parts: a) Initial histogram and color difference thresholding; b) Improving the initial masks; c) geometric operations; d) finding cytoplasm or myelin and e) labelling the image objects and comparing them with an object model. Parts (a-e) are used to segment the image at each single focus level. Quality judgement f) combines the calculated masks of each focus setting and, finally, g) silver grains, if any, are detected.

4.1. Initial Histogram and Color Difference Thresholding

Histograms and typical grey value thresholds (T1,T2,T3,T4) from the histograms, in addition to characteristic color difference thresholds, are used to locate the most certain areas in an image:

if $A(x,y) < T1$	the pixel is definitely part of a dark nucleus or myelin
if $T1 < A(x,y) < T2$	the pixel might be either part of a nucleus or myelin
if $T2 < A(x,y) < T3$	the pixel is uncertain
if $T3 < A(x,y) < T4$	the pixel might be cytoplasm, myelin or background
if $T4 < A(x,y)$	the pixel is light cytoplasm, myelin, axon, or background, depending on the biological material

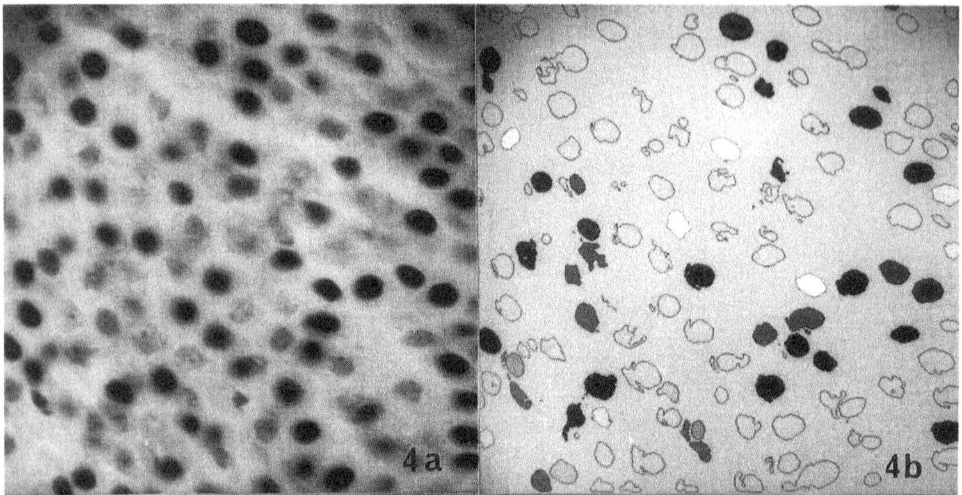

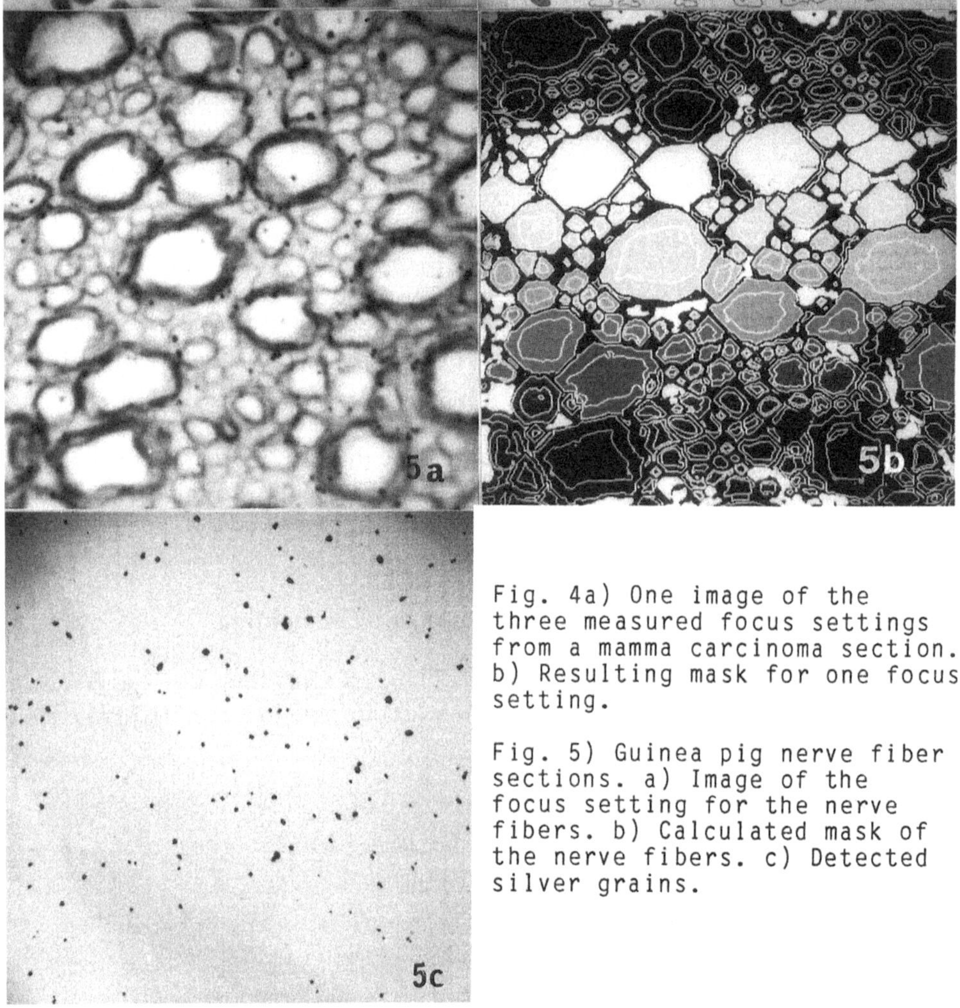

Fig. 4a) One image of the three measured focus settings from a mamma carcinoma section. b) Resulting mask for one focus setting.

Fig. 5) Guinea pig nerve fiber sections. a) Image of the focus setting for the nerve fibers. b) Calculated mask of the nerve fibers. c) Detected silver grains.

where: A(x,y) = gray value of the image at a pixel with coordinates (x,y). A(x,y) is the red channel image for nerve fibers and the green channel image for cells.

Thresholding with these grey values only is insufficient for tissue section images. Therefore characteristic color difference (CD) and color difference thresholds (CDT) are also calculated [3,4]:

$$CD(x,y) = \text{Color Difference, a Function of } \{(R-B), (G-B), (R-G)\}$$

where R,G,B = the original scanned Red, Green, Blue TV image.

The specific color difference images and thresholds depend on the staining and microscope magnification. With the thresholds T1 to T4 and the various CDTs, the differently stained regions are easier to locate. The most certain regions to identify are:

if $CD(x,y) < CDT$ and $A(x,y) > T4$	then pixel is definitely background or axon
if $CD(x,y) > CDT$ and $A(x,y) < T2$	then pixel is definitely part of a nucleus
if $CD(x,y) > CDT$ and $A(x,y) < T4$	then pixel is myelin or cytoplasm, for (B–R)

At this step, the most certain regions of nuclei, axons and background have been marked. The marked areas may be smaller or larger than the corresponding areas in the image. Nonetheless, they form the starting points, or the first coarse masks, in the segmentation process.

4.2. Improving the Initial Masks

In the improvement step, new masks are generated using equidistance isograms calculated according to [7]. The size of one mask is larger (arrow "1" in Figure 2.b), and the other mask is smaller (arrow "2" in Figure 2.b) than each initial mask found above. For each new mask, the color difference histograms (CDH) are calculated. The relative shift in the CDH (labelled with 1 and 2 in Figure 2.b) indicates whether the first mask is too big or too small. An improved nuclear or axon mask is estimated in combination with a probability function. The likelihood of a pixel belonging to the final mask is greater at the center than at the boundary of the region. A pixel belongs to the improved mask if:

$$CD(x,y) > CDTnew - P$$

where: P is the probability function and

$$CDTnew = CDTold + \text{color shift in the two rings in Figure 2.b.}$$

4.3. Geometric Operations

Geometric operations estimate whether subregions should be combined. The radii of the regions and the distances between their centers are the criteria for combining two regions and labelling them with the same number. Two subregions are combined if:

$$(R1+R2)\ K > D$$

where: R1,R2 = radii associated with centers
D = distance between these centers
K = variable from 0.3 to 0.6, depending on the size of R1,R2

K is variable because larger objects must be located closer together, relative to the radii, than smaller objects before they are marked as one object [5].

For very heterogeneous nuclei with incomplete borders, as found in rat liver sections, the last part of Figure 2.c must also be incorporated in the segmentation process. The mean coordinates of the centers of each detected small part of a nuclear region are taken as center of the whole nucleus. A probability function is used in the same way as described above to calculate the entire nuclear mask. The algorithm does not trace boundaries. Only areas and thresholds define the criteria for locating the boundaries.

4.4. Finding Cytoplasm or Myelin

Any cytoplasm or myelin is most certain to be located in 5 pixel wide rings nearest the nuclei or axons. In these 5 pixel wide rings, the characteristic color differences for each cytoplasm or myelin sheath are calculated. Using characteristic color difference thresholds, a larger ring surrounding the nucleus can be segmented. Once again, a probability function is included in the segmentation algorithm. This is necessary in order to process unstained holes, such as vacuoles, correctly. The shape of the probability function, Figure 2.d, reflects the simple fact that one is more certain to find cytoplasm or myelin near the nuclear, or axon regions, than farther away. The width of the probability function, Pn, is the maximum radius of the cell plus a delta pixel space which depends on the magnification and the cell material. In myelin sheaths, the criterion estimating Pn is a function of the ratio of the ring sizes, color differences, and intensities of 3 pixel wide rings surrounding the axons. First, 10 three pixel wide rings are calculated outside the axon masks using equidistance isograms [7]. Then the mean color difference and intensity of each ring is calculated from the RGB image. These mean values are compared to the mean values from the 5 pixel wide ring nearest the axon. The value of Pn is the pixel distance from the axons mask boundary to a 3 pixel wide ring in which the mean values are substantially different from those in the 5 pixel ring. A pixel belongs to the cytoplasm or the myelin if color and intensity are in the range of the 5 pixel wide ring's mean color ± delta and intensity ± delta. In most applications, delta is two times the standard deviation of the color or intensity, respectively. Curve b in Figure 2.d shows the probability function in the case of myelin sheath detection. In nerve fiber processing, pixels belong to the myelin if:

R(x,y) > T2 in the ring from P1 to P2
B(x,y) − G(x,y) > CDT1 or R(x,y) − IM1 < T2 in the ring from P2 to Pn/2
B(x,y) − G(x,y) > CDT2 or R(x,y) − IM1 < T2 in the ring from Pn/2 to 3 Pn/4
B(x,y) − G(x,y) > CDT3 and R(x,y) − IM1 < T2 in the ring from 3 Pn/4 to Pn
B(x,y) − G(x,y) > CDT3 and R(x,y) < T2 − fk2 in the rest of the image (IM>Pn)
where:

T2	=	the threshold between the axon/myelin (Figure 2.a)
CDT1	=	mean B–G color difference calculated in a 5 pixel wide ring nearest surrounding the axon
B(x,y)	=	pixel of the blue channel image
G(x,y)	=	pixel of the green channel image
IM1	=	distance in the ring to the axon border multiplied by the probability function b) in Figure 2.d.
CDT2	=	CDT1 + fk1
CDT3	=	CDT2 + fk1

fk1 and fk2 are determined experimentally and depend on the magnification and preparation methods.

4.5. Labelling Each Object

Each part of a nucleus, cytoplasm, axon, and myelin sheath is labelled with its own number. A nuclear mask does not necessarily correspond to a single complete biological object as viewed in the light microscope. Consequently, the labelled masks are compared with an object model and combined if required. Different nuclear regions can belong to one cytoplasm, but two or more different cytoplasms can not belong to one cell. There are also limits on size, shape and color of each cellular object [5].

4.6. Quality Judgement

A quality judgement for the segmented cell masks is necessary because tissue sections are located in a 3-D space and cells are cut during the preparation process. Cells which are too small are removed from the segmented scene [4].

4.7. Detecting Silver Grains

In autoradiographs, silver grains are typically located in those pixels where either the color difference {G(x,y) + fk3} > B(x,y) or B(x,y) is darker than the surrounding area. The algorithms are nearly the same as those used in segmentation of nuclear regions. Only size and color limits are different.

5. Examples

The capabilities of the segmentation procedure are shown in Figures 3,4,5 for three different biological applications. Figures 3 a,b are photographs of two of the five focus settings used to segment an image from a rat liver section. All cell masks have been detected and labelled with different numbers in Figure 3.c. Cells indexed with "A" do not meet the quality judgement and their masks are removed from the image. Figure 4 shows one of the three focus level images from a breast carcinoma (4.a) and the calculated corresponding nuclear mask (4.b). The darker nuclear masks are marked as being optimum masks at this focus setting. The lighter nuclear masks, with the labelled borders, will be analyzed at another focus setting. Figure 5.a shows the image of a nerve fiber section with superimposed silver grains; Figure 5.b contains the nerve fiber masks and Figure 5.c the automatically detected silver grain distribution.

6. Conclusion

The possibility of segmenting stained tissue section images in more than one focus setting is demonstrated. Color and color differences, geometric area operations, an object model, and quality judgement are the basic components of the segmentation procedure. The general strategy can be applied to images of different biological material, which have been prepared by different routine preparation methods.

The nature of histological specimens necessitates 3-D analysis and quality judgement as an integral part of the segmentation. The object model and the correlation of the object masks with the model are important steps in the method. As described in [4,5] the method does not rely on contour following techniques as used in [2]. The specimens consist of routine preparations from the clinical laboratory with the usual variations in staining and general quality. The color difference thresholding technique permits such normal variations in the specimen.

Acknowledgments

The technical assistance of Ms. M.Haucke is greatly appreciated. This work was supported by the Deutsche Forschungsgemeinschaft and the Bundesministerium für Forschung und Technologie,Bonn, West Germany.

References

[1] Aus HM, Harms H, Gunzer U, Haucke M, Baumann I, Hinterberger J, ter Meulen V: Validierung von Zellparametern zur computergestützten Diagnostik leukämischer Blutbildveränderungen, Forschungsbericht, Technologische Forschung und Entwicklung, Medizin, Jan. 1986

[2] Brenner JF, Necheles TF, Bonacossa IA, Fristensky R, Weintraub BA and Neurath PW: Scene Segmentation Techniques for the Analysis of Routine Bone Marrow Smears from Acute Lymphoblastic Leukemia Patients. J. Histochem Cytochem vol 25, 7:601 - 613, 1977

[3] Hall EL: Computer Image Processing and Recognition Academic Press, New York, 1979,pp 8-73,458 - 459

[4] Harms H, Aus H M: Computer Colour Vision: Automated Segmentation of Histological Tissue Sections, In: Pattern Recognition in Practice II, Gelsema E A, Kanal L N, Editors, Elsevier Science Publishers, pp 323-330, 1986

[5] Harms H, Haucke M, Aus H M, Gunzer U: Segmentation of Stained Blood Cell Images Measured at High Scanning Density with High Magnification and High Numerical Aperture Optics. Cytometry in press.

[6] Preston K: High-Resolution Image Analysis, J Histochemistry and Cytochemistry, vol 34, 1:67-74, 1986

[7] Rosenfeld A, Kak AC: Digital Picture Processing. Academic Press, 1976, pp 352-361

METHODS FOR COMPUTER ANALYSIS AND COMPARISON OF TWO-DIMENSIONAL PROTEIN PATTERNS OBTAINED BY ELECTROPHORESIS

Reinhold C. Mann, Betty K. Mansfield and James K. Selkirk[1]

Biology Division, Oak Ridge National Laboratory, Oak Ridge, TN 37831 USA
[1]National Toxicology Program, NIEHS, Research Triangle Park, NC 27709 USA

1. Introduction

Mammalian cells contain thousands of proteins each representing an important function for maintaining the homeostasis of the cell at the biochemical, genetic, or structural level. Two-dimensional gel electrophoresis is uniquely sensitive in its ability to separate these proteins in the first dimension by isoelectric focusing as a function of net charge, and in the second dimension as a function of molecular weight ([13]). The presence of a certain radioactively labeled protein in a preparation is indicated by a spot that is produced on a film. The intensity of the spot is indicative of the amount of protein. Usually several hundred, even up to a few thousand spots, *i.e.*, proteins, can be distinguished in a gel image, which makes rigorous quantitative analysis by simple visual inspection impossible. Analysis of the voluminous information inherent in a gel image requires localization, quantitation and possibly identification of each protein. In addition, and equally importantly, it is necessary to make local and global comparisons between multiple gels that reflect potential changes in protein patterns from various disease states or after carcinogen or mutagen treatment, in order to demonstrate subtle changes that occur in the progression to the diseased state.

The importance of computer analysis and pattern recognition methodology for quantitative two-dimensional electrophoresis is being recognized, as documented in several reports on analysis systems that appeared in the literature during the past few years ([1], [3], [6], [8], [9], [10], [14], [15], [17], [19]). However, no data are available from systematic studies that would allow a critical assessment of the relative advantages and disadvantages as well as potential intrinsic limitations of the different methods described so far. The purpose of this article is to summarize some results that we obtained from experiments designed to compare the performance of different methods for gel image analysis. Our goal is to identify algorithms that are suitable for gel image analysis and comparison.

2. Parametric Versus Non-Parametric Gel Image Analysis

A typical image obtained with radiolabeled cytoplasmic proteins of a Friend erythroleukemia cell line [5] is shown in Figure 1.

NATO ASI Series, Vol. F30
Pattern Recognition Theory and Applications
Edited by P. A. Devijver and J. Kittler

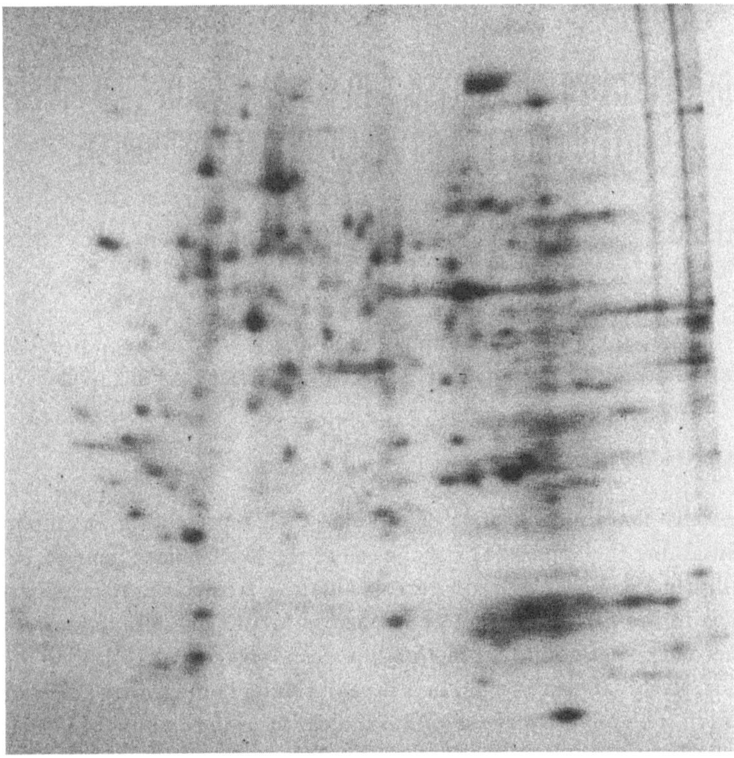

Figure 1: Typical gel image obtained with cytoplasmic proteins of Friend erythroleukemia cells.

The corresponding X-ray film was digitized with an Optronics P1000 scanner (Optronics International Inc., Chelmsford, MA) at 100μ intervals, covering an intensity range of 3 OD at 8 bits resolution. Gels in our laboratory are approximately 15cm×15cm resulting in images with 1536 × 1536 pixels. Sometimes the analysis can be confined to 512 × 512 pixel sections of the images, as was done for the examples shown in this article, thereby reducing processing time often considerably. By exposing areas containing known amounts of radioactivity incorporated in the gel, lookup tables can be set up that are used to convert optical density, *i.e.*, greyvalues to radioactivity. This is necessary because of the non-linear film response. The goal in quantitative gel image analysis is to reduce the pictorial data to a list of protein spots, each spot being defined by a triplet, quintuplet or a different but usually small amount of numbers, *e.g.*, location (x, y), spread in x and y, integrated density, and sometimes boundary coordinates. The analysis is preceeded by a processing step, generally a bandpass operation that eliminates high and very low frequencies, the latter corresponding to a locally varying image background that would make simple thresholding inadequate for image segmentation. Some systems use a local thresholding technique for background elimination ([3], [8]), others a non-linear min/max filter ([1], [17]) first described in the context of "mathematical morphology" [16].

Although the algorithms for spot detection and quantification that have been described so far, differ in many details, partially because of different hardware configurations, we can categorize these methods in two sets: parametric methods that operate on the basis of some model for the spots ([1], [6], [9], [10]), and non-parametric methods that do not rely on any assumptions as to the shape of the spots ([8], [17], [19]). We will subsequently refer to these sets as P and NP respectively. Methods in P usually assume Gaussian spot profiles. This can be justified considering the diffusion processes involved in electrophoresis combined with the sieving effect produced by the concentration gradient in the polyacrylamide gel medium. Each spot is characterized numerically by at most six parameters: location, spread in x and y, maximal intensity, and angle of principal component if the Gaussian is not assumed to be separable. A synthetic image produced by the superposition of all Gaussians is fitted optimally, usually in the least squares sense, to the bandpass-filtered image.

As with parametric methods the details of implementation for methods in NP differ considerably between the systems described in the literature. The common feature of NP methods is that time-consuming surface fitting is not performed. Overlap between spots is resolved by examining spatial derivatives of the image. Spots are characterized by their location and volume, and often boundary coordinates are stored in order to allow for display of a contour map depicting the result of computer analysis.

NP methods cannot achieve the amount of data reduction obtained with P methods without sacrificing the frequently important capability of displaying a synthetic gel image, based on the numerical information on the spots, that resembles the original image. Obviously, non-Gaussian spot profiles can be handled better by NP methods.

We performed experiments designed to compare the accuracy and consistency of quantification obtained with 2 typical methods, subsequently referred to as A and B, from P and NP respectively. Method A was described in detail in [10]. Briefly, it involves the removal of image background using a non-linear min/max filter ([16]), followed by spot search and estimation based on the assumption that the spots can be adequately described by separable Gaussians. It follows that images can be analyzed in the 2 dimensions separately, which reduces analysis times to acceptable ranges (ca. 1h for 1536 $\times$ 1536 images) on our hardware configuration (commercial pipelined image processor, minicomputer host).

Figure 2 illustrates some of the processing and analysis steps. Method B uses the same filters for smoothing and background removal as method A. In this study, the analysis part of method B was implemented to be executed interactively, the user selecting a rectangular area around an isolated spot within which super-threshold pixel values are added to give a spot volume estimate.

Computer-generated images containing 5 isolated Gaussian spots of different sizes were distorted by additive Gaussian noise, and analyzed by methods A and B. Noise parameters were chosen to simulate realistic conditions (Kodak SB X-ray film, preflashed to 0.5 OD). Maximum spot intensities were 50, 100, 150, 235 greyvalues. A detailed account of results is beyond the scope of this article, and will be reported elsewhere. Relative errors in spot volume estimates ranged from 0% to 27% for method A, and were between 0% and 15% for method B, with the median of the relative errors for individual spots ranging from 1% to 11% for A and from 0.1% to 9% for B. The coefficients

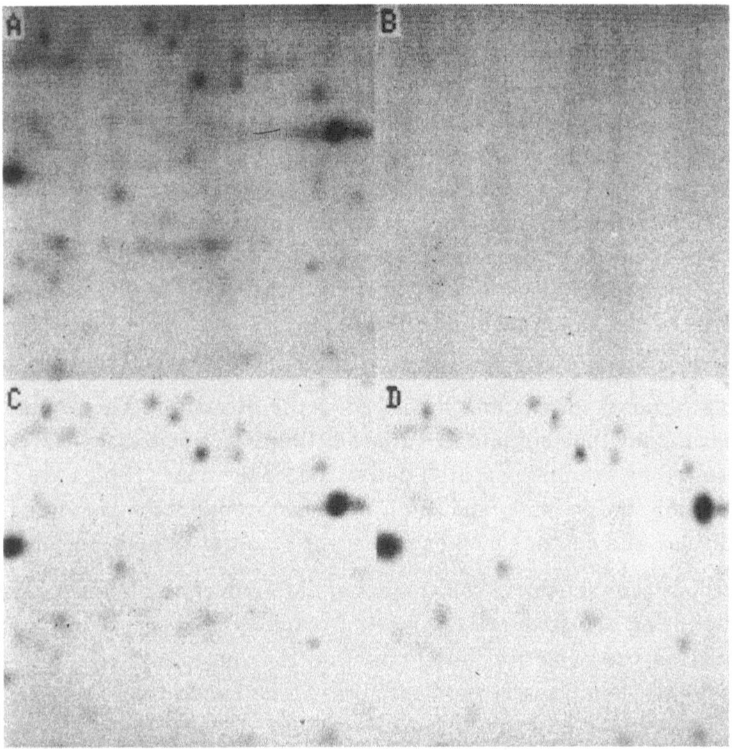

Figure 2: Processing and parametric analysis of a gel image: (A) original image, (B) background determined by non-linear greyvalue erosion/ dilation filter, (C) background removed, (D) synthetic image, result of parametric analysis.

of variation (CV), an indication of the spread in the estimates for individual spots when the analysis was repeated 10 times for each intensity level with independent noise realizations, varied between 1% and 14.6% for method A, 0.2% and 7.6% for method B, the medians of 6.5% and 0.8% being significantly different ($P < 0.001$). The results indicate that, for isolated spots, fitting of Gaussian surfaces to the spot profiles, if performed sub-optimally for reasons of computational economy, can be inferior to a very simple non-parametric method that only involves a threshold operation and summation of greyvalues. Work is underway to adapt method B to non-interactive operation, and to compare methods A and B when applied to overlapping spots.

One of the unresolved problems in gel image analysis is the sensitivity of results to changes in the image processing parameters, notably the choice of filter windows for background computation. With the non-linear filter we are using [10], the window should be chosen larger than the maximum extension of the biggest spot. A range of window sizes fit this rule, due to difficulties in defining spot sizes, and optimal window selection for this class of filters has not been described to date. Therefore, we analyzed

7 gel images (selecting 20 well-defined, isolated spots in each) after background removal with 4 different window sizes: 55, 75, 95, 105 pixels. In summary, we observed that the CVs of spot estimates ranged from 0% to 50% without a significant difference between methods A and B. The background filter should be kept constant for a series of images that are to be compared to each other. An objective procedure that estimates the filter parameter from the image data should be developed.

3. Gel Image Comparison

Comparison of gel images is complicated by the fact that substantial spatial distortions can result from small variations in the electrophoresis procedure that are beyond the experimenter's control. Global or local image warping, based on a number of interactively selected, well-matching spots, is generally applied in order to register images. These transformations are applied after image analysis is completed. The degree of required user interaction varies among different implementations of this approach ([1], [8], [11], [12], [14]). Polynomial warping can be executed quite quickly by special hardware and software that are readily available. However, it is often necessary to specify a rather large number (> 30) of matches, so-called "landmarks", in order to achieve adequate registration of the spot patterns. The quality of fit is limited by the kind of transformation used for warping (usually polynomials of maximum degree 2 or 3). Comparison is myopic in the sense that single spots instead of characteristic spot constellations are used to orient the registration algorithm. Constellations are considered by the algorithms of Miller *et al.* [12], performing a nearest neighbor analysis that attempts to match clusters of spots, and Skolnick's method [18] that compares graphs associated with spot patterns.

No comparative data are available on the performance of these methods. However, it is expected that the algorithms that search for spot constellations rather than individual spots, and are not limited to a certain class of spatial transformations, result in more accurate and reliable gel image comparisons. Figure 3 illustrates a typical situation in gel image comparison. The images in panels A and B cannot be matched by simple translations and/or rotations. Panel C shows how a polynomial transformation based on 37 "landmarks" to register these images would deform a rectangular grid. For the 13 isolated well-defined spots shown in panel D this warping results in an average Euclidean distance between matching spots of 9 pixels (CV = 56%). For spots that are not that well isolated, this can lead to a considerable number of mismatches. The approach sketched in panel D, the matching of spot constellations, leads to exact matches. However, difficulties arise with missing or newly emerging spots that slightly alter a constellation.

Minimum spanning trees appear to be rather sensitive to insertions or deletions of nodes, *i.e.*, spots. Skolnick [18] reports that Gabriel graphs can be useful data structures for gel image comparison.

Once adequate image registration is achieved, explicitly as in the case of warping methods or implicitly as with graph structures, it is possible to perform local, *i.e.*, spot by spot, and global spot image comparisons. Principal component analysis was described in [2] as a tool for global comparison and classification of spot patterns. After matching and introduction of a common spot numbering system, each gel image is de-

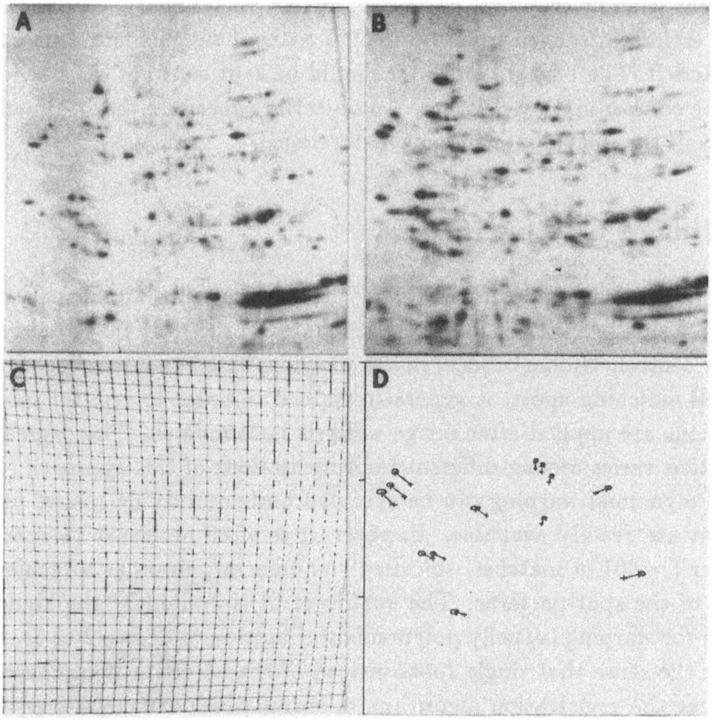

Figure 3: Registration of gel images: (A), (B) images to be compared, (C) effect of polynomial warping on a rectangular grid, (D) matching spot constellations (spots from panels A and B shown as crosses and ellipses respectively)

fined by a vector whose elements are the intensities (volumes) of all the spots in the image. Dimensionality reduction by principal component analysis is performed in order to obtain image features with good discriminatory power. Other, more robust projection pursuit methods [7] should be considered in this context.

4. Discussion

Automated analysis of gel images is an important part of the quantitative study of proteins that have been separated by two-dimensional gel electrophoresis. In order to establish the sensitivity of assays relying on this separation technique it is crucial to know how accurately and reliably information can be extracted from gel images. We have examined some of the main factors that influence the results of quantitative gel image analysis. These include the choice of parameters for image processing procedures to remove high and low spatial frequencies, and the selection of appropriate methods for analysis as well as comparison. From our experiments with simulated images as well as gel images we conclude that an analysis procedure that does not rely on assumptions regarding the greyvalue distribution within spots, *i.e.*, Gaussian spot profiles, appears to result in slightly more accurate and significantly more reproducible spot volume estimates than a parametric method that involves suboptimal surface fitting. We have also seen that analysis results can be quite sensitive to image processing parameters. CVs of up to 50% were observed when the window size for our background subtraction filter was varied within a range selected according to the rule of thumb to choose the window larger than the biggest spot in the image.

It is obvious that the 3 different tasks of (1) bandpass filtering, (2) spot detection and analysis, and (3) image comparison that are performed sequentially and independently of each other by current analysis systems, are not mutually independent. The choice of filter in (1) influences the results of (2), which is potentially critical for the reliable detection of significant differences between gel images. Based on experiments that we carried out earlier [10] to assess spot detection error rates, we anticipate greatly enhanced performance of a system in which the analysis of an image can be guided by a priori knowledge obtained from gels already analyzed in the course of an experiment. The interdependence of (2) and (3) will be taken into account by this system. Moreover, it is expected that the results reported by Young *et al.* [20] on the choice of optimal parameters for non-linear filters will be extended to greyvalue images, thereby rendering filter selection for task (1) more rigorous.

As pointed out in [17], many of the operations involved in gel image analysis, including image comparison, can be performed in spatially separated image regions at the same time. The increased processing speed associated with this parallel execution of the tasks allows one to implement a knowledge-based gel image analysis system with acceptable execution times. Recent developments in rapid electronic autofluorography [4] make it possible to generate images from electrophoresis gels in a matter of minutes versus hours or days when exposing gels to film. Therefore, the speed of analysis becomes an important factor in selecting algorithms and hardware. We have started using an NCUBE general-purpose 64-processor computer (NCUBE Corp., Beaverton, Oregon) for the non-linear image processing involved in our method. Without major code modifications or optimizations we observed increases in processing speeds up to 2 orders of magnitude with the NCUBE compared to the pipelined image processor/minicomputer host hardware we have been using so far. Multi-processor boards are becoming available at very moderate cost for personal computers. Thus, the prospects are promising for affordable computer-assisted rapid quantitative two-dimensional gel electrophoresis for an increasing number of laboratories.

Acknowledgement
We are grateful to Dr. M.C. Hall, ORNL Engineering Physics and Mathematics Division, for his advice and assistance in using the NCUBE multi-processor. This research was sponsored by the Office of Health and Environmental Research, U.S. Department of Energy, under contract DE-AC05-840R21400 with the Martin Marietta Energy Systems, Inc.

References

[1] Anderson N.L., J. Taylor, A.E. Scandora, B.P. Coulter, N.G. Anderson, "The TYCHO system for computer analysis of two-dimensional gel electrophoresis patterns,"

Clin. Chem., 27, 1807-1820, (1981).

[2] Anderson N.L., J.P.Hofmann, A.Gemmell, J.Taylor, "Global approaches to quantitative analysis of gene expression patterns observed by use of two-dimensional gel electrophoresis," *Clin. Chem.*, 30/12, 2031-2036, (1984).

[3] Bossinger J., M.J. Miller, K.P. Vo, E.P. Geiduschek, N.H. Xuong, "Quantitative analysis of two-dimensional electrophoretograms," *J. Biol. Chem.*, 254, 7986-7998, (1979).

[4] Davidson J.B., "Electronic autofluorography: principles, problems, and prospects," in: *Electrophoresis '84*, V.Neuhoff, ed., Verlag Chemie, 235-251, (1984).

[5] Friend E., W. Scher, J.G. Holland, T. Sato, "Hemoglobin synthesis in murine virus-induced leukemic cells in vitro: Stimulation of erythroid differentiation by dimethyl sulfoxide," *Proc. Natl. Acad. Sci. USA*, 68, 378-382, (1971).

[6] Garrels J.I., "Two-dimensional gel electrophoresis and computer analysis of protein synthesized by clonal cell lines," *J. Biol. Chem.*, 254, 7961-7979, (1979).

[7] Huber P.J., "Projection pursuit," *Annals of Statistics* 13:435-475, 1985.

[8] Lemkin P.F., L.E. Lipkin, "GELLAB: A computer system for 2d gel electrophoresis analysis, Parts I, II, III," *Comp. Biomed. Res.*, 14, 272-297, 335-380, 407-446, (1981).

[9] Lutin W. A., C.F. Kyle, J.A. Freeman, "Quantitation of brain proteins by computer analyzed two-dimensional electrophoresis," in: *Electrophoresis '78*, N. Catsimpoolas, ed., Elsevier/North Holland, Amsterdam-New York, 1979.

[10] Mann R.C., B.K. Mansfield, J.K. Selkirk, "Automated analysis of digital images generated by two-dimensional gel electrophoresis," in: *Pattern Recognition in Practice II*, E.S.Gelsema, L.N.Kanal (eds.), Elsevier/North Holland, Amsterdam, 1986, pp. 301-311.

[11] Miller M.J., P.K. Vo, C. Nielsen, E.P. Geiduschek, N.H. Xuong "Computer analysis of two-dimensional gels: Semi-automatic matching," *Clin. Chem.*, 28, 867-875, (1982).

[12] Miller M.J., A.D. Olson, S.S. Thorgeirsson, "Computer analysis of two-dimensional gels: automatic matching," *Electrophoresis 5*, 297-303, (1984).

[13] O'Farrell P.H., "High resolution two-dimensional electrophoresis of proteins," *J. Biol.Chem.*, 250, 4007-4021, (1975).

[14] Pardowitz I., H.G. Zimmer, V. Neuhoff, "Spot identification in two-dimensional patterns by a least-squares template matching," *Clin. Chem.*, 30, 1985-1988, (1984).

[15] Ridder G., E. Von Bargen, D. Burgard, H. Pickrum, E. Williams "Quantitative analysis and pattern recognition of two-dimensional electrophoresis gels," *Clin. Chem.*, 30, 1919-1924, (1984).

[16] Serra J., *Image Analysis and Mathematical Morphology*, Academic Press, London-New York, 1982.

[17] Skolnick M.M., S.R. Sternberg, J.V. Neel, "Computer programs for adapting two-dimensional gels to the study of mutation," *Clin. Chem.*, 28, 969-978, (1982).

[18] Skolnick M.M., "Automated comparison of image similarities and differences," PhD Thesis, University of Michigan 1984, University Microfilms International, Ann Arbor, Michigan.

[19] Vo K.P., M.J. Miller, E.P. Geiduschek, C. Nielsen, A. Olson, N.H. Xuong, "Computer analysis of two-dimensional gels," *Anal. Biochem.*, 112, 258-271, (1981).

[20] Young I.T., G.L. Beckers, L. Dorst, A. Boerman, "Choosing filter parameters for non-linear image filtering," in: *Pattern Recognition in Practice II*, E.S. Gelsema, L.N. Kanal (eds.), Elsevier/North Holland, Amsterdam, 1986, pp. 5-14.

LIST OF PARTICIPANTS

Dr. Emile H. L. Aarts
Philips Research Laboratories
P.O.Box 80.000 - 5.600 JA Eindhoven
The Netherlands

Dr. Xavier Aubert
Philips Research Laboratory
Avenue Em. Van Becelaere 2, Box 8
B-1170 Brussels, Belgium

Dr. Hans-Magnus Aus
Biomedical Image Processing Lab.
Institute of Virology
Versbacher Strasse 7, 8700 Wurzburg
West Germany

Professor Eric Backer
Delft University of Technology
Department Electrical Engineering
4 Mekelweg 2628 GA Delft
The Netherlands

Dr. Gerald J. Bakus
University of Southern California
University Park
Los Angeles, California 90089-0371, USA

Monsieur Didier Billard
L.E.P. Division 32
3, Avenue Descartes BP 15
94450 Limeil-Brevannes, France

Mr. Thomas Bjerch
Norwegian Computing Center
BP. 335, N-0314 Blinderen
Oslo 3, Norway

Dr. Richard E. Blake
Department of Computer Science and Electrical Engineering
University of Tennessee
Knoxville TN 37996, USA

Mr. Leo Böhmer
Hollandse Signaalapparaten B.V.
Zuidelijke Havenweg, 40
Postbus 42, 7550 GD Hengelo
The Netherlands

Mr. Hervé Bourlard
Philips Research Laboratory
Avenue Em. Van Becelaere 2, Box 8
B-1170 Brussels, Belgium

Dr. John S. Bridle
Royal Signal & Radar Establishment
St Andrews Road, Great Malvern, Worcs
WR14 3PS United Kingdom

Professor Horst Bunke
University of Bern
Department of Informatics
Langgassstrasse 51, CH-3012 Bern, Switzerland

Mr. Antonio Miguel de Campos
DEE - LNETI
Azinhaga dos Lameiros
1699 Lisboa Codex, Portugal

Mr. Stephen J. Cheetham
University of Sheffield
Department of Mechanical Engineering
Mappin Street, Sheffield
United Kingdom

Mr. Xiang S. Cheng
Delft University of Technology
Department Electrical Engineering
4 Mekelweg 2628 GA Delft
The Netherlands

Professor Darrel L. Chenoweth
Dept. Electrical Engineering
University of Louisville
Louisville, Kentucky 40292, USA

Professor Renato De Mori
School of Computer Science
McGill University
805 Sherbrooke Street West
Montréal, PQ., Canada H3A 2K6

Mr. Michel Dekesel
Philips Research Laboratory
Avenue Em. Van Becelaere 2, Box 8
B-1170 Brussels, Belgium

Dr. Sylvana Dellepiane
DIBE - Universita' di Genova
via All'Opera Pia 11a
16145 Genova, Italia

Madame Anne-Marie Derouault
Centre Scientifique IBM France
36, Avenue Raymond Poincare
75116 Paris, France

Monsieur Jacques Destine
Institut Montéfiore, B-28
Université de Liège
Sart Tilman, 4000 Liège, Belgium

Dr. Pierre A. Devijver
Philips Research Laboratory
Avenue Em. Van Becelaere 2, Box 8
B-1170 Brussels, Belgium

Professor Luc Devroye
School of Computer Science
Burnside Hall
McGill University
805 Sherbrooke Street West
Montréal, PQ., Canada H3A 2K6

Dr. Michel Dhome
LERM UA 830 du CNRS
Université de Clermont II
B.P. 45, 63170 Aubière, France

Professor Vito Di Gesù
I.F.C.A.I.
Via Mariano Stabile 172
90100 Palermo, Italy

Dr Hubert Emptoz
I.N.S.A.
Centre de Mathématiques
20 Avenue Albert Einstein
69621 Villeurbanne Cedex, France

Dr. Hector B. Epelbaum
MPI fur biophys. Chemie
Abt. Molekulare Biologie
Postach 968, 3400 Goettingen, West Germany

Dr. Olivier Faugeras
INRIA, BP 105
78153 Le Chesnay Cedex, France

Professor Jerome A. Feldman
University of Rochester
Department of Computer Science
Ray P. Hylan Building
Rochester, New York, 14627, USA

Madame F. Fogelman-Soulie
Laboratoire de Dynamique des Réseaux
C.E.S.T.A.
5, rue Descartes, F-75005 Paris, France

Monsieur Patrick Gallinari
Laboratoire de Dynamique des Réseaux
C.E.S.T.A.
5, rue Descartes, F-75005 Paris, France

Professor Donald Geman
Department of Mathematics
University of Massachusetts
Amherst, MA 01003, USA

Ms. Sadiye Güler
Earth Resources Laboratory
M.I.T. Bld.E–34, Rm 34–570
42-44 Carleton Street
Cambridge, MA 02142, USA

Mr. Charles D. Hansen
Department of Computer Science
The University of Utah
Salt Lake City, UT 84112, USA

Dr. Harry Harms
Biomedical Image Processing Lab.
Institute of Virology
Versbacher Strasse 7, 8700 Wurzburg
West Germany

Mr. John Haslett
Department of Statistics
Trinity College, Dublin 2, Ireland

Professor Thomas C. Henderson
Department of Computer Science
The University of Utah
Salt Lake City, UT 84112, USA

Mr. John Hyde
MARCONI Command and Control
Systems, Technology Group
Chobham Road, Frimley, Camberley,
Surrey, United Kingdom

Dr. John Illingworth
Rutherford Appleton Laboratory
Chilton, Didcot, Oxfordshire OX11 0QX
United Kingdom

Professor Anil K. Jain
Department of Computer Science
Michigan Sate University
East Lansing, Michigan 48823, USA

Mr Jean-Michel Jolion
I.N.S.A.
20 Avenue Albert Einstein
69621 Villeurbanne Cedex France

Mr. Michel Jourlin
Université de Saint-Etienne
C.N.R.S. 996
23, rue du Docteur P. Michelon
42023 Saint-Etienne Cedex, France

Madame Agnès Jousselin-Grenier
Electricité de France
Direction des Etudes et Recherches
6, quai Watier, B.P. 49
F-78400 Chatou, France

Dr. Yves Kamp
Philips Research Laboratory
Avenue Em. Van Becelaere 2, Box 8
B-1170 Brussels, Belgium

Professor Laveen Kanal
University of Maryland
Computer Science Department
College Park, MD 20742, USA

Mr. Alex Kashko
Queen Mary College
Mile End Road, London E1 4NS
United Kingdom

Professor Leonard Kaufman
Department of Statisitcs
Vrije Universiteit Brussel
Pleinlaan 2, 1050, Brussels, Belgium

Ms. Anne Keuneke
Computer & Inform. Sciences Dept.
The Ohio State University
2036 Neil Avenue Mall
Columbus, Ohio 43210-1277, USA

Mr. Ian Kerr
MARCONI Command and Control
Systems, Technology Group
Chobham Road, Frimley, Camberley,
Surrey, United Kingdom

Dr. Josef Kittler
Dept. Electronic & Electrical Engrg.
University of Surrey
Guilford GU2 5XH, United Kingdom

Dr. Jan Korst
Philips Research Laboratories
P.O.Box 80.000 - 5.600 JA Eindhoven
The Netherlands

Dr. George Kouroupetroglou
University of Athens
Department of Physics
Panepistimioupoli - Ktiria T.Y.P.A.
157 71 Athens, Greece

Ms. Vinciane Lacroix
Philips Research Laboratory
Avenue Em. Van Becelaere 2, Box 8
B-1170 Brussels, Belgium

Monsieur Michel Lamure
Université Lyon I
Département de Mathématiques
Bd. du 11 Novembre 1918
F-69.621 Villeurbanne, France

Ms. Violet Leavers
Department of Physics
King's College London
Strand, London WC2R 2LS
United Kingdom

Dr. Wolfgang Lellmann
Computer Gesellschaft Konstanz MBH
Postfach 1142, D-7750 Konstanz
West Germany

Professor Murray H. Loew
Dept. Electr. Engrg. & Comput. Sci.
Georges Washington University
Washington D.C. 20052, USA

Dr. Robert L. Manicke
U.S. Naval Academy
Annapolis MD 21402, USA

Dr. Reinhold C. Mann
Oak Ridge National Laboratory
Biology Division
P.O.Box Y, Oak Ridge, TE 37831, USA

Dr. John Mantas
National Center of Medical
Documentation
14-16 Aristidou Street, P. Faliro
GR-17563 Athens, Greece

Mr. Botbol Meir
ELBIT Computer Ltd.
Advanced Technology Center
P.O.B. 5390, Haifa 31051, Israel

Dr. Jean-Vincent Moreau
Department of Computer Science
Michigan Sate University
East Lansing, Michigan 48823, USA

Ir. Arno M.M. Muijtjens
Dept. Medical Informatics & Stat.
University of Limburg
P.O.Box 616, 6200 MD Maastricht
The Netherlands

Professor H. Bacelar Nicolau
Faculdade de Ciencias
Universidade de Lisboa
Rua da Escola Politecnica, 58
1294 Lisboa Codex, Portugal

Professor Erkki Oja
Department of Applied Mathematics
Kuopio University
P.O.Box 6, 70221 Kuopio, Finland

Professor John A. Orr
Worcester Polytechnic Institute
100 Institute Road, Worcester, MA
01609, USA

Professor Erdal Panayırcı
Department of Electrical Engineering
Technical University Istanbul
Istanbul, Turkey

Mr. Keith Ponting
Royal Signal & Radar Establishment
St Andrews Road, Great Malvern,
Worcs, United Kingdom WR14 3PS

Monsieur Serge Raes
Institut Montéfiore, B-28
Université de Liège
Sart Tilman, 4000 Liège, Belgium

Professeur J-P. Rasson
Faculté Universitaire Notre Dame de la
Paix
Rempart de la Vierge 8, 5000 Namur,
Belgium

Mrs Ana Paula Rocha
Grupo de Matematica Aplicada
Rua das Taipas 135, 4000 Porto,
Portugal

Mr. Hector Rulot
Centro de Infomatica
Universidad de Valencia
Burjasot, Valencia - Spain

Monsieur Marc Saerens
Université Libre de Bruxelles
Institut de Phonétique
Avenue F.-D. Roosevelt 50, 1050
Bruxelles

Mr. Richard Saunders
Department of Computing Sciences
University of Stirling
Stirling FK9 4LA, Scotland

Professor Ishwar K. Sethi
Department of Computer Science
Wayne State University
Detroit MI 48202, USA

Professor Michael Shalmon
Université du Québec
INRS - Télécommunications.
3, Place du Commerce, Ile des Soeurs
Verdun, Québec, Canada

Mr. Dominique Snyers
Philips Research Laboratory
Avenue Em. Van Becelaere 2, Box 8
B-1170 Brussels, Belgium

Mr. Ahmet C. Sonmez
University Engineering Department
Trumpington Street
Cambridge CB2 1PZ, United Kingdom

Mr. Torfinn Taxt
Norwegian Computing Center
BP. 335, N–0314 Blinderen, Oslo 3, Norway

Professeur Michel Terrenoire
Université Lyon I
Département de Mathématiques
Bd. du 11 Novembre 1918
F–69.621 Villeurbanne, France

Madame Sylvie Thiria
Laboratoire de Dynamique des Reseaux
C.E.S.T.A.
5, rue Descartes, F-75005 Paris, France

Professor Michael G. Thomason
Department of Computer Science and Electrical Engineering
University of Tennessee
Knoxville, TN 37917, USA

Prof. Godfried Toussaint
School of Computer Science
Burnside Hall
McGill University
805 Sherbrooke Street West
Montréal, PQ., Canada H3A 2K6

Mr. Panagiotis Trahanias
Greek Atomic Energy Commission
NRC "Democritos"
Aghia Paraskevi, Attiki Greece

Dr. Thomas Tsao
University of Maryland
Computer Science Department
College Park, MD 20742, USA

Dr. Thierry Van Cutsem
Université de Liège
Institut Montéfiore
Sart Tilman B-28, 4000 Liège, Belgium

Dr. Andrew Webb
Royal Signals and Radar Establishement
St Andrews Road, Great Malvern
Worcs WR14 3PS, United Kingdom

Professor Harry Wechsler
University of Minesota
Dept. Electrical Engineering
123 Church Street S.E.
Minneapolis, Minesotas 55455, USA

Dr. Christian Wellekens
Philips Research Laboratory
Avenue Em. Van Becelaere 2, Box 8
B-1170 Brussels, Belgium

Professor Andrew K.G. Wong
Faculty of Engineering
University of Waterloo
Waterloo Ontario N2L 3G1, Canada

Professor H.-J. Zimmermann
Lehrstuhl fur Unternehmensforschung
RWTH Aachen
Templergraben 64, D-51 Aachen
West Germany

NATO ASI Series F

Vol. 1: Issues in Acoustic Signal – Image Processing and Recognition. Edited by C. H. Chen. VIII, 333 pages. 1983.

Vol. 2: Image Sequence Processing and Dynamic Scene Analysis. Edited by T. S. Huang. IX, 749 pages. 1983.

Vol. 3: Electronic Systems Effectiveness and Life Cycle Costing. Edited by J. K. Skwirzynski. XVII, 732 pages. 1983.

Vol. 4: Pictorial Data Analysis. Edited by R. M. Haralick. VIII, 468 pages. 1983.

Vol. 5: International Calibration Study of Traffic Conflict Techniques. Edited by E. Asmussen. VII, 229 pages. 1984.

Vol. 6: Information Technology and the Computer Network. Edited by K. G. Beauchamp. VIII, 271 pages. 1984.

Vol. 7: High-Speed Computation. Edited by J. S. Kowalik. IX, 441 pages. 1984.

Vol. 8: Program Transformation and Programming Environments. Report on an Workshop directed by F. L. Bauer and H. Remus. Edited by P. Pepper. XIV, 378 pages. 1984.

Vol. 9: Computer Aided Analysis and Optimization of Mechanical System Dynamics. Edited by E. J. Haug. XXII, 700 pages. 1984.

Vol. 10: Simulation and Model-Based Methodologies: An Integrative View. Edited by T. I. Ören, B. P. Zeigler, M. S. Elzas. XIII, 651 pages. 1984.

Vol. 11: Robotics and Artificial Intelligence. Edited by M. Brady, L. A. Gerhardt, H. F. Davidson. XVII, 693 pages. 1984.

Vol. 12: Combinatorial Algorithms on Words. Edited by A. Apostolico, Z. Galil. VIII, 361 pages. 1985.

Vol. 13: Logics and Models of Concurrent Systems. Edited by K. R. Apt. VIII, 498 pages. 1985.

Vol. 14: Control Flow and Data Flow: Concepts of Distributed Programming. Edited by M. Broy. VIII, 525 pages. 1985.

Vol. 15: Computational Mathematical Programming. Edited by K. Schittkowski. VIII, 451 pages. 1985.

Vol. 16: New Systems and Architectures for Automatic Speech Recognition and Synthesis. Edited by R. De Mori, C.Y. Suen. XIII, 630 pages. 1985.

Vol. 17: Fundamental Algorithms for Computer Graphics. Edited by R.A. Earnshaw. XVI, 1042 pages. 1985.

Vol. 18: Computer Architectures for Spatially Distributed Data. Edited by H. Freeman and G. G. Pieroni. VIII, 391 pages. 1985.

Vol. 19: Pictorial Information Systems in Medicine. Edited by K. H. Höhne. XII, 525 pages. 1986.

Vol. 20: Disordered Systems and Biological Organization. Edited by E. Bienenstock, F. Fogelman Soulié, G. Weisbuch. XXI, 405 pages.1986.

Vol. 21: Intelligent Decision Support in Process Environments. Edited by E. Hollnagel, G. Mancini, D.D. Woods. XV, 524 pages. 1986.

Vol. 22: Software System Design Methods. The Challenge of Advanced Computing Technology. Edited by J.K. Skwirzynski. XIII, 747 pages. 1986.

NATO ASI Series F

Vol. 23: Designing Computer-Based Learning Materials. Edited by H. Weinstock and A. Bork. IX, 285 pages. 1986.

Vol. 24: Database Machines. Modern Trends and Applications. Edited by A.K. Sood and A.H. Qureshi. VIII, 570 pages. 1986.

Vol. 25: Pyramidal Systems for Computer Vision. Edited by V. Cantoni and S. Levialdi. VIII, 392 pages. 1986.

Vol. 26: Modelling and Analysis in Arms Control. Edited by R. Avenhaus, R.K. Huber and J.D. Kettelle. VIII, 488 pages. 1986.

Vol. 27: Computer Aided Optimal Design: Structural and Mechanical Systems. Edited by C.A. Mota Soares. XIII, 1029 pages. 1987.

Vol. 28: Distributed Operating Systems. Theory und Practice. Edited by Y. Paker, J.-P. Banatre and M. Bozyiğit. X, 379 pages. 1987.

Vol. 29: Languages for Sensor-Based Control in Robotics. Edited by U. Rembold and K. Hörmann. IX, 625 pages. 1987.

Vol. 30: Pattern Recognition Theory and Applications. Edited by P.A. Devijver and J. Kittler. XI, 543 pages. 1987.

MIX
Papier aus verantwortungsvollen Quellen
Paper from responsible sources
FSC® C105338

If you have any concerns about our products,
you can contact us on
ProductSafety@springernature.com

In case Publisher is established outside the EU,
the EU authorized representative is:
Springer Nature Customer Service Center GmbH
Europaplatz 3, 69115 Heidelberg, Germany

Printed by Libri Plureos GmbH
in Hamburg, Germany